BESTSELLING Annual Bible Commentary

Standard LESSON COMMENTARY®

KJV SEPTEMBER–AUGUST 2022–2023

KING JAMES VERSION

Editorial Team

Jane Ann Kenney
Ronald L. Nickelson
Taylor Z. Stamps

Volume 70

Standard®
PUBLISHING
part of the David C Cook family

In This Volume

Index of Printed Texts

The printed texts for 2022–2023 are arranged here in the order in which they appear in the Bible.

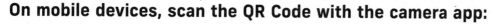
We are committed to serving you by providing excellent resources that inspire, educate, and motivate you in a growing relationship with Jesus Christ. Please tell us about your experience with Standard Lesson Commentary by completing the survey at: StandardLesson.com/survey.

On mobile devices, scan the QR Code with the camera app:

Don't forget the visuals!

The thumbnail visuals in the lessons are small reproductions of 18″ x 24″ full-color posters that are included in the *Adult Resources* packet for each quarter. Order numbers 1629122 (fall 2022), 2629123 (winter 2022–2023), 3629123 (spring 2023), and 4629123 (summer 2023) from either your supplier, by calling 1.800.323.7543, or at www.standardlesson.com.

Asking the Right Questions

by Ronald L. Nickelson

Do this right now: rate yourself on your level of Bible knowledge on the following point-scale:

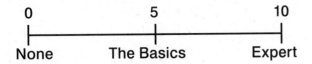

Next, suppose that you had to take the following essay test in order to justify a ranking of no less than "5":

1. Describe the person and work of Christ.
2. Define repentance from sin and give examples.
3. Explain the significance of baptism.
4. List situations that call for laying on of hands.
5. Relate resurrection to eternal judgment.

To justify a "5" ranking, you must answer all five test items correctly. Were you to take this test, would you be able to get that "5"?

What Excuses Tempt You?

If you're now feeling uncomfortable by the possibility (or likelihood) of not being able to justify claiming at least a "5," perhaps you're beginning to think of excuses—excuses such as *I haven't been to Bible college, and I'm not a theologian.* But Hebrews 5:11–6:3 won't allow you that easy way out. That text describes all the subjects covered in the above test as foundational to faith (5:12; 6:1); they fall in the category of "milk" rather than "meat" (5:12-13). Milk is important for babies (compare 1 Peter 2:2), but milk is to be a temporary staple in one's growth process, whether physical or spiritual.

Why Are You Stalled?

There are many enticing answers to this question. There are so many, in fact, that you might be tempted to put the excuses in categories such as issues of the church's fault, your family situation, etc. But all blame-shifting aside, it boils down to one thing: *priorities.* The reason you're not a "5"—let alone being a "10"—is that you have prioritized your time elsewhere. And the reason you've done

so is that you have rationalized your level of Bible knowledge as being adequate. (If you had not so-deemed it, then your priorities would have been different.)

That was my own problem for about the first 16 years after accepting Christ at age 10. When my church started a challenge for everyone to read the entire Bible through in a year, I (age 26) rationalized that in all the years I had attended Sunday school, surely I had read the entire Bible in that span of time.

But I eventually realized that I was fooling no one but myself. We're good at doing that, aren't we? Do the math. There are 31,102 verses in the Bible. For me to have read every verse over the course of 52 Sundays for 16 years would have required lessons of about 38 words each, with no verses repeated. In short, I had pledged my life to value the words of a book that I had not even read!

What Can Must We Be Better At?

You won't prioritize your time toward intensive, comprehensive Bible study until you're convinced of the need to do so. A good starting point is to consider the lives of those who did just that along with their reasons (see Ezra 7:10; Psalm 119:11; Hosea 4:6; 1 Timothy 1:8-11; 3:14-17; 4:6; 2 Timothy 2:15; Titus 2:1; etc.). Be open to the Spirit's leading you to seek this knowledge (John 16:13; etc.).

As you begin the road to greater Bible knowledge, trust that God desires not only to work *within* you but also *through* you. That means not keeping your task private to yourself. When my church began that through-the-Bible-in-a-year program, the enthusiasm in January was high. But by late February, about half the people had dropped out. Each succeeding month saw more drop outs. By December 31, probably no more than 20 percent had finished the task. Accountability partners would have helped. Recruit one—

and be one! The stakes are too high to do otherwise (2 Timothy 4:10a; Jude 23).

Is This a Mentor-Protégé Relationship?

No. The accountability partner concept differs from that of a mentor-protégé relationship in that the latter involves a novice being guided by an expert. But two people who agree to hold each other accountable can be at the same level of spiritual growth. The idea is to function as a source of encouragement to stay on track. And the roles must continually be reversed as the encourager becomes the one encouraged in a reciprocal way.

The distinction between the two kinds of relationships can be illustrated by how family life works. Ten-year-old twin girls can cheer each other on in a game of baseball as each gives her best effort, knowing that the other is watching. But that's not a mentor-protégé relationship since neither has more expertise than the other. A mentor appears when their baseball-wise father steps in as their personal coach.

Which Relationship Should I Seek?

Eventually, you will reap benefits from both an accountability partner and a mentor-protégé relationship in your spiritual growth. The apostle Paul recognized this. On the one hand, he functioned as an encourager of encouragers (1 Thessalonians 3:2; 4:18; 5:11, 14; etc.), recognizing in the process the value of himself being encouraged (3:7). On the other hand, he also functioned as a mentor, using an analogy to family life (1 Timothy 1:2; Titus 1:4).

What Else Will Foster Spiritual Growth?

Everything we've talked about so far boils down to a two-word phrase: *behavior modification*. In our faith context, modifying our behavior must begin with asking the Spirit to guide and bless our efforts. These efforts can be summarized with three techniques, each of which starts with the letter *M*. One of those three is *Make a commitment to another*, which is the accountability partner approach just discussed.

The second *M* is *Monitor your behavior*. Someone who is trying to lose weight might keep a daily log of "calories in vs. calories out" and bathroom-scale weighings. Monitoring one's own behavior for the purpose of spiritual growth could involve having a daily Bible-study listing for the year with boxes to check off as readings are completed.

The third *M* is *Modify your environment*. This can involve inclusion as well as exclusion. I'm very much an out of sight, out of mind person. So I include in my living space a set of weights where I see them frequently. Thus I have a daily, visual reminder to lift weights for exercise. In the same way, seeing my Bible out and waiting nudges me to open its pages and study.

Why Is This Important?

Spiritual growth is connected with increasing knowledge; spiritual backsliding, however, goes hand in hand with the opposite (see Hosea 4:6; Matthew 13:18-23; 2 Timothy 2:15; 3:14–4:5; 2 Peter 1:5-9; etc.). Marvelous tools exist online for helping one grow in the knowledge of the Word of God. But for every one such tool, there also seems to be a tool, forum, video channel, etc., that opposes the truth of Christianity.

> *You won't prioritize your time toward . . . Bible study until you're convinced of the need to do so.*

The painful irony here is that the current Information Age in which we live is just as rightly called the Disinformation Age (compare Colossians 2:8; Revelation 2:24). This calls for being "wise as serpents, and harmless as doves" (Matthew 10:16) as we seek tools for Bible study. Such godly wisdom not only is able to recognize and reject anti-Christian material, it also resists the old problem known as *means/end reversal*. That problem arises when we get so enamored with a tool that it becomes an end in itself rather than a means to an end.

Such are the challenges of growing in Christ. But overcoming these challenges will reap eternal dividends. May the Spirit guide you in your seeking.

On Divine Discontent

by Ronald L. Nickelson

With this edition of the Standard Lesson Commentary, my status changed from that of Senior Editor to being Senior Editor Emeritus. That's a fancy way of saying that I have elected retirement from my 20-year ministry in curriculum publishing. The lower energy level that advancing age brings, as complicated by Parkinson's disease, was the main driver of this decision.

Reflecting on those 20 years, I can hardly think of any job or ministry that would have been more fulfilling to me than to be in a position to influence the eternal destinies of many thousands of people! The old saying "Find a job you love, and you'll never work a day in your life" certainly applies here. But what brought me to this ministry was a series of jobs and events that I did not especially love or was otherwise ill-suited for. I call these my "series of divine discontents." I share that series on the possibility—even likelihood—that it may inspire others who are themselves in the throes of divine discontent.

Divine Discontent 1

Armed with a bachelor's degree in accounting, my post-college working days began with me on active duty in the US Air Force, crunching numbers. Finding my then-future wife was the brightest spot during those seven years, during which I became discontent with my occupation—I was bored. I also came under conviction during that time that, although I accepted the Bible as the Word of God, I had never actually read it! Thus began a journey to read the Bible cover-to-cover in a year—which I ended up doing every year for at least a dozen years.

Divine Discontents 2 & 3

I quit the Air Force and enrolled in seminary. My goal was to reenter the Air Force as a chaplain after graduation. That I did, but as a part-time Reservist, not full-time active duty. So I took a pulpit ministry to wait for an opening. After about two years, however, I sensed divine discontents two and three: seeing the kinds of pressures that active-duty chaplains were under and being somewhat ill-suited for pulpit ministry dissuaded me from both. So I enrolled in a post-graduate program with intent to eventually teach in a Bible college, which I did.

Divine Discontents 4 & 5

At the same time, my job as a USAF Reservist changed: I transitioned out of base-level ministry to become one of two Reservist historians working at the Air Staff to document policy and procedure changes within the USAF Chaplain Service. But after several years at both that part-time job and the full-time teaching ministry, I again began to feel that itch—neither seemed to be what I thought God was preparing me for. On top of all that, the college where I taught needed someone with different credentials for accrediting purposes.

Then something startling happened: without researching ministry openings, doing personal networking, or otherwise beating the bushes, a new opportunity appeared out of nowhere, from an unlikely source: the manager of the college bookstore informed me that a sales rep had told her that Standard Publishing needed an editor on the Standard Lesson Commentary. I instantly knew that was the task that God had been preparing me for all those years.

Divine Contentment

I am amazed anew whenever I reflect on the multi-decade chain of events and experiences that prepared me for this position. They all seemed rather random as I faced them at the time. But hindsight reveals a sequence of preparation in God's providential time line. And so it may be with you!

Discover Free Lesson Helps & Tips at StandardLesson.com

In the World

Connect the timeless truth with today's news. *In the World* connects a current event—something your students are probably talking about that very week—with each week's lesson. Use *In the World* to introduce or to wrap up your lesson.

Activity Pages

These completely reproducible pages engage your students in the Involvement Learning plan suggested on the final page of each lesson. One page is available for every lesson throughout the year! (These pages are also available in print with the *Standard Lesson Commentary Deluxe Editions* and in the *Adult Resources* digital access download.)

Weekly Teacher Tips

Insights and ideas for effective teaching from the editors of the Standard Lesson® will help you present each lesson with variety and creativity. The learning never ends with our archive of helpful articles!

Standard Lesson Monthly

Every issue will help deepen your study of God's Word and bring out the best in *Standard Lesson Commentary* and *Standard Lesson Quarterly*. Get these great features emailed to you each month in our information-packed newsletter:

- Our monthly Classroom Tips article to help you become a more effective teacher

- An overview of the lesson content that will be covered in the upcoming month

- A featured resource (with free sample!) each month

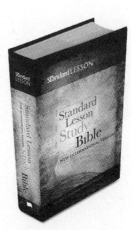

Fall 2022
King James Version

God's Exceptional
Choice

Special Features

Lessons
Unit 1: God Calls Abraham's Family

Unit 2: Out of Slavery to Nationhood

Unit 3: We Are God's Artwork

Quarterly Quiz

Use these questions as a pretest or as a review. The answers are on page iv of This Quarter in the Word.

Lesson 1

1. Lot was Abram's _____? (father, brother, nephew) *Genesis 12:5*

2. Who did Abram think might become his heir? (Ebed, Ehud, Eliezer)? *Genesis 15:2*

Lesson 2

1. Esau grabbed Jacob's heel at birth. T/F. *Genesis 25:26*

2. What did Esau sell to his brother for a meal? (birthright, servant, wild game) *Genesis 25:33*

Lesson 3

1. After wrestling a man, Jacob's name was changed to _____. *Genesis 32:28*

2. What name did Jacob give to the location where he wrestled? (Pithom, Peniel, Pirathon) *Genesis 32:30*

Lesson 4

1. Jacob's sons by Rachel were Joseph and Benjamin. T/F. *Genesis 35:24*

2. Judah proclaimed that Tamar was "more _____ than I." *Genesis 38:26*

Lesson 5

1. Moses' father was from the tribe of _____. *Exodus 2:1*

2. Pharaoh's daughter named the child Moses because she "drew him out of the _____." *Exodus 2:10*

Lesson 6

1. The song describes God as what? (the Sea, the Rock, the Sky) *Deuteronomy 32:4*

2. The song likens God's care to an eagle caring for its young. T/F. *Deuteronomy 32:11-12*

Lesson 7

1. God handed Israel over to be ruled by whom? (Magog, Midian, Mesopotamia) *Judges 6:1-2*

2. Under what did the angel of the Lord sit while visiting Gideon? (an oak, a shelter, a winepress) *Judges 6:11*

Lesson 8

1. Samuel was pleased to hear that Israel desired a king. T/F. *1 Samuel 8:6*

2. According to Samuel, Israel had _____ God. *1 Samuel 10:19*

Lesson 9

1. From whose sons did the Lord choose Israel's next king? (Samuel, Saul, Jesse) *1 Samuel 16:1*

2. Upon further questioning it was found that David was working with _____. *1 Samuel 16:11*

Lesson 10

1. Redemption and forgiveness come in accordance to the riches of God's _____. *Ephesians 1:7*

2. All people, regardless of their belief, are marked with the Holy Spirit. T/F. *Ephesians 1:13*

Lesson 11

1. Paul gives thanks for the faith and love of the Ephesians. T/F. *Ephesians 1:15-16*

2. God placed Jesus to be the _____ over the church. *Ephesians 1:22*

Lesson 12

1. God is described as being "rich" in what? (grace, mercy, love) *Ephesians 2:4*

2. Believers are created in Christ Jesus to do good works. T/F. *Ephesians 2:10*

Lesson 13

1. The primary opponents of believers in spiritual struggle are flesh and blood. T/F. *Ephesians 6:12*

2. The sword of the Spirit is described as "the _____ of God." *Ephesians 6:17*

Quarter at a Glance

by Christopher Cotten

From a mountain in the wilderness of Sinai, God told Moses, "If ye will obey my voice indeed, and keep my covenant, then ye shall be a peculiar treasure unto me above all people . . . and ye shall be unto me a kingdom of priests, and an holy nation" (Exodus 19:5-6a). God's words declare one of the central themes of Scripture: God's freedom to choose a people to be His own.

Our limited understanding will not fully comprehend God's choices. His selections may defy our standards for determining who is considered "choice." Ultimately, He is in no way bound by our human standards. This quarter's Scripture texts unpack the exceptional nature of God's choice.

An Obscure Choice

The quarter begins by looking at the narratives in Genesis set amid the nomadic life of the ancient Near East. God demonstrated His choice by calling a descendant of Noah to experience blessing and a new land (Genesis 12:1-7). God's choice was demonstrated through this family as He chose certain individuals for service to His name (25:19b-34).

God's choice is not reserved for the notable or the powerful. These Scripture texts show that He may choose people not widely recognized. His choice is not based on any criteria other than His desire and freedom to choose.

Sometimes our expectations do not align with God's choice. We should practice humility and show attentiveness to God's purposes—He might work in ways that catch us unaware. Are you in a position to notice?

A Surprising Choice

Through the second unit of lessons, God's choice is shown, even through the centuries. These lessons highlight the development of God's choice of His people, from a child born of a slave (Exodus 2:1-10) to a shepherd turned king (1 Samuel 16:1-13). God's call can be unexpected—He may even choose people who are trying to avoid His call altogether (Judges 6:7-16a)!

God choice will often be in spite of human expectations. Moses' path to fulfilling God's choice was marked by uncertainty and risk (Exodus 2:3-4). Gideon had no reputation aligned with the tasks God called him to do (Judges 6:15). David's fitness as king was overlooked by his own family (1 Samuel 16:7-12). Have you felt incompatible with God's choice over your life? Remember that God is "the Rock, his work is perfect" (Deuteronomy 32:4).

A Life-Changing Choice

The final unit of lessons highlights how God continues to choose people for His will. These four lessons explore Paul's teaching to Christians in the city of Ephesus regarding the life-changing nature of God's choice over their lives—and ours.

> God's choice is not reserved
> for the notable or the powerful.

Paul explained the life-changing nature of God's choice when he wrote that God's people are blessed "according as he hath chosen us in him before the foundation of the world, that we should be holy and without blame before him in love" (Ephesians 1:4). For God's people, being chosen comes with responsibility. Their actions and choices will be changed in light of God's choice.

God's people must live with obedience and good works in Christ (Ephesians 2:1-10). Evil in the world desires to tear down God's chosen people. Therefore, God's people must prepare (see 6:10-18)!

We can encourage and support other believers through prayer, preaching, teaching, discipleship, and mentoring. God's exceptional choice can never be doubted. He desires that His people live in a manner that reflects His choice. Let us turn our eyes toward that goal.

Get the Setting

by Mark S. Krause

Throughout Scripture, cities often served as the backdrop for God's work among His people. In some instances, God called people to leave a thriving city in order to follow Him. However, in other instances God called people to live in these cities in order to serve Him.

Ancient Wealth in Ur

During the era of Abraham (about 2167–1992 BC), one of the largest cities in Mesopotamia was Ur. Archaeologists have identified the city's ruins located on the Euphrates River, about 220 miles southeast of modern-day Baghdad. The ruins provide evidence of human occupation dating back to approximately the third millennium BC.

Ur was one of the premier cities of its day. Its location near the Persian Gulf and the confluence of the Tigris and Euphrates Rivers allowed the city to develop a thriving economy. Archaeological findings provide insight into the city's wealth. For example, the city's royal tombs have been found to have been filled with numerous riches, thus reflecting the wealth of the city and its inhabitants.

The city has been traditionally held as the ancestral home of Abraham's family (see Genesis 11:28, 31; compare Acts 7:2). However, the family did not stay in Ur—they traveled to Canaan. Scholars have tried to recreate their journey and estimate the exact route from Ur to Canaan. The most direct route would have taken the family directly up the Euphrates River valley. This route would have proven to be dangerous as the travelers would have forded tributaries, skirted marshlands, maneuvered through desert lands, and negotiated with hostile peoples.

The travels of Abraham's family were highly unusual during that time period. Many people stayed in the same geographic region for most of their lives. Cities, like Ur, were the home of much known wealth. That God promised blessing and greatness for Abraham (see Genesis 12:2-3) outside Ur (15:7) would have been unparalleled. Abraham's contemporaries might have considered that he would find blessing in the thriving metropolis, not in unknown foreign lands.

Pagan Temples in Ephesus

During the first century AD, thriving cities were situated on critical trade routes, shipping corridors, or both. These cities served as ideal locations for the gospel message to take root and spread throughout the Roman Empire. Ephesus, a city on the western coast of Asia Minor (modern-day Turkey), was no exception.

A large harbor provided the city access to key shipping routes in the Mediterranean Sea. Highways connected the city to the rest of Asia Minor and, thereby, the far reaches of the empire. Therefore, the city was crucial for trade across the region.

Further, Ephesus was also important for pagan religious practices. During the era of the apostle Paul, the city was home to a large temple dedicated to the pagan goddess Diana (see Acts 19:35). The temple was more than a location for pagan rituals; it also provided a financial benefit for the city (see 19:24-27).

As a result, Ephesus was an ideal stop for the apostle Paul during his missionary journeys across the Mediterranean region (see Acts 18:19-21; 19:1-10). From this city, the message of Jesus Christ spread throughout the Roman Empire and, perhaps, through the known world.

Ambassadors to the World

In some instances, God called His people to leave large cities—like He called the family of Abraham to leave the city of Ur. However, in other instances, God called people to live and serve in large, influential cities—like Paul in Ephesus. Each context provided God's people with unique challenges as they were to be His ambassadors to the world.

This Quarter in the Word

Mon, Aug. 29	The Faith of Abraham	Hebrews 11:8-19
Tue, Aug. 30	Blessed Are They Who Dwell in Your House!	Psalm 84
Wed, Aug. 31	God Reckons Righteousness	Romans 4:1-12
Thu, Sep. 1	A Promised Inheritance	Romans 4:13-25
Fri, Sep. 2	Abraham Rejoiced in the Day	John 8:51-59
Sat, Sep. 3	First Steps of Faith	Genesis 11:27-32
Sun, Sep. 4	Called to Be a Blessing	Genesis 12:1-7; 15:1-7
Mon, Sep. 5	The First Will Be Last	Luke 13:23-30
Tue, Sep. 6	God Is Great and Gracious	Psalm 147:1-6, 12-20
Wed, Sep. 7	God Judges Rightly	Psalm 75
Thu, Sep. 8	God's Word Does Not Fail	Romans 9:6-16
Fri, Sep. 9	Who Can Argue with God?	Romans 9:17-29
Sat, Sep. 10	God Blesses Jacob	Genesis 28:10-22
Sun, Sep. 11	God Is Free to Choose	Genesis 25:19-34
Mon, Sep. 12	Partake in God's Holiness	Hebrews 12:7-17
Tue, Sep. 13	A Blessing Bestowed	Genesis 27:18-29
Wed, Sep. 14	A Blessing Forsaken	Genesis 27:30-41
Thu, Sep. 15	God Will Be Merciful to All	Romans 11:25-32
Fri, Sep. 16	Praise for God's Wonderful Works	Psalm 105:1-11
Sat, Sep. 17	Seeking Favor in God's Sight	Genesis 32:3-12
Sun, Sep. 18	Wrestling for a Blessing	Genesis 32:22-32

Mon, Nov. 14	Grace Overflowed for Service	1 Timothy 1:1-4, 12-17
Tue, Nov. 15	Live in Peace and Godliness	1 Timothy 2:1-8
Wed, Nov. 16	Qualifications for God's Servants	1 Timothy 3:1-13
Thu, Nov. 17	Do Justice, Love Mercy, Walk Humbly	Micah 6:1-8
Fri, Nov. 18	Trust in God and Do Good	Psalm 37:1-9, 37-40
Sat, Nov. 19	A Prayer for Boldness	Acts 4:23-31
Sun, Nov. 20	Created for Good Works	Ephesians 2:1-10
Mon, Nov. 21	Remembrance and Repentance	Revelation 2:1-7
Tue, Nov. 22	The Mystery of Christ	Ephesians 3:1-13
Wed, Nov. 23	Build Up the Body of Christ	Ephesians 4:1-8, 11-16
Thu, Nov. 24	Put On the New Self	Ephesians 4:17-27
Fri, Nov. 25	God Is Our Refuge	Psalm 91
Sat, Nov. 26	God Rebuilds the Afflicted	Isaiah 54:6-17
Sun, Nov. 27	Strength in the Lord	Ephesians 6:10-24

Answers to the Quarterly Quiz on page 2

Lesson 1—1. nephew. 2. Eliezer. Lesson 2—1. false. 2. birthright. Lesson 3—1. Israel. 2. Peniel. Lesson 4—1. true. 2. righteous. Lesson 5—1. Levi. 2. water. Lesson 6—1. the Rock. 2. true. Lesson 7—1. Midian. 2. an oak. Lesson 8—1. false. 2. rejected. Lesson 9—1. Jesse. 2. sheep. Lesson 10—1. grace. 2. false. Lesson 11—1. true. 2. head. Lesson 12—1. mercy. 2. true. Lesson 13—1. false. 2. word.

iv

i

Lesson Cycle Chart

International Sunday School Lesson Cycle, September 2022–August 2026

Year	Fall Quarter (Sep, Oct, Nov)	Winter Quarter (Dec, Jan, Feb)	Spring Quarter (Mar, Apr, May)	Summer Quarter (Jun, Jul, Aug)
2022–2023	**God's Exceptional Choice** Genesis, Exodus, Deuteronomy, Judges, 1 Samuel, Ephesians	**From Darkness to Light** 2 Chronicles, Isaiah, Joel, Luke, 1 Corinthians, 2 Timothy, James, 1 Peter	**Jesus Calls Us** Matthew, Mark, Luke, John, Acts	**The Righteous Reign of God** Prophets, Matthew, Romans, 1 Corinthians, Galatians
2023–2024	**God's Law Is Love** Luke, John, Acts, Romans, 1 Corinthians, Galatians, Colossians	**Faith That Pleases God** Ruth, 1 Samuel, 2 Chronicles, Proverbs, Prophets, Matthew, Luke, Romans, Hebrews	**Examining Our Faith** Matthew, Mark, Luke, Acts, Romans, 2 Corinthians, 1 Peter, Jude	**Hope in the Lord** Psalms, Lamentations, Acts, Epistles
2024–2025	**Worship in the Covenant Community** Genesis, Exodus, 2 Samuel, 1 & 2 Kings, 2 Chronicles, Psalms, Isaiah, John	**A King Forever and Ever** Ruth, 2 Samuel, Psalms, Matthew, Luke	**Costly Sacrifices** Exodus, Leviticus, Numbers, Deuteronomy, 1 & 2 Chronicles, Ezra, Matthew, Hebrews, 1 John, Revelation	**Sacred Altars and Holy Offerings** Genesis, Gospels, Romans, 1 Corinthians, Ephesians, Hebrews, 1 Peter
2025–2026	**Judah, From Isaiah to Exile** 2 Kings, 2 Chronicles, Isaiah, Jeremiah, Ezekiel	**Enduring Beliefs of the Church** Exodus, Psalms, Gospels, Acts, Epistles, Revelation	**Social Teachings of the Church** Genesis, Exodus, Deuteronomy, Nehemiah, Psalms, Prophets, Gospels, Acts, Epistles	**Faithful Witnesses** Judges, 1 Samuel, Amos, Gospels, Acts, 2 Timothy, Philemon

The Power of Acrostics

Teacher Tips by Mary T. Lederleitner

Because adult learners live busy, distracted lives, you may find it challenging to make a memorable teaching point. Further, many adults are convinced that they are not good at memorization, so they don't make any attempt to improve in that regard.

The use of acrostics can be an effective way for teachers to make a lasting impression with students. An acrostic is a piece of writing in which the first letter of each word, line, or paragraph spells out another word or phrase. By remembering one specific word or phrase, students are able to then remember other words and phrases. Acrostics engage the mind in unique ways, thus making memorization more accessible.

Neural Pathways

Neuroscientists who study the human nervous system in regard to human learning have found a connection between learning and neural pathways. These pathways serve as connections between different parts of the human nervous system. The more utilized the connections, the stronger the pathways might become.

Through the repetitive use of these pathways, memory and learning are established and strengthened. Various memory devices, like acrostics, are helpful for teachers to use because these devices build on learners' existing neural pathways and serve to reinforce teaching points.

A Useful Example

Acrostics have been used to educate believers on ways to share their faith. Some believers feel ill-prepared to share their faith—perhaps due to a sense of intimidation or fear. To encourage and strengthen believers in this regard, the following model of evangelism was created.

The *BLESS* model utilizes an acrostic to highlight five steps to help believers share their faith. *B* stands for "begin with prayer." The work of evan-gelism all begins with God. *L* stands for "listen." Active listening is an important aspect in building evangelistic relationships. *E* stands for "eat." Finding space to share a meal with a person is a way by which the evangelistic relationship can grow. *S* stands for "serve." Evangelism involves service: the willingness to serve others or let them serve you. The final *S* stands for "share." Evangelism culminates when believers share the story of how their lives changed because of Jesus.

This acrostic helps believers learn and internalize the steps of evangelism. What could be an elaborate approach is streamlined as believers learn to bless others via the *BLESS* approach.

The Power of Linking

An acrostic's power lies in its ability to link one word with other words. *BLESS* links a single, easy-to-remember word to the activities of evangelism.

However, acrostics can be more potent for your class when the acrostic links Scripture texts to your teaching points. In this quarter, as you teach on God's choice of His people, what acrostics can you create based on the word *CHOICE*?

Playing with Words

To help spur your creativity in using acrostics, consider the following questions: What words do learners use in your context? What phrases might your learners consider to be commonplace, funny, or serious? Are there ways to employ frequently used key words or phrases? At the end of the day, what do you want learners to remember?

Pray and ask God for creativity and wisdom regarding the use acrostics in your teaching. You will not want to use acrostics all the time, lest they start to feel recycled and stale. However, the timely use of acrostics will cause learners to perk up and pay attention. While developing acrostics may take some effort on your part, the long-term impact for your learners is worth the investment!

The Call of Abram

Devotional Reading: Hebrews 11:8-19
Background Scripture: Genesis 12:1-7; 15:1-7

Genesis 12:1-5, 7

1 Now the LORD had said unto Abram, Get thee out of thy country, and from thy kindred, and from thy father's house, unto a land that I will shew thee:

2 And I will make of thee a great nation, and I will bless thee, and make thy name great; and thou shalt be a blessing:

3 And I will bless them that bless thee, and curse him that curseth thee: and in thee shall all families of the earth be blessed.

4 So Abram departed, as the LORD had spoken unto him; and Lot went with him: and Abram was seventy and five years old when he departed out of Haran.

5 And Abram took Sarai his wife, and Lot his brother's son, and all their substance that they had gathered, and the souls that they had gotten in Haran; and they went forth to go into the land of Canaan; and into the land of Canaan they came.

7 And the LORD appeared unto Abram, and said, Unto thy seed will I give this land: and there builded he an altar unto the LORD, who appeared unto him.

Genesis 15:1-7

1 After these things the word of the LORD came unto Abram in a vision, saying, Fear not, Abram: I am thy shield, and thy exceeding great reward.

2 And Abram said, Lord GOD, what wilt thou give me, seeing I go childless, and the steward of my house is this Eliezer of Damascus?

3 And Abram said, Behold, to me thou hast given no seed: and, lo, one born in my house is mine heir.

4 And, behold, the word of the LORD came unto him, saying, This shall not be thine heir; but he that shall come forth out of thine own bowels shall be thine heir.

5 And he brought him forth abroad, and said, Look now toward heaven, and tell the stars, if thou be able to number them: and he said unto him, So shall thy seed be.

6 And he believed in the LORD; and he counted it to him for righteousness.

7 And he said unto him, I am the LORD that brought thee out of Ur of the Chaldees, to give thee this land to inherit it.

Key Text

The LORD appeared unto Abram, and said, Unto thy seed will I give this land: and there builded he an altar unto the LORD, who appeared unto him. —**Genesis 12:7**

God's Exceptional Choice

Unit 1: God Calls Abraham's Family
Lessons 1–4

Lesson Aims

After participating in this less, each learner will be able to:

1. List key features of Abraham's call and subsequent covenant vision.

2. Explain the relationship between that call and vision.

3. Identify one or more ways that Abraham's obedience will serve as a model to his or her obedience under the new covenant.

Lesson Outline

Introduction

A. Answering the Call

"When 'the Mouse' offers you a job, you say yes," an executive chef on a Disney cruise declared. Prior to his work with Disney, the chef had worked in an executive capacity at several successful restaurants. He enjoyed the line of work but had not considered doing so on the seas.

However, his name was suggested to the cruise line for a position. Eventually someone from the company called him, conducted an interview, and made an offer. The chef accepted, and for over a decade he has served in several upscale restaurants at sea. The chef answered the call, and the decision changed his life forever.

How much more so with God! When He calls, He expects a faith-filled response. His call may feel rather demanding, even overwhelming. In today's lesson, God called someone to a new context so that God's promises could be fulfilled.

B. Lesson Context

The first 11 chapters of Genesis look at humanity broadly—from their creation and fall (Genesis 1–3), to their acts of violence (4:2-12) and wickedness (6:5-6, 11-12), to their judgment and rescue (6:7–9:17). Despite all this, people still made vain attempts to focus attention on themselves (11:1-9).

As Genesis is the first book of the Old Testament, such a broad focus is understandable. This prepares readers of all eras to hear how God worked through humanity generally and specifically through one family.

After the flood narrative (Genesis 6–10), the text lists the descendants of Noah's son Shem (11:10-25). This genealogy culminated with Terah, the father of Abram, Nahor, and Haran (11:26).

Terah outlived Haran, the father of Lot (Genesis 11:27-28). Terah's other sons, Abram and Nahor, were both married. However, Abram and his wife Sarai were unable to conceive (11:29-30).

The family lived in Ur of the Chaldees (Genesis 11:31). This ancient Mesopotamian city was located on the banks of the Euphrates River. Modern archaeological discoveries have provided insight into the city's wealth, culture, and pagan religious practices. The family's connections to the city likely ran deep, and at one time they took part in the city's pagan religious practices (see Joshua 24:2).

However, the family did not stay in Ur. Terah led Abram, Sarai, and Lot toward Canaan, a land bordering the western edges of the Mediterranean Sea (see Genesis 10:19). But Terah did not complete the journey. He settled and died in Haran (11:31b-32), an important city on a major trade route between Mesopotamia and Canaan.

Today's Scripture text continues narrowing the focus as it highlights the family of Abram. (Note that Abram is the same man who later had his name changed to Abraham; see Genesis 17:5.)

I. The Call Announced
(Genesis 12:1-5, 7)
A. God's Declaration, Part 1 (vv. 1-3)

1. Now the LORD had said unto Abram, Get thee out of thy country, and from thy kindred, and from thy father's house, unto a land that I will shew thee.

As *the Lord* addressed *Abram*, the focus of the text turns to the life of this man. The text gives no clues regarding the way through which God spoke. All that is noted is that God called to Abram.

That God told Abram to *get thee out* emphasized that God expected His imperative to be followed. Toward the end of Abram's narrative, God would show similar urgency by telling Abram to "get thee" to a certain place to sacrifice his son (Genesis 22:2).

If Abram had stayed in Haran, the livelihood of his *kindred* could have been jeopardized. In a culture of polytheism (meaning "many gods"), the act of worshipping the one true God could have required Abram to detach from the larger community. This may be part of the reason that God ordered Abram to leave everything behind and proceed to a new *land*.

In the ancient world, a person's identity and social standing were attached to family and ancestry. For this reason, genealogies and ancestral records were of great importance (examples: Genesis 5; 11:10-32; Nehemiah 7:6-64). Additionally, inheritance claims and family responsibilities were tied to a person's family lineage.

By calling Abram to leave his *father's house*, God called him to a new identity. As he followed God's imperative, Abram would demonstrate trust, even if uncertainties remained (see Hebrews 11:8).

Grieving and Going

As the child of a military service member, I learned to relocate every few years. This constant churn is one reason why moving to a new country sounded appealing. I didn't have a strong attachment to any particular "home"—or so I thought.

Recently, I found myself weeping at my parents' house. My wife and I were staying with my parents before leaving to become missionaries abroad. I was emotional because I realized that my nuclear family—regardless of their location—had always been my "home." They were a stabilizing force during every move. As I prepared to move abroad, I felt the significance of not living near my family.

Perhaps Abram experienced similar grief as he left his family to follow God's call. He might have never seen them again. When God calls you to follow Him, will you go no matter the cost? —N. G.

2. And I will make of thee a great nation, and I will bless thee, and make thy name great; and thou shalt be a blessing.

Blessing would result if Abram obeyed God: the childless Abram would become *a great nation*. Nothing from this promise indicated human power. Abram's descendants would become great only because of the Lord's steadfast love and promises (Deuteronomy 7:7-8).

His descendants were not to be like other nations. Instead, they were to be a "holy people . . . above all the nations" (Deuteronomy 14:2; see Leviticus 20:26). Their unique establishment

How to Say It

Chaldees	*Kal*-deez.
Eliezer	El-ih-*ee*-zer.
Haran	*Hair*-un.
Moreh	*Moe*-reh.
Nahor	*Nay*-hor.
Sichem	*Sigh*-kem.
Terah	*Tair*-uh.

would cause God's name to be glorified and made great among the peoples of the earth (see Isaiah 29:23; 60:21-22; Ezekiel 36:23).

Abram and his descendants were tasked with living among other nations in a manner that would result in the *blessing* of both groups. In a way, Abram's descendants were to serve as a "kingdom of priests" for the whole world (Exodus 19:5-6).

3. And I will bless them that bless thee, and curse him that curseth thee: and in thee shall all families of the earth be blessed.

Abram would not have to face trials alone—God would give protection as He would *curse* all people *that curseth* Abram. As a result, blessing would continue for generations (compare Exodus 23:22).

God's choice was not to the exclusion and rejection of other people. The apostle Paul interpreted God's promise of blessing to apply also to people who expressed faith in Jesus Christ (see Romans 4; Galatians 3:7-9, 14). Further, this blessing included making salvation available to all people, regardless of ancestry, through Abram's seed (see 3:26-29).

As Abram followed God, he would be a witness of God's grace and mercy to the peoples of the world. As *all families of the earth* saw how Abram's descendants obeyed God and saw the blessings that resulted, they would want to follow the same God and *be blessed* themselves (Acts 3:25).

> **What Do You Think?**
> In what ways has God provided blessings for you?
> **Digging Deeper**
> How might believers live in a way that blesses their unbelieving family and friends?

B. Abram's Response (vv. 4-5)

4. So Abram departed, as the LORD had spoken unto him; and Lot went with him: and Abram was seventy and five years old when he departed out of Haran.

One might expect *Abram* to have discussed the issue with God or provided pushback. (Compare Abraham's discussion with God regarding Sodom's pending judgment, Genesis 18:16-33.)

But there is no record that Abram did so. He obeyed and *departed out of Haran*. Abram showed faith trusted that God would not renounce His promises.

By allowing *Lot* to go *with him*, Abram acted honorably (see Genesis 11:27-28). Given this act, combined with Abram's advanced age (*seventy and five years old*) and his childless reality (11:30), one might expect the promised blessing to come through Lot. However, that was not the case (see 17:19). Lot would cause great difficulty and heartache for Abram (see 13:2-13; 14:1-16).

> **What Do You Think?**
> How can believers ensure their obedience to God's commands?
> **Digging Deeper**
> What is the connection, if any, between obedience to God and resulting blessing from Him?

5. And Abram took Sarai his wife, and Lot his brother's son, and all their substance that they had gathered, and the souls that they had gotten in Haran; and they went forth to go into the land of Canaan; and into the land of Canaan they came.

While God called *Abram* specifically, the call apparently included more than him alone. Thus we see him taking his wealth (Genesis 13:2) and extended household on the trip.

Abram's journey *into the land of Canaan* brought the travelers to Moreh of Sichem (Genesis 12:6, not in our printed text). This region would become a significant place for Abram's descendants (see 35:4; Joshua 24:25). Its importance among Abram's descendants resulted from his obedience.

C. God's Declaration, Part 2 (v. 7)

7a. And the LORD appeared unto Abram.

Abram's obedience brought him to a new land and to a new interaction with *the Lord*. Several other times he experienced God's self-disclosure (see Genesis 17:1; 18:1). Other patriarchs had similar experiences (see 26:2; 35:1; 46:2; 48:3). The means by which God appeared is not the most important aspect. Instead, most important is His desire to reveal and the content of His words.

7b. And said, Unto thy seed will I give this land.

The content of God's declaration reveals a new aspect of the previously given promises. The manner through which Abram would become "a great nation" (Genesis 12:2, above) would be through his descendants (his *seed*) and *this land* of Canaan. These two are often mentioned in discussion of God's promises to His Old Testament people (see Genesis 13:15; 15:18; 17:8; 24:7; 48:4; Exodus 32:13; 33:1; etc.).

7c. And there builded he an altar unto the LORD, who appeared unto him.

Abram's act of building *an altar* in response to God's words was of significance. Other cultures built altars to their pagan gods (see Deuteronomy 12:2-3). But Abram did not reuse a pagan altar.

Instead, Abram built a new altar to *the Lord*. By doing so, Abram announced the focus of his worship to the one true God. This altar served as a tangible reminder of God's faithfulness and presence (compare Genesis 8:18-20; 13:14-18; 35:7; Exodus 17:15; 24:3-4; etc.).

> **What Do You Think?**
> How can believers tangibly remember and celebrate God's work?
>
> **Digging Deeper**
> How might Exodus 20:8-11; 31:12-18; Joshua 4; and 1 Corinthians 11:23-25 provide believers with examples of tangible remembrance?

II. The Call Affirmed
(Genesis 15:1-7)

A. Protection Pledged (v. 1)

1. After these things the word of the LORD came unto Abram in a vision, saying, Fear not, Abram: I am thy shield, and thy exceeding great reward.

Abram's first interactions in the land were challenging. For a time, Abram and Lot lived separately (Genesis 13:10-18). Eventually, the two were reunited when Abram saved Lot from captivity

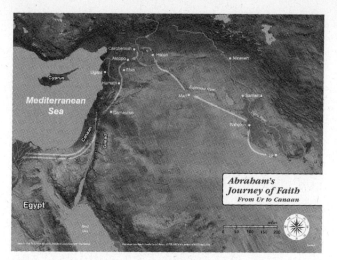

Visual for Lesson 1. *Show this map as you teach on the locations, events, and people of the first unit of lessons.*

(14:11-16). Additionally, Abram met with a mysterious king and offered him a tithe (14:18-20; Hebrews 7:1-10). It was *after these things* that God appeared again to Abram.

The underlying Hebrew translated here as *vision* occurs only three other times in the Old Testament. The word's stress is not necessarily on the revelation's visual component, but that a specific utterance from God had arrived (see Numbers 24:4, 16).

It was the vision's content that was most important for Abram. That God promised to be Abram's *shield* is indicative of His care and protection for His people (see Deuteronomy 33:29; 2 Samuel 22:3, 31; Psalms 3:3; 28:7; 84:11; 115:9-11). In a dangerous new land, Abram could take comfort in God's protection.

During an encounter with the king of Sodom, Abram refused riches and financial gain from the king (Genesis 14:22-24). Abram did not want to depend on the wealth of others. Instead, he trusted that the Lord himself would be an *exceeding great reward*.

"But Jesus Is with You!"

"Come see this really cool thing!" I heard my 8-year-old implore his 4-year-old brother. The older son is frequently afraid to go upstairs by himself. He often comes up with creative ruses to entice his younger brother to accompany him up the stairs. Most of the time the ruses work, and the younger brother happily complies.

However, if my older son revealed his fear, the younger son would answer, "But Jesus is with you!" The 4-year-old is unwavering on this point. He explains he isn't afraid because "Jesus is with me!"

Our youngest seems to grasp the truth of God's exhortation to Abram: "Fear not" (Genesis 15:1). What are you most afraid of right now? Can you say with confidence "Jesus is with me"—and let Him be your shield?   —N. G.

B. Challenge Offered (vv. 2-3)

2. And Abram said, Lord GOD, what wilt thou give me, seeing I go childless, and the steward of my house is this Eliezer of Damascus?

For the first time, we have a record of *Abram* responding directly to the *Lord God*. The response was filled with concern. God's promises would not come to fruition unless Abram had a child of his own. His words reflected an awareness of the Lord's promise to make of him "a great nation" (Genesis 12:2). Yet at this point Abram remained *childless*, and his wife was past the age of child-bearing (see 12:4; 17:17). How could God truly be Abram's "exceeding great reward" (15:1) under these circumstances?

The steward . . . Eliezer may have joined the journey during travel from Haran to Canaan (Genesis 12:4-5) since *Damascus* is situated between the two locations.

The act of transferring the heir's rights to the steward of Abram's *house* would have been a last resort to ensure Abram's legacy. The transference of an heir's blessing from a firstborn to another person was not unusual in the narrative of Abram's descendants (see Genesis 25:31-33; 48:13-14; 49:3-4).

3. And Abram said, Behold, to me thou hast given no seed: and, lo, one born in my house is mine heir.

Ancient adoption practices allowed for a childless couple to adopt another man as household servant or steward. This person would then care for the couple in their old age and provide a proper burial when they died. As a result, this person would then inherit the family property. This allowed for an *heir* and continuation of the family line.

Familial love and care, while possible, were not the primary reason for many ancient adoptions. Instead, this relationship was more like a business contract between adults. Considering the likelihood of this result, Abram vented his frustrations to God. How could the God who promised so much also provide *no seed* to Abram?

C. Promise Confirmed (vv. 4-5)

4. And, behold, the word of the LORD came unto him, saying, This shall not be thine heir; but he that shall come forth out of thine own bowels shall be thine heir.

In response to Abram's frustration, *the Lord* spoke to him with assurance. God's promises would not be diverted—*this* man, Eliezer, would *not* become Abram's *heir*. God declared that a child from Abram's *own bowels* would instead be his heir. When God makes a promise, He will keep it, although its fulfillment may not align with earthly expectations. This heir would be the first of many "children of promise" (see Galatians 4:28).

5. And he brought him forth abroad, and said, Look now toward heaven, and tell the stars, if thou be able to number them: and he said unto him, So shall thy seed be.

God had previously compared the number of Abram's descendants to "the dust of the earth" (Genesis 13:16). The numerous *stars* in the sky also served to illustrate God's promise. The assertion that Abram's descendants would be as numerous as the stars is one of the most prevalent promises in Scripture (see Genesis 22:17; 26:4; Exodus 32:13; Deuteronomy 1:10; 10:22; 28:62; 1 Chronicles 27:23; Nehemiah 9:23; Hebrews 11:12).

God did not dismiss Abram's frustration, nor did He give an explanation. Instead, God merely reaffirmed His promises. If God had kept His promises thus far, Abram could trust that God would keep His promises in full.

D. Righteousness Reckoned (vv. 6-7)
6a. And he believed in the LORD.

That Abram *believed* did not simply mean he felt good about his relationship with God. Rather Abram demonstrated faith when he trusted that these promises would come to pass; he trusted in the guarantor of those promises. Abram knew what his descendants would someday find out: *the Lord* is faithful and keeps His promises (Deuteronomy 7:9).

6b. And he counted it to him for righteousness.

Abram's belief did not go unnoticed—it would become the model for all others (see Hebrews 11:8-10, 12). His belief led to his being *counted . . . for righteousness*—being viewed in right standing with God.

Because God's own nature is righteous and perfect (see Deuteronomy 32:4; Psalm 103:6, 17; Zephaniah 3:5; Zechariah 8:8; etc.), He desires that His people be righteous as well. They could live righteously and justly, with God and with others, as they did "that which is lawful and right" (Ezekiel 18:5).

The text utilizes an accounting metaphor: God counted Abram's faith as the foundation for righteousness. The underlying Hebrew verb gets at the idea of regarding something or someone as having a certain characteristic, although that thing or person may not actually have that characteristic (compare Genesis 31:15; Numbers 18:27; Job 18:3; Proverbs 17:28; etc.). Abram's faith was enough for God to consider Abram in right standing with Him.

For the apostle Paul, this verse provided background on the nature of salvation. As righteousness came to Abraham (Abram's later name) through his faith, all people who follow his example and demonstrate faith will be counted as righteous (Romans 4:1-8, 13-15, 22). People who demonstrate faith in God are considered "children of Abraham" (Galatians 3:7) regardless of their ancestry (3:8-9).

The apostle James furthers the narrative regarding the faith of Abram. Not only was he counted righteous, but he was also called "the Friend of God" (James 2:23). His words and deeds exhibited the presence of his faith.

What Do You Think?
What is the relationship between belief and right action (see James 2:14-24)?
Digging Deeper
How would you explain righteousness to a person unfamiliar with Scripture?

7. And he said unto him, I am the LORD that brought thee out of Ur of the Chaldees, to give thee this land to inherit it.

The Lord brought Abram from his homeland in *Ur* to the *land* that He promised. Abram could be encouraged because the one who would declare himself "*I am*" (Exodus 3:14) was guiding him.

Conclusion
A. Abram Answered. Will You?

Abram had to answer a difficult call with boldness, courage, and faith. God had placed the call, and Abram answered by way of relocating his family. This decision would radically change his life and the lives of others for centuries.

There will be times in the life of a believer when the challenge is not to *find* God's will but to *follow* God's call. This call may lead to a different job, a new neighborhood, or even to an unknown land. Yet if we remain faithful to God and trust in His steadfast promises, He will bless us deeply.

B. Prayer

God, throughout history You have shown yourself to be faithful. Give us faith to follow Your call and patience to trust You. In Jesus' name. Amen.

C. Thought to Remember

God calls us—we only need to follow His directions!

Visuals FOR THESE LESSONS

The visual pictured in each lesson (example: page 13) is a small reproduction of a large, full-color poster included in the *Adult Resources* packet for the Fall Quarter. Order No. 1629122 from your supplier.

Involvement Learning

Enhance your lesson with KJV Bible Student (from your curriculum supplier) and the reproducible activity page (at www.standardlesson.com or in the back of the KJV Standard Lesson Commentary Deluxe Edition).

Into the Lesson

Begin class by saying, "You have been faced with a call and offered a prestigious job. How will you answer?" Instruct participants to give a thumbs-up sign if they would accept or a thumbs-down sign if they would decline.

Continue adding conditions to the job offer: "You will have to move away from family and friends." "You can expect to work an average of 65 hours a week." "You will be 100 percent vested in company stock options at the beginning of the job." After stating each condition, allow time for students to give a thumbs-up or thumbs-down sign.

After the activity ask for volunteers to discuss why they accepted or declined the call and what conditions affected their decision in this regard. Transition to Bible study by saying, "In today's lesson we will see how God placed a call on the life of Abram. The conditions of God's call required life-changing decisions from Abram."

Into the Word

Divide the class into three groups, giving each group a handout (you prepare) according to the following: **Nation Group:** Genesis 12:1-2; 15:1 / **Blessing Group:** Genesis 12:3-4; 15:2-4 / **Provision Group:** Genesis 12:5, 7; 15:5-7.

Ask the group to read their assigned Scripture passages and answer the following questions: 1–Identify the promise(s) that God made to Abram. 2–How did God fulfill the promise(s) during Abram's life? 3–How would the fulfilled promise(s) affect Abram's descendants? 4–How would the fulfilled promise(s) affect the world?

After 10 minutes, reconvene the class and have a volunteer from each group read their responses.

Transition to the second part of the activity by saying, "God's promises and Abram's responses were seen as important by the New Testament writers. Let's see how the apostle Paul and the author of Hebrews refer to the events of today's lesson."

Have students remain in the same groups as before, and assign one of the following New Testament passages to each group: Romans 4:1-5; Galatians 3:6-9; Hebrews 11:8-12.

Have each group answer the following questions on a handout that you prepare beforehand: 1–What promise does the New Testament passage highlight? 2–How does the New Testament writer interpret God's promise(s)? 3–How does the New Testament writer interpret Abram's (Abraham's) response(s)?

After 10 minutes have a volunteer from each group read the group's responses for each question.

Alternative. Distribute copies of the "God's Promises Fulfilled" exercise from the activity page, which you can download. Have students work in pairs to complete the activity as indicated. After 10 minutes, ask volunteers to share their conclusions.

After either activity, make the transition to Into Life by saying, "The narrative of Abram can inform us greatly regarding obedience and emboldened faith. The next practice will demonstrate how today's Scripture passage is more than a good story for us to read."

Into Life

Write two headers on the board: "Abram" and "Us." Through whole-class discussion, have students work together to make a list under the "Abram" header regarding how Abram lived in obedience, faith, trust, and right action regarding the commands of God. Through the same discussion model, have students work together to make a list under the "Us" header of how believers might live in obedience, faith, trust, and right action regarding the commands of God. These answers should be based on Scripture and personal testimony.

Alternative. Distribute copies of the "Emboldened and Obedient" activity from the activity page. Have learners complete the activity individually in a minute.

God Chooses the Younger Twin

Devotional Reading: Psalm 75
Background Scripture: Genesis 25:19-34

Genesis 25:19b-34

19b Abraham begat Isaac:

20 And Isaac was forty years old when he took Rebekah to wife, the daughter of Bethuel the Syrian of Padanaram, the sister to Laban the Syrian.

21 And Isaac intreated the LORD for his wife, because she was barren: and the LORD was intreated of him, and Rebekah his wife conceived.

22 And the children struggled together within her; and she said, If it be so, why am I thus? And she went to enquire of the LORD.

23 And the LORD said unto her, Two nations are in thy womb, and two manner of people shall be separated from thy bowels; and the one people shall be stronger than the other people; and the elder shall serve the younger.

24 And when her days to be delivered were fulfilled, behold, there were twins in her womb.

25 And the first came out red, all over like an hairy garment; and they called his name Esau.

26 And after that came his brother out, and his hand took hold on Esau's heel; and his name was called Jacob: and Isaac was three-score years old when she bare them.

27 And the boys grew: and Esau was a cunning hunter, a man of the field; and Jacob was a plain man, dwelling in tents.

28 And Isaac loved Esau, because he did eat of his venison: but Rebekah loved Jacob.

29 And Jacob sod pottage: and Esau came from the field, and he was faint:

30 And Esau said to Jacob, Feed me, I pray thee, with that same red pottage; for I am faint: therefore was his name called Edom.

31 And Jacob said, Sell me this day thy birthright.

32 And Esau said, Behold, I am at the point to die: and what profit shall this birthright do to me?

33 And Jacob said, Swear to me this day; and he sware unto him: and he sold his birthright unto Jacob.

34 Then Jacob gave Esau bread and pottage of lentiles; and he did eat and drink, and rose up, and went his way: thus Esau despised his birthright.

Key Text

The LORD said unto her, Two nations are in thy womb, and two manner of people shall be separated from thy bowels; and the one people shall be stronger than the other people; and the elder shall serve the younger.
—Genesis 25:23

God's Exceptional Choice

Unit 1: God Calls Abraham's Family
Lessons 1–4

Lesson Aims

After participating in this lesson, each learner will be able to:

1. Summarize the account and result of Rebekah's pregnancy.

2. Contrast the motives of Jacob and Esau.

3. Identify a character quality to demonstrate this week in handling a conflict.

Lesson Outline

Introduction

A. Unhappy in Its Own Way

A popular English translation of Leo Tolstoy's novel *Anna Karenina* begins with the following observation: "Happy families are all alike; every unhappy family is unhappy in its own way." The statement highlights an important concept for the novel: numerous factors might affect a family's relationship and well-being. Any of these factors might go awry and lead to a family's dysfunction.

From my experience ministering to families, I have seen Tolstoy's generalization lived out. I have seen that a family's happiness correlates to its levels of commitment, love, and respect for one another.

Conversely, I have seen that unhappy families experience turmoil in a variety of ways: bad attitudes, unfaithfulness, favoritism, anger, and addiction. Regardless of what may have caused the families to experience these things, the negative effects were noticeable.

God is at work, even in unhappy families. This week's lesson introduces us to a family that experienced strife and conflict. As a result, the direction of whole nations would forever be affected.

B. Lesson Context

The second half of Genesis introduces audiences to Abraham (originally known as Abram) and his family line. God promised that this family would be the way by which He would bless the world (Genesis 12:1-3; see lesson 1). Despite Abraham and Sarah's fertility issues and their advanced age (11:30; 12:4), God provided them with a son, Isaac (21:1-7).

However, Abraham would have other sons by other women. Hagar, a servant of wife Sarah, gave birth to Ishmael (Genesis 16:1-4, 15-16). After Sarah died, Abraham took another wife, Keturah, who bore him other sons (25:1-2). However, Abraham held Isaac in the highest regard (25:5-6). Isaac eventually married Rebekah (24:67). Together they settled in the southern part of Canaan, near the Sinai Peninsula (25:11; see 16:14).

Throughout Genesis, family lines and the concept of generations serve as transition points in the text. For original audiences, these served as markers for moments of great significance, and each marked a new focus in the narrative (see Genesis 5; 6:9-10; 11:10-27; 25:12-18).

The underlying Hebrew word translated as "generations" (Genesis 5:1; 6:9; 10:1, 32; 11:10; etc.) reminds audiences to focus their attention on the upcoming narrative and the individuals depicted. This lesson focuses on "the generations of Isaac, Abraham's son" (25:19a).

I. Unexpected Declaration
(Genesis 25:19b-23)
A. Two Generations (vv. 19b-22)
19b. Abraham begat Isaac.

God had promised *Abraham* that he would become "a great nation" (Genesis 12:2) with numerous descendants (15:5). The fulfillment of this promise seemed impossible. However, God was gracious to the couple, and He fulfilled His promise: Sarah gave birth to *Isaac* (21:2-3).

20. And Isaac was forty years old when he took Rebekah to wife, the daughter of Bethuel the Syrian of Padanaram, the sister to Laban the Syrian.

Abraham sent a servant to his ancestral homeland, Mesopotamia, to find a *wife* for *Isaac* (Genesis 24:1-10). At *forty years old*, Isaac might be considered an elderly bachelor. However, considering the marriage practices of the era (compare 26:34) and his eventual length of life (35:28), his seemingly advanced marital age was likely not uncommon.

Rebekah, the daughter of Abraham's nephew *Bethuel* (Genesis 22:20-23; 24:15), was chosen to marry Isaac. Her family—especially her brother *Laban*—would be important for Abraham's descendants (see 29:10-12; 30:25–31:55).

The region of *Padanaram* was in northwest Mesopotamia. One of the principal cities of the region was Haran, the place where Abraham (as Abram) began his journey (Genesis 12:4; see lesson 1). As this was the patriarch's ancestral homeland, Padanaram serves as a critical location in the family's narrative (see 28:1-7; 31:18; 35:9).

The repetition of the title *Syrian* differentiated Rebekah's family from neighboring Canaanite families (see also Genesis 31:20, 24; compare Deu-

teronomy 26:5). Abraham considered Canaanite women inappropriate for Isaac to marry (Genesis 24:1-4; compare 27:46–28:2).

21a. And Isaac intreated the LORD for his wife, because she was barren.

Although a suitable *wife* for *Isaac* was found, that was no guarantee regarding the continuation of the family line. Infertility had also affected Isaac's mother, Sarah (Genesis 11:30). Both generations had to depend on God's power in order to conceive.

Just as his father had done years before (see Genesis 15:1-4), Isaac *intreated the Lord* through prayer. Unlike other women in the Old Testament, there is no record of Rebekah's approaching the Lord in prayer regarding her infertility (compare 30:22; 1 Samuel 1:10-11).

All That's Humanly Possible

My heart broke as a I heard my friends describe their trials. They desired children of their own, but they were unable to conceive. They conferred with doctors and specialists, costing the couple time and money. After many failed attempts to conceive, the couple determined that they had done all that was humanly possible. They placed their struggle in God's hands and would await His answer.

This couple is not alone in their struggles to conceive. You probably know several couples who are facing struggles regarding fertility and conception, whether you realize their struggles or not!

When Rebekah faced fertility challenges, Isaac approached God in prayer. Do you pray for the couples in your life who face fertility struggles? More broadly, how do you pray for the invisible struggles that others experience?   —C. R. B.

> **What Do You Think?**
> How can churches support families who may be dealing with infertility?
>
> **Digging Deeper**
> How can your church be sensitive to the experiences of childless adults among your congregation?

21b. And the LORD was intreated of him, and Rebekah his wife conceived.

However, Isaac's prayers were answered as *the*

Lord was intreated of him (compare Judges 13:8-9). That *Rebekah . . . conceived* highlighted God's work in doing what people might consider impossible.

22. And the children struggled together within her; and she said, If it be so, why am I thus? And she went to enquire of the LORD.

The underlying Hebrew word translated *struggled* is fairly common in the Old Testament, but its rare construction in this verse alludes to conflict that is more intense than ordinarily expected. Rebekah's physical distress was more than would be anticipated by a pregnant woman; something deeper and more serious was at hand.

Hagar experienced a divine interaction during her pregnancy (see Genesis 16:7-14). That interaction provided her with hope and encouragement. Perhaps Rebekah was trying *to enquire of the Lord* and experience the same kind of comfort that Hagar received.

B. Two Nations (v. 23)

23a. And the LORD said unto her, Two nations are in thy womb, and two manner of people shall be separated from thy bowels; and the one people shall be stronger than the other people.

The Lord's response set up future conflict between Rebekah's children (see Genesis 27). The internal conflict she experienced would someday continue outside her *womb* as her children would become *two nations*. God was not necessarily addressing the conflict that would immediately occur, but conflict between the *people* of their descendants (see commentary on 25:30, below).

The text does not immediately describe how the two people groups would come from her two unborn children. *The Lord* was not directing Rebekah regarding her future parenting practices. Further, the text is not describing a form of divine predeterminism by which people have no role and responsibility. Instead, God was describing the future realities of generations and thereby reinforcing the promise that Abraham would "be a father of many nations" (Genesis 17:4).

23b. And the elder shall serve the younger.

Primogeniture—the right or inheritance of the firstborn—was a crucial element of the ancient Near East's social and legal systems (see Genesis 27:19; Deuteronomy 21:15-17). Rebekah, along with the text's original audience, would have anticipated that her first child would receive greater status and acclaim than the second child.

However, the Lord overturned those expectations. Rebekah's *elder* child would not receive the expected firstborn blessing. Instead, the blessing would be given to (actually, taken by) *the younger* child (compare Genesis 17:18-21; 49:3-4).

God did not provide details regarding the younger child's acquisition of power. God's intentions will come to pass, regardless of human structures (see 1 Corinthians 1:27-31). He transforms broken situations because His ways are superior to ours (see Isaiah 55:8-9). As a result, humans are to respond to Him in love and faith (see Deuteronomy 7:7-9; John 3:16-18; Ephesians 1:3-14).

The apostle Paul elaborates on today's text in Romans 9:10-12. The significance of this text for Paul was that God chose the younger child (Jacob) before he was even born. God's purpose for the world resulted in His call of Jacob as the individual through whom God's promises would be fulfilled.

> **What Do You Think?**
> What prayers are appropriate for a parent to say for their quarreling children?
>
> **Digging Deeper**
> What prayers are appropriate for a believer to say for parents who may be dealing with quarrelsome children?

II. Undeniable Differences
(Genesis 25:24-28)
A. Physically (vv. 24-26)

24-25. And when her days to be delivered were fulfilled, behold, there were twins in her womb. And the first came out red, all over like an hairy garment; and they called his name Esau.

Scripture describes instances when a child's name indicated something about the parents' relationship with God (see 1 Samuel 1:20; 4:21) or the circumstances surrounding the child's birth (see Genesis 35:18). The naming of Rebekah's *twins* reflected similar practice.

The *name Esau* reflected a physical attribute of the *first* child: his skin, hair, or both appeared *red*. The pronunciation of this underlying Hebrew word sounds similar to another name given to Esau (see commentary on Genesis 25:30, below). This Hebrew word was also used to describe David's "ruddy" health (1 Samuel 16:12; see lesson 9). Esau's *hairy* physique would become key in how he would lose his firstborn blessing (see Genesis 27:11).

26a. And after that came his brother out, and his hand took hold on Esau's heel; and his name was called Jacob.

The name of Esau's *brother* also demonstrates wordplay and foreshadowing. The underlying Hebrew word for *Jacob* has multiple connections. It is related to a verb concerning the act of grasping—either for protection or restraining movement, like using a *hand* to take *hold* of something (see Hosea 12:3). Another similar sounding Hebrew verb describes fraud or trickery (see Jeremiah 9:4). Later texts would describe how Jacob demonstrated the latter sense (see Genesis 27:35-36).

Further, Jacob's name has similarities to the Hebrew word for "heel," thus relating his name to his actions during his birth. Jacob's act of grabbing *Esau's heel* during birth foreshadows future dealings between the brothers and Jacob's interactions with others—Jacob would be shrewd and cunning as he took what he desired.

26b. And Isaac was threescore years old when she bare them.

That *Isaac* was *threescore years old* (that is, age 60) highlights the 20 year period that the couple had to wait before having children (see Genesis 25:20). This time was reminiscent of the long wait Isaac's parents endured before his own birth (see 21:5). God was faithful to this family, even if His timing was not what they desired or expected.

B. Personality (vv. 27-28)

27a. And the boys grew: and Esau was a cunning hunter, a man of the field.

The brothers' differences became apparent as *the boys grew* up. In a nomadic culture, having a family member serve as a *hunter* was important for the family's livelihood (compare Genesis 10:8-

9). That he was *cunning* alluded to his knowledge of the land: the surrounding *field* and its resources (see 27:3, 5). Considering his perception, pulling a fast one on Esau would be difficult—or so one might think.

27b. And Jacob was a plain man, dwelling in tents.

One meaning of the Hebrew word translated here as *plain* describes a guiltless and upright person who was not liable for wrongdoing (see references to Job in Job 1:1, 8; 2:3). Its usage regarding Jacob was an ironic descriptor, considering that his future actions were anything but guiltless.

In contrast to his outdoorsman brother, Jacob preferred to live a life *dwelling in* the *tents* of the home camp. As a result, he may have had a propensity for administration, an aptitude later demonstrated by his son Joseph (see Genesis 39:4, 22-23; 41:33-40, 46-49).

28. And Isaac loved Esau, because he did eat of his venison: but Rebekah loved Jacob.

The favoritism demonstrated in that each parent *loved* a particular son would be repeated years later by *Jacob* (renamed Israel; Genesis 37:3-4). Isaac's love for *Esau* and his hunting would be a factor in how Jacob and *Rebekah* plotted against Esau and *Isaac* regarding the father's blessing (see 27:2-13).

What Do You Think?
How can parents avoid showing favoritism toward one of their children?

Digging Deeper
What practices ensure that believers do not show favoritism in their congregations?

Family Feud?

When you think of the title above, the first image that may come to mind is that of the long-running TV game show of the same name. And while that show is all in good fun, some bitter rivalries between families, such as that of the Hatfields and the McCoys in the nineteenth century, exist. Those two families spent decades in violent conflict.

But that was an *interfamily* feud, while the text

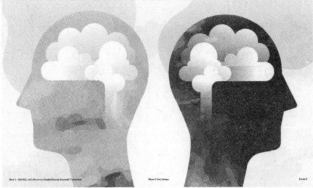

JACOB VS ESAU:
A POWER STRUGGLE FROM THE WOMB

Visual for Lesson 2. *Show this visual as you ask the class what part of God's words in Genesis 25:23 is most surprising.*

at hand presents us with an *intrafamily* rivalry. The distinction is important because causes, effects, and dynamics are often quite different. As an example, feuds *between* families are usually overt—highly visible. Feuds *within* families, on the other hand, are often hidden from public view as individuals maneuver against one another in subtle ways to form or destroy alliances. Parental favoritism magnifies the problem.

Do you see yourself in any of this? If your answer is no, would you be willing to check for blind spots by asking others if they agree with your self-assessment?   —C. R. B.

III. Unruly Disregard
(Genesis 25:29-34)
A. Desperate (vv. 29-32)

29. And Jacob sod pottage: and Esau came from the field, and he was faint.

That *Jacob sod pottage* implied that he was preparing a stew. The stew might have consisted of herbs, vegetables, and lentils (see Genesis 25:34, below; compare 2 Kings 4:38-40).

This encounter might have occurred at a shepherding camp where the brothers tended livestock. That *Esau* was an outdoorsman made it natural for him to go out into *the field*. This left Jacob to manage the chores around camp, including meal preparation. As a result of Esau's hard work, he felt *faint* with exhaustion (compare Judges 8:5).

30. And Esau said to Jacob, Feed me, I pray thee, with that same red pottage; for I am faint: therefore was his name called Edom.

Esau's pleading made him appear impulsive as he focused on immediate physical concerns. His request to *feed me, I pray* could be read as exasperated begging. Instead of making a level-headed request, Esau sounded like a beggar.

The Hebrew word translated here as *red* was used to describe Esau at his birth (see commentary on Genesis 25:25, above). An alternative *name* for Esau sounded similar: *Edom* (see 36:1, 8, 19).

Esau's descendants were the Edomites (Genesis 36:9, 43). They would eventually settle in the region of Seir (Deuteronomy 2:22), southeast of the Dead Sea. During the era when kings ruled Israel, a constant state of tension and frequent warfare existed between the Edomites and the Israelites (see 1 Samuel 14:47; 1 Kings 11:14). As a result, God's promise to Rebekah regarding her sons (Genesis 25:23b, above) came to pass. The descendants of her older son would serve the descendants of her younger son (see 2 Samuel 8:14; 2 Kings 14:1, 7).

31. And Jacob said, Sell me this day thy birthright.

In contrast to Esau's desperate pleading, *Jacob* is portrayed as opportunistic and manipulative. It is unknown whether Rebekah revealed to him the nature of God's promises. But what is certain is that Jacob drove a hard bargain. This was an expensive bowl of soup—it would cost Esau the rights that only a firstborn would enjoy.

The firstborn's *birthright* would include a double portion of the father's estate (Deuteronomy 21:15-17). Isaac was a wealthy man (Genesis 26:12-14), therefore the birthright would have been sizable.

> **What Do You Think?**
> What things might believers consider to be their "birthright" that may instead hinder their relationship with God?
>
> **Digging Deeper**
> How might these things affect relationships among believers?

32. And Esau said, Behold, I am at the point

to die: and what profit shall this birthright do to me?

Esau was driven by his physical urges. It is doubtful that he was *at the point to die*. Surely someone known as "a cunning hunter" (Genesis 25:27) would have been better prepared for hunger! His desire for immediate gratification led him to disregard the most important earthly thing that was his to lose: his *birthright*.

The writer of Hebrews depicts Esau's attitude and action here as "profane" (Hebrews 12:16-17). Esau was so focused on immediate *profit* and pleasure that he gave up lifelong blessing.

B. Despised (vv. 33-34)

33. And Jacob said, Swear to me this day; and he sware unto him: and he sold his birthright unto Jacob.

Jacob made the deal permanent by having Esau *swear* an oath. Esau risked divine judgment, should he later try to deny or break the agreement.

The act of swearing an oath or vow was not uncommon. Abraham swore that he would deal truthfully and kindly with Abimelech and his descendants (Genesis 21:22-24). Additionally, Abraham's servant swore that he would not procure a wife for Isaac from among the Canaanites (24:3-9). These vows were irrevocable and would result in a curse if broken (see Nehemiah 10:29). While God allowed for His people to take oaths and vows, He had certain stipulations (see Numbers 30).

> **What Do You Think?**
> How should believers consider the practice of swearing an oath?
>
> **Digging Deeper**
> How might Leviticus 19:12; Matthew 5:33-37; James 5:12; and Revelation 10:5-6 inform your answer?

34. Then Jacob gave Esau bread and pottage of lentiles; and he did eat and drink, and rose up, and went his way: thus Esau despised his birthright.

Following the oath, the exasperated *Esau* received his temporary relief—*bread and pottage of lentiles*. However, the shrewd *Jacob* received per-

manent blessing—the transferred *birthright*. The older brother would continue to be at the mercy of his younger brother (see Genesis 27).

Conclusion

A. Unworthy but Chosen

Readers should be unimpressed with the attitudes and actions of the individuals described in this lesson. Isaac and Rebekah each favored one of their sons over the other. Esau desired immediate relief over long-term benefits. Jacob schemed and manipulated his brother for personal gain. A story that began with God's love and power transitions into a story of people pursuing selfish interests.

However, we need not idealize any one human character, because the Lord is the protagonist of this story. He alone can make good out of less than ideal circumstances and less than ideal people (see Romans 8:28; compare Genesis 50:20).

God worked through this deeply flawed family, and He will work in the lives of all people whom He has called. People of God should not strive to force His hand. Instead, we should trust that His plans and purposes will be fulfilled, regardless of any attempts to circumvent or force those plans.

B. Prayer

Father, we celebrate that You have chosen to work through us. Thank You for Your faithfulness to us, even when we fail to live holy lives. Prepare us so that we can live out Your purposes. In Jesus' name. Amen.

C. Thought to Remember

God's plans will be fulfilled, either through or despite your efforts.

How to Say It

Abimelech	Uh-**bim**-eh-lek.
Bethuel	Beh-*thew*-el.
Keturah	Keh-*too*-ruh.
Laban	*Lay*-bun.
Padanaram	*Pay*-dan-a-ram.
Seir	*See*-ir.
Syrian	*Sear*-ee-un.

Involvement Learning

Enhance your lesson with KJV Bible Student *(from your curriculum supplier) and the reproducible activity page (at www.standardlesson.com or in the back of the* KJV Standard Lesson Commentary Deluxe Edition*).*

Into the Lesson

On the board write, "I would _____ for _____." Explain that the first blank will be filled in with an extreme action, while the second blank will be filled in with a favorite food. (For example: "I would swim an icy river for my mother's apple pie.")

Instruct all students to complete their own version of this phrase on a slip of paper that you will provide. After one minute, have students pass their slips to you. Randomly select one slip and read it aloud. Invite the class to guess the author. Have the author indicate when the group guesses correctly.

After this activity, lead into Bible study by saying, "In today's story, notice what each character desires and what they do to fulfill that desire."

Into the Word

Ask a volunteer to read aloud Genesis 25:19b-23. Divide the class into two groups: **Isaac Group** and **Rebekah Group**. Instruct each group to create a character sketch of their namesake. The sketches could be written out or drawn (with supplies you provide). After no more than 10 minutes, have a representative from each group present their sketch to the class.

Alternative. Distribute copies of the "Get What You Want" exercise from the activity page, which you can download. Have learners work in small groups to complete rows 1 and 2.

Ask a volunteer to read aloud Genesis 25:24-28. Divide the class into two new groups: **Esau Group** and **Jacob Group**. Instruct each group to create a character sketch of their namesake. Just as before, the sketches could be drawn or written out. After no more than 10 minutes, have a representative from each group present their sketch to the class. Update the Isaac and Rebekah character sketches with any new characteristics or insights.

Ask the class, "How does God's reply to Rebekah in verse 23 seem to be playing out?" Allow for no more than three minutes of whole-class discussion.

Ask a volunteer to read aloud Genesis 25:29-34. Set up a debate about which brother was "right" regarding his actions. In the same groups as previously, have each group represent and defend their namesake. Encourage each group to develop two arguments and one example to reinforce their argument. Allow no more than 10 minutes for each group to prepare.

Give each group two minutes to make their case. Allow time for each group to give a rebuttal and response. Encourage friendly discussion, but step in if discussion becomes heated.

Afterward, have the class respond to these questions in whole-class discussion: 1–Were either of the brothers truly in the right? 2–Why or why not? 3–How did their selfish desires affect their actions?

Alternative. If groups completed rows 1 and 2 of the "Get What You Want" activity, have the same groups complete rows 3 and 4 now.

Into Life

Write on the board three headers: *Desires / Consequences / James 3:17-18*. Lead the class in brainstorming selfish desires and resulting negative consequences that may lead to conflict with others. Jot down responses in the appropriate column. If necessary, encourage students not to be too specific.

Have a volunteer read James 3:17-18 aloud. Have students use the qualities named in these verses to address the selfish desires and negative consequences listed on the board. Jot down responses in the final column.

Alternative. Distribute copies of "The Situation" activity from the activity page. Have learners complete it with a partner.

Close class with a prayer based on Psalm 75, a psalm composed to provide reassurance of God's victory. Begin the prayer by reading verse 1 aloud. Allow students to pray silently regarding the conflicts they may face, asking God for His wisdom. End the prayer by reading verse 9 aloud.

Jacob Called Israel

Devotional Reading: Romans 11:25-32
Background Scripture: Genesis 32:22-32

Genesis 32:22-32

22 And he rose up that night, and took his two wives, and his two womenservants, and his eleven sons, and passed over the ford Jabbok.

23 And he took them, and sent them over the brook, and sent over that he had.

24 And Jacob was left alone; and there wrestled a man with him until the breaking of the day.

25 And when he saw that he prevailed not against him, he touched the hollow of his

thigh; and the hollow of Jacob's thigh was out of joint, as he wrestled with him.

26 And he said, Let me go, for the day breaketh. And he said, I will not let thee go, except thou bless me.

27 And he said unto him, What is thy name? And he said, Jacob.

28 And he said, Thy name shall be called no more Jacob, but Israel: for as a prince hast thou power with God and with men, and hast prevailed.

29 And Jacob asked him, and said, Tell me, I pray thee, thy name. And he said, Wherefore is it that thou dost ask after my name? And he blessed him there.

30 And Jacob called the name of the place Peniel: for I have seen God face to face, and my life is preserved.

31 And as he passed over Penuel the sun rose upon him, and he halted upon his thigh.

32 Therefore the children of Israel eat not of the sinew which shrank, which is upon the hollow of the thigh, unto this day: because he touched the hollow of Jacob's thigh in the sinew that shrank.

Key Text

He said, Thy name shall be called no more Jacob, but Israel: for as a prince hast thou power with God and with men, and hast prevailed. **—Genesis 32:28**

God's Exceptional Choice

Unit 1: God Calls Abraham's Family
Lessons 1–4

Lesson Aims

After participating in this lesson, each learner will be able to:

1. Recount the reason for Jacob's trip.
2. Explain the text's focus on names.
3. List attitudes and actions of Jacob to emulate and to avoid.

Lesson Outline

Introduction

A. Defining Struggle

The image of Jacob wrestling under the night sky with a mysterious individual has captivated thinkers, artists, and writers through the centuries. The sheer number of artistic endeavors that depict this event speaks to the text's influence. Renaissance painters and modern alternative musicians have all used this event from Scripture to inform their art.

However, Jacob's struggle is more than a provocative backdrop for creating art. Nor is Jacob's struggle merely a stand-in for the battle between good and evil. Instead, the struggle would define Jacob and his descendants.

B. Lesson Context

Today's text comes from the larger set of narratives regarding Isaac's son Jacob and his conflicts with others. Jacob's struggle with his brother Esau began at their birth (Genesis 25:26, lesson 2). Their conflict became more intense by Jacob's scheming (and meal preparation) when he acquired his brother's birthright (25:29-34). Later Jacob tricked his father into giving him the blessing set aside for firstborn Esau (27:6-36). Jacob's scheming destroyed his relationship with Esau; Jacob was "hated" and threatened by his brother (27:41). In response, Jacob fled to the household of his uncle Laban (28:5).

Jacob worked seven years for his uncle to gain the hand of Laban's daughter Rachel in marriage (Genesis 29:18). However, Laban required that Jacob first marry Leah, leading Jacob to another seven years in service to marry Rachel (29:26-27).

Jacob flourished during his time in Laban's land, but the relationship between the two men soured (Genesis 31:2). This was due to Jacob's perception of unfair treatment regarding his payment from Laban (31:6-7). In response, Jacob and his wives took all that they owned and left Laban's household in secret (31:17-21). Ultimately, Laban confronted Jacob and the two agreed to a covenant (31:44). Jacob's struggle with his uncle had subsided.

Today's text comes as a part of Jacob's preparation to meet his brother. If Jacob returned to the land promised by God, then he would have to be on good terms with Esau. Jacob initiated contact by sending messengers to request grace from Esau (Genesis 32:5). Esau responded with a promise to appear—along with 400 of his men (32:6).

This response brought fear and distress to Jacob. It would appear that the time had come for Esau's threats to be fulfilled. Jacob responded with alarm: he divided his camp (Genesis 32:7-8), prepared gifts for Esau (32:13-20), and approached God in prayer (32:9-12). Jacob's fear was understandable; God had promised him descendants (28:14). An enraged Esau would likely not only kill Jacob but also Jacob's household. Jacob, known for his scheming ways, openly admitted fear of someone else's scheme.

Throughout his life, Jacob's clever planning had generally paid off in his favor, often to the detriment of others. A mysterious struggle would now define Jacob in unimaginable ways.

I. The Struggle
(Genesis 32:22-25)

A. Jacob's Situation (vv. 22-23)

22. And he rose up that night, and took his two wives, and his two womenservants, and his eleven sons, and passed over the ford Jabbok.

That Jacob *rose up* to travel during the *night* could indicate that he desired secrecy regarding his movements. Esau might have been made aware of Jacob's presence (see Genesis 32:20). As a result, Jacob may not have wanted his exact movements to be noticed. Nomadic travelers in the desert, similar to Jacob and his household, may have preferred to travel during the cool of the night.

While unnamed here, Jacob's *two wives* were Leah (Genesis 29:21-23) and Rachel (29:28). Jacob also had *two womenservants* turned surrogate wives: Bilhah (30:4) and Zilpah (30:9). At this point in his life, the four women had given him a total of *eleven sons*. Another son (Benjamin) would later be born to Rachel (35:16-18), giving Jacob a total of 12 sons (35:22b-26, see lesson 4).

The text does not mention Jacob's daughter, Dinah (Genesis 30:21). While she was likely present with the family at this time (34:1), her exclusion from the narrative could be because she did not participate in the night expedition *over the ford Jabbok.*

The Jabbok is identified as an eastern tributary of the Jordan River. The river served as a boundary for non-Israelite kingdoms (see Numbers 21:24; Deuteronomy 2:37; Joshua 12:2) and Jacob's descendants (see Deuteronomy 3:16).

23. And he took them, and sent them over the brook, and sent over that he had.

By sending his wives, servants, and children *over the brook*, Jacob planned for their protection. He was concerned that his upcoming interaction with his brother would prove to be dangerous for his family (see Lesson Context).

B. Jacob's Injury (vv. 24-25)

24. And Jacob was left alone; and there wrestled a man with him until the breaking of the day.

As the night progressed, *Jacob* prepared to meet his brother. Scripture describes instances when God spoke to His people in their solitary moments (see Exodus 24:2; Daniel 10:8). Though Jacob's family had left, he was anything but *alone* in the night.

Out of the night's stillness, a figure who appeared as *a man* approached Jacob. This occurrence is an example of a theophany, a specific appearance or manifestation of God to humanity. Some theophanies consisted of what appeared to be God in human form (see Genesis 18; Exodus 24:10; 33:11, 18-23; etc.). However, other theophanies demonstrated God's self-disclosure through non-human manifestations (see Exodus 3:2; 19:18; Numbers 22:28; etc.). These events confirmed a person's relationship with God and provided confidence of His work (see Genesis 16:13; Exodus 4:10-12; Numbers 22:22; Joshua 5:15; Judges 6:16-17).

This appearance consisted of more than

How to Say It

Bilhah	*Bill*-ha.
Elohim *(Hebrew)*	El-o-*heem*.
Jabbok	*Jab*-uck.
Peniel	Peh-*nye*-el.
theophany	the-*ah*-fuh-nee.
Zilpah	*Zil*-pa.

dialogue. Instead, a skirmish between Jacob and the so-called man resulted. The pronunciation of the Hebrew word translated as *wrestled* sounds similar to the pronunciations of the Hebrew words for Jabbok and Jacob. The repetition of sounds would have been evident to original audiences and would have reminded them that Jacob jostled at the Jabbok!

A Nocturnal Struggle

At my family's encouragement, I scheduled an appointment with my doctor regarding a possible case of sleep apnea. The doctor questioned my sleeping and breathing habits and put me through a variety of tests. The results proved my family's concern—I suffered from sleep apnea. The doctor suggested that I begin using a breathing device known as a CPAP machine when I slept.

The device delivers pressurized air through a mask fitted over the nose or mouth. The first night I used the device, the mask triggered a sense of claustrophobia in me. The second night was worse. While dreaming that I was using the mask incorrectly and that my doctor was trying to communicate with me, I struggled with the actual mask and ripped it off.

Jacob struggled throughout his life—with his brother and with God. These struggles came to a head as Jacob jostled at the Jabbok. What life struggles are affecting your relationships? Have you made plans to resolve those issues?   —C. R. B.

25. And when he saw that he prevailed not against him, he touched the hollow of his thigh; and the hollow of Jacob's thigh was out of joint, as he wrestled with him.

Jacob had reason to be confident in his physical strength. He had spent 20 years in hard service to his uncle (Genesis 31:38-41; compare 29:2, 10). The mysterious man *saw* Jacob's strength firsthand and *prevailed not against* him. This was no ordinary wrestling match; each wrestler was unable to gain an edge over the other!

However, Jacob suffered an injury when his assailant *touched* him. Win or lose, this experience affected Jacob's body. That the injury occurred after the assailant could not gain an upper hand might emphasize a level of equal physical ability between the two, or that the man was holding back for Jacob's sake.

The exact nature of Jacob's injury is unclear because the underlying Hebrew words are difficult to translate. The word translated *thigh* could refer to a person's side (Exodus 32:27) or upper leg (28:42; Judges 3:16, 21). It could also refer to procreation or descendants (see Genesis 46:26; Exodus 1:5). The *hollow* region would describe the part that joins with another part of the body.

The severity of Jacob's injury is unclear. This is one of only four times in three passages where the Hebrew verb translated as *out of joint* is used in this particular manner. The other uses speak to God's Spirit departing (Jeremiah 6:8) and to the alienation experienced by Jerusalem at the hands of the Babylonians (Ezekiel 23:17-18). While the exact details of Jacob's injury are unclear, his hip separated in a way not intended for a hip to move.

II. The Debate
(Genesis 32:26-29)
A. Dual Demands (v. 26)

26a. And he said, Let me go, for the day breaketh.

Despite striking a blow to Jacob, the assailant demanded that Jacob *let* him *go*. That *the day breaketh* gives insight on the duration of the struggle—the night had passed without resolution. Perhaps the assailant was concerned that dawn would reveal his identity, to the detriment of Jacob (compare Exodus 33:20; Judges 13:22).

26b. And he said, I will not let thee go, except thou bless me.

Risking further injury, Jacob would *let* his assailant *go* only on one condition. Jacob held on and made a certain demand—he wanted something he was not entitled to receive (compare Genesis 25:29-34; 27:35-36; see lesson 2).

Jacob's demand does not provide further detail regarding the reason or nature of the request. Perhaps Jacob desired divine blessing as he prepared for his upcoming interaction with his estranged brother. Or perhaps Jacob desired confirmation of the viability of God's promises (see Genesis 28:13-14). The scheming Jacob again sought to swing things in his favor.

B. Different Designation (vv. 27-28)

27. And he said unto him, What is thy name? And he said, Jacob.

Names in the Bible often reveal insight on a person's character (1 Samuel 25:25; compare Proverbs 22:1) or their characteristics (Genesis 25:25; Luke 8:30). Names can even describe the situations surrounding a person's birth (Genesis 41:51-52; Exodus 2:22; 1 Samuel 1:20; 4:21; 1 Chronicles 4:9). That the mysterious man asked for Jacob's *name* forced Jacob to reveal an insight regarding his nature (see below). In this instance, Jacob answered honestly (contrast Genesis 27:19).

The underlying Hebrew for the name *Jacob* sounds like a Hebrew verb for the act of grasping (see Genesis 25:26, see lesson 2). The pronunciation was also similar to a Hebrew word regarding acts of deception (27:35-36; see Jeremiah 9:4). Both descriptors were fitting for Jacob.

28a. And he said, Thy name shall be called no more Jacob, but Israel.

In Scripture, the change of a person's name signaled a personal change for that person (Genesis 17:5, 15; 2 Kings 24:17; Acts 13:9; compare Isaiah 62:2). *No more* would *Jacob* be known as a deceiver who grasped for personal gain. Abra-

ham's descendant, a recipient of God's covenant promises, received a new name.

The meaning of Jacob's new name, *Israel*, reflects his life of struggle. The *el* syllable found in the Hebrew language is often used as a referent to the Hebrew word *Elohim*, a name for the God of Israel. (This is the underlying word for God in Genesis 1.) When that syllable is found in Hebrew names, it speaks to something regarding God. For example, the name "Bethel" (Genesis 35:15) means "house of God"; the name "Elimelech" (Ruth 1:1-2) means "God is my king"; the name "Ishmael" means "heard by God" (Genesis 16:11).

Jacob's renaming also gives us insight into the poetic passages where both names are used. Such dual usage indicates parallelism, where one thought is expressed in two ways (examples: Psalms 22:23; 78:21; Isaiah 10:20; Jeremiah 2:4; Micah 3:1).

28b. For as a prince hast thou power with God and with men, and hast prevailed.

The Hebrew word used to indicate a struggle of *power* (see also Hosea 12:3-4) sounds very similar to the first two syllables of Jacob's new name. Jacob's new name reflected his struggles in life—*with God and with men*. Like a powerful *prince*, Jacob had found and would find success in both contexts. Even so, the proclamation did not condone his methods (see Genesis 27:23-33).

The declaration that Jacob *prevailed* serves as a bit of foreshadowing. Jacob had not yet found favor in his brother's eyes. The success that Jacob found in this wrestling match was the preface to a successful reunion with his brother.

What's in a Name?

Your family name may give insight into the possible occupation of a distant relative who had

CHOOSE YOUR OPPONENTS WISELY!

Visual for Lesson 3. *Start a discussion by pointing to this visual as you ask, "Was Jacob in the right to ask his opponent for a blessing?"*

the same name. A person named Smith may have a blacksmith in their ancestry. Or a person named Cooper may have descended from a person who repaired wooden casks or barrels. However, names are not always indicative of present realities. For example, I may be named Boatman, but I have never owned a boat!

Jacob was known as a trickster who took advantage of others through deception. His name was appropriate (see lesson 2). However, Jacob was given a new name and the possibility of a new legacy. Would he be known for his scheming ways or for his relationship with the Lord? What legacy would you like future generations to recall when they consider your name? —C. R. B.

C. Divine Delight (v. 29)

29. And Jacob asked him, and said, Tell me, I pray thee, thy name. And he said, Wherefore is it that thou dost ask after my name? And he blessed him there.

Jacob desired a more intimate knowledge of God. However, this was not the time for God to self-disclose more fully (compare Exodus 3:14; 6:3). The mysterious figure scolded Jacob for asking his *name*. Instead, the figure *blessed* Jacob in that moment. This would not be the only time Jacob would experience a blessing from God (see Genesis 35:9; 48:3).

Centuries later, Manoah, the father of Samson, had a similar divine interaction and requested the

name of the mysterious figure (Judges 13:9-17). In response, the figure declared that his name was "secret" (13:18; translated "too wonderful" in Psalm 139:6).

III. The Results
(Genesis 32:30-32)
A. Protected at Peniel (v. 30)

30. And Jacob called the name of the place Peniel: for I have seen God face to face, and my life is preserved.

Jacob recognized the significance of the night's events. In the struggle, he had encountered and *seen God*. Very few individuals could claim to see God *face to face*. However, this expression did not necessarily indicate a physical face-to-face interaction with God (see Exodus 33:20; compare John 1:18). Instead, the expression was an idiom to speak to the intimacy of the experience (see Exodus 33:11; Numbers 14:14; Deuteronomy 5:4; 34:10).

The prophet Hosea described this "man" (Genesis 32:24, above) as an "angel" (Hosea 12:4). This interpretation alludes to the sense of mystery experienced during divine interactions. However, Jacob's declaration indicates that he saw this mysterious assailant as more than a man or an angel.

If a particular location was spiritually meaningful for the people of God, a significant name was provided for that location (see Genesis 22:13-14; 28:18-19; 35:15). The name Jacob gave this location reflected the relational closeness of his experience. The Hebrew word *Peniel* means "the face of God." The exact location of Peniel is unknown, but it can be assumed to be east of the Jordan River.

This is the only mention of Peniel in the Old Testament. However, the variation "Penuel" (Genesis 32:31, below) likely referred to the same location. In the era of the judges (about 1370–1050 BC), this location served as a critical juncture in the narrative of Gideon (see Judges 8:5-9, 17). Jeroboam I, king of Israel (reigned 921–910 BC), would later rebuild the city (1 Kings 12:25).

Dual meanings are possible regarding Jacob's declaration on the status of his *life*. On the one hand, Jacob could have been reflecting on his survival despite believing he had seen the face of God (compare Judges 6:22-23; 13:22).

On the other hand, Jacob could have been proclaiming an answered prayer. Previously, Jacob requested that God rescue him from his brother Esau (Genesis 32:11). The underlying Hebrew root for this request is used again when Jacob proclaimed this his life was *preserved* (compare 33:10). Jacob could trust that the rescue he desired would come to pass because he had been blessed by God.

What Do You Think?

What feelings arise when you think about seeing God face-to-face one day?

Digging Deeper

How might 2 Corinthians 3:18 and 1 John 3:19-24 describe the transformed life of a follower of Jesus?

B. Remembered by Relatives (vv. 31-32)

31. And as he passed over Penuel the sun rose upon him, and he halted upon his thigh.

The turning of a new day as *the sun rose upon him* marked newness surrounding Jacob: his name and his physical affliction. As Jacob left *Penuel* (see commentary on 32:30, above), his walk was *halted* as he limped. The injury he suffered to *his thigh* during the night continued to affect him. Perhaps the injury stayed with Jacob for the rest of his life, a permanent reminder of his interaction with God.

What Do You Think?

How should believers respond to a mental or physical ailment for which healing doesn't seem to have occurred?

Digging Deeper

How might Psalm 41:3; 2 Corinthians 4:7-12; 12:6-10; and Revelation 21:4 inform your answer in this regard?

32. Therefore the children of Israel eat not of the sinew which shrank, which is upon the hollow of the thigh, unto this day: because he touched the hollow of Jacob's thigh in the sinew that shrank.

An editorial comment clarifies the significance of Jacob's injury for future generations of *the children of Israel*. A sinew is a tendon, a connective tissue that joins bone and muscle (see Job 10:11; Ezekiel 37:8). Later Jewish tradition interprets the *sinew which shrank* as the sciatic nerve that runs through the muscles of the hip and into the upper *thigh*. The command *eat not of* this body part is not found elsewhere in Scripture. However, the prohibition is found in later Jewish commentary. The dietary practices of Jacob's descendants bore witness to his encounter that night.

Conclusion
A. The Clenched Hand of Prayer

English poet Christina Georgina Rossetti (1830–1894) used the example of Jacob's struggle in her poem "Alas My Lord." Rossetti interpreted Jacob's struggle as a demonstration of "the clenched hand of prayer" that she desired her readers to practice. The poem concludes with a petition to the Lord "to hold Thee fast, until we hear Thy Voice" and "see Thy Face."

We may be tempted to judge Jacob's stubbornness because of our familiarity with his story. However, we can admit that we need "the clenched hand of prayer" to sustain us during our struggles. God is present—we only need to open our eyes.

Jacob's struggle humbled him and gave him a new identity before God and man. When we struggle—spiritually or physically—our faithfulness to God will point others to Him. He is the one who can give true rest (see Matthew 11:28).

B. Prayer

O God of Jacob, You are present in our struggles. We ask that You use those moments to reveal yourself to us in a unique way. We want to better understand Your will and direction and follow it in our lives. In Jesus' name. Amen.

C. Thought to Remember

Despite the darkness and amid our struggles, God is present.

Involvement Learning

Enhance your lesson with KJV Bible Student *(from your curriculum supplier) and the reproducible activity page (at www.standardlesson.com or in the back of the* KJV Standard Lesson Commentary Deluxe Edition*).*

Into the Lesson

Ask for volunteers to participate in a thumb wrestling contest. Set clear rules. For example, before the match begins, both contestants must chant "one, two, three four, I declare a thumb war." A contest is over when one contestant's thumb is pinned by the other contestant's thumb. Match up men against men and women against women. Pair the winners of the first round with other winners, continuing until a class champion is declared.

Alternative. Ask volunteers to share a decision or situation they have "wrestled with" during the past week. Invite them to share how they held on to God in the middle of the struggle.

After either activity, say, "We all struggle with difficult thoughts, feelings, and actions. Through today's Scripture text, we will consider our struggles, who or what we struggle against, and what we stand to lose or gain in the struggle."

Into the Word

Explain the background for today's lesson using material from the Lesson Context section. If possible, recruit a class member ahead of time to present a three-minute lecture based on this material to set the stage for today's Bible study.

Announce a Bible-marking activity. Provide copies of Genesis 32:22-32 for those who do not want to write in their own Bibles. Provide handouts (you create) with these instructions:

- Underline each statement of Jacob.
- Double-underline every descriptor of Jacob and his situation.
- Draw a circle around every mention of the names Jacob, Israel, and Peniel/Penuel.
- Draw a question mark above any word or phrase that you find difficult to understand.

Read the Scripture aloud slowly (or ask volunteers to do so) at least twice and as many as four times. As the Scripture is read, class members are to mark their copies in the ways noted.

After the final reading, divide class members into three groups for class discussion. Have groups answer the following questions that you will write on the board: 1–What do these verses tell us about who Jacob is? 2–Why do you think Jacob demanded a blessing? 3–What is the meaning and significance of the names Jacob, Israel, and Peniel/Penuel? (Students might need to access lesson commentary, study Bible notes, or online resources to answer adequately.)

After 10 minutes, have a representative from each group provide a response to each question. Finally, ask volunteers to share what they found helpful, challenging, or confusing from the text.

Option. Distribute copies of the "What's in a Name?" exercise from the activity page, which you can download. Have learners work in pairs to complete as indicated. After 10 minutes, provide the correct answers for the class and ask volunteers to share their answers to the final three questions.

Into Life

Place students in pairs and ask them to share a struggle they have experienced, how they dealt with the struggle, and how they experienced God's presence in the struggle. Have each pair list Jacob's attitudes and actions as described in the lesson and whether those should be emulated or avoided. Have each student consider how the experience of their own struggle might differ if they were to follow Jacob's actions.

Encourage pairs to consider how to apply Jacob's imitation-worthy actions to a struggle they are currently facing. Ask pairs to pray together, praising God for His presence and asking Him for perseverance, faithfulness, and submission through current struggles.

Option. Distribute copies of the "Count Your Blessings" exercise from the activity page as a take-home. To encourage completion, promise to discuss the results at the beginning of the next class.

The Scepter Given to Judah

Devotional Reading: Numbers 24:2-9, 15-17
Background Scripture: Genesis 35:22b-26; 38:12-19, 24-26; 49:8-12

Genesis 35:22b-26

22b Now the sons of Jacob were twelve:

23 The sons of Leah; Reuben, Jacob's first-born, and Simeon, and Levi, and Judah, and Issachar, and Zebulun:

24 The sons of Rachel; Joseph, and Benjamin:

25 And the sons of Bilhah, Rachel's handmaid; Dan, and Naphtali.

26 And the sons of Zilpah, Leah's handmaid; Gad, and Asher: these are the sons of Jacob, which were born to him in Padanaram.

Genesis 38:24-26

24 And it came to pass about three months after, that it was told Judah, saying, Tamar thy daughter in law hath played the harlot; and also, behold, she is with child by whoredom. And Judah said, Bring her forth, and let her be burnt.

25 When she was brought forth, she sent to her father in law, saying, By the man, whose these are, am I with child: and she said, Discern, I pray thee, whose are these, the signet, and bracelets, and staff.

26 And Judah acknowledged them, and said, She hath been more righteous than I; because that I gave her not to Shelah my son. And he knew her again no more.

Genesis 49:10-12

10 The sceptre shall not depart from Judah, nor a lawgiver from between his feet, until Shiloh come; and unto him shall the gathering of the people be.

11 Binding his foal unto the vine, and his ass's colt unto the choice vine; he washed his garments in wine, and his clothes in the blood of grapes:

12 His eyes shall be red with wine, and his teeth white with milk.

Key Text

The sceptre shall not depart from Judah, nor a lawgiver from between his feet, until Shiloh come; and unto him shall the gathering of the people be. —**Genesis 49:10**

Photo © Getty Images

God's Exceptional Choice

Unit 1: God Call's Abraham's Family
Lessons 1–4

Lesson Aims

After participating in this lesson, each learner will be able to:

1. Summarize the structure of Jacob's family.

2. Explain the connections among the three sections of the lesson text.

3. State a way to overcome a family dysfunction for increased service to the Lord.

Lesson Outline

Introduction

A. The Royal House

Eight European monarchs trace their lineage back to one man: George II (1683–1760), king of Great Britain and Ireland. Over the course of 300 years, his descendants intermarried with other European royals, and a complicated web of family relations resulted. Now the monarchs of eight European countries—the United Kingdom, the Netherlands, Spain, Sweden, Norway, Denmark, Monaco, and Luxembourg—claim a common ancestor.

In the modern era, a monarch's power is largely ceremonial. However, this week's lesson introduces a common ancestor to a royal genealogy, who still reigns in power and has forever changed the course of history.

B. Lesson Context

At the beginning of the patriarchal narratives in Genesis, God promised to make Abraham "a father of many nations" (Genesis 17:5). From these descendants God declared that "kings shall come" (17:6; see 17:16, 20).

However, situations regarding offspring (see Genesis 16:1; 18:13; 30:1) and family conflict (see 16:4-5; 25:19-34; 27:1-41) arose. These situations might have led Abraham's family to doubt God's promises. Yet God remained faithful, even repeating His promises (see 35:11).

Abraham's grandson Jacob fathered 12 sons; the descendants of these sons became the tribes of Israel. Scripture provides two primary methods of counting the tribes. The first method lists tribes with an inheritance of land (see Numbers 1:5-15; 2:3-32; Joshua 13–19). Under this method, Joseph's sons (Manasseh and Ephraim) were counted as tribes. The descendants of Levi were not included in this numbering of the 12 tribes since they were not to receive an inheritance of land (13:33).

The second method lists tribes by the name of each tribe's patriarch (Genesis 46:8-25; 49:3-27; Deuteronomy 27:12-14; 1 Chronicles 2:2). Under this method, the descendants of Manasseh and Ephraim were instead listed as the tribe of Joseph. Through Jacob's family, God's promise of royalty would come. He would choose neither Jacob's oldest son (Reuben) nor his favorite son (Benjamin) to be the ancestor of the royal line. Rather, out of Judah would come an eternal kingdom.

I. Jacob's Family
(Genesis 35:22b-26)
A. Twelve Sons (vv. 22b)

22b. Now the sons of Jacob were twelve.

God had promised *Jacob* (also known as Israel; lesson 3) that his descendants would be like "the dust of the earth" (Genesis 28:14) and "the sand of the sea" (32:12). The existence of Jacob's *twelve* sons (and their offspring) displayed God's faithfulness to fulfill these promises.

B. Four Mothers (vv. 23-26a)

23. The sons of Leah; Reuben, Jacob's firstborn, and Simeon, and Levi, and Judah, and Issachar, and Zebulun.

The listing of Jacob's 12 sons here is not in overall birth order. Instead, the sons are listed from oldest to youngest according to their respective mothers.

Although *Leah* was Jacob's first wife, he had not intended to marry her (Genesis 29:23-26). Despite her numerous *sons*, Leah never experienced the love from Jacob that her sister received (29:30).

The scandalous behavior of *Reuben* (Genesis 35:22) caused him to lose the *firstborn* privilege (49:3-4). His descendants would never rise to the same level of importance as would the descendants of his brothers.

Simeon and *Levi* fell out of their father's favor because of their violence (Genesis 49:5). Upon hearing of profane treatment toward their sister, the brothers had responded with violence (34:25). Jacob was concerned that their actions would cause him to experience poor treatment by the surrounding nations (34:30).

Judah would rise to a position of leadership among his brothers (Genesis 37:25-28; 44:14-18; 46:28). While Judah acted unrighteously at times (see Genesis 38), he was uniquely blessed (49:8-12).

Issachar was conceived during a unique situation involving the use of mandrakes (see Genesis 30:15-18), a plant with seemingly aphrodisiac properties.

Warriors of the tribe of *Zebulun* fought valiantly in the days of the judges (see Judges 4:6; 6:35).

24. The sons of Rachel; Joseph, and Benjamin.

Jacob's love for *Rachel* was unparalleled (Genesis 29:30). God miraculously worked to allow her to conceive *Joseph* (30:22-24).

The favor that Joseph experienced from his father led his brothers to hate him (Genesis 37:3-4). They would sell him for 20 pieces of silver (37:28). Due to the wisdom God granted him, Joseph rose to a position of leadership in Egypt (41:39-41). In this situation, he was prepared to deal with a famine—for the good of the whole known world, including his family (42:1-2).

Jacob blessed Joseph's sons, Ephraim and Manasseh, as his own (Genesis 48:5). The descendants of these sons would later be counted as tribes of Israel (Numbers 1:32-35, see Lesson Context).

As the youngest son of Rachel, *Benjamin* received extra concern from his father (see Genesis 42:4). Though Benjamin's descendants were relatively few in number (see Numbers 1:36), Israel's first king came from them (1 Samuel 9:21).

25. And the sons of Bilhah, Rachel's handmaid; Dan, and Naphtali.

When Rachel was unable to conceive, she gave *Bilhah* to Jacob to bear him children (Genesis 30:4). Rachel named Bilhah's first child *Dan* (30:6). His descendents, though many in number (see Numbers 1:39; 2:26), were not powerful militarily (see Joshua 19:47; Judges 1:34-35).

Descendants of *Naphtali* were lauded for their valor (Judges 5:18). They joined with descendants

How to Say It

Bilhah	*Bill*-ha.
Ephraim	*Ee*-fray-im.
Ephrath	*Ef*-rath.
Gad	*Gad* (a as in *bad*).
Issachar	*Izz*-uh-kar.
Manasseh	Muh-*nass*-uh.
Naphtali	*Naf*-tuh-lye.
Shiloh	*Shy*-low.
Tamar	*Tay*-mer.
Zebulun	*Zeb*-you-lun.
Zilpah	*Zil*-pa.

of Asher and Manasseh to drive the Midianites from the land (7:23-25).

26a. And the sons of Zilpah, Leah's handmaid; Gad, and Asher.

When Leah was unable to conceive, she allowed Jacob to continue fathering children, through *Zilpah* (Genesis 30:9).

The descendants of *Gad* settled east of the Jordan River (Numbers 32:1-33; Joshua 13:8). This land was well suited for raising livestock.

Jacob proclaimed the richness of the food produced by *Asher* (Genesis 49:20). Perhaps this declaration foreshadowed the tribe's settlement of the fertile regions of Canaan (Joshua 19:24-31).

What Do You Think?

How have previous generations of believers informed and influenced your spiritual growth?

Digging Deeper

What steps will you take to influence future generations of believers so that they might spiritually grow and mature?

C. One Father (v. 26b)

26b. These are the sons of Jacob, which were born to him in Padanaram.

Not all *sons of Jacob* were *born* in *Padanaram*; Benjamin was born in Ephrath, which is Bethlehem (Genesis 35:16-19). Perhaps the inclusion of Padanaram referred to the location where Benjamin was conceived (compare 35:9).

Judging Ancestors

Through DNA testing and online records, exploring one's ancestry has become quite accessible. One family member traced our family's ancestry back to slave owners in the American South. Despite my disgust, I am unable to change who my ancestors are.

Scripture's genealogies always list people who erred—look at Jacob's family! We would not consider many of their actions to be admirable. God still used them for His plan. Their lives are evidence of God's faithfulness. Will future generations see that *you* were following God?   —C. R. B.

II. Judah's Humbling

(Genesis 38:24-26)

The oldest of Judah's sons, Er, married Tamar. However, Er acted wickedly and was struck dead (Genesis 38:6-7). Judah directed his second son to father children with Tamar (38:8). But that son refused and was also killed (38:10).

With two sons dead, Judah sent Tamar to live with her father while waiting for Judah's third son to reach the age of marriage. This placed the marginalized widow in a grievous situation. She had no husband or son to care for her. Years passed, but Judah did not allow his daughter-in-law to marry his third son (Genesis 38:14b).

Tamar took matters into her own hands: she would have a child with her father-in-law. Tamar disguised herself and went to a location where Judah would see her. Judah failed to recognize her and considered her to be a prostitute (Genesis 38:13-16). Before they had intercourse, she requested from him a pledge to confirm his promised payment (38:17a). After he provided these things, Tamar became pregnant by him (38:17b-18).

A. Tamar's Situation (v. 24)

24a. And it came to pass about three months after, that it was told Judah, saying, Tamar thy daughter in law hath played the harlot; and also, behold, she is with child by whoredom.

Judah had sent a friend to take back his pledge (see above), but the woman could not be found (Genesis 38:22). *Three months* would *pass* before Judah would discover her identity.

Though *Tamar* lived in her father's household, *Judah* still claimed her as a part of his family. As long as his third son was alive, Judah would take an interest in her well-being, even if from a distance. Since she was widowed and lived in her father's house, there was no other way she could be *with child* except through immorality.

24b. And Judah said, Bring her forth, and let her be burnt.

Judah's judgment was striking and harsh. The Law of Moses did not exist during the time of Judah. It would later prescribe being *burnt* as a form of punishment (see Leviticus 20:14; 21:9).

Judah's declaration highlighted the horrific irony of the situation. He demanded capital punishment for his daughter-in-law because of her presumed prostitution. However, he was the one who had impregnated Tamar. Further, Judah might have considered Tamar's act to be one of unfaithfulness to his son Shelah, who was still next in line to be given as her husband (Genesis 38:11).

What Do You Think?

How can people respond fairly and in good time to an unjust situation?

Digging Deeper

How would your response differ if you or someone you loved was experiencing the unjust situation?

B. Tamar's Revelation (v. 25)

25. When she was brought forth, she sent to her father in law, saying, By the man, whose these are, am I with child: and she said, Discern, I pray thee, whose are these, the signet, and bracelets, and staff.

Tamar did not have to state publicly the extent of Judah's involvement. Instead, she forced *her father in law* to confront his hypocrisy and consider how he had failed to provide for her (see Genesis 38:14b). Tamar had no need to state the obvious. The personal items left behind would reveal *the man* who caused her to be *with child* (38:18).

A *signet* was an engraved stone that would leave a unique imprint when pressed on a surface (see Exodus 28:11). Signets were worn as rings (see Jeremiah 22:24; Daniel 6:17) or could have been on *bracelets* or chains around Jacob's neck. A *staff* was a necessary tool when working with herds. A staff's owner would sometimes be identified by an inscription on it (Numbers 17:2). Tamar's shrewdness revealed her intentions. She had requested and retained these items not because of their financial value, but because of their identifying capabilities.

C. Tamar's Righteousness (v. 26)

26. And Judah acknowledged them, and said, She hath been more righteous than I;

because that I gave her not to Shelah my son. And he knew her again no more.

The revealing of the personal items would have brought great shame on *Judah*. To his credit, he *acknowledged* the items and their implications regarding his own failures. Whether because of his own shame or to hide his immoral act, Judah turned the discussion to Tamar.

His statement that *she hath been more righteous than I* did not fully justify her. Rather, the statement indicated that Judah's behavior was relatively worse. He had acted unfaithfully and unjustly toward Tamar by preventing his son *Shelah* from marrying her (Genesis 38:1-14). He failed to care for his widowed daughter-in-law. Tamar was in the right to want Judah to honor his obligations. She desired just treatment and forced Judah's hand so that she would receive it. But that doesn't mean that the end justified the means.

That Judah *knew* Tamar *again no more* indicates that he had no further sexual relations with her. Tamar gave birth to sons (Genesis 38:29-30) who would continue the line of Judah (Ruth 4:12). Both Judah and Tamar were counted in a later genealogy of Jesus (Matthew 1:3).

What Do You Think?

How should a person respond when confronted with their unrighteous or sinful decisions?

Digging Deeper

How might confrontation differ when with believers (see Matthew 18:15-20)?

III. Judah's Ruler
(Genesis 49:10-12)

At the end of his life, Jacob called together his sons and described their future (Genesis 49:1-2). Much of what he stated would unfold when the descendants of his sons settled in the promised land centuries later.

Jacob's lengthy speech regarding Judah spoke to that son's preeminence. Judah's brothers would someday praise him and bow down to him (Genesis 49:8). Judah would become like a lion, bringing fear to those "who shall rouse him up"

Promised to Judah. Fulfilled by Jesus.

Visual for Lesson 4. *Have this visual displayed prominently as a backdrop as you discuss the Scripture passages in the Conclusion.*

(49:9). Jacob's words began by addressing Judah directly, but shifted to talk *about* Judah and his descendants.

A. The King's Reign (v. 10)

10. The sceptre shall not depart from Judah, nor a lawgiver from between his feet, until Shiloh come; and unto him shall the gathering of the people be.

Jacob's dying proclamation demonstrated his trust in the Lord's promise that kings would come from his descendants. A *sceptre* symbolized the presence of royalty and authority (see Esther 4:11; 5:2; Isaiah 14:5; Zechariah 10:11; Hebrews 1:8).

The declaration described Jacob's hope: a ruler would come from his descendants (see also Numbers 24:17, 19). Specifically, this ruler would come *from Judah* (1 Chronicles 5:2; compare Psalm 60:7). The ruler and His kingdom would be permanent and would *not depart*.

This prophesied individual would be in a position of leadership and authority—*a lawgiver* for the people. He would be so because God himself is the ultimate "lawgiver" (Isaiah 33:22; James 4:12).

The underlying Hebrew word translated here as *feet* is used elsewhere to refer indirectly to genitalia (Ezekiel 16:25) or the womb (Deuteronomy 28:57). The royal authority would come from Judah's offspring.

The phrase *until Shiloh come* provides unique translation challenges. A major reason for this comes from the fact that the original Hebrew text was written without vowels. Later scribes added notation in the text to indicate vowel sounds. Different vowel notations can result in different readings of the text.

One possible reading of the text includes a mention of the city Shiloh. The city was the location of the tabernacle (Joshua 18:1; contrast Psalm 78:60) and the place for key administrative decisions (Joshua 18:9-10; 19:51). Shiloh did not maintain importance during the era of the kings when the tribe of Judah would exhibit prominence.

However, a different vowel notation (and word break) leads to a different possible translation. The text could refer to the timing of the arrival of the royalty. The prophet Ezekiel alludes to this translation when proclaiming the rightful heir, following the destruction and exile of the tribe of Judah. The prophet proclaimed that the crown "shall be no more, until he come whose right it is" (Ezekiel 21:27).

Despite the translation difficulties, Jacob's prophetic intention is evident. *The people* of the nations would be impacted by Judah's descendant. This individual will gather people under His rule and require their obedience (compare Psalms 2:8-11; 72:8; Isaiah 11:10-12; Zechariah 9:10).

B. The King's Abundance (vv. 11-12)

11a. Binding his foal unto the vine, and his ass's colt unto the choice vine.

The king's abundance is on display through the imagery of grape *vine* and livestock (compare Deuteronomy 8:7-8). One can imagine that the king's abundance was so much that he would allow his *foal* and *colt* to be tied to the vine. Even if the animals ate some of the fruit of the vine, the loss would not have been an issue because of the king's bountiful and fertile crops.

11b. He washed his garments in wine, and his clothes in the blood of grapes.

The king's wealth would be on display because *wine* would be as common as laundry water for *his garments*. His winepresses would be full so that *his clothes* would be saturated in freshly pressed grape juice (compare Isaiah 63:2), *the blood of grapes* (compare Deuteronomy 32:14).

12. His eyes shall be red with wine, and his teeth white with milk.

Prosperity is further evident on the king's face. Some writers of Scripture attribute shades of *red*, like those seen in *wine* or rubies, to a person's physical vigor (example: Lamentations 4:7). *White* and straight *teeth* were a desirable physical trait (see Song of Solomon 4:2; 6:6).

> **What Do You Think?**
> How has God's abundance been demonstrated in your life?
>
> **Digging Deeper**
> What spiritual blessings have you experienced?

A Vision Fulfilled

Early in my career I felt called to lead a small Bible college. The college had an aging campus, a shrinking donor base, and a dated curriculum model. If the college could not attract new students, it would not survive. I spent five years leading the college, but found little success. I left the position convinced that someone else was needed for the college to flourish.

Years later the college had relocated, enrollment had increased, and a new curriculum had been established. My successor informed me that the plans made during my tenure had become the blueprint for his administration. The vision that God had given my administration had been fulfilled—just later than I had anticipated.

Generations after Jacob, God fulfilled His promise of a king. We may never understand in this life how God accomplishes His plans. We may sometimes doubt that they'll come to fruition when we don't see immediate results. Which of God's promises provide encouragement during moments of doubt?　　　　　—C. R. B.

Conclusion

A. Wrecks into Royals

Promises regarding the royal descendant of Judah were fulfilled in two ways. First, they were fulfilled through the Davidic monarchy. David, a descendant of Judah, ruled Israel in power given by God (see 2 Samuel 7:5-15).

David partially fulfilled the prophecy; his rule was a shadow of the royalty to come. The second way Judah's promises were fulfilled was through the promised eternal king (2 Samuel 7:13, 16; Jeremiah 33:17; see Psalm 45:6). The Old Testament prophets looked for "a rod out of the stem of Jesse" (Isaiah 11:1) who would gather all people (11:10-16). His rule would be one of peace and righteousness from the throne of David (9:7) and the tribe of Judah (Jeremiah 23:5-6; Micah 5:2).

The New Testament writers interpreted these promises to apply to Jesus (see Matthew 2:1-6; Luke 1:32; Hebrews 7:14). As king, Jesus would bring salvation to the world (Luke 2:29-32). His kingdom, inaugurated at His first coming, would be fulfilled in His second coming to earth (see Revelation 2:26-27; 5:5; 19:15).

Judah and his family were by no means ideal ancestors for royalty—they were marked by rivalry, strife, and dysfunction. Judah's life, in particular, was filled with unrighteous acts. He was a wreck and an unlikely choice to be the ancestor of royalty.

However, God's plan of redemption is transformative. He led a dysfunctional family to become the nation of Israel. From this family would emerge the Savior of the world. He turns wrecks into royals!

> **What Do You Think?**
> In what ways are this lesson's Scripture texts applicable to modern audiences?
>
> **Digging Deeper**
> How do the other lessons of this unit reinforce the main idea of this lesson's Scripture text?

B. Prayer

God of Jacob and Judah, we praise You for Your kingdom in Christ Jesus. Thank You for inviting us to partake in Your kingdom, despite our failures. Show us how we might live as citizens of Your kingdom. In the name of King Jesus we pray. Amen.

C. Thought to Remember

God transforms wrecks into royals!

Involvement Learning

Enhance your lesson with KJV Bible Student *(from your curriculum supplier) and the reproducible activity page (at www.standardlesson.com or in the back of the* KJV Standard Lesson Commentary Deluxe Edition*).*

Into the Lesson

In the week before class, ask three volunteers to bring an object to the next class. Tell volunteers that the object should be unique and meaningful to them and should represent something about their family identity.

At the beginning of class, have each volunteer showcase their object. They should explain it, how they attained it, and why it represents them.

After the volunteers share, say, "In today's lesson, Judah's possessions are used to bring shame—and honor—to him and his family."

Into the Word

Ask a volunteer to read aloud Genesis 35:22b-26. Divide the class into four groups: **Leah Group, Rachel Group, Bilhah Group,** and **Zilpah Group.** Have each group prepare a three-minute presentation regarding their group's namesake and her children. Have each group include details about the mother and her children, even details not mentioned in the lesson. Students can use study Bible notes and online resources to prepare.

After 10 minutes, have each group present their findings. Ask the groups to notice which sons they knew more about than the others.

Alternative. Distribute copies of the "Jacob's Family" exercise from the activity page, which you can download. Have learners work in pairs to complete as indicated.

In the same groups, have each student read Genesis 38:1-30 silently. Then ask a volunteer to reread aloud Genesis 38:24-26.

Have groups summarize the events of the chapter, then answer the following questions (which you will write on the board): 1–What actions of Judah were considered unjust? 2–Why was Tamar considered to be "more righteous" (Genesis 38:26)? 3–What are possible interpretations and applications of this story for modern audiences?

Ask a volunteer to read aloud Genesis 49:10-12.

Divide the class into three groups: **Scepter Group (49:10) / Vine Group (49:11) / Physical Traits Group (49:12).**

Have each group interpret the imagery in their assigned verse. Ask the groups to answer the following questions that you will write on the board: 1–To what could your group's verse be referring? 2–Have these things already been fulfilled? 3–How do the other verses inform your interpretation?

After five minutes, ask a volunteer to share their answers and respond to other groups in order to get a more complete understanding of Jacob's words.

Option. Distribute copies of the "Family Tree" activity from the activity page. Have learners complete it as indicated, in small groups. After no more than five minutes, ask for volunteers to share their group's insights from the discussion questions.

Into Life

Write these words on the board: *hide, deny, resign,* and *ignore.* Have students work in pairs to consider how these words might describe a family's response to conflict or dysfunction. (Encourage pairs to use anonymous examples.)

After five minutes, have students each write on a index card (you provide) a family conflict where peace and reconciliation are needed. Inform students to keep the index cards private.

After one minute, have pairs discuss how to respond to family conflict and dysfunction in a God-honoring manner. After three minutes, have students call out words that are opposite of the words on the board. Write those words on the board.

Have students each use one of the new words to write a response to the conflict or dysfunction written on their index card.

Invite students to use their cards during their prayer time in the coming week. Have students ask God to guide how they might work to overcome the family conflict written on their card.

The Birth of Moses

Devotional Reading: Acts 7:17-29
Background Scripture: Exodus 1:15–2:10

Exodus 2:1-10

1 And there went a man of the house of Levi, and took to wife a daughter of Levi.

2 And the woman conceived, and bare a son: and when she saw him that he was a goodly child, she hid him three months.

3 And when she could not longer hide him, she took for him an ark of bulrushes, and daubed it with slime and with pitch, and put the child therein; and she laid it in the flags by the river's brink.

4 And his sister stood afar off, to wit what would be done to him.

5 And the daughter of Pharaoh came down to wash herself at the river; and her maidens walked along by the river's side; and when she saw the ark among the flags, she sent her maid to fetch it.

6 And when she had opened it, she saw the child: and, behold, the babe wept. And she had compassion on him, and said, This is one of the Hebrews' children.

7 Then said his sister to Pharaoh's daughter, Shall I go and call to thee a nurse of the Hebrew women, that she may nurse the child for thee?

8 And Pharaoh's daughter said to her, Go. And the maid went and called the child's mother.

9 And Pharaoh's daughter said unto her, Take this child away, and nurse it for me, and I will give thee thy wages. And the woman took the child, and nursed it.

10 And the child grew, and she brought him unto Pharaoh's daughter, and he became her son. And she called his name Moses: and she said, Because I drew him out of the water.

Key Text

The woman conceived, and bare a son: and when she saw him that he was a goodly child, she hid him three months. —**Exodus 2:2**

God's Exceptional Choice

Unit 2: Out of Slavery to Nationhood
Lessons 5–9

Lesson Aims

After participating in this lesson, each learner will be able to:

1. Retell the account of Moses' infancy.

2. Explain how an injustice was avoided.

3. Make a concrete plan to act in response to an identified or potential injustice.

Lesson Outline

Introduction
   A. Operation Varsity Blues
   B. Lesson Context
I. Unique Response (Exodus 2:1-4)
   A. Hidden at Home (vv. 1-2)
   B. Sheltered in the Stream (vv. 3-4)
II. Unexpected Rescue (Exodus 2:5-10)
   A. Daughter's Discovery (vv. 5-6)
     The Power of Papyrus
   B. Sister's Suggestion (vv. 7-9)
     A Fish Out of Water
   C. Son's Significance (v. 10)
Conclusion
   A. Aggressive Compassion
   B. Prayer
   C. Thought to Remember

Introduction

A. Operation Varsity Blues

For many teenagers, the college admission process is the culmination of their many years of hard work. High school students spend years preparing in hopes of being accepted into their dream college or university. Entrance exams, scholarship essays, amateur athletic camps, and local community service all factor into the process, on top of a student's course load and GPA.

However, for other teenagers, the college admissions experience is all about their family's money and connections. In 2019, a scandal rocked the college admission world, revealing the ways that people were unjustly and illegally working the college admission process for their children. An FBI investigation—named Operation Varsity Blues—revealed that dozens of parents conspired to lie, bribe, and cheat in order to get their children into elite colleges and universities. By doing so, other students who had worked hard and earned their spot would be denied admission.

Evidence of life's injustices is all around us. When faced with these realities, the people of God are to respond with boldness and trust in the God who will, in His time, set injustices right

B. Lesson Context

Centuries before the events of this lesson's Scripture text, God had promised Abraham, a nomadic herdsman from Mesopotamia, that his descendants would be numerous (Genesis 15:5, see lesson 1). One such descendant, Joseph (25:24), was removed from his ancestral land and taken to Egypt. Through God's power and directives, Joseph ended up in a position of high regard in service to the Egyptian pharaoh (41:41-57).

Ultimately, Joseph brought his extended family to live with him in Egypt (Genesis 50:22; Exodus 1:1-5). His descendants would become the Israelites. Centuries later, they "were fruitful, and increased abundantly, and multiplied . . . and the land was filled with them" (1:7). God's promise of numerous descendants had become a reality.

Jacob's descendants would be in the land of Egypt for a total of 430 years (see Exodus 12:40).

Eventually, a new pharaoh came to power and was concerned regarding the growth of the Israelite population (1:8-10).

The exact identity of the pharaoh in question is unknown. The construction of cities "Pithom and Raamses" (Exodus 1:11) has led some scholars to estimate that the pharaoh in question was Rameses II (approx. 1290–1224 BC). He oversaw vast construction projects and kept numerous slaves, realities that align with the first chapters of Exodus.

However, Scripture describes how Solomon began construction on the temple 480 years after the Israelites left Egypt (1 Kings 6:1). This timing would place the exodus at approximately 1447 BC, outside of the reign of Rameses II (compare Exodus 12:40-41; Galatians 3:17). Specific details regarding the exact timing of the exodus and the pharaoh involved may never be recovered.

The pharaoh in question saw the growing presence of Israelites as a threat. To suppress their increase in number and to exert power over them, the pharaoh established hard labor for the Israelites and placed slave masters over them (Exodus 1:11-14). The pharaoh's oppressive treatment intensified in his declaration that "every son that is born ye shall cast into the river" (1:22).

Despite this oppression, God blessed Jacob's descendants. Because of the shrewdness of Hebrew women (see Exodus 1:15-20), more Hebrew boys survived infancy than the pharaoh intended. Today's Scripture text highlights the response of several women to the pharaoh's unjust declaration. A seemingly small event—the birth of a child and his upbringing—served as the way by which God provided a just response to an unjust situation.

I. Unique Response
(Exodus 2:1-4)

A. Hidden at Home (vv. 1-2)

1. And there went a man of the house of Levi, and took to wife a daughter of Levi.

A later genealogical account provides the names this *man* and his *wife*: Amram and Jochebed (Exodus 6:20). Both were from the lineage *of Levi* (see Numbers 26:57-59).

Moses: From Protected to Protector

Visual for Lesson 5. *Conclude the lesson by asking the class how Moses was both protected and a protector for God's people.*

After the people left Egypt, descendants of Levi would become priests (Exodus 28–30) and religious leaders (Deuteronomy 10:8-9) for the Israelites. This child would be in that same lineage.

2. And the woman conceived, and bare a son: and when she saw him that he was a goodly child, she hid him three months.

The survival of the woman's *son* would be in doubt, considering the cruel decree from the pharaoh (Exodus 1:22; see Lesson Context). The text before us does not speak to the birth order of this child. Later texts indicate the presence of an older brother, Aaron (7:7), and an older sister (2:4, below).

The description of the *child* as *goodly* could speak to a variety of attributes. The underlying Hebrew word is elsewhere translated as "good"—a descriptor of God's intentions in His creation (Genesis 1:4, 10, 12, etc.). In this sense, the word could be describing how this child fulfilled God's plans. The Septuagint, the Greek translation of the Old Testament, translates that same Hebrew word into a Greek word that is used in the New Testament to describe the child as "fair" (Acts 7:20) and "proper" (Hebrews 11:23).

Furthermore, the word could also be speaking of the health of the child (compare 1 Samuel 9:2). However, physical appeal or beauty is not a measure for God's call on a person (16:7, see lesson 9).

The child faced the infanticide of Pharaoh's tyrannical declaration of Exodus 1:16. The fact that a nursing mother could hide her child for *three months* implied her ability to avoid long hours of outdoor labor described in Exodus 1:13-14. The author of Hebrews reflects on the actions of the child's parents: "By faith Moses . . . was hid three months of his parents, because they saw he was a proper child; and they were not afraid" (Hebrews 11:23).

What Do You Think?
How should believers respond to human laws that contradict God's moral law?
Digging Deeper
How do Exodus 1:15-21; Esther 3:12–4:17; Daniel 3; 6; Romans 13:1-7; and Titus 3:1 inform a believer's response to civil obedience or disobedience?

B. Sheltered in the Stream (vv. 3-4)

3. And when she could no longer hide him, she took for him an ark of bulrushes, and daubed it with slime and with pitch, and put the child therein; and she laid it in the flags by the river's brink.

After three months, the baby could *no longer* stay hidden. The time had come for his parents to deal with the unjust realities of the pharaoh's command.

Ironically, the child's mother did follow the letter of the law of the pharaoh: she *did* cast her son into the river (compare Exodus 1:22). However, she did so in a manner that allowed for the child's survival, thus going against the *spirit* of the pharaoh's law.

The underlying Hebrew word translated as *ark* appears in one other Old Testament narrative: the ark of Noah (Genesis 6–9). In this verse, the ark was built to hold a small child; it was like a basket. In both instances, God provided for His people through an ark. Just as an ark saved Noah and his family from the waters of a flood, this ark would save a child from waters of the river.

The child's mother built the basket using common materials found in the region of the Nile River delta. *Bulrushes* of papyrus would have been obtained from the marshy wetlands of the river delta (compare Job 8:11). These were also used in the construction of seafaring vessels (Isaiah 18:2).

In order to seal the basket, the child's mother *daubed* the basket *with slime*—a sticky substance used in construction (see Genesis 11:3). Here, the substance served to bind the papyrus reeds together to form the vessel. *Pitch* was added as a waterproofing agent, fit to keep the interior of water-borne vessels and their passengers dry (compare 6:14).

In the harsh desert climate, the Nile River served as a key component of daily Egyptian life. The river provided water for drinking (Jeremiah 2:18), bathing (Exodus 2:5), irrigating (Isaiah 19:7), and livestock (Genesis 41:1-4). The river provided sustenance for daily life in general, and God would use the Nile to provide for Moses' life specifically.

Amid the slow moving, marshy waters of the *brink* of this river, *she laid* the papyrus basket. She would have to trust that God would protect her son.

Along the *river's* shore would have grown *flags* of reeds. By placing the basket here, the reeds provided protection and concealed the basket.

4. And his sister stood afar off, to wit what would be done to him.

We learn that the child had a *sister* (Miriam; Numbers 26:59). At this point in the narrative, specific details about her life are unknown. In this instance, she *stood afar* of the basket to keep an eye on her brother and take note of his eventual outcome: survival or death.

What Do You Think?
When, if ever, might it be better for a believer to wait and see God's provision before addressing a situation?
Digging Deeper
In what ways does this absolve a believer from action? In what ways does it not?

II. Unexpected Rescue
(Exodus 2:5-10)

A. Daughter's Discovery (vv. 5-6)

5. And the daughter of Pharaoh came down to wash herself at the river; and her maidens

walked along by the river's side; and when she saw the ark among the flags, she sent her maid to fetch it.

The pharaoh would have had many partners, "wives," and children. The relative power of any one child in the pharaoh's kingdom would have depended on the importance of that child's mother to the pharaoh. This *daughter of Pharaoh* may or may not have been a powerful woman in her father's kingdom (see Lesson Context). In any case, she was far more powerful than Moses' family—for better or worse.

Surely a royal princess would have more appropriate locations *to wash herself*—including royal bathhouses. Her motivations for bathing *at the river* are not obvious. Perhaps she was following the example of her father (see Exodus 7:15).

Most importantly, she noticed *the ark* floating *among the flags* of papyrus. Whether the child's mother and sister intended for him to be found by Egyptian royalty is unknown. The pharaoh's daughter was faced with a problem: abide by her father's commands regarding the treatment of Hebrew sons, or not.

The Power of Papyrus

Have you considered the importance of papyrus? The plant flourishes in marshy areas like the lands surrounding the Nile River. On first glance, the tall, reed-like plant may not seem to be a valuable natural resource. However, the ancient Egyptians maximized the plant's use.

The plant's husk would be peeled, and the remaining parts would be cut into thin strips. The strips were flattened and left to dry under the sun. The resulting sheets, similar to modern paper, were used for writing. But the use of papyrus was not limited to the creation of paper. Ancient texts speak to its use in making shoes, in decorating buildings, and even during the mummification process.

If not for the papyrus basket and the papyrus rushes, the baby might have been killed. This insignificant plant protected this child through God's saving plan. What "insignificant" part of your daily life has God used to advance His plan? Are your eyes open to noticing it?   —T. Z. S.

6. And when she had opened it, she saw the child: and, behold, the babe wept. And she had compassion on him, and said, This is one of the Hebrews' children.

Given that the previous verse refers to both the pharaoh's daughter and "her maid," the antecedent of *she* who *had opened* the basket is unclear. Even if the pharaoh's daughter was not the specific individual who opened the basket, she would have been aware of the resulting interaction. Like any other 3-month-old child, *the babe wept*—perhaps he was startled, fearful, or even hungry.

Despite the ethnic and cultural differences between the child and the princess, a natural response to a vulnerable child is evident. Her privilege and position of power did not diminish her sense of *compassion* for the child. She recognized the child's ethnicity, whether because of his circumcision (see Genesis 17:10-13) or assumed heritage based on his abandonment. The recognition of their cultural differences did not prevent her from helping the child.

Throughout the Old Testament, calling an individual a Hebrew often came from a Gentile person (Genesis 39:14, 17; 41:12; Exodus 1:15-16; 1 Samuel 14:11, 21). Other times, the title was used in regard to the people's experience of slavery (Deuteronomy 15:12; Jeremiah 34:9, 14).

What Do You Think?
What apparent need in your community fills you with a sense of compassion to respond?

Digging Deeper
What is one action step that you can take to help address this need?

B. Sister's Suggestion (vv. 7-9)

7. Then said his sister to Pharaoh's daughter, Shall I go and call to thee a nurse of the Hebrew women, that she may nurse the child for thee?

From her outpost, the child's *sister* appeared. Her appearance presented a conundrum: why would *Pharaoh's daughter* listen to this strange girl? Further, why choose *a nurse of the Hebrew women* when Egyptian nurses were available for the pharaoh's daughter?

In ancient cultures a mother did not always have the ability to nurse and care for her child. In this case, a nurse was chosen to help both the child and the mother (compare Genesis 24:59). Powerful women might acquire a nurse to avoid the inconveniences of motherhood. However, the precise motives of the pharaoh's daughter desiring a nurse is unknown. In any case, if she was not recently pregnant, she could not have nursed the child.

This interaction linked the child's sister and mother with the Hebrew midwives—women who saved vulnerable babies (Exodus 1:15-17). Further, this text speaks to the resilience of the child's family as they made efforts to survive under hostile and unjust conditions.

By asking whether a Hebrew *may nurse the child*, the pharaoh's daughter was placed in a difficult position. Would she resist the pharaoh's tyranny and take pity on the child and the Hebrew woman who stood before her? Or, instead, would she follow the dehumanizing practices of her powerful father?

8. And Pharaoh's daughter said to her, Go. And the maid went and called the child's mother.

The irony of *the child's mother* sending him away, and then having the chance to nurse him would not have escaped the text's audiences. The vulnerable slave woman outwitted the imperial, death-bent system that desired the death of her son. Even more ironic was that this was achieved through the daughter of the very man who instituted the death decree. Audiences of all eras can appreciate the cleverness of the Hebrew women in this narrative.

9. And Pharaoh's daughter said unto her, Take this child away, and nurse it for me, and I will give thee thy wages. And the woman took the child, and nursed it.

The attention of *Pharaoh's daughter* turned to the mother of *this child*. Whether the pharaoh's daughter suspected the true identity of this woman is unknown. By telling the baby's mother to *take* him could indicate that the pharaoh's daughter was filled with compassion and desired that the baby boy return to his people.

Because Moses' mother trusted God, she was

rewarded. Not only would she raise her own *child*, but she would be given *wages* to care for him, paid out of the royal coffers. She would provide for her family, all while she preserved her son's life.

What Do You Think?

What needs do you see in your community that are too challenging for you to tackle alone?

Digging Deeper

Who will you recruit to assist you in this regard?

C. Son's Significance (v. 10a-b)

10a. And the child grew, and she brought him unto Pharaoh's daughter, and he became her son.

Not only did Jochebed provide for his emotional well-being, but *the child* also *grew*—in a physical sense, and perhaps in understanding of the God of his ancestors. This same God would one day appear to him and direct him (see Exodus 3:4–4:17).

However, the child's time with his mother had a limit. At a prescribed time, unstated by the text, his mother *brought him* to the royal house. The text does not explain the means by which *Pharaoh's daughter* adopted the child. The fact that no one else is mentioned as *he became her son* highlights the moral courage of these two women in the midst of an oppressive system.

As young Moses grew, he would live in the house of the pharaoh, away from his own people (see Exodus 2:11; Acts 7:23). The longer he remained in the pharaoh's household, the more familiar he became with the cultural mores of the Egyptians. At times he was assumed to be an Egyptian (see Exodus 2:19).

What Do You Think?

How might you "adopt" a young person from your community with the intention of listening to their possible plight?

Digging Deeper

What steps will you take regarding the appropriate action in response to your active listening?

A Fish Out of Water

Have you ever had a "fish out of water" experience? I sure did when I moved to California. Before the move, I had lived my entire life in the Midwestern United States. I had a certain perspective on life—all based on the Midwestern culture.

After the move, I was ill-prepared for the cultural change. The West Coast culture felt faster and more tense than I was familiar with. After some time, the differences were too much for me to handle. I was ready to move back to a more comfortable culture. I wondered whether my discomfort was based on biblical principles or was a matter of preference.

Moses lived among three different cultures: the Israelites, the Egyptians, and the Midianites (see Exodus 2:11-25). God used each culture to shape him for future work. Are you attentive to how God might use different cultural contexts—even ones that you feel ill-prepared to handle—to shape you to better serve Him? —C. R. B.

10b. And she called his name Moses: and she said, Because I drew him out of the water.

At last, the name of this child is revealed. Undoubtedly the child's birth mother had given him a name. The text only tells us the *name* he was *called* by the pharaoh's daughter: *Moses*. The meaning and history of the name is unclear.

As he was given this name by an Egyptian, we can assume connections to the Egyptian language. The Egyptian word for "son" sounds similar to his name. (This name can be seen in the endings of other Egyptian names like Ahmose and Thutmose.)

The name could have connections to the Hebrew language. A Hebrew word indicating being drawn *out of* and rescued from *the water* also sounds like the name (see 2 Samuel 22:17; Psalm 18:16).

Despite these uncertainties, the child's name provides theological significance. Moses was rescued from certain death, and with God's guidance, he would rescue his people from future dangers (see Exodus 6:1; 13:3).

Conclusion

A. Aggressive Compassion

The story surrounding Moses' birth and upbringing triggers more questions than answers. One of the biggest unknowns concerns the motives of the pharaoh's daughter and her desire to help. Scripture does not indicate whether she feared God or not.

Despite her connection to the governing power, she was not overcome by its brutal demands. She was a beneficiary of the same system that allowed the pharaoh to act oppressively. But she managed to defy her upbringing and provided a just response to an unjust situation.

However, the real heroines of this story are the child's mother and sister. They took great risk to protect Moses. They trusted that God would see their response to the injustice and provide a way out. Their bold actions gave way to the bold actions from the daughter of Egyptian royalty.

God provides justice where injustice reigns. He invites His people to reflect His character by taking bold (and sometimes risky) steps to protect and care for vulnerable individuals. The justice that God requires of His people is not hypothetical—it is active and embodied.

B. Prayer

God of justice, we ask that You strengthen our compassion to respond to the vulnerable members of our community. Show us how we might be instruments of Your justice and peace to those who experience injustice. In the name of Jesus. Amen.

C. Thought to Remember

Reflect God's just character by responding to your most vulnerable neighbors.

How to Say It

Ahmose	*Ah*-mohs.
Amram	*Am*-ram.
Jochebed	*Jock*-eh-bed.
Mesopotamia	*Mes*-uh-puh-**tay**-me-uh.
Miriam	*Meer*-ee-um.
Midianites	*Mid*-ee-un-ites.
Pithom	*Py*-thum.
Rameses	*Ram*-ih-seez.
Thutmose	Thut-*mo*-se.
Pharaoh	*Fair*-o or *Fay*-roe.

Involvement Learning

Enhance your lesson with KJV Bible Student *(from your curriculum supplier) and the reproducible activity page (at www.standardlesson.com or in the back of the* KJV Standard Lesson Commentary Deluxe Edition*).*

Into the Lesson

Before class, write the following continuum on the board:

Easy **0 1 2 3 4 5** *Difficult*

Explain that you will give the class several decisions, and students will decide the level of difficulty to make the decision. Students will indicate the decision's difficulty by holding a piece of paper with the corresponding number from the continuum.

Ask the class to consider the following decisions: 1–Your neighbor needs some flour. 2–A friend requests your help for their move. 3–Your church wants you to oversee a special offering for a local charity. 4–Your pastor asks you to go on an overseas mission trip. 5–You have been nominated to lead a local citizens' group to address a neighborhood concern.

After the activity, ask volunteers to share what factors made making the decision easy or difficult. Lead into Bible study by saying, "Today we will look at the story of a family that was faced with a difficult decision. God used their response to accomplish great things for a whole nation."

Into the Word

Ask a volunteer to read aloud Exodus 2:1-10. Divide the class into three groups, designating them: **Jochebed Group**, **Miriam Group**, and **Pharaoh's Daughter Group**. Distribute handouts (you prepare) to each group with the following questions for small-group discussion:

Jochebed Group: 1–How did Jochebed deal with the danger of having a son? 2–Why do you think she created an "ark of bulrushes" (Exodus 2:3) for her son? 3–What do her actions teach us about justice and compassion?

Miriam Group: 1–What dangers were possible for Miriam as she approached the pharaoh's daughter? 2–How did Miriam help ensure that her brother would continue to live instead of dying as the pharaoh had decreed? 3–What do her actions teach us about justice and compassion?

Pharaoh's Daughter Group: 1–In what ways did the actions of the pharaoh's daughter oppose her father? 2–How did her adoption of Moses show God's plan to deliver His people? 3–What do her actions teach us about justice and compassion?

Alternative. Distribute copies of the "An Unforgettable Day" exercise from the activity page, which you can download. Have learners work in pairs to complete as indicated.

After calling time for either exercise, have groups present their findings for whole-class discussion.

Into Life

Transition by saying, "Moses' mother, his sister, and the pharaoh's daughter were all faced with complex and unjust situations. In their own way, they each responded with justice and compassion. As God's people, we are to honor Him and be used to enact His justice in the world."

Write on the board: *Situations That Require Justice and Compassion*. Ask the class to work in pairs to determine possible answers to the header. Challenge pairs to include individual and global injustices that they believe God wants His people to address. After no more than five minutes of discussion, ask pairs to state their answer(s). Write responses on the board.

Based on the responses, discern one situation of particular concern for the class. Through whole-class discussion, ask what steps your students can take to address the perceived injustice. (You might appoint a group of students to provide an all-class response for the next class period. If you do so, allow time in the next class session to discuss and make a plan based on the presented suggestion.)

Alternative. Distribute copies of the "Decisions, Decisions" activity from the activity page. Because of the personal nature of the activity, students may wish to complete this as a take-home.

Song of Moses

Devotional Reading: Exodus 14:21-31
Background Scripture: Deuteronomy 31:30–32:47

Deuteronomy 32:3-6, 10-14, 18

3 Because I will publish the name of the LORD: ascribe ye greatness unto our God.

4 He is the Rock, his work is perfect: for all his ways are judgment: a God of truth and without iniquity, just and right is he.

5 They have corrupted themselves, their spot is not the spot of his children: they are a perverse and crooked generation.

6 Do ye thus requite the LORD, O foolish people and unwise? is not he thy father that hath bought thee? hath he not made thee, and established thee?

10 He found him in a desert land, and in the waste howling wilderness; he led him about, he instructed him, he kept him as the apple of his eye.

11 As an eagle stirreth up her nest, fluttereth over her young, spreadeth abroad her wings, taketh them, beareth them on her wings:

12 So the LORD alone did lead him, and there was no strange god with him.

13 He made him ride on the high places of the earth, that he might eat the increase of the fields; and he made him to suck honey out of the rock, and oil out of the flinty rock;

14 Butter of kine, and milk of sheep, with fat of lambs, and rams of the breed of Bashan, and goats, with the fat of kidneys of wheat; and thou didst drink the pure blood of the grape.

18 Of the Rock that begat thee thou art unmindful, and hast forgotten God that formed thee.

Key Text

He said unto them, Set your hearts unto all the words which I testify among you this day, which ye shall command your children to observe to do, all the words of this law. —**Deuteronomy 32:46**

God's Exceptional Choice

Lesson Aims

After participating in this lesson, each learner will be able to:

1. Recall ways that the Lord had blessed His people.

2. Determine the identity of "they" in Deuteronomy 32:5.

3. Compose a personal song of thankfulness to the Lord.

Lesson Outline

Introduction
  A. Sing and Remember
  B. Lesson Context
I. **God's Faithfulness (Deuteronomy 32:3-6)**
  A. Because of His Greatness (vv. 3-4)
  B. Despite a Crooked Generation (vv. 5-6)
II. **God's Goodness (Deuteronomy 32:10-14)**
  A. Through Protection (vv. 10-12)
    Apple of His Eye
  B. By Provision (vv. 13-14)
III. **People's Apostasy (Deuteronomy 32:18)**
  A. Disregarding Their Rock (v. 18a)
    Maternal Care
  B. Forgetting Their Birth (v. 18b)
Conclusion
  A. Creative Praise
  B. Prayer
  C. Thought to Remember

Introduction

A. Sing and Remember

A friend spent years caring for his mother as she experienced the debilitating effects of Alzheimer's. Over time she lost her recollection of events and decades-old relationships—even relationships with her own children.

Despite the loss of certain memories, my friend's mother retained some ability to sing. As a devoutly religious woman, she had sung hymns all her life. Those hymns were deeply embedded; so even as she experienced the dramatic symptoms of Alzheimer's, she could still sing of her comfort and hope in God. Her faith—and the faith of her children—was strengthened by hymns and songs of worship. The destructive nature of Alzheimer's could not dismiss the eternal truths found in hymns, deeply instilled through years of singing and recitation.

Worship, lament, praise, and joy are reflected through the songs of Scripture. These songs give voice for people of God to express complex feelings about life and the nature of following God. In the concluding chapters of Deuteronomy, the Israelites were taught a song for their future.

B. Lesson Context

As the book of Deuteronomy comes to a close, Israel's leader, Moses, was on the verge of death. As a result of the impending change of leadership, Moses spoke publicly for the final time. The result is several smaller speeches and songs (found in Deuteronomy 29:2–33:29) that serve as the dramatic conclusion to Moses' ministry.

At first Moses reminded the Israelites to remember and accept the stipulations of God's covenant (Deuteronomy 29–30). This covenant was based on God's love for His people and their responding love and commitment to Him (see 4:37-40; 5:2-3; 6:5-6; 7:9; 11:1; 13:4). A failure to adhere to God's requirements would result in dramatic negative consequences for Israel (see 28:15-68). In addition, Moses' speech included a statement on his successor (31:1-8), a recitation of the law (31:9-13), and a prediction of the future (31:14-29).

In the midst of Moses' speeches, he presented a

song for the people (Deuteronomy 31:30–32:43). The song is reminiscent of psalms that celebrate the people's relationship with God (examples: Psalms 78; 105; 106). Just as the psalms were meant for singing, so was this song of Moses (Deuteronomy 31:19, 21-22).

The three divisions of the song speak to the scope of the Israelites' relationship with God. God's loyalty is contrasted with their sinfulness (Deuteronomy 32:1-14). As a result, negative consequences are certain (32:15-35). However, forgiveness, healing, and protection can still be attained (32:36-43).

I. God's Faithfulness
(Deuteronomy 32:3-6)

The song begins by calling the heavens and the earth as witnesses to the unfolding word of warning from God (Deuteronomy 32:1-2).

A. Because of His Greatness (vv. 3-4)

3. Because I will publish the name of the LORD: ascribe ye greatness unto our God.

The object that all creation should bear witness to was the proclamation of God's holy name. For the people of God, the centrality of *the name of the Lord* was crucial for their worship (Deuteronomy 12:5-6). God's name reflected the very nature of His being (see Exodus 33:19). To misappropriate His name brought great consequences (Deuteronomy 5:11).

As God's name was proclaimed, His *greatness* would be celebrated. God's greatness is not an abstract principle, but is a specific reality. The people of Israel experienced divine greatness firsthand as they saw how *God* treated them during their most vulnerable moments (Deuteronomy 3:24; 9:26; see Psalm 150:2). Even the angels in Heaven will sing of God's greatness upon seeing His victory over evil (Revelation 15:1-4).

4a. He is the Rock.

Because of God's greatness, He is the anchor for His people—*the* one and only *Rock*, the Savior and ruler of His people (see Deuteronomy 32:15, 18; 2 Samuel 23:3).

Other biblical texts describe God a "R/rock,"

referring to His stability and unchanging nature (see 1 Samuel 2:2; 2 Samuel 22:3, 32, 47; Psalms 18:2, 31; 28:1; 62:2, 6-7). Later parts of this song contrast the Rock of Israel with the weak gods of Israel's enemies (Deuteronomy 32:31, 37). The God of Abraham, Isaac, and Jacob was "the stone of Israel" (Genesis 49:24), steadfast for His people.

4b. His work is perfect: for all his ways are judgment.

The people of God can take refuge in God as their Rock because His *work* in the world is *perfect* (see 2 Samuel 22:31). Even when humans act unfairly and unjustly, God is flawless. His law "is perfect, converting the soul" of humans to walk in His ways of righteousness (Psalm 19:7; see 23:3).

Even when humans question, God's acts of *judgment* are just and right (see Job 34:12; 37:23; Psalm 33:5; Isaiah 5:16). As a result, God requires that His covenant people live with the same high regard for just living in the world (see Deuteronomy 16:19; 24:17; Isaiah 1:17; 56:1; etc.).

4c. A God of truth and without iniquity, just and right is he.

The song continues to laud the greatness of *God*. The *truth* of His name is fulfilled in His faithfulness to His people (Isaiah 25:1; see Psalm 33:4). His true faithfulness is demonstrated as He is holy, *without iniquity*, in all that He does (Zephaniah 3:5).

This song makes clear that God is worthy to be worshipped because of His holiness and perfection. These attributes are displayed through His *just and right* ways. His ways are to be imitated by His people (Hosea 14:9; see Exodus 23:1-9).

What Do You Think?
What are some attributes of God's greatness that you can discern?
Digging Deeper
How might Psalms 90:1-2; 147:5; Isaiah 66:1-2; Jeremiah 10:10; Mark 4:35-41; John 4:24; 5:26; Acts 17:24-25; and Revelation 21:6 inform your answer?

B. Despite a Crooked Generation (vv. 5-6)

5. They have corrupted themselves, their

spot is not the spot of his children: they are a perverse and crooked generation.

God's people would be noticed for their lack of spiritual blemish (see Leviticus 21:17-23 for a physical reality). This implied that God desired that they live upright and righteous lives. This would include their relationships with each other and the land, and their worship of the one true God.

Certain livestock without spot were required by Israel for sacrifices (Numbers 19:2; 28:3, 9, 11; 29:17, 26). These livestock were considered to be without corruption and were set aside.

However, as the people of God *corrupted themselves* with unholy influences (Exodus 32:7; Deuteronomy 4:16, 25; 9:12), *they* took on the *spot* of corruption. As a result, they ran the risk of being excluded as *children* of God.

The opposite of God's just ways are the *perverse and crooked* ways of humans. When a person is unable to make sense of the way he or she should go, wickedness thrives (see Proverbs 2:12-15). Israel had placed itself in a self-destructive position from which it could not easily escape. Despite all of Israel's experiences of God's divine redemption, the people of Israel had abandoned their redeemer (compare Jeremiah 32:30).

While this song refers to a specific *generation*, the song's truths are timeless and applicable to God's children in all eras. Jesus used a similar phrase to describe the unbelieving nature of some people in His audience (Matthew 17:17).

Ultimately, the children of God are tasked with living in an upright manner—obedient to the commands of God. Believers can do so as they are redeemed by the blood of Christ, the "lamb without blemish and without spot" (1 Peter 1:19). As a result, their lives can shine in the dark, crooked ways of the world (Philippians 2:14-16).

6. Do ye thus requite the LORD, O foolish people and unwise? is not he thy father that hath bought thee? hath he not made thee, and established thee?

The relationship between *the Lord* and Israel was based on Israel's loyalty and trust (Exodus 19:5-6; Deuteronomy 7:6-16). However, the *people* of Israel would betray the relationship by their reliance on foreign gods (31:16). The people would be *foolish* and *unwise* when they disregarded God's faithfulness. As a result of their foolishness, this song described how God would respond with a harsh warning and disastrous consequences (32:21-27, not in our printed text).

God cared for Israel as a father would care for his child (Deuteronomy 1:31; Hosea 11:1-2). The song's tenderness at this point contrasts the monstrous nature of Israel's ingratitude to God's covenant love.

Israel's whole identity came into existence because of the Father's love as He *bought* them into His inheritance (Exodus 15:16). He *made* and *established* Israel to be His own covenanted people (Genesis 17:7-8; Exodus 6:7-8). The song reminded Israel of the source of their high value: the God who established His covenant with them.

II. God's Goodness
(Deuteronomy 32:10-14)

The intervening verses describe how God would "set the bounds" of His people (Deuteronomy 32:8). God brought His people—"the lot of his inheritance" (32:9)—into safety.

A. Through Protection (vv. 10-12)

10a. He found him in a desert land, and in the waste howling wilderness; he led him about, he instructed him.

This song depicts God's people—referred collectively as *him*—as being lost in an inhospitable, barren *land*. In a metaphorical sense, the Israelites' slavery in Egypt served as a *desert*, an inconducive place for their flourishing. Following their exodus from Egypt, the Israelites wandered in an actual *wilderness*.

Yet in these trying places, God was always present for His people. He *led* them to places of care and rest (see Hosea 13:4-5; Jeremiah 31:2). The deserts in the Sinai peninsula, south of Judah, are quite inhospitable to travelers. The ancient singer knew the dangers to someone lost in the desert.

10b. He kept him as the apple of his eye.

The eye is one of the smallest and most sensitive parts of the human body. Yet it is also one of the most important parts of the body. Eyelashes, eyelids, eyebrows, blinking reflexes, nearly invisible membranes, and the eye socket all serve to protect the sensitive organ. Israel's importance is reflected in the way the song describes God protecting His people as though protecting *the apple of his eye*.

The phrase addresses a certain level of intimacy and care between God and His people (see Psalm 17:8-9; Zechariah 2:8-9). God gave attention to Israel's needs and took the necessary steps to protect and provide for them, all out of His love for them. Though Israel was like a wandering traveler, they would no longer fear—because God provided through the inhospitable wildernesses of life.

Apple of His Eye

If there is adequate lighting, clear vision, and appropriate proximity, I might see my reflection in the eyes of another person. By no means is this reflection clear—it's only a glimmer. Some details in the reflection may be lacking, and clarity may linger for only a few seconds.

Rarely do I stand close enough to another person to see my reflection in their eyes. My children, however, are among the few people whose eyes I get close enough to gaze into. I wonder if they see their reflection in my eyes—for they are the apple of my eye.

The intimate relationship between God and His people leads the songwriter to speak of God's people as the apple of God's eye. God's people reflect a sliver of God's character to the world. In order for that to occur, God's people must be close to Him. What prevents you from being close to God? You are the apple of His eye!   —L. M. W.

11. As an eagle stirreth up her nest, fluttereth over her young, spreadeth abroad her wings, taketh them, beareth them on her wings.

The second metaphor relates God's care for

His people to an *eagle* caring for its *young*. As the eaglets grow up, the parent eagle will protect them with the expanse of its *wings* over the *nest*. By describing God's care and protection of His people in this manner, this song reflects the sentiment of the psalmist regarding God's protection (Psalm 91:4).

Further, when eaglets learn to fly, they glide behind their mother's wings as she *beareth them* in flight. The young birds learn as they express their own autonomy with the safety of the mother's wings to catch and carry them should they fail.

By using this imagery, not only does the song highlight God's protection but also His guidance for His people. God brought them out of Egypt and brought them to a place where they might flourish (see Exodus 19:4). They were "flying solo," but their hope for survival was in relying heavily on the Lord God (Isaiah 40:31).

> **What Do You Think?**
> How might analogies and metaphors help readers better understand God?
> **Digging Deeper**
> What are some weaknesses or dangers of using analogies and metaphors to describe God?

12. So the LORD alone did lead him, and there was no strange god with him.

The identity of the Israelites was based in their core confession (Deuteronomy 6:4), their covenant, and the stipulations for life that resulted (5:1-10; see Exodus 20:1-6). This song celebrates the Israelites' unique identity and relationship with *the Lord*; they were like a flock of sheep that their shepherd *did lead*.

As a part of this unique identity, Israel was not to follow any *strange* (that is, foreign) *god*. As the people followed the one true God, they maintained their freedom. However, they would not always stay on this path (see Deuteronomy 31:16).

B. By Provision (vv. 13-14)

13a. He made him ride on the high places of the earth.

The song transitions to refer to Israel's hope for

What treasure does your heart hold?

Visual for Lessons 6 & 9. *Allow learners one minute to silently reflect on situations when they have not given God first place in their hearts.*

their future and the many blessings that followed. If the people followed God, they would experience safety from destructive forces. They would dwell *on the high places*, safe from an enemy's invasion.

Other texts describe high places as being significant locations where an interaction with God occurred (see 1 Samuel 9:12-13, 19; 1 Kings 3:2-3). However, many of these so-called high places became locations of improper worship for Israel (see Leviticus 26:30; Numbers 33:52; 1 Kings 11:7; 2 Kings 23:19; Psalm 78:58; Hosea 10:8; etc.).

13b. That he might eat the increase of the fields; and he made him to suck honey out of the rock, and oil out of the flinty rock.

From this advantageous location, the people of God could be positioned above good farmland. The *increase* of crops from *the fields* would be so fruitful, they would never experience famine (see Ezekiel 36:30).

God had promised the Israelites that they would live in "a land flowing with milk and *honey*" (Exodus 13:5), a land of agricultural blessing (Deuteronomy 8:7-9). That *oil* and honey flowed *out of the rock* implied abundance and satisfaction, even in inhospitable terrain (see Psalm 81:16).

14. Butter of kine, and milk of sheep, with fat of lambs, and rams of the breed of Bashan, and goats, with the fat of kidneys of wheat; and thou didst drink the pure blood of the grape.

The land and the people's livestock would provide sustenance. The livestock would provide enough extra *milk* to produce *butter* and perhaps cheese for the people (see 2 Samuel 17:29).

A certain *breed* of *rams* from the *Bashan* region was highly prized. This region was likely located northeast of the Sea of Galilee and east of the Jordan River (Deuteronomy 4:47). During the time of Moses, the region consisted of 60 cities (see 3:4-6). In addition, the region was known for its other livestock (Ezekiel 39:18) and oak trees (Isaiah 2:13; Ezekiel 27:6; Zechariah 11:2).

The song returns to celebrate the agricultural blessing of the land (compare Deuteronomy 32:13b, above). The best quality of wheat—indicated by the idiom *the fat of kidneys of wheat*—would be accessible. Further, the vines would produce *pure blood*: unfermented *grape* juice. The land would produce abundant blessing, beyond the bare necessities needed. This section of the song describes God's care for His people. Provision and sustenance were celebrated.

> **What Do You Think?**
> How can God's people honor God as the source of all provisions?
> **Digging Deeper**
> What steps can you take in the coming week to share God's provision with your neighbors?

III. People's Apostasy
(Deuteronomy 32:18)

A. Disregarding Their Rock (v. 18a)

18a. Of the Rock that begat thee thou art unmindful.

Despite the promises of vast blessing and numerous provisions, the song details how Israel would grow comfortable and careless. Their prosperity would lead them to a state of "waxed fat, . . . grown thick, . . . [and] covered with fatness" (Deuteronomy 32:15). In their complacency, they ignored God as the source of their blessing. Their comfort and willful ignorance would lead them to worship false gods instead of the one true God who provided for them and blessed them (32:16-17).

The song refers again to two previously used metaphors: God as a *Rock* (see commentary on

Deuteronomy 32:4, above) and God as a parent who *begat* children (see commentary on 32:5, 11, above). This verse is a mixed metaphor—rocks do not have children! The resulting point is the scope of God's relationship with Israel. He was their source of life and their sustainer.

> **What Do You Think?**
> How can believers ensure that they do not disregard God as their Rock, the source of salvation and blessing?
>
> **Digging Deeper**
> Who will you invite to provide accountability in this regard?

Maternal Care

As children, my sister and I had a cat named Fluffy. Some of my fondest childhood memories revolve around Fluffy and her kittens. I remember watching her care for her kittens by protecting, cleaning, and nursing them.

One afternoon a stray kitten wandered into our yard. I wanted to keep the kitten, but my parents reminded me that Fluffy would often chase away other cats—even stray kittens. Albeit with warnings, my parents agreed to let the stray cat stay. The next morning we found Fluffy sprawled out, nursing and caring for the kitten. Fluffy's maternal instincts had replaced her territorial tendencies.

Scripture describes how God cares for His people like a mother's comfort (see Isaiah 66:13). What steps are you taking to remember the one who has promised to never forget you (49:15)? —L. M. W.

B. Forgetting Their Birth (v. 18b)
18b. And hast forgotten God that formed thee.

Corporate memory can create a community identity as it allows the group members to recollect, rehearse, and codify their most important experiences together. From the remembrance the community can draw conclusions regarding how its members should act, think, and feel in the future.

Throughout Deuteronomy, the Israelites are told to remember their history and how God brought them out of slavery (Deuteronomy 5:15; 7:18; 8:2; 15:15; 16:12). The people were to go to great lengths to not forget their history. This would ensure that future generations would not have forgotten the ways God formed and maintained them (see 11:2-7; 18-21).

Conclusion
A. Creative Praise

Throughout church history, believers have expressed their joys, doubts, fears, and hopes in songs. These songs of worship have shaped believers into spiritually mature disciples of Jesus. Singing should not be a kind of sedative that numbs us. Rather, our singing should include repentance with praise and self-examination with satisfaction. Only in that way can singing shape us as people of God.

On the surface, the nature of the song in today's text is rather cynical; it highlights the failure of the people of Israel. Yet the song's pointed nature leads to a declaration of hope. God's salvation will transform and sustain, if only people remember His steadfast commitment to them. As a result, God's people can sing of His mighty deeds, all while confessing our their own failure to appreciate them.

That same sort of forgetfulness can plague Christians today when we forget that our salvation is a gift from God as He draws us into His kingdom. We did not earn that citizenship; it was given to us freely. God sustains us when we recite the story of our faith and live out its implications in our lives.

B. Prayer

God, You are the Rock in whom we can find provision and protection. Lead us in Your ways so that we will not turn away from You. In Jesus' name. Amen.

C. Thought to Remember
God's people sing of His
provision and protection!

How to Say It

Bashan	*Bay*-shan.
Deuteronomy	Due-ter-*ahn*-uh-me.
Zephaniah	Zef-uh-*nye*-uh.

Involvement Learning

Enhance your lesson with KJV Bible Student (from your curriculum supplier) and the reproducible activity page (at www.standardlesson.com or in the back of the KJV Standard Lesson Commentary Deluxe Edition).

Into the Lesson

Before class, prepare a set of five index cards for each anticipated small group. (Each group should consist of no more than five students.) Each set of five index cards should show the following prompts, one per index card:

My earliest memory is . . .
A person I'll always remember is . . .
A past experience that still affects me is . . .
What I'd like others to remember about me is . . .
A moment that I want to always remember is . . .

As the class convenes, put students in small groups. Give a set of the premade index cards to each group, but tell the group members not to look at the prompts on the index cards.

Once you have distributed all the sets of index cards, say, "Each person in your group should choose one of the index cards at random and give an answer to the prompt." After no more than five minutes, allow volunteers to share their responses.

Alternative. Write on the board, "What role does memory play in the Christian life?" Allow for whole-class discussion.

Lead into the lesson by saying, "Today's lesson is about the importance of memory and remembrance. Let's see how Moses told the entire congregation of Israel what they must never forget."

Into the Word

Help students understand the setting for today's Bible study by briefly summarizing material found under the Lesson Context for this lesson. (You may want to recruit a class member ahead of time to prepare this two-minute lecture.)

Before class prepare handouts with the following questions, each as a header of a column: 1–What God's people were supposed to remember. 2–Signs of the people's disobedience. 3–Evidence of God's faithfulness.

Have students stay in the original groups from the Into the Lesson portion. Have each group read Deuteronomy 32:3-6, 10-14, 18. Then, have each group work together to write down the answers to the prompts on the handout. Allow 10 minutes to complete the activity before reconvening the class for discussion.

Option. Distribute copies of the "Goodness and Rebellion" exercise from the activity page, which you can download. Have groups work together to complete the activity as indicated before discussing their findings with the whole class.

Into Life

Write on the board the following questions that will serve as headers to three columns: 1–What are we supposed to remember? 2–What signs of disobedience do we see in our world? 3–What evidence do we have of God's faithfulness? (You may point out that each of the questions corresponds to the questions used earlier during Into the Word.)

Invite class members to work in their original groups to answer the three questions. As they work, encourage the groups to consider how the scriptural truths of the lesson text compel us to live in faithful action today.

After no more than 10 minutes, ask for a volunteer from each group to report their answers to the whole class. Write each group's answers on the board under the corresponding questions.

Then say, "Now try writing new words to a familiar hymn melody. The new words should contain ideas from these lists. Let's compose our own songs of praise to God."

After no more than 10 minutes, reconvene the class and encourage the groups to sing their new songs for the whole class.

Alternative. Distribute copies of the "Images of Praise" activity from the activity page. Have learners work in pairs to complete the activity as indicated. After five minutes, have volunteers give their answer to the third prompt on the activity.

The Call of Gideon

Devotional Reading: 2 Corinthians 12:1-10
Background Scripture: Judges 6:1-27

Judges 6:1-2, 7-16a

1 And the children of Israel did evil in the sight of the Lord: and the Lord delivered them into the hand of Midian seven years.

2 And the hand of Midian prevailed against Israel: and because of the Midianites the children of Israel made them the dens which are in the mountains, and caves, and strong holds.

7 And it came to pass, when the children of Israel cried unto the Lord because of the Midianites,

8 That the Lord sent a prophet unto the children of Israel, which said unto them, Thus saith the Lord God of Israel, I brought you up from Egypt, and brought you forth out of the house of bondage;

9 And I delivered you out of the hand of the Egyptians, and out of the hand of all that oppressed you, and drave them out from before you, and gave you their land;

10 And I said unto you, I am the Lord your God; fear not the gods of the Amorites, in whose land ye dwell: but ye have not obeyed my voice.

11 And there came an angel of the Lord, and sat under an oak which was in Ophrah, that pertained unto Joash the Abiezrite: and his son Gideon threshed wheat by the winepress, to hide it from the Midianites.

12 And the angel of the Lord appeared unto him, and said unto him, The Lord is with thee, thou mighty man of valour.

13 And Gideon said unto him, Oh my Lord, if the Lord be with us, why then is all this befallen us? and where be all his miracles which our fathers told us of, saying, Did not the Lord bring us up from Egypt? but now the Lord hath forsaken us, and delivered us into the hands of the Midianites.

14 And the Lord looked upon him, and said, Go in this thy might, and thou shalt save Israel from the hand of the Midianites: have not I sent thee?

15 And he said unto him, Oh my Lord, wherewith shall I save Israel? behold, my family is poor in Manasseh, and I am the least in my father's house.

16a And the Lord said unto him, Surely I will be with thee.

Key Text

The Lord said unto him, Peace be unto thee; fear not: thou shalt not die. —**Judges 6:23**

God's Exceptional Choice

Lesson Aims

After participating in this lesson, each learner will be able to:

1. Describe the historical context of Israel's oppression.

2. Articulate the presupposition behind Gideon's first question.

3. Determine one or more ways to avoid false thinking regarding whether God is *with* or *not with* him or her.

Lesson Outline

Introduction

A. Getting into Action

Rather than sitting at home and worrying during the pandemic of 2020, retirees Ted and Ellen decided to act. Many families in their community had been unemployed or underemployed as a result of the pandemic, so Ted and Ellen "adopted" seven families and brought them food each week. Some of the food was from a local food bank and some from their own kitchen.

This couple took the initiative to do something for others. While food matters, human connection matters more. Their work and presence brought a bit of God's deliverance to those who needed it.

When we read the "big" stories of the Bible, we may be tempted to imagine that God works only or primarily through dramatic events. But countless "small" stories of generosity and faith have occurred through the centuries as God has worked through the hands and feet of believers (compare Mark 9:41; 12:42). When people of faith answer God's call, the blessings of unexpected opportunities to serve follow.

B. Lesson Context

The book of Judges features accounts of a series of leaders ("judges") who arose to rescue Israel from foreign oppressions during the era 1380 to 1050 BC. These stories fit together to paint a picture of a dreary pattern: the Israelites sinned, God punished them with foreign oppression, the Israelites repented, a deliverer came, and peace followed. Gideon, the deliverer-judge of today's lesson, was the fifth of perhaps 14 judges; he served in that capacity during the first half of the twelfth century BC. The Midianites, the oppressors whom Gideon was to confront in today's text, came from what is now northern Saudi Arabia or southeastern Jordan. They had created a sophisticated society based on trade across the Arabian Peninsula with the cultures around its perimeter (Egypt, Syria, Palestine, and Mesopotamia; compare Genesis 37:28). They were not barbarians. The Midianites shared a history with Israel (see Exodus 18:1; etc.), a history that included conflict (see Numbers 25:14-18; Psalm 83:9-12).

I. Midianite Oppression

(Judges 6:1-2)

A. Punishment (v. 1)

1. And the children of Israel did evil in the sight of the LORD: and the LORD delivered them into the hand of Midian seven years.

The book of Judges often begins the accounts of deliverer-judges by referring to the *evil* that the nation of Israel had engaged in (Judges 3:7, 12; 4:1; 10:6; 13:1). Their evil actions are the first part of a pattern of sin → servitude → supplication → salvation that structures most of the book of Judges. The length of the suffering of *seven years* is relatively short when compared to oppressions lasting 8 (3:8), 18 (3:14; 10:8), 20 (4:3); and 40 years (13:1).

The nature of the evil that *the children of Israel did* is not specified. But in other instances where the phrase "evil in the sight of the Lord" occurs, the evil is idol worship (Judges 2:11-13; 3:7; 10:6).

> ### What Do You Think?
> How can you tell whether hard times are God's judgment for sin or simply the result of living in a fallen world?
>
> ### Digging Deeper
> How will your reactions differ between the two?

B. Hiding (v. 2)

2. And the hand of Midian prevailed against Israel: and because of the Midianites the children of Israel made them the dens which are in the mountains, and caves, and strong holds.

The land of Israel features large and small *caves*, both natural and man-made. When people felt vulnerable, they might flee to one of them for refuge (see 1 Samuel 13:6; 1 Kings 18:4; compare Revelation 6:15; compare the nonbiblical 2 Maccabees 6:11). *Strong holds* are fortresses with difficult access (1 Samuel 23:14, 19; Ezekiel 33:27).

Fight, Flight, or Freeze?

I saw my sister's hair spread on the pillow behind her on the couch. I was angry because of an insult she had hurled at me, so I grabbed a handful of hair and pulled. Incensed, she jumped up and lunged at my own hair, pulling a handful. I screamed, and a fight ensued. This was a rare occurrence since we usually got along well. For some reason, we overreacted, and we had the biggest fight of our lives.

The fight did not last long. I knew if I told my parents about the fight, we would both get in trouble. I did not want to be in trouble myself, and deep down I did not want her to get punished. So, confronted with the options of fight, flight, or freeze, I chose the middle option—running away and hiding in the other room.

We may struggle to know whether fight, flight, or freeze is best; the Scriptures offer many right and wrong examples of all three choices (compare and contrast Genesis 19:17, 26; 27:43; Exodus 14:13; Psalm 46:10; John 18:10-11; Hebrews 6:18; etc.). One thing we know: God's Word guides us in these choices (Matthew 10:23; etc.). But one other issue comes before all that: How do we ensure that the opposition we face is not God's response to our own sin?   —L. M. W.

II. Divine Deliverance

(Judges 6:7-16a)

A. Prophetic Warning (vv. 7-10)

7. And it came to pass, when the children of Israel cried unto the LORD because of the Midianites.

The pattern of deliverance involved Israel pleading for help. The prayers may have resembled the

How to Say It

Abiezrite	A-by-**ez**-rite.
Amorites	**Am**-uh-rites.
Gilead	**Gil**-ee-ud (G as in get).
Habakkuk	Huh-**back**-kuk.
Maccabees	**Mack**-uh-bees.
Manasseh	Muh-**nass**-uh.
Ophrah	**Ahf**-ruh.
Sivan	See-**vahn**.
Zechariah	**Zek**-uh-**rye**-uh.
Zephaniah	**Zef**-uh-**nye**-uh.

Visual for Lesson 7. Show this image and discuss how being in God's will allows believers to live without fear.

petitions found elsewhere in Scripture (see Psalm 44; Lamentations 5). In such compositions, the writers both complained to God about their situations and asked for help in relieving them.

8. That the LORD sent a prophet unto the children of Israel, which said unto them, Thus saith the LORD God of Israel, I brought you up from Egypt, and brought you forth out of the house of bondage.

The 17 prophetic books of the Old Testament do not always state the precise occasion that prompted their prophetic oracles. However, some texts do speak of prophets appearing on the scene in order to warn their audience or to call them to action (examples: 1 Samuel 2:27-36; 1 Kings 13:1-10).

The unnamed *prophet* in the verse before us, however, brings a word of challenge that will ultimately bring about the people's deliverance. Prophets were not all that unusual in the life of Israel. God had spoken through Moses regarding His will that the people listen to His prophet (Deuteronomy 18:14-22). God used both men and women (see Exodus 15:20; Judges 4:4; 2 Kings 22:14) to serve as prophets and declare His directives for His people.

This prophet's message is grounded in Israel's core story: the story of the exodus. The phrase *house of bondage* always shows up in stories about Israel's departure *from Egypt* (Exodus 13:3, 14; 20:2; Deuteronomy 5:6; 6:12; 7:8; 8:14; 13:5, 10; Joshua 24:17; etc.). By the time of the events of

today's text, the exodus was more than 250 years in the past. Generations had come and gone. But the Israelites did not need a reminder of what it was like to be oppressed—they were being oppressed by the Midianites at the time! Rather, the prophet was reminding the people of Israel of the one who had delivered their ancestors.

9. And I delivered you out of the hand of the Egyptians, and out of the hand of all that oppressed you, and drave them out from before you, and gave you their land.

The deliverance had two parts: exodus and settlement. God's gift of the *land* (Exodus 23:31; etc.) had made it possible for the people to enjoy their relationship with God in the rhythms of holy life.

Appeal to the story of the settlement appears also in Amos 2:9-11. According to that prophet, God had driven out the pagan population in order to make possible the delivered people's place in their land. The Israelites, however, ultimately imitated the people they had displaced by engaging in idol worship, thereby disowning their redeemer (see commentary on Judges 6:1, above).

10. And I said unto you, I am the LORD your God; fear not the gods of the Amorites, in whose land ye dwell: but ye have not obeyed my voice.

The foundational story of the exodus always should have pointed the Israelites toward loyalty to *the Lord*. His displacement of *the Amorites* to make room for the Israelites should have done so as well. Amorites are mentioned dozens of times in the Old Testament, along with numerous other "-ites" whose lands were given to Israel. The Amorites seemed to have been particularly sinful, in light of Genesis 15:16 (compare 2 Kings 21:11). Whether the writer is referring to Amorites specifically or just using that designation to refer to all the dispossessed "-ites" in general is uncertain.

Since the Lord had demonstrated His power in forming and settling Israel as a nation, it made no sense to *fear* other gods. But for ancient peoples, worship was less about matters of pro and con arguments than it was about not leaving any gods accidentally unworshipped (examples: 2 Kings 17:24-41; Acts 17:23). The idea of worshipping one and only one God, no matter where one lived, was highly unusual. This outlook is reflected in the fact that the plural word *gods* occurs more than 200 times in the Old Testament.

But commonly accepted cultural practices do not necessarily have God's approval. Idolatry was an act of disloyalty. When Israel adopted pagan cultural practices, they abandoned the religion that Moses had led them in decades earlier.

> **What Do You Think?**
> What are some ways to warn people of God's judgment while "speaking the truth in love" (Ephesians 4:15)?
>
> **Digging Deeper**
> What do you do if people then dismiss you as being judgmental?

B. Angelic Assurance (vv. 11-12)

11a. And there came an angel of the LORD, and sat under an oak which was in Ophrah.

The second scene in this story involves a different sort of messenger, a heavenly being, who appears near a certain *oak* tree. Large trees—whether solitary or in a grove—were often used as landmarks and significant places for the people (Genesis 12:6; 18:1; 35:4; Joshua 19:33; Judges 4:11; etc.). They also served as shade and so places of rest and conversation for people who had worked all day and wanted a break. For various references to oak trees specifically, see Joshua 24:26; 2 Samuel 18:9-10; 1 Kings 13:14; Ezekiel 6:13.

There are two biblical towns named Ophrah. One was located in the tribal territory of Benjamin, about a dozen miles north-northeast of the city later known as Jerusalem (Joshua 18:21-24). The other *Ophrah*, the one under consideration here, was in the tribal territory of Manasseh; some students propose that the name is another designation for the town of Gilead mentioned in Judges 10:17. In any case, this is "Ophrah of the Abiezrites" (Judges 6:24; also see 6:11b, next).

11b. That pertained unto Joash the Abiezrite: and his son Gideon threshed wheat by the winepress, to hide it from the Midianites.

This half verse reveals that the oak tree under which the heavenly messenger was sitting was on the property of father *Joash* which would pass to *son Gideon.* To be an *Abiezrite* was to be of the tribe Manasseh (see Joshua 17:2). For Gideon to be threshing *wheat* is a time indicator: the wheat harvest in this region occurs in the month of Sivan, which is late May or early June. *The winepress* won't be used for its intended purpose until the grapes ripen later in the summer months.

Gideon could have been threshing either by striking sheaves with a flail or by having oxen pull a threshing sledge on a hard outdoor surface (compare 1 Chronicles 21:20-23). Threshing is different from winnowing, the latter occurring after the former, although they occur in the same place (compare Ruth 3:2; Matthew 3:12; Luke 3:17). That Gideon felt the need *to hide* the wheat indicates the oppressive treatment from *the Midianites* regarding Israel's crops (Judges 6:3-6).

12. And the angel of the LORD appeared unto him, and said unto him, The LORD is with thee, thou mighty man of valour.

The heavenly messenger greeted Gideon not on the basis of his past achievements (as far as we know), but as a foreshadowing of what he was to become: a *mighty man of valour.* The statement that *the Lord is with thee* is not a cliché; it occurs rather rarely in the Bible. The only other place a heavenly messenger uttered this phrase unconditionally is in Luke 1:28, to Mary. The phrase was used presumptively by Nathan the prophet (2 Samuel 7:3). The longer, conditional use of the phrase is found in 2 Chronicles 15:2: "The Lord is with you, while ye be with him; and if ye seek him, he will be found of you; but if ye forsake him, he will forsake you."

More common is the assurance that "God is with thee" (Genesis 21:22; 1 Samuel 10:7; 1 Chronicles 17:2). Combining the words *God* and *Lord* in such an assurance occurs elsewhere (see 22:18; 28:20; Zephaniah 3:17).

C. Gideon's Response (v. 13)

13. And Gideon said unto him, Oh my Lord, if the LORD be with us, why then is all this befallen us? and where be all his miracles which our fathers told us of, saying, Did not the LORD bring us up from Egypt? But now the

LORD **hath forsaken us, and delivered us into the hands of the Midianites.**

Gideon's cynical response reflected a sense of despair as he pointed out the gap between his then-current experience and the age-old stories of deliverance. The reader knows that the Midianite oppression was the due punishment brought on by Israel's sins (see Judges 6:1, above). Did Gideon not realize this?

This sort of protest appears often in the Bible as various people wonder about God's apparent lack of involvement or concern (examples: Joshua 7:7; Lamentations 2; Habakkuk 1:2-3). Gideon's question should not strike us as rude, much less unfaithful, but as a heartfelt attempt to make sense of his experiences.

Questions about the message of predecessors seem especially important. Moses encouraged parents to teach their children about the experiences of deliverance (Exodus 13:14-16). Israel's poetic literature proclaimed the importance of remembering God's deeds (Psalm 78:1-8). Gideon has trusted the message of his ancestors. At the time, however, he could not resolve the apparent disconnect between "then" and his "now."

D. God's Clarification (vv. 14-16a)

14. And the LORD looked upon him, and said, Go in this thy might, and thou shalt save Israel from the hand of the Midianites: have not I sent thee?

Gideon's call to become the deliverer bears similarities to those of Moses (Exodus 3:1–4:17) and Joshua (Joshua 1:1-9).

The reference to *this thy might* seems strange. What so-called might did Gideon have? The text says nothing of his political intelligence or past military experience. His skills as a farmer might have prepared him for the physical rigors of warfare, but little else.

Perhaps the answer lies in the previous verse. Gideon knew the ancient story of Israel's deliverance as told in the exodus story. He dared to question God as to why his present realities seemed so different. The strength that Gideon desired would fill him as he went where God *sent* him (see Judges 6:34).

An Unexpected Christmas Sermon

I like shaking people out of long-held and complacent expectations. One time when I did so was in using Judges 6:14 as a text for a Christmas sermon. For those who expected a sermon from Matthew 1, 2, or Luke 2, the shock was rather total!

My impetus for using Judges 6:14 at Christmas was the oft-heard lament that Christ was being taken out of Christmas. The greeting "Merry Christmas" was being replaced with "Happy Holidays." Stores stocked increasing numbers of lawn displays of Santa Claus and decreasing numbers of Nativity scenes. Christmas was ever more becoming commercialized. It seemed as if the truth of Emmanuel, meaning "God with us" (Matthew 1:23; compare Judges 6:12), was disappearing by means of secular commercialism.

My answer and challenge to the problem was an extended application of Judges 6:14: Go in your might and save your Christmas! Begin first at home: prioritize the placement of Nativity scenes. Replace expectations of receiving things with gratitude of having already received. Identify and avoid provocations that cause the season of love to become a season of shove.

The challenge of Judges 6:14 can apply to many areas of Christian life. The most important area right now is the one where you need to set aside the complaint of "If the Lord be with us, why then is all this befallen us?" (Judges 6:13). Otherwise, you won't be able to hear God's declaration "Go in this thy might" and solve the problem.   —R. L. N.

> ### What Do You Think?
> What unused spiritual gifts has God given you that you can begin to use this week?
>
> ### Digging Deeper
> Would you seek the counsel of a fellow Christian before doing so? Why, or why not?

15. And he said unto him, Oh my Lord, wherewith shall I save Israel? behold, my family is poor in Manasseh, and I am the least in my father's house.

Gideon objected to the call on the basis of insignificant lineage (compare Isaiah 6:5; Jeremiah 1:6). A leader in antiquity needed family connections and alliances with other families. When Gideon pointed to the insignificance of his *family*, he was not simply being modest. He knew that political leaders needed a power base of connections.

16a. And the LORD said unto him, Surely I will be with thee.

The explicit promise *I will be with thee* is the strongest assurance Gideon can receive! This promise is all the more striking given the phrase's rarity in the Old Testament (see Genesis 26:3; 31:3; Exodus 3:12; Joshua 1:5; 1 Kings 11:38; Isaiah 43:2). These can be contrasted with the opposite, the Lord's promise elsewhere to *not* be present (see Deuteronomy 1:42; Numbers 14:43; Joshua 7:12).

Conclusion

A. From Why to What's Next

Today's text begins an account of how Israel experienced deliverance from an oppression. It draws on the most important Israelite story—the exodus—by pointing out the gap between the memory of the story and the present experience. God had delivered in the past, but He seemed no longer willing to do so. As with many stories of the call of prophets or kings, the hero here (Gideon) gets to express the confusion that the readers must also feel and that we may still feel when our beliefs and our experiences seem to clash.

When that happens, we can get stuck brooding in an endless cycle of asking why, as Gideon did (compare Jeremiah 5:19; 13:22; 16:10; etc.). In that regard, it is important to note what is missing in Judges 6:14: the Lord did not answer Gideon's why question of Judges 6:13. We are answerable to the Lord, not He to us (compare Job 38–41). Our why questions will not always be answered; sometimes the Lord will only tell us what's next. Sometimes trouble can result when we try to run ahead of the Lord by assuming we know what's next (examples: Numbers 14:39-45; Joshua 7:1-12). Gideon also seems to have allowed himself to fall into this trap later (Judges 8:24-28).

Yet on balance Gideon was attentive to the Lord's will. He refused to become king, insisting that God alone should rule Israel (Judges 8:22-23). Like all of us, Gideon experienced both successes and failures. When he heard the call to act, he stated his doubts openly, asking God for answers. But when God did not answer those questions, Gideon wanted miraculous signs (see 6:17-22, 36-40).

It's been said that there are two ways to learn things: by wisdom and by experience. Wisdom is when we learn from the mistakes of others; experience is when we learn from our own mistakes. The life of Gideon is recorded that we might learn from his successes and failures (compare Romans 15:4; 1 Corinthians 10:11; 2 Timothy 3:16). While his call differs from that of Christians, Gideon's life still has much to teach us. The Lord still calls us to serve. He still says that He is with us (Matthew 28:19-20). But are *we* with *Him*?

B. Prayer

Oh God who warns and challenges, raise us up to be Your hands and feet in Your saving work. May our questions reflect direction as You remind us of Your presence. We pray in the name of Your Son, Jesus. Amen.

C. Thought to Remember

Let God work through your faith.

Involvement Learning

Enhance your lesson with KJV Bible Student *(from your curriculum supplier) and the reproducible activity page (at www.standardlesson.com or in the back of the* KJV Standard Lesson Commentary Deluxe Edition*).*

Into the Lesson

Distribute in random order 10 sheets of paper (you prepare), each displaying one letter of the word *insecurity*. Ask recipients to stand before the class and display their letters. Encourage other class members to voice suggestions regarding the order of the letters. (Smaller classes can distribute two sheets to each participant, who hold one in each hand.)

After the correct order of letters is established, write the letters on the board in correct order in a vertical column. Ask the class to work with you to create an acrostic, where letters of horizontally written words intersect with the letters in the vertical column.

Take a poll by asking: "How many of you remember a time when you felt insecure?" Ask for a show of hands. Then ask, "How many of you experienced a situation when insecurity made the problem worse?" Ask for another show of hands.

Lead to Bible study by saying, "Today we'll look at a Bible story showing how God called someone who may have been characterized by one or more of the words in our acrostic—or maybe not!"

Into the Word

Divide the class into four groups, designating them **Israelites Group / Prophet Group / Angel Group / Gideon Group**. Ask all groups to listen as today's text is read-aloud to discover and take notes on what the namesake(s) of their groups said and did. After the reading, have participants work within their groups to write a monologue spoken by a representative of each group that retells what their namesakes said and did. Instruct that in the retelling, groups can use their "sanctified imaginations" to fill in gaps with additional material that is consistent with the nature of the character(s) they will be portraying.

After several minutes, call for monologues to be delivered to the whole class. After each monologue, allow the rest of the class to ask questions.

Write *Surprised by God* on the board as a stimulus for whole-class discussion as you ask, "How does that phrase make a good title for the story of Gideon?"

Into Life

Distribute copies of a handout (you prepare) that features these three column headings:

Tough Situation! / God's Work? / God's Silence?

Have the following instructions printed on the handout: "Jot down a word or phrase under each heading to describe a situation when you prayed for God to intervene. Note whether you saw how God worked or that He seemed silent." State that they have a maximum of one minute to finish, and no one will be put on the spot to reveal what they've written. After the minute, allow sharing within groups for those who desire to do so.

Then pose this question for whole-class discussion: "When we as Christians go into action to help resolve tough situations of our country, how do we know whether God is *with* or *not with* us?" (If you think the question will cause the discussion to turn political, rephrase it to minimize that possibility.) After responses, ask, "What about tough situations we are facing as a congregation?" Following the ensuing discussion, ask members to return to their groups to discuss personal situations. As they ponder various courses of action or inaction, how do they determine whether God is *with* or *not with* them?

Option. Close the class by distributing copies of the "Help!" exercise on the activity page, which you can download. Allow one minute for participants to complete as indicated individually before voluntary sharing. Or use this activity as a take-home prayer prompt for the week ahead.

Option. Distribute copies of the "Called to Rescue" crossword puzzle on the activity page as a take-home.

Who Is King?

Devotional Reading: Psalm 93
Background Scripture: 1 Samuel 8:1-9; 10:17-26

1 Samuel 8:4-7

4 Then all the elders of Israel gathered themselves together, and came to Samuel unto Ramah,

5 And said unto him, Behold, thou art old, and thy sons walk not in thy ways: now make us a king to judge us like all the nations.

6 But the thing displeased Samuel, when they said, Give us a king to judge us. And Samuel prayed unto the LORD.

7 And the LORD said unto Samuel, Hearken unto the voice of the people in all that they say unto thee: for they have not rejected thee, but they have rejected me, that I should not reign over them.

1 Samuel 10:17-24

17 And Samuel called the people together unto the LORD to Mizpeh;

18 And said unto the children of Israel, Thus saith the LORD God of Israel, I brought up Israel out of Egypt, and delivered you out of the hand of the Egyptians, and out of the hand of all kingdoms, and of them that oppressed you:

19 And ye have this day rejected your God, who himself saved you out of all your adver-sities and your tribulations; and ye have said unto him, Nay, but set a king over us. Now therefore present yourselves before the LORD by your tribes, and by your thousands.

20 And when Samuel had caused all the tribes of Israel to come near, the tribe of Ben-jamin was taken.

21 When he had caused the tribe of Benja-min to come near by their families, the family of Matri was taken, and Saul the son of Kish was taken: and when they sought him, he could not be found.

22 Therefore they enquired of the LORD fur-ther, if the man should yet come thither. And the LORD answered, Behold, he hath hid him-self among the stuff.

23 And they ran and fetched him thence: and when he stood among the people, he was higher than any of the people from his shoul-ders and upward.

24 And Samuel said to all the people, See ye him whom the LORD hath chosen, that there is none like him among all the people? And all the people shouted, and said, God save the king.

Key Text

Ye have this day rejected your God, who himself saved you out of all your adversities and your tribulations; and ye have said unto him, Nay, but set a king over us. —**1 Samuel 10:19a**

God's Exceptional Choice

Unit 2: Out of Slavery to Nationhood
Lessons 5–9

Lesson Aims

After participating in this lesson, each learner will be able to:

1. List circumstances that caused the nation of Israel to demand a king.

2. Explain why Israel's wanting a king was a rejection of the Lord.

3. Identify one item that represents a rejection of the Lord in his or her life and write a plan for changing this.

Lesson Outline

Introduction
  A. The Ultimate Authority
  B. Lesson Context
I. The Call for a King (1 Samuel 8:4-7)
  A. Rejection of Samuel (vv. 4-5a)
    Wayward Sons
  B. Rejection of the Lord (vv. 5b-7)
II. The Acclamation of a King
                  (1 Samuel 10:17-24)
  A. Gathering the Tribes (vv. 17-19a)
    "The Ultimate Fulfillment"
  B. Choosing Benjamin (vv. 19b-20)
  C. Choosing Saul (vv. 21-24)
Conclusion
  A. Planning in the Priesthood
  B. Prayer
  C. Thought to Remember

Introduction
A. The Ultimate Authority

Parents wear many hats. One of these requires rendering judgment between siblings on the basis of parental authority in the household. When siblings disagree, they can seek a word straight from the top that might fall in their favor.

For instance, in the case of two daughters, their mother might have to decide whether the older had the right to donate a hoodie from her ex-boyfriend, even though the younger desired to keep it for herself. The older daughter would argue that it was hers to do with as she pleased; and furthermore, she had a right not to see it in her own home as a reminder of her former boyfriend. The younger would counter, saying it was still a good hoodie, no matter where it came from. Their mother would rule to decide the fate of the hoodie.

When Samuel gathered the people together, the fate of an entire nation was at stake. But would the people recognize his authority? And would they recognize the authority *behind* Samuel—the Lord himself?

B. Lesson Context

In the Christian arrangement of the books of the Old Testament, 1 and 2 Samuel are included with the 12 historical books (Joshua–Esther). They record the transition from theocracy (being governed by the Lord) to monarchy (being governed by an earthly king). The books of 1 and 2 Samuel can be divided into these sections:
I. End of judges' period (1 Samuel 1–8)
II. God's selection and rejection of Saul
    (1 Samuel 9–15)
III. God's selection of David and Saul's fall
    (1 Samuel 16–31)
IV. Establishment of David's throne (2 Samuel
    1–10)
V. David's sin and flight from Jerusalem
    (2 Samuel 11–18)
VI. Reestablishment of David in Jerusalem
    (2 Samuel 19–20)
VII. David's legacy (2 Samuel 21–24)

The period of the judges lasted more than 300 years, from 1380 to 1050 BC (see lesson 7 Lesson Context). The judges administered justice and served as God's chosen military leaders when the people were oppressed by foreign invaders. This is told briefly in Judges 2:6-19 and recorded in detail in the rest of that book (see lesson 7). Samuel's prophetic ministry began during the latter part of those deplorable years, in 1067 BC; this was a time when Israel had no king (Judges 18:1; 19:1). This was also a time when moral conditions among the people were chaotic: "every man did that which was right in his own eyes" (21:25).

In his transitional role, Samuel is sometimes referred to as the last of the judges (1 Samuel 7:6, 15-17) and the first of the prophets (3:20; Acts 3:24; 13:20). Samuel was one of the greatest of Israel's judges. After freeing the country from oppressors, he established a circuit court to administer justice (1 Samuel 7:16). His decisions were respected, for they were according to the law.

I. The Call for a King

(1 Samuel 8:4-7)

The events recounted in this section were precipitated by the desire to avoid a crisis of leadership in Israel, such as was often seen following the death of a judge (example: Judges 3:7–4:7).

A. Rejection of Samuel (vv. 4-5a)

4. Then all the elders of Israel gathered themselves together, and came to Samuel unto Ramah.

Ramah was a village in the hill country belonging to the tribe of Benjamin (Joshua 18:20b, 25). Its exact location is unknown, though it was likely 5–12 miles north of Jerusalem, which was still a Jebusite stronghold (15:8, 63). Ramah was Samuel's birthplace and served as one of his primary sites for judging (1 Samuel 1:19-20; 7:16-17). He offered sacrifices on behalf of Israel (7:9) and served as a "seer," one who received words from the Lord directly (9:19).

It's unclear whether *the elders of Israel* went straight to Ramah or met elsewhere and traveled together after an initial meeting about their shared concerns. As their title suggests, these men were the heads of families and leaders in their clans

and so were older, seen as having gained wisdom throughout their lives. They formed the councils that governed day-to-day life in the tribes of Israel. Describing this group as *all* the elders suggests there were representatives from each of the 12 tribes (Exodus 3:16-18; Numbers 11:16-30; Joshua 8:33). Though we frequently think of a united Israel, in many ways the tribes operated independently, making their uniform desire all the more remarkable (see 1 Samuel 8:5a-b, below).

5a. And said unto him, Behold, thou art old, and thy sons walk not in thy ways.

Samuel's age caused the elders (rather ironically) to worry about the future following his death. Perhaps they knew the stories of how Israel repeatedly fell into sin and was overtaken by enemies following a judge's death (example: Judges 2:6-19). Maybe they simply wanted to be sure, before Samuel died, of the leadership they would inherit.

Or the elders could have been primarily concerned for their children and grandchildren, not wanting to see them under the leadership of Samuel's *sons*. These two, Joel and Abiah, were acting as judges. But they failed spectacularly in their roles because of their greed (1 Samuel 8:1-3, not in our printed text; compare 3:11-14). They did not follow in their father Samuel's *ways* and could not be trusted to guide with righteousness and justice.

Wayward Sons

King George III (1738–1820) reigned in England during the American Revolution. For all his flaws, King George III led a pious life and took his role as king seriously. After all, he believed God had put him in his position.

In contrast, his son George IV (1762–1830) proved an immoral and vain ruler. He fathered numerous illegitimate children with multiple women. He was a heavy drinker and threw lavish, expensive parties. King George IV was known as a cavorting, wasteful ruler who cared more about himself than his people.

Like George IV, Samuel's sons were immoral men. Their ungodly leadership led the elders to ask for a king, which led to the division of Israel and finally to becoming exiles in Assyria and Babylon.

Think of the leaders in your life. Do they show

DON'T BLEND IN. BE *HOLY!*

Visual for Lesson 8. *While discussing the questions associated with verses 5b-6a, ask how identity in Christ is connected to holiness.*

the fruit of the Spirit, growing in relationship with God and leading in a Christlike manner? Or are they grasping for power, money, and influence? Who you follow determines where you're going. Choose wisely. —L. M. W.

B. Rejection of the Lord (vv. 5b-7)

5b-6a. Now make us a king to judge us like all the nations. But the thing displeased Samuel, when they said, Give us a king to judge us.

Even before Israel's entry into the land of Canaan, the Lord knew there would be a time when the people would desire a king. This was foreseen by Moses, who warned Israel of the consequences (Deuteronomy 17:14-20). To have a king made the nation more like their neighbors instead of less (1 Samuel 8:20, not in our printed text). The elders' stated desire to be *like all the nations* disturbs the reader. God specifically chose Israel and made the nation holy so that it *wouldn't* be like the nations (Exodus 19:5-6)! Trying to blend in by having *a king* as other peoples was a faithless response (see 1 Samuel 8:7, below).

In the time of the judges, Israel functioned as a theocracy (see Lesson Context). But the eldership was not interested in waiting for God to raise up another judge as He had been doing for many generations. Their demand to Samuel can very well be seen as one of grave disrespect toward the prophet. They needed him to act because no one else in Israel had the gravitas of Samuel and hope to unify

the nation behind a new king. But they did not want the benefit of his wisdom regarding whether or not to have a king, having come to him with a solution already in mind. *Samuel* was understandably *displeased* by this, as he saw the elders' desire as a rejection of the Lord's intentions for them.

> **What Do You Think?**
> What situations tempt you to embrace cultural norms that contradict your identity in Christ?
>
> **Digging Deeper**
> How can you strengthen your sense of identity in Christ in order to resist the temptations you named?

6b. And Samuel prayed unto the LORD.

Rather than engage with the elders in a shouting match or shut his door in disgust, *Samuel prayed unto the Lord*. This was a pause with purpose rather than an avoidance of conflict. Samuel's displeasure and anger would not get the best of him. We do well to follow his example—not avoiding conflict or simply giving in to demands, nor responding in the heat of the moment, but seeking the Lord and His will.

> **What Do You Think?**
> What strategies can you employ to go to the Lord with your anger and frustrations instead of losing your temper in the moment?
>
> **Digging Deeper**
> How do you ensure that these strategies are not simply ways to avoid needed confrontation?

7a. And the LORD said unto Samuel, Hearken unto the voice of the people in all that they say unto thee.

This was not the first time God adjusted His plan to accommodate the actions or desires of His chosen people (example: Genesis 21:13). Even so, God had never chosen a king for Israel (compare Judges 9), so the Lord's command to *hearken unto the voice of the people* represented a break from their entire history of governance. The Law of Moses had included guidelines for an eventual king, assuming a monarchy one day would be formed (Deuteronomy 17:14-20; contrast 28:15, 26-27).

7b. For they have not rejected thee, but they have rejected me, that I should not reign over them.

This rejection may have felt like a referendum on how Samuel raised his sons, if not also on how he had led Israel. Such personal affront is easy to understand. But the Lord set the prophet straight: the people's demanding a king was primarily about rejecting God's reign as it had been carried out to that point (compare Judges 8:22-23; 1 Samuel 8:8, not in our printed text).

Then as now, trusting in God's governance requires great faith in the face of all that sin has wrought in the world. It is much easier to look to a king or president for direction than to wait on the Lord. Even the apostles feared what would happen when Jesus was no longer physically with them (see John 14–17). Resting in the uncertainty of when and how God will choose to act is not for the faint of heart (Isaiah 40:28-31; 2 Timothy 1:7).

What follows in 1 Samuel 8:10-20 reveals the elders' lack of comprehension concerning what it would mean to be ruled by a monarch. They failed to consider that a king or dynasty was likely to become tyrannical. They thought a king would give the nation more stability, especially in terms of military might—forgetting that the only source of true strength is the Lord (Exodus 14:12-31; Isaiah 12:2). Although God had delivered Israel from Egypt, He would not hear their cry when the king they wanted oppressed them. With these warnings, the men went back to their homes.

> **What Do You Think?**
> What implications does Israel's rejection of God in favor of a king have for your attitudes toward national leaders?
>
> **Digging Deeper**
> What other biblical texts inform your thinking about your responsibility as a citizen of an earthly nation and possible tensions with your citizenship in the kingdom of Heaven?

II. The Acclamation of a King
(1 Samuel 10:17-24)

After Israel's elders expressed their desire for a king, Samuel met Saul, whom God had revealed to be His choice for their first king (1 Samuel 9:15-19a). Samuel secretly anointed Saul (10:1-16, not in our printed text).

A. Gathering the Tribes (vv. 17-19a)

17. And Samuel called the people together unto the LORD to Mizpeh.

How much time passed between the meeting with the elders and this one with *the people* is unclear, though the events did not happen back-to-back (see 1 Samuel 8:8–10:16). Perhaps several thousand people would be expected to come. *Mizpeh* was where Samuel had orchestrated a victory over the Philistines that solidified his leadership role as the judge of Israel (7:6). Specifying that the meeting was *unto the Lord* suggests that *Samuel* did not call this gathering of his own volition.

18. And said unto the children of Israel, Thus saith the LORD God of Israel, I brought up Israel out of Egypt, and delivered you out of the hand of the Egyptians, and out of the hand of all kingdoms, and of them that oppressed you.

Samuel's address echoed Moses' own farewell speech, giving *the children of Israel* insight and instruction for a future without Samuel (compare Deuteronomy 1:1-5; 7:12-24). The people were not vulnerable without a king; look at all that God had done without one! Not only had He *brought up Israel out of Egypt* (compare Numbers 21:1-3, 21-26); He had protected them from *all kingdoms* since then that had threatened His people (examples: Joshua 10; Judges 3:12-30).

> **What Do You Think?**
> What memories of God's goodness have encouraged you in times when trusting the Lord was especially difficult?
>
> **Digging Deeper**
> How does sharing these stories with others strengthen both their trust in the Lord and your own?

19a. And ye have this day rejected your God, who himself saved you out of all your adversities and your tribulations; and ye have said unto him, Nay, but set a king over us.

Israel would receive what they asked of God, but it wasn't ideal. So why didn't the Lord stop Israel from this folly? The answer comes back to how we understand God's working out His will. There are events that the Lord desires and works to establish (we think especially of Jesus' incarnation, ministry, death, and resurrection); that He desires and calls people to accomplish with Him; and that people desire and God chooses to work through. Giving Israel a king falls in the latter category, and we see that God used it to pave the way for Christ (2 Samuel 7:5-16; Luke 1:30-33; Acts 13:21-23).

Samuel could not in good conscience proceed without reminding the nation of God's great deeds and of their rejection of Him. This was likely a call to repentance. At the very least, Samuel would have hoped the people would not forget the Lord, even when they had an earthly king.

"The Ultimate Fulfillment"

"If you asked me, my life was hijacked by the lottery," Donna Mikkin wrote in her article "How Winning the Lottery Led to Emotional Bankruptcy." Before she won the New York State Lottery—then worth $34.5 million—she was basically a happy person. When she won, she believed the money was "the ultimate fulfillment." Donna did not realize how winning would affect her emotional health. She became preoccupied with others' perception of her and felt guilty for winning out over others.

The Israelites believed a king would be their ultimate fulfillment. God told Samuel to give the people what they wanted, knowing it was not what they really needed. How many times do we get what we want in life, only to realize it does not satisfy us? The dream job, relationship, or possessions can't take the place of God in our lives. Don't be fooled! Ultimate fulfillment is found only in the Lord. —L. M. W.

B. Choosing Benjamin (vv. 19b-20)
19b-20. Now therefore present yourselves before the LORD by your tribes, and by your thousands. And when Samuel had caused all the tribes of Israel to come near, the tribe of Benjamin was taken.

Casting lots was a way of recognizing that God was making His choice (see 1 Samuel 10:20-21 and compare 10:22-23, below; Joshua 7:14; Jonah 1:7; Acts 1:26). Proverbs 16:33 gives the view that it is the Lord who controls the outcome. In such a situation, one marked object was placed in a container with other items that were similar. The marked item identified God's choice.

Benjamin was an unexpected choice, for it was the smallest and least influential of Israel's *tribes*—Saul himself said as much (1 Samuel 9:21). Furthermore, Benjamin had been punished and ostracized by the rest of the nation in its recent history for a particularly notorious episode of savagery (Judges 19–21). From our vantage point, however, Saul's connection to this tribe might be the first twinge of foreboding we experience.

C. Choosing Saul (vv. 21-24)
21. When he had caused the tribe of Benjamin to come near by their families, the family of Matri was taken, and Saul the son of Kish was taken: and when they sought him, he could not be found.

Nothing more is known of *the family of Matri*, lending credence to Saul's protest of being from an insignificant family. But *Kish* was "a mighty man of power," which could be understood to mean he was wealthy (1 Samuel 9:1), especially as he had both livestock and servants (9:3). Still, the choice of *the tribe of Benjamin* was strange due to its small size and checkered history (Judges 20–21).

22. Therefore they enquired of the LORD further, if the man should yet come thither. And the LORD answered, Behold, he hath hid himself among the stuff.

If Saul had simply not come to Mizpeh, he potentially would have retained some measure of dignity. Instead, Saul was hiding *among the stuff*, likely luggage the visitors brought with them for their stay. The text does not tell us why, leaving us to wonder—was he feeling great humility and the weight of responsibility falling on him (consider

1 Samuel 9:21)? Or was he afraid of the challenge before him, unsure that God would guide him (17:1-11)? It could be a mix of both. Whatever the reason, it was a strange place to begin his reign.

23. And they ran and fetched him thence: and when he stood among the people, he was higher than any of the people from his shoulders and upward.

Despite this inauspicious beginning, Saul's stature would have been a reassuring sight for people hoping for a military leader. Judging by the outside, Saul was literally "head and *shoulders*" the best candidate for the job (contrast 1 Samuel 16:7; see lesson 9).

24a. And Samuel said to all the people, See ye him whom the Lord hath chosen, that there is none like him among all the people?

Samuel's words can be taken as praise and delight in Saul, or they can be taken simply as a statement of fact regarding Saul's imposing physical stature. Samuel probably intended this ambiguity, not speaking out directly against God's chosen man but not giving him a glowing endorsement either.

What Do You Think?

What ratio of your compliments are in regard to a person's outward appearance versus his or her inward qualities?

Digging Deeper

What benefits can you anticipate in shifting this ratio to favor inward qualities? Do these benefits change based on the age of the recipient?

24b. And all the people shouted, and said, God save the king.

God save the king is a prayer to the Lord. Though the people's desire was at its heart a rejection of the Lord, they did not desire to lose the Lord's blessings and protection. We may be tempted to judge the people for these mixed and seemingly opposing desires. But we need only observe our own mixed motives to realize how infrequently we act from totally righteous or totally flawed motivations. At such times, we do well to still cry out to God, who sees our hearts and can work to cleanse us of desires that are counter to the life of faith.

Conclusion

A. Planning in the Priesthood

Despite having been rejected by the people, the Lord chose not to abandon them. He sometimes punished them (2 Chronicles 36:15-21), but He continued to love His people and work through them (see Genesis 12:1-3). The same goes for us. Though we make decisions that grieve God, He does not abandon us or stop working through the church. He has the power to use even our worst decisions for His glory (Romans 8:28).

Samuel and the elders were concerned for Israel's future, though they had very different plans to alleviate that worry. In the same way, leadership in churches—whether ministers, elders, or other leaders—do well to look to the future of their congregations and of the worldwide church. When considering our plans, however, we must not discount the warnings of godly people who do not share a majority opinion. We have an ally in this endeavor that Israel did not: the presence of the Holy Spirit in the life of every believer (Acts 2:17-21). May we seek clarity from the Lord in every decision, resisting worldly wisdom so that we can continue to live out our calling as the priesthood of believers (1 Peter 2:4-12).

B. Prayer

Lord God, forgive us when we value our judgment over Yours. Help us examine our hearts and overcome those motivations that are a rejection of You. In Jesus' name we pray. Amen.

C. Thought to Remember

There is room for only one King in our hearts.

How to Say It

Kish	*Kyesh.*
Matri	*May-try.*
Mizpeh	*Miz-peh.*
theocracy	*thee-ah-cruh-see* (*th* as in *thin*).

Involvement Learning

Enhance your lesson with KJV Bible Student *(from your curriculum supplier) and the reproducible activity page (at www.standardlesson.com or in the back of the* KJV Standard Lesson Commentary Deluxe Edition*).*

Into the Lesson

Write on the board *Things Are Not What They Seem to Be*. Divide your class into groups of five members or fewer. Ask each group to think of at least one example from current events, from history, or from a personal experience. After five or six minutes, ask each group to share one example. As a whole class, talk about what perspective and choices keep people from seeing something as it really is.

Say, "Today we will look at a pivotal incident from Israel's history, when outside influences and perspectives led God's people to make a decision that didn't honor God."

Into the Word

Ask the class what they already know about Samuel. Write their answers on the board, consulting the Lesson Context to fill in any gaps.

Divide the class into small groups. Have the groups study today's text, from 1 Samuel 8:4-7; 10:17-24, and decide whether each statement below is true or false. If the statement is false, they should rewrite it to make it true. (Note: every statement is false.) Distribute a handout (you create) with the following nine statements:

1. The elders knew that Samuel's sons, although competent, were not available.

2. Samuel wanted to be king, but the people didn't want him.

3. The Lord was happy to be the heavenly King while the people also had an earthly monarch.

4. God didn't want to give them a king, but Samuel talked Him into doing so.

5. The Israelites' deliverance from Egypt would have happened sooner if only they'd had a king.

6. Samuel didn't want to tell the people how God really felt about their desire for a king.

7. Saul seemed to all the people to be the obvious choice for king.

8. Saul was as eager to be king as the people were eager to make him king.

9. The people couldn't accept such a little man to be their king, and they rejected Samuel's choice.

Give groups several minutes to work; then review as a whole class.

Alternative. Distribute copies of the "Diary of an Old Man" exercise from the activity page, which you can download. Have learners work together to complete as indicated. After a few minutes, invite volunteers to read what they've written.

After completing either activity, have the class draw conclusions about how Israel's choices reflected their relationship with God and His standards.

Into Life

Distribute handouts (you prepare) of the following list of principles:

• God loves us in spite of our bad decisions.

• External appearances may not indicate God's preferences.

• The will of the people or majority rule is not a clear indicator of God's will.

• God works through government when the governed give first allegiance to Him.

• God allows us to go our own way, even when it leads to disaster.

• God uses imperfect people to do His work on earth.

In their groups, students choose at least two of the statements. Ask them to discuss how today's lesson illustrates the statements or principles. After several minutes, allow each group to report.

Alternative. Distribute copies of the "What Do You Say?" exercise from the activity page. Have learners complete it in pairs before discussing conclusions as a whole class.

Have students identify one item in today's lesson that represents a rejection of the Lord in his or her life and take one minute to plan how to change this behavior or thought pattern. End class with prayer.

David Anointed as King

Devotional Reading: Acts 13:21-31
Background Scripture: 1 Samuel 16:1-13

1 Samuel 16:1-13

1 And the LORD said unto Samuel, How long wilt thou mourn for Saul, seeing I have rejected him from reigning over Israel? fill thine horn with oil, and go, I will send thee to Jesse the Bethlehemite: for I have provided me a king among his sons.

2 And Samuel said, How can I go? if Saul hear it, he will kill me. And the LORD said, Take an heifer with thee, and say, I am come to sacrifice to the LORD.

3 And call Jesse to the sacrifice, and I will shew thee what thou shalt do: and thou shalt anoint unto me him whom I name unto thee.

4 And Samuel did that which the LORD spake, and came to Bethlehem. And the elders of the town trembled at his coming, and said, Comest thou peaceably?

5 And he said, Peaceably: I am come to sacrifice unto the LORD: sanctify yourselves, and come with me to the sacrifice. And he sanctified Jesse and his sons, and called them to the sacrifice.

6 And it came to pass, when they were come, that he looked on Eliab, and said, Surely the LORD's anointed is before him.

7 But the LORD said unto Samuel, Look not on his countenance, or on the height of his stature; because I have refused him: for the LORD seeth not as man seeth; for man looketh on the outward appearance, but the LORD looketh on the heart.

8 Then Jesse called Abinadab, and made him pass before Samuel. And he said, Neither hath the LORD chosen this.

9 Then Jesse made Shammah to pass by. And he said, Neither hath the LORD chosen this.

10 Again, Jesse made seven of his sons to pass before Samuel. And Samuel said unto Jesse, The LORD hath not chosen these.

11 And Samuel said unto Jesse, Are here all thy children? And he said, There remaineth yet the youngest, and, behold, he keepeth the sheep. And Samuel said unto Jesse, Send and fetch him: for we will not sit down till he come hither.

12 And he sent, and brought him in. Now he was ruddy, and withal of a beautiful countenance, and goodly to look to. And the LORD said, Arise, anoint him: for this is he.

13 Then Samuel took the horn of oil, and anointed him in the midst of his brethren: and the Spirit of the LORD came upon David from that day forward. So Samuel rose up, and went to Ramah.

Key Text

The LORD seeth not as man seeth; for man looketh on the outward appearance, but the LORD looketh on the heart —**1 Samuel 16:7b**

God's Exceptional Choice

Unit 2: Out of Slavery to Nationhood
Lessons 5–9

Lesson Aims

After participating in this lesson, each learner will be able to:

1. Describe the selection process of David as king.

2. Compare and contrast that process with that of the choosing of Saul as king.

3. Write a prayer asking God for a clean heart and eyes of faith.

Lesson Outline

Introduction
  A. The Unlikely President
  B. Lesson Context
I. God Chooses a New King (1 Samuel 16:1-3)
  A. Rejection (v. 1)
    Pity Party for One
  B. Direction (vv. 2-3)
II. God Chooses David (1 Samuel 16:4-13)
  A. Coming to Bethlehem (vv. 4-5)
  B. Rejecting Older Sons (vv. 6-10)
  C. Selecting the Shepherd Son (vv. 11-13)
    Picture Perfect
Conclusion
  A. Walking by Faith
  B. Prayer
  C. Thought to Remember

Introduction

A. The Unlikely President

Abraham Lincoln's birth in 1809 in a Kentucky log cabin was a sign of his family's nineteenth-century situation. His education was unimpressive. As an adult, Lincoln did not attend college but studied on his own to pass the bar exam and become a lawyer. Drawn to politics, he was defeated for election to the Illinois state legislature in 1832 but then elected to four terms beginning in 1834. Looking to the serve in Congress, he lost his first attempt at gaining his party's nomination to the U.S. House of Representatives in 1843. Running again, he was elected in 1846 but limited himself to one term in that office. He then twice lost in his quest to be elected a senator from Illinois—first in 1855, then again in 1858. He became his party's surprise nominee for the 1860 presidential election, and he changed the course of the nation.

Did all that happen by random chance, or was it by providential intervention? Only God knows! But the Lord always reserves the right to intervene in matters involving human leadership, as today's text affirms.

B. Lesson Context

Much of the context for this lesson is shared with that of lesson 8. Israel's first king, Saul, was identified by the Lord and anointed by Samuel. But Saul overstepped his role and failed to obey the Lord (1 Samuel 13:7b-14; 15:2-33). Saul increasingly demonstrated the downfalls of having a king at all. As a result the Lord regretted choosing Saul and decided to find another king (15:35).

The events in this lesson occurred sometime during Saul's 40-year reign, which lasted from 1050 to 1010 BC. David's reign would not begin until 1010 BC, but it was known to Saul and his family long before then that they were not the start of a dynasty in Israel (1 Samuel 23:16-17).

I. God Chooses a New King
(1 Samuel 16:1-3)
A. Rejection (v. 1)

1a. And the LORD said unto Samuel, How

long wilt thou mourn for Saul, seeing I have rejected him from reigning over Israel?

Samuel's mourning over Saul's failures and rejection was not inappropriate. After all, Saul's success would have been success on behalf of Israel. And the last time Samuel would ever meet Saul was to tell him that God had rejected him as king (1 Samuel 15:20-23, 35). But Saul demonstrated that he looked the part (9:2) without being able to carry out the office of king in the manner desired by the Lord (15:1-11). God's word to *Samuel* was that the time for mourning was past (compare Ecclesiastes 3:1, 4).

1b. Fill thine horn with oil, and go, I will send thee to Jesse the Bethlehemite: for I have provided me a king among his sons.

The *horn* is likely that of a ram (see Genesis 22:13). Though horns were often used to produce sound (example: Joshua 6:5), they could also make excellent containers for *oil* (compare 1 Kings 1:39; Psalm 92:10).

Jesse was the grandson of Boaz and Ruth (Ruth 4:21-22). Jesse and his family made their living as shepherds (see 1 Samuel 16:11, below). Their hometown, Bethlehem, was located in Judah, south-southeast of Samuel's home in Ramah in the territory of Ephraim (compare 7:17). There are perhaps five towns named Ramah in the Old Testament, so we take care not to get them mixed up. The journey of more than 20 miles to Bethlehem required crossing through the territory of Benjamin. The New Testament village of Arimathaea is likely this same place renamed (John 19:38).

Pity Party for One

"I'm going to my room and I'm never com-

ing out!" The bedroom door slammed shut. That agony-filled hyperbole came from our 15-year-old daughter, who had asked to go to a concert with her friends and then stay the night in a hotel. While she thought that was a perfectly reasonable request, her father and I knew it was asking for trouble.

We wondered how long it would take her to resume the normalcy of life; it was during dinner the next evening. A friend called and asked her to the movies, and we gladly gave the OK. While she still wasn't happy with our decision about the concert, she was moving on.

God's rejection of Saul as king was valid, but Samuel mourned that decision deeply. But God stood fast and told Samuel it was time to move on. How long will you sit and mourn when God tells you no?

—P. M.

B. Direction (vv. 2-3)

2a. And Samuel said, How can I go? if Saul hear it, he will kill me.

The most likely road to Bethlehem went through Gibeah, the hometown of *Saul* (1 Samuel 15:34). The odds were high that Saul or his family might realize what Samuel was doing, which could prove to be a grave danger. Without an innocuous reason to travel, suspicion or curiosity could be aroused.

2b. And the LORD said, Take an heifer with thee, and say, I am come to sacrifice to the LORD.

Samuel was known for offering sacrifices while traveling (1 Samuel 7:9; 9:12-13; 10:8; etc.). While this was not the primary reason for Samuel to be traveling this time, it was a legitimate reason—and quite an appropriate one when anointing a king chosen by God.

A *heifer* is a young female cow. Heifers were not typically sacrificed, although precedent and instruction existed (Genesis 15:9; Numbers 19:2-10; Deuteronomy 21:3-6). Generally male animals were sacrificed (Leviticus 1:5; 4:3-21; Numbers 8:8; Deuteronomy 18:3; etc.). This may have been in recognition that female animals were more valuable for reproduction. While one male could significantly increase an entire herd, one female was unlikely to be so fruitful.

The Law of Moses specified several types of animal sacrifices (examples: Leviticus 12:6-8; 16:3-28). Samuel's sacrifice was not connected to any specific festival, so it should likely be considered a peace offering. The beast could be male or female so long as it was "without blemish" (3:1). A key difference in this case is that neither the tabernacle nor priests play a part. But Samuel had been instructed by the Lord himself to make this sacrifice as part of his errand to Bethlehem, so these absences are no cause for concern.

3. And call Jesse to the sacrifice, and I will shew thee what thou shalt do: and thou shalt anoint unto me him whom I name unto thee.

The Lord did not give Samuel detailed instructions at this point, though Samuel might have appreciated a step-by-step guide in advance. All he needed to know to proceed was to take a *sacrifice* and to invite *Jesse* to be present for it. Samuel would walk by faith, eager for God's next instruction (compare Romans 1:17).

II. God Chooses David
(1 Samuel 16:4-13)

A. Coming to Bethlehem (vv. 4-5)

4-5a. And Samuel did that which the LORD spake, and came to Bethlehem. And the elders of the town trembled at his coming, and said, Comest thou peaceably? And he said, Peaceably.

It's unclear why *the elders* immediately *trembled at* Samuel's approach. Their reaction may be evidence that Samuel had a reputation for bringing punishment and bad news—a reputation that many prophets later earned (1 Kings 18:17-19; Jeremiah 38:1-4; Amos 7:10-17; etc.). The Hebrew word translated *peaceably* has more to do with positive connotations of peace—like wholeness and well-being—than simply an absence of violence. Regarding their question *Comest thou peaceably?* compare 1 Kings 2:13 and 2 Kings 9:17-29.

5b. I am come to sacrifice unto the LORD: sanctify yourselves, and come with me to the sacrifice. And he sanctified Jesse and his sons, and called them to the sacrifice.

Israel did not yet have a temple (1 Kings 6:1), and the ark of the covenant was located in Kirjathjearim (1 Samuel 7:1-2). Though in later generations, sacrifices offered outside Jerusalem and the temple where the ark was housed were often associated with idolatry (examples: 1 Kings 13:32-33; 14:23; 15:14), at this time it was the norm (example: 1 Samuel 9:11-25). Sacrifices such as Samuel's could be given on an altar that was built to God's specifications (Exodus 20:24-26).

Sanctification was an act of preparation that involved ceremonial washing to remove any ritual uncleanness and the donning of freshly washed clothes (example: Exodus 19:14-15; compare Numbers 6:1-21). The ritual of cleaning oneself for a sacrifice was an acknowledgment that ultimately no gift could be given to God that was "good enough," but He would accept what came from a clean heart (contrast Leviticus 26:41).

B. Rejecting Older Sons (vv. 6-10)

6. And it came to pass, when they were come, that he looked on Eliab, and said, Surely the LORD's anointed is before him.

Eliab was Jesse's oldest son (1 Chronicles 2:13). Being the firstborn son entitled him to high honor. He could expect to inherit double what his brothers would receive when Jesse died (Deuteronomy 21:15-17). Possibly Samuel noticed markers of Eliab's favored status, though this is by no means a necessary conclusion. More likely Jesse brought his firstborn in front of Samuel first, assuming this was another honor for the oldest son (see 1 Samuel 16:8-10, below). For whatever reason, Samuel jumped to the conclusion that his search was done.

7a. But the LORD said unto Samuel, Look not on his countenance, or on the height of his stature; because I have refused him.

Eliab was apparently tall and handsome, reason enough for Samuel to be impressed at first glance. But such outward measures had already failed as valid criteria regarding whether Saul was up for the job (1 Samuel 10:23-24; see lesson 8).

7b. For the LORD seeth not as man seeth; for man looketh on the outward appearance, but the LORD looketh on the heart.

The Lord would later tell Isaiah, "My thoughts are not your thoughts, neither are your ways my ways. . . . As the heavens are higher than the earth, so are my ways higher than your ways, and my thoughts than your thoughts" (Isaiah 55:8-9). The evidence supporting this truth is overwhelming, present from Genesis 1 to Revelation 22. Here God cites the key difference in the way He sees things. Society often judges a person based on his or her appearance (example: Esther 2:17-18; compare Isaiah 53:2-3), and Christians are not immune to making the same assessments (James 2:1-4). But *the Lord* looks past this—is not even distracted by *appearance*—and seeks out the deepest recesses of our hearts (Psalm 139).

Samuel could not possibly be expected to know Eliab's character on sight. But God's knowledge went beyond sight. We catch a glimpse of Eliab's heart when he fails to stand up to Goliath *and* chastises David (see 1 Samuel 17:28). That encounter gives us a clue as to why Eliab was not God's next choice for king (contrast 17:32-37a).

8-9. Then Jesse called Abinadab, and made him pass before Samuel. And he said, Neither hath the LORD chosen this. Then Jesse made Shammah to pass by. And he said, Neither hath the LORD chosen this.

Jesse called his second- and third-born sons,

Abinadab and *Shammah*, respectively. Little more is known about these brothers beyond that they were in Saul's military facing Goliath and the Philistines (1 Samuel 17:13).

10. Again, Jesse made seven of his sons to pass before Samuel. And Samuel said unto Jesse, The LORD hath not chosen these.

Only *seven* of Jesse's *sons* (and both of his daughters) are named in 1 Chronicles 2:13-15. But David was the eighth son (see 1 Samuel 16:11, below; 17:12). The likeliest explanation for this difference is that Jesse had another son who unfortunately died before reaching adulthood. Because a genealogy documented lineage, especially from father to son, a son who died before marrying and without heirs might not be named.

What Do You Think?

What do you learn from situations in which you have been passed over for a promotion or other position of authority?

Digging Deeper

How do you serve effectively when you have not been called to be a leader?

C. Selecting the Shepherd Son (vv. 11-13)

11a. And Samuel said unto Jesse, Are here all thy children? And he said, There remaineth yet the youngest, and, behold, he keepeth the sheep.

Jesse apparently considered his *youngest* too insignificant to be called home. Or maybe there was no one to relieve that son from his work watching *the sheep* (contrast 1 Samuel 17:20), and he seemed an unlikely choice regardless. Jesse's description of the missing son as the youngest could also be understood as the "smallest," suggesting that Jesse hadn't called this son home because he wasn't a grown man (compare 17:42). Exclusion for this reason clearly contradicts the Lord's admonition to Samuel that the physical qualities of a candidate were of no consequence (see 16:7, above).

Though shepherding was not a profession of great esteem, the imagery of a shepherd was used

How to Say It

Abimelech	Uh-*bim*-eh-lek.
Abinadab	Uh-*bin*-uh-dab.
Eliab	Ee-*lye*-ab.
Gibeah	*Gib*-ee-uh (*G* as in *get*).
Kirjathjearim	*Kir*-jath-**jee**-uh-rim or jee-*a*-rim.
Ramah	*Ray*-muh.
Shammah	Shuh-*muh*.

to describe the caliber of a leader. When a priest or king was unfaithful, the people were like defenseless, directionless sheep (Jeremiah 10:21; 23:1-2; Matthew 9:36). When the people were led well, it was like having a good shepherd guiding them (Psalm 23; Isaiah 40:11; John 10:1-18). The man God chose would be in the latter category (Ezekiel 34:23; 37:24).

11b. And Samuel said unto Jesse, Send and fetch him: for we will not sit down till he come hither.

Jesse and all his sons but one had been sanctified for the sacrifice (1 Samuel 16:5b, above). Still, Samuel insisted that the remaining son arrive before they sat down to eat the sacrifice (see 16:2b, above). Samuel needed to see the youngest son before his task was finished.

Picture Perfect

My husband is a part-time photographer with a very good eye. After one particular wedding shoot, he edited the proofs and picked out a few for the album. He left others out, thinking they would have little sentimental meaning to the bride and groom. When he met with the couple, they asked him if any pictures were missing and requested to see the ones he hadn't included. One of those missing photos became the main cover of their wedding album. My husband realized he was not the best judge of what others would find valuable in his photographs.

Like my husband, Jesse and Samuel both tried to make a decision that was better left to another—in their case, the Lord. But you have never done that, have you?　　　—P. M.

12a. And he sent, and brought him in. Now he was ruddy, and withal of a beautiful countenance, and goodly to look to.

Even though the Lord does not look at the outward appearance (1 Samuel 16:7, above; compare 2 Corinthians 10:7), the youngest was a good-looking young man. Just as we cannot assume that an attractive person is also a good person, neither can we assume that the opposite must be true (example: Isaiah 53:2b). Truly the outside is no measure, one way or the other.

Ruddy is a rare word in Hebrew for physical description that implies the color red. Elsewhere it described Esau's appearance at birth (Genesis 25:25; see lesson 2). This has been interpreted to mean Esau looked healthy and robust or, alternatively, that he had red hair and rosy cheeks. We cannot be sure of this, but if David had red hair, he would have been a conspicuous sight. Red hair is found among most of the peoples of the earth, but is rare in all.

12b. And the LORD said, Arise, anoint him: for this is he.

Though David had not been sanctified with his father and brothers for the sacrifice, the Lord indicated that not only would David participate, but he was to be anointed as Israel's next king (see 1 Samuel 16:13a, next).

13a. Then Samuel took the horn of oil, and anointed him in the midst of his brethren: and the Spirit of the LORD came upon David from that day forward.

Here all David's brothers stood, freshly washed and in their best clothes, ready for a feast. In from the fields came this youngster, unwashed, smelling like sheep . . . and *he* was the honored one! While this might be puzzling or even troubling to the brothers or other onlookers, we know that God had chosen David based on the state of the man's heart. Though he hadn't cleaned the outward dirt, inside David had a heart turned to God and ready to do His will.

Jesus later said to the scribes and Pharisees, "Ye make clean the outside of the cup and of the platter, but within they are full of extortion and excess. Thou blind Pharisee, cleanse first that which is within the cup and platter, that the outside of them may be clean also" (Matthew 23:25-26). We can conclude here that God considered David clean on the inside already; an outer washing would just have been for appearances.

Before the anointing of Saul and then David as kings in Israel, the act had been used primarily for ordaining priests or sanctifying an object as holy to the Lord (examples: Exodus 28:41; 30:22-33; Numbers 7:1; 35:25). From Abimelech's attempt to become king (Judges 9), anointing shifted to focusing more often on a king than a priest.

Significantly, *David* was not *anointed* only with *oil* but also with *the Spirit of the Lord* (compare 1 Samuel 10:6, 9-10; contrast 16:14, not in our printed text). This image reminds us of Jesus' own baptism in water and the Spirit's coming to Him "like a dove" (Luke 3:22; compare 4:18; Acts 10:38). Echoes of David are appropriate and even intentional in Jesus' life. After all, Jesus is the fulfillment of the promise to David of an eternal throne (2 Samuel 7:11b-16; Hebrew 1:8-9). And if David was an imperfect, fallen example of a man after God's own heart, Jesus is the perfect example, the very image of God (Colossians 1:15-20).

What treasure does your heart hold?

Visual for Lessons 6 & 9. *Ask the class to consider how they answered this question in lesson 6 and how it may have shifted since then.*

> **What Do You Think?**
> In what ways do you experience the presence of the Holy Spirit?
>
> **Digging Deeper**
> What you intentionally do this week to help you follow the Spirit's lead more closely (see Galatians 5:25)?

13b. So Samuel rose up, and went to Ramah.
The saga ends with no drama. The next king was anointed, so *Samuel* simply left to continue his usual work in *Ramah* (see 1 Samuel 7:17).

Conclusion

A. Walking by Faith

God's choice transcended human expectations of royalty and testifies to the Lord's knowledge of the human heart. We are at a disadvantage when we make decisions based on what we see. And sight may not be limited to what we sense right before our eyes. We fear that war and persecution may come to us, that violence is blossoming all around; we dread the next hurricane or tornado or earthquake. We mourn the moral failings of our secular leaders and, especially, of Christian leaders.

But like David, we have been anointed with the Spirit (2 Corinthians 1:21-22). And this Spirit leads us not into fear of what we see but with confidence in what we cannot see, hope in what we know by faith (5:7). Like Samuel, we do not often know the whole story or what we are meant to do

many (or even a few) steps into the future. For the prophet, as for us, the Lord gives the information needed in order to be able to act in faith. We can work confidently when we are focused on becoming more like Jesus and calling others to love Him as we do.

When you look at the world, do not trust only your senses. Ask God for the heart to see what He sees, to see past all the terror and sin to His redeeming work and desire for the hearts of all people. May we pray as David did, "Create in me a clean heart, O God" (Psalm 51:10).

> **What Do You Think?**
> What takeaways from lessons 8 and 9 are most challenging to you?
>
> **Digging Deeper**
> What changes do these insights require of you in thought, speech, and action?

B. Prayer

Lord God, teach us to value the heart over the outward appearance of a person. Purify our own hearts so that when others see us, they will see that You have chosen us and are forming us in the image of Jesus. It is in His name that we pray. Amen.

C. Thought to Remember

What does God see in your heart?

Involvement Learning

Enhance your lesson with KJV Bible Student *(from your curriculum supplier) and the reproducible activity page (at www.standardlesson.com or in the back of the* KJV Standard Lesson Commentary Deluxe Edition*).*

Into the Lesson

Give participants time to talk about how it worked during the past week to make choices by leaning on godly principles.

Distribute a handout (you prepare) with each of the following statements. Put the continuum at the top of the page or on the board.

Not at all important   Extremely Important

0   1   2   3   4   5

1. My reputation among my coworkers
2. The way I look when I go out to run errands
3. How clean and neat my clothes are
4. Whether my outfits reflect current styles
5. What my family members think of me
6. My ability to be "the best" in at least one area
7. The style reflected by the car I drive

Give students one minute to jot their answer beside each statement. Then ask volunteers to tell which statements they rated 4 or 5 and which they rated 1. Talk as a whole class about why people often rely on outward appearances.

Alternative. In groups of three, class members should search media for evidence of our culture's emphasis on outward appearances. If they find contrasting examples—an emphasis on internal character—they should note those also. Allow at least five minutes for group study before asking them to share examples with the whole class.

After either activity, lead into the Bible lesson by saying, "Samuel listened to what God was telling him—despite wanting to depend on appearances."

Into the Word

Divide the class into groups of three. Ask half the groups to skim 1 Samuel chapters 10–11 and 13–15 to understand why Saul (the subject of last week's lesson) was rejected as king by God. The other groups should use study Bibles or online Bible reference tools to prepare a brief report on Bethlehem. Allow six to eight minutes for research. Have groups report their findings to the whole class.

Send class members back to their groups to look at 1 Samuel 16:1-13. Write *God's sight is not human sight* on your board and ask class members to list how today's text shows that statement to be true.

After calling time, compare the lists as a whole class. Ask a volunteer to read Acts 13:22. Discuss how their findings agree with what Paul says about David.

Alternative. Distribute copies of the "Samuel's Tough Assignment" exercise from the activity page, which you can download. Have learners work in pairs or small groups to complete as indicated.

Into Life

Draw a large outline of a heart on your board or on a piece of newsprint taped to the wall. Distribute self-stick notes to class members, and ask them to write descriptions, each on a note, of the heart of God—what He values most. Invite them to attach their notes inside the heart you've drawn. Distribute sheets of paper. Ask each class member to draw a heart in the center of their sheet and write, in the center of it, one or two of the qualities on display inside the heart on the wall.

Alternative. Distribute copies of the "Leaders You Know" exercise from the activity page. Have learners work independently for one minute before working with others in their groups of three to complete the activity.

After either activity, end with sentence prayers from class members asking God to help them develop a clean heart and eyes of faith, as well as the specific qualities they wrote down. You may ask students to jot down their prayers on their sheets. Plan time next week to talk about how God is working to develop godly leadership qualities in your learners.

God Picked You!

Devotional Reading: Esther 4:5-17
Background Scripture: Acts 19; Ephesians 1:1-14; Revelation 2:1-7

Ephesians 1:1-14

1 Paul, an apostle of Jesus Christ by the will of God, to the saints which are at Ephesus, and to the faithful in Christ Jesus:

2 Grace be to you, and peace, from God our Father, and from the Lord Jesus Christ.

3 Blessed be the God and Father of our Lord Jesus Christ, who hath blessed us with all spiritual blessings in heavenly places in Christ:

4 According as he hath chosen us in him before the foundation of the world, that we should be holy and without blame before him in love:

5 Having predestinated us unto the adoption of children by Jesus Christ to himself, according to the good pleasure of his will,

6 To the praise of the glory of his grace, wherein he hath made us accepted in the beloved.

7 In whom we have redemption through his blood, the forgiveness of sins, according to the riches of his grace;

8 Wherein he hath abounded toward us in all wisdom and prudence;

9 Having made known unto us the mystery of his will, according to his good pleasure which he hath purposed in himself:

10 That in the dispensation of the fulness of times he might gather together in one all things in Christ, both which are in heaven, and which are on earth; even in him:

11 In whom also we have obtained an inheritance, being predestinated according to the purpose of him who worketh all things after the counsel of his own will:

12 That we should be to the praise of his glory, who first trusted in Christ.

13 In whom ye also trusted, after that ye heard the word of truth, the gospel of your salvation: in whom also after that ye believed, ye were sealed with that holy Spirit of promise,

14 Which is the earnest of our inheritance until the redemption of the purchased possession, unto the praise of his glory.

Key Text

Blessed be the God and Father of our Lord Jesus Christ, who hath blessed us with all spiritual blessings in heavenly places in Christ. —**Ephesians 1:3**

God's
Exceptional Choice

Unit 3: We Are God's Artwork
Lessons 10–13

Lesson Aims

After participating in this lesson, each student will be able to:

1. List spiritual blessings mentioned by Paul.
2. Compare and contrast physical adoption with spiritual adoption.
3. Make a plan to change one area of his or her lifestyle in light of adoption in Christ.

Lesson Outline

Introduction
A. The Love of the Father
B. Lesson Context
I. Greetings (Ephesians 1:1-2)
A. From Paul (v. 1a)
B. To the Faithful (vv. 1b-2)
II. Unbridled Blessing (Ephesians 1:3-14)
A. Of God (v. 3)
B. Through Christ (vv. 4-12)
   To the Praise of His Glory?
C. In the Spirit (vv. 13-14)
   Inheriting Well
Conclusion
A. Praise Him!
B. Prayer
C. Thought to Remember

Introduction
A. The Love of the Father

Completing the paperwork for an international adoption is a grueling process. The prospective parents must assemble birth certificates, medical affidavits, financial statements, etc. The family doctor and social worker must include copies of their licenses. Every signature must be notarized, and the county courthouse must verify the authenticity of the notary stamps. The county seal is "apostilled" at the state capital, a fancy way of describing another level of certification. The whole portfolio then goes overseas to be translated, with a new series of stamps added to verify the translation.

Now imagine if it were possible instead for just one person of great authority to look at the portfolio and put one stamp on the whole thing to approve the adoption. God himself has already placed His seal of adoption on us. Our text today celebrates our Father and His great love for us.

B. Lesson Context

The book of Ephesians is one of what we often call Paul's prison letters. As in Philippians, Colossians, and Philemon, Paul presented himself as "the prisoner" (Ephesians 3:1; compare 2 Timothy 1:8). It is reasonable to conclude that he wrote this letter while he was a prisoner in Rome (see Acts 22–28) in about AD 63.

Paul's letter to the Ephesians has many of the features of his other letters. But unlike the others, Ephesians does not clearly address a problem or issues that arose in a particular church. Rather, it reads as a general reminder and instruction in the nature of the gospel and the Christian life. This is one reason some believe it was a circular letter that was sent to the city of Ephesus (in present-day Turkey) to be read and then shared in the surrounding region (see Ephesians 1:1b, below; see lesson 11 for more information about Ephesus).

Ephesians includes challenging language and ideas. Our scripture text mentions many concepts that long have been debated. But when we remember the challenges that Christians of both Jewish and Gentile backgrounds faced, we can reframe those difficult concepts.

I. Greetings
(Ephesians 1:1-2)
A. From Paul (v. 1a)

1a. Paul, an apostle of Jesus Christ by the will of God.

A Roman apostle was an official messenger who conveyed messages from authority figures to the public. On the road to Damascus, *Jesus* claimed *Paul* as His own messenger (Acts 26:12-16). Paul's zeal, previously misdirected toward murderous ends (9:1-2; Galatians 1:13-14), was put to use *for* the making of disciples for *Christ*. All this happened according to *the will of God* (1:15-24).

The word *Christ* is a translation of the Hebrew word *messiah*. Both designations refer to the anointed one, associated since David's days with God's chosen kings in Israel (1 Samuel 16:1, 12-13; 2 Samuel 7:8-16; compare John 1:41; 4:25). Before that, the term was not used but could have been appropriately applied to priests, who were anointed for their service in the tabernacle (Exodus 28:41; etc.). Jesus fulfills the roles of both priest and king (Hebrews 8:1-6; Revelation 17:14), making Him uniquely positioned to be *the* Christ.

B. To the Faithful (vv. 1b-2)

1b. To the saints which are at Ephesus, and to the faithful in Christ Jesus.

This greeting is descriptive but generic. Since Paul's greetings are often very specific, this is one piece of evidence that the letter was meant for circulation instead of intended only to address those in *Ephesus*. Paul seemed intent to explain his doctrine succinctly, looking to what it means to be part of those who are *the faithful in Christ Jesus. Saints* simply means "holy ones," affirming that these people were set apart from others because they belonged to God. This word had referred only to Israel until Jesus' time (Deuteronomy 28:9; Isaiah 62:12; etc.). Paul used the word to emphasize that Gentiles were welcomed into faith in Jesus, on equal standing with their Jewish brothers and sisters who had also accepted Christ. It was not enough or even necessary to claim heritage in Abraham, because faith was and is the primary condition for determining whether one is a saint. The lives of saints are different, even out of place in the world, because our identity is found in Christ, not in human families, clans, or nations (Galatians 3:27-29).

2a. Grace be to you, and peace.

The greeting *grace* plays on the more typical Greek greeting *rejoice*. The words sound similar in Greek. Paul's choice emphasizes the Christian nature of this letter (compare 1 Peter 1:2; 2 Peter 1:2; Revelation 1:4). *Peace* was a typical greeting in Hebrew, a prayer for God's blessing to fall on His people. Far from the mere absence of violence or discord, the word has the much more positive connotation of wholeness and wellness. Grace acknowledges that asking for peace is totally based on God's good desires, not on anything a person or people have done to earn His favor. Together grace and peace turned an otherwise unremarkable greeting into an expectant expression of God's blessing.

2b. From God our Father, and from the Lord Jesus Christ.

Naming *God our Father* in parallel with *the Lord Jesus Christ* highlights the Christian revelation of the Son's equality with the Father. Unbelieving Jews considered this new Christian belief a sin against the command to love the Lord alone (Deuteronomy 6:4-5). However, naming Jesus Christ as Lord makes clear that Paul and other Christians understood that Jesus was well worthy of love and praise, just as God the Father is (Galatians 2:8-11).

II. Unbridled Blessing
(Ephesians 1:3-14)
A. Of God (v. 3)

3. Blessed be the God and Father of our Lord Jesus Christ, who hath blessed us with all spiritual blessings in heavenly places in Christ.

We sense Paul's joy conveyed in the length of this sentence—in the Greek it doesn't end until verse 14! This is the longest sentence in the New Testament at just over 200 words in the Greek. We can imagine his scribe (likely Tychicus; see Ephesians 6:21) frantically taking down Paul's breathless praise.

Paul's presentation of God as the *Father of our Lord Jesus Christ* (compare 2 Corinthians 1:3; 1 Peter 1:3) is in keeping with Jesus' emphasis on God "our Father" (Matthew 6:9). The Jews of Paul's day had many ways to describe God, but God as Father is not found very often. Yet God as Father is an understanding that runs throughout Jesus' teachings (examples: 23:9; John 4:23; compare Romans 1:7; 8:15; 1 Corinthians 8:6).

Paul's repetition conveys his overwhelming awe. He was a scholar in the Hebrew Scriptures, and his writings' content and style both show Hebrew influences. One way Hebrew poetry strengthens a statement is by repeating it, either with the same phrase (example: Psalm 136) or with synonyms and other slight changes (examples: 1:1; 5:3). Paul's multiple use of forms of *bless* suggests (by word and by repetition) the greatness of our *God* and our *blessings*. To call God *blessed* is to acknowledge that He is praiseworthy and exalted. To call His people *blessed* is to acknowledge the reality that God gives us good gifts (James 1:17) and works out all things for our good (Romans 8:28).

In heavenly places refers to the throne room of God (Ephesians 1:20; 2:6; 3:10; 6:12). Because we are already part of God's family, we experience blessing in His presence now, though we still suffer because of the fallen world around us.

B. Through Christ (vv. 4-12)
4. According as he hath chosen us in him

before the foundation of the world, that we should be holy and without blame before him in love.

Before the foundation of the world focuses on God's plan before creation (compare 2 Thessalonians 2:13). Though God's choosing *us* may seem like a statement of predestination (see Ephesians 1:5, below), it is actually a much broader statement of God's loving intent for all people. We were all meant to *be holy and without blame before him*. The fall threw all people into a sinful tailspin outside of God's good plan (Genesis 3:16-24; 6:5-6, 11; etc.).

But God was unwilling to let sin take its natural course and condemn all people to death. So God set in motion the plan that would call us back to him *in love*. Jesus was that plan. And through His death He conquered both sin and death, doing what we could not accomplish for ourselves. Our status changes as a result. We are counted as being holy (set apart in a godly way) and without blame (having our sins forgiven). We gain these attributes because of God's efforts through Christ.

5. Having predestinated us unto the adoption of children by Jesus Christ to himself, according to the good pleasure of his will.

This verse implies that Paul's audience is primarily Gentile, as they would identify with being adopted into the "natural" family Israel. The practice of adoption goes back thousands of years. Properly motivated, adoption is an act of grace toward orphans or children whose parents are unable to care for them. In the Roman world of Paul's day, there was another important consideration when it came to adoption: a father who had no sons might adopt someone to be his heir. This allowed the father's assets to be distributed according to his will—and for his family line and name to continue.

Predestinated echoes God's pre-creation choice for people (see Ephesians 1:4, above; also 1:11, below). Some scholars believe this means that everyone's eternal status was decided by God before anyone was born. However, we should not fall into fatalism—the belief that free will does not exist, that we can make no choices that influence the outcome. God has chosen us by His grace; we must choose Him through our faith (John 1:12).

The emphasis here is not on predestination but on *adoption*. God's plan to adopt humans as His *children* in holiness was fulfilled only in *Jesus Christ*. Nothing that happened around Christ's coming or in His ministry, death, and resurrection was haphazard, a fluke, or a mistake. This act of loving mercy is described as coming from *the good pleasure of his will*. Our adoption is not done grudgingly or under compulsion. God's desire is for us to be reconciled to Him, to be included among His people. Inclusion into God's family is a marvelous demonstration of God's love (see 1 John 3:1).

6. To the praise of the glory of his grace, wherein he hath made us accepted in the beloved.

God's pre-creation plan, when put into action, produces worship. Believers of all nations worship the God who made them His people (Revelation 15:4). Angels worship the God whose plan has been fulfilled (5:11-12). In Heaven and on earth, through both time and space, we are one congregation glorifying God (compare 5:13-14).

This blessed acceptance cannot be separated from the grand act of love that characterizes God's work in Jesus Christ. He is referred to here as *the beloved* (compare Matthew 3:17). Christ is the Son of God in a unique way, but God's love is extended to all who believe and are adopted as sons and daughters in Christ (John 1:12; Galatians 3:26). Our adoption results in full acceptance as children of God, with all the rights of an heir (4:7).

To the Praise of His Glory?

"Your daughter has no heartbeat." Eleven and a half minutes with no heartbeat post-birth would leave my daughter with severe brain injuries—if she lived. Was this God's plan, leading "to the praise of the glory of his grace" (Ephesians 1:6)?

Three days later, with few answers, I wrote one of the most difficult prayers of my life: "I want her to be able to run and sing and laugh. But I entrust her into Your care and infinite wisdom. If she dies tomorrow, or if she can't play or eat or breathe on her own, I trust that her life still will result in many people loving You. Be glorified, Lord. Amen."

Six years later, my daughter requires extensive care. She can't walk or eat on her own, but she laughs and plays in her own way. And many people have shared how my daughter has strengthened their faith in God. He has indeed glorified himself through my daughter—and how I thank Him for doing so! What have you thanked God for today?   —N. G.

7-8a. In whom we have redemption through his blood, the forgiveness of sins, according to the riches of his grace; wherein he hath abounded toward us.

Redemption and forgiveness are both terms used to speak of the liberation of slaves. The Ephesian believers were familiar with both words as they related to slavery in the Roman world. Redemption means to be "bought back," as a slave might be repurchased. Forgiveness means "letting go" and can refer to the release of a slave. Paul drew on this cultural example to describe the passage from a sinful life into one of *forgiveness* in Christ (compare Colossians 1:14, 20).

The word translated *sins* is translated "trespasses" in Jesus' explanation of the Lord's Prayer (Matthew 6:14-15). The idea behind the word is "to stray from the correct path while traveling." We are reminded of the common biblical depiction of life as a journey made up of choices (see Deuteronomy 30:15-18). Through the *blood* of Jesus, we have the means to be delivered from wrong choices and be put back on the path of God's choosing (Romans 2:4; 3:24-25). *The riches of his grace* (also Ephesians 2:7) are truly marvelous!

What Do You Think?
In light of the fact that God has forgiven you for *all* your sins, who do you need to forgive for sinning against you?

Digging Deeper
How can you forgive a person when reconciliation is either impossible or unwise?

8b-9. In all wisdom and prudence; having made known unto us the mystery of his will, according to his good pleasure which he hath purposed in himself.

All wisdom and prudence describes God's way of dealing with His wayward children. Wisdom conveys the sense of knowing the difference between right and wrong and making the choice to do the right thing (compare Proverbs 1:10). In this context, prudence refers to correct thinking.

In the Bible there are various ways that God makes His will known to humans. One is that of a mystery being revealed, something initially hidden from human understanding but now being shown (Ephesians 3:9). We understand God as a self-revealing God, for we cannot unravel the deep things of God by our own deep thinking (Romans 16:25). A god that people can fully comprehend is more likely made in their *own* image rather than the other way around (Genesis 1:27).

10. That in the dispensation of the fulness of times he might gather together in one all things in Christ, both which are in heaven, and which are on earth; even in him.

God's fulfilled plan restores and unites *all* of creation (Romans 8:19-22). Everything God created suffers because of the effects of sin. And because God loves all of His creation—from people created in His image to deep-sea creatures we will never see to mountains we can't miss— He will *gather together in one all things in Christ* (Colossians 1:20). A key part of this is the reunification of humanity, which is divided into hostile groups. The barrier between Jews and Gentiles is broken down through Christ (Ephesians 2:14); these groups can be brought together in Christ according to God's will and purpose (3:4-6).

All this is according to God's plan, for it takes place at *the fulness of times* (see Galatians 4:4). Bringing everything together in Jesus will not be fully realized until He returns. But let us not miss how Christ is already accomplishing this promised future. Whenever by God's mercy a sinner becomes a saint, whenever through the gospel the estranged are reconciled, whenever through their lives of loving service Christians bring a greater measure of justice to the world, we see God's plan already being fulfilled (Mark 1:15; Romans 5:6).

11-12. In whom also we have obtained an inheritance, being predestinated according to the purpose of him who worketh all things after the counsel of his own will: that we should be to the praise of his glory, who first trusted in Christ.

Once again Paul reassures the reader that nothing happens without God's allowing it (Romans 8:28; see Ephesians 1:5, above). Regardless of believers' physical circumstances, we are experiencing already the blessings of God. The proper response following redemption is giving *praise* and *glory* to God. This concept is once again couched in adoption language. Our adoption results in the *inheritance* (Romans 8:29-30; Hebrews 6:17-20). We do not inherit money or property, though, but the spiritual treasures of God (Ephesians 1:18-21).

What Do You Think?
How can you better demonstrate the unity you have with fellow Christians?

Digging Deeper
How does your answer apply to Christians who hold doctrinal beliefs that differ from your own?

C. In the Spirit (vv. 13-14)

13. In whom ye also trusted, after that ye heard the word of truth, the gospel of your salvation: in whom also after that ye believed, ye were sealed with that holy Spirit of promise.

Roman officials affixed wax seals to documents to indicate their authenticity and authority. Paul used this image to help us understand the nature of the gift of God's Spirit to the believer. After we accept *the word of truth, the gospel*, we are in line for a marvelous inheritance (Colossians 1:5). We do not wait to begin to enjoy the blessings of this inheritance, for we are *sealed* by God through the gift of the *holy Spirit* (Ephesians 4:30).

Paul pictures this spiritual sealing as a *promise* (compare Acts 2:16-18). This gift of the Holy Spirit is bestowed *after* faith (John 14:16-17). While the Holy Spirit plays a role in drawing people to faith, the Spirit's presence in the heart is a gift promised to believers (Acts 2:38-39).

14. Which is the earnest of our inheritance until the redemption of the purchased possession, unto the praise of his glory.

The gift of the Holy Spirit is not our full inheritance, but is *the earnest of our inheritance.* The key word *earnest* is a legal term that refers to a down payment in a transaction. The idea is that of a "first installment" (compare 2 Corinthians 1:22; 5:5). The Spirit is a gift promising more gifts to come. Through the Holy Spirit, believers experience God's presence and power now, a taste of what we will experience in full when Christ returns. The future holds not only the final defeat of sin and its effects but also spiritual fulfillment and completion.

Paul finished this long, complex, Greek sentence (which began in verse 3 of our text) with an observation regarding praise. Praise of God is our recognition of His mighty works and person. When Paul said that God acts for *the praise of his glory* (see Ephesians 1:6, 12, above), the apostle was not implying that God somehow needs human approval. Humans should praise God because it is good, proper, and part of our created nature.

> **What Do You Think?**
> What prevents you from wholly trusting the Holy Spirit?
>
> **Digging Deeper**
> Who are believers you trust to mentor you in deepening your dependence on the Spirit?

Inheriting Well

After 45 years of marriage, George's wife passed away, leaving him alone and lonely. One day he decided to do something special for his daughter and two daughters-in-law. He carefully divided his late wife's jewelry into three piles, then wrote notes explaining how much his wife had loved them. George packaged and mailed the gifts. But his daughter was furious. How *dare* her father give her mother's jewelry to her brothers' wives? The conflict left George even more heartbroken than before.

Such squabbles certainly don't honor the giver. Response to the inheritance that Paul describes should be different. God grants this inheritance both to Jewish and Gentile believers, to "the praise

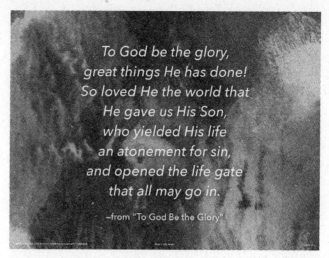

To God be the glory,
great things He has done!
So loved He the world that
He gave us His Son,
who yielded His life
an atonement for sin,
and opened the life gate
that all may go in.

—from "To God Be the Glory"

Visual for Lesson 10. *Consider singing or playing a recording of "To God Be the Glory" as your students enter the classroom.*

of his glory." How will you honor your Father's decision in celebrating the inheritance He leaves for you *and* your brothers and sisters?   —N. G.

Conclusion
A. Praise Him!

The ability to praise and worship God freely and properly is indeed a part of our inheritance and a manifestation of the Holy Spirit in our lives. While all His works offer opportunity to worship, our adoption into God's own family is an especially joyful reason for praise. May we, who have been brought into the Father's family through His loving Son and His trustworthy Spirit, erupt in praise for our salvation.

B. Prayer

Glorious Father, we are in awe of Your grace! Remind us always of our standing before You, even as we wait for Your Son to return in glory. In Jesus' name we pray. Amen.

C. Thought to Remember
Rejoice in God's plan for your salvation.

How to Say It

Ephesus	*Ef*-uh-sus.
Messiah	Meh-*sigh*-uh.
Tychicus	*Tick*-ih-cuss.

Involvement Learning

Enhance your lesson with KJV Bible Student *(from your curriculum supplier) and the reproducible activity page (at www.standardlesson.com or in the back of the* KJV Standard Lesson Commentary Deluxe Edition*).*

Into the Lesson

Before class, collect magazines related to business, sports, and entertainment. Have students form pairs (or groups of three), and distribute the magazines. Instruct participants to look through the magazines for articles and advertisements that suggest criteria for success, like ads for expensive cars or an article about winning a lifetime achievement award. *Option.* Instead of using magazines, give each group a few minutes to create a list for success.

Invite them to call out words, phrases, and images as you write them on the board. After five minutes, stop building the list and label it "Worldly Lens."

Alternative. Distribute copies of the "Winning Qualities" exercise from the activity page, which you can download. Allow three minutes for pairs to complete the activity.

After either activity, discuss how our criteria for choosing a winner or determining success affects how we see ourselves and how we interact with others. Consider pressures as well as possible positive outcomes of a culture focused on winning awards. Wrap up by saying, "Today's lesson allows us to expand beyond a popular worldview and think about who we are in Christ."

Into the Word

Distribute an index card and a pen to each participant. Invite volunteers to take turns slowly reading aloud Ephesians 1:1-14. Learners should listen closely to Paul's statements and write down any words describing who they are in Christ like *holy, without blame, chosen, redemption, adoption as God's children*, and *forgiven*. Compile these words in a list on the board next to the "Worldly Lens" list from the previous activity. Label the new list "Godly Lens." Take a few minutes as a whole class to compare and contrast the lists.

Instruct participants to flip over their index cards and take one minute to jot down how any of the words, from either list, impact their daily lives. Then ask: "How can understanding the differences between the world's expectations and God's truth affect how you see yourself?"

Alternative. Participants might have children or other loved ones who also need to hear Paul's message. Invite them to consider this secondary audience and write a modern-day letter to that person, using the passage from Ephesians as a model.

Into Life

Ask participants to consider what criteria they would use for success in their spiritual lives. Extend the discussion by asking: "What is your identity in Christ?"

Allow time for reflection on challenges participants anticipate in the week ahead. Encourage note-taking. Then ask learners to consider what type of outcomes they'd like to have for their challenges. Ask these questions to help their brainstorming: 1–How can you create a successful outcome? 2–Why does our understanding of our identity in Jesus Christ affect how we approach day-to-day life?

Encourage students to make connections about themselves as part of God's family and how this impacts the way they approach relationships and goals for their lives. Allow one minute for silent reflection on one change that each student could make in light of his or her adoption in Christ.

Alternative. Distribute copies of the "Adopted in Christ" exercise from the activity page. Allow a minute for students to work individually; then let them work together to complete the puzzle. Discuss ideas for how to implement this message into their lives this week when they are faced with challenges.

Plan time during next week's lesson to see how learners are dealing with their challenges from the perspective of being God's children. Close with a prayer of praise for adoption into Christ's family.

Christ Is Wisdom

Devotional Reading: Psalm 16
Background Scripture: Acts 19; Ephesians 1:15-23; Revelation 2:1-7

Ephesians 1:15-23

15 Wherefore I also, after I heard of your faith in the Lord Jesus, and love unto all the saints,

16 Cease not to give thanks for you, making mention of you in my prayers;

17 That the God of our Lord Jesus Christ, the Father of glory, may give unto you the spirit of wisdom and revelation in the knowledge of him:

18 The eyes of your understanding being enlightened; that ye may know what is the hope of his calling, and what the riches of the glory of his inheritance in the saints,

19 And what is the exceeding greatness of his power to us-ward who believe, according to the working of his mighty power,

20 Which he wrought in Christ, when he raised him from thc dead, and set him at his own right hand in the heavenly places,

21 Far above all principality, and power, and might, and dominion, and every name that is named, not only in this world, but also in that which is to come:

22 And hath put all things under his feet, and gave him to be the head over all things to the church,

23 Which is his body, the fulness of him that filleth all in all.

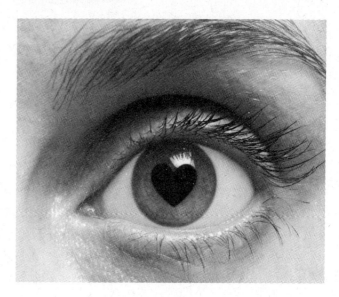

Key Text

The eyes of your understanding being enlightened; that ye may know what is the hope of his calling, and what the riches of the glory of his inheritance in the saints. —**Ephesians 1:18**

God's Exceptional Choice

Unit 3: We Are God's Artwork
Lessons 10–13

Lesson Aims

After participating in this lesson, each learner will be able to:

1. List things for which Paul prayed.

2. Explain the meaning and significance of the "eyes of your" statement.

3. Make a list of people he or she will promise to pray for as Paul did.

Lesson Outline

Introduction

A. Everything Looks So Different!

When my father was in grade school, he was perpetually cutting up in class, distracting other students, and generally causing a ruckus. While looking for solutions to the issues, it was discovered that his eyesight was very poor. His whole world changed after receiving his first pair of glasses! He could see so clearly, and his lifelong love of reading was born. The once rambunctious troublemaker could now sit quietly for hours with his books, enjoying a wider perspective thanks to the sharpness of his sight.

Perhaps you have had a similar experience, either literally or figuratively. The world that seemed normal to you became somehow different when finally the right "glasses" corrected your sight. In Christ, everything looks so different!

B. Lesson Context

Ephesus was a leading city of the Roman Empire. It was a large administrative center, perhaps 200,000 in population. Its Jewish population was substantial (some estimate more than 10,000), with many synagogues. Ephesus was a bustling seaport at the time, the point of contact for trade from the eastern and the western parts of the empire. Its harbor eventually filled with silt and became unusable, however, so the site was abandoned within a few hundred years. Ephesus was home to the Temple of Diana (the goddess's Roman name; Artemis in Greek), one of the Seven Wonders of the Ancient World (Acts 19:35).

Paul's first contact with the Ephesians was on his second missionary journey (AD 52–54). After his lengthy ministry in Corinth (Acts 18:11), Paul, accompanied by Priscilla and Aquila, set sail for Ephesus. He remained there only a short time and then departed for Jerusalem, leaving Priscilla and Aquila behind (18:18-21).

Paul's second visit to Ephesus was on his third missionary journey, the account of which is recorded in Acts 18:23–21:6 (about AD 54–58). He spent about two and a half years in that city (compare the chronological references in 19:8, 10 and 20:31). Those converted under Paul's ministry gave up their magic practices and burned their magic books—worth 50,000 pieces of silver, which is estimated to be equal to the yearly income of more than 130 men (19:18-19). The impact of his ministry had such an effect in the city that Demetrius, a leader of the local silversmiths, incited a mob at the theater against Christian teaching (19:23-41).

Demetrius's motive was less religious than economic. The problem was that, due to Paul's ministry, widespread conversion to Christianity occurred. This meant that people were not purchasing the cultic paraphernalia of Diana, and this created a significant income loss for the silversmiths. So Demetrius persuaded the crowds that Christianity was not only detrimental to their business but also brought disrepute to the goddess Diana, who was worshipped throughout "Asia and the world" (Acts 19:27).

The message of Christianity was making inroads in a great trade city of the Roman Empire, upsetting the status quo in the process. Paul's message reached both Jews and Greeks (Acts 19:10, 17; 20:21). After leaving Ephesus, he ministered in Macedonia and Achaia. And on his return Paul visited the Ephesian elders at Miletus, where he reminded them of his ministry, warned them about false teachers, and prayed with them before his departure (20:15-38). The letter we call Ephesians came about some five years later, while Paul was imprisoned (Ephesians 3:1; 4:1; 6:20).

Our text picks up exactly where lesson 10 (Ephesians 1:1-14) left off. Most letters in Paul's time offered a brief word of thanks to whatever god the writer worshipped. Paul followed this practice in most of his letters in the New Testament, praising only the true God. And he used the thanksgiving not just as a formality—part of good letter writing—but as a way to introduce ideas that he would develop later in the letter.

I. Prayer for the Present
(Ephesians 1:15-16)
A. Because of Faith and Love (v. 15)
15a. Wherefore I also, after I heard of your faith in the Lord Jesus.

Wherefore signals that the new thought beginning here is a result of what Paul has already written (Ephesians 1:1-14; see lesson 10). Paul was present with Priscilla and Aquila when the Ephesian church was planted (see Lesson Context). Despite cultural pressures, the Ephesians had maintained their *faith in the Lord Jesus.* Receiving this report from messengers or other missionaries put Paul's mind at ease to some degree (compare 2 Corinthians 11:28-29).

15b. And love unto all the saints.

The greatest expression of faith in Christ is loving one another (Matthew 22:37-40; 1 Corinthians 13; 1 John 2:10-11). Christians are called to love others because Christ has loved them at the cost of His own life (4:9-10). The love of Christ knows no boundaries.

Despite popular usage today, the word *saints* in the Bible refers not to a select number of believers but to all those who put their faith in Christ. Loving every saint meant the Ephesians saw through the past divisions to cherish each believer they met (Galatians 3:26-28).

B. Of Thanksgiving (v. 16)
16. Cease not to give thanks for you, making mention of you in my prayers.

Paul practiced what he preached: "Pray without ceasing. In every thing *give thanks*" (1 Thessalonians 5:17-18). His time in prison likely afforded Paul time to spend in extended prayer. Even so, the phrase *cease not* does not mean he was praying 100 percent of the time. Instead, prayer was Paul's faithful habit (compare Romans 1:9-10; 12:12; Philippians 1:4; etc.).

Though Jesus warned about heaping up words

How to Say It

Achaia	Uh-*kay*-uh.
Aquila	*Ack*-wih-luh.
Demetrius	De-*mee*-tree-us.
Miletus	My-*lee*-tus.
Orual	*Oh*-roo-awl.
Pax Romana *(Latin)*	*Pahks* Ro-*mah*-nah.
Priscilla	Prih-*sil*-uh.
Psyche	*Sigh*-kee.

when we pray (Matthew 6:7-8), what Paul models here certainly is a positive example. Indeed, in many aspects Paul's habitual prayers for churches and believers (example: Colossians 1:3; 1 Thessalonians 1:2) fulfilled Jesus' own model of prayer, beginning with the expectation that God would be glorified and that His kingdom would come and His will would be done "in earth, as it is in heaven" (Matthew 6:10). Prayers that come from sincere faith and love are never inappropriate and bear repeating regularly. God always deserves our praise, and giving Him praise affirms that we treasure Him above all else (compare 6:21).

What Do You Think?

How do you incorporate thanks for fellow believers into your prayer life?

Digging Deeper

How does the state of your relationship with those believers—whether friends, "competitors," or strangers—affect your thanksgiving for them?

A Gracious Cycle

My wife and I thank God every time we remember the refugees who lived by us in northern Africa. At night next to the campfire, they patiently taught us their language. We worshipped with the small group of believers in their hand-built church building. They paged through the Arabic and English Bibles, trying to understand the truth presented in their second or third languages. Even their non-Christian neighbors were excited about the first Scripture portions in their own language.

The small refugee church kept growing. Our missionary teammates launched discipleship groups, a Bible translation team, and a literacy program. In 2020 the native believers numbered over 1,000 and led their congregations—planting more and discipling everywhere.

We already thanked God every time we remembered these believers, and we still with very great reason! This thanks naturally led us into even more prayer for them. I've heard of a *vicious* cycle, but this was a *gracious* cycle. Who ignites your heart in a gracious cycle? —N. G.

II. Prayer for Growth
(Ephesians 1:17-19)
A. To Know Him (v. 17)

17. That the God of our Lord Jesus Christ, the Father of glory, may give unto you the spirit of wisdom and revelation in the knowledge of him.

Paul has already spoken repeatedly of *the God of our Lord Jesus Christ* and expounded on the Father's *glory* (see Ephesians 1:6, 12, 14; lesson 10). This inspires believers to praise.

The spirit of wisdom and revelation in the original Greek can be taken, grammatically, to refer to the human spirit. In other words, Paul asked God to give each person wisdom and revelation *in the knowledge of* God in his or her own spirit. Elsewhere the Holy Ghost, or the Spirit, is associated with wisdom (Acts 6:3) and spiritual knowledge (1 Corinthians 2:4, 13). Ultimately the Holy Spirit gives wisdom (knowledge of how to live rightly applied to living) and revelation (the uncovering of knowledge that cannot be achieved by humans, no matter how hard we think or meditate, without the Spirit's intervention).

Paul did not pray that the Ephesian believers receive the Holy Spirit for the first time. They were sealed already with the Holy Spirit as their guarantee of a future inheritance from God (Ephesians 1:13-14; see lesson 10). But the Holy Spirit has a role in applying the truth of the gospel to the life of the believer (1 Corinthians 2:10-13; Colossians 1:9-10).

The Bible itself is a Spirit-directed revelation of God (2 Timothy 3:16). Jesus is the most direct revelation of God that we have—God in the flesh (John 14:6-9). The Spirit is given to believers so that we can continue to grow in our knowledge of the Lord, and thus love Him and follow in His paths (14:23-27).

The wise person does not simply know the truth but lives it out (examples: Proverbs 3:7; Matthew 7:24-27). True wisdom and revelation come through knowledge of what God in Christ has done (1 Corinthians 1:20-25). No true wisdom, knowledge, or revelation contradicts the Lord's.

B. To Be Enlightened (vv. 18-19)

18a. The eyes of your understanding being enlightened.

The result of receiving "wisdom and revelation" (Ephesians 1:17, above) is godly enlightenment. Our physical senses allow us to make sense of the physical world around us. Our *eyes* can be similarly attuned to spiritual reality. This metaphor reminds us of Jesus' words about those who have eyes that see or don't see (Matthew 13:14-17; see Isaiah 6:10). Having our eyes wide open gives us a different perspective from which to interpret the world. What once seemed most important is now placed below seeking God's kingdom (Matthew 6:33).

18b. That ye may know what is the hope of his calling, and what the riches of the glory of his inheritance in the saints.

Christian *hope* is more than a wish for the future, because it is based on the actions of our trustworthy God. Specifically, our expectant hopes are based on Jesus' ministry and especially His death and resurrection. Because of this work, the penalty for our sins is paid and we receive eternal life (1 Corinthians 15:1-4, 20-28). These are part of *the riches of the glory of his inheritance* for us (Ephesians 1:14; see lesson 10). We have confidence that no matter what happens in the short term, we will experience the fullness of God's blessings.

The biblical concept of calling can be specific (like the call of a prophet to ministry; example: 1 Samuel 3:10) or general (like the call of Israel to be God's holy people; example: Joshua 24:1-18). The *calling* here is general, issued to all people to believe the gospel and put their hope in Christ (Matthew 28:18-20). Responding to this call results in some immediate blessings, such as forgiveness and reconciliation with God (John 3:16-21) as well as the presence of the Holy Spirit

(Romans 5:5). Continuing in faithfulness to the call results in growth in the Spirit toward greater godliness (examples: 2 Corinthians 4:16; Galatians 5:16-18, 22-25). No matter where we are in our spiritual walk, we can always be encouraged by the hope we have and continue to appreciate the fullness of the life we have in Christ (John 10:10).

Rags or Riches?

C. S. Lewis's novel *Till We Have Faces* is a creative retelling of the myth of Cupid and Psyche. The woman Psyche was spirited away to a mountain to be wedded to the god Cupid. But her sudden and unexplained disappearance caused her family to believe Psyche was dead. Yet her sister Orual found her alive. When Psyche gave Orual a handful of berries and a palmful of water, claiming they were fine food and wine, Orual began to worry. Psyche also thought that her rags were elegant clothes and saw her palace in place of the desolate mountains her sister perceived. Despite the rags Orual saw, Psyche really *was* surrounded by the riches Cupid had given her, his bride.

Lewis retold this myth as an allegory of what life is like for Christians. Like Psyche, we see spiritual blessing where others see only physical circumstance. Paul prayed for the Ephesians to see the hidden, glorious reality of life in Christ. Do you see it? Are you echoing Paul's prayer for those around you to see it too?

—N. G.

19. And what is the exceeding greatness of his power to us-ward who believe, according to the working of his mighty power.

In this verse Paul used several Greek words that can indicate *power* as a way of emphasizing *the exceeding greatness of* God's own power. The greatest examples of God's power are found in Christ's resurrection (see Ephesians 1:20, below), in the

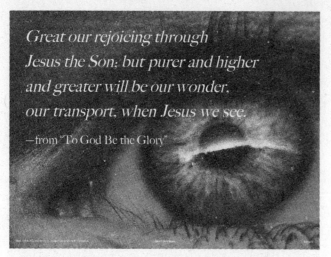

Great our rejoicing through Jesus the Son: but purer and higher and greater will be our wonder, our transport, when Jesus we see.

—from "To God Be the Glory"

Visual for Lesson 11. *Play a recording of this hymn or ask the class to sing this verse together before ending the class with prayer.*

Father's giving us new life in the Spirit now (see 1:17, above), and in our hope for our own future resurrection (1:13-14; see lesson 10). No force—not even sin and death—can stand against our Lord!

III. Praise of God's Power
(Ephesians 1:20-23)
A. Glorified Christ (vv. 20-21)

20. Which he wrought in Christ, when he raised him from the dead, and set him at his own right hand in the heavenly places.

Power throughout the ages is often expressed as military might, political domination, and the unchecked use of wealth and privilege for one's own ends. But the power of God (see Ephesians 1:19, above) is seen in the cross and empty tomb of Christ. No amount of earthly power or wealth can restore life to the dead.

When David was king in Israel (1010–970 BC), he wrote, "The Lord said unto my Lord, Sit thou at my right hand, until I make thine enemies thy footstool" (Psalm 110:1). This poem celebrated (in anticipation of) God's rule that would come through the king He had promised to David. Jesus referred to this verse when He asked the Pharisees who the Messiah is (Matthew 22:41-46) and again when on trial before the Jewish leaders (Luke 22:66-70). At Pentecost, Peter explained David's words as they referred to Jesus (Acts 2:29-36). Now Paul affirms that Jesus is indeed at the

Father's *right hand in the heavenly places*, a clear sign that Jesus is *Christ*, the Greek translation of the Hebrew word *messiah* (John 1:41).

What Do You Think?
How do you experience Jesus' rule as a current reality?
Digging Deeper
How does the knowledge that Jesus has already defeated evil empower you in situations for which Jesus' rule has not yet been made complete?

21a. Far above all principality, and power, and might, and dominion, and every name that is named.

Listing *principality, and power, and might, and dominion* is not meant to be an exhaustive list of every possibility but, instead, a list that covers all possibilities succinctly in a few phrases. These terms have slightly different connotations—but taken altogether—indicate that Jesus' reign and power are *far above* any competing entity. A *name* was considered another mark of power; invoking a name was thought to imbue a person with the power of the name they spoke (example: Acts 19:13-16). Jesus' name and power and dominion are above all spiritual and physical powers that are opposed to His reign (compare Ephesians 6:12; see lesson 13).

When considering powers or names that stood against Christ, Ephesian believers would likely have had two entities in mind: Rome and the goddess Diana. Roman emperors had not always claimed to be deities, but when they started to do so, they were loathe to give up their god-like status. Terms like *lord* or *savior* were titles the Roman emperors used in reference to themselves. The Pax Romana—when many peoples and nations were forced into peace, or at least a cessation of hostilities (mostly)—seemed to the emperors reason enough to be hailed as saving the people. This caused issues for Christians who refused to call the emperors by these titles. Though the emperors liked to think they had brought peace throughout the Roman Empire, what they had actually done was conquer in the same way that every other empire has ever done: with violence.

Christ the Savior, however, brings a kingdom that spreads by and with peace (Isaiah 9:7; contrast Matthew 10:34). Though the emperor might claim to be the ultimate authority on earth and to be a son of a god, only Christ is *the* Son of God.

Especially in Ephesus, the mythical goddess Diana was named as a power opposed to Christ (see Lesson Context). Paul could have listed Diana or Rome specifically, but kept his list general and therefore all-encompassing. We do well today to recognize those powers or entities—whether objectively real (like a government) or real only in terms of consequences (like a false god/false teaching)—that still try to exert power opposed to Christ's own.

21b. Not only in this world, but also in that which is to come.

This phrase speaks to two realities. Certainly we understand that after Christ returns, His authority will be recognized as supreme (Philippians 2:10-11). But Paul first insists that the same is true *in this world* right now. Those who seem to have ultimate power in our world in fact only have whatever power God allows them to exert (see John 19:10-11).

B. Body of Christ (vv. 22-23)

22-23. And hath put all things under his feet, and gave him to be the head over all things to the church, which is his body, the fulness of him that filleth all in all.

Once again Jesus' power is emphasized. *All things* are *under his* control, though this present reality is best seen in the church. Only believers willingly submit to Christ at this time and accept His leadership in all things. In Paul's day some thinkers like the Stoic philosophers sought fullness through a complete, direct experience of the creator. By connecting to the god who created all (so they thought), they would gain fullness in their lives. Against this, Paul asserted that *fulness* is found in the church and God is experienced through His Son.

This is the first time in Ephesians that Paul refers to *the church* as Christ's *body*, a metaphor he uses frequently in his writing (Romans 12:1-5; 1 Corinthians 12:12-27; Colossians 1:18-24; etc.).

Growing in unity in faith and knowledge of Jesus causes the church—Jesus' body—to grow toward "the fulness of Christ" (Ephesians 4:13). As Jesus' body, the church expresses *the fulness of him that filleth all in all*. As Jesus revealed the Father (John 14:9-10), so we the church are to reveal Christ. Growing to spiritual maturity together yields a healthy body (Ephesians 4:15-16) that is equipped not only to reveal Christ but also to act in place of His physical presence on earth.

> **What Do You Think?**
> How has your experience in the church led you to a fuller understanding of who Christ is?
>
> **Digging Deeper**
> How can you address failures of fellow believers while still loving the worldwide church as the body of Christ?

Conclusion
A. Live a Full Life

Even the best of times can be very challenging. Paul's thanksgiving prayer in today's lesson is a reminder that in Christ we have an eternal reality, already begun, that transforms our lives. We can experience the fullness of living because Jesus gives that fullness to His body, the church.

The call to action for this lesson is quite simple—but quite difficult: rest in the truth of what Paul has taught. We do nothing to create the reality: that the Father has chosen to reveal himself in the Son and bring us to greater knowledge of Him through the Spirit. All we can do is give thanks for this reality and constantly strive to live worthy of the calling. Our Lord is the Lord of the universe, and He gives us life to the fullest.

B. Prayer

Thank You, Father, that You have chosen to show the fullness of Your love through Jesus. We ask that Your Spirit continue to enlighten and guide us. In Jesus' name we pray. Amen.

C. Thought to Remember

Nothing can stand against Christ our Lord.

Involvement Learning

Enhance your lesson with KJV Bible Student *(from your curriculum supplier) and the reproducible activity page (at www.standardlesson.com or in the back of the* KJV Standard Lesson Commentary Deluxe Edition*).*

Into the Lesson

Ask students to recall a time when they were part of a group that had a clearly defined mission and purpose. Be prepared with an example of your own to get them started. As a whole class, reflect on how the mission and/or purpose impacted the energy and unity of the groups being discussed: 1–In what ways did the group's actions align with its words and its stated mission? 2–How did a lack of a well-communicated mission statement impact people's commitment levels? 3–In contrast, how did a well-communicated mission statement impact the commitment of the members? 4–What is the connection between a group's actions and its mission statement? Encourage discussion about both positive and negative experiences.

Alternative. Distribute copies of the "Mission Accomplished?" exercise from the activity page, which you can download. Have learners work in pairs to complete as indicated. After several minutes of work time, invite volunteers to share what they've discovered.

After calling time for either activity, say, "Today we'll look at how Paul encourages Christians to do God's work."

Into the Word

Divide the class in half, designating one half as the **Ephesus Church Group** and the other half as the **Ephesian Group**. Distribute handouts of the questions below for in-group discussions.

Ephesus Church Group: Read Acts 19:1-10. 1–What picture do you have of the church in Ephesus? 2–How did the Holy Spirit work through Paul? Read Ephesians 1:15-23. 3–What is Paul saying about Jesus and the Ephesian church? 4–Reread Ephesians 1:15-16. Think about our church. What are some examples of faith in Jesus Christ and love for others that are hallmarks of our congregation? 5–How does applying Christ's wisdom help us as a church?

Ephesian Group: Read Acts 19:11-20. 1–What picture do you have of Ephesus? 2–How did the word of God spread throughout Ephesus? Read Ephesians 1:15-23. 3–What is Paul saying about Jesus and the Ephesian church? 4–Reread Ephesians 1:15-16. Think about our church. What are some examples of faith in Jesus Christ and love for others that are hallmarks of our congregation? 5–How does applying Christ's wisdom help our church reach out to our community?

Be prepared with examples in case participants struggle to come up with examples on the spot. After several minutes of small group discussion, allow time for the whole group to discuss the last question.

Into Life

Allow a couple of minutes for learners to think about people they know who have different prayer needs. Encourage each of them to choose one of those people (or a group) whose needs resonate with them. Then encourage participants to pray for those people. Distribute inexpensive note cards with envelopes. Allow approximately five minutes for learners to write encouraging notes to the people they prayed for. Close with a time of praise and thanks to God for His care for your church. Commit to God's care the people who have been lifted up in prayer. Encourage everyone to send or deliver their cards

Alternative. Distribute copies of the "Show Me the Love" activity from the activity page. Have students work in pairs to complete the chart and action plan. It is important to follow up on this activity next week. Make a plan to discuss (at that time) ways they saw God at work through their initiatives. Remind students to be prepared for this discussion. Then remember to praise and thank God together for the blessings—and to commit to God's care anything that did not turn out as expected.

We Are God's Handiwork

Devotional Reading: 1 Timothy 2:1-8
Background Scripture: Acts 19; Ephesians 2; Revelation 2:1-7

Ephesians 2:1-10

1 And you hath he quickened, who were dead in trespasses and sins;

2 Wherein in time past ye walked according to the course of this world, according to the prince of the power of the air, the spirit that now worketh in the children of disobedience:

3 Among whom also we all had our conversation in times past in the lusts of our flesh, fulfilling the desires of the flesh and of the mind; and were by nature the children of wrath, even as others.

4 But God, who is rich in mercy, for his great love wherewith he loved us,

5 Even when we were dead in sins, hath quickened us together with Christ, (by grace ye are saved;)

6 And hath raised us up together, and made us sit together in heavenly places in Christ Jesus:

7 That in the ages to come he might shew the exceeding riches of his grace in his kindness toward us through Christ Jesus.

8 For by grace are ye saved through faith; and that not of yourselves: it is the gift of God:

9 Not of works, lest any man should boast.

10 For we are his workmanship, created in Christ Jesus unto good works, which God hath before ordained that we should walk in them.

Key Text

We are his workmanship, created in Christ Jesus unto good works, which God hath before ordained that we should walk in them. —**Ephesians 2:10**

Photo © Getty Images

God's Exceptional Choice

Unit 3: We Are God's Artwork
Lessons 10–13

Lesson Aims

After participating in this lesson, each learner will be able to:

1. Identify the basis of salvation.

2. Contrast salvation by works with salvation by grace.

3. Write a prayer of gratitude for the salvation available through grace.

Lesson Outline

Introduction
    A. Leaving Hospice
    B. Lesson Context
I. Dead in Sin (Ephesians 2:1-3)
    A. Living for the Enemy (vv. 1-2)
    B. Ensnared by Selfishness (v. 3)
        From Condemnation to Comfort
II. Alive in Christ (Ephesians 2:4-10)
    A. Loved by God (vv. 4-7)
    B. Saved by Grace (vv. 8-9)
    C. Prepared for Work (v. 10)
        Write Your Story
Conclusion
    A. Reacting to the Call
    B. Prayer
    C. Thought to Remember

Introduction

A. Leaving Hospice

A hospice is a wonderful but sobering place. For terminally ill patients, today's hospice facilities provide care that brings comfort for the patient and the patient's family and friends. But no ill person looks forward to going to hospice, for few patients leave the hospice alive.

Because hospice patients expect death, the few who are discharged describe the experience with amazement and words like, "I was ready to die, but here I am alive. It is like I *was* dead and now I'm resurrected or something. I guess God has more for me to do."

"From death to life" is how in our text Paul describes becoming a Christian. The old life was really death, but the new life is real life, a fundamentally different existence. And it is really true that God made us alive in Him because He has work for us to do.

B. Lesson Context

Paul wrote his letter to the Ephesians as a prisoner of the Roman Empire (see Ephesians 3:1; 4:1; 6:20; also Lesson Context of lesson 10). If he wrote during his imprisonment in Rome mentioned in Acts 28:30-31, then he was living in his own rented house and could receive visitors, both his fellow Christian workers and those interested in hearing about Jesus. He was not in a dark dungeon, as we might imagine a prisoner to be.

However, his situation still was not pleasant. Being a prisoner meant he could not move about as he pleased. It meant that he faced the threat of a judgment against him that could even mean his execution. Confinement, worry, shame—these were his experience.

But Paul's prison letters do not suggest that the misery of Paul's condition dictated his outlook. Even as a prisoner, Paul repeatedly emphasized that Christians have an exalted place in God's plan. Being a prisoner might seem like death, but Paul could only speak of being *raised* from the dead.

Paul's readers, though not prisoners, were also in a difficult position. Their new faith put them at odds with the world around them. Many of their familiar relationships had been cut off: Christians of Jewish background were sometimes no longer welcome in the synagogue; Christians of Gentile background were no longer to participate in the worship rites of paganism. Each group was under additional scorn for associating with the other. Christians were suspected of wanting to undermine the foundations of their communities.

Paul's message to the Ephesians emphasizes a different perspective, the perspective of God. From God's throne, Christians are not downtrodden but victorious. They are not rebels against the community but God's agents of renewal for the world. Despite rejection by neighbors or even those in authority, Christians—then and now—are the grateful recipients of everything God has done. We're already experiencing God's eternal blessings and anticipating a still greater future when Christ returns. We live together as God's temple (Ephesians 2:11-22). And Paul himself, proclaiming the gospel despite his confinement, exemplified what the lives of his audience were truly like (3:1-19).

But this status was not something they deserved or had earned. The work was all God's. They needed God's work in Christ to rescue them from the helpless state of death and make them alive to all that God had for them.

I. Dead in Sin
(Ephesians 2:1-3)
A. Living for the Enemy (vv. 1-2)

1. And you hath he quickened, who were dead in trespasses and sins.

Ephesians 1:18-23 (see lesson 11) spoke forcefully of Jesus' resurrection. With the opening *and you* here, Paul moves from God's display of power in Christ to the results for humanity. God has also given us a resurrection from death. This is summarized with the older word *quickened* (compare Colossians 2:13).

The immediate result of this transaction is not immunity to physical death (such death is overcome later; see 1 Corinthians 15). Rather, the new life at issue in the passage before us is spiritual

Visual for Lesson 12. *Follow up the final set of discussion questions by asking how growing in grace blesses the Lord.*

in nature. Spiritual death is a consequence of our *trespasses and sins.*

Only here and in Romans 5:20-21 do the Greek nouns behind this phrase occur in such proximity to one another (there as "offence" and "sin"). It's as if Paul was making sure the Ephesians didn't miss the point: they were guilty of rebellion against God, deserving of death. Death is the consequence of sin (Romans 6:23).

To be a sinner is to be spiritually dead: without true life, without connection to God, without hope. And to die in one's sins is to be eternally separated from the Lord, with no hope of life following death. We may not want to admit it, but we are committing spiritual suicide when we sin. Those having been made alive in Christ should entertain no longing for that previous state.

2. Wherein in time past ye walked according to the course of this world, according to the prince of the power of the air, the spirit that now worketh in the children of disobedience.

Before coming to faith in Christ, Paul's readers lived under the sway of the trends and influences of a world in rebellion against God. Though this might have felt like freedom, it certainly was not. Before Christ they actually were in bondage to three closely related influences.

Before they came to love and submit to Christ, Paul's readers may have believed themselves to be free. But such was not the case. First, they had lived *according to the course of this world.* That means they had acted as if God's standards for living were not valid. Today we still hear voices that call us to selfish sin, to moral failure, and to dishonesty. The world wants to direct us by its standards. If we let it, we are neither free nor godly.

Second, Paul connected this with serving *the prince of the power of the air*. Paul and his readers were acutely aware of the evil influences that attacked them. The prince of these spiritual forces of evil is unnamed here but corresponds with "the devil" later (Ephesians 6:11-12). The spiritual beings who are in rebellion against God are not our friends, but seek to destroy us and keep us far from fellowship with the Lord. The phrase *of the air* does not refer to a specific location, but to the spiritual nature of this evil. The letter to the Ephesians addresses this reality more than any other writing of Paul.

Even so, Paul was confident that Jesus has authority (and therefore victory) over all the spiritual forces that are in rebellion against God (see Ephesians 1:21; lesson 11). But this is an ongoing battle (see 6:12). This leads to Paul's third element.

B. Ensnared by Selfishness (v. 3)

3a. Among whom also we all had our conversation in times past in the lusts of our flesh, fulfilling the desires of the flesh and of the mind.

The third element that promotes sin lies within us. *We all* (Paul includes himself) had been driven *in times past* by personal *lusts of our flesh*. (*Conversation* in this older sense refers to one's conduct.) Paul clarifies by indicating that such behavior includes both *desires of the flesh and of the mind*. If one's body indicates that something feels good, the person may do it despite moral consequences. We can blame our sinfulness on our bodily desires. But the problem begins deep inside us, in how we think and what we want.

3b. And were by nature the children of wrath, even as others.

Paul's summary of that former life includes the fact that he and his readers had been *even as others*. That *children of wrath* characterization of unbelievers is quite striking (compare Ephesians 5:6). We should note that the word *others* is inclusive.

It is not just pagan Gentiles who deserve God's wrath. Jews outside of Christ do not get a pass. Without Christ they too are children of wrath.

Paul's use of the word *nature* indicates something fundamental about us. As a result of our inherent tendency to sin, "there is none righteous, no, not one" (Romans 3:10). We need not debate the possibility of living a perfect life and thereby earning our salvation. Although that is the standard (Matthew 5:48), it does not happen. It *will not* happen.

Such was our former life: infatuated by the sinful world, beset by temptations from the evil one, and controlled by out-of-control passion for the forbidden fruits desired by body and mind. When drawn to the influences of the world and the devil, people mired in sinful desires think themselves to be in control, but they are not. They are slaves to passion and lust.

What Do You Think?

How can reflecting on the sinful patterns of your past contrasted with your grace-filled present encourage you as you face uncertain times?

Digging Deeper

Who can you share your personal testimony with to encourage that person's own faith journey?

From Condemnation to Comfort

One Christmas I offered to spend a Saturday making cookies with my friend and her two toddlers. She is a single mom, and I love making cookies—so the fact that I'd also be helping her out was a bonus. After a few hours, the boys got bored "helping," which gave us two moms time to chat.

The conversation turned to parenting, and I found myself confessing my shortcomings. My friend admitted the same, with relief in her voice and demeanor. In my days as a young mother, I hadn't had friends to whom I could admit such mistakes in a loving environment. I was so happy to be that sort of friend to her.

We've all fallen short—sometimes sinfully—in

every role we fill. Paul included himself as a sinner, no better than anyone else by nature. As Paul did, we all lived under condemnation until Christ. When the opportunity arises, will you offer comfort rather than condemnation? —P. M.

II. Alive in Christ
(Ephesians 2:4-10)
A. Loved by God (vv. 4-7)

4. But God, who is rich in mercy, for his great love wherewith he loved us.

Having characterized one's pre-Christian past as consisting of infatuation with worldly influences, devil-driven disobedience, and indulgence in sinful passions, Paul moved the discussion to his readers' future life. This shift is signaled by movement from the "and you" (Ephesians 2:1, above) to the *but God* of the verse before us.

If God had no wrath, the world would have no justice. But if God had no mercy, the world would have no hope. Left to ourselves, we are rebels deserving of ruin and judgment, of death and all that it entails. But thanks be to God, we are not left to ourselves. God is not merely merciful, but *is rich in mercy,* just as He is rich in grace (Ephesians 1:7; see lesson 10). Because of God's infinite wisdom, utter righteousness, and richness of grace, His eternal plan is to be merciful through the self-sacrificial work of Christ. God's justice is satisfied by Christ's righteous life and self-sacrificial death, the innocent Lord himself willingly taking the place of the guilty. By this amazing means, God can be both righteous and gracious, both just and merciful (Romans 3:25-26).

Any hope for us must begin with God's mercy and love. Even while deserving God's wrath, people still bear His image and likeness (Genesis 1:26-27). God has gone to great effort to save His lost image-bearers (Luke 19:10; etc.).

Paul is given to large statements when it comes to the nature of God. We see a great example in the description here of God's attribute of being rich in mercy (compare Romans 2:4; also Ephesians 2:7, below). Paul expands on this imagery by describing God's mercy as a *great love wherewith he loved us.* Paul used repetition for emphasis.

He was barely able to contain his excitement! God spends His inexhaustible supply of mercy on us freely and lovingly. "His mercy endureth for ever" is the repeated refrain of Psalms 118 and 136.

5. Even when we were dead in sins, hath quickened us together with Christ, (by grace ye are saved).

Life before Christ was one of being *dead in sins.* But as Christ has been raised from death to resurrected life, so too are we *quickened* (also Colossians 2:13). When through faith we are joined with Christ, we are joined in His resurrection. That means we are already transferred from death to life. But it also promises a resurrection to come (1 Corinthians 15:20-26). Resurrection life is both present and future. Salvation is both present and future.

The parentheses around the statement *by grace ye are saved* may lead us to believe that this affirmation is somehow secondary to the thought at hand. But what is mentioned so briefly here serves two purposes: (1) it anticipates a fuller explanation of salvation by grace a bit later; and (2) it helps paint the larger picture of God's attitude toward His wayward children as His grace is considered alongside His mercy and love.

6. And hath raised us up together, and made us sit together in heavenly places in Christ Jesus.

Our spiritual resurrection from the death of sin is followed by an "ascension." Christ's story is now our story; Christ's life is our life. Christ ascended to Heaven after His resurrection (Luke 24:50-51; Acts 1:1-9; etc.); and following our resurrection from spiritual death, we are positioned *in heavenly places in Christ Jesus* (compare Colossians 3:1-3). By God's grace we share Christ's victory and are agents of Christ's rule. Having front-row seats in the glorious light of the presence of Christ and His victories means we no longer fear the spiritual darkness.

7. That in the ages to come he might shew

How to Say It

Ephesians   Ee-*fee*-zhunz.
Gentiles   *Jen*-tiles.

the exceeding riches of his grace in his kindness toward us through Christ Jesus.

Paul gives an eternal reason for God's rescue of sinners from spiritual death: that we might serve as a demonstration of His marvelous grace forever. The era that begins with salvation through faith in Christ is not an intermediate stage in God's plan. Rather, it is for all time, a plan for *the ages to come.* Again, Paul pictures God's grace as inexhaustible *riches.* To this is added the element of God's kindness, a word that implies essential goodness (compare Romans 2:4). *His grace in his kindness* is not God's response to anything meritorious we have done; rather, it is an offer that should draw a response from us.

> **What Do You Think?**
> Would you describe yourself as being "rich in mercy"? Why or why not?
>
> **Digging Deeper**
> How can meditating on God's character—including His mercy—encourage you to seek growth in that area in your own life?

B. Saved by Grace (vv. 8-9)

8a. For by grace are ye saved through faith.

The concept of *by grace are ye saved*, introduced in Ephesians 2:5 (above), is now explored in greater depth. Salvation by grace expects and requires a response. The salvation God offers is of no effect unless accepted *through faith* on the part of the one who is dead in sins. Faith is often defined as "assent plus trust." In other words, assent is accepting the gospel facts as true. Trust, on the other hand, is surrendering control of one's life to Jesus on the basis of who He is and what He has done (John 3:16; Acts 10:43; 16:31; 1 Timothy 1:16).

8b. And that not of yourselves: it is the gift of God.

A technical issue of the original Greek must be considered, an issue that is not apparent in our English translation. Every Greek noun and pronoun has a grammatical gender: either masculine, feminine, or neuter. So the gender of one or both pronouns *that* and *it* in verse 8b here must match the gender of one or both nouns *grace* and *faith* in verse 8a to determine the antecedent.

But there is no match. The nouns are both feminine, while the pronoun *that* is neuter. The pronoun *it* does not actually exist in the Greek text; it has been supplied in English for smooth reading.

We conclude, then, *that not of yourselves* is not referring to any one particular element of verse 8a, but to God's system of salvation as a whole. Salvation is a gift; it cannot be earned. We are not partners with God in bringing salvation. We are recipients of this rich *gift of God.*

> **What Do You Think?**
> Who in your life would benefit from receiving grace from you as a taste of God's willingness to extend grace?
>
> **Digging Deeper**
> What prevents you from extending grace (which is undeserved) to that person?

9. Not of works, lest any man should boast.

If salvation resulted from our own efforts, we could be justifiably proud. Paul knows well the danger here. Before he met Christ, Paul's seemingly spotless life was a source of pride to him, evidence of his moral superiority (see Philippians 3:4-6).

But there are no *works*, no actions we can take, that make us worthy of being self-excused from our sins. The best among us still have lapses and failures; we still yield to self-centeredness and gratification of lusts. We have no room for boasting, only for humility.

C. Prepared for Work (v. 10)

10. For we are his workmanship, created in Christ Jesus unto good works, which God hath before ordained that we should walk in them.

In the spiritual world of righteousness, there is no such thing as a self-made woman or man. Our spiritual resurrection is God's *workmanship.* We are the very people whom God has made—His deliberate, artful product.

Our new life has purpose, and this is part of

God's design. We have been rescued from spiritual destruction so that we might be instruments of *good works*. Yet we must realize that living the life that pleases God is not how we are saved. Good works are not a payment for our salvation, nor are they the condition of our receiving the gift. The gift is free. But the effect of the gift is transformation. Though the struggle against "the prince of the power of the air" (Ephesians 2:2, above) will continue, in Christ we have new motivation to serve and obey. And through God's Holy Spirit, we have new power to do so. As our sin made the old creation spin toward destruction, so by God's grace our new creation sets us on a course to do God's will on earth "as it is in heaven" (Matthew 6:10). Our aim becomes bringing our lives into line with the gift we have received, so that we reflect our new identity as God's people (Ephesians 4:1).

> **What Do You Think?**
> What biblical texts reveal the good works that God has prepared for *all* Christians to do?
>
> **Digging Deeper**
> How do you discern what good works God has prepared in advance for *you* to do?

Write Your Story

I always knew I wanted to be a writer when I grew up. I wrote my first book at 13 (it's cringeworthy to think about now!) and spent my young adult years honing my skills and learning the craft. I began to have success by the time I was married with children.

At the same time, my heart was yearning to be closer to God. The closer I got to Him, the clearer it became that writing was a talent He gave me. I had a choice to make: Do I continue the path I'm on, publishing more stories and establishing myself with worldly success, or do I focus the talent God gave me to bring others closer to Him? God was asking me to tell people about Him. What will your choice be, when you're faced with how to use the gifts that God gave you? —P. M.

Conclusion
A. Reacting to the Call

If we are new to faith, we may feel overmatched by our calling. How can we measure up to expectations? How can we possibly overcome all the wrong in our lives? Paul reminds us to put our focus not on our inadequacy but on Christ's abundance. In Christ God has done everything for us. Forgiveness is full, and His power is sufficient. We need only continue to receive and trust, doing moment by moment what the Spirit directs and enables.

If we have followed Christ for a long time, we may fall into a habit of thinking we deserve any good things or benefits we have. Paul reminds us that our best was never good enough; that we stand with Christ by *His* action, not ours; and that whatever is good in our lives is now the result of freely receiving God's gift.

And if we are still considering faith in Christ, Paul gives us a powerful introduction to what God offers us. God has done all for us. But as we receive His gift, we will be forever different, set on a path to become what God, the good God of grace and mercy, has intended for us since before the beginning.

> **What Do You Think?**
> What truth from this text challenges one of your patterns of thinking, speaking, or acting?
>
> **Digging Deeper**
> What truth encourages you to continue in your faithful efforts and habits?

B. Prayer

O God, Your mercy is everlasting, and Your truth endures through the ages. May we receive Your gracious gift afresh. And may we, as Your handiwork, live lives that fit the richness of Your grace. In Jesus' name we pray. Amen.

C. Thought to Remember

We live now and forever by accepting God's gift through Christ's victory.

Involvement Learning

Enhance your lesson with KJV Bible Student (from your curriculum supplier) and the reproducible activity page (at www.standardlesson.com or in the back of the KJV Standard Lesson Commentary Deluxe Edition).

Into the Lesson

Option. If group members did the "Show Me the Love" take-home exercise (from the last class), discuss and give thanks for what they experienced.

Have participants form four teams: **Kindness Team, Goodness Team, Gentleness Team,** and **Self-Control Team.** Each team will need a sheet of paper and a pen or pencil; teams should assign the role of scribe to one person. Explain that teams will have three minutes to create a list of ways they showed God's love to others in the past week. These should be specific actions they took. Avoid referring to this activity as a competition, although it's fine to let the forming of teams serve to imply it as such. Use a stopwatch and have teams begin.

At the end of three minutes, call time. Invite teams to share several examples from their lists. Ask for their total number of listed actions. Write each team's name and total number on the board. Then ask, "So, which team won?" Naturally, the team with the most "points" will declare themselves the winner. Act confused and look around for a set of "rules" or "goals" of the activity, finding none. Say, "Today we'll look Ephesians 2 and discover that showing God's love to others isn't a competition, and God isn't keeping score."

Into the Word

Have participants close their eyes and visualize their own life in Christ as you slowly read aloud today's Scripture passage, Ephesians 2:1-10.

Distribute paper and colored pencils; include additional art supplies if you'd like. Give the learners one minute to sketch how they imagine their lives in Christ based on Ephesians 2. Ask them to continue sketching or jotting down thoughts, pictures, or words that stand out as you read the text once more.

Have learners continue the contemplative activity as they reflect on the following: 1–Take inventory of the gifts of God at work in you: mercy, love, life, grace, being raised with Christ, faith. What difference do these gifts of God make in your life? 2–How do you show these gifts daily?

Ask learners to define *initiative* (example: a procedure that starts with one's discretion without any outside influence). Have learners contemplate the initiative God takes for His people: 1–Why does God take this initiative? 2–What is our response to God's work in our lives? 3–How about in our world?

Option. Consider playing instrumental music as adults draw and write. (Check your church's library or licensing rights to online music.)

Alternative. Distribute copies of the "Rich in Mercy" exercise from the activity page, which you can download. Have learners work in pairs to complete as indicated. Allow time for group discussion before continuing with the next part of the lesson.

Into Life

Distribute paper and pens or pencils. Divide the group into pairs. Have them discuss the following as they jot down notes: 1–What are the gifts God has given you? 2–How could you use them to show gratitude to God that He gives us salvation by grace—not salvation by works?

After a couple of minutes, ask for volunteers to share their ideas for the second question. Allow one minute for learners to express that gratitude as they write a prayer of thanks for salvation through grace.

Alternative. Distribute copies of the "Pass It On" exercise on the activity page. Allow one minute for the quick brainstorming exercise. Have individuals share their commitments with a partner for accountability.

After calling time for either activity, end the lesson with a prayer time, praising God for the love and grace experienced in being God's workmanship.

God Gives Tools for Our Protection

Devotional Reading: Psalm 91
Background Scripture: Acts 19; Ephesians 6:10-24; Revelation 2:1-7

Ephesians 6:10-18

10 Finally, my brethren, be strong in the Lord, and in the power of his might.

11 Put on the whole armour of God, that ye may be able to stand against the wiles of the devil.

12 For we wrestle not against flesh and blood, but against principalities, against powers, against the rulers of the darkness of this world, against spiritual wickedness in high places.

13 Wherefore take unto you the whole armour of God, that ye may be able to withstand in the evil day, and having done all, to stand.

14 Stand therefore, having your loins girt about with truth, and having on the breastplate of righteousness;

15 And your feet shod with the preparation of the gospel of peace;

16 Above all, taking the shield of faith, wherewith ye shall be able to quench all the fiery darts of the wicked.

17 And take the helmet of salvation, and the sword of the Spirit, which is the word of God:

18 Praying always with all prayer and supplication in the Spirit, and watching thereunto with all perseverance and supplication for all saints.

Key Text

Take unto you the whole armour of God, that ye may be able to withstand in the evil day, and having done all, to stand. —**Ephesians 6:13**

God's
Exceptional Choice

Unit 3: We Are God's Artwork
Lessons 10–13

Lesson Aims

After participating in this lesson, each learner will be able to:

1. List elements of the armor of God.

2. Distinguish between offensive and defensive elements of that armor.

3. Make a plan to use one of those elements more effectively.

Lesson Outline

Introduction
  A. All the Toys
  B. Lesson Context
I. Empowered by God (Ephesians 6:10-12)
  A. Divine Protection (vv. 10-11)
  B. Unseen Enemies (v. 12)
    The True Enemy
II. Outfitted by God (Ephesians 6:13-18)
  A. Fully Equipped (vv. 13-17)
    Reflect, Create, Share
  B. Faithful Prayer (v. 18)
Conclusion
  A. Strong in the Lord
  B. Prayer
  C. Thought to Remember

Introduction
A. All the Toys

Though we probably hope to have a car that is reliable and safe, we are drawn to the extra features that the manufacturers build in to keep us buying their products. New styles, new colors, new electronics . . . these options get us into the showroom and thinking about a new or new-to-me automobile.

People who sell cars have their own term for those options: toys. A car with lots of optional features is, to the sales force, a car with "all the toys." And such a car is usually the first car you see when you enter the dealership.

There is little about the Christian faith that is like shopping for a car. But our text today does have a list of equipment. Unlike a car's optional features, though, these are not toys but standard tools, the means God supplies for a victorious life in Christ. The Lord gives these to every follower of Jesus at no cost and with no exceptions.

B. Lesson Context

Paul wrote his letter to the Ephesians when he was especially conscious of the stakes in the battle between good and evil. Most of his letters addressed specific issues within a congregation. Ephesians is unique, however, in presenting the gospel more generally, without taking on any specific problems this church faced. This may be due in part to Paul's intention that this letter begin circulating from Ephesus into the wider territory, what is now Turkey.

Having planted churches across the Roman world over the course of more than two decades, the apostle had been arrested in Jerusalem during a riot (Acts 21:26-35). A corrupt governor refused to resolve his case (24:27); so after sitting in jail for two years, Paul appealed to Caesar. This appeal resulted in a trip to Rome to stand trial (25:1-12).

Paul then spent two years under house arrest in Rome, waiting for a hearing before the emperor (Acts 28:30). During this time (about AD 61–63) Paul wrote letters to his churches in cities back east, including the one in Ephesus. Doubtless the circumstances of his arrest and the daily frustrations of his imprisonment led Paul to greater awareness of Satan's schemes and the preparation necessary for defeating them.

I. Empowered by God
(Ephesians 6:10-12)

A. Divine Protection (vv. 10-11)

10. Finally, my brethren, be strong in the Lord, and in the power of his might.

The last two chapters of the book of Ephesians focus on ways that true faith in Christ expresses itself in daily living. This includes pursuing unity among believers (Ephesians 4:3-4), speaking truthfully and dealing with people honestly (4:25, 28), extending forgiveness (4:32), avoiding sexual sin (5:3), being a good spouse and parent (5:22-33; 6:4), and demonstrating a strong work ethic (6:5-9). These imperatives are not always easy to carry out, so Paul reminded the reader of the true source of power to be able to do so: *the Lord*.

It may seem impossible to remain consistently faithful to Christ in every (or even any) area of life. From a human perspective, this is indeed the case. Left to our own devices, we cannot become the people God has called us to be. But God has not left us to our own devices. In commanding us to live rightly, He also provides us with the resources to do so. *The power of his might* is available to us in the battle against evil.

11. Put on the whole armour of God, that ye may be able to stand against the wiles of the devil.

Paul's illustration has prophetic precedent: Isaiah said that "righteousness shall be the girdle of his loins, and faithfulness the girdle of his reins" (Isaiah 11:5)—referring to the Messiah, who is of course Jesus (see 59:17). His treatment emphasizes the thoroughness with which *God* has equipped His people for spiritual protection. In full equipment for battle, a Roman soldier was an imposing figure. Legions of these soldiers were a common sight throughout the Roman Empire. Even more than any earthly leader, God does not leave us defenseless or send us into situations where we are unequipped for success.

Paul did not describe Christians' duty as conquering territory or taking prisoners, though these have been the objectives of many an earthly military, especially Rome. The enemy we face is not other human beings but Satan, the spiritual accuser and adversary who tempts and torments humanity (2 Corinthians 2:11; 1 Peter 5:8; etc.). Only by relying on God are we *able to stand against the wiles of the devil*. The false ideas that might move us from steadfast faith have their origins not in humans but with the spiritual being who inspires those ideas. The main question is whether we will avail ourselves of what God provides.

B. Unseen Enemies (v. 12)

12. For we wrestle not against flesh and blood, but against principalities, against powers, against the rulers of the darkness of this world, against spiritual wickedness in high places.

Judaism and other ancient religions taught that good *and* evil spirits all live in the heavens above the physical world, with human beings living in the bottom layer of a massive cosmic hierarchy. (Sheol—the place of the dead—was thought of as below the earth [example: Ezekiel 32:27].) Elsewhere, Paul describes a visionary experience of his own as a trip to "the third heaven" (2 Corinthians 12:2), the place where God himself dwells beyond the sky (the first heaven) and the stars (the second heaven).

A similar outlook is reflected in the verse before us, which envisions Satan and other evil spirits living skyward (*in high places*; compare "heavenly places" in Ephesians 3:10), between the earth and God's abode. From the vantage point we're picturing, demons can descend to move quickly among humans to threaten and tempt us in various ways

How to Say It

Judaism	Joo-duh-izz-um or Joo-day-izz-um.
Pax Romana (Latin)	Pahks Ro-mah-nah.
scutum (Latin)	skyoo-tuhm.
Sheol	She-ol.

(Job 1:7). As "the prince of the power of the air" (Ephesians 2:2; compare John 14:30), Satan's influence extends from certain high places to the world in which we live.

As a result *flesh and blood* people, including some who have influence over our lives and livelihoods, can serve as tools of Satan to bring the powers of darkness to bear in concrete ways. But they are not our true adversaries. Such people are not always even aware that their actions are serving the devil's purposes, and many do not even believe in Satan at all. This does not change the fact that their actions can present serious challenges to us as believers, challenges that we must be prepared to face. These challenges can take the form of outright threats, persecution, ridicule, and rejection, but also (and more often) of more indirect temptations to join in their sin.

Even so, people are never the real enemy. Every person—no matter how their lives have been twisted by sin—was created in the image of God. These image-bearers of the Father are victims of the real enemy: Satan, along with the *principalities* and *powers* and *rulers* that willingly follow his lead. Against these spiritual forces is our struggle.

What Do You Think?

How would you interact with others differently if you paused to remember that Satan and his demons—and not other people—are the true enemy?

Digging Deeper

In what ways does this insight make it easier for you to obey Jesus' command to love your enemies (Matthew 5:44)?

The True Enemy

Anger burned in my gut as I drove. I imagined myself throwing log after log onto a fire as I recalled everything my fellow missionaries had done. *How could* they *be my fellow Christians?* It didn't occur to me to pray for them.

Anger flared up again recently, fueled by heated political exchanges with friends and family alike. For several weeks it became an obsession, robbing me of all joy and peace. *How could* they *be so wrongheaded?*

Then I remembered the lesson I'd learned on the mission field: we do not wrestle against flesh and blood. I asked a friend to pray for me. And then everything changed for me. The obsessive anger cooled down as the fruit of the Spirit began to emerge again in my heart. Who is the "they" you think is your enemy? Pray for "they" now, and remember who your real enemy is.   —N. G.

II. Outfitted by God
(Ephesians 6:13-18)
A. Fully Equipped (vv. 13-17)

13. Wherefore take unto you the whole armour of God, that ye may be able to withstand in the evil day, and having done all, to stand.

This statement expands on what Paul already said (see Ephesians 6:11, above), thus emphasizing its importance. Because we cannot predict when, where, or how the enemy will strike, we must be dressed and ready for conflict at any moment. The goal of such preparation is repeated in the phrases *that ye may be able to withstand* and *having done all, to stand*. No matter what comes our way, we must be prepared to stand against every challenge. The ground on which we stand firm is our faith in the Lord and faithfulness to a godly lifestyle.

The armor that God provides—"the armour of light" (Romans 13:12)—will protect us *in the evil day* from assaults on our beliefs and from temptations to sin. This is an end-times term that anticipates a time when evil forces mount a terrible assault on God's people just before God vanquishes them entirely, ushering in the fullness of His promised reign.

With Christ's death and resurrection, the promises of God are being fulfilled. God's kingdom is breaking into the world, and so we can appropriately say that the end times have begun (note the phrase "in these last days" in Hebrews 1:2). This means that Paul's first-century audience was already facing the evil day; we still face it today. We do not put on the armor of God out of paranoia but to stand firm against the very real forces that already assail us.

14a. Stand therefore, having your loins girt about with truth.

The word *truth* emphasizes both the content of our faith (the propositions of the true gospel message) and the way we live out that faith (our lifestyle). God has provided His people with the foundational gift of truth, a right understanding of reality (John 14:6; 2 Timothy 3:16; etc.). The gospel shows us our true selves: rebels against God in desperate need of His mercy. And it shows us that mercy is ours through faith in the crucified and risen Jesus. Truth is our defense against Satan's lies (compare John 8:44). By thinking and living in ways consistent with God's truth, we prepare ourselves for periods of trial that would take us along false paths.

What Do You Think?
In what specific areas of your life may you be vulnerable to shame-based attacks? What in your past, present, or future causes you to doubt the gift of righteousness given to you by God?
Digging Deeper
How can putting greater trust in Jesus help you overcome feelings of shame?

14b. And having on the breastplate of righteousness.

Roman armor included a *breastplate,* a large leather or metal covering that protected the torso from frontal assault. Paul connected this piece of equipment with *righteousness* (compare Isaiah 59:17), the quality of living correctly in God's eyes. We protect ourselves from Satan's assaults by living rightly with the help of the Spirit. Being in the habit of living in the Spirit and growing in righteousness forms our character. In turn, that character serves as a defense against temptations of any kind.

15. And your feet shod with the preparation of the gospel of peace.

Travel of any kind instantly becomes more treacherous without the proper footwear. We note that the spiritual footwear of which Paul speaks is not *the gospel of peace* itself, but *the preparation of* that gospel. The meaning of this phrase as structured in the original language is not easy to interpret. What exactly is this *preparation of*? There are several suggestions, but probably the best one is that the word *of* should be taken to mean something like "that results from." In this case, it is the gospel itself that prepares our feet for the day of spiritual battle (compare Psalm 37:31; Romans 16:20).

The Roman Empire claimed that it brought peace to all its subjects, referred to as the Pax Romana. But this peace was oftentimes merely a cessation of hostility with the possibility of violence never far off. The good news of Jesus' reign is that He brings perfect and lasting peace. Strife is replaced with goodwill among the subjects of the kingdom, wholeness of life for all who live under Christ's rule. But most of all, it's peace with God.

What Do You Think?
What are the key truths of the gospel?
Digging Deeper
What might be the effects of sharing this simple gospel with people without expanding with other doctrinal concerns?

16. Above all, taking the shield of faith, wherewith ye shall be able to quench all the fiery darts of the wicked.

This verse evokes images from ancient warfare to describe our conflict with Satan. *The shield* to which Paul referred was the large, semicylindrical *scutum* (Latin for "shield") of the frontline Roman soldier. These shields were locked together by soldiers standing shoulder-to-shoulder, which formed a protective wall of wood and leather.

Paul's application of this imagery makes two key points. First, *faith* is our protective shield. Faith is more than mere agreement to a creed or a statement about who Jesus is. It's more than how we were raised. It is the trusting commitment of our lives to the truth of that statement, placing our lives in God's all-mighty hands to provide, protect, and direct. Obedient faith shields us from temptations and difficulties, symbolized as *the fiery darts* of Satan. Second, the typical Roman use of the *scutum* reminded Paul's readers that there is strength in numbers. As God's faithful people stand together, we become better able to protect ourselves.

What Do You Think?

How can you cooperate with the Holy Spirit to strengthen your faith against the fiery attacks of the evil one?

Digging Deeper

If an arrow of doubt hits its mark in your life, what is your plan for recovering from this lapse of faith? Consider Ecclesiastes 4:12 and 1 John 1:9.

17a. And take the helmet of salvation.

Salvation in our thinking is sometimes reduced to the assurance of life after death. But salvation is not just future, but present. It's not just overcoming death, but restoration to a life of meaning, purpose, joy, and love in everyday experience. Paul also called this *helmet* "the hope of salvation" (1 Thessalonians 5:8).

The helmet also proclaims our allegiance to Christ. Roman soldiers' helmets were fashioned to declare their nationality wordlessly but vividly. So too the hope of our salvation should shine in our lives, making clear to those who have eyes to

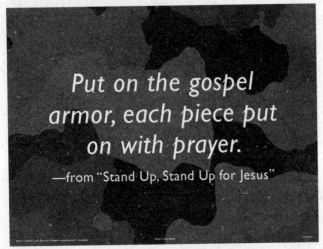

Put on the gospel armor, each piece put on with prayer.
—from "Stand Up, Stand Up for Jesus"

Visual for Lesson 13. *Discuss with the class how a kingdom that spreads in peace (Isaiah 9:7) offers a different perspective on spiritual armor.*

see that we are under the Lord's command (Matthew 13:16-17).

Reflect, Create, Share

I recently wrote some poems inspired by the description of the armor of God in Ephesians 6. I began with the helmet of salvation:

> let Accuser's voice grow weary
> let it tear and crack with strain
> while I, heedless, never tarry
> poisoned thoughts to entertain.
> filled instead with grateful wonder
> hast'ning to my Father's call
> gracious to myself and others
> showing love to Him and all.

This poem helps me remember that our true enemy is an accuser. If I find myself entertaining too many accusatory thoughts about myself or others, then I am poisoning myself and those around me. But realizing that I possess the helmet of salvation—knowing that I am saved by grace—helps me repel such thoughts when they arise.

Creating art is a wonderful way to reflect on Scripture and apply its truths. If you're not a poet, maybe you enjoy woodworking, knitting, baking, or some other craft. How can your hobbies help you meditate on the gospel and create something that inspires others as well?   —N. G.

17b. And the sword of the Spirit, which is the word of God.

Paul's audience did not have the entire collection we call the Bible. Instead they relied on Israel's sacred Scriptures, what we call the Old Testament. And they did have this letter of Paul and perhaps a few others that had been copied and shared by other churches. They had learned the story of Jesus through the testimony of Paul and others, and they remembered and repeated those stories. For them *the word of God* was primarily the oral message of how God had acted in history through Israel to bring about fulfillment in Jesus.

The sword of the Spirit is the only armament that can be used offensively as well as defensively. But we must be careful not to use biblical knowledge as a weapon against the lost and hopeless. When we remember that we are not fighting against people (see Ephesians 6:12, above), we are reminded that our knowledge and love of the Lord protects us but is not intended to harm the lost and hopeless. Following the nudges of the Spirit will guide us as we actively proclaim the gospel.

What Do You Think?

How does the Word of God function as more than a book to be studied? How is it a living and active part of your life?

Digging Deeper

What specific steps of obedience do you need to take in response to your knowledge of the Word of God (James 1:22-25)?

B. Faithful Prayer (v. 18)

18. Praying always with all prayer and supplication in the Spirit, and watching thereunto with all perseverance and supplication for all saints.

The armament illustrations above emphasize ways that Christians are equipped for spiritual battle. Success in spiritual battle requires a unified effort. One manifestation of Christian unity is found in prayer. Believers should be *praying always* (1 Thessalonians 5:17). Our prayers are to include *supplications*, requests for aid against spiritual dangers. The context suggests that Paul was not thinking of prayers for personal desires, but rather of requests for endurance and assistance against trials and temptations—like a soldier would call for supplies, reinforcements, and support. We will be much more successful at resisting the powers of evil when we have the assistance of faithful brothers and sisters in Christ. By praying for one another, we ask God to supply all of us with what we need to keep fighting.

Prayer *in the Spirit* does not refer to speaking in some mystical language but rather to the channel by whom we communicate with God. Paul here portrays the Holy Spirit as a sort of messenger, carrying requests from the front lines. And because we pray in the Spirit, we should find our-selves more and more often asking for God's will to be done, not our own, as Jesus demonstrated (Matthew 26:39, 42, 44).

Conclusion

A. Strong in the Lord

God's people are always under attack from the adversary. Made new in Christ, our lives are at odds with the world around us, the world that Satan steadfastly tries to align with his evil ways. We always feel the tension of living in a world battered by evil forces; we feel the pressure that the forces of evil press on us. It is easy and natural to feel weak when it seems that darkness surrounds us.

But by God's provision we are strong. There are no flaws in His armor, no gaps in the protection it supplies. Reviewing all that God has provided, we have renewed strength to stand firm in every circumstance. Though the spiritual battle may often seem bleak, we know that God holds victory in His hand. He will choose the moment to overturn all that opposes Him and His people. What seems slow to us is the patience of our Lord, giving each person time to accept the gospel and turn from the darkness of their previous lives.

So put on your armor! And remember who the real enemy is. Then, knowing your enemy, do no harm to anyone who is not your enemy—namely every creature that bears the image of God. Instead, recruit those who need God's armor. Offer them the protection that comes from accepting the truth about Jesus. Pray for those who join you in the fight. And keep praying for all who choose to remain defenseless against the devil's attacks.

B. Prayer

O God, You have met our every need through Christ. By Your power may we stand faithfully and firmly as Your people, no matter what we may encounter. In Jesus' name we pray. Amen.

C. Thought to Remember

Outfitted with God's armor, we overcome every attack of Satan.

Involvement Learning

Enhance your lesson with KJV Bible Student *(from your curriculum supplier) and the reproducible activity page (at www.standardlesson.com or in the back of the* KJV Standard Lesson Commentary Deluxe Edition*).*

Into the Lesson

Option. Begin with participants sharing about how they have experienced God's grace and mercy during the last week.

Divide the class into pairs or trios and have them choose a scribe for the group. Distribute paper and pens or pencils to the scribes. Ask the groups to brainstorm a list of valuables we protect; the scribes should write down the ideas. While groups are working, create a column on the board labeled "Valuables." After two minutes, write suggestions from the groups in this column.

Create a second column called "Protection." Have groups brainstorm methods for protecting each of these valuables. After a couple of minutes, again gather ideas from the groups, writing them in the second column.

If no one included "heart and soul" in their list of valuables, add that to the board and gather a bit of feedback. Allow the whole group a minute or two to talk about why it is important to protect something valuable.

Alternative. Distribute copies of the "Seeking Security" exercise from the activity page, which you can download. Have learners work in pairs to complete as indicated. Allow time for group discussion.

Lead into Bible study by saying, "The apostle Paul uses the imagery of a suit of armor to show how God protects believers from evil."

Into the Word

Distribute paper and pens. Ask a volunteer to read aloud Ephesians 6:10-18. Then allow five minutes for participants to write about two issues: 1—ways they personally feel a sense of spiritual warfare in their lives, and 2—ways they sense that spiritual warfare is affecting society at large (given that Satan is a liar, deceiver, accuser, etc.). Let people know when half the time has passed; give another alert with one minute remaining.

Read Ephesians 6:10-18 aloud again slowly. This time, have group members list on their papers each of the elements of the armor of God. Ask: 1—Which of the elements are weapons for offense? 2—Which are for defense? (Note: only the Word of God is an offensive weapon; all others are defensive.)

Form three or four groups, making sure each group has at least one mobile phone or tablet. *Alternative.* Distribute current newspapers and magazines to each group.

Instruct groups to search for stories about some of the societal issues they wrote about. Allow up to 10 minutes for groups to research and choose one issue to present. Ask them to consider these: 1—the worldly challenges, 2—the world's protections, and 3—the ways the armor of God can lift the burdens of the situation. Give each group two minutes to present their results to the group.

Into Life

Brainstorm actions the class can take to defend against at least one of the examples of oppression, injustice, and evil presented in the previous activity. Select one activity for your group to battle Satan's agenda in your community.

Then turn to individual concerns. Ask, "Which of the pieces of armor from Ephesians can most help you defend against this pressure?" Allow a minute for reflection on how we overcome every attack of Satan when outfitted with God's armor. Repeat Ephesians 6:10-18 as a closing prayer, replacing verse 12 with "We bring you our individual struggles, Lord. Hear them now," and pause for students to silently share their hearts with God. Then read verses 13-18 to finish the prayer.

Alternative. Distribute copies of the "Dress Me in Armor" activity from the activity page. Allow one minute for participants to complete the exercise.

Winter 2022–2023
King James Version

From Darkness
to Light

Special Features

Lessons
Unit 1: God's Preparation

Unit 2: God's Promises

Unit 3: God's Call

Quarterly Quiz

Use these questions as a pretest or as a review. The answers are on page iv of This Quarter in the Word.

Lesson 1

1. The mother of John the Baptist was named _____. *Luke 1:13*

2. The angel caused Zacharias to become deaf. T/F. *Luke 1:20*

Lesson 2

1. Some people expected the child to be named after his father. T/F. *Luke 1:59*

2. The child would be called a "_____ of the Highest." *Luke 1:76*

Lesson 3

1. John preached about the baptism of _____. *Luke 3:3*

2. Where was the prophesied voice said to call? (the wilderness, the valley, the mountain) *Luke 3:4*

Lesson 4

1. What would people of "all generations" call Mary? (humbled, blessed, dignified) *Luke 1:48*

2. Mary declared that God's mercy extends to those people who _____ Him. *Luke 1:50*

Lesson 5

1. Who did the Lord make a covenant with to establish the throne? (Saul, David, Solomon) *2 Chronicles 7:18*

2. The people would remain in the land, regardless of their actions. T/F. *2 Chronicles 7:20*

Lesson 6

1. The Lord promised to give Egypt, Seba, and _____ for His people. *Isaiah 43:3*

2. The people were chosen as what? (Choose two: warriors, priest, witnesses, servant) *Isaiah 43:10*

Lesson 7

1. In one way, Israel's stubbornness was described as what? (burning nose, iron neck, twisted tongue) *Isaiah 48:4*

2. The Lord praised Israel for having open ears. T/F. *Isaiah 48:8a*

Lesson 8

1. Included as a part of Isaiah's chosen fast was to "break every _____." *Isaiah 58:6*

2. When God's people provide and care for others, what will go before them? (righteousness, honor, praise) *Isaiah 58:8*

Lesson 9

1. The land itself is told to "be glad and rejoice." T/F. *Joel 2:21*

2. God's provision for His people meant that they would no longer be _____. *Joel 2:26*

Lesson 10

1. For believers, the preaching of the cross is like what of God? (power, wisdom, peace) *1 Corinthians 1:18*

2. Paul observed that preaching Christ crucified was _____ to the Greeks. *1 Corinthians 1:23*

Lesson 11

1. The name of Timothy's grandmother was _____. *2 Timothy 1:5*

2. Through the putting on of hands, Timothy received the "gift of God." T/F. *2 Timothy 1:6*

Lesson 12

1. God chose the poor of the world to be rich in _____. *James 2:5*

2. The "royal law" of Scripture consists of loving one's neighbor as oneself. T/F. *James 2:8*

Lesson 13

1. Believers are to offer physical sacrifices acceptable to God. T/F. *1 Peter 2:5*

2. Which of the following was not given by Peter to describe believers? (priesthood, nation, body) *1 Peter 2:9*

Quarter at a Glance

by Mark W. Hamilton

The lessons of this quarter give evidence of cause-and-effect relationships at work. God's call serves as the cause, with the effect being the presence of His salvation available for all people. As a result, all humanity is invited to live in reverence to the merciful and saving God.

God's Preparation

The quarter begins with four lessons from Luke's Gospel. These lessons highlight faithful people of God who longed to experience God's salvation. These people longed not merely for spiritual salvation, but for God's reign on earth. They desired a world where God would bring mercy and justice to his people (see Luke 1:46-55).

Luke's Gospel describes the ways that God's people came boldly to Him in prayer. The expectant hope that "all flesh shall see the salvation of God" (Luke 3:6) was the foundation for their eagerness to pray. Through their prayers, the people were prepared to hear God's peculiar and unique call.

God's Promises

The second unit of lessons, from the Old Testament historical books and prophets, describes God's promises to His prepared people. The Old Testament writers reminded the people that God's promises were reliable and trustworthy.

At the dedication of the temple in Jerusalem, God promised to be a present help for Solomon (2 Chronicles 7:12-22). God's promises of presence and deliverance would apply as long as the people acted justly and worshipped God purely.

Likewise, by way of the prophet's words, God responded to the people's experience of exile. The people's situation came as a result of their failure to live faithfully and justly as God's called people.

Through the words of the prophet Isaiah, God promised to teach and direct His people (Isaiah 48:17). If they followed God, received Him, and obeyed His commands, the people would expe-

rience the promised redemption and restoration (Isaiah 43:1-4, 10-12; 48:3-8a, 17).

Another Old Testament prophet, Joel, proclaimed a similar message to God's people. God promised to be among His people and restore their land. As long as they followed Him, they would never again experience shame (Joel 2:27).

God's promises, given through His prophets, addressed the people during their moments of need. The prophets offered an avenue for the community to hear and understand God's promises of renewal. However, the people would be required to change their behavior. They were to consider how they might serve others and avoid acting oppressively in any sense (Isaiah 58:6-10).

> *God's assessment does not always match human evaluation.*

God's Call

The quarter's final lessons take us to the New Testament epistles and their teachings on the inclusive nature of God's call. God's assessment does not always match human evaluation. As a result, He may call those people whom the world considers lowly and unremarkable (1 Corinthians 1:26-28).

God's call may lead to suffering in the lives of the called. This is not suffering for suffering's sake. Instead, God's people can experience His presence in their trials. Since God "hath abolished death" (2 Timothy 1:10), His promises bring hope.

The ultimate effect of God's promises is holiness in His people through the marvelous light of His salvation (1 Peter 2:9-10). Some people may consider God's call to be peculiar at best or a cause for stumbling at worst (2:8). Nonetheless, God remains faithful through His merciful call (2:10) that leads to holiness and salvation.

Get the Setting

by Mark W. Hamilton

For many of the Scripture texts of this quarter, the temple serves as the backdrop for the events and teaching emphasis. In some instances, the physical temple in Jerusalem was the location where God revealed His will to His people (example: Luke 1:8-20, lesson 1). In other instances, it was the redefinition of the temple to include the people of God (example: 1 Peter 2:1-10, lesson 13).

In the case of the former, the temple was more than a building for religious practices; it served as a sign of God's work among His people. Though the physical temple in Jerusalem was destroyed in AD 70, God's people had access to another temple.

Paul reminded followers of Jesus that their own bodies are the "temple of the Holy Ghost" (1 Corinthians 6:19). Though the temple as a physical building was no more, God's reign and presence among His people continued.

Ancient Temples

Humans built temples long before the era of ancient Israel. The plans for Solomon's temple (see 1 Kings 6–7) have parallels in its contemporaneous pagan temples. Modern archaeologists have excavated pagan temples from across the region and from the same time period that have floor plans that match the temple of Solomon.

Despite the identity of the gods worshipped in these temples, they were places where humans made sacrifices, sang hymns and laments, celebrated festivals, and generally interacted with the divine in ways not possible outside of the temple.

For example, worshippers of the pagan Babylonian god "Merodach" (Jeremiah 50:2) came to their temple to request help during a time of distress. The worshippers promised to praise Merodach after their deliverance. The pagan worshippers and diviners offered cedar resin, apricots, and grain as sacrifices to Merodach. The worshippers praised Merodach for his mercy and likely aimed to both please and appease the god. Ancient temples were places to seek the help of the gods.

The Temple of the True God

On the surface, the practices at the temple of the Israelites differed little from the practices at the pagan temples of Israel's neighbors. However, Israel's temple was different in an important way: It honored and worshipped the one true God of Israel. This was the God who brought Israel out of slavery and into the land that He had given them.

Israel's temple did not belong to a human monarch. Instead, it belonged to the people of God and to God himself. The temple was the location for the people's worship of the one true Creator God, who alone was all-powerful and who sought to make His presence known to His people.

Israel's temple represented God's commitment to His people. With the temple as a backdrop, God's people came to understand this divine commitment (example: Luke 1:8-20), even when they failed to follow Him (see 2 Chronicles 7:12-22).

The Temple in Our Imagination

However, Israel's temple—the former "house of God" (Luke 6:4)—would be replaced by a new house of God, the church (see 1 Timothy 3:15; Hebrews 3:6; 10:21). Now the church as the community of God's people became the place where God's presence with His people was evident.

In Israel's temple, only a particular person from a particular lineage could serve as a priest. However, in this redefined house of God, any follower of Jesus becomes a member of the "holy priesthood," with the Lord as the "chief corner stone" of that temple (1 Peter 2:5-6). The temple of the one true God symbolized God's presence with humanity, and it continues the same today through the "chosen generation, a royal priesthood, an holy nation, [and] a peculiar people" (2:9) of the church of God's people.

Answers to the Quarterly Quiz on page 114

Lesson 1—1. Elisabeth. 2. False. **Lesson 2**—1. True. 2. prophet. **Lesson 3**—1. repentance. 2. the wilderness. **Lesson 4**—1. blessed. 2. fear. **Lesson 5**—1. David. 2. False. **Lesson 6**—1. Ethiopia. 2. witnesses, servant. **Lesson 7**—1. an iron neck. 2. False. **Lesson 8**—1. yoke. 2. righteousness. **Lesson 9**—1. True. 2. ashamed. **Lesson 10**—1. power. 2. foolishness. **Lesson 11**—1. Lois. 2. True. **Lesson 12**—1. faith. 2. True. **Lesson 13**—1. False. 2. body.

Chart Feature

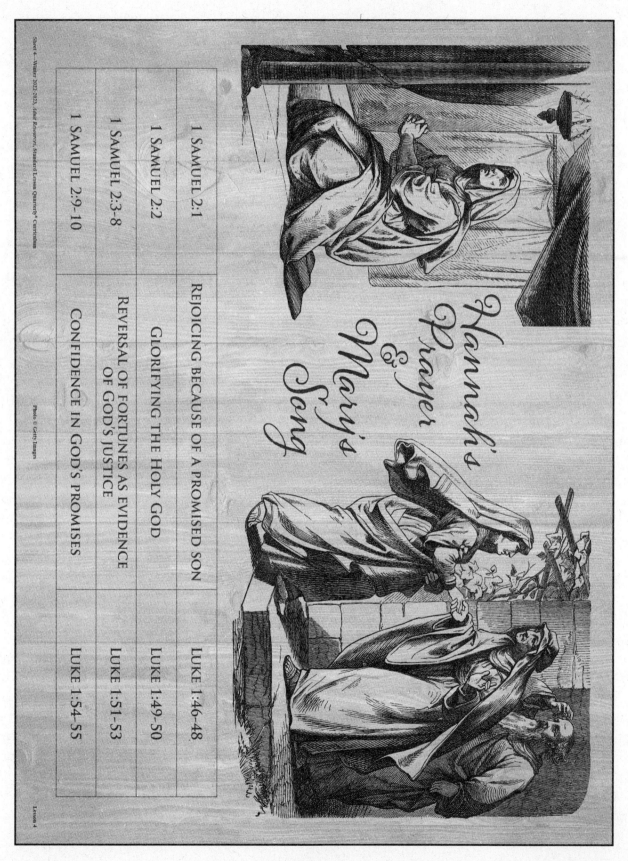

Hannah's Prayer & Mary's Song

1 SAMUEL 2:1	REJOICING BECAUSE OF A PROMISED SON	LUKE 1:46-48
1 SAMUEL 2:2	GLORIFYING THE HOLY GOD	LUKE 1:49-50
1 SAMUEL 2:3-8	REVERSAL OF FORTUNES AS EVIDENCE OF GOD'S JUSTICE	LUKE 1:51-53
1 SAMUEL 2:9-10	CONFIDENCE IN GOD'S PROMISES	LUKE 1:54-55

Sheet 4 • Winter 2022–2023, Adult Resources, Standard Lesson Quarterly® Curriculum

Photo © Getty Images

Lesson 4

People Think Faster Than You Speak

Teacher Tips by Mary T. Lederleitner

Have you ever found your mind wandering as you listened to a sermon or a presentation? When this happens, you might tell yourself to pay attention and pull your focus back to the presentation.

If this has been your experience, you are not alone. One of the biggest challenges for teachers is holding the attention of their students. An increased pace of life is now the reality for most students. Some of your students may be balancing several jobs, requiring that they monitor their phones or computers at all times. Further, students are more distracted. They may feel the need to check in with family, friends, or the news at all times of the day—even during class. As the teacher, it is your job to teach in a way that conveys the life-changing information of Scripture in a manner that holds your students' attention.

Neuroscience and Teaching

Another challenge facing teachers is that the human mind can process information faster than a person can speak. Since the mind likes to stay busy, having nothing to occupy this additional mental-processing power can leave learners feeling bored or restless. This might even occur if the topic is incredibly important.

A key to keeping students attentive during a lesson involves engaging any additional mental bandwidth they might have. The following learning tasks can be assigned, regardless of the Scripture text you may be teaching on.

Relating to the Text

Research has shown that if a teacher can trigger emotion in students, they will retain the teaching longer. The following practice can help students consider the Scripture passage by way of using emotion. To begin this practice in your class, say, "As we read our lesson's Scripture passage, I want you to think about this question."

Then provide a question that you believe will be most helpful in light of your teaching point. Here are a few examples:

- How would you have responded if you were a primary character in the text?
- What surprises you about the actions of the main character in this Scripture?
- How does this Scripture help believers understand God's work with people?

There are many types of questions that you could ask. The key is to ask a question that will invite an emotional response from the students.

Planning Your Next Step

Another simple, yet powerful, learning task involves planning the next step for your students. Consider creating a handout to guide your students' next steps. This handout might include take-home questions that would connect key teaching points to personal application. As you distribute these handouts, you might say, "James 1:22 tells us that we need to be more than hearers of God's Word. Instead, we are to live in a way that follows Scripture's teaching." Seeing your students' lives transformed is evidence that they are paying attention and taking to heart Scripture's lessons.

Remember As You Plan

A key principle of teaching is the reminder that *telling* students something is not the same as their *learning*. Teachers might focus on the wording of their lesson, thinking that is where learning occurs.

However, learning occurs when the student hears and internalizes the teacher's words. By doing so, students draw connections between the content of what they are hearing and their specific lives. This will maintain their focus to the lesson, broaden their understanding of Scripture, and challenge them to live in a new way.

When you practice these strategies for your class, you are creating an environment that fosters attentive and focused disciples of Jesus.

Zacharias Hears from God

Devotional Reading: John 10:22-30
Background Scripture: Luke 1:5-23

Luke 1:8-20

8 And it came to pass, that while he executed the priest's office before God in the order of his course,

9 According to the custom of the priest's office, his lot was to burn incense when he went into the temple of the Lord.

10 And the whole multitude of the people were praying without at the time of incense.

11 And there appeared unto him an angel of the Lord standing on the right side of the altar of incense.

12 And when Zacharias saw him, he was troubled, and fear fell upon him.

13 But the angel said unto him, Fear not, Zacharias: for thy prayer is heard; and thy wife Elisabeth shall bear thee a son, and thou shalt call his name John.

14 And thou shalt have joy and gladness; and many shall rejoice at his birth.

15 For he shall be great in the sight of the Lord, and shall drink neither wine nor strong drink; and he shall be filled with the Holy Ghost, even from his mother's womb.

16 And many of the children of Israel shall he turn to the Lord their God.

17 And he shall go before him in the spirit and power of Elias, to turn the hearts of the fathers to the children, and the disobedient to the wisdom of the just; to make ready a people prepared for the Lord.

18 And Zacharias said unto the angel, Whereby shall I know this? for I am an old man, and my wife well stricken in years.

19 And the angel answering said unto him, I am Gabriel, that stand in the presence of God; and am sent to speak unto thee, and to shew thee these glad tidings.

20 And, behold, thou shalt be dumb, and not able to speak, until the day that these things shall be performed, because thou believest not my words, which shall be fulfilled in their season.

Key Text

The angel said unto him, Fear not, Zacharias: for thy prayer is heard; and thy wife Elisabeth shall bear thee a son, and thou shalt call his name John. —**Luke 1:13**

From Darkness to Light

Unit 1: God's Preparation
Lessons 1–4

Lesson Aims

After participating in this lesson, each learner will be able to:

1. List elements of Zacharias's doubt and fear.
2. Explain why his doubt was inexcusable.
3. Voice or write a sentence of repentance for harboring an inexcusable doubt.

Lesson Outline

Introduction

A. Does History Rhyme?

A popular claim is that history repeats itself. But does that claim hold up? Perhaps a more accurate claim is that history does not repeat itself, but it rhymes. This means that while no one historical event is exactly like any other, similarities may exist between the two events.

Events in God's plan of salvation are frequently similar to His earlier work among His people. These similarities can help people understand the singular, focused plan of God. His work consists of more than isolated events in history. Instead, His work is a grand epic to turn rebellious, hostile humanity into His holy people.

Today's Scripture text highlights one of these rhythms of God's plan. Would the recipient of this good news trust that God would be faithful to His promises?

B. Lesson Context

The Gospel of Luke is one of two Gospel accounts that describe Jesus' birth and its context. The other account comes from the Gospel of Matthew (Matthew 1:18–2:23).

Luke's account is distinct in at least two ways. First, Luke's account is interwoven with events regarding the birth of Jesus' cousin John (Luke 1:5-25, 57-80). Both pregnancies were announced by an angel (1:13, 30-33), were accompanied by great wonders (1:62-66; 2:13-15), and had prepared the people for God's salvation (1:32-33, 67-79).

Second, Luke's account highlights the significance of these parallel birth narratives through depictions of worship. Mary (Luke 1:46-55; see lesson 4), Zacharias (1:67-79; see lesson 2), a heavenly host (2:13-14), and Simeon (2:28-32) all give praise to God for His work.

Luke's account opens by way of introducing Zacharias, the father of John and a priest in the division of Abia (Luke 1:5). Zacharias and other priests descended from Aaron, the brother of Moses (see Exodus 28:1). Over the centuries, Aaron's descendants became numerous to the point that they could not all serve in the temple at the same time. King David had organized the priests into 24 divisions for service (1 Chronicles 24:1-19). The divisions required adjustment following a season of captivity (see Ezra 2:36-39). These divisions apparently continued into the New Testament era.

Every division would serve in the temple for roughly two nonconsecutive weeks each year. The assigned priests would complete the necessary tasks for the temple, including accepting and offering sacrifices, burning incense, and leading prayers.

Zacharias and his wife Elisabeth, also a descendent of Aaron, were "righteous before God" and "blameless" regarding obeying His commandments (Luke 1:6). The couple was without children due to their ages and Elisabeth's barrenness (1:7).

I. Holy Occasion
(Luke 1:8-10)
A. Post of the Priest (vv. 8-9)

8. And it came to pass, that while he executed the priest's office before God in the order of his course.

The time had arrived for Zacharias and his priestly *order* to begin their service in the temple (see Lesson Context). The events that followed would take place against the backdrop of a priest performing his duties *before* the presence of *God*.

9. According to the custom of the priest's office, his lot was to burn incense when he went into the temple of the Lord.

The renovation and expansion of *the temple of the Lord* in Jesus' day began during the reign of Herod the Great (ruled 37–4 BC). Herod's efforts in this regard took at least 46 years (see John 2:20). He used the temple as a political and religious tool to gain support from the Jewish people. The layout of Herod's temple paralleled its predecessors. The temple complex consisted of a series of outdoor courts, a large porch (see 10:23), and a building that housed the inner sanctuaries (compare 1 Kings 6:2-10, 16-36)—the center of the entire complex.

Twice daily, a priest would enter the outer sanctuary and *burn incense* on the altar of incense (compare Exodus 30:1-8; 40:26-27; 1 Kings 6:20-22; 7:48). The rising smoke and the fragrant aroma represented the people's prayers going up to God (compare Psalm 141:2; Revelation 5:8; 8:3).

Because of the numerous priests, *the custom* of drawing lots determined the priest who would fulfill this particular duty. The practice was not intended as a pagan lottery (compare John 19:24). Rather, it was a way to determine God's will (compare Proverbs 16:33; Acts 1:21-26). The chosen priest would fill this role one time in his lifetime. We can imagine the sense of awe and reverence that Zacharias felt as he received *his lot* and entered the sanctuary.

B. Prayers of the People (v. 10)

10. And the whole multitude of the people were praying without at the time of incense.

Because only the chosen priest entered the Holy Place where the altar of incense was located, *the whole multitude of the people* was scattered throughout the temple's courts as the priest burned the incense. The people were restricted to the various outer courts because of God's requirements regarding who could enter that space. It was not as though the people were unholy—their acts of *praying* highlighted their commitment to the Lord.

The content of the crowd's prayer *at the time of incense* is unknown. The worshippers would bring their requests before God. One request was probably paramount: that God restore Israel and free them from their bondage to foreign empires (compare Isaiah 2).

II. Profound Announcement
(Luke 1:11-17)
A. Fearful Reaction (vv. 11-12)

11. And there appeared unto him an angel of the Lord standing on the right side of the altar of incense.

How to Say It

Abia	Ab-*ee*-ah.
asceticism	uh-*set*-uh-sizz-um.
Elias	Ee-*lye*-us.
Gabriel	*Gay*-bree-ul.
Herod	*Hair*-ud.
Johanan	Jo-*hay*-nan.
Zacharias	Zack-uh-*rye*-us.

Frequently in the writings of Luke, a declaration that someone *appeared* indicates a supernatural presence (see Luke 9:30; 22:43; 24:34; Acts 9:17). This appearance to Zacharias was no exception.

A heavenly visitor, such as *an angel of the Lord,* was a representative of God (see Judges 6:11-22; Matthew 2:19). Though not used here, when Scripture includes the definite article *the* with "angel of the Lord," the reference can be to the presence of God himself (example: Exodus 3:2-4). Zacharias did not have to wait long to discover the identity of this mysterious heavenly visitor (Luke 1:19, below).

12. And when Zacharias saw him, he was troubled, and fear fell upon him.

This feeling of *fear* meant a sense of deep respect combined with sheer terror. Such a reaction was common when a person experienced the appearance of a messenger of God (see Judges 6:22-23; 13:21-22; Daniel 8:16-17; Luke 1:29-30; 2:9).

> **What Do You Think?**
> How can a believer respond with joy rather than fear to God's unexpected acts?
>
> **Digging Deeper**
> How does love serve as an antidote to fear? (See 1 John 4:18.)

B. Future Realities (vv. 13-17)

13a. But the angel said unto him, Fear not, Zacharias: for thy prayer is heard.

The first words of *the angel* provided comfort to the troubled priest. Other depictions of heavenly visitors also include the imperative *fear not* (examples: Daniel 10:5-12; Matthew 28:5; Luke 1:30; 2:10). The command reassured God's people of His presence and calmed their nerves.

The text is unclear which particular *prayer* of *Zacharias* had been *heard* by God. Zacharias and Elisabeth had likely prayed countless times for a child of their own. However, it is unknown whether they continued praying that request. Perhaps they felt that because of their advanced ages (Luke 1:7) having a child of their own was out of the question. Such a prayer, however, would have been consistent with the prayers of their ancestors (examples: Genesis 25:21; 30:22; 1 Samuel 1:10-11).

Other students of the text have proposed that the prayer in question was a prayer of Zacharias at the altar of incense concerning Israel's salvation. However, Scripture is silent on this point. This proposal assumes that it would have been inappropriate for a priest to offer personal prayers while serving in the temple on behalf of the people. Perhaps Zacharias prayed along the lines that Israel would see the "horn of salvation" (Luke 1:69) and that they would "be saved from [their] enemies, and from the hand of all that hate [them]" (1:71).

Whatever the content of Zacharias's prayer, God answered the prayer in a way that possibly addressed both the desire for a child and a desire to see Israel's salvation (see commentary on Luke 1:16, below).

> **What Do You Think?**
> How can believers remain faithful in prayer even if their prayers are not answered on their preferred timetable?
>
> **Digging Deeper**
> How can Romans 5:1-5 and 8:18-27 provide encouragement to believers to exercise patience in this regard?

13b. And thy wife Elisabeth shall bear thee a son, and thou shalt call his name John.

The angel's declaration that *Elisabeth* would *bear . . . a son* was likely surprising to Zacharias. However, the announcement of a child to an elderly, childless couple is not without precedent in Scripture (example: Genesis 17:17-19). Only the one, true God could work such a miracle.

The *name John* was common among men in the New Testament era (see Matthew 10:2; John 1:42; Acts 4:6). However, the name likely came from the Hebrew name Johanan (see 1 Chronicles 3:15, 24, etc.), the meaning of which describes God's graciousness. Zacharias and Elisabeth were to experience God's graciousness firsthand in the birth of their son.

14. And thou shalt have joy and gladness; and many shall rejoice at his birth.

Feelings of *joy and gladness* would replace feelings of fear (see Luke 1:13a, above). But the birth of this child would have a much wider impact than on just this couple. *Many* other people would *rejoice* because of the role this child would have in declaring God's plan for His people (compare 2:10). John would not bring the long-awaited salvation to God's people. Instead, he would be a forerunner, preparing the way for that salvation (3:15-18; see lesson 3).

15a. For he shall be great in the sight of the Lord.

John's *great* standing would not be measured by worldly standards of success. Years later, Jesus affirmed the angel's prophecy: "Among those that are born of women there is not a greater prophet than John the Baptist" (Luke 7:28). John's greatness *in the sight of the Lord* would come from his role as the person who would announce the good news of the arrival of God's salvation (Mark 1:14-15; Luke 3:1-6).

15b. And shall drink neither wine nor strong drink.

Alcoholic beverages were common in the biblical world. *Wine* was served by itself (see John 2:3-10) or mixed with other substances and served for pain relief (see Mark 15:23). Any other fermented alcoholic beverage made with natural sugars was a *strong drink*. The alcohol content of these beverages is unknown. At no point in John's life would he *drink* these beverages (see Luke 7:33). Because of his chosen sobriety, John would be marked as someone who had a distinct role for God.

The Law of Moses described two specific situations when a person would make a vow of abstinence from alcohol. First, priests were to avoid alcohol during their service to God (Leviticus 10:8-11; Ezekiel 44:21). Second, Israelites who had taken the vow of a Nazarite were also to avoid alcohol (Numbers 6:1-3; compare Judges 13:2-7). Both priests and Nazarites were set apart from others in order to serve God and His people.

However, John would not become a priest like his father, and it is unknown whether John became a Nazarite. Either way, John practiced asceticism, a self-denial of earthly pleasures, in order to focus on a lifelong service to God (see Luke 7:24-28).

15c. And he shall be filled with the Holy Ghost, even from his mother's womb.

Instead of being filled with alcohol, John would *be filled with the Holy Ghost* (compare Ephesians

Visual for Lesson 1. *Before closing the class with prayer, encourage the class to consider how they might silence their fears regarding God's work.*

5:18). A characteristic of God's prophets in Scripture was that they were filled with God's Spirit (see Isaiah 61:1; Ezekiel 11:5; Micah 3:8). John would serve as a prophet of God, *even from his mother's womb*, where he "leaped . . . for joy" in the presence of the unborn Savior (Luke 1:44).

16. And many of the children of Israel shall he turn to the Lord their God.

The angel's message transitions from *who* John would become to *what* he would do. As God's messenger, John would call his own people, *the children of Israel*, to return to God. Part of this message warned the people that their being Abraham's descendants was no indicator of the presence of true repentance (Luke 3:7-9).

In the Old Testament, God's people showed true repentance when they put away their lives of sin and returned *to the Lord their God* (Deuteronomy 30:2-3; 1 Samuel 7:3; Hosea 3:5; 7:10; compare Acts 11:21; 26:20; 1 Peter 2:25). John would call people to turn from their wickedness and enter the life of God's salvation. In this way, John was like Israel's prophets who proclaimed the "law of truth" and "did turn many away from iniquity" (Malachi 2:6).

Influencer Marketing

Have you ever heard someone claim to be an influencer? An influencer is a person with whom brands collaborate to sell a product on the influencer's social media platforms. The more followers an influencer has on social media, the more valuable that influencer's platform will be to brands. And so, brands and businesses pay to be showcased on that influencer's social media platform.

Through social media, the influencer can advertise brand-name makeup, trendy clothing, or the latest electronic device. One influencer has even reported being offered thousands of dollars to place a brand-name beverage in the background of a video that he filmed for his social media!

While an influencer's advertisements appear innocent, they are essentially pointing people to consume—perhaps mindlessly. Followers of Jesus, however, should be *spiritual* influencers for the world. John the Baptist would influence many of his peers to turn to the Lord. He would be an influencer for spiritual matters and would point others to the Lord's salvation. Are you living as a spiritual influencer, advertising a life changed because of God's salvation?   —P. L. M.

17. And he shall go before him in the spirit and power of Elias, to turn the hearts of the fathers to the children, and the disobedient to the wisdom of the just; to make ready a people prepared for the Lord.

John would not be unique as a prophet of God's salvation; many other prophets had gone *before* the Lord and had proclaimed the hope of God's salvation. John came in the type, *the spirit*, and the *power of* the prophet *Elias* (Elijah; see Matthew 11:12-14). As God's prophet, Elijah had confronted the people's unfaithfulness (see 1 Kings 18:16-46).

Similarly, John would confront the people's unfaithfulness as he called them to repentance. His teaching would lead to changes in the lives of those who listened to and heeded his message. The reconciliation of *fathers to* their *children* (compare Malachi 4:6) and the turning of *the disobedient* to the way of *wisdom* (compare Proverbs 1:2-3; 10:23-24) would confirm John's prophetic message.

John would not be the source of God's salvation. Instead, he would get people *ready* and *prepared* for God's salvation. His role would be like that of a "voice . . . that crieth in the wilderness, Prepare ye the way of *the Lord*" (Isaiah 40:3; see John 1:23).

III. Skeptical Exchange
(Luke 1:18-20)
A. Desiring a Sign (v. 18)

18. And Zacharias said unto the angel, Whereby shall I know this? for I am an old man, and my wife well stricken in years.

In the Old Testament, requesting a sign from God was common and seen in a positive or neutral light (see Genesis 15:8-9; Exodus 4:1-5; Judges 6:17-18, 36-40; 2 Kings 20:8-11; Isaiah 7:11-17). In the New Testament, however, requests for signs are depicted in a negative light (see Mark 8:11-13; Luke 11:16, 29-30; 1 Corinthians 1:22-23), unless God initiated the sign (Luke 2:12).

The angel's promises appeared impossible to *Zacharias*. He desired a sign to *know* if these promises would come true. If a couple could not become pregnant before, then surely they could not do so when they were *old* and *well stricken in years*.

B. Embodying the Sign (vv. 19-20)

19. And the angel answering said unto him, I am Gabriel, that stand in the presence of God; and am sent to speak unto thee, and to shew thee these glad tidings.

Scripture frequently leaves angels unnamed (see Genesis 19:15; Exodus 14:19; Luke 2:13-14; Acts 10:1-3). However, this *angel* revealed his name (compare Jude 9; Revelation 9:11; 12:7). *Gabriel* also appeared in and interpreted the visions of the prophet Daniel (Daniel 8:16; 9:21). The same angel would later appear to Mary to announce the pending arrival of the Son of God and the eternal rule of God on earth (Luke 1:26-37). The lowly virgin Mary accepted Gabriel's message to her with faith, humility, and rejoicing (1:38, 46-56). However, the knowledgeable priest Zacharias responded to Gabriel's message with skepticism and doubt.

Zacharias's skepticism toward Gabriel's message was called out. When God speaks through His messenger, there is no uncertainty with regard to that message. Instead, God's people are to submit to the message that brings *glad tidings*.

A Messenger of Life

A little after midnight local time on July 30, 1945, an enemy submarine torpedoed the USS *Indianapolis*. Twelve minutes later, the ship sank in the Philippine Sea.

This was a tragedy for my family—my great-uncle was among the hundreds of sailors who died on the ship. Several days after the ship sank, an official military messenger informed my great-aunt of her husband's death. Military families fear the worst possible message from these messengers.

Not all messengers bring news of death. Through a heavenly messenger, Zacharias received a message of life. Now God has spoken to us through His Son (Hebrews 1:1-2). God has brought us life through His Son. How can you be a messenger of this life in the Son to someone else? —P. L. M.

20. And, behold, thou shalt be dumb, and not able to speak, until the day that these things shall be performed, because thou believest not my words, which shall be fulfilled in their season.

Zacharias himself would embody the sign that he desired. This sign was the result of his unbelief regarding God's words through Gabriel. A demonstration of God's power and Zacharias's failure to believe was for Zacharias to be *not able to speak*.

But Gabriel's sign also came with mercy and promise: on *the day* that Gabriel's promises were *fulfilled*, Zacharias's sign would lift (see Luke 1:57-66, lesson 2). At that point, Zacharias's unbelief

would be replaced with praise to God for fulfilling His promises (1:67-79).

Conclusion
A. Rhythms of God's Plan

Zacharias expected that God would use someone exceptional, not ordinary, to work out His divine plan of salvation. However, God frequently calls the unassuming or the seemingly ill-equipped. Zacharias and his family were the latest iteration of God's working through people who least expected it. Though Zacharias served as a priest, he was skeptical that God would work though him and his wife.

Of course we are not the parents of the forerunner of Christ, but Zacharias's story shows us that God will work through our lives as well. Will we doubt that God is serious when He calls us to fulfill His plan? Or will we believe and trust that God, who often has worked through ordinary people, will work through ordinary us?

B. Prayer

God of our salvation, we acknowledge that we sometimes doubt Your work and that You would choose us. Strengthen our faith so that we can be ready when You call us. In Jesus' name. Amen.

C. Thought to Remember
God works extraordinarily through the ordinary.

Visuals FOR THESE LESSONS

The visual pictured in each lesson (example: page 125) is a small reproduction of a large, full-color poster included in the *Adult Resources* packet for the Winter Quarter. Order No. 2629123 from your supplier.

Involvement Learning

Enhance your lesson with KJV Bible Student (from your curriculum supplier) and the reproducible activity page (at www.standardlesson.com or in the back of the KJV Standard Lesson Commentary Deluxe Edition).

Into the Lesson

Ask two volunteers to each share a story about an event that happened in their lives during the past week. After selecting the volunteers, flip a coin to determine how each volunteer will tell his or her story. If the coin lands on heads, the volunteer will act out their story without using any words. If the coin lands on tails, the volunteer will draw images (no words!) on the board to depict the story. Each volunteer is allowed one minute to "tell" their story while the class guesses the story.

Alternative. Distribute copies of the "An Astonishing Story" exercise from the activity page, which you can download. Have learners complete the exercise as indicated.

After either activity, say, "Communicating without speaking words is a challenge. In today's lesson, we will consider how Zacharias's inability to speak was both a punishment and an expression of mercy."

Into the Word

Ask a volunteer to read Luke 1:8-20 aloud. Divide the class into three groups: **"Who?" Group** / **"What?" Group** / **"Why?" Group**. Distribute handouts (you prepare) with the following questions:

"Who?" Group: 1–Based on Exodus 30:1-9; 1 Chronicles 6:48-49; and 2 Chronicles 26:16:18, who was supposed to burn incense on the altar of incense? 2–How do these Scriptures help us understand today's passage? 3–How is Genesis 17:1-8, 15-19 similar to or different from Gabriel's announcement to Zacharias? 4–What do these Scriptures tell us about God and His work?

"What?" Group: 1–Based on Exodus 30:1-8, what was the priest's duty at the altar of incense? 2–How does knowing this help us understand Zacharias's role in today's passage? 3–How is Judges 13:2-14 similar to or different from Gabriel's announcement to Zacharias? 4–What do these Scriptures tell us about God and His work?

"Why?" Group: 1–Based on Revelation 8:2-4, why was the burning of incense considered significant? 2–How does knowing this help us understand Zacharias's role in today's passage? 3–How is 1 Samuel 1:1-18 similar to or different from Gabriel's announcement to Zacharias? 4–What do these Scriptures tell us about God and His work?

Have groups present their findings from the first two questions for whole-class discussion. After no more than 10 minutes of discussion, say, "Since Zacharias was a priest and followed God, he would have been familiar with these stories from the Old Testament. What should Zacharias have known about God and His work?" Have groups present their findings from the last two questions for whole-class discussion.

Alternative. Distribute copies of the "Baby Announcement" exercise from the activity page. Have students work in pairs to complete the activity as indicated.

After calling time under either activity, ask each group or pair to write two alternative endings to today's Scripture text. Have them consider the following prompts when imagining the alternative endings: 1–How could Zacharias have responded differently to the angel's news? 2–What other consequences could Zacharias have received for his doubts?

After 10 minutes, have each group or pair present their alternative endings for whole-class discussion.

Into Life

Distribute an index card and pen to each student. Ask them to consider a recent doubt they have felt toward God or His work and write that doubt on the index card. Have students write down a plan to deal with the doubt.

Have students turn over their index cards and write a prayer of repentance for harboring inexcusable doubts toward God. Encourage students to pray their prayers during the upcoming week.

Zacharias Speaks

Devotional Reading: Malachi 4:1-6
Background Scripture: Luke 1:57-80

Luke 1:57-66, 76-79

57 Now Elisabeth's full time came that she should be delivered; and she brought forth a son.

58 And her neighbours and her cousins heard how the Lord had shewed great mercy upon her; and they rejoiced with her.

59 And it came to pass, that on the eighth day they came to circumcise the child; and they called him Zacharias, after the name of his father.

60 And his mother answered and said, Not so; but he shall be called John.

61 And they said unto her, There is none of thy kindred that is called by this name.

62 And they made signs to his father, how he would have him called.

63 And he asked for a writing table, and wrote, saying, His name is John. And they marvelled all.

64 And his mouth was opened immediately, and his tongue loosed, and he spake, and praised God.

65 And fear came on all that dwelt round about them: and all these sayings were noised abroad throughout all the hill country of Judaea.

66 And all they that heard them laid them up in their hearts, saying, What manner of child shall this be! And the hand of the Lord was with him.

76 And thou, child, shalt be called the prophet of the Highest: for thou shalt go before the face of the Lord to prepare his ways;

77 To give knowledge of salvation unto his people by the remission of their sins,

78 Through the tender mercy of our God; whereby the dayspring from on high hath visited us,

79 To give light to them that sit in darkness and in the shadow of death, to guide our feet into the way of peace.

Key Text

Thou, child, shalt be called the prophet of the Highest: for thou shalt go before the face of the Lord to prepare his ways. —**Luke 1:76**

From Darkness to Light

Unit 1: God's Preparation
Lessons 1–4

Lesson Aims

After participating in this lesson, each learner will be able to:

1. List the significant events that occurred during the first eight days of the life of John the Baptist.

2. Explain elements of cause and effect regarding the reactions of neighbors and relatives.

3. Identify one way he or she can help prepare someone's heart to receive the Lord.

Lesson Outline

Introduction

A. Dramatic Pause

Skilled performers and communicators will harness the power of an aptly timed silence to capture the attention of their audience. Musicians might stop playing for two beats before playing the next section of music. Actors might stand in silence for an extended moment before continuing their dialogue. Magicians might pause to build the audience's sense of anticipation before revealing the illusion's climax. Preachers might take a silent breath after reading Scripture, allowing the congregation time to consider Scripture's imperatives. A well-timed, sometimes dramatic pause has the power to affect audiences.

The power of a dramatic pause comes in what follows the pause; silence frequently precedes the high point. Today's Scripture text continues a dramatic pause that began in the last lesson. We will understand how this pause highlights the fulfillment of God's promises to a family and to the whole world.

B. Lesson Context

The first chapters of Luke's Gospel tell the stories of two important births. Luke presents the events surrounding the births of John and Jesus in a way that connects them to each other. In both accounts, the angel Gabriel announced an approaching pregnancy and promised birth. Gabriel first appeared to a priest named Zacharias and prophesied regarding the pregnancy of his wife, Elisabeth, and the birth of their son, John (Luke 1:8-19; see lesson 1). Then the angel appeared to Mary and announced that she was "highly favoured" in the eyes of God (1:28) and that she would give birth to a son (1:31-33).

Mary and Elisabeth were related (Luke 1:36). Later, when Mary visited Elisabeth, the unborn John "leaped" in his mother's womb, and Elisabeth "was filled with the Holy Ghost" (1:41). Elisabeth proclaimed her relative to be blessed because of Mary's demonstration of faith and belief in God's words through Gabriel (1:45). The proclamation led Mary to rejoice through a song of worshipful adoration and prophetic expectation (1:46-56, lesson 4). Luke's Gospel emphasizes

God's work in the world by way of Elisabeth, Mary, and their experiences while pregnant.

This lesson's Scripture depicts the second half of a type of pause that affected John's father. When Zacharias received Gabriel's revelation regarding Elisabeth's pregnancy, he questioned whether God's promise could come true (see Luke 1:18, lesson 1). Gabriel gave a sign to Zacharias: he would be mute until Gabriel's words were fulfilled (1:19-20). Zacharias would have to endure this sign for the length of Elisabeth's pregnancy.

Elisabeth recognized that God was at work in and through her pregnancy. She proclaimed that "the Lord dealt with me in the days wherein he looked on me, to take away my reproach among men" (Luke 1:25). Would Zacharias feel the same on the other side of his dramatic pause?

I. Joyous Occasion
(Luke 1:57-63)
A. Birth of a Son (vv. 57-58)

57. Now Elisabeth's full time came that she should be delivered; and she brought forth a son.

Beyond Zacharias's and Elisabeth's interactions with the crowds and with Mary (see Luke 1:21-22, 39-45), Luke's Gospel does not provide further insight regarding any other interactions they had with others. Whether others knew of Elisabeth's pregnancy or Zacharias's loss of speech is unknown. Elisabeth's seclusion for five months (1:24) may have contributed to Luke's silence regarding this period.

Luke's sparse narration until this point focuses the reader's attention on the fulfillment of Gabriel's promise to Zacharias. After the *full time* of *Elisabeth's* pregnancy, she gave birth to *a son*, just as God promised through Gabriel (Luke 1:13, lesson 1).

58. And her neighbours and her cousins heard how the Lord had shewed great mercy upon her; and they rejoiced with her.

One family member had known that Elisabeth was pregnant (see Luke 1:36). Although Zacharias had limited capacity for communication (1:20), others among their *neighbours* and *cousins heard* of and celebrated the birth as a work of God. Only God could give a child to an elderly couple who

were previously considered barren (compare Genesis 18:11-13).

Elisabeth's experience of the Lord's *great mercy* was a taste of the mercy that God would show toward all His people (see Luke 1:50, 54). This display of mercy led the people to rejoice *with* Elisabeth, thus fulfilling Gabriel's promises (see 1:14). Communal celebration replaced Elisabeth's former feelings of disgrace (1:25).

> **What Do You Think?**
> How have you experienced joy that resulted from God's acts of mercy?
> **Digging Deeper**
> In what ways did you share these feelings of joy with other believers?

B. Affirming His Name (vv. 59-63)

59. And it came to pass, that on the eighth day they came to circumcise the child; and they called him Zacharias, after the name of his father.

Zacharias and Elisabeth desired to live in righteousness and in adherence to the Lord's commands (Luke 1:6). They would demonstrate willingness to obey God and His commands as they raised their *child*.

Circumcision of infant males *on the eighth day* after birth was a practice that dated back to the time of Abraham (see Genesis 17:9-14) and to the Law of Moses (Leviticus 12:3). The practice continued into the first century (see Luke 2:21; Philippians 3:5). Circumcision served as a sign that the infant son was included in the covenant with God.

Tradition is unclear regarding the cultural norms of naming a baby in the New Testament era. The Old Testament provides no explicit example

How to Say It

Benedictus	Ben-eh-*dik*-tus.
Jerusalem	Juh-*roo*-suh-lem.
Judaea	Joo-*dee*-uh.
Malachi	*Mal*-uh-kye.
Septuagint	Sep-*too*-ih-jent.
Zealots	*Zel*-uts.

of a baby boy being named at his circumcision (compare Genesis 21:1-3; 25:24-26). However, the practice of naming a son on the day of his circumcision seems to have become the norm by the time of Zacharias and Elisabeth (compare Luke 2:21). The gathered crowd was unfamiliar with Gabriel's proclamation regarding the name of the child (see 1:13). They desired to honor the priest Zacharias when *they called* his child *after* him.

What Do You Think?
How can believers determine whether or not a tradition follows God's will?

Digging Deeper
How do Mark 7:1-15; 1 Corinthians 11:23; Colossians 2:8; 2 Thessalonians 2:13-15; and 1 Peter 1:18-19 inform your determination in this regard?

60. And his mother answered and said, Not so; but he shall be called John.

The crowd's consensus regarding the baby's name was immediately contradicted by the baby's *mother.* Scripture does not indicate exactly how Elisabeth knew that her child would *be called John.* Perhaps Zacharias informed her in writing (see commentary on Luke 1:63, below).

61. And they said unto her, There is none of thy kindred that is called by this name.

The crowd did not understand Elisabeth's insistence on that *name.* John was a common name in the New Testament era (see Matthew 10:2; John 1:42; Acts 4:6). However, the crowd's response indicates that no other member of the baby's family (*kindred*) was named John. They were obviously not privy to the rationale behind Elisabeth's proclamation of his name.

62. And they made signs to his father, how he would have him called.

Because Zacharias was "not able to speak" (Luke 1:20; see lesson 1), he resorted to making signs with his hands to communicate (1:22). The crowd on this day *made signs to* him, perhaps indicating that he was both mute *and* deaf (compare Mark 7:32). His impairment would continue until the fulfillment of Gabriel's promises.

63. And he asked for a writing table, and

wrote, saying, His name is John. And they marvelled all.

A writing table was a stone or board coated with wax—a smooth surface on which letters and words were etched using a writing object, like a pen (compare Isaiah 30:8). After short messages were etched on the waxy surface, the wax was heated and smoothed, creating a new surface on which a new message could be written.

As Zacharias was a priest (Luke 1:8), he was likely trained in various methods of writing. Space for a brief message was all that Zacharias required as he *wrote* on the tablet, *His name is John.* Zacharias simply reiterated the name that had been given to him by God, communicated through the angel Gabriel, and stated to the crowds by Elisabeth.

The crowd was amazed at the consistent message between Elisabeth and the impaired Zacharias. Luke's Gospel frequently portrays people as being *marvelled* (see Luke 20:26) and in wonder (24:12) when faced with the results of God's work (examples: 2:33; 9:43; 11:14).

II. Astonishing Restoration
(Luke 1:64-66)
A. The Speech (v. 64)

64. And his mouth was opened immediately, and his tongue loosed, and he spake, and praised God.

Zacharias's inability to speak resulted from his expression of doubt regarding God's plan (Luke 1:20; see Lesson Context). However, God's mercy is greater than human doubt. Zacharias experienced this mercy firsthand when *his mouth was opened* and *his tongue* was *loosed.* God's mercy, demonstrated through His power over the physical world, is expedient and effective (see 5:24-25; 8:43-44; 13:10-13; 18:35-43).

As Zacharias *praised God,* God's Spirit filled him (Luke 1:67; not in this week's Scripture text). This same Spirit worked dramatically in the events and people of the early chapters of Luke's Gospel (see 1:15, 35, 41, 67, 80; 2:25-27).

License to Believe

When it was time for my oldest son to learn

to drive, he wanted no pointers from me. I tried to warn him of certain challenges, like residential speed limits and laws regarding school zones, but he wanted none of my advice. Pridefully, he did not believe that he needed to learn anything from his parents regarding safe driving.

Unfortunately, he failed his driving test three times and had to wait six months before taking the test again. While his peers were driving, he had hit a "speed bump" and lost out on months of driving. During those months, he studied the driving rules and regulations like he was cramming for a school final exam. After this period, he took the test again and passed. No one was happier—or celebrated more—than my son!

Zacharias's unbelief resulted in his being unable to speak—he had to wait until the birth of his son before that ability returned. When it did return, Zacharias responded with celebratory praise. Do pride and unbelief prevent you from worshipping God? Don't hit a spiritual speed bump! Celebrate God and His salvation.   —P. L. M.

B. The Reaction (vv. 65-66)

65. And fear came on all that dwelt round about them: and all these sayings were noised abroad throughout all the hill country of Judaea.

Feelings of *fear* arise in a person because of an awareness of danger (see Matthew 14:26; John 7:13). However, fear can also refer to the awe felt when witnessing God's work (see Luke 5:25-26; 7:15-16). The people that day were in awe and fear when they saw a man who had previously been mute now be able to speak.

News of John's birth and Zacharias's restored ability did not stay in the temple area or even in Jerusalem. *The hill country of Judaea* was the rural region around Jerusalem. Because of its mountainous terrain, travel in this region was difficult. Despite these challenges, news of Zacharias, Elisabeth, and their baby spread *throughout* the region. People sensed that God was at work!

66. And all they that heard them laid them up in their hearts, saying, What manner of child shall this be! And the hand of the Lord was with him.

The miraculous nature of these events stayed with the people *that heard* or saw the events firsthand. They had a sense of wonder, awe, and anticipation *in their hearts* regarding the miraculous nature of the events (compare Luke 2:19, 51).

Though years passed before John's ministry formally began (see Luke 3:1-3), God's presence *was with him*. Old Testament writers described God's presence and power as *the hand of the Lord* working for the protection and flourishing of His people (Deuteronomy 2:15; 1 Chronicles 4:10; Isaiah 31:3; 66:14; compare Acts 11:21).

What Do You Think?
How can you provide spiritual leadership to the children in your congregation?
Digging Deeper
To whom among younger generations will you share the good news that the Lord is with him or her?

III. Promise-Filled Song
(Luke 1:76-79)

The same Spirit that filled Elisabeth (Luke 1:41) then filled Zacharias (1:67). His Spirit-filled life led him to praise God and to prophecy regarding God's future work through John. Zacharias's prophetic song—sometimes called the Benedictus—announced the presence of God's "horn of salvation" (1:69) that brings promised mercy (1:72-73) and deliverance (1:74). The second part of the song (1:76-79) highlights John's unique role within God's plan of salvation.

A. Announcing a Prophet (vv. 76-77)

76. And thou, child, shalt be called the prophet of the Highest: for thou shalt go before the face of the Lord to prepare his ways.

The future tense of the statement *shalt be called* indicates that God had a specific role for this *child* that would be fulfilled according to God's timing.

Prophets, as depicted in Scripture, gave promises and warnings regarding the future and proclaimed God's commands for His people. These two tasks are sometimes referred to as *foretelling* and *forthtelling*. John would become a *prophet*

Visual for Lesson 2. *Have this visual on display as you discuss the commentary associated with Luke 1:76-78.*

of the Highest in both senses. He spoke regarding God's warnings and of the coming Messiah (Luke 3:7-18). However, he would be different from other prophets in that he would be the climax of God's prophets (see Matthew 11:13; Luke 7:24-28; 16:16; Hebrews 1:1-2).

By going *before . . . the Lord*, John fulfilled a role described by the prophet Isaiah. John became "the voice . . . that crieth in the wilderness" to "*prepare . . .* the way of the Lord" (Isaiah 40:3; compare Malachi 3:1; Mark 1:1-4; Luke 7:26-27). John's prophetic work prepared the world to receive God's glory (see Isaiah 40:4-5) and the *ways* of God's salvation (see Matthew 3:3).

Preparing for Arrival

Before I began a new job, my new employer went to great lengths to welcome me. I received several gifts before my first day of work. On my first day, my office was arranged based on my preferences so that I could start work with ease. The company prepared a way for me to be a successful team member from the moment I arrived in the position.

John would prepare people for the arrival of the Lord (Luke 1:76). He did so by preparing people's hearts to receive Jesus' proclamation of salvation —a reality far greater than a new job.

Though Jesus' first coming has passed, believers can prepare themselves and others for His second coming! The needed preparation is found in Luke 18:8: "When the Son of man cometh, shall he find

faith on the earth?" Keep in mind that you can't prepare others to have what you don't!—P. L. M.

77. To give knowledge of salvation unto his people by the remission of their sins.

The kind of salvation that some Jews of the first century expected was that of a political freedom and an end to oppression under foreign empires. Those Jews who were most militant in holding this desire were the Zealots. One of Jesus' 12 apostles was called a "Zelotes" (Luke 6:15; Acts 1:13), likely for his identification with this group. They believed that God's kingdom and the people's salvation would come through military and political power, sometimes requiring violence.

John would *give knowledge* of a *salvation* beyond a political one. His own *people*, the Jews, would be shown a spiritual salvation. John was not the first to proclaim God's salvation; prophets before him proclaimed similarly (see Isaiah 25:9; Jeremiah 3:23; etc.). The hope and mercy that God's people desired would come not from an act of human warfare but from God's redemption and salvation in Christ (see Psalm 130:7-8; Acts 4:8-12; 2 Timothy 3:15; Hebrews 9:28; etc.).

The underlying Greek word for *remission* is translated elsewhere as "forgiveness" (see Mark 3:29; Acts 5:31; Ephesians 1:7; Colossians 1:14). John would be "preaching the baptism of repentance for the remission of *sins*" (Luke 3:3).

Zacharias's prophetic song reveals that God's plan of salvation is bigger than political salvation. People, regardless of their ethnicity or nationality, would experience salvation when they had their sins forgiven by God.

What Do You Think?

How can believers share "knowledge of salvation" in a way that would be attractive to unbelievers?

Digging Deeper

How might Paul's gospel presentations (Acts 17:16-34; 22:2-21; Romans 1:14–2:16) inform your own approach?

B. Proclaiming God's Mercy (vv. 78-79)

78. Through the tender mercy of our God;

whereby the dayspring from on high hath visited us.

Zacharias had acclaimed God's promise to show mercy (Luke 1:72). That same *mercy of our God* is the foundation for God's act of salvation for His people. Its *tender* nature describes the care that comes from His compassion (see Psalm 51:1; James 5:11). God does not base His giving of salvation on people's perceived worthiness. His salvation flows out of His mercy and kindness (Isaiah 63:7)!

A form of the underlying Greek word translated *daypring* appears several times in the Septuagint, the Greek version of the Old Testament. The word is used to refer to the "Branch" of the Lord (Jeremiah 23:5; Zechariah 3:8; 6:12). A verb form of the same word is used to speak of the rising of "the Sun of righteousness" (Malachi 4:2) and the coming of "a Star out of Jacob" (Numbers 24:17).

Because of the mention of the visitation *from* Heaven *on high*, we interpret that Christ is the subject of this verse and the next. Jesus is the king from "a Branch" of Jesse (Isaiah 11:1), who would shine His salvation for the world to see (see Ephesians 5:14). The resurrected and ascended Lord proclaimed later that He is "the root and the offspring of David, and the bright and morning star" (Revelation 22:16).

79. To give light to them that sit in darkness and in the shadow of death, to guide our feet into the way of peace.

When people live in opposition to God and His salvation, they live in a state of spiritual *darkness* (see John 3:19; 1 Corinthians 4:5; Ephesians 5:8; 6:12). In this state, both physical and spiritual *death* are inevitable (Romans 5:12; 6:23).

God's salvation brings spiritual *light* into spiritual darkness. The people in spiritual darkness and in death's *shadow* will "have seen a great light" (Isaiah 9:2): the long-awaited Messiah. Jesus fulfilled this proclamation as He taught on the need for repentance and of the presence of the kingdom (Matthew 4:12-17; compare Acts 26:15-18).

Peace means not just the absence of hostility, but God's people living in unity, new in Him (Ephesians 2:15). The fulfillment of Zacharias's hope came about in God's salvation brought through Christ Jesus.

What Do You Think?
How is God's mercy evident to both believers and unbelievers?

Digging Deeper
How do Psalm 86:15; Lamentations 3:22-23; Ephesians 2:4-5; and Hebrews 4:16 inform your answer in this regard?

Conclusion

A. Dramatic Praise

Zacharias's so-called dramatic pause—his inability to speak—came before the high point of his depiction in Scripture. When he recovered his voice, his first act was to praise God! Though Zacharias had previously expressed doubt, God remained faithful to him and Elisabeth. The dramatic pause prepared Zacharias to give dramatic praise; God showed His goodness to the couple by giving them a son. This son would someday prepare people to receive the goodness of God's salvation.

We all have seasons of life when we face dramatic pauses—when we may not have words to praise God or give Him our prayers. When this occurs, we may wonder if our failures have ruined us or if the presence of God has left us.

But as Zacharias discovered, God is faithful and merciful despite our unbelief. His faithfulness invites us to give Him praise. His mercy calls us to embrace His forgiveness. With lives of praise, we can proclaim His faithfulness for the whole world to hear. When we find ourselves facing a dramatic pause, we can offer praise that proclaims God's salvation for the world. Where God's salvation is present, darkness and death will turn to light and life.

B. Prayer

God, thank You for Your display of mercy to us: the forgiveness of our sins through Your Son, Jesus Christ. Though we may not often have adequate words, we praise You. Show us how we might prepare the way in the hearts of others to receive Your forgiveness. In Jesus' name. Amen.

C. Thought to Remember

God's faithfulness will lead us to praise.

Involvement Learning

Enhance your lesson with KJV Bible Student *(from your curriculum supplier) and the reproducible activity page (at www.standardlesson.com or in the back of the* KJV Standard Lesson Commentary Deluxe Edition*).*

Into the Lesson

Write a common male first name on an index card and a common female first name on a second index card. Do not use names of any people in your class. Give the cards to two participants, one card each. Instruct them to look at the name on the card, think of one word that they associate with that name, and write that word on the back of the card. Participants should pass the card to the next person. Repeat this pattern until every student has written on both cards. Have a volunteer read aloud the list of words written on the back of each card. Have the students discuss what was associated with the names on the cards.

Alternative. Distribute copies of the "What's in a Name?" activity from activity page, which you can download. Have learners work in small groups to complete as indicated.

After calling time under either activity, say, "Sometimes a name's significance is in its meaning. Other times its significance is related to our experiences with people who have that name—no matter how fair or accurate those perceptions are. In today's lesson, consider how the name John was significant for Elisabeth and Zacharias."

Into the Word

Ask a volunteer to read aloud Luke 1:57-66. Ask two volunteers to stand at the front of the class. One volunteer will play the part of Elisabeth while the other volunteer will play the part of Zacharias. Tell the rest of the class that they will play all the neighbors and relatives.

Guide the class to act out the scene depicted in Luke 1:57-66. Then ask the following questions: 1–How did God show that He was faithful to Elisabeth and her friends and family? 2–Did Zacharias's response to his healing surprise you? 3–Did the crowd's response to Zacharias's healing surprise you?

Write two headers on the board: *John / Jesus*.

Divide students into two groups: **John Group** and **Jesus Group**. Distribute handouts (you prepare) of the text of Luke 1:76-79 to each group.

Ask each group to read the Scripture and underline which parts of the text are prophecies about John and which parts are prophecies about Jesus. After five minutes, ask a volunteer from each group to come to the board and write, under the appropriate header, the lines of Scripture that their group underlined.

Ask, "How did John and Jesus each fulfill these prophecies?" Allow students time to respond and discuss. (Note: You may need to prepare other Scripture passages in advance to reference the ways that they each fulfilled their prophecies.)

Alternative. Distribute copies of the "Prophecies" activity from the activity page. Have learners work in pairs to complete as indicated.

After calling time, ask how Zacharias's prophecy showed God's faithfulness and prepared the hearts of the people to receive the Lord.

Into Life

Distribute an index card and pen to each student. Ask students to write down how they would prepare for a visit by an important guest. After one minute, have students share what they wrote with a partner.

Ask, "John prepared the way for the Lord. How did he do this?" Have students work in their pairs to write down some ways John prepared the way for Jesus. After five minutes, have a volunteer read John 1:19-39 aloud. Give students the opportunity to compare this text to what they wrote.

Have students work in their pairs to identify one way that they can prepare someone's heart to receive the Lord and become His disciple. Have each pair share their findings for the whole class.

End class by having each pair pray for courage and opportunities to prepare people to become disciples of Jesus.

John the Baptist Appears

Devotional Reading: John 1:29-42
Background Scripture: Luke 3:1-20; John 1

Luke 3:2b-6, 15-18

2b The word of God came unto John the son of Zacharias in the wilderness.

3 And he came into all the country about Jordan, preaching the baptism of repentance for the remission of sins;

4 As it is written in the book of the words of Esaias the prophet, saying, The voice of one crying in the wilderness, Prepare ye the way of the Lord, make his paths straight.

5 Every valley shall be filled, and every mountain and hill shall be brought low; and the crooked shall be made straight, and the rough ways shall be made smooth;

6 And all flesh shall see the salvation of God.

15 And as the people were in expectation, and all men mused in their hearts of John, whether he were the Christ, or not;

16 John answered, saying unto them all, I indeed baptize you with water; but one mightier than I cometh, the latchet of whose shoes I am not worthy to unloose: he shall baptize you with the Holy Ghost and with fire:

17 Whose fan is in his hand, and he will throughly purge his floor, and will gather the wheat into his garner; but the chaff he will burn with fire unquenchable.

18 And many other things in his exhortation preached he unto the people.

Key Text

He came into all the country about Jordan, preaching the baptism of repentance for the remission of sins.
—Luke 3:3

From Darkness to Light

Unit 1: God's Preparation
Lessons 1–4

Lesson Aims

After participating in this lesson, each learner will be able to:

1. Identify the Old Testament passage John quoted.

2. Compare and contrast Luke 3:15-18 with Matthew 3:11-12; Mark 1:7-8; and John 1:24-28.

3. Articulate whether he or she should or should not intentionally seek to have a personal wilderness experience.

Lesson Outline

Introduction

A. Wilderness Experiences

For a season I worked as an intern at a church located in the Navajo Nation in Arizona. I learned that living in a new location gave me new opportunities to deepen my relationship with God. The internship became a wilderness experience—both physically and spiritually. As I served the congregation, I better understood my personal limitations regarding ministry. Though the experience challenged me, it also led me to grow as a servant of the body of Christ.

So-called wilderness experiences are memorable because of how they have the potential to change a person. Though these experiences might be disorienting and filled with challenges, God can use them to draw people closer to Him for greater service, as in the examples of Elijah (1 Kings 19:1-9) and Paul (Galatians 1:17-18). In what may be called a ripple effect, a person's wilderness experience has the potential to change many others as well, not just the person with the experience.

B. Lesson Context

All four Gospels tell the story of John the Baptist, a forerunner of Jesus (Matthew 3:1-12; Mark 1:1-8; Luke 1:5-25, 57-66; John 1:19-34; 3:22-36). We take care not to confuse him with the John who wrote the Gospel that bears that name.

The Gospels describe John the Baptist and his preaching as coming in the type of the prophet Elias (that is, Elijah; see Matthew 11:13-14; 17:11-13; Mark 9:11-13; Luke 1:17; compare John 1:21-27). John came as the last prophet of Israel. As such, his task was to "turn the hearts of the fathers to the children, and the disobedient to the wisdom of the just; to make ready a people prepared for the Lord" (Luke 1:17, lesson 1; compare Malachi 4:5-6).

John spent his formative years in the wilderness (Luke 1:80). Some students of the New Testament propose that while in the wilderness John interacted with a Jewish sect known as the Essenes. Unlike the parties of the Sadducees and the Pharisees, the Essenes are not mentioned in the New Testament. However, historians of the first century AD, including Josephus, attest to their existence and ascetic practices. Though similarities exist between the practices of the Essenes and those of John, Scripture is silent regarding any association that John may have had with that group.

John's birth is described in Luke 1:57-66 (see lesson 2). After pausing to tell of the birth of Jesus (Luke 2), Luke reintroduces his audience to John. He does so by setting the context of John's public ministry within the political and religious context of the day (see 3:1-2a). Luke mentions, among others, Tiberius Caesar (Roman emperor, AD 14–37), Pontius Pilate (governor of Judaea, AD 26–36), Herod Antipas (tetrarch of Galilee and Perea, 4 BC–AD 39), and two high priests (variously served, AD 7–36). Luke states that the narrative of John the Baptist in today's text occurred in the "fifteenth year of the reign of Tiberius Caesar" (3:1), which dates to either AD 28 or 29.

Luke's references to these leaders do more than merely establish a time frame for events recorded in his Gospel. The inclusion of these rulers reminds Luke's intended audience (which may be primarily Gentile in background) that the Jewish people of this time lived under foreign Roman occupation. They were waiting for a savior who would free them from foreign occupation (compare Luke 24:21; John 6:15; Acts 1:6). John, however, came into this context preaching a message of a different sort of salvation. Matthew 3:1-2, 11-12; Mark 1:4-8; and John 1:24-28 are parallel to the two segments of today's text.

I. The Prophet Appears
(Luke 3:2b-6)
A. In the Wilderness (vv. 2b-3)

2b. The word of God came unto John the son of Zacharias in the wilderness.

The word of God came to Old Testament prophets and led them to action (see 1 Chronicles 17:3-4). Those prophets based their proclamations on having received "the word of the Lord" (examples: Jeremiah 1:2; Hosea 1:1; Micah 1:1; Haggai 1:1).

Jesus later proclaimed, however, that John was much more than a prophet (Luke 7:24-28). John brought a message that earlier prophets could not.

As *the son of Zacharias*, John was in the lineage of Israel's priesthood (see Luke 1:8-9, lesson 1). Scripture does not indicate that John pursued a priestly role like his father.

The parallel passage in Matthew's Gospel adds that John was "preaching *in the wilderness* of Judaea" (Matthew 3:1). This remote and mountainous region is found around the Jordan River and the Dead Sea.

In Scripture, the wilderness was significant for God's people. A wilderness served as the backdrop for their chastisement (see Ezekiel 20:35-38) and for their renewal (see Hosea 2:14-23). Jesus even spent time in the wilderness before His public ministry (Matthew 4:1-11; Mark 1:12-13; Luke 4:1-13). The wilderness also served as the context that prepared John the Baptist for his public ministry.

> **What Do You Think?**
> How can you be attentive to God's Word when you feel "in the wilderness" because of life's challenges?
>
> **Digging Deeper**
> How will you continue to memorize God's Word (see Psalm 119:11) so that it will be readily available to you at all times?

3. And he came into all the country about Jordan, preaching the baptism of repentance for the remission of sins.

The country in which John preached included the town of Bethabara beyond the *Jordan* (see John 1:28; 10:40). John's work fulfilled the prophecy of John's father that John would "give knowledge of salvation unto his people by the remission of their sins" (Luke 1:77). Long after John's death, the leaders of the first-century church continued to preach a message of repentance and baptism (Acts 2:38).

The act of repentance requires that people acknowledge their sin and turn to God (see Jeremiah 31:19). Showing repentance is the first step that a person can make to receive God's forgiveness and salvation (see 2 Corinthians 7:10). Calling sinful humans to repentance was a central component of Jesus' earthly ministry (see Luke 5:32; Acts 5:31).

The Greek word translated *remission* is elsewhere

translated "forgiveness" (Acts 13:38; 26:18; Ephesians 1:7; Colossians 1:14), and that is the sense here. When people repent of their sins, they receive forgiveness from God (compare Acts 5:31).

The practice of water baptism to indicate spiritual cleansing did not originate with John. The prophet Ezekiel described how water would metaphorically cleanse God's people from their moral impurities and would show the presence of God's Spirit (Ezekiel 36:25-28; compare Psalm 51:2). Further, the immersion of a person into water served as a way for non-Jews (Gentiles) to signify their conversion to Judaism. Archaeological findings reveal that first-century Jewish neighborhoods and homes sometimes included large ritual baths where this practice took place.

John's baptism prepared his audience to receive God's coming salvation. The act of baptism served as a tangible and outward presentation of an inward change of heart. But since John's *baptism of repentance* was preparatory in nature, believers who had received that baptism needed also to be baptized again "in the name of the Lord Jesus" after His ascension. This baptism affirmed their belief in Him and resulted in their receiving the Holy Spirit (Acts 19:1-6).

We see the longer, Trinitarian formula of "in the name of the Father, and of the Son, and of the Holy Ghost" in Matthew 28:19. Unlike John's baptism, Christian baptism pantomimes the historical facts of Jesus' death and resurrection (see Romans 6:4; Colossians 2:12; 1 Peter 3:21).

> **What Do You Think?**
> How is repentance for sins necessary in the life of an already baptized believer?
> **Digging Deeper**
> How can you incorporate the practice of repentance into your daily rhythms?

B. Fulfilling an Ancient Message (vv. 4-6)

4. As it is written in the book of the words of Esaias the prophet, saying, The voice of one crying in the wilderness, Prepare ye the way of the Lord, make his paths straight.

Luke quoted *the words of Esaias the prophet* (Isaiah) in order to show that John's message fulfilled the Old Testament prophets. A close word-by-word comparison between Isaiah 40:3-5 and Luke 3:4-6 will show differences between the two texts. This is because Luke quoted from the Septuagint, the Greek version of the Old Testament. The differences between the texts highlight how Luke interpreted the words of the prophet.

The context of what was *written* by the Old Testament prophet celebrated the return of captive Israelites to a restored Jerusalem (see Isaiah 40:1-2). The people were to declare God's faithfulness to Jerusalem (40:9-11) and to all people who "wait upon the Lord" (40:31). God's restoration and salvation was seen to be at hand for His people.

Luke took the premise of the prophet's text and applied its proclamation to John—he would call people to prepare for God's work of salvation. John provided spiritual direction in light of God's salvation.

John was like *one crying in the wilderness,* preaching a message of repentance, forgiveness, and baptism (see Luke 1:80; 3:2-3). He proclaimed a message of hope to *prepare* the people to repent and accept God's redemptive work. Luke's audience would have understood the immediate connection between *the Lord* and Christ Jesus (compare 1:43, 76; 2:11).

> **What Do You Think?**
> How will you follow the example of John and "prepare . . . the way of the Lord" (Luke 3:4) among your neighbors?
> **Digging Deeper**
> What are possible "wilderness experiences" that have prepared you to communicate the gospel to other people?

5. Every valley shall be filled, and every mountain and hill shall be brought low; and the crooked shall be made straight, and the rough ways shall be made smooth.

All four Gospel accounts quote sections of Isaiah 40:3 to describe John's ministry (see Matthew 3:3; Mark 1:3; Luke 3:4-6; John 1:23). The other Gospel accounts do not include the material from Isaiah 40:4-5 that is found in Luke 3:5-6.

The metaphor of land being *filled* and *brought low* is an image for the humbling nature of repentance (compare Luke 1:52; 14:11; 18:14). Children of God, those people who express repentance for their sin, will have the *crooked* and perverse ways of their lives *made straight* (see Philippians 2:15).

By quoting the prophet in this manner, Luke illustrates the scope of God's salvation (see Luke 2:30-32). His salvation serves to "guide our feet into the way of peace" (1:79; see lesson 2).

Filling Potholes

When I lived overseas, springtime was pothole season. After months of winter freezes, giant potholes would appear in our city's streets. As temperatures warmed and ice melted, these holes grew and posed a danger to vehicles and drivers.

The local government did not prioritize road maintenance. Once in a while, citizens would take issues into their own hands and fix the ever-deepening chasms. They would sometimes gather large tree branches and place them in the potholes. The branches filled the craters and warned unaware drivers regarding the danger to their vehicles. The fix was temporary, but it protected drivers until the city could provide a more permanent fix.

God's salvation is a permanent fix for humanity. When people accept God's salvation, the "crooked" and "rough ways" of sinful humanity will be made "straight" and "smooth" (Luke 3:5). Are you making temporary fixes to your life, or have you accepted the permanent fix of God's salvation?

—L. M. W.

6. And all flesh shall see the salvation of God.

Luke passed over Isaiah's mention of "the glory of the Lord" (Isaiah 40:5). Instead, Luke interpreted God's glory as *the salvation of God*, an interpretation supported by the Greek version of Isaiah's text. *All flesh* describes the reach of God's salvation. People from all the earth would someday experience God's plan of salvation (see Psalm 98:2; Isaiah 52:10; compare Acts 28:28). God's salvation will be proclaimed throughout the world, though not all people will accept it (see Matthew 7:14).

II. The Prophet's Identity
(Luke 3:15-18)
A. The Crowd's Expectation (v. 15)

15. And as the people were in expectation, and all men mused in their hearts of John, whether he were the Christ, or not.

First-century expectations regarding the Jewish Messiah—the anointed Jewish king (compare 2 Samuel 7:16; 22:48-51; Daniel 9:25; Acts 1:6; etc.)—varied greatly. Some Jews expected that the Messiah would be a military leader who would free the Jewish people from foreign oppression. Other Jews anticipated that the Messiah would come in the form of a prophet like Moses (compare Deuteronomy 18:18). The title *Christ* is the Greek equivalent of *Messiah* (see John 1:41; 4:25). Both terms mean "the anointed one."

Both Romans and Jewish religious leaders considered zealous messianic expectations to be dangerous because those beliefs might lead to violence or rebellion. Religious zealots at that time frequently attracted violent followers (see Acts 5:36-37). The *expectation* of the crowd before John was not one of mild interest. The crowd had a deep curiosity regarding the possible presence of the Messiah.

When Jesus proclaimed something that only a Messiah could proclaim—like the forgiveness of sins—people considered the implications of the teaching *in their hearts* (see Matthew 21:25; Mark 2:6-8; Luke 5:21-22). John's proclamation

How to Say It

Esaias	Ee-*zay*-yus.
Essenes	*Eh*-seenz.
Herod Antipas	*Hair*-ud *An*-tih-pus.
Herodias	Heh-*roe*-dee-us.
Pentecost	*Pent*-ih-kost.
Pharisees	*Fair*-ih-seez.
Pontius Pilate	*Pon*-shus or *Pon*-ti-us *Pie*-lut.
Sadducees	*Sad*-you-seez.
tetrarch	*teh*-trark or *tee*-trark.
Tiberius Caesar	Tie-*beer*-ee-us *See*-zer.

Visual for Lesson 3. *Start a discussion by pointing to this visual as you ask, "What does it mean to be baptized with water and fire?"*

regarding God's plan of salvation brought many people to wonder about the extent of God's plan. The crowds were also likely curious of the identity of the person who would inaugurate that plan.

Determining whether *John* was the promised Messiah was the central concern of the crowd. By the time of his public ministry, he had a following of disciples (see Luke 5:33; 7:18-19). His following continued even after his death (see Acts 18:24-25; 19:1-3). John, however, denied that he was the long-awaited *Christ*, the Messiah (see John 1:20).

B. The Coming Messiah (vv. 16-18)

16a. John answered, saying unto them all, I indeed baptize you with water; but one mightier than I cometh, the latchet of whose shoes I am not worthy to unloose.

John picked up on the crowd's thoughts regarding his possible identity. He *answered* the crowd and offered a contrast between his work and the work of the Messiah that would come.

John affirmed that the baptism *with water* had value. However, John's baptism was temporary; it merely prepared for the baptism by the *one mightier than* John: the Messiah. The apostle Paul interpreted John's baptism of repentance as a sign "that they should believe on him which should come after [John], that is, on Christ Jesus" (Acts 19:4).

Ancient roads, especially in the far reaches of the Roman Empire, were likely made of dirt. As a result, the feet of pedestrians would become quite

dirty, even if they wore shoes or sandals. Because of these unsanitary conditions, the act of undoing *the latchet* of another person's footwear would have been considered disgusting at best. A servant may not even have removed the footwear of his master.

John does not consider himself to be *worthy to unloose* the sandals of the coming Christ—he considered himself too lowly for the "honor" of this task for the Christ. John's humility would point people to the coming Christ, while confirming to first-century believers the presence of God's promised Savior (see Acts 13:23-25).

16b. He shall baptize you with the Holy Ghost and with fire.

John acknowledged the difference between the baptism that he brought and the baptism that Christ was to bring. Whereas John baptized with water, Christ baptizes His followers into God's Spirit to form "one body" of God's people (1 Corinthians 12:13).

Jesus promised that the "Comforter, which is *the Holy Ghost*" would come to "teach you all things, and bring all things to your remembrance" (John 14:26). This promise expanded the teachings of Israel's prophets that God's Spirit would be "poured . . . from on high" (Isaiah 32:15; see 44:3-4; Joel 2:28-29). The fulfillment of these promises came at Pentecost (see Acts 2:1-41).

Fire is a tool for creation or destruction. On one hand, the fire to which John referred could point to the visible representation of God's Spirit at Pentecost (compare Acts 2:3). In this sense, fire indicated the establishment of an expanded people of God.

On the other hand, Luke frequently refers to fire as a tool of divine punishment (see Luke 3:9; 9:54; 12:49). Considering what follows in Luke 3:17, this *fire* is likely one of judgment (compare John 15:6).

17. Whose fan is in his hand, and he will throughly purge his floor, and will gather the wheat into his garner; but the chaff he will burn with fire unquenchable.

A *fan* is a shovel-like tool used to toss grain into the air to separate its parts. The useful *wheat* would fall to the threshing *floor* to be gathered. *Chaff*, however, would float in the wind (see Psalm 1:4), eventually falling to the ground where it was gathered and burned (compare Isaiah 5:24).

John's audience was warned: the coming Christ would remove impurity from among His people. With fire—metaphorical and real—Christ would sanctify the people of God (see 1 Peter 1:7). He would also provide a final judgment to those people who turn their backs on Him (see Isaiah 66:22-24; Matthew 25:41-43; Jude 7; Revelation 14:9-11).

What Do You Think?
How would you respond to a person who says that Luke 3:17 describes a wrathful and unloving God?

Digging Deeper
What Scriptures come to mind as you consider how you would address that concern?

18. And many other things in his exhortation preached he unto the people.

Luke provides an editorial statement: that John said *many other things* regarding the coming Christ. As John *preached*, he rebuked the political leaders of the day, particularly Herod Antipas, for their immorality (see Luke 3:19). This led to John's beheading at the prompting of Herod's wife, Herodias (see Matthew 14:1-12; Mark 6:14-29).

John understood his role as a servant of God. He proclaimed the message of God's plan of salvation that was arriving in Christ Jesus. This message was good news and told that a way out of sin and spiritual condemnation had arrived for all people!

What Do You Think?
In what ways can believers exhort others to know and follow Jesus Christ?

Digging Deeper
What steps will you take to be better prepared to urge other people regarding the gospel of Jesus?

Not-So-Secret Service

Preparing for a visit from the president of the United States requires numerous Secret Service agents. They arrive months before the president's visit. Their task is simple: ensure the safety of the president and oversee the security of the visit.

Agents meet with local law enforcement, plan the route of the president's motorcade, and complete background checks of anyone who might interact with the president. During the president's visit, Secret Service agents are on high alert for every contingency. A pouch of blood that matches the president's blood type is even kept in the heavily armored presidential limousine.

John's service for God was *not* secretive. He preached and exhorted people to listen to his message of repentance. Through what not-so-secretive way might you prepare other people to receive God's salvation through Christ Jesus? —L. M. W.

Conclusion
A. Prepare the Way

John came as a forerunner for Christ and a prophet to the people. He served the cause of Christ by baptizing people into a life of repentance and proclaiming the imminent arrival of God's salvation. Throughout the ministry of John the Baptist, he proclaimed good news, encouraged the downtrodden, and upset powerful leaders. Though Scripture is mostly silent regarding his time in the wilderness (see Matthew 3:4), he came from that place with a message that would change the world.

How might a wilderness experience prepare you to proclaim God's message of salvation through Jesus Christ? These experiences may cost you; wilderness experiences may not bring you a life filled with the world's measures of comfort, power, wealth, or honor. Instead, Jesus' followers are called to follow Him and proclaim the good news of His salvation. In this sense, all believers prepare the world for the way for the Lord.

B. Prayer

God, as we wait for Jesus' return, show us how to prepare others to receive Your salvation. Help us be attentive to the workings of Your Spirit in our "wilderness." In the name of Jesus. Amen.

C. Thought to Remember
Prepare the way for the Lord!

Involvement Learning

Enhance your lesson with KJV Bible Student *(from your curriculum supplier) and the reproducible activity page (at www.standardlesson.com or in the back of the* KJV Standard Lesson Commentary Deluxe Edition*).*

Into the Lesson

Write the names of famous people (living or dead) on sticky notes, one per note. Place one note on the back of each learner. Tell the class that the goal is for each learner to figure out the name written on their note. Have the learners mingle, asking each other questions to learn about their names. Learners can ask up to 10 yes-or-no questions about the name written on their note, but they cannot ask someone to reveal the name. Likewise, they can answer any question about someone else's name but cannot reveal the other person's name. After five minutes, have learners take turns guessing the name on their note. After their guess, they can check their note.

Alternative. Distribute copies of the "Always Be Prepared" exercise from the activity page, which you can download. Have learners work in their groups to complete as indicated.

Transition into the Scripture text by saying, "In today's Scripture, notice how John the Baptist introduced people to the Lord and how he answered their questions regarding the Lord's identity."

Into the Word

Ask a volunteer to read aloud Luke 3:2b-6 and list the main metaphors of Isaiah's prophecy. (Expected answers: valleys filled, mountains and hills lowered, crooked roads made straight, and the rough ways made smooth)

Divide the class into four groups. Distribute handouts (you prepare) of the following questions for in-group discussion: 1–What could these metaphors mean? 2–How do they relate to preparing human hearts for salvation? 3–How was John the Baptist interpreting Isaiah's words? Have groups present their findings in whole-class discussion.

Option. Have students form groups. Give each group five index cards. Write these Scriptures references on the board: Romans 3:10; Romans 3:23; Romans 5:8; Romans 6:23; Romans 10:9; Romans 10:13. Instruct groups to write a summary from each verse on a card, one verse per card. Then have them lay the cards in the order that would lead someone to salvation.

Ask a volunteer to read aloud Luke 3:15-18. Say, "This account is recorded in all four Gospels." Divide learners into groups of three. Assign each group member one of the following passages to read to their group: Matthew 3:11-12; Mark 1:6-8; John 1:24-28. Then have each person review their assigned passage within their group by answering this question: Did John fulfill these words? After 10 minutes, compare and contrast each passage through whole-class discussion.

Into Life

Distribute a sheet of paper and a pencil to each learner. With the longest side of the paper facing them, have them write *Today* on the left side of the paper and *One Year from Now* on the right side of the paper. Ask learners to draw a line across the page, connecting the two titles. Say that the paper represents a time line of the upcoming year. Allow one minute to write on the time line upcoming life events that they anticipate might be a challenge or lead to a possible wilderness experience.

After calling time, have learners form pairs to discuss their time lines by answering the following questions: 1–In light of your time line, how would you define a "wilderness experience"? 2–What experiences "in the wilderness" have you had before today? 3–Should people intentionally seek to have a personal wilderness experience?

Option. Distribute copies of the "Relating to Jesus" exercise from the activity page. Have learners work in pairs to complete as indicated. After calling time, invite pairs to share their responses to the last question. Encourage everyone to share their metaphors with a neighbor during the upcoming week and be prepared to report on the experience at the beginning of the next class.

Mary Rejoices

Devotional Reading: Isaiah 9:1-7
Background Scripture: Luke 1:46-55

Luke 1:46-55

46 And Mary said, My soul doth magnify the Lord,

47 And my spirit hath rejoiced in God my Saviour.

48 For he hath regarded the low estate of his handmaiden: for, behold, from henceforth all generations shall call me blessed.

49 For he that is mighty hath done to me great things; and holy is his name.

50 And his mercy is on them that fear him from generation to generation.

51 He hath shewed strength with his arm; he hath scattered the proud in the imagination of their hearts.

52 He hath put down the mighty from their seats, and exalted them of low degree.

53 He hath filled the hungry with good things; and the rich he hath sent empty away.

54 He hath holpen his servant Israel, in remembrance of his mercy;

55 As he spake to our fathers, to Abraham, and to his seed for ever.

Key Text

Mary said, My soul doth magnify the Lord, and my spirit hath rejoiced in God my Saviour.
—Luke 1:46-47

From Darkness to Light

Unit 1: God's Preparation
Lessons 1–4

Lesson Aims

After participating in this lesson, each learner will be able to:

1. List key reasons for Mary's rejoicing and praise.

2. Compare and contrast Mary's Song with Zacharias's Song (Luke 1:67-79; see lesson 2).

3. Compose two to four lines of a song of personal praise, using Mary's Song as a model.

Lesson Outline

Introduction
    A. Boasting or Celebrating?
    B. Lesson Context
I. **Worshipping the Almighty (Luke 1:46-50)**
    A. Virgin Rejoices (vv. 46-49)
       Spontaneous Song
    B. Generations Receive Mercy (v. 50)
       Faithful Generations
II. **The Work of the Almighty (Luke 1:51-55)**
    A. Exalting the Lowly (vv. 51-53)
    B. Remembering His Servant (vv. 54-55)
Conclusion
    A. Self-Exaltation or Salvation?
    B. Prayer
    C. Thought to Remember

Introduction

A. Boasting or Celebrating?

No one likes a braggart, but most people like to celebrate accomplishments. We celebrate athletes when they win, employees when they receive the long-awaited promotion, and parents after the birth of their child.

Many people consider it to be rude for a person to congratulate his or her own successes publicly. Even worse, we are disgusted by people who exaggerate their own accomplishments. These people frequently congratulate and celebrate themselves more than doing the same for others. When people become braggarts, others may cringe.

Instead, it is far more acceptable to celebrate the accomplishments of *another* person. In this context, even over-the-top bragging and praise are tolerated.

Two forms of bragging are evident in today's Scripture: one directed toward God and His work, and one found among the powerful people of the world. After reading this Scripture, will your life follow Mary's example, as well as remaining on alert to the dangers of being filled with empty pride?

B. Lesson Context

Two of the four New Testament Gospels tell the story of Jesus' birth: Luke and Matthew. Whereas Matthew's account emphasizes the story of Jesus' birth from the perspective of Joseph (see Matthew 1:18-25; 2:13, 19), Luke's account is from the perspective of Mary.

Luke's narrative begins with the angel Gabriel appearing to Mary and proclaiming that she was "highly favoured" and "blessed . . . among women" (Luke 1:28). Though she was a virgin, she became pregnant through the power of the Holy Spirit (1:31, 35). Gabriel proclaimed that Mary's son would be called "the Son of the Highest" and would someday rule as king (1:32; see Isaiah 9:6-7).

Though Mary questioned Gabriel's promises (Luke 1:34), she identified herself as a servant of the Lord (1:38). She submitted to God's will, however unexpected or seemingly unrealistic His will might have been.

After Mary received Gabriel's message, she visited her relative Elisabeth (Luke 1:36, 39-40). During the visit, Elisabeth proclaimed that Mary and the "fruit of [her] womb" would be "blessed" (1:42). This unlikely virgin received blessing because she believed that God would fulfill the promises that He made to her (1:45).

In response to Gabriel's promise and Elisabeth's blessing, Mary worshipped God (Luke 1:46-55). Though not explicitly described as a song in Scripture, many students consider her worship in this text to be similar to that of a song. As such, students call her song the Magnificat, a title taken from the first line of the Latin version of the text.

Scripture includes several songs of praise from God's people. These songs give glory to God for who He is and what He has done for them. Such songs include those from Moses (Exodus 15:1-18), Miriam (15:21), Deborah and Barak (Judges 5), Asaph (1 Chronicles 16:7-36), and Simeon (Luke 2:28-32).

The prayer of Hannah (1 Samuel 2:1-10) lifts up themes similar to Mary's Song. Hannah's prayer followed her request that the Lord "remember . . . and not forget" her by giving her a son (1:11). After she became pregnant and gave birth to Samuel (1:20), Hannah dedicated him to the Lord and prayed a word of thanksgiving to God. Hannah's prayer rejoices in God's power and might (2:1-4, 9-10) and in His concern for the poor and needy (2:7-8). As this lesson unfolds, Mary's Song will echo these themes, with an extra inclusion regarding the all-encompassing aspect of God's salvation.

I. Worshipping the Almighty
(Luke 1:46-50)

A. Virgin Rejoices (vv. 46-49)

46. And Mary said, My soul doth magnify the Lord.

The song of *Mary* begins with her worship of God for His greatness. Her *soul* included the non-physical part of her person—the invisible part that continues even after a person's physical death (see Matthew 10:28). Mary's whole being praised God.

To *magnify the Lord* means to honor His name (see Psalm 34:3) and to give thanks for His work (69:30). Mary honored God and praised Him

because of the revelation she received regarding her pregnancy (Luke 1:30-37; see Lesson Context). She likely did not yet know exactly how God would work through her child. All she had on which to base her worship were Gabriel's promises and Elisabeth's blessing (1:42-45). Mary knew she was a favored part of God's plan, no matter how that plan would come to pass. As a result, she praised God.

47. And my spirit hath rejoiced in God my Saviour.

By way of parallelism, this verse repeats the intent of the previous verse. The practice of referring to both a person's soul and *spirit* was common in Hebrew writings (see Job 7:11; Isaiah 26:9). Though there are subtle differences between the two, readers should not become distracted. Every part of Mary magnified and *rejoiced in* the Lord *God*.

During the New Testament era, powerful military figures and pagan gods were proclaimed to be saviors of people. The Old Testament, however, uses the title to refer to the God of Israel. God is called Savior because of His work of deliverance (see 2 Samuel 22:3; Isaiah 43:3, 11; 45:21). Mary acknowledged that the deliverance she desired would not come from a military leader or pagan god. Instead, the one true God who had rescued the people of Israel would be her *Saviour*. All people can receive the Savior's salvation when they respond according to the biblical plan of salvation.

God's greatness evokes joy and gladness among His people. God and His plans will not fail, and so His people can depend on Him. They need not fear; they celebrate and worship Him as the one who brings salvation (see Habakkuk 3:18).

How to Say It

Advent	Ad-vent.
anthropomorphic	an-thruh-puh-*mawr*-fik.
Asaph	Ay-saff.
Barak	Bair-uk.
Habakkuk	Huh-back-kuk.
Magnificat	Mag-nif-ih-cot.
Miriam	Meer-ee-um.
patriarchs	pay-tree-arks.
Simeon	Sim-ee-un.

48a. For he hath regarded the low estate of his handmaiden.

This verse provides Mary's reason *for* praising God as her Savior. She glorified her Savior, who saw her in her place of lowliness. The song portrays God as a king who looks on His lowliest subjects and still regards them with favor (see Psalm 138:6).

Mary's *low estate* was because of her position in the world. She was a young, unmarried, and pregnant woman. Her hometown, Nazareth (Luke 1:26-27), was held in low regard by other Jews (John 1:46). Her ancestors had a history of living under foreign rule (see Deuteronomy 26:7; 2 Kings 14:26). By the world's standards, Mary resided in a state of insignificance.

An attitude of humility can be found in the people whom God chooses to use. Jesus describes himself as "meek and lowly in heart" (Matthew 11:29). His followers are called to a life of humility (1 Peter 3:8; 5:5-6). God promises to lift up the humble and lowly (Luke 14:11; 18:14) and offer them grace (James 4:6). When His people live in humility, they can be attentive to His call.

As a *handmaiden* of the Lord (compare Luke 1:38a), Mary placed herself in obedience to Him. She pledged to follow the Lord's commands so that His promises might be fulfilled in and through her (see 1:38b). God's people are not servants ignored or mistreated. Instead, His people are the recipients of His favor and blessing.

> **What Do You Think?**
> What do you need to take up or give up in order to better practice humility?
>
> **Digging Deeper**
> What connection exists between living with humility and being attentive to God's call?

Spontaneous Song

When my sister was a preschooler, she developed an eye infection. The infection worsened, and our parents took her to the emergency room. While in the waiting room, my sister—with one eye puffy and red—spontaneously started singing a song from her favorite movie, *The Jungle Book*. She repeatedly sang the same song, seemingly unconcerned about the issue that brought her to the emergency room. She sang as a child who trusted her caregivers.

As an unmarried and pregnant young woman from first-century Nazareth, Mary likely faced difficulties (see Matthew 1:19). However, an angel proclaimed her highly favored by God, and her relative called her blessed by God. As a result, Mary sang her worship to God! The holy and powerful God was working with her and through her. What song of praise will you sing when you face challenging situations in service to Him? Let Mary's Song inform your own song of praise!

—L. M. W.

48b. For, behold, from henceforth all generations shall call me blessed.

Future *generations* would *call* Mary *blessed*—not because of her own efforts but because of the ways that the Lord used her. She gave birth to Jesus, the one who brings blessing to all generations. Though Mary's proclamation came to pass (see Luke 11:27), all people can be considered blessed by God when they "hear the word of God, and keep it" (11:28).

49a. For he that is mighty hath done to me great things.

Throughout Scripture, God's people proclaim His might as they worship Him (Deuteronomy 3:24; Joshua 4:24; Psalm 24:8; Ephesians 1:19-20; etc.). God shows His might by working *great things* for His people (see Deuteronomy 10:21; Judges 2:7; 1 Samuel 12:24; Job 37:5). These works involve the redeeming of His people from slavery (see Deuteronomy 11:1-7) and saving them from oppression (see Joel 2:19-21). In response, God's people experience gladness (see Psalm 126:3) and respond with worship (see 71:19). Through His *mighty* power, God worked exceptionally in Mary when she gave birth to Jesus, "the Son of the Highest" (Luke 1:32).

49b. And holy is his name.

In Scripture, a person's name sometimes refers to an attribute of that person (example: Genesis 25:24-26, 30). Mary knew that God is *holy*, so she proclaimed *his name* to be the same (compare

Psalms 103:1; 111:9). God's holiness speaks to His moral perfection (see Job 34:12; Habakkuk 1:13). Although humans commit sin, God cannot; He is at all times morally pure and upright (James 1:13). He desires that His people practice holiness as well (see Leviticus 11:44-45; Joshua 24:19; 2 Corinthians 6:14–7:1; Ephesians 1:4; 1 Peter 1:15-16).

B. Generations Receive Mercy (v. 50)

50. And his mercy is on them that fear him from generation to generation.

Mary previously proclaimed how God did a mighty work "to me" (Luke 1:49a, above). In this verse, the song changes focus to tell of God's mercy to *them*, the people who *fear* and follow God. The almighty God shows His love toward His people when they come to Him with humility and keep His commands (see Psalm 103:17-18). When the people live in this manner, they have knowledge of His work and His blessings (see Proverbs 3:7-8; 9:10-12).

Experiences of God's *mercy* are a central theme in the first chapter of Luke's Gospel (Luke 1:54, 58, 72, 78). When people love God and follow His commands, He promises His presence and mercy (see Exodus 20:6; Deuteronomy 4:31). God's promises to His people endure. His promises will not fail *from generation to generation* of His people (see Exodus 20:4-6; Psalm 33:11; Isaiah 34:17).

What Do You Think?
How do you follow God so that His mercy will be displayed through you to future generations?

Digging Deeper
How have previous generations of believers provided an example for you in the same regard?

Faithful Generations

In an unassuming rural church, God's people displayed their faithfulness to Him. Though this congregation was small in number of members, they desired for God to work through them to accomplish His mission for the world.

Members of the congregation became like fam-

Visual for Lesson 4. *Point to this visual as you discuss the Lesson Context. Ask a volunteer to read aloud Hannah's prayer in 1 Samuel 2:1-10.*

ily to each other. They gathered during holidays, celebrated key moments in their church, and shared life's highs and lows.

Over time, younger generations of church members moved away. Some entered college, others went into ministry, and others moved overseas. Because of the faithful example of the congregation's older generations, many from the younger generations strove to become faithful members of the universal body of Christ. No matter where the younger people lived, they feared and honored God because of the example of previous generations of believers.

Because of the faithfulness of generations of believers, God demonstrated His mercy to this small congregation. Their influence had far-reaching results on generations of believers throughout the world. How will future generations see the evidence of God's mercy in your life? —L. M. W.

II. The Work of the Almighty
(Luke 1:51-55)

A. Exalting the Lowly (vv. 51-53)

51. He hath shewed strength with his arm; he hath scattered the proud in the imagination of their hearts.

Though God is spirit (John 4:24), Scripture frequently describes His attributes in terms of human characteristics (Exodus 7:5; Leviticus 20:6; Deuteronomy 3:24; 2 Kings 19:16; Psalm 34:15; etc.). This is known as anthropomorphic language. The *arm* of God describes His might and control in the world (see Exodus 6:6; Deuteronomy 26:8; Psalm 89:10; Isaiah 40:10; 51:5; Jeremiah 32:21).

Previously, Mary proclaimed God's might (Luke 1:49), but His *strength* would also be directed toward people who exalt themselves. In contrast to the people who "fear" God and follow His commands (1:50, above) are *the proud* people. Because of their pride, these people disregard God and His authority (see Deuteronomy 8:14). They rely on their own ability, power, and name to find success in the world's eyes (example: Genesis 11:1-8).

Scripture lists pride as a sin found in people who refuse to follow God (2 Timothy 3:1-5). God "resisteth the proud, and giveth grace to the humble" (1 Peter 5:5; see Proverbs 3:34). He does not tolerate prideful people (Psalm 101:5), and He promises to punish them for their sin (Isaiah 13:11). Mary's Song portrays prideful people as God's enemies. He would strike down the proud and scatter them in defeat (see Psalm 68:1).

Not only is pride evident in a person's actions, but it can also be found in *their hearts* (see Genesis 6:5; 2 Chronicles 12:14). The Greek word behind *imagination* can also refer to a person's "mind" (Luke 10:27) and "understanding" (Ephesians 4:18). Prideful people express arrogance through their actions and in their hearts and minds.

> **What Do You Think?**
> How can believers avoid pride in their thoughts, words, and deeds?
>
> **Digging Deeper**
> Who would you recruit to serve as an accountability partner in this regard?

52. He hath put down the mighty from their seats, and exalted them of low degree.

Mighty rulers in the world frequently show pride when they appeal to their own power and authority. However, these rulers fail to recognize the true source of their power: the God who "removeth kings, and setteth up kings" (Daniel 2:21; see Job 12:19; Isaiah 40:23). When prideful people fail to acknowledge God as the one who allows and/or provides their authority and influence, He will *put* them *down . . . from their seats* of power.

The same God who brings down proud and mighty rulers also shows concern toward the people whom the world would consider to be of *low degree*. God has *exalted* the humble by promising them grace (James 4:6). Mary sang this promise because she experienced these promises firsthand. Though she was lowly, God "highly favoured" and "blessed [her] . . . among women" (Luke 1:28). One part of God's work in the world is to debase the proud while providing salvation to the humble (see Job 5:11; Ezekiel 21:25-27; etc.).

53. He hath filled the hungry with good things; and the rich he hath sent empty away.

Scripture describes how God provided for His people in their moments of need. In the Garden of Eden (Genesis 2:9), in the wilderness wanderings (Exodus 16:4), and even by providing land itself (3:8), God *filled* the needs of His people. Because of His mercy and salvation, *the hungry* will have sustenance (1 Samuel 2:5; Psalm 107:9).

People still experience hunger and poverty today (compare Matthew 26:11). Mary's Song looks forward to the day when those who hunger will be filled and will hunger no more (see 1 Samuel 2:8; Luke 6:21; Revelation 7:16).

The song serves as a warning. When *the rich* and powerful refuse to care for others (see Luke 16:19-31) and instead focus on their accumulation of wealth (12:13-21), they are *sent empty away*. God's kingdom does not make room for such selfish and prideful people (see Matthew 25:31-46).

> **What Do You Think?**
> How would you answer someone who says that Luke 1:53 argues that God does not want people to be rich?
>
> **Digging Deeper**
> How do Proverbs 22:2; Luke 6:24; 16:8-14; 1 Timothy 6:9-10, 17-19; and James 5:1-6 inform your answer?

B. Remembering His Servant (vv. 54-55)

54. He hath holpen his servant Israel, in remembrance of his mercy.

Throughout the Old Testament, *Israel* was identified as the *servant* of the Lord (Psalm 136:22; Isaiah 41:8-9; 44:21). As such, the people of Israel had a special role in God's plan of salvation: they would be "a light to the Gentiles" (49:6). Out of them the light of God's salvation would shine for the world (see Luke 2:32; John 1:9).

Mary was confident that the prophetic implications of her song would be fulfilled because of God's history of remembering His promises (see Exodus 2:24; 1 Chronicles 16:15; Psalm 105:42; Micah 7:20). God's plan was not to forget Abraham's descendants. Instead, His plan was to reveal the way of salvation through them.

Mary's Song reflects the heart of the psalmist: God "hath remembered his mercy and his truth toward the house of Israel: all the ends of the earth have seen the salvation of our God" (Psalm 98:3). God showed help toward (*he hath holpen*) His people in the advent of Christ Jesus. Though the people had disregarded God and His commands, God still showed them mercy. He provided a way for their salvation as well as for the salvation of the world.

55. As he spake to our fathers, to Abraham, and to his seed for ever.

Mary's Song makes an appeal to the patriarchs, the *fathers*, of Israel. The promises that God *spake . . . to Abraham* would be fulfilled by way of Mary's child. God promised Abraham that his family would be a blessing to all the earth (Genesis 12:1-3). Through Mary's child and Abraham's descendant, the promise of blessing had arrived (see Galatians 3:16-19, 29). This was not a new work of salvation by God, but a continuation of the promise that He had made (see Genesis 22:18).

The mention of Abraham introduces a common theme in Luke's Gospel and the book of Acts. Both texts connect God's promises to Abraham with the expansion of the people of God to include both Jew and Gentile. Not all people who claimed to be descendants to Abraham would receive God's blessing (see Luke 3:8-9; 13:28; 16:19-30; Acts 3:25). Instead, as the apostle Paul would write, faith in Jesus as the Savior would define God's people (Romans 4:16-17; 9:7-8; Galatians 3:7).

The song's conclusion invites its audience to imagine the scope of God's work of salvation and the resulting blessing. Though Mary was considered lowly in the world's regard, God would use her to give birth to the Christ, the actual seed through whom salvation came. Mary recognized her blessedness in this regard. She envisioned the fulfillment of God's salvation. This would be a world where the downtrodden would be lifted up and where God's mercy would extend to generations of people.

> **What Do You Think?**
> How is Mary's Song different from and similar to popular contemporary praise and worship songs?
>
> **Digging Deeper**
> Would Mary's Song be appropriate for congregational worship?

Conclusion

A. Self-Exaltation or Salvation?

On special occasions like birthdays, anniversaries, and holidays, we may take a moment to consider our blessings and achievements. However, this practice runs the risk of becoming an opportunity for self-exaltation; we might make God's gifts sound like something we achieved by our own strength and power.

Today's Scripture reminds us of the futility of self-exaltation. God will choose whom He wants to work through, regardless of the world's perception of that person. Further, today's Scripture also warns of what can happen when people are driven by pride and selfish desires. God will inevitably humble people who exalt themselves. If we seek salvation through our power, wealth, or acclaim, God will remove us from those positions.

Self-exaltation will not lead to salvation. In fact, it will lead a person to emptiness and an existence without God's salvation. We have a choice.

B. Prayer

Mighty God, just as You worked in Your people throughout history, we ask that You do a mighty work in us. Show us how we might better proclaim Your salvation. Fill us with humility so that we can be attentive to You. In the name of Jesus. Amen.

C. Thought to Remember

God's salvation lifts the lowest to the highest.

Involvement Learning

Enhance your lesson with KJV Bible Student *(from your curriculum supplier) and the reproducible activity page (at www.standardlesson.com or in the back of the* KJV Standard Lesson Commentary Deluxe Edition*).*

Into the Lesson

Ask learners to form pairs. Each person is to think about a family member or friend whom they could brag about. (Possible ideas: a spouse who completed a challenging work project; a friend who was accepted into a prestigious school) Give learners a moment to brag about this person to their partners. Then ask learners to think about a situation in which they might brag about themselves. Give everyone a moment to brag on themselves to their partners.

After no more than two minutes, ask, "Who was it easier to brag about: yourself or someone else? Why is that?" Allow a few moments for whole-class discussion.

Alternative. Distribute copies of the "Awards Show" exercise from the activity page, which you can download. Have learners complete it individually in a minute or less. Ask volunteers to share their responses to the final question.

After either activity, transition to the lesson by saying, "Although Mary was shown favor by God, she did not brag about herself at all. Instead, she praised God for the work that He had done."

Into the Word

Announce a Bible-marking activity. Provide copies of Luke 1:46-55 for those who do not wish to write in their own Bibles. Provide four different colored pencils to each learner and provide handouts (you create) with these instructions:

- Underline with one color the words that describe Mary.
- Underline with a second color the words that describe Mary's actions.
- Underline with a third color the words that describe God.
- Underline with a fourth color the words that describe God's actions.

Read the Scripture aloud (or ask a volunteer to do so) slowly two to four times. As the Scripture is read, class members are to mark their copies of the Scripture text in the ways noted.

Write on the board *Descriptions of Mary / Mary's Actions / Descriptions of God / God's Actions.* Ask volunteers to share the underlined words for each category. Write responses under the correct headers.

After all responses to the underlining activity have been given, ask the following questions for whole-class discussion: 1–What is notable about how Mary describes herself? 2–In light of her self-description, how does Mary respond in action? 3–What is notable about Mary's descriptions of God? 4–How have you experienced Mary's descriptions of God in your own life? 5–What part of Mary's Song do you find most challenging?

Into Life

Give each learner a sheet of paper and pencil. Ask them to write down an attribute of God that they have experienced. Then ask them to write down a time when God fulfilled His promises to them.

Say, "What poured out of Mary's heart was a song of praise. Let's use Mary's Song as a model to write our own songs of praise to God." Have learners use their earlier responses to each compose their own song of praise to God. Instruct them to focus more on content and meaning of the song than on its rhyme or rhythm. Caution against hurrying, and challenge them to use the experience of writing a song as an act of praise in itself. Learners will complete the activity as a take-home. To encourage completion, explain that you will be asking for volunteers to share their completed songs at the beginning of the next class.

Alternative. Distribute copies of the "Song of Praise Template" exercise from the activity page. Assign this as a take-home activity. To encourage completion, ask learners to consider sharing their completed songs at the beginning of the next class.

God Promises to Hear and Forgive

Devotional Reading: Deuteronomy 30:1-10
Background Scripture: 2 Chronicles 7:1-22

2 Chronicles 7:12-22

12 And the LORD appeared to Solomon by night, and said unto him, I have heard thy prayer, and have chosen this place to myself for an house of sacrifice.

13 If I shut up heaven that there be no rain, or if I command the locusts to devour the land, or if I send pestilence among my people;

14 If my people, which are called by my name, shall humble themselves, and pray, and seek my face, and turn from their wicked ways; then will I hear from heaven, and will forgive their sin, and will heal their land.

15 Now mine eyes shall be open, and mine ears attent unto the prayer that is made in this place.

16 For now have I chosen and sanctified this house, that my name may be there for ever: and mine eyes and mine heart shall be there perpetually.

17 And as for thee, if thou wilt walk before me, as David thy father walked, and do according to all that I have commanded thee, and shalt observe my statutes and my judgments;

18 Then will I stablish the throne of thy kingdom, according as I have covenanted with David thy father, saying, There shall not fail thee a man to be ruler in Israel.

19 But if ye turn away, and forsake my statutes and my commandments, which I have set before you, and shall go and serve other gods, and worship them;

20 Then will I pluck them up by the roots out of my land which I have given them; and this house, which I have sanctified for my name, will I cast out of my sight, and will make it to be a proverb and a byword among all nations.

21 And this house, which is high, shall be an astonishment to every one that passeth by it; so that he shall say, Why hath the LORD done thus unto this land, and unto this house?

22 And it shall be answered, Because they forsook the LORD God of their fathers, which brought them forth out of the land of Egypt, and laid hold on other gods, and worshipped them, and served them: therefore hath he brought all this evil upon them.

Key Text

If my people, which are called by my name, shall humble themselves, and pray, and seek my face, and turn from their wicked ways; then will I hear from heaven, and will forgive their sin, and will heal their land. —2 Chronicles 7:14

From Darkness to Light

Unit 2: God's Promises
Lessons 5–9

Lesson Aims

After participating in this lesson, each learner will be able to:

1. Summarize the Lord's promises of blessing and discipline spoken to Solomon.

2. Categorize those promises in terms of their enduring or temporary nature.

3. State one or more "lessons learned" from times of being personally blessed or disciplined.

Lesson Outline

Introduction

A. Forgiveness as a Lifestyle

Brian and Candy's 40th wedding anniversary was a hard-won victory. As their children, grandchildren, in-laws, and friends gathered, some people remembered another time, years earlier, when that marriage had almost ended. The family's spending had become so extravagant that Brian had involved himself in illegal business practices to cover the costs. When he was found out, he had faced possible jail time.

As a result, Brian and Candy spent time talking through the issues that had led the family to such overspending. They changed the spending habits that had led Brian to search for money in unethical ways. And over time, Brian and Candy rebuilt their marriage—they chose forgiveness as a lifestyle. Divine forgiveness is also a choice, requiring action from both God and His people.

B. Lesson Context

Ancient Jewish sources attribute much of 1 and 2 Chronicles (originally one document) to Ezra, with the events after his time being recorded by Nehemiah. These two men writing Chronicles would date the document between 539 and 515 BC. However, there are several pieces of evidence within the book that date its writing to a later time—425 BC or after. Because of this, the writer is just called "the Chronicler."

One reason for a later dating of 1 and 2 Chronicles is that the text quite unapologetically used the earlier 1 and 2 Kings as source material. In places, the text has been changed very little or not at all. Second Chronicles 7:12-22 (today's text) repeats 1 Kings 9:1-9 almost word for word. This makes differences between the texts more interesting.

One of the key differences between Kings and Chronicles concerns the Davidic dynasty (see discussion on 2 Chronicles 7:18, below). Our text today harkens back to the first temple and Solomon's dedication prayer (6:21-39; compare 1 Kings 8:30-51). Solomon asked God to forgive Israel even when its sinfulness would lead God to carry out the curses of the covenant (see Deuteronomy 28). This prayer linked three important concepts: the Davidic monarchy, the temple, and the land (2 Chronicles 6:4-11). The Chronicler's audience had returned from Babylonian captivity (538 BC) and the second temple had been built (516 BC). But the Davidic monarchy had not been reestablished. What this meant regarding God's faithfulness to His people and His promises was a burning concern in Judah.

I. On Turning Back
(2 Chronicles 7:12-16)
A. God's Affirmation (v. 12)

12. And the LORD appeared to Solomon by night, and said unto him, I have heard thy prayer, and have chosen this place to myself for an house of sacrifice.

God's acknowledging that He *heard* Solomon's *prayer* set up the expectation that God was about to act as Solomon had requested (2 Chronicles 6:14-42). While 1 Kings 9:2 refers to Solomon's earlier dream at the high place Gibeon, 2 Chronicles 7 omits that reference entirely (see 1 Kings 3:4-15). And to the degree this incident is mentioned in 2 Chronicles, the Chronicler chose to clarify that the tabernacle was at Gibeon—Solomon was not simply visiting a high place (2 Chronicles 1:3-7). This is in keeping with the Chronicler's emphasis on the temple itself as God's *chosen* earthly home after the tabernacle (compare 5:7-14; 6:6, 34, 38). Given God's promise to David that one of his sons would build the temple (1 Chronicles 17:11-13), it comes as no surprise that the Lord accepted *this place* as His own *house*.

God's choosing a permanent home within Jerusalem cemented the promised land as the place He had chosen for Israel (Exodus 23:27-33). Until this point, God had been content with the tabernacle (2 Samuel 7:5-7). The temple Solomon built replaced the tabernacle as the center of worship in Israel, signified by the relocation of the ark of the covenant to the temple (2 Chronicles 5:2-14).

The phrase *house of sacrifice* occurs only here in the Old Testament. All sacrifices to the Lord were to be made here, at the temple. Sacrifices reaffirmed the relationship between God and worshippers (example: Leviticus 16). And since the worshippers often ate the sacrificed animal together, the meal deepened the relationships among the people as well. Sacrifice could mark an apology for unintentional sins (chapters 4–5) or express gratitude for blessings received (7:11-15).

Later, for returned exiles, it was important to reinstate the priests in the rebuilt temple so that sacrifices could once again be offered (Ezra 6:14-18). Emphasizing the sacrifices offered in the temple assured the returned exiles that the Lord heard them. The temple was important, yes, but the Lord was not dependent on the people having a temple in their midst for *Him* to be present with them (compare Acts 17:24).

What Do You Think?

What, if any, circumstances cause you to wonder whether the Lord has heard your prayers?

Digging Deeper

When you or someone you love experiences these doubts, what Bible passages encourage you?

B. God's Attention (vv. 13-16)

13. If I shut up heaven that there be no rain, or if I command the locusts to devour the land, or if I send pestilence among my people.

God named some punishments for apostasy. Drought is caused by extended periods without *rain*. At the opposite end of this spectrum, we might expect to find flooding, but *locusts* can also represent the devastation of very wet conditions. A subset of grasshoppers, these insects experience a drastic change when heavy rains fall. Instead of being solitary creatures of little impact in their "grasshopper phase," the locusts enter a "gregarious phase," finding each other and swarming crops in groups as large as tens of *billions* of the flying insects. They can destroy thousands of square miles of farmland, bringing famine in their wake (see lesson 9). *Pestilence* refers to a variety of infectious diseases that can ravage a population; the bubonic plague is one example.

We should note that hardships can and do occur without being punishment from God. For instance, several barren women named in the

Seek only the Lord.

Visual for Lesson 5. *Ask students to silently contemplate this phrase before you pose the questions associated with verse 22.*

pride, "goeth before destruction, and an haughty spirit before a fall" (Proverbs 16:18). Second, prayer can be specifically of repentance, but its true importance is in renewing the relationship with the Lord. It is one way to *seek* God's *face*, which in turn is a way to speak of knowing God's character. Interestingly, all of this comes (at least grammatically) *before* turning from *wicked ways* (contrast Isaiah 55:7). Too much can be made of this order of events, but as written it suggests that the process of owning one's sins, seeking to repair the relationship with God, and learning more of who God is prepares the person to repent fully of evil.

> **What Do You Think?**
> How do you identify situations that are calling for your repentance?
>
> **Digging Deeper**
> Who are spiritual leaders you trust to help you with any blind spots you might experience?

Bible (and countless nameless others) experienced their childlessness as a grave lack but with no indication that God was punishing them (examples: Genesis 16:1-2; 21:1-7; 1 Samuel 1:5-8, 20). When Jesus was speaking to a great crowd, He declared that neither the Galilaeans whom Pilate had killed nor the 18 people killed by the tower in Siloam were more or less guilty than all the people of the crowd (Luke 13:1-5a). We also do well to be wary of those who declare such and such a disaster to be what "those people" had coming to them. Instead, we all ought to heed Jesus' warning and repent of our own sins (13:5b).

14a. If my people, which are called by my name, shall humble themselves, and pray, and seek my face, and turn from their wicked ways.

Using the phrase *my people* twice in quick succession (see 2 Chronicles 7:13, above) emphasizes the desired close relationship between Israel and the Lord. *Which are called by my name* adds weight to what it means to be God's people. Names in the ancient Near East carried not only the importance we give them today but also a sense of the power of a person or the honor due that person. To call the nation of Israel by God's own name was to assert that "I Am" was their protector and Lord (Exodus 3:14).

The actions listed are necessary for the people to be renewed as those called by God's own name. First, humility allows us to acknowledge when we have wronged God and one another. Its opposite,

14b. Then will I hear from heaven, and will forgive their sin, and will heal their land.

Only God can replace "the stony heart" with "an heart of flesh" (Ezekiel 36:26). Everything we do in turning toward Him is simply what opens the door to our renewal. Once again God hears before acting—and that *from heaven*! Although the temple was later razed, seemingly indicating that God dwelt far from His people, in fact He still listened and heard from "the heavens of heavens" (Psalm 68:33; contrast Lamentations 3:44). God never literally resided in the temple. Solomon acknowledged as much when he dedicated the temple (2 Chronicles 6:18). The phrasing also draws on the image of God as king, since God's throne is in Heaven (18:18). Although the Chronicler's audience no longer had a king in the land, their true king had always been sovereign over their nation and their world.

God's response would be forgiveness of *sin* and healing for the *land*. Old Testament writings overtly acknowledge that the people's way of living affected not only themselves but also the land in which they lived (example: Deuteronomy 11:12-15; compare Romans 8:19-22). In this case, we assume that God would reverse the effects of disease, famine, and drought in order to *heal* both people and nonhuman creation.

15. Now mine eyes shall be open, and mine ears attent unto the prayer that is made in this place.

The temple was always meant to be a "house of prayer" (Isaiah 56:7; Mark 11:15-17). For the post-exilic returnees who were to rebuild the temple in the days of Ezra (see Lesson Context; 2 Chronicles 7:12, above), it would be especially reassuring that God had promised His attention.

16. For now have I chosen and sanctified this house, that my name may be there for ever: and mine eyes and mine heart shall be there perpetually.

The temple's sanctification did not come about by the human rituals of prayer and sacrifice but by God's own divine action. By choosing to meet Israel at the temple, God made it holy. And while God would not literally live in *this house* (Isaiah 66:1), allowing the temple to be associated with His *name* meant He was tying His reputation to the temple and to His people who worshipped there (see 2 Chronicles 7:14a, above). Adding that God's *heart* would be in the temple speaks both to the care and the attention that God would give His people.

We can think of this in the parallel way that Christians are God's chosen temple (1 Corinthians 3:16-17). Our mode of conduct reflects on our holy God who has chosen us as His people and the dwelling place of the Holy Spirit (2 Timothy 1:14).

What Do You Think?

How do you take care of God's temple —both your own body and the larger church—as acts of dedication to God?

Digging Deeper

Does your house or church building require a similar care? Provide biblical evidence to back up your answer.

Temple Turmoil

In his book *Jerusalem Besieged*, archaeologist Eric H. Cline notes that Jerusalem has been "destroyed at least twice, besieged 23 times, attacked an additional 52 times, and captured and recaptured 44 times." That's a lot of turmoil over 3,000 years!

Instead of focusing on Jerusalem in general, it is more insightful to focus on the first two temples in particular. Solomon's temple stood for nearly 400 years until 586 BC. The second temple, dedicated by Zerubbabel, stood for several centuries more, until it was destroyed by the Romans in AD 70.

By promising His presence in the temple, God offered the people protection and stability if they were willing to follow Him. But God also made promises about what would happen if the rulers and people failed to follow Him. Are we on high alert as we follow God, remaining under His protection? Or are we a bit too casual about our "temples"?

—B. H.

II. On Turning Away
(2 Chronicles 7:17-22)

A. David's Blessing (vv. 17-18)

17. And as for thee, if thou wilt walk before me, as David thy father walked, and do according to all that I have commanded thee, and shalt observe my statutes and my judgments.

Walk is a common biblical metaphor for a way of life (examples: Deuteronomy 5:33; Proverbs 2:13; Zechariah 3:7). *David thy father* was an apt role model for his heir Solomon. When David sinned, he humbled himself, prayed, sought God's face, and turned from his sinful ways (examples: 2 Samuel 12:13; 24:10, 14-17; Psalm 38; see 2 Chronicles 7:14a, above). For this reason, we see over and over again that God did not hold David's sins against him, even when the man experienced the effects of his failings (examples: 2 Samuel 13:21, 32-33; 24:15-16, 24b-25).

The phrase *my statutes and my judgments*, virtual synonyms (see 2 Chronicles 7:19, below), uses the terminology of Deuteronomy. First and 2 Kings constantly refer to Deuteronomy, and the Chronicler carried over that language here. The phrase in combination with being *all that* God *commanded* could be understood narrowly as laws to be obeyed. More likely, however, the entire Law of Moses—Genesis through Deuteronomy—was in mind, as a requirement for how to live a life pleasing to the Lord (see 2 Kings 22:8-13).

18. Then will I stablish the throne of thy kingdom, according as I have covenanted with David thy father, saying, There shall not fail thee a man to be ruler in Israel.

The promise to maintain David's family on *the throne* of Israel was paradoxically both conditional and unconditional (see 2 Samuel 7). It was unconditional in the sense that God would preserve the dynasty even when its rulers practiced idolatry and unjust behaviors. However, Solomon's own sins resulted in 10 of the 12 tribes being taken from his son Rehoboam (1 Kings 11:9-11; 12:1-24). And when Judah fell to Babylon in 586 BC, the monarchy was destroyed.

The Chronicler was keenly aware that the Davidic monarchy had fallen, and as he wrote Chronicles, there was no reason (from an earthly point of view) to believe the royal line would be restored. The writer correctly attributed the failure of the line to the kings' faithlessness. The land and people could be restored, but it would be many centuries before a new kind of king from David's line would take up the crown (John 18:33-37). How God chose to keep this promise to David was greater than anyone in the Chronicler's day could anticipate: Jesus would live as a man and be proclaimed in His rightful place as king over the entire world (12:12-16; Revelation 17:14).

> ### What Do You Think?
> In what ways do you hope your faithfulness to God will become a blessing to future generations?
>
> ### Digging Deeper
> What are you doing now in hopes that God will bring it to fruition later (1 Corinthians 3:5-7)?

B. People's Punishment (vv. 19-22)

19-20a. But if ye turn away, and forsake my statutes and my commandments, which I have set before you, and shall go and serve other gods, and worship them; then will I pluck them up by the roots out of my land which I have given them.

Verse 19 shifts the addressee from Solomon himself to the people as a whole (the Hebrew word for *ye* is plural in verse 19, but singular in verses 17-18). While all sin severs the relationship between Israel and God, the root of many sins is idolatry—allowing some non-god to take God's place. False gods' ways are never God's ways, and in fact these imaginary gods often demand or condone wickedness (we think of human sacrifice as an extreme example). Worshipping any God but the Lord violates the first two commandments (Exodus 20:2-6) and ensures that a people will be led further to *forsake* God's *statutes* and *commandments*.

The result of Judah's continued idolatry was exile (2 Chronicles 36:15-20). There is a certain logic to this: if people desire to put something else in God's place, they may find that God allows them to have what they desire, knowing it is not what is really needed. Plucking Israel *up by the roots out of* God's *land* might bring to mind a gardener removing weeds or unfruitful plants (see Luke 13:6-9). The sins of Israel polluted the land, so God took the people away to allow healing to begin (example: 2 Chronicles 36:21).

Uprooted

A few minutes after midnight on March 3, 2020, a tornado ripped through my neighborhood in Nashville, Tennessee. The tornado stayed on the ground for over an hour and traveled more than 60 miles. According to estimates, it was the sixth most destructive tornado in US history.

More than a year later, most of the devastation was no longer visible, with one glaring exception: the utter lack of trees. On multiple occasions in the first few months after the tornado, I found myself wondering if I had gotten lost in my own neighborhood. Uprooting the trees changed everything.

This image comes to mind when I read that God warned the Israelites that He would uproot them from the land if they were unfaithful. This happened in an act that left the land and the people forever changed. How will God respond if *we* turn away and forsake Him? —B. H.

20b. And this house, which I have sanctified for my name, will I cast out of my sight.

While people can be *cast out* into exile, surely God's *house* could not. This is best understood as regarding the destruction of the temple that occurred in 586 BC alongside the final deportation of exiles into Babylon. The razing of the temple signified God's presence leaving (compare Ezekiel 10:18-19; contrast 43:1-5).

20c-21. And will make it to be a proverb and a byword among all nations. And this house, which is high, shall be an astonishment to every one that passeth by it; so that he shall say, Why hath the LORD done thus unto this land, and unto this house?

One consequence of exile would be finding that God's people had become *a proverb and a byword*. Israel's exile would serve as an example of how God disciplines sinful people. Even worse, their destruction would be so widely known that it would become a kind of shorthand to describe horrible misfortune. Foreigners rather surprisingly would assess correctly that *the Lord* had not been powerless to protect His people but instead had *done thus unto this land, and unto this house.*

22. And it shall be answered, Because they forsook the LORD God of their fathers, which brought them forth out of the land of Egypt, and laid hold on other gods, and worshipped them, and served them: therefore hath he brought all this evil upon them.

Answering *why* God had done this would be an opportunity for Israelites to rehearse their history and assert the fact of God's holiness amid their own checkered past of serving Him.

This response emphasizes Israel's ingratitude for their deliverance from Egypt (Exodus 12:31-42; contrast 16:1-2). Israel's core identity came from the Lord who chose them and liberated them from Egyptian bondage (12:14-20). Worshipping and serving *other gods* was a rejection of what God had done (example: 32:2-8). We do well to remember that the Lord does not do moral *evil* (James 1:13-14; 1 John 1:5). But the exiles experienced the siege and destruction of Jerusalem and the temple and later living in Babylon as *physical* evil (compare Joshua 23:15; 2 Samuel 24:16). Outsiders who saw what happened in Israel would explain it as evil from the Lord.

Conclusion
A. God's Forgiveness

While sin has consequences, often dire, neither sin nor its consequences can utter the final word about the relationship between chosen people and the choosing God. Even when sin seems to have ruined God's plans entirely—as with the apostasy of the Davidic line—we do well to remember that God's promises and plans move forward. The loss of David's kingdom led to the greatest gift of all: salvation through Jesus' blood, bringing us out of our exile in sin and into God's kingdom.

We cannot anticipate how God will choose to work through our "exilic" experiences (Romans 8:28). Still, when asking for God's mercy, we must remember our own responsibility: to humble ourselves, to offer honest prayer, and to seek God's face as we turn from evil. He honors our repentance when we honor Him.

B. Prayer

O God who hears and sees, to You we turn when our sins consume us. Please forgive and heal us. In Jesus' name we pray. Amen.

C. Thought to Remember

Repent to experience forgiveness and healing.

How to Say It

Chronicler	*Krahn*-ih-kler.
Davidic	Duh-*vid*-ick.
Gibeon	*Gib*-e-un (G as in *get*).
Rehoboam	Ree-huh-*boe*-um.

Involvement Learning

Enhance your lesson with KJV Bible Student *(from your curriculum supplier) and the reproducible activity page (at www.standardlesson.com or in the back of the* KJV Standard Lesson Commentary Deluxe Edition*).*

Into the Lesson

Ask learners to split into pairs, and assign each pair a site that was called holy in the Bible. (Possibilities come from Exodus 3, 19, 26, etc.) Pairs could also discuss the Sabbath and Israel in terms of their holiness. Allow 5 to 10 minutes before reconvening the class. Ask each pair to briefly describe what they learned. Then facilitate a whole-class discussion by asking what characteristics were shared by places (or days or people) that are holy. List these on the board as they are named.

Alternative. Distribute copies of the "A Holy Place" exercise from the activity page, which you can download. Have learners complete it individually (in one minute) before sharing their creations with a partner. As a whole group, discuss what is required for a place to be considered holy. Continue the discussion by asking, "Why do we seek sacred spaces?"

After either activity, say, "With God's approval and guidance, Solomon built the temple, and with God's presence it became a holy place to worship and pray to God. But consequences would follow if the people forsook their faithfulness to Him."

Into the Word

Write on the board *Ifs / Thens* as the headers of two columns. Ask a volunteer to read aloud 2 Chronicles 7:12-22. Divide the class in half, designating one half as the **Ifs Group** and the other half as the **Thens Group**. Tell each group the role they will play as you read the passage again: The **Ifs Group** should raise their hands when a verse mentions responsibilities or actions that God asks us to take. The **Thens Group** should raise their hands when a verse mentions the promises or consequences from God. Jot these answers on the board, noting if a verse contains more than one *If* or *Then*. (Possible answers for *Ifs*: vv. 14, 17, 19. Possible answers for *Thens*: vv. 15-16, 18, 20.)

Lead a whole-group discussion on how the lists show God's covenant with His people. Ask: 1–How do you see God's promises in this passage? 2–Are His promises here unconditional or conditional? Explain. (See commentary for further guidance.)

Alternative. Read through today's passage aloud once. Distribute copies of the "If/Then Covenant" activity from the activity page. Have learners work in pairs to complete as indicated. (This exercise may be more time-consuming than it appears at first glance.) Then reconvene the whole class to discuss their work.

After calling time for either alternative, have the whole group discuss how this passage confirms or challenges our belief in God's unconditional love. As a whole group, discuss how 2 Chronicles 7:19-22 came true in Israel's history. See commentary for examples.

Into Life

Discuss examples of modern-day idolatry and the visible consequences to them. Then hand out paper and pencils. Give learners time to reflect and note how God's covenant has been true in their own lives by way of being either personally blessed or disciplined. Challenge learners to think about choices they have made and ways that God's promises and consequences were fulfilled. Allow several minutes for writing.

Give learners one minute to think individually of one or more lessons they learned from times of being personally blessed or disciplined. Then ask volunteers to share what change they would like to make to continue to benefit from those lessons. Invite learners to use that change as they take one minute to compose a prayer of personal consecration to God for the new year. Allow time at the end for volunteers to pray their prayers aloud. Encourage them to pray about their changes as they go through the week.

God Promises to Restore

Devotional Reading: 2 Thessalonians 3:1-5, 13-17
Background Scripture: Isaiah 43:1-21

Isaiah 43:1-4, 10-12

1 But now thus saith the LORD that created thee, O Jacob, and he that formed thee, O Israel, Fear not: for I have redeemed thee, I have called thee by thy name; thou art mine.

2 When thou passest through the waters, I will be with thee; and through the rivers, they shall not overflow thee: when thou walkest through the fire, thou shalt not be burned; neither shall the flame kindle upon thee.

3 For I am the LORD thy God, the Holy One of Israel, thy Saviour: I gave Egypt for thy ransom, Ethiopia and Seba for thee.

4 Since thou wast precious in my sight, thou hast been honourable, and I have loved thee: therefore will I give men for thee, and people for thy life.

10 Ye are my witnesses, saith the LORD, and my servant whom I have chosen: that ye may know and believe me, and understand that I am he: before me there was no God formed, neither shall there be after me.

11 I, even I, am the LORD; and beside me there is no saviour.

12 I have declared, and have saved, and I have shewed, when there was no strange god among you: therefore ye are my witnesses, saith the LORD, that I am God.

Key Text

Thus saith the LORD that created thee, O Jacob, and he that formed thee, O Israel, Fear not: for I have redeemed thee, I have called thee by thy name; thou art mine. —**Isaiah 43:1**

Photo © Getty Images

From Darkness to Light

Unit 2: God's Promises
Lessons 5–9

Lesson Aims

After participating in this lesson, each learner will be able to:

1. List parallel elements in the lesson text—elements that say the same thing in different words.

2. Compare and contrast the use of the word *ransom* in Isaiah 43:3 with that word's usage in Matthew 20:28; Mark 10:45; and 1 Timothy 2:6.

3. List ways to recognize God's protection when it is occurring today.

Lesson Outline

Introduction

A. A Trustworthy Witness

Many citizens think of jury duty as an onerous task to be avoided. But for one man, actually serving on a jury made a world of difference in his attitude. In the case before him and his peers, a young woman was charged with theft, forgery, assault, and attempted murder. She testified truthfully, admitting freely to the first two charges and proving to be a reliably truthful witness in her own defense. It became obvious in the course of proceedings that she was innocent of the two more serious charges.

After rendering their verdict, the man learned that one of his peers had decided after the first day of the trial that the defendant was guilty on *all* charges. This explained why it had taken several hours to persuade that juror that the evidence did not support her predetermined verdict. That's when the man realized his privilege: serving on that jury gave him opportunity to work with his peers to prevent a young woman from spending several unwarranted years in prison.

Israel was called as a witness to tell the truth about God's loving faithfulness. But unlike the young woman, Israel was not always a reliable witness. Isaiah's call was for people to act as reliable, truthful witnesses of all that God had done.

B. Lesson Context

As we open today's study from Isaiah 43, time has moved forward about 300 years since last week's lesson about King Solomon. Various kings have come and gone, and the nation of Israel has been split into two parts. The Israelites have been through multiple cycles of sin and repentance.

Isaiah 1:1 allows us to date Isaiah's lengthy prophetic ministry to between 740 and 680 BC. Hosea, an older contemporary of Isaiah, warned the northern kingdom of Israel to repent and recommit their ways to the Lord (examples: Hosea 1:1; 3:4-5). Sadly, the Israelites refused. Within a few years after Hosea's ministry, the northern kingdom was defeated and dispersed by the Assyrian Empire in 722 BC. Isaiah's ministry to the southern kingdom of Judah had only slightly better prospects. Isaiah 36–39 tells of Jerusalem's deliverance from the Assyrian army of King Sennacherib, as well as other events from the time of King Hezekiah (ruled approximately 727–695 BC). Those were dark days for the little nation of Judah. Unfortunately, the original readers in Judah mistook the miraculous deliverance from the Assyrian army in 701 BC as a sign that God would never allow Judah to fall (Jeremiah 7:2-26).

This narrative section ends in Isaiah 39 with an ill-advised action by Hezekiah: the king welcomed Babylonian envoys to Jerusalem and gave them a private viewing of all his wealth. Isaiah then gave Hezekiah a dire prophecy that the Babylonians would carry Judah and all its treasures into captivity (Isaiah 39:5-7; compare 2 Kings 20:12-19).

Beginning in Isaiah 40 (considered the start of the second section of the book, sometimes called "The Book of Comfort"), Assyria, so prominent in the first 39 chapters, is no longer a threat to God's people; Babylon is the new menace. There is also a greater emphasis in Isaiah 40–66 on promises of hope and a brighter future for God's people, in contrast with the theme of judgment that is so prevalent in the previous chapters. In this second section, Isaiah developed an important theme of God's people acting as God's witnesses to the other nations of the earth (Isaiah 45:20-21; 48:20; etc.). This was not witness in the sense of "evangelism" but that of "testimony" (see 43:10, below).

Just so we don't get too confused by terminology, we should point out that sometimes the word *Israel* in the book of Isaiah means only the northern kingdom of that name, as distinct from the southern kingdom of Judah. At other times, however, the word *Israel* refers to all the Jewish people in both northern and southern kingdoms together. The context will tell us what is meant at any one time.

I. The Lord Acts
(Isaiah 43:1-4)
A. God Creates (v. 1)

1. But now thus saith the LORD that created thee, O Jacob, and he that formed thee, O Israel, Fear not: for I have redeemed thee, I have called thee by thy name; thou art mine.

But now marks Isaiah's transition from a declaration of judgment (Isaiah 42:18-25) to an assurance of mercy. Examples from the past provide solid reason for hope that God had not abandoned His people (see 43:2a-2b, below). For this reason, the Lord commanded the people *fear not*—one of the most frequent commands in the Bible (examples: Genesis 15:1; Joshua 1:9; Luke 1:30; Revelation 1:17).

God's relationship to *Israel* (also called *Jacob*; see Genesis 32:28; Isaiah 41:8) is described with four verbs. First, the Lord *created* them. This concept is poetically repeated by saying that God *formed* them. This is a familiar theme throughout the Old Testament: Israel was created and chosen by the Lord God, not the other way around (see Ezekiel 20:5). Third, the Lord *redeemed* Israel. To redeem has the sense here of deliverance by paying a price. In combination to references of God's forming the people, this alludes most clearly to Israel's rescue from Egyptian bondage (see Exodus 6:6). The exodus from Egypt was the beginning of the nation of Israel, a redemption from slavery. Fourth, the Lord *called* and named Israel as His chosen nation, and the call and escape from Egypt was the foundation of this relationship (see Hosea 11:1).

What Do You Think?

How have these key verbs shaped your identity as God's child: created, formed, redeemed, and called?

Digging Deeper

Which of these four strikes a chord with you today, and why?

Save Us!

I still remember hearing Kate Smith sing "God Bless America" during the early days of World War II. Throughout the war, the song was offered as a prayer for God to protect America from the ravages of the war. In the years since then, the song's title has been used as a dubious shorthand to express both patriotism and faith.

God announced that He was the savior of the nation of Israel . . . and He *was*, but not always in the way (or at the time) in which the Israelites expected Him to be. I suspect the same could be true of us. We want God to save our country. But we do well to consider what we're *really* asking for when we ask for God's salvation for any particular nation. Do we seek protection from evil, from political enemies, from discomfort? And is our nation of origin or citizenship *really* the nation God should bless?   —C. R. B.

B. God Protects (vv. 2-4)

2a. When thou passest through the waters, I will be with thee; and through the rivers, they shall not overflow thee.

Allusion to the exodus continues with reference to passing *through the waters*, as in the miraculous Red Sea event (Exodus 14:15-31; compare Psalm 78:13). The promise that the floodwaters of *rivers* will not *overflow* recalls Israel's experience at the Jordan River (Joshua 3:15-17).

Similar flooding language was used earlier in Isaiah to speak figuratively of King Shalmaneser V (ruled 727–722 BC; see Isaiah 8:6-8). This Assyrian king overtook the northern tribes of Israel (2 Kings 17:1-6; 18:9), stopping short of taking the two southern tribes of Judah and Benjamin. The Assyrian King Sennacherib (ruled 705–681 BC) would further threaten them (18:13-17; Isaiah 36:1–37:38), though Jerusalem would not fall until 586 BC to the Babylonian King Nebuchadnezzar (ruled 605–562 BC; see 43:2b, below).

Such dangers were not to be feared, because the Lord promised He would *be with* the people (compare Psalm 124:1, 4-5). This echoes God's similar promises elsewhere (examples: Exodus 3:12; Joshua 1:5; Judges 6:16). This promise proves to be the key not only to Israel's deliverance but also to our own. Immanuel, meaning "God is with us" (Isaiah 7:14; compare Matthew 1:23), has come to save us from every sin that ensnares, reconcile us

to our Lord, and give us life eternal (2 Corinthians 5:18-19; Colossians 1:19-23a).

2b. When thou walkest through the fire, thou shalt not be burned; neither shall the flame kindle upon thee.

Whereas protection from waters recalled the past, the same was not literally true of *fire* and *flame* (see Deuteronomy 4:20; Jeremiah 11:4). Looking into the nation's future in Babylonian captivity, however, we remember Shadrach, Meshach, and Abednego's miraculous salvation in King Nebuchadnezzar's superheated furnace (Daniel 3:19-27)! Israel could faithfully, hopefully expect to experience this kind of supernatural protection in God's hands, even as they experienced punishment for their sins in a foreign land.

> **What Do You Think?**
> What events from your life give you confidence that God is always with you?
> **Digging Deeper**
> What verses in addition to Isaiah 43:2 can you turn to when your confidence wavers?

3a. For I am the LORD thy God, the Holy One of Israel.

This first title again hearkens back to the exodus from Egypt, as this is how God introduced himself when He gave the Ten Commandments (Exodus 20:2; the exact Hebrew expression appears also in Isaiah 41:13 and 48:17). *Lord* brings to mind the personal name by which He revealed himself to Moses at the burning bush— "I Am That I Am" (Exodus 3:14). This designation speaks to God's eternal, unchanging nature. Jesus would later also tie this name to the hope of resurrection because God is the Lord of the living, not the dead (compare 3:16; Matthew 22:32).

God is a more generic Hebrew word that could be used to speak of the Lord (as here) or of false gods (example: Genesis 31:30-32; Isaiah 21:9), with context determining which. Though Israel was called to worship the Lord God only, they were surrounded by people who venerated other, fictitious gods, and most often many such gods at once.

How to Say It

Nebuchadnezzar	*Neb*-yuh-kud-**nez**-er.
Seba	*See*-buh.
Sennacherib	Sen-*nack*-er-ib.
Shalmaneser	Shal-mun-*ee*-zer.

Isaiah especially emphasized that God is not one among many, but the only God (example: 45:6).

To claim to be Israel's only God was necessarily to claim to be *the Holy One of Israel*. Though we can think of holiness as a set of characteristics like purity, sinlessness, and so on, the basic claim here is of uniqueness. The Holy One is the special One, unlike any other. And God is not bound to Israel because of something the people did but, instead, by His own promises. Because the holy God chose Israel, the people were called to be holy as well (Exodus 19:6; Leviticus 19:2)—not just pure, but also unique in the world. The same call holds for Christians today (1 Peter 1:16; Revelation 1:6). We are to serve our unique God in unique ways that will often run counter to cultural expectations (Romans 12:2).

3b. Thy Saviour: I gave Egypt for thy ransom, Ethiopia and Seba for thee.

Though the word *Saviour* takes on an overtly spiritual definition in Christianity (example: John 3:16-21), Isaiah's audience would likely have thought of physical deliverance (example: Psalm 18:3). Even in Jesus' day, the term frequently was applied to Roman military victors or emperors. The Lord saved Israel from its enemies because of His great mercy (example: 13:5; compare Romans 5:8).

Three nations are listed as examples of the Lord's saving Israel. First is *Egypt,* the great enslaver and oppressor of the people of Israel. Second and third are *Ethiopia*, a region south of Egypt, and *Seba,* which is near Ethiopia and with a likely association with Sheba (Psalm 72:10). The effect of naming these three countries is to emphasize the extent of the *ransom* that God paid for His people. After King Cyrus of Persia (ruled 539–530 BC) released the Jews to return to Judah (2 Chronicles 36:22-23; Ezra 1:1-4), his son King Cambyses II (ruled 530–522 BC) took control of Egypt and the surrounding areas. In this way, the Jews were given relative freedom in Judah because Persian attention was diverted elsewhere (see lesson 5).

After the Babylonians took Jerusalem, many inhabitants, including an unwilling Jeremiah, fled to Egypt (Jeremiah 43:4-7)—and some likely beyond to those other nations as well. This began what is known as the Diaspora. Everywhere they

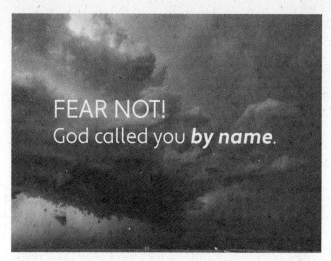

FEAR NOT!
God called you *by name*.

Visual for Lesson 6. *Before discussing verse 1, ask learners to spend one minute silently considering the value of being known by name.*

went, the Jewish refugees took their religion with them (examples: James 1:1; 1 Peter 1:1). Hundreds of years after today's text, when the gospel began to spread throughout the Greco-Roman world, these pockets of Jewish believers would aid its spread—whether in spite of ill-considered attempts to squash the good news (example: Acts 8:1b-8) or their own evangelistic efforts (example: 18:2, 26). In large part, this fulfills Isaiah 43:5-7 (not in our printed text; compare Matthew 8:11).

4. Since thou wast precious in my sight, thou hast been honourable, and I have loved thee: therefore will I give men for thee, and people for thy life.

The grand biblical story is that God chose Israel to be the nation that received His laws to prepare the way for the Messiah (Galatians 3:24). Because Israel was chosen by God out of all the nations, they were counted as both *precious* and *honourable*. These terms should be understood as closely related to the concept of holiness (see Isaiah 43:3a, above). Israel's identity was given to them by ransom, not through their own efforts—a concept that we who follow Christ are intimately acquainted with (Mark 10:45; 1 Timothy 2:6).

Held for Ransom

In 75 BC, one of the most famous kidnappings in history took place. Cilician pirates captured a young Julius Caesar and held him for ransom. Reportedly, they demanded 20 talents of gold. Julius scoffed at them, thinking this ransom demand did not represent his true value, so he suggested that they more than double their demand to 50 talents. Julius Caesar's supporters raised this incredible sum, paid the ransom, and the already famous Roman was released. The freed Julius Caesar then raised a small naval fleet, captured the pirates, and had them all crucified. Presumably, he recovered most of the ransom money too.

In a perverse way, a ransom demand quantifies society's valuation of a person. When considered in this way, we see that the Lord was willing to pay a steep price indeed for Israel. And *this* price only foreshadowed the price He would pay for the entire world: His own Son's blood (Mark 10:45). Like Julius and Israel, you have a choice: What are you going to do with your freedom now that your ransom is paid in full? —M. S. K.

II. The Lord Calls
(Isaiah 43:10-12)
A. Israel Must Testify (v. 10a)

10a. Ye are my witnesses, saith the LORD, and my servant whom I have chosen.

The concept of using a witness to verify legal claims is very ancient, and the integrity of witnesses is the foundation of all legal systems (compare Exodus 20:16). The wisdom writers of Israel saw the honest witness as "faithful" in contrast to the "false witness" (see Proverbs 14:5). The people of antiquity were very aware of the great damage a false witness could bring (see 25:18).

Ancient law courts were different from modern ones, but many roles are similar. It is important to identify the role that each character may represent (judge, plaintiff, defendant, witness, etc.) and the purpose for the scene (to level charges, to prove guilt, to announce a verdict, to impose a sentence). The figurative courtroom before us is packed with "all the nations" (Isaiah 43:9, not in our printed text). As the Lord's *witnesses*, the Israelites must be able to give testimony of their experiences of God's saving actions, such as those described above.

The witness of the people is magnified by the Lord's *servant*, the one whom He has *chosen*.

Sometimes Isaiah applies the idea of the servant to an individual yet to come. This future servant will be identified as Jesus (Matthew 12:17-21, quoting Isaiah 42:1-4). But here the servant refers broadly to Israel as a collective singular for the plural *ye* (compare Isaiah 41:8-9; 45:4). God's mighty acts made Israel the witness for the Lord to all other nations. The law required two or three witnesses to convict someone of a crime (Deuteronomy 19:15; compare John 8:17). In Israel, God had a whole nation of witnesses.

B. The Truth to Be Believed (vv. 10b-12)

10b. That ye may know and believe me, and understand that I am he: before me there was no God formed, neither shall there be after me.

The content of the servant's testimony is tied to things that the original readers could *know*, *believe*, and *understand*. The servant Israel is called to testify about the holiness of the Lord (see Isaiah 43:3a, above). Doing so requires rehearsing their own history and also embracing the nature of God—that *before me there was no God formed*. This eternal, uncreated state is as far from our creaturely experience as can be. We have both ancestors who came before and descendants who come after us. Not so with God. There is no god who existed before the Lord. He is the uncreated Creator. Furthermore, there is no being like the Lord and *neither shall there be* (see Revelation 1:4). Logically this follows, for how could another uncreated being or god come into being?

> **What Do You Think?**
> How does witnessing about the Lord deepen your knowledge, faith, and understanding?
>
> **Digging Deeper**
> In what ways does it remain relevant to witness against false gods, both for your own spiritual health and others' edification?

11. I, even I, am the LORD; and beside me there is no saviour.

The Lord had always insisted on Israel's

acknowledging that He was their only *saviour*. Worshipping other gods was only one way that Israel betrayed a lack of trust in the Lord to save them. Another seemingly more pragmatic way was to ally with foreign nations. These two means cannot be totally separated—the ancient world did not separate the world into religious and secular the way we in the Western world do today. We might think of Solomon's many foreign wives and allies and his resulting walk away from the Lord as one key example (1 Kings 11:1-8). Turning to other, foreign gods could not save Israel, but only kindle the wrath of the Lord (example: 11:9-11). As the psalmist rightly asserted, "[The Lord] only is my rock and my salvation" (Psalm 62:6).

> **What Do You Think?**
> What modern "saviors" do people depend on instead of the Lord?
> **Digging Deeper**
> How does your life testify that the Lord is your only Savior?

12. I have declared, and have saved, and I have shewed, when there was no strange god among you: therefore ye are my witnesses, saith the LORD, that I am God.

Should the Israelites balk and ask how they were qualified to act as God's *witnesses*, here it is spelled out for them. Because God *declared* and *saved* and *shewed*—in other words, because God chose to be knowable to these people, to reveal himself in actions—the people were meant to be witnesses to all that they had learned (see Isaiah 43:3, above, on the implications of God's names).

We can make too fine a difference between what it meant for God to declare, save, and show; all of these are interconnected. However, we may think of declaration as God's giving knowledge of His intentions (example: Genesis 12; 15) and of His expectations (example: Exodus 20). His saving deeds have been rehearsed throughout this lesson (see especially Isaiah 43:3b, above). And finally, God did not do these things in secretive ways but openly, where other nations could see them and speak of them (examples: Joshua 2:8-13; Jeremiah 40:2-3).

In Isaiah 44, which follows, the prophet speaks at length on what has been called the "folly of idols." This reinforces the foundational truths that there is no God but the Lord and that all other gods are human creations. Israel's witness was greatly diminished by dalliances with *strange* gods, in part because knowledge of the Lord is tied to devotion to Him. Forsaking God for a false god erodes the knowledge a person already had and prevents growth toward God.

Conclusion

A. Do I Have a Witness?

Much as we might be tempted to judge Israel's efforts to witness, we do well to appreciate that though Isaiah was not believed in his own ministry, his words were written down. These were considered precious enough (by God) to be preserved throughout generations, and Isaiah's words undergird the Christian's witness today.

As disciples of Christ, we are to be witnesses to the unbelieving world (see Acts 1:8). And though we might think of ourselves individually as witnesses, the church is the primary witness (John 13:34-35; Colossians 3:12-17). What do our worship services say about our God? How does our presence in the community tell the truth about our Lord? What are our relationships and work and pastimes saying about our holy God?

> **What Do You Think?**
> Which concept in today's lesson do you find most challenging?
> **Digging Deeper**
> Which concept do you find most encouraging?

B. Prayer

Lord, give us hearts and minds to be true witnesses of Your mighty works. Thank You for how You have revealed yourself throughout history. In Jesus' name we pray. Amen.

C. Thought to Remember

Remember God's works, and witness faithfully.

Involvement Learning

Enhance your lesson with KJV Bible Student *(from your curriculum supplier) and the reproducible activity page (at www.standardlesson.com or in the back of the* KJV Standard Lesson Commentary Deluxe Edition*).*

Into the Lesson

Distribute magazines featuring current events and advertisements. Have each learner find at least one image that provokes fear and at least one that provides comfort. Have learners share their images or stories, along with feelings they provoked, in groups of three. Then as a whole class, discuss the role that faith should play in reacting either way. Ask, "What effect does faith have on us when we are in a fearful situation? How much do we rely on faith when we are feeling comfortable?"

Alternative. Distribute copies of the "Fear-o-Phobia" exercise from the activity page, which you can download. Have learners work in pairs to complete as indicated. As time allows, ask learners to talk about how faith can help people overcome their fears.

After either activity, say, "In today's text, Isaiah shares promises God gave to Israel, and us, to help calm fears."

Into the Word

Read through today's passage: Isaiah 43:1-4, 10-12. As a class, talk about how a ransom is a payment for the release of someone or something held captive. Discuss how Egypt was given as a "ransom" for Israel historically. Use the commentary to correct misconceptions.

Ask a volunteer to reread verses 2 and 3. Lead a short discussion on who the promise applies to—just Old Testament Israel or Christians as well? Encourage learners to share their reasoning.

Have participants form groups of three. In each group, have one person look up Matthew 20:28, another look up Mark 10:45, and the last person find 1 Timothy 2:6. Ask the groups to read the passages and talk about how the word "ransom" is used in these passages. Then have the groups compare the use of "ransom" in Isaiah 43:3 with those passages. Have groups determine what "price for freedom" was paid, according to these Scriptures.

Allow time for learners to discuss in their groups before taking responses as a whole class. Read Isaiah 43:10-12. As a class, consider how God described not only what He has done in today's passage, but also what He will do.

Alternative. Before your group meets, enlist a volunteer (either from within the group or another member of your church community) to share a brief testimony of how God delivered him or her from a peril. Ask your volunteer to compare his or her level of trust in God before, during, and after the experience. Invite discussion about the impact of both sharing and hearing this story. Say: "In verse 11, God reveals that He is the Lord and that besides Him, there is no Savior." Ask: 1–How does sharing our stories about God's saving grace align with that message? 2–Think about our own roles in proclaiming the restoration that comes from the price Jesus paid. Why might we sometimes shy away from our call to witness to others?

Into Life

Distribute a handout of the questions below (you prepare) to help learners think through their roles as witnesses for the Lord. 1–Where in current global or national events do you see God protecting his people? 2–Where in your local community or church do you see God's protection? 3–Where do you or have you seen God's protection in your own life? Give learners a few minutes to journal on those questions. Have participants share what they have written with a partner and discuss how recognizing God's protection prepares them to witness to others.

Alternative. Distribute copies of the "God's Protection" activity from the activity page. Have learners complete as indicated.

After either alternative, read Isaiah 43:1, replacing the words "O Jacob" and "O Israel" with a pause. Ask learners to silently say their own names in place of the pause.

God Promises to Guide

Devotional Reading: Psalm 119:81-96
Background Scripture: Isaiah 48:1-22

Isaiah 48:3-8a, 17

3 I have declared the former things from the beginning; and they went forth out of my mouth, and I shewed them; I did them suddenly, and they came to pass.

4 Because I knew that thou art obstinate, and thy neck is an iron sinew, and thy brow brass;

5 I have even from the beginning declared it to thee; before it came to pass I shewed it thee: lest thou shouldest say, Mine idol hath done them, and my graven image, and my molten image, hath commanded them.

6 Thou hast heard, see all this; and will not ye declare it? I have shewed thee new things from this time, even hidden things, and thou didst not know them.

7 They are created now, and not from the beginning; even before the day when thou heardest them not; lest thou shouldest say, Behold, I knew them.

8a Yea, thou heardest not; yea, thou knewest not; yea, from that time that thine ear was not opened.

17 Thus saith the LORD, thy Redeemer, the Holy One of Israel; I am the LORD thy God which teacheth thee to profit, which leadeth thee by the way that thou shouldest go.

Key Text

Thus saith the LORD, thy Redeemer, the Holy One of Israel; I am the LORD thy God which teacheth thee to profit, which leadeth thee by the way that thou shouldest go. —**Isaiah 48:17**

From Darkness to Light

Unit 2: God's Promises
Lessons 5–9

Lesson Aims

After participating in this lesson, each learner will be able to:

1. List words that indicate a time element.

2. Explain the ideal relationships between hearing, seeing, and acknowledging.

3. Identify a personal disconnect among hearing, seeing, and acknowledging—and make a plan for change.

Lesson Outline

Introduction

A. "Psychohistory"

In 1942, science fiction author Isaac Asimov created a fictitious world, in his Foundation series of books, in which a scientist developed an accurate model for predicting future events based on a discipline he called "psychohistory." While this seemed fantastic at the time, current computer programmers use "big data" collected on web and smartphone activity to predict all sorts of things. Ads are created, based on this information, to motivate you to make a purchase for something you're likely interested in. Elsewhere, computer data analytics are widely used in professional sports leagues to predict future performance of players, which influences player drafts, trades, and contracts.

There is a marked difference, though, between discerning a likely future and knowing the future infallibly and in detail. This lesson will examine why God sometimes reveals the future to people.

B. Lesson Context

As we noted last week, the Babylonians had taken full control of the southern kingdom of the Israelites, called Judah, by 586 BC. The temple was destroyed, its vessels were confiscated, and many people were deported to Babylon. That was about 136 years after Assyria had done the same to the northern kingdom, called Israel.

The various sections of the book of Isaiah are unified by their repeating of important themes about the Lord and His relationship to Israel. One such section that refers to the "servant" of the Lord is often recognized as Isaiah 40–55. Beyond seeing the role of the Lord's servant (sometimes understood to be the nation of Israel, sometimes as an individual to come), the reader of this section will notice some consistent messages.

First, Isaiah points out the absurdity of worshipping idols (example: Isaiah 41:22-24). The idolater takes a piece of wood, uses part of it to make a fire and bake bread. And then with the rest of the wood he makes a "god" that he worships (44:14-17)! Second and closely related to the first, Isaiah emphasizes that there is no other God but the Lord (44:6; 45:6).

Third, Isaiah frequently notes the Lord's knowledge and control of the future. He knows the "end from the beginning" and "will do all [His] pleasure" (Isaiah 46:10). Furthermore, the Lord challenges the false gods to match Him by revealing the future (41:22; 43:9; 44:7; 45:21; 48:14).

Fourth, the role of the Lord as the Creator of all things is also prominent (Isaiah 40:28). God laid the earth's foundation and stretched out the heavens above (48:13; 51:13). Included in His activity is the creation of the nation of Israel (43:15), often expressed as childbirth (example: 66:7-13).

I. The Knowing God
(Isaiah 48:3-8a)

Isaiah 48 begins by listing the various ways the people identified themselves as people of God, but it asserts that their identity was "not in truth, nor in righteousness" (48:1). God's faithfulness stood in stark contrast to the inconsistency and hypocrisy of Israel.

A. Former Things (vv. 3-6a)

3. I have declared the former things from the beginning; and they went forth out of my mouth, and I shewed them; I did them suddenly, and they came to pass.

In contrast to all the false arts Israel had used to try to foretell the future (Isaiah 44:25; Jeremiah 27:9; 29:8), the Lord asserted in no uncertain terms that *He* was the one who *declared the former things.* The phrase *from the beginning* is not fatalistic. Instead, it gives confidence that God's plan was not haphazardly thrown together as He encountered fresh disobedience from His people. Much evidence could be gathered for Israel to understand that God was in charge and was not caught off guard by anything the people said or did. Two key moments would be (1) promising that Abram—despite his and Sarai's childless and aged condition (Genesis 15:2-3; 17)—would become the father of a great nation (12:1-3); and (2) reassuring Jacob (also called Israel; 46:2) that God would bring Jacob's descendants out of Egypt and back to the promised land (48:21). Isa-

iah's prophecies themselves are examples, foretelling both Judah's exile in Babylon (Isaiah 39:6-7) and the people's return in the days of the Persian King Cyrus (45:13).

Although God's plans are not haphazard, promises like these two can seem to take a long time to be fulfilled. But after God *shewed them,* they truly did seem to happen *suddenly.* So much waiting could make the people doubtful of the promises (compare 2 Peter 3:3-10), but each one *came to pass* just as the Lord had said (see Isaiah 48:5a, 6b-7, below).

4a. Because I knew that thou art obstinate.

Israel's obstinacy is a common thread in the nation's history (examples: Judges 2:19; Matthew 23:37; Acts 7:51), and Isaiah's prophecy echoes other descriptions of the people's being stiffnecked (examples: Exodus 33:3, 5; Deuteronomy 31:27). A related metaphor is the language of a hard heart (examples: 2 Chronicles 36:13; Psalm 95:8), as is refusing to hear or see (examples: Zechariah 7:11-12; Matthew 13:15; Acts 7:51, 57-58).

We can also look at the consequences of Israel's stubbornness. For instance, the people's refusal to trust in the Lord after He delivered them from Egypt resulted in His preventing the first generation from entering the promised land (Deuteronomy 1:32-40). Much later, King Rehoboam's insistence on following his friends' foolish advice led directly to the division of Israel into two kingdoms (1 Kings 12:8-21).

4b. And thy neck is an iron sinew, and thy brow brass.

Iron and brass were the hardest metals known at the time Isaiah ministered. Beginning sometime before 1000 BC, the Iron Age marked the time when iron began to be smelted to create steel. The Hittites in Turkey may have been the first to discover how to make steel by heating iron with carbon. This innovation quickly became known throughout the ancient Near East, and by the time Isaiah wrote, the people would recognize that iron was a formidable material. Brass was still widely used, especially in the beginning of the Iron Age; the Bronze Age came to an end around 1200 BC.

This illustration evokes the image of a beast of burden as hardheaded as these metals. A beast of burden wears a wooden yoke and leather harness strapped tightly around its *neck*. The obedient animal allowed itself to be directed by the reins of its driver. If the driver pulled on the right rein, the animal's head should turn right, and the beast would walk to the right. But an animal with a neck of *iron sinew* would not turn or respond to the commands or will of its driver. The *brow of brass* emphasizes this stubbornness, suggesting a will so set that no new information or knowledge could cause the creature to change course. Together, a stiff neck and a brass brow prove completely unalterable, even to the creature's own harm—much as Israel had often demonstrated.

What Do You Think?

In what situations would your best friend or spouse say you can become especially stubborn?

Digging Deeper

In those moments of stubbornness, are you honoring God? If not, what will you do to address the issue of your stubbornness?

Whoa!

My grandfather, Andrew Boatman, spent much of his working life managing citrus groves. Back then, smudge pots were used in the groves on cold nights. These oil-burning devices were placed between the rows of trees to prevent frost from harming the fruit. In warmer weather the pots were moved back into the rows so a plow could renew the irrigation furrows. But sometimes the plow would catch and turn over a smudge pot. Grandpa would yell "Whoa!" to the mules and rush to set the pot upright before the tree-killing oil leaked out.

Years went by, and Grandpa replaced the mules with a tractor. Soon after, Grandpa was plowing and tipped over a smudge pot. Grandpa yelled "Whoa!" but the tractor didn't "whoa!" It only stopped several yards further when the plow hooked itself on a tree trunk.

We usually think of stubborn mules, not tractors! But when Grandpa gave a command, the tractor never would whoa! When God says "Whoa!" will you obey, or will you plow ahead in your own way?   —C. R. B.

5a. I have even from the beginning declared it to thee; before it came to pass I shewed it thee.

The first half of this verse largely repeats the thought from Isaiah 48:3 (above). Far from being merely redundant, repetition was a typical Hebrew writing convention. Whether word for word, with synonymous parallelism, or in other ways, repetition was used frequently to emphasize the importance of a point. Verse 4b (above) is an example of nearly synonymous ideas being used to strengthen an image. Watch for this repetition in the rest of Isaiah 48.

When we consider that most of Isaiah's audience would have been illiterate, and even those who could read wouldn't have a copy of his prophecies *to* read, it makes sense to lean into repetition like this. What one hears over and over again tends to stick and form one's thoughts and actions. It's no wonder that God gave the Israelites words to repeat to themselves and their children—words to form who they would be (example: Deuteronomy 6:4-9; see Isaiah 48:8a, below).

5b. Lest thou shouldest say, Mine idol hath done them, and my graven image, and my molten image, hath commanded them.

Mine idol, my graven image, and *my molten image* are another example of repetition (see Isaiah 48:5a, above); all these are ways to speak of false gods, created by human hands. Some idols were made of wood (example: 44:13-17), while others could be made of or plated with gold and silver (examples: 2:20; 30:22).

Attributing any action—good, bad, or indifferent—to an idol is pure lunacy (Isaiah 44:18-19). And yet Israel fell into this trap time after time (example: 1 Kings 17:7-17). While the Ten Commandments prohibit worshipping other gods or making images of them (Exodus 20:3-5), Moses descended the mountain after receiving this command to find that his brother, Aaron, had already broken it! He'd facilitated the making of a golden calf idol that the people were worshipping as Moses walked back into their camp (32:1-6). This was a dark blot on the history of Israel. Not only were the people worshipping things they made by hand; they were also attributing God's great works to those false gods (Isaiah 46:5-13). Nothing is more foolish than this.

> ### What Do You Think?
> What are modern-day equivalents of idols that receive credit that is due to God alone?
>
> ### Digging Deeper
> How can you guard against either taking too much credit for your own blessings or attributing them to something other than God's grace?

6a. Thou hast heard, see all this; and will not ye declare it?

Relating back to Isaiah 48:5a (above), God once again challenged the people to admit that He had told them what was to come. And what He said, they had *heard* and even seen. Still, they were unwilling to *declare* that God had done this (see lesson 6 on Isaiah 43:10-12 for more on being a witness).

B. New Things (vv. 6b-8a)

6b-7. I have shewed thee new things from this time, even hidden things, and thou didst not know them. They are created now, and not from the beginning; even before the day when thou heardest them not; lest thou shouldest say, Behold, I knew them.

The people did not want to admit that the gods they worshipped were imaginary beings and thus completely powerless. If Israel would not be convinced that this was the case even though God had told them what would happen (see Isaiah 48:3, above), would they be swayed when God *didn't* tell them in advance? The *new things* and *hidden things* were completely without prophetic warning or any other means of anticipation. No amount of foretelling would allow the people to *know* what God was going to do next.

The new things are truly novel, for they have been *created now*. Only God can create something

that has never been before (contrast Ecclesiastes 1:10). We think of the physical universe (Psalm 148:4-5), a man and a woman (Genesis 1:27), or a new heart (Psalm 51:10). Isaiah also proclaims that the Lord created the nation of Israel (Isaiah 43:1). This activity, then, is not so much the revealing of hidden things, but the display of God's creative power at any time according to His pleasure. Knowledge of such things comes at the time they are revealed and implemented, so no one can claim, *Behold, I knew them.* Impossible!

Seeing and Not Knowing

I was called years ago to lead a Christian ministry that was in decline. I caught the vision of what I believed God wanted to happen, but only a few of those plans became reality. I discerned that God was showing me new things, but I did not see them come to pass. After several years, I resigned in frustration. Under my successor's leadership, the ministry multiplied in number, strength, and outreach.

Thirty years later, I was talking with that man and was surprised when he said, "The things you said and wrote became my vision for what the ministry has become." To paraphrase God's words through Isaiah, the growth did not take place in my time, so I could not say, "Look what I have done!" But looking back over those decades, I marvel at how God has accomplished what I had dreamed of—in the way He wanted it to happen.

Visual for Lesson 7. *After discussing Isaiah 48:8a, allow one minute for self-reflection in answer to this question.*

Have you had similar experiences? Are you undergoing such challenges now? —C. R. B.

8a. Yea, thou heardest not; yea, thou knewest not; yea, from that time that thine ear was not opened.

A foundational principle for Israel's relationship with God was that Israel was to "hear" (Deuteronomy 6:4a). And what they were to hear was that "the Lord our God is one Lord" (6:4b) and to "love the Lord thy God with all thine heart, and with all thy soul, and with all thy might" (6:5; compare Mark 12:29-30). Furthermore, they were to teach what they heard to one another and their children (Deuteronomy 6:6-9).

Not to hear the Lord (and therefore not to know; see Isaiah 48:6-7, above) violates this foundational law in God's covenant with Israel. The act of truly hearing the Lord always has included obedience to what He commands (see 30:9). Because Israel had hearing that did not result in understanding (6:9), it was as though *from that time*—the beginning of their relationship with God—their *ear was not opened*. This resulted in the people's reputation of dealing "treacherously" with the Lord and being "called a transgressor from the womb" (48:8b, not in our printed text). Jesus would pick up on this language concerning those who would not or could not understand His ministry and identity (example: Matthew 13:10-15).

What Do You Think?

How can you motivate a friend or family member to listen to (obey) God's Word?

Digging Deeper

What self-reflection might be necessary to ensure that you are not trying to clear the "mote" from another's eye before addressing the "beam" in yours (Matthew 7:3)?

II. The Living God
(Isaiah 48:17)

In Isaiah 48:9-11 (not in our printed text), God asserted that it was for His own glory that He had not already punished Israel for all their disobedience. Verses 12-16 (not in our printed text) go on to assert that God would not leave Babylon unpunished for what the empire had done to Judah (compare Isaiah 13). This is another example of God's showing His previously hidden plans with the intent of demonstrating that He carries out what He promises.

A. Of Israel (v. 17a)
17a. Thus saith the LORD, thy Redeemer, the Holy One of Israel; I am the LORD thy God.

Thus saith the Lord (and variations on the phrase) is a very common way of emphasizing that God, not the prophet, is the source of the prophet's words (examples: Exodus 4:22; Joshua 24:2; Jeremiah 2:2). Going on to add *thy Redeemer, the Holy One of Israel* emphasizes the relationship between God and the people (see lesson 6; Isaiah 12:6; 44:24; 47:4; 54:5, 8). We might say that *Redeemer* reflects closeness while *Holy One* reflects distinctiveness in that relationship.

B. Who Teaches the Way (v. 17b-c)
17b. Which teacheth thee to profit.

The source and content of correct teaching is the Lord himself (see Psalm 119:68). This teaching came to Israel first in the form of the Law of Moses. We learn and grow when we do the right thing, but we also can benefit when we learn from our past sins (see 119:71).

God is not often depicted as a teacher in the Old Testament, though of course it would be appropriate to do so. But we do see Jesus called "rabbi" (John 1:38, 49; 3:2, 26; etc.). And while this is *also* appropriate, it does not reflect a complete understanding of Jesus' role. He is not only a teacher but also the Christ (Matthew 1:1). Jesus still teaches us for our own good; we do well when we obey Him (Luke 9:23-26).

17c. Which leadeth thee by the way that thou shouldest go.

The Bible frequently pictures living as a way that we travel (Genesis 6:12; Psalm 1:6; compare Matthew 7:13-14). There are good paths and bad paths, roads that lead to prosperity and those that lead to destruction (see Deuteronomy 30:15). Isaiah pictures the only wise pathway as following the Lord, living according to His teachings. The Lord is both the teacher of Israel and the way-maker for His people.

Whereas we might think a teacher would take a hands-off approach—"I've taught you, and now you must take your test"—God chooses to both teach *and* lead. The Lord does not tell His people the right way to live and then retreat to the background. This is a popular but erroneous understanding of who God is and how He chooses to interact with people. Instead, God leads His people *by the way that* they should *go*. He is like a shepherd who leads his flock of sheep to safe pastures (Psalm 23:2).

In the New Testament, it is even more striking that Jesus claims himself to be the only "way," the exclusive pathway to the Father (John 14:6). And the image from John 10 of Jesus as our shepherd resonates because we know the lengths He went to for us. This too is an imperfect metaphor. But taken with other images—including that of teacher—we get a fuller picture of who God is, and how Jesus lived as God incarnate among us (Philippians 2:6-8).

The book of Acts also refers to the Christian faith as the way. Paul's momentous trip to Damascus was occasioned by his desire to detain Jews who had begun to follow "this way" (Acts 9:2). Toward the end of Acts, Paul appeared before the Roman Governor Felix, who had a rather thorough knowledge of "that way" (24:22). Far from being a theoretical framework, our faith is the very way that we live. When our lives are in step with Jesus and the Spirit, we find ourselves traveling by the way that we should go.

What Do You Think?
Who or what is your secondary teacher of "the way" you should go?
Digging Deeper
What can you do to develop "the mind of Christ" (1 Corinthians 2:16) in order to adhere ever more closely to the correct way?

Conclusion
A. Living, Learning

The tragedy of Israel's history is that God had revealed many things to them: His law, His will for their nation, His choices of leaders, and so on. Despite the long history of such revelations, the nation often acted as though the people did not have ears to hear. Time after time, Israel ignored the Lord's directives and warnings.

Iron-necked Judah would not change its course of action despite the warnings of the Lord's prophets, making punishment inevitable. We have a major advantage: we are empowered by the Spirit to grow in our relationship with the Father and become more like Jesus each day. When we do so, we will be better able to hear warnings when we are following a way not set out by the Lord. And we will have ears hearing what the Lord is doing as He calls to us to join His work. Listen for the call!

What Do You Think?
Which concept in today's lesson do you find most challenging?
Digging Deeper
Which concept do you find most encouraging?

B. Prayer

Lord God, forgive us for the times we have been too stubborn to seek You and Your will for our lives. Please give us ears to hear so that we can follow Your way. All this we pray in Jesus' name. Amen.

C. Thought to Remember
Learn from the Lord and follow in His ways.

How to Say It

Cyrus	*Sigh*-russ.
Hittites	*Hit*-ites or *Hi*-tites.
Isaiah	Eye-*zay*-uh.
Messiah	Meh-*sigh*-uh.
Persian	*Per*-zhen
rabbi	*rab*-eye.

Involvement Learning

Enhance your lesson with KJV Bible Student *(from your curriculum supplier) and the reproducible activity page (at www.standardlesson.com or in the back of the* KJV Standard Lesson Commentary Deluxe Edition*).*

Into the Lesson

Write *Stubborn* on the board as a header. Below this header write *Positive / Negative* as the headers of two columns. Begin the lesson by having learners divide into pairs to look up the word *stubborn* in a digital thesaurus. Have pairs brainstorm situations when stubbornness can be an asset and when it can be a liability. Allow time for pairs to discuss together which definitions feel negative (such as "cantankerous" and "pigheaded") and which suggest a positive trait (such as "determined" and "steadfast"). Have them jot down examples of the negative (when stubbornness can be a liability) and examples of the positive (when it can be an asset).

After several minutes, convene the whole group for discussion on their findings, and follow up asking how to recognize a spiritual fork in the road. What is necessary to choose wisely? Say, "Today we'll learn about God's warnings for Israel and for us about being stubborn against His warnings."

Alternative. Distribute copies of "The Googles Know" exercise from the activity page, which you can download. Have learners work in pairs to complete as indicated. Discuss conclusions as a group. Say: "While technologies may seem to 'know' us, today's passage illustrates how nothing is hidden from God and that only He controls and reveals the future—at His pleasure."

Into the Word

Have a volunteer read aloud Isaiah 48:3-8a, 17. Divide the class into pairs. Distribute handouts of the questions below (you create) for in-group discussion. Instruct pairs to find a verse or phrase from the lesson text that relates to each statement. Then they are to indicate who they think is speaking.

1. "You have ears to hear, but you are not using them!"
2. "If I want another good harvest, I'd better pray to my fertility idol."

3. "God said He would send a plague of hail on the Egyptians, and He did just like He said—on them, but not on us."
4. "I am your Redeemer, and I will teach you what you need to know and guide you on the right path."
5. "You are stiff-necked and stubborn and keep refusing to listen to me."
6. "Sure, it sounds like new information, but I already knew that!"
7. "Why can't you admit that when I tell you something is going to happen, it always does?"

(*Answers*: 1. God [v. 8a]; 2. idol-worshiping Israelite [v. 5b]; 3. Israelite slave in Egypt [v. 3]; 4. the Lord God [v. 17]; 5. God to Israelites [v. 4]; 6. Israelite [v. 7]; 7. God [v. 6].)

After learners have completed this exercise, ask for pairs to volunteer their answers. As a whole class discuss together, "What are some ways God's people were being stubborn and not listening to Him or not giving God credit for the things He had done?"

Into Life

Ask learners to read Isaiah 48:4 and Ezekiel 3:10. Use a minute of silence for individual reflection regarding which of the two verses better reflects the nature of each person's response to the words of the Lord. With a partner, allow each learner time to identify a personal disconnect with hearing, seeing, or acknowledging God's words and outline a plan for change.

Ask learners to read Isaiah 48:17 again. Have them discuss ways they can learn God's leading and teaching. Distribute index cards and ask learners to write down one way they will lean into God's leading this week.

Alternative. Distribute copies of the "Win or Learn" activity from the activity page. Have learners complete it individually (in one minute) before discussing conclusions in small groups.

God Promises Light

Devotional Reading: Ephesians 5:11-20
Background Scripture: Isaiah 58:1-14

Isaiah 58:6-10

6 Is not this the fast that I have chosen? to loose the bands of wickedness, to undo the heavy burdens, and to let the oppressed go free, and that ye break every yoke?

7 Is it not to deal thy bread to the hungry, and that thou bring the poor that are cast out to thy house? when thou seest the naked, that thou cover him; and that thou hide not thyself from thine own flesh?

8 Then shall thy light break forth as the morning, and thine health shall spring forth speedily: and thy righteousness shall go before thee; the glory of the LORD shall be thy rereward.

9 Then shalt thou call, and the LORD shall answer; thou shalt cry, and he shall say, Here I am. If thou take away from the midst of thee the yoke, the putting forth of the finger, and speaking vanity;

10 And if thou draw out thy soul to the hungry, and satisfy the afflicted soul; then shall thy light rise in obscurity, and thy darkness be as the noonday.

Key Text

If thou draw out thy soul to the hungry and satisfy the afflicted soul; then shall thy light rise in obscurity, and thy darkness be as the noonday. —**Isaiah 58:10**

From Darkness to Light

Unit 2: God's Promises
Lessons 5–9

Lesson Aims

After participating in this lesson, each learner will be able to:

1. Identify what results in light breaking forth.

2. Explain the context of the three undesirable actions of Isaiah 58:9b.

3. Propose a way to honor Isaiah 58:10a personally today.

Lesson Outline

Introduction

A. Persistent Poverty

Government agencies and academic researchers have good reason to study why poverty persists. Their studies have produced specialized vocabulary, with terms such as "food insecurity," "persistent poverty regions," and "economic blight." The official poverty rate in America consistently hovers at around 10 percent of the population, with some counties having rates over 30 percent. Every community has poor people in its midst, folks struggling to have adequate food, clothing, and housing.

Isaiah repeatedly addressed care for *all* people, exhorting his hearers to recognize the poor among them and offer relief. This week's lesson has wonderful, timeless teaching for us as we consider the Christian's obligations to the poor in our churches and communities.

B. Lesson Context

This is now our third lesson from the book of Isaiah, so the Lesson Contexts of the previous two lessons apply to this one as well. Our text, found in Isaiah 58, focuses on fasting, though not as the audience would have expected.

The essence of fasting is self-denial. The intent behind this practice is typically understood as being reminded of complete dependence on the Lord, as Jesus expressed during His temptation (Matthew 4:1-4; compare Luke 12:22-31). Fasting on a regular and devout basis could earn the respect of the community. For example, a heroine of the Jews who lived in the intertestamental times, Judith, was renowned for her extensive fasting practices, said to have occurred all the days of her widowhood (see the non-biblical Judith 8:6). Community fasting was a solemn event for the people of Israel (1 Samuel 7:6; Esther 4:1-3, 15-17; 9:31-32; Joel 1:14-15; contrast 1 Kings 21:9-12). Fasting could be an appropriate personal condition for a dedicated time of prayer (2 Samuel 12:16, 21-23; Nehemiah 1:4; Daniel 9:3). It was for the humbling of the soul (Psalm 35:13).

Unfortunately, fasting could easily become an empty ritual, more about recognition for Judah's own piety than as a spiritual discipline (see Zechariah 7:5-6; Matthew 6:16-18; Luke 18:9-14). In that vein, Isaiah begins chapter 58 by loudly declaring the rebellion and hypocrisy of Israel (Isaiah 58:1-2). The people invited that critique by pointing to their fasts (58:3a) as evidence of their humility, only for God to point out what should have been the obvious error in their way: fasting gave the appearance of humility, but it actually resulted in exploitation (58:3b) and violence (58:4)! "Wilt thou call this a fast, and an acceptable day to the Lord?" (58:5). What kind of fast does God *really* desire?

I. God's Chosen Fast
(Isaiah 58:6-7)
A. Break Every Yoke (v. 6)

6a. Is not this the fast that I have chosen?

Isaiah 58:7 (below) begins with a similar question. *This* refers to what follows rather than what came before, which is demonstrably not what God desires (58:1-5, not in our printed text). The resulting lines of parallel thoughts help our understanding, as those parallels serve to interpret each other. The overall effect is to make crystal clear the kind of *fast* God desires.

And sadly, this might offer insight into the wickedness of the people Isaiah was addressing. Is it possible that to this audience, actively pursuing righteousness amounted only to "fasting" from the evil habits they enjoyed? After all, unscrupulous and unrighteous actions were (and still are) one way to become and remain wealthy or powerful. Giving up wickedness as a fast speaks to how the people benefitted from their injustice and to the pain they would feel giving it up.

6b. To loose the bands of wickedness.

Although the actions are named as the Lord's chosen fast for Israel (see commentary on Isaiah 58:6c-7a, below), the list does not read as things to avoid doing. Instead, these actions have more to do with adding righteous actions and actively obeying the law than with giving up negative or neutral actions.

Hebrew poetry often uses parallelism of thoughts or phrases to emphasize a point, so we can assume that the actions listed here through Isaiah 58:7 are tightly connected and will help interpret each other. *Wickedness* is a broad category and can describe any sinful habits that need to be repented of and discarded. Given Isaiah's preaching against idolatry (example: 2:8, 18, 20), we might think of all the wickedness that false gods were thought to condone. The first evil of idolatry is giving any credit to an idol when *all* credit belongs to the Creator and Lord alone (example: 40:18-26). All other idolatrous sins grow out of this.

To describe wickedness as *bands* to be loosened suggests that the people were entrapped by wickedness, whether of their own doing or that of society at large. Such restraints could only be escaped with outside help. Ultimately only the Lord could *loose* these restraints, though the people are called to participate in the work. In order to experience freedom granted by God, the people needed to repent of the sinful thoughts and actions that prevented them from having God's blessing.

6c. To undo the heavy burdens.

The word translated *heavy burdens* is also translated "cords" elsewhere in the *King James Version* (Job 36:8; Psalms 129:4; 140:5; Proverbs 5:22; Isaiah 5:18; 54:2), and that is the sense here. This phrase might turn our thoughts to the exodus, when the pharaoh gave the people more and more work to do, out of fear that they would escape or become powerful in their own right (Exodus 5:4-18). This injustice explained the command to follow Sabbath regulations—time when each man, woman, child, and even *animal* was to be given rest (Deuteronomy 5:12-15; see Isaiah 58:6e, below). Jesus' so-called woes pronounced to the Pharisees and other legal experts is evidence that, sadly, the problem of legalistic adherence to *some* laws (or human traditions; see Mark 7:8-13) would persist. And often the laws set aside were those concerned with justice and mercy (see Matthew 23:4; Luke 11:37-54).

6d. And to let the oppressed go free.

Letting *the oppressed go free* sounds like Year of Jubilee language, when slaves were to be emancipated and familial lands returned from essentially being rented out for up to 50 years (Leviticus

25:10-13). This language is closely related to sabbath-year language (25:4), though the Jubilee was intended to occur only every 50 years. This concept also relates to the exodus; the reason Israel was to care for the stranger (a vulnerable person because of the lack of familial ties to Israel) was because of their own experience in Egypt (19:34; compare Luke 4:18). Zechariah 7:10 lists various categories of oppressed people.

A Spirit That Oppresses Others

After the Japanese attack on Pearl Harbor on December 7, 1941, intense fear of and violence against Americans of Japanese descent living in the United States exploded. One result was internment camps erected in California and other states. At the time, it was argued that such a measure was necessary for America's defense—although a much smaller number of Americans of German and Italian descent received such treatment.

After the war was over, my wife developed friendships with several Japanese people who had been forcibly relocated to one such camp in the barren desert of eastern California. She heard their sad stories.

In a verse just preceding today's text (Isaiah 58:4), God says anger and violence destroy our relationship with Him. Can there be any doubt what God thinks about us if we claim to be Christians yet hate others—as evidenced by discrimination (James 2:1-13) and violence (Galatians 5:15)? What steps do you take to silence your own evil thoughts (2 Corinthians 10:5) and so prevent sinful actions against those who are different from you?   —C. R. B.

> ### What Do You Think?
> How can you identify oppression in your community?
> ### Digging Deeper
> What resources are available to you to 1) identify oppression and 2) discover who to learn from and work with to address the problem?

6e. And that ye break every yoke?

Sometimes the yoke symbolized an invading nation that gained control over the people of Israel (example: Isaiah 14:25). In that regard, a yoke symbolized oppression, compelled obedience to a master (example: Jeremiah 27:2). While yoking farm animals often was necessary for them to do their work, the image of yoking people was one of grave cruelty. It suggested that the yoked ones were less than human and could be treated as such.

But the Lord had commanded that even animals be allowed to rest from their work on the Sabbath (Exodus 20:10; Deuteronomy 5:14). If He cared for the beasts, how much more the people (Matthew 10:29-31)? And all people are created in the image of God (Genesis 1:27). Treating even one person by lower standards than the standards for a beast of burden is a failure to recognize God's great care for those made in His image. The culmination of God's fast entails breaking the metaphorical *yoke* so that it could not be used again to oppress anyone (see lesson 7).

B. Provide for Any Need (v. 7)

7a. Is it not to deal thy bread to the hungry, and that thou bring the poor that are cast out to thy house? when thou seest the naked, that thou cover him.

Withholding food from *the hungry* results in an ironic, horrifying, forced fast. The appropriate fast would be to turn from these evils (see commentary on Isaiah 58:6b-6e, above) and care for *the poor* and *the naked*. In each instance, the solution is to care appropriately for the need of the person. The people should "fast" from the active wickedness of the sins of commission and "gorge" on opportunities that, if ignored, would be sins of omission.

Jesus took this a step further, teaching that what was done to the hungry, thirsty, etc., was also done to *Him* (Matthew 25:31-46). We show love for God by loving those who are made in His

How to Say It

Immanuel	Ih-*man*-you-el.
Isaiah	Eye-*zay*-uh.
pharaoh	*fair*-o or *fay*-roe.

image (example: Luke 10:25-37; see commentary on Isaiah 58:6e, above). And while we are saved only by faith in Jesus rather than works of the law (Romans 3:21-26), the fruit of the Spirit and the works of our hands are evidence of that faith (Galatians 5:22-23; James 2:14-20).

What Do You Think?

What resources do you currently devote to caring for impoverished people?

Digging Deeper

Considering that this care is one way of expressing devotion to God, are there any other resources you would consider devoting to aid the poor?

7b. And that thou hide not thyself from thine own flesh?

The family unit has been the basic building block of societies since ancient times. When we can count on no one else, we expect to be able to call on our family members for help. Even when this is not the case, deep down we feel we *should* be able to call on our relatives. Hiding *from thine own flesh* thus represents a particularly painful example of refusing to offer appropriate aid. In a community where not even families care for one another, what hope is there for the widow, the orphan, or the foreigner who lives without the same safety net? Loving one's own people is basic righteousness, something Jesus says even the publicans do (Matthew 5:46)!

A Growing Crisis

Homelessness has proven a difficult problem to solve in many countries. People end up being homeless for a variety of reasons, including untreated mental illness, addiction, and catastrophic financial reversals. If people experiencing homelessness have "housing" at all, it may begin with expensive motel stays and move on to their living under bridges, in shelters, in tent cities, or even in cardboard boxes.

My good friend Brad sensed the call of God to minister to these souls. Many are elderly, with no family support system. Brad sees firsthand the despair and loneliness his homeless friends feel.

Visual for Lesson 8. *While discussing verse 10, ask the class to consider the difference between walking in the light and living as (shining) the light.*

They testify to feeling invisible as we more fortunate ones avert our eyes when we walk by them.

God, through the prophet Isaiah, reminded Israel of the burden of caring for the needy. We also carry this weighty responsibility. Consider James 1:27: "Pure religion and undefiled before God and the Father is this, To visit the fatherless and widows in their affliction." Realizing that the word *visit* in the *King James Version* signifies "care for," how is your congregation involved in ministry to the homeless? How can you become more involved personally?
—C. R. B.

II. A Bright Future
(Isaiah 58:8-10)
A. God's Protection (vv. 8-9a)

8a. Then shall thy light break forth as the morning.

Light has long been associated with right conduct and knowledge thereof (see especially 2 Samuel 23:4). When the Israelites lived, or walked, in the light as fresh and bright *as the morning* (Psalms 36:9; 37:6; see commentary on Isaiah 58:10, below), they were shown to have nothing to hide. And by living as light they could fulfill their calling: to be a priestly nation ministering to a dark world, revealing the righteous God through word and deed (Exodus 19:6).

The blessing and calling to live as light continues into the church. Jesus saw himself as a light to a dark world (John 12:46). Paul admonished the Ephesians to live as "children of light" (Ephesians 5:8), and Peter reminded his readers that their faith had the effect of bringing them from the darkness to the light (1 Peter 2:9; see lesson 13). Living as light should be the desire of every Christian; such a life does away with selfishness and hypocrisy.

8b. And thine health shall spring forth speedily.

It would be easy to over-spiritualize restoration of *health* and assume that this *only* applies to spiritual healing. Undoubtedly there is a strong element of spiritual care and health here. However, we know that God is concerned with the whole person—mind, body, and spirit—and this is made evident in Jesus' own ministry (see examples in Mark 5). By extension, this relates to the health of God's chosen community as well. When the most vulnerable people are cared for, society has the potential to function well. This is God's desire for all people, and this is what was promised to Israel if they turned back to God in sincerity.

8c. And thy righteousness shall go before thee.

Israel's *righteousness* here is a metaphor for the Lord himself, similar to His military might (Exodus 15:3; Psalm 18:1-2, 13-14; etc.). He would once again be the advance guard, as armor against the wicked (compare Exodus 13:21-22; 14:19-25).

8d. The glory of the LORD shall be thy rereward.

The vanguard of righteousness would be complemented by the rearguard protection of *the glory of the Lord* (see Isaiah 52:12). *Rereward* is an old English term referring to the rearguard of an advancing army (compare Joshua 6:9, 13). This strengthens the apparent allusion to the exodus (see commentary on Isaiah 58:8c, above). The people would be protected on all sides and in all ways by the Lord himself.

9a. Then shalt thou call, and the LORD shall answer; thou shalt cry, and he shall say, Here I am.

It is easy to assume that a feeling of God's absence or silence is evidence that He "hidest . . . in times of trouble" (Psalm 10:1). The biblical evidence is mixed regarding God's attention when we feel He is far away. On the one hand, Job experienced the loss of his fortune and family as God's absence, even though we know by reading the book that God was present throughout Job's heartbreak (Job 1:1–2:10; 42:7-17). But God himself asserted that He would punish the people when they sinned and failed to repent (Deuteronomy 31:16-21; Lamentations 5:19-22); examples of this are found not only in the exile when repentance came too late but also in the cycles of repentance found in the book of Judges (example: Judges 2:10-19).

In the case at hand, the Lord had deliberately turned away from the people. So His choosing to *answer* their *call* really would be evidence that He was choosing to hear and to bless once again. And the ultimate fulfillment of God's answering with *Here I am* was to come in Immanuel—Jesus—about whom Isaiah had prophesied (Isaiah 7:14; Matthew 1:23). In Jesus and through the Spirit we experience God among us.

What Do You Think?

In what ways can you expect the blessings of Isaiah 58:8-9a to come about as a consequence of righteousness in action?

Digging Deeper

How can you continue to do what is right without becoming overly motivated by your own expected blessing?

B. God's Promise (vv. 9b-10)

9b. If thou take away from the midst of thee the yoke, the putting forth of the finger, and speaking vanity.

This is the first time that fasting language—*take away*—is used in place of affirmative commands. Still, this language echoes what has already been stated (see commentary on Isaiah 58:6, above). This is a reaffirmation of the need for justice in the community at all levels and active easing of the effects of grinding poverty.

The putting forth of the finger—a Hebrew phrase unique to this verse—seems to be the pointing of an accusing finger at someone, an insulting sign of disrespect (compare Proverbs 6:13). In context, it is another mark of arrogance and hypocrisy in the wicked in their treatment of unfortunate members of their society.

The word translated *vanity* is often found in Isaiah as "iniquity" (Isaiah 1:13; 31:2; 59:6-7, 12). It can have the sense of emptiness, but also of a falseness with evil intent. The heart saturated with iniquity blocks the prayers of such a person (Psalm 66:18). A society that becomes a slave to falsehood is an evil place and will not be blessed by the Lord. It becomes a chaotic, self-destructive place (see 7:14-16).

10. And if thou draw out thy soul to the hungry, and satisfy the afflicted soul; then shall thy light rise in obscurity, and thy darkness be as the noonday.

This verse echoes the fast that God desired, starting with the *if* statement (see commentary on Isaiah 58:6a-7, above), and the blessings that would follow according to the *then* clause (see commentary on 58:8a-9b). The result of getting these priorities in order would be lives of *light*. The image of *darkness be as the noonday* is one of the complete dispelling of all that darkness represents: selfishness, insincere worship, hypocritical fasting, and all manner of other sinfulness.

The chapter closes with positive metaphors of Israel as a garden and a rebuilt city (Isaiah 58:11-12, not in our printed text).

> **What Do You Think?**
> Which "if" statement of Isaiah 58:9b-10 is more compelling to you? Why?
> **Digging Deeper**
> What is a concrete example of working toward greater justice by shining brightly as a light from the Lord?

Conclusion

A. Fasting Today

Isaiah pushed Israel to understand that what God deems important is not a temporary willingness to fast from food, but a spiritual health that leads to righteous behavior. So we might ask ourselves two questions: Do I go through ritualistic motions on a regular basis instead of allowing my heart to really be turned toward God during those practices? What "fast" might I need to undertake to align myself with the type of fasting God desires?

A just and caring community will consider the "hungry" in all aspects Isaiah has already defined: food, clothing, and housing (Isaiah 58:7). How can we feel comfortable in our abundance if we know there is suffering in our neighborhoods (1 John 3:17)? It may be impossible for any one individual to meet every community need, but this does not excuse us from keeping our eyes open to the plight of others or striving to meet the needs we see.

Experience has taught me that I am most successful with fasting if I practice it in community, with at least one partner. Then the limits of the fast are mutually agreed on and there is an accountability that helps keep me focused and faithful to the practice. Maybe you should seek a "fasting partner" who will share the experience and grow with you. That way you can grow in grace and truth together (see John 1:14, 17).

> **What Do You Think?**
> Which concept in today's lesson do you find most challenging?
> **Digging Deeper**
> Which concept do you find most encouraging?

B. Prayer

Lord God, give us hearts that seek a lifelong "fast" from the pleasures of sin and an ongoing "feast" of obedience to You. May we not be guilty of making a show out of our religious actions while having hearts of stone. Give us a character that cares about the needy, abstains from pointing fingers at others, loves and practices truth, and reflects the light of Your Word. We pray in Jesus' name. Amen.

C. Thought to Remember

Fasting is meaningless without a heart of repentance and humility.

Involvement Learning

Enhance your lesson with KJV Bible Student *(from your curriculum supplier) and the reproducible activity page (at www.standardlesson.com or in the back of the* KJV Standard Lesson Commentary Deluxe Edition*).*

Into the Lesson

Before class, prepare the following four placards and post them on the wall in the four corners of your classroom: "I've not had much contact with people living in poverty." "I've found ways to help people living in poverty." "When I or someone I know was living in poverty, here's how help came." "I saw someone lift themselves out of poverty."

To begin today's session, read the four placards aloud and ask class members, "Which of these statements best applies to you?" Ask learners to go stand in the corner for the statement they chose. (If your group might be reluctant to move around, position the placards at four different tables or locations.) Give them several minutes to share their stories with those near the same placard, each explaining why they chose that statement.

After discussions are completed, ask volunteers to share with the whole class something they said or something they heard in their group.

Lead into Bible study by saying, "Today we'll consider one passage that tells God's people how to respond to poverty and need. As we study, reflect on how your experience resonates with God's instruction."

Into the Word

Distribute blank sheets of paper. Ask learners to write two headings across the top: *To Do* and *To Receive*. Down the left side of their sheets, they should write the verse numbers in today's text (6, 7, 8, 9, 10).

Divide the class into groups of three or four. Ask groups to read Isaiah 58:6-10 and then complete the sheet. All the instructions to God's people from this text should be noted under the first heading. The resulting blessings God's people can receive should be noted under the second heading. Each entry should be beside the verse number that corresponds. Give class members about eight minutes for their study before allowing volunteers to report to the whole class. Write the two headings on the board and complete the chart as the group discusses so everyone can see the same conclusions at the same time.

Alternative 1. Distribute copies of the "Compare the Passages" exercise from the activity page, which you can download. Have groups work to complete as indicated.

Alternative 2. Distribute copies of the "Passage Prompts" activity from the activity page. Have groups complete as indicated.

Into Life

Ask, "How contemporary do the concerns in today's Scripture sound to you? How do these Bible verses shed light on the experiences you shared at the beginning of class?"

Write on the board (or on a large poster) these headers of three columns: *How can our church help those living in poverty? / How could our group help those living in poverty? / How can you personally help those living in poverty?* Lead the class to complete three brainstorming lists, allowing two minutes for each column. Note any responses that appear under more than one heading. As a group, talk about why those actions should be in more than one column.

Ask members to work in pairs to decide which of the items on your lists would be best to choose first. After a few minutes, reconvene the class and either decide on a project for the class to pursue or allow volunteers to share how they will follow up on ideas under the third brainstorming list.

Alternative. Ask a representative from a local food bank, shelter, or clothing ministry to share about their work and what needs they have for volunteer support. Provide plenty of time for questions and answers. Come to a decision about how your learners as a group can serve this ministry. Otherwise, make sure the representative describes the ways individuals could choose to get involved.

God Promises His Presence

Devotional Reading: Exodus 33:12-23
Background Scripture: Joel 1:1-4; 2:18-31

Joel 2:21-27

21 Fear not, O land; be glad and rejoice: for the LORD will do great things.

22 Be not afraid, ye beasts of the field: for the pastures of the wilderness do spring, for the tree beareth her fruit, the fig tree and the vine do yield their strength.

23 Be glad then, ye children of Zion, and rejoice in the LORD your God: for he hath given you the former rain moderately, and he will cause to come down for you the rain, the former rain, and the latter rain in the first month.

24 And the floors shall be full of wheat, and the fats shall overflow with wine and oil.

25 And I will restore to you the years that the locust hath eaten, the cankerworm, and the caterpiller, and the palmerworm, my great army which I sent among you.

26 And ye shall eat in plenty, and be satisfied, and praise the name of the LORD your God, that hath dealt wondrously with you: and my people shall never be ashamed.

27 And ye shall know that I am in the midst of Israel, and that I am the LORD your God, and none else: and my people shall never be ashamed.

Key Text

Ye shall know that I am in the midst of Israel, and that I am the LORD your God, and none else: and my people shall never be ashamed. —**Joel 2:27**

Photo © Getty Images

From Darkness to Light

Lesson Aims

After participating in this lesson, each learner will be able to:

1. List elements of cause and effect.
2. Compare and contrast the positive and negative imperatives in today's text.
3. Express confident assurance of God's presence in his or her life now.

Lesson Outline

Introduction

A. Rebuilding After Loss

In 1874, swarms of grasshoppers swept through parts of the Great Plains of North America and laid waste to crops, wood, paper, and even people's clothing. These kinds of insects measure no more than one-and-a-half inches long, but when numbered in the billions, they have the potential to destroy thousands of acres of crops. The result of the destruction was total; people reported that land appeared as if it had been ravaged by wildfire.

Immigrants to Kansas were among the hardest hit by the swarms. People's livelihoods depended on bountiful crops, but the crops had been devoured and were no more. The renewal of the land and the restoration of the people took years and required assistance from the entire nation.

A natural disaster of this level feels foreign for modern readers who have never experienced it. However, many people in today's world still suffer hardship because of destructive plagues of insects. The people of Judah and the prophet Joel could report on this type of destruction firsthand. Both the people *and* their land needed wondrous and miraculous renewal.

B. Lesson Context

Several uncertainties surround the composition of the book of Joel. The book opens by stating that what follows is "the word of the Lord that came to Joel the son of Pethuel" (Joel 1:1). The name Joel was common in the Old Testament era (examples: 1 Chronicles 4:35; 5:4, 12; 6:33, 36; 7:3; 11:38; 15:7; 27:20; 2 Chronicles 29:12; Ezra 10:43; Nehemiah 11:9). Beyond the prophet's name and the name of his father, other personal details regarding this specific Joel are unavailable to us.

Several possibilities exist regarding the composition date of the book of Joel. Traditional interpretations date it to the ninth century BC. The era of King Joash (ruled 835–795 BC) is frequently listed as a possible backdrop for Joel's prophecy (see 2 Kings 12; 2 Chronicles 24).

However, other theories place the book in a postexilic context, after 538 BC. If Joel wrote in this context, then he was lamenting what had happened to Jerusalem (Joel 3:17) and held hope for God's vengeance against foreign aggressors (3:1-16). Some details behind the composition of the book of Joel may never be discovered. That fact should not dissuade modern readers from taking seriously the prophet's warnings and promises.

Joel directed his prophetic message to the people of Judah and the city of Jerusalem (Joel 2:21). The book opens by describing a plague of insects that destroyed the crops of Judah (1:2-12, 17-20; 2:1-11). The once fruitful land of Judah became barren by the destructive insects. Because of the land's desolation, the people of Judah lived in famine and in want. Joel interpreted the destruction as the consequences of Judah's sin, and he called his audience to return to the Lord and repent (2:12-14; compare 2 Chronicles 6:28-31; Amos 4:6-11).

The Lord saw the turmoil in the land and the suffering of His people. Though the people had sinned, He had compassion for them (compare Exodus 34:6; Nehemiah 9:17). The Lord was "jealous for his land" and showed "pity" for His people (Joel 2:18). He demonstrated His care by promising His people renewed sustenance (2:19) and protection from foreign enemies (2:20). His renewal would cause His people and their land to prosper. Because of His compassion, His greatness would be on display for His people and the whole world.

I. God's Renewal
(Joel 2:21-25)
A. Fearless Occasion (v. 21)

21. Fear not, O land; be glad and rejoice: for the LORD will do great things.

The command to *fear not* appears at least 50 times in the Old Testament. Sometimes this command came directly from God (Genesis 15:1; 21:17; Joshua 8:1; Isaiah 41:14; etc.). At other times, the command came from God's prophet (Exodus 20:20; 1 Samuel 12:20; etc.). Despite the people's hardship, they could take comfort in knowing that God was present; they had no reason to fear their situation (Isaiah 41:10-14; 43:1, 5; 54:14; etc.).

However, the command was not directed toward a person, but toward the *land* of Judah. The land had become distressed through a series of disasters (Joel 1:4, 6-7, 10-12; see Lesson Context), brought about on "the day of the Lord" (1:15; 2:11). God's promised redemption, however, would undo the results of those disasters and bring renewal to the land of Judah.

Though the land's desolation was evident, it was commanded to *be glad and rejoice* (compare Zephaniah 3:14-15). The greatness and might of *the Lord* would be on display through His acts of restoration (see 3:16-17). God had done *great things* for the people as they came out of bondage in Egypt (Exodus 7–14; 2 Samuel 7:21-23; Psalm 106:21). God would continue to do the same for His people and their land.

B. Fruitful Land (vv. 22-25)

22. Be not afraid, ye beasts of the field: for the pastures of the wilderness do spring, for the tree beareth her fruit, the fig tree and the vine do yield their strength.

Joel described how the beasts of the field "groan" (Joel 1:18) and "cry" (1:20) because of the destruction of their habitats. Fire, drought, and swarms of insects had destroyed the land; *the pastures* and the fields were laid waste (1:10). The land was uninhabitable for all of creation (compare Jeremiah 9:10-11).

However, the Lord's great work of restoration (Joel 1:21, above) would come to the creatures of the land—they had no reason to fear! The Lord's restoration of *the wilderness* reflects the connectedness among God's creation. Only a fruitful land could sustain animals, livestock, and humans. Centuries later, Jesus taught that God provides for all of His creation, even the smallest animals (see Matthew 6:26; Luke 12:24-28).

Previously, vines were wasted and dried up, while the bark of the fig trees was stripped, leaving the trees to decay (Joel 1:7, 11). However, the land's restoration brought renewed provision for the people. A fruitful *vine* and *fig tree* showed that the people lived in safety and flourished (see 1 Kings 4:25; Micah 4:4; Zechariah 3:10). An ideal and good land easily supported grapevines and fig trees (see Deuteronomy 8:8). The agricultural renewal would bring about a settled population and would mark the end of the season of destruction (see Joel 1:11-12, 16-20).

> **What Do You Think?**
> How can believers praise God for His care over creation?
>
> **Digging Deeper**
> How can believers engage in creation care as an act of worship to God without worshipping creation itself?

23. Be glad then, ye children of Zion, and rejoice in the LORD your God: for he hath given you the former rain moderately, and he will cause to come down for you the rain, the former rain, and the latter rain in the first month.

This verse and the surrounding verses do not merely provide information regarding the climate and planting practices of the time. Instead, this verse directed the celebration of the land and the inhabitants of Jerusalem. *Zion* is another name for the city of Jerusalem (see 1 Kings 8:1; Joel 2:1).

Because of the Lord's restoration, the people would experience joy and gladness, feelings that were lost because of the turmoil (see Joel 1:16). The *Lord . . . God* who seemed absent during disaster would deliver His people and be present with them as their true king (see Psalm 149:2).

The underlying Hebrew word translated *moderately* is translated elsewhere as "righteousness" (example: Amos 5:7) or "justice" (example: Isaiah 56:1). God showed justice to His people by allowing the return of the rains, thus bringing an end to the drought. When the people returned to God, His justice would be fulfilled, and He would show compassion (Joel 2:13).

The types of rains described in this verse reversed the land's harsh drought (Joel 1:17). The previously described agricultural growth (2:21-22, above) would be the result of renewed seasons of rain (see James 5:7). *Former rain* came in the late

fall season during the month of Tishri (also known as Ethanim; see 1 Kings 8:2), and it helped soften the ground for sowing new crops. *Latter rain* fell during Nisan, *the first month* of Israel's religious calendar (corresponding to parts of March and April). This springtime rain brought necessary moisture to the ground prior to the harvest season. The land would return to a natural cycle of rainy and dry seasons and would experience no more drought (see Leviticus 26:4; Deuteronomy 11:14).

What is in view here is drought that came as a result of the people's failure to follow God (compare Jeremiah 50:38; Haggai 1:11). Drought results in famine, which was also a consequence for the people's failure to follow God (Ezekiel 5:17; Amos 8:11). By promising a return to consistent rainy seasons, God showed that He is faithful to care for His people and their land. He would treat His people rightly, as His justice poured down on the people and led to salvation (see Isaiah 45:8).

The Year Without a Summer

The year 1816 has been declared the Year Without a Summer. Mount Tambora, a volcano located in Indonesia, had erupted violently a year before. The resulting volcanic ash circled the globe and obstructed sunlight as far away as Europe and North America. Daily average temperatures dropped. A New York newspaper noted that parts of the state saw hard frosts during every month of that summer. Food shortages were unavoidable, leading some people to call that year "eighteen-hundred and starve-to-death." The world would recover, but only after several years passed.

During the time of Joel's proclamation, the people of Judah experienced a locust plague and famine. However, the prophet proclaimed that God's people should rejoice. Restoration would come and rains would return to the land.

Joel's words were intended as comfort to God's people—their restoration was at hand! What prevents you from hearing God's promises? Might your own sinful attitudes stand in the way? —C. R. B.

24. And the floors shall be full of wheat, and the fats shall overflow with wine and oil.

Rather than experience famine, the people

would see tangible examples of the Lord's blessing (compare Deuteronomy 7:13; Jeremiah 31:12).

A person would separate usable grain from husks and chaff at threshing *floors* (see commentary on Luke 3:17, lesson 3). Grains like wheat and seed like corn supplied the people with the means for sustenance. The land's restoration would be evident as the people contrasted previously "wasted" fields (Joel 1:10) with threshing floors *full of wheat*.

The underlying Hebrew word translated here as *fats* elsewhere speaks of presses for *wine* (Isaiah 16:10; Jeremiah 48:33). The first step in the creation of both olive *oil* and wine was to crush the fruit by a press or underfoot (Micah 6:15). The presses would *overflow* because of the bountiful harvest (see Proverbs 3:10). No longer would God's people have to live hand to mouth. Malachi prophesied of a similar blessing as God promised to "pour you out a blessing, that there shall not be room enough to receive it" (Malachi 3:10).

Wine and oil were an important part of everyday life of God's people. The two liquids were used for offerings to God (Exodus 29:40; Leviticus 23:13; Ezra 6:9) and indicated the presence of His blessing (Deuteronomy 7:13). They were also used at military defenses (2 Chronicles 11:11), perhaps for their medicinal properties (see Luke 10:34). The goodness of the Lord was displayed for His people through wine, oil, and wheat (Jeremiah 31:12).

Visual for Lesson 9. *Show this visual as you discuss the commentary and Digging Deeper question associated with Joel 2:21.*

What Do You Think?

How can you share with your neighbors from the overflow of your life's blessings?

Digging Deeper

How can believers avoid a "we won't have enough left" mindset in regard to such sharing?

25. And I will restore to you the years that the locust hath eaten, the cankerworm, and the caterpiller, and the palmerworm, my great army which I sent among you.

Joel's prophecy began by describing the land's destruction by several types of insects (Joel 1:4). In the ancient Near East, as in the current day, invasive insects could number in the billions as their swarms came on a particular land. These swarms would "spoileth" the land by eating the entirety of a land's vegetation, before swarming elsewhere (Nahum 3:16). Complete destruction followed these swarms: vines destroyed, vegetation ruined, and tree bark stripped (Joel 1:7). As a result, the people living in these lands frequently experienced famine (see Psalm 105:34-35).

The text's distinctions regarding the insects are not entirely clear to modern readers. Students have proposed that *the cankerworm, the caterpiller,* and *the palmerworm* are all different stages of *locust* development. Another interpretation is that the described insects may be distinct species of invasive creatures, like "worms" (Deuteronomy 28:39) and "locust" or "grasshoppers" (1 Kings 8:37).

Through the imagery of a *great army*, Joel described two major invasions: destructive insects (Joel 1:6) and foreign armies (2:20). Scripture is unclear regarding the exact identity of the foreign invaders, "the northern army" of Joel 2:20 (compare Jeremiah 1:14-15). Joel describes God's warning to Tyre, Zidon, and "all the coasts of Palestine" (Joel 3:4). Along with Egypt and Edom (3:19), these nations received a warning because of their action toward Judah (3:21).

Although Joel portrayed two destructive forces, insect and human, these may very well be two descriptions of the same locust plague. God's people could rejoice because God had not disregarded their suffering.

For God to renew the land and the people involved the people's receiving restitution for the *years* that they had lost. A form of the Hebrew verb translated here as *I will restore* appears in the Law of Moses to instruct a person who has harmed another person to make restitution for the wrongdoing (Exodus 22:1-14; Leviticus 24:18, 21).

God did no wrongdoing—the people were experiencing the consequences of their sins (compare 2 Chronicles 7:13-14, lesson 5). But God, "gracious and merciful, slow to anger, and of great kindness" (Joel 2:13), acknowledged their suffering and pitied His people (2:18). When God's people repented of their sinful and selfish ways, then they would experience comfort and restoration (see Isaiah 40:1-2).

II. God's Reminders
(Joel 2:26-27)
A. His Wondrous Work (v. 26)

26a. And ye shall eat in plenty, and be satisfied, and praise the name of the LORD your God, that hath dealt wondrously with you.

The famine would be reversed. A time of celebration would follow as the people gathered to *eat in plenty* and *be satisfied*. The atmosphere would be like that of a celebration following a successful harvest season. The people would gather to *praise the name of the Lord* who provided the harvest (see Leviticus 26:5; Deuteronomy 16:10-15).

The restoration followed God's history of working *wondrously* for His people. Though the people experienced harsh and dehumanizing treatment while living as slaves in Egypt, God dealt miraculously with the Egyptians to free the people (Exodus 3:20; see Psalm 78:12; Micah 7:15). Isaiah described how God would complete a marvelous work to confound the ways of sinful humans (Isaiah 29:14). God demonstrated His covenant love to His people—despite their sinfulness—through marvelously kind ways (see Psalms 17:7; 31:21).

26b. And my people shall never be ashamed.

In the Old Testament era, to be *ashamed* had a communal dimension. Shame was not merely an individual's feelings of inadequacy or worthlessness. Instead, it was a social state in which a group of people were considered by others as lacking honor

or dignity. Famine, drought, and infertile crops were shameful occurrences (see Jeremiah 12:13; 14:4) and were frequently the result of covenant disobedience (Deuteronomy 28:15-24). The land's destruction put the people in the shameful position of not being able to take care of their basic needs.

Further, shame had a spiritual component. Prophets warned that shame would be experienced by those people who practiced idolatry (Isaiah 42:17; 44:9-11; 45:16) and opposed God (41:11; Jeremiah 17:13) and His word (8:9). The psalms, however, frequently declare the deliverance from shame as one of God's blessings (example: Psalm 25:2-3, 20). The people of Judah could be encouraged that, despite their shameful circumstances, God had not left them.

What Do You Think?

How do you differentiate feelings of guilt from feelings of shame?

Digging Deeper

How can focusing on Jesus' promises (2 Corinthians 12:9-10), provision (Philippians 4:19), forgiveness (1 John 1:9), and humility (Hebrews 9:26) serve to break the power of shame?

Wrong Ingredients

My sugar cookie dough looked like cake batter—slightly runny and less dense than cookie dough should be. I added more of the contents from the flour tin to the dough, hoping to thicken the runny mixture. After adding several heaping spoons from the tin, my cookie dough had not changed.

I tasted the dough and realized that I had made a horrible mistake! I had switched my tin of powdered sugar with my tin of flour. No wonder the cookie dough was the consistency of cake batter; it contained almost no flour and over twice the intended amount of sugar! Only after I threw out that batch of dough and remade it with correct ingredients did the cookies turn out as I planned. I ate *plenty* of those cookies!

The people of Judah failed to follow God's commands. They tried to add the wrong ingredients of idolatry and selfishness. After they experienced the consequences of their sin, God worked wondrously and gave them the opportunity to start over. They were to be a renewed people with plenty. What "wrong ingredients" prevent you from noticing God's wondrous work? Are you ready to throw those out and follow Him?　　　—M. L. E.

B. His Commitment (v. 27)

27. And ye shall know that I am in the midst of Israel, and that I am the LORD your God, and none else: and my people shall never be ashamed.

At the center of the relationship between God and the people was the reality that God was present and active *in* their *midst* (see Leviticus 26:12; Deuteronomy 23:14). When their suffering was reversed and they saw the renewal of their land, they would *know* that God was present as He promised.

The uniqueness of this relationship was its exclusivity. *None else* could rightly claim Israel's allegiances and worship (see Exodus 20:3; Isaiah 45:5-6, 18; Hosea 13:4). God's presence with His people led to their rejoicing (Isaiah 12:6) for His mercies (Hosea 11:9). The people were to live without fear of being *ashamed*, because "the king of Israel" was in their midst (Zephaniah 3:15).

> ### What Do You Think?
> What do you need to remove from your life so that you will be better aware of the Lord's presence?
>
> ### Digging Deeper
> Who will you invite as an accountability partner to help in this regard?

Conclusion

A. Total Restoration

A plague of destructive insects with the accompanying feelings of terror—like the one described in this lesson's text—might be incomprehensible to modern audiences. Therefore, the feelings of joy from God's promised renewal might seem equally as foreign.

However, modern audiences of Joel's prophecy can take away two applications. First, the text serves as an ancient reminder regarding a present reality:

the importance of maintaining hope during seasons of suffering. Joel's words, directed to a people in the midst of hardship, reoriented their expectations. Disaster and shame changed to flourishing and celebration, all because of God's great work of renewal. Joel promised the people that hope was possible in the midst of disaster and suffering.

Although sin brings consequences, as it did for the people of Judah, God will not ignore or disregard His people. Instead, God can bring joy to replace sorrow. His timetable may not be ours, and He may not immediately bring joy or fix our suffering. However, His people can take comfort in knowing His presence.

Second, this passage serves as a reminder of God's promises to renew all creation. Joel promised that not only would the people be restored, but creation—the land and the animals—would also be restored. God's plan of restoration is not only focused on the spiritual realm but also the physical realm (see Romans 8:18-21). All things—spiritual and physical—belong to the God who created them. Joel calls us to embrace all aspects of God's restoration and renewal. As a result, God's people of all eras can celebrate His presence in their midst.

B. Prayer

Heavenly Father, we trust that You will bring restoration to our world, despite our sinful actions and inactions. Renew us so that we might better follow and praise You. Show us how to live as Your people, free from shame. In Jesus' name. Amen.

C. Thought to Remember

God's people need not be ashamed—
He brings renewal!

How to Say It

Ethanim	*Eth*-uh-nim.
Joash	*Jo*-ash.
Nisan	*Nye*-san.
Pethuel	Peth-*you*-el.
Tishri	*Tish*-ree.
Tyre	Tire.
Zidon	*Zye*-dun.

Involvement Learning

Enhance your lesson with KJV Bible Student *(from your curriculum supplier) and the reproducible activity page (at www.standardlesson.com or in the back of the* KJV Standard Lesson Commentary Deluxe Edition*).*

Into the Lesson

Bring a stack of recent newspapers or news magazines to class. Divide students into groups of four and distribute the resources to each group.

Write two headers on the board: *Enemies of Hope / Signs of Hope.* Ask groups to search through the newspapers and magazines for stories, opinion pieces, or ads that could fit under either heading.

Option. Have students use their smart phones to look through popular news websites for examples.

Alternative. Distribute copies of the "Hope Quotes" exercise from the activity page, which you can download. Divide learners into four groups and have them complete the activity.

After calling time for either activity, have students present their findings to the class. Then ask the following questions as part of whole-class discussion: 1–How do you define *hope*? 2–Why is hope important? 3–When is having hope difficult? 4–What happens when people give up hope?

Lead into the lesson by saying, "Today's Scripture text was written to people who needed hope that God's presence would be evident. We'll examine the prophet's message and consider how helpful his message was to them and to us."

Into the Word

Help students understand the setting for today's Bible study by briefly summarizing material found under the Lesson Context for this lesson. (You may want to recruit a class member ahead of time to prepare this two-minute lecture.)

Before class, select a student to role-play as a person from ancient Judah who received Joel's message. Bring the person to the front and interview him or her by asking these three questions: 1–What was your experience before receiving Joel's message? 2–What do Joel's words mean to you? 3–How will God's promises change your outlook on life? (Note: You may want to give the student the questions before class.)

Divide students into equal groups. Give each group a handout (that you prepared beforehand) with the following three headers: *What God Promised / Why God Promised / Results of God's Promises.* Each group should read Joel 2:21-27, then fill out the three headers based on their reading. While groups work, write the same headers on the board.

After five minutes, reconvene and have groups share their lists. Write responses on the board. Discuss similarities or differences between these responses and the responses provided during the earlier interview.

Alternative. Distribute copies of the "Hope's Foundation" activity from the activity page. Have learners work in pairs to complete as indicated. (This exercise will be more time-consuming than it appears at first glance.) After 10 minutes, ask pairs to share their paraphrases with the whole class.

Into Life

Write the following open-ended sentence on the board:

Hope is hard for me to have because . . .

Distribute slips of paper to each student and ask them to complete the sentence. Their responses should be such that they would be willing to share with the whole class. Collect the slips and read them aloud one at a time. Ask, "How can today's Bible study help us in these situations?" Allow one minute for the class to give an answer to each response.

Write the following open-ended sentence on the board:

Because God is present, I have hope that . . .

Distribute new slips of paper to each student. Ask them to complete the sentence, indicating how they will practice having hope in the promise of God's presence. Challenge students to keep this slip in a place where it can be a daily reminder to hope in God, His presence, and His promises.

Résumé of Those Called

Devotional Reading: Psalm 25:1-15
Background Scripture: 1 Corinthians 1:18-31

1 Corinthians 1:18-31

18 For the preaching of the cross is to them that perish foolishness; but unto us which are saved it is the power of God.

19 For it is written, I will destroy the wisdom of the wise, and will bring to nothing the understanding of the prudent.

20 Where is the wise? where is the scribe? where is the disputer of this world? hath not God made foolish the wisdom of this world?

21 For after that in the wisdom of God the world by wisdom knew not God, it pleased God by the foolishness of preaching to save them that believe.

22 For the Jews require a sign, and the Greeks seek after wisdom:

23 But we preach Christ crucified, unto the Jews a stumblingblock, and unto the Greeks foolishness;

24 But unto them which are called, both Jews and Greeks, Christ the power of God, and the wisdom of God.

25 Because the foolishness of God is wiser than men; and the weakness of God is stronger than men.

26 For ye see your calling, brethren, how that not many wise men after the flesh, not many mighty, not many noble, are called:

27 But God hath chosen the foolish things of the world to confound the wise; and God hath chosen the weak things of the world to confound the things which are mighty;

28 And base things of the world, and things which are despised, hath God chosen, yea, and things which are not, to bring to nought things that are:

29 That no flesh should glory in his presence.

30 But of him are ye in Christ Jesus, who of God is made unto us wisdom, and righteousness, and sanctification, and redemption:

31 That, according as it is written, He that glorieth, let him glory in the Lord.

Key Text

Base things of the world, and things which are despised, hath God chosen, yea, and things which are not, to bring to nought things that are: that no flesh should glory in his presence. —**1 Corinthians 1:28-29**

From Darkness to Light

Lesson Aims

After participating in this lesson, each learner will be able to:

1. Identify an appropriate context in which a first-century Christian might boast.

2. Explain the difference between the world's wisdom and God's wisdom.

3. Share a personal example of worldly wisdom that he or she has rejected.

Lesson Outline

Introduction

A. Source of Sermons

Experienced preachers use many sources to develop sermons: their study of the Bible, illustrations from their readings, and personal experiences. The need to preach weekly can create a lot of pressure, causing preachers to "borrow" sermons from other preachers. The internet makes thousands of new sermons available on a weekly basis. A friend of mine has cynically hypothesized that it will not be long until there are only four or five preachers left who construct original sermons that all other preachers will copy!

The apostle Paul had no internet sources for his sermon preparation. He preached the best that he could, drawing on his great knowledge of Scripture, his observations of life, and his personal experience in encountering the risen Jesus. Paul did not consider himself to be a gifted or highly trained public speaker, and apparently neither did others (1 Corinthians 2:1-4; 2 Corinthians 10:10). Even so, his preaching resulted in a church being planted in the city of Corinth, which impacted hundreds of lives for many years. The struggles of that church have much to teach us yet today.

B. Lesson Context

The city of Corinth lies about 50 miles west of Athens. That's about a one-hour train ride today, but in the first century AD, the "distance" was much greater in terms of culture and history. Athens had been the Greek center for philosophy, religion, education, and government for centuries (compare Acts 17:18-21). Names of Athenian philosophers are still recognized, especially those of Socrates, Plato, and Aristotle.

Corinth, on the other hand, was an industrial, working-class city. Located strategically near the four-mile-wide Isthmus of Corinth, the city thrived because of its Diolkos, an ancient railway system that transported small boats and cargo overland between the Aegean Sea and the Gulf of Corinth. The fees for using it were high (making Corinth a wealthy city), but the railway saved merchants many days of sailing around the Peloponnesian Peninsula with its treacherous coastline and plentiful pirates. A modern canal cutting through the isthmus was not completed until 1893.

Acts 18 records Paul's first visit to Corinth, after a disappointing time in Athens. Historical clues in Acts allow us to date this time as an 18-month period in AD 51–52, not quite 20 years after Paul's conversion (Acts 9:1-31).

Paul wrote the letters we call 1 and 2 Corinthians sometime between AD 54 and 57 while in Ephesus (1 Corinthians 16:5-9). Paul had received reports of several issues troubling the Corinthian congregation (1:10-17).

In the section of verses preceding today's lesson, Paul identified one of those problems: factions. Members of the congregation had been rallying around specific leaders in an unhealthy way (1 Corinthians 1:12). One of the factions had named Paul as its guiding light, and he objected, unwilling to countenance church divisions (1:13-16). He reminded his readers that he had come to Corinth to preach the gospel—period (1:17). This led him to recount the motives and actions of his initial visit to Corinth, today's text.

I. Word of the Cross
(1 Corinthians 1:18-25)
A. God's Power (vv. 18-19)

18a. For the preaching of the cross is to them that perish foolishness.

The Greek word translated *preaching* is "logos," often rendered as "word" (example: Matthew 12:32) or "Word" (John 1:1, 14). Paul was speaking of the word *of the cross*. The historical reality of Jesus' death by Roman crucifixion had drawn different reactions, and Paul assessed people by their responses. Those who interpreted the message of Jesus' death as *foolishness* (compare 1 Corinthians 1:21-23; 2:14; 3:19) are lost and perishing in their unforgiven sins (compare Romans 2:12; 2 Corinthians 2:15; 4:3). Paul had encountered this mindset in Athens (see Acts 17:32).

18b. But unto us which are saved it is the power of God.

On the other hand, those who see *the power of God* to forgive sins through such a seemingly shameful event are the ones who *are saved*. This

forms the centerpiece of Paul's discussion: the culturally shameful execution of Jesus on the cross in fact demonstrated the power and wisdom of God.

> **What Do You Think?**
> How would you explain why the message of the cross is foolishness to the world, but power for the believer?
> **Digging Deeper**
> How can you help others understand this through your attitudes and actions?

19. For it is written, I will destroy the wisdom of the wise, and will bring to nothing the understanding of the prudent.

Paul condemns human-based wisdom by drawing on Isaiah 29:14. In its context, that verse reveals the Lord's agenda: to show that those who believe that their human reasoning is impeccable will be devastated. Our greatest systems of human thought will collapse if they do not include the works and ways of the God of the Bible (compare 1 Corinthians 3:19).

B. World's Foolishness (vv. 20-23)
20a. Where is the wise?

This is the first of four rhetorical questions as Paul begins his salvo against the so-called wisdom of the world (see also 1 Corinthians 2:6; 3:18-20). *The wise* likely referred to those steeped in the Greek philosophical tradition (see Acts 17:18-21). The word *philosopher* means "lover of wisdom" and is in view here (compare Isaiah 19:11-12; Matthew 11:25; Luke 10:21; Romans 1:22; Colossians 2:8).

How to Say It

Aegean	A-*jee*-un.
Aristotle	**Air**-*uh*-staw-tul.
Athenian	Uh-*thin*-e-un.
Athens	*Ath*-unz.
Corinth	*Kor*-inth.
Crispus	*Kris*-pus.
Diolkos	Dih-*awl*-koss.
Plato	Play-tow.
Socrates	*Saw*-kruh-teez.
Sosthenes	*Soss*-thuh-neez.

20b. Where is the scribe?

This question targets the Jewish scholars who often opposed Jesus (example: Mark 11:18).

20c. Where is the disputer of this world?

This question points to people who always seek to argue a point, to prove themselves right. Such an argumentative spirit resulted in condemnation from Jesus, who warned those who were scrupulous in their tithing but ignored the "weightier matters" (Matthew 23:23). The implied answer to the questions we have seen to this point is this: the wise, the scribes, and the disputers are among those who are perishing.

20d. Hath not God made foolish the wisdom of this world?

The lesson within this question is taught many times in the Old Testament. It is Job's conclusion (Job 12:17). It is a conclusion of the book of Ecclesiastes, which includes the pursuit of wisdom as meaningless if it does so without God (Ecclesiastes 1:16-17). It is the story line of several episodes in the book of Daniel, which teaches that true wisdom must come from God (Daniel 1:17).

21. For after that in the wisdom of God the world by wisdom knew not God, it pleased God by the foolishness of preaching to save them that believe.

Paul contrasts *the wisdom of God* and the *wisdom* of *the world*. Although the same word *wisdom* is used, the gulf between the two concepts is great. God's wisdom is perfect, and He knows "the end from the beginning" (Isaiah 46:10).

The wisdom of the world does not lead to a knowledge of God. Paul discusses this flaw in human attempts at wisdom in Romans 1:18-23. There he declares that human ways of thinking that exclude God are futile and that such thinkers are "without excuse" (Romans 1:20).

We should not miss the irony in Paul's tone here. Human "wisdom" that does not acknowledge God is not wisdom at all. It is the opposite. Paul extends the irony to say that the magnificent *preaching* of the cross seems like *foolishness* to the self-appointed wise of the world. The height of this foolishness, in their eyes, would be to proclaim a message of God's salvation. How can they believe the message of salvation from God if they do not even acknowledge God, let alone any need to be saved?

22. For the Jews require a sign, and the Greeks seek after wisdom.

Paul moves to more specific accusations, identifying two groups he interacted with in Corinth and elsewhere: *Jews* and *Greeks* (Acts 18:4), Greeks being the same as Gentiles. The desire of the Jewish people to see an undue amount of signs before they committed to believing in Jesus is well documented in the Gospels. Repeatedly, Jewish leaders came to Jesus and demanded that He show them a miraculous sign (Matthew 12:38; Mark 8:11; etc.).

However, even the miracles of Jesus were not sufficient for some, who remained unbelievers (John 12:37). Jesus provided signs to prove who He was (20:30-31); to have considered those signs inadequate or to interpret them wrongly (as in Luke 11:14-15) is the opposite of a move toward faith. The Greeks' search for *wisdom*, like the Jewish demand for signs, was flawed from the start and unable to find faith if (or since) it denied God.

> **What Do You Think?**
> What are examples of modern wisdom that people pursue to find meaning and purpose apart from God?
>
> **Digging Deeper**
> How can you model God's true wisdom for your unbelieving neighbors?

23a. But we preach Christ crucified, unto the Jews a stumblingblock.

Paul returns to the simplicity of his appeal: *we preach Christ crucified* (also 1 Corinthians 2:2). Those who cannot accept a crucified Savior will never come to saving faith. The idea that a Jewish peasant-teacher from the obscure village of Nazareth could have accomplished anything by dying on a Roman cross was a *stumblingblock* to *Jews*. They expected a powerful, military Messiah who would free Israel from its oppressors and usher in the Day of the Lord. Jesus was a failure in their eyes, no more than a populist preacher of an earlier decade. We get our English word *scandal* from the Greek word translated "stumblingblock." The cross was scandalous because most Jews could not accept that God's Messiah would be shamefully executed like a notorious criminal. Paul knew that this aspect of the Messiah was expected by God and prophesied (see Isaiah 8:14; Romans 9:33).

23b. And unto the Greeks foolishness.

Paul characterizes the pagan Greek response to the message of the cross as cursory dismissal. *The Greeks* considered that message a waste of time and thought an execution in Jerusalem 20 years earlier was *foolishness*. Such an attitude is found today. Some refuse to consider the implications of the cross because it does not fit their preconceived notions of how God should act in history.

The Scandal of the Cross

I was reading my Bible on a park bench in Israel one day when a man stopped to talk to me. I didn't speak Hebrew, so he switched to English. When I told him I was reading the Bible, he seemed interested. He even showed me a certain verse in Exodus that contained his name.

As the conversation went on, it became clear that he did not hold traditional Jewish beliefs. He spoke of New Age philosophies and beliefs. Then he asked about my beliefs. When I mentioned Jesus dying on the cross to save us, he exploded in profanity. He forced himself to calm down before changing the subject, and he soon went on his way.

The conversation had been peaceful until I mentioned Jesus' death on a cross. If you never have had that kind of experience, how would you respond in such a moment?   —N. G.

C. God's Wisdom (vv. 24-25)

24. But unto them which are called, both Jews and Greeks, Christ the power of God, and the wisdom of God.

Various forms of the translation *called* occur hundreds of times in the Bible. But meaning often boils down to one of four usages, depending on context. In that regard, the word *call* and its derivatives can refer to (1) speaking out in prayer, as in Jeremiah 33:3; (2) summoning, as in 2 Kings 4:36; (3) naming someone or something, as in Genesis 1:5; and (4) indicating a summoning in terms of appointing by God, as in the text before us. The latter can be a summoning to salvation

Visual for Lessons 10 & 11. *Show this visual as you discuss the lesson commentary associated with 1 Corinthians 1:23a.*

(example: 1 Corinthians 1:9) or a calling to a specific task (example: Acts 13:2).

The calling to receive salvation through Christ comes to everyone (John 12:32; compare Romans 1:6; 8:28-30; 9:24) as the Holy Spirit confronts the world about sin through the proclaimed Word of God (John 15:26; 16:8; Romans 10:17; 2 Peter 1:21). This call can be resisted, and indeed it often is (Acts 7:51; compare Isaiah 63:10; Luke 13:34).

Even so, Paul encountered *Jews* who embraced Jesus as *the power of God* beyond any sign-miracle they could expect. Paul also preached to *Greeks* (Gentiles) who abandoned their worldly philosophies and accepted Jesus as *the wisdom of God*. Faith sometimes comes to those whom we least expect.

25. Because the foolishness of God is wiser than men; and the weakness of God is stronger than men.

Paul's irony now comes full circle in one of the most powerful verses in the New Testament. God is great and His greatness is not hidden. God's *foolishness*, what seems impossibly unwise to human observers, is *wiser* than anything philosophers have ever dreamed up. The plans of God exceed any human expectations.

Paul surely personalizes this. In his youth, he had sought to be the greatest of the Jewish scholars, studying at the feet of the finest teacher of his day (Acts 22:3). Paul's learning and mental capacity were well-known (see 26:24). Paul understood that he could never compare with the divine wisdom of God displayed in the cross of Jesus Christ.

Furthermore, Paul's opponents would say that he did not recognize the death of Jesus as *weakness*, the failure to overcome His enemies. Paul's insight, though, is that if those who crucified Jesus had truly understood who He was, they would never have killed Him (1 Corinthians 2:8). Strength in weakness is a great paradox, one that Paul celebrates elsewhere (see 2 Corinthians 12:10).

The Deceptive Plant

I bought a succulent plant for my wife on her birthday. Its cascading purple leaves looked lovely on the kitchen windowsill. But to her dismay, the leaves began falling off the very next day.

Had she overwatered or underwatered the plant? Did it need more or less sunlight?

I found myself questioning the wisdom of its Creator. Why create something so fragile? How did this picky plant ever survive in the wild?

My wife did some research and laid out the fallen leaves on a damp paper towel. A few days later, tiny roots sprouted out of the base of each dismembered leaf. Then came perfect miniature succulent plants, each growing from a single leaf.

What I had dismissed as foolishness was actually an ingenious process of reproduction. How many "foolish" things that you see around you are actually God's intricate designs?   —N. G.

II. Calling of the Humble
(1 Corinthians 1:26-31)
A. Confounding the Wise (vv. 26-27)

26. For ye see your calling, brethren, how that not many wise men after the flesh, not many mighty, not many noble, are called.

Paul asked the Corinthians to evaluate their own ranks. Did they see a church filled with recognized *wise men*—from the *mighty*, powerful people of the community; or with those who were *noble* (literally, "well-born")—the aristocratic class of wealth and privilege? Maybe a few people in the Corinthian church could be described in this

manner (see the example of Crispus, 1 Corinthians 1:14; Acts 18:8), but that was not the case of this church generally.

27. But God hath chosen the foolish things of the world to confound the wise; and God hath chosen the weak things of the world to confound the things which are mighty.

The application of this verse defies logic. Wouldn't God want a church full of the rich, powerful, and highly educated? Choosing the community's humble serves *to confound* the elite citizens of Corinth. Historically, we see this in Gallio, who served as the Roman deputy of the city and region. When Sosthenes was brought before Gallio to be judged, the governor brushed the matter aside as if it involved people not worthy of his time or consideration. When Sosthenes was savagely beaten in this Roman noble's presence, Gallio was unconcerned (Acts 18:12-17).

> **What Do You Think?**
> What beliefs of believers might some people consider to be foolish?
> **Digging Deeper**
> How might Jesus' acts of humility (Philippians 2:5-11) be considered foolish to the world?

B. Choosing the Despised (vv. 28-29)

28-29. And base things of the world, and things which are despised, hath God chosen, yea, and things which are not, to bring to nought things that are: that no flesh should glory in his presence.

Paul insisted that *God*, rather than favoring the godless world's elite, had *chosen* the *base things of the world* to effect His plans. The word translated "base" is the opposite of the word in 1 Corinthians 1:26 that is translated "noble." God does not recognize human traditions of noble birth to find His servants. Our Lord calls those who would be considered ignoble, the *despised* by worldly standards. Does this mean the church should not seek to add the influential members of its community? Of course not. But all must come to the cross in humility, recognizing their spiritual poverty. There is no place for anyone to claim personal *glory in his presence.* This is the great reversal, the upending of human expectations and standards. God chooses those who are of no account in the world's reckoning and gives them importance and value. In so doing, God takes the world's estimation of greatness and brings it *to nought.*

The verb translated *glory* is also translated "boast" in Romans 2:23; 2 Corinthians 9:2; etc. Boasting is a display of pride rather than humility. Our salvation through the cross of Jesus is a matter worked out without our prior approval. We had nothing to do with it, so we have no place for boasting about saving ourselves.

What Do You Think?
How can believers use earthly prestige, like wealth or education, in a way that glorifies God instead of themselves?

Digging Deeper
What might prevent believers from acting in this manner?

C. Focus of Boasting (vv. 30-31)

30-31. But of him are ye in Christ Jesus, who of God is made unto us wisdom, and righteousness, and sanctification, and redemption: that, according as it is written, He that glorieth, let him glory in the Lord.

We do not boast pridefully about ourselves, but about our Lord. We *glory in the Lord* alone (Galatians 6:14) and leave behind personal claims. Paul sums this up by listing four things we gain by faith in Christ, none of which is our own accomplishment. Through Christ we learn true *wisdom,* the ways of God in our world (1 Corinthians 2:6-16). We find *righteousness,* being made right with God (2 Corinthians 5:21). We enjoy *sanctification,* the cleansing of our sins by the Holy Spirit (1 Corinthians 6:11). And we experience *redemption,* being bought back from the power of sin (Romans 3:24).

Paul does not boast of his greatness but of his weakness and the power of God. This is a glorying based in humility, not seeking acclaim but offering thanksgiving and praise to the one who has saved us from the futility of human attempts to deny God.

What Do You Think?
How would you describe the doctrines of righteousness, sanctification, and redemption in your own words?

Digging Deeper
How do these doctrines fulfill God's "treasures of wisdom and knowledge" (Colossians 2:3) for the believer?

Conclusion
A. Doctrine of the Cross

Martin Luther, the sixteenth-century reformer, was inspired by this text in his doctrine of the cross. Luther found contrasts between this way ordained by God and the human way, the doctrine of glory. He argued that the human doctrine of glory is centered on human wisdom that leads to the blinding of hearts. However, he stated that the divine doctrine of the cross is centered on God's self-revelation of His suffering Son, which softens hearts.

The Christian message is still a scandalous stumbling block. The central historical fact is that Jesus of Nazareth was executed as a criminal would be: on a shameful cross. It was a brutal affair. It did not seem like a victory at the time, but a colossal defeat. Yet without the cross, there is no salvation!

Today's church still confronts the dangers Paul warned about: the church may seek the world's approval. As Luther and Paul taught, the true way of salvation will seem foolish, weak, and shameful to the world. This Scripture text challenges us to examine how much we have accommodated our priorities to the world. What elements of the world's "doctrine of glory" have we adopted? Instead, we should look to God, who can be found in sufferings and the cross.

B. Prayer

Father, we bow our hearts before You. Your ways are far beyond the ways of human wisdom. May we rely on Your strength and wisdom as we put our trust in Your Son. It is in His name we pray. Amen.

C. Thought to Remember
God's ways seem foolish to a world impressed by cleverness and success.

Involvement Learning

Enhance your lesson with KJV Bible Student *(from your curriculum supplier) and the reproducible activity page (at www.standardlesson.com or in the back of the* KJV Standard Lesson Commentary Deluxe Edition*).*

Into the Lesson

Begin class by reading the following statements. After each statement, ask students to raise their hands if they agree with it; then ask students to raise their hands if they disagree with it. Ask volunteers to indicate why they answered so.

I'm wiser today than I was 10 years ago.
I've grown in wisdom by listening to others.
I'm wiser because of my chosen friends.
Wisdom is inherent, but foolishness is inherited.

Transition to Bible study by saying, "People have many opinions about the nature of wisdom and how people can become wise. Let's look for a biblical solution to this dilemma as we learn what Paul has to say to a group of first-century believers."

Into the Word

Distribute a handout (you prepare) with the following prompts or write the prompts on the board:

Wisdom is . . .
Wisdom is not . . .
Wisdom does . . .
We need wisdom because . . .

Divide the class into equal groups. Ask each group to read 1 Corinthians 1:18-31. Have students complete each prompt based on the Scripture reading. Explain that they may write similar phrases under more than one heading.

Option. Ask each group to complete one prompt. Ensure that every prompt is considered by at least one group.

Alternative. Distribute copies of the "Word Web" exercise from the activity page, which you can download. Have learners work in pairs to complete the activity as indicated.

After calling time for either activity, have groups present their findings in whole-class discussion. Conclude the activity by asking, "Why do the implications of the cross seem foolish to some people?"

Into Life

Have students gather in small groups. Distribute handouts (you create) of the prompts below for discussion. Ask each group to apply one of the verses from today's Scripture to each statement.

Option. Assign multiple prompts to each group.

1–We've observed instances when the world's wisdom was debunked.
2–We've interacted with people who do not accept the wisdom that comes from God.
3–We've experienced how God uses insignificant things to show His wisdom and strength.
4–We've experienced the futility of chasing after the world's wisdom.
5–We've experienced how the gospel of Christ Jesus offers people help and strength in their moments of need.
6–We've experienced how God's wisdom overcomes our own weaknesses.

After five minutes, have each group present their findings for whole-class discussion. If different groups discussed the same prompt, point out similarities and differences in the groups' responses.

Alternative. Distribute copies of the "Praying for Wisdom" activity from the activity page. Have students complete the activity as indicated (in a minute or less) before sharing with a partner.

Close class with a guided prayer. Encourage students to pray aloud regarding their own short prayers after you state the following prayers:

God, help us know and understand the wisdom that comes from the gospel of Christ Jesus.

God, fill us with Your wisdom so that we might best love and serve our neighbors.

God, help our neighbors know and understand the wisdom that comes from the gospel of Christ Jesus.

Reminder of the Call

Devotional Reading: John 15:1-14
Background Scripture: 2 Timothy 1:3-14

2 Timothy 1:3-14

3 I thank God, whom I serve from my forefathers with pure conscience, that without ceasing I have remembrance of thee in my prayers night and day;

4 Greatly desiring to see thee, being mindful of thy tears, that I may be filled with joy;

5 When I call to remembrance the unfeigned faith that is in thee, which dwelt first in thy grandmother Lois, and thy mother Eunice; and I am persuaded that in thee also.

6 Wherefore I put thee in remembrance that thou stir up the gift of God, which is in thee by the putting on of my hands.

7 For God hath not given us the spirit of fear; but of power, and of love, and of a sound mind.

8 Be not thou therefore ashamed of the testimony of our Lord, nor of me his prisoner: but be thou partaker of the afflictions of the gospel according to the power of God;

9 Who hath saved us, and called us with an holy calling, not according to our works, but according to his own purpose and grace, which was given us in Christ Jesus before the world began,

10 But is now made manifest by the appearing of our Saviour Jesus Christ, who hath abolished death, and hath brought life and immortality to light through the gospel:

11 Whereunto I am appointed a preacher, and an apostle, and a teacher of the Gentiles.

12 For the which cause I also suffer these things: nevertheless I am not ashamed: for I know whom I have believed, and am persuaded that he is able to keep that which I have committed unto him against that day.

13 Hold fast the form of sound words, which thou hast heard of me, in faith and love which is in Christ Jesus.

14 That good thing which was committed unto thee keep by the Holy Ghost which dwelleth in us.

Key Text

Hold fast the form of sound words, which thou hast heard of me, in faith and love which is in Christ Jesus. —2 Timothy 1:13

From Darkness to Light

Unit 3: God's Call
Lessons 10–13

Lesson Aims

After participating in this lesson, each learner will be able to:

1. Identify ways that Paul, Lois, and Eunice influenced Timothy's faith.

2. Explain Paul's mentoring technique.

3. Develop a personal plan to guard sound doctrine.

Lesson Outline

Introduction

A. Call to Action

Those who have been believers for any amount of time are probably familiar with the stories of Christian martyrs: men and women cruelly killed by orders of Nero, Domitian, or some other Roman emperor. We may think of being thrown to the lions in the Coliseum at Rome or being burned alive. Turning to modern times, we may be aware of missionaries in various parts of the world who have faced arrest, imprisonment, and even death because of their faith.

For most of us, though, those pressures are not a part of our daily experience. Neither was it part of the daily experience of many first-century Christians. Even so, for every martyr who died at the hands of a Roman soldier or in the mouth of a lion, there were many more who faced much less dramatic forms of persecution. These included social exclusion, financial penalties, and the like (compare John 9:22). Loss of social status brought with it feelings of shame or embarrassment, particularly when a prominent Christian leader, like Paul in today's lesson, was imprisoned. Although our circumstances are generally different, most of us have experienced something like this at some point: having others think us odd or strange for our way of life, feeling a sense of embarrassment or shame in certain social situations. Often we will try to avoid these sorts of situations, but today's text shows us the better way.

B. Lesson Context

Two recognized groupings of some of the apostle Paul's writings are the Prison Epistles (Ephesians, Philippians, Colossians, and Philemon) and the Pastoral Epistles (1 Timothy, 2 Timothy, and Titus). The letter of 2 Timothy could actually fit in either category since Paul wrote it while imprisoned (2 Timothy 1:16; 2:9).

The New Testament presents 2 Timothy in an uncomplicated fashion: as a letter written by the apostle Paul to the younger evangelist Timothy. We are introduced to the person of Timothy in Acts 16:1-3. That introduction occurs in the context of Paul's second missionary journey, which extends from Acts 15:36 to 18:22. Over time, Paul came to think quite highly of Timothy as a protégé, referring to him four times as a "son" in a spiritual sense (1 Corinthians 4:17; Philippians 2:19-22; 1 Timothy 1:2; 2 Timothy 1:2).

We know certain things about Timothy in a personal sense: he was relatively young (1 Timothy 4:12), probably had a reserved personality (1 Corinthians 16:10), and was frequently ill (1 Timothy 5:23). His ancestry was that of both Judaism and paganism (Acts 16:1; see further commentary below), and he had a good reputation among the believers of his native region (16:2). Paul's trust in him increased over time (see 19:22), so much so that Timothy is named as the co-sender of some of Paul's letters (example: 2 Corinthians 1:1). Timothy's dedication to the gospel resulted in his having been imprisoned at some point (Hebrews 13:23). The two dozen occurrences of his name in the New Testament indicate the importance of his role in the spread of the gospel. Following his days as a traveling missionary with Paul, Timothy seems to have settled into a ministry located in Ephesus (1 Timothy 1:3).

We date the letter of 2 Timothy to about AD 67, as Paul's final New Testament writing before his execution in Rome (see 2 Timothy 4:6-8). Persecution under Emperor Nero (reigned AD 54–68) was underway. But internal problems of the church at Ephesus and Timothy's leadership in that regard there were Paul's main concerns.

I. Reminder of Heritage
(2 Timothy 1:3-7)

A. Thankfulness, Conscience, Prayer (v. 3)

3. I thank God, whom I serve from my forefathers with pure conscience, that without ceasing I have remembrance of thee in my prayers night and day.

Following the standard address found in almost all of Paul's letters, we see the importance with which he views *prayers* of thankfulness and intercession (also Romans 1:8-10). The phrases *without ceasing* and *night and day* indicate relentlessness in this regard (compare Luke 2:37; 1 Thessalonians 1:2; 3:10; 1 Timothy 5:5). This is not mere formu-

laic language; rather, it speaks to a primary practice of Paul.

A second touchstone for Paul is his *conscience*, a word occurring more than 20 times in his letters and in addresses attributed to him. Conscience deals with moral sensitivity, an inner awareness of the quality of one's actions (see 1 Corinthians 10:25, 27). The New Testament presents conscience in both positive and negative senses (examples: Acts 23:1; 24:16; 1 Timothy 4:2; Titus 1:15).

> **What Do You Think?**
> What words would you use to describe your prayer life as it is now? As you would like it to be?
>
> **Digging Deeper**
> How might your daily habits need to change in order for your prayer life to be described as "relentless"?

B. Desire, Sorrow, Joy (v. 4)

4. Greatly desiring to see thee, being mindful of thy tears, that I may be filled with joy.

This verse continues the theme of the close bond seen in the previous verse. What is added is a clue about Timothy's sensitive nature, as Paul noted *being mindful of* Timothy's *tears*. To have served alongside Paul was to subject oneself to strong emotions (compare Acts 20:36-38; 2 Corinthians 7:13). Paul himself experienced such emotions (examples: Acts 20:19, 31; 2 Corinthians 2:4; 7:4; Philemon 7).

We might naturally ask here about the specific reason for Timothy's distress. It probably refers to the earlier urgent need for Timothy to remain in Ephesus (1 Timothy 1:3), which resulted in a tearful farewell when Paul left for Macedonia. Given that Paul would request a personal visit in 2 Timothy 4:9, he hoped that the two would yet be reunited and that tears would be replaced *with joy*.

Leaving Friends Behind

When I lived in Ukraine as a missionary, I would return to the United States every summer to visit friends and family. And every fall, I headed back to Ukraine. I had deep friendships in both locations, and each time I left one place, I felt sad leaving the people I loved there.

After having moved back to the United States permanently, I still remember my friends in Ukraine. When the weather changes, I feel a certain type of chill in the air and wonder what my Ukrainian friends are doing. I look at photos my friends post and remember the good times we had.

As we consider Paul's remembrance of Timothy's tears, perhaps we should ask ourselves, *When was the last time I had a shared-ministry friendship so deep that separation resulted in weeping?* If the answer is "never," what does that imply?
—L. M. W.

C. Lois, Eunice, Paul (vv. 5-6)

5. When I call to remembrance the unfeigned faith that is in thee, which dwelt first in thy grandmother Lois, and thy mother Eunice; and I am persuaded that in thee also.

This verse reveals that Timothy was not an absolute newcomer to godliness when Paul had recruited him some dozen years earlier. Although Timothy's father was "a Greek" (Acts 16:1), the two devout women mentioned here had instructed Timothy in *unfeigned faith*. Such faith is characterized by a complete lack of hypocrisy (contrast Matthew 23:23). *Lois* and *Eunice* are both Greek names, suggesting the women were ethnically Greeks. But their faith was rooted in the Old Testament before learning about and accepting Jesus as the promised Messiah.

> **What Do You Think?**
> Who are the faithful women in your life who helped shape your faith?
>
> **Digging Deeper**
> How can you glorify God while celebrating these women or their memories?

A Faithful Grandma

My grandma grew up in Appalachia. The oldest of many children, she helped raise her younger siblings and held quite a bit of adult responsibility. On a trip back to that area one time, she and I stood on a hillside overlooking the valley where she had lived as a child. She pointed out where landmarks used to be and told me about the people who had lived there.

"Down that way was an old church, and on the other end of the holler was another church, and over the hill was another one. When I was a teenager, my friends and I used to spend the whole day every Sunday going to each one," she explained. "We'd go to one in the morning, another in the afternoon service, and the third in the evening." They made a day of worshipping God together, building relationships in the process. My grandma's dedication to God did not end when she reached adulthood; she brought up her children and grandchildren to follow Jesus as well.

What will be your legacy in terms of discipling someone younger?
—L. M. W.

6. Wherefore I put thee in remembrance that thou stir up the gift of God, which is in thee by the putting on of my hands.

Having set the tone by describing the nature of their relationship, Paul turned to a purpose in writing this letter: Timothy needed to exert leadership in the face of the challenges before him. That leadership would become manifest as Timothy stirred *up the gift of God, which* was already internal to him.

Perhaps Timothy was wavering (or in danger of wavering) in the face of the challenges before him, which Paul went on to specify as the letter continued. No matter if Paul's imprisonments were a source of embarrassment to his younger colleague, Paul had been the conduit through which that gift was bestowed. But what exactly was that gift?

Elsewhere Paul used similar phrasing in connection with grace (Romans 5:15; Ephesians 3:7), eternal life (Romans 6:23), salvation (Ephesians 2:8), and spiritual gifts (1 Corinthians 7:7; 12:28). The first three of those four all deal with salvation from different angles, so the choices would seem to boil down to just two: Paul, by *the putting on of* his *hands,* conferred on Timothy either salvation or a spiritual gift.

But two other possibilities should be mentioned. Grammatically, the sentence could mean that God himself was the gift, but this seems unlikely. Also, 1 Timothy 4:14 should be taken into account: "Neglect not the gift that is in thee, which was given thee by prophecy, with the laying on of the hands of the presbytery." A laying on of hands is also noteworthy (1) as part of commissioning ceremonies in Acts 6:6 and 13:3; (2) as accompanying receptions of the Holy Spirit in 8:17; 9:17; and 19:6; (3) in a cautionary sense in 1 Timothy 5:22; and (4) as one of the "principles of the doctrine of Christ" in Hebrews 6:1-3.

It's tempting to see a commissioning ceremony as being solely in view, but we would not speak of an ordination as being "in" someone. Ultimately, it seems that the best understanding is a combination of Timothy's having received some spiritual gift (the inward) during an ordination ceremony (the outward). We should understand Paul's ministry as being Spirit-driven (see also 1 Timothy 1:18).

D. Power, Love, Soundness (v. 7)

7. For God hath not given us the spirit of fear; but of power, and of love, and of a sound mind.

Although the gift of God that Paul had in mind may be unclear to us today, what Paul does *not* refer to is certain: the gift is not *the spirit of fear* (see also Romans 8:15). A challenge for us modern readers of the Bible is that the Greek word translated *spirit* is capitalized as *Spirit* in places where the Holy Spirit is being discussed. But the ancient Greek manuscripts are no help in this regard because capitalized and uncapitalized texts do not occur together. Context usually makes clear whether "Spirit" or "spirit" is meant, but not always. Some verses where this uncertainty presents itself are Romans 1:4; Ephesians 1:17; 1 Peter 4:14; and Revelation 19:10. Regarding the text at

hand, does *the spirit* refer to a human disposition that is characterized by *power, and . . . love, and . . . a sound mind*, or does it refer to the Holy Spirit proper? Other passages have this kind of language both ways (consider Luke 4:14; Romans 8:15; 15:19, 30; Colossians 1:8).

Whatever conclusion is reached, one thing is clear: the assets on which Timothy can depend are supernatural in origin—from God. Fear cripples strength and love, and it makes sound judgment very difficult. Fear draws us to focus on our inadequacy; but realization of divinely provided power, love, and a sound mind draws us to focus on God's strength and character.

> **What Do You Think?**
> How do your actions differ when you are unafraid versus when you feel great fear?
>
> **Digging Deeper**
> How do the spiritual gifts listed in 2 Timothy 1:7 help prevent being overcome in the first place?

II. Reason for Faithfulness
(2 Timothy 1:8-12)
A. Power, Not Shame (v. 8)

8. Be not thou therefore ashamed of the testimony of our Lord, nor of me his prisoner; but be thou partaker of the afflictions of the gospel according to the power of God.

Shame and power are also contrasted in Romans 1:16. *The afflictions of the gospel* refer to—or at least include—Paul's imprisonment. Consider Timothy's dilemma: he had pledged allegiance to the message of a leader who is awaiting execution! So how could that message have any credibility?

Paul offered the surprising way out of the dilemma: *be thou partaker of the afflictions*. To be a faithful witness of the gospel, Timothy would have to come to terms with this imperative. He would have to accept the fact that his teacher and mentor had been imprisoned because of the message Timothy was tasked to preach. He would have to understand that Paul's imprisonment did not invalidate or otherwise discredit the truth of

How to Say It

Domitian	Duh-*mish*-un.
Ecclesiasticus	Ik-*leez*-ee-**as**-ti-kuhs.
Eunice	U-*nye*-see or *U*-nis.
Maccabees	*Mack*-uh-bees.
Nero	*Nee*-row.
Sirach	*Sigh*-rak.

the gospel. Indeed, the opposite was true (compare Philippians 3:10). So Paul told Timothy much the same thing that he had told the church in Corinth: the power and wisdom of God, revealed in Jesus Christ, will always look shameful and weak to the world (1 Corinthians 1:25-31).

B. Grace, Not Works (v. 9)

9a. Who hath saved us, and called us with an holy calling.

This half verse touches on two vital doctrines of the church: those of justification (what happens for a person's salvation to occur) and sanctification (what happens—or should happen—after salvation occurs).

9b. Not according to our works, but according to his own purpose and grace, which was given us in Christ Jesus before the world began.

Paul stressed anew what he had made clear in Ephesians 2:8-9: we are saved by God's *grace*, not by *our works* (see also Titus 3:5). The power of God, manifested in the redemptive work of Jesus Christ, existed *before the world began* (John 1:1). Such power never retreats in the face of false teachers, no matter how eloquent or socially acceptable they are.

> **What Do You Think?**
> Given that we are not called or saved based on our works, what reasons can you suggest for holy living?
>
> **Digging Deeper**
> What Scriptures do your answers draw on?

C. Life, Not Death (vv. 10-12)

10. But is now made manifest by the appearing of our Saviour Jesus Christ, who hath abolished death, and hath brought life and immortality to light through the gospel.

Perhaps the best antidote to Timothy's fear was a robust restatement of the sheer, awe-inspiring glory of *the gospel*. That gospel presented itself in the flesh and blood *appearing of our Saviour Jesus Christ;* His appearance was not some kind of unseen abstraction (1 John 1:1-3). The verse before us might be seen as a summary of Paul's extensive thoughts in 1 Corinthians 15.

11. Whereunto I am appointed a preacher, and an apostle, and a teacher of the Gentiles.

Paul had absolutely no shame in acknowledging the three roles mentioned here, and they are interesting to compare and contrast. The Greek noun translated *preacher* is relatively rare in the New Testament, occurring only here, in 1 Timothy 2:7, and in 2 Peter 2:5. This noun is also rare in the Greek version of the Old Testament (the Septuagint), occurring only in Genesis 41:43 and Daniel 3:4. The noun is also found in the nonbiblical Jewish texts of Sirach (Ecclesiasticus) 20:15 and 4 Maccabees 6:4. In all cases, the idea is that of loud public proclamation. By numeric contrast, the verbal forms of this noun occur 19 times in Paul's letters (plus 45 times elsewhere in the New Testament). This may indicate that the *act* of preaching is to be stressed over the *position* of preacher.

By further contrast, the nouns translated *apostle* and *teacher*, occurring dozens of times each in the New Testament, are much more common than the noun translated *preacher*. The three roles overlap in meaning since an apostle was called to preach and teach (Mark 3:14; 6:30; Acts 4:2, 33; 8:25; etc.). When we see the word *apostle*, we may naturally think of the original 12 (Luke 6:13-16), plus the replacement for Judas (Acts 1:15-26), plus Paul (formerly known as Saul). We may be surprised to see that designation also applied to several others as well (see Acts 14:14; 1 Thessalonians 1:1; 2:6; possibly Romans 16:7).

12. For the which cause I also suffer these things: nevertheless I am not ashamed: for I know whom I have believed, and am persuaded that he is able to keep that which I have committed unto him against that day.

For the which cause refers back to Paul's overlapping roles as a preacher, apostle, and teacher of the gospel; he suffers what he suffers because of exercising those roles (compare 2 Corinthians 6:2-10; 11:23-33). He had every reason to feel ashamed from a cultural perspective. But he was *not ashamed*. Shame has its place in the Christian life (see Romans 6:21; 2 Corinthians 9:4; 2 Thessalonians 3:14; Titus 2:8). But the task of gospel presentation is not in that category (also Romans

1:16; 2 Corinthians 10:8; Philippians 1:20; 2 Timothy 1:16; 2:15).

What Do You Think?

How can you encourage new Christians to be bold and unashamed in living out their faith?

Digging Deeper

How will you apply this encouragement to your own life?

III. Requirement of Soundness
(2 Timothy 1:13-14)
A. What to Do (v. 13)

13. Hold fast the form of sound words, which thou hast heard of me, in faith and love which is in Christ Jesus.

Having reflected on his own life and ministry, Paul returned to addressing Timothy directly. The phrase *the form of sound words* undoubtedly strikes our ears as odd. The only other place in the New Testament where the Greek word behind the word *form* occurs is 1 Timothy 1:16, there translated "pattern." Regarding the translation *sound*, the three Pastoral Epistles have 8 of the 12 occurrences of New Testament usages of the underlying Greek word (here and 1 Timothy 1:10; 6:3; 2 Timothy 4:3; Titus 1:9, 13; 2:1, 2). Elsewhere in the *King James Version*, the translation of the Greek behind *words* is "utterance" (2 Corinthians 8:7), "speech" (10:10), and "communication" (Ephesians 4:29). The same sense is present here; compare the "sound words" in the text at hand with "sound doctrine" in 1 Timothy 1:10 (translating a different word that overlaps in meaning). In sum, Paul required Timothy to maintain his *faith and love* in the gospel of *Christ Jesus.*

B. How to Do It (v. 14)

14. That good thing which was committed unto thee keep by the Holy Ghost which dwelleth in us.

The same gospel (*that good thing*) that had been entrusted to Paul to proclaim (2 Timothy 1:11, above) had been *committed* to Timothy as well. The charge here is quite similar to that in 1 Tim-

Visual for Lessons 10 & 11. *Have learners discuss how preaching Christ crucified encourages the boldness called for in verse 12.*

othy 6:20, but here with the added mention of the strength available through the power of *the Holy Ghost.* Some argue that the word *us* refers specifically to Paul and Timothy in their capacities as ministers of the gospel, carriers of the ministerial gift received through ordination (see commentary on 2 Timothy 1:6, above). But there is nothing apparent in the text that requires this.

Conclusion
A. Sound Words

In our media-saturated environment, it can be hard to find the space for sound, healthy teaching. Even in Christian circles, it is easy to get carried away with worries over the state of the world and of society. May today's text remind us to center our focus on the life-altering power of the gospel. Let us resolve to make Paul's charge to Timothy his charge to us as well!

B. Prayer

Heavenly Father, guard our hearts and our minds from despair and shame. Through the power of the Holy Spirit, who dwells within us, show us how to live courageously and proclaim the gospel fearlessly. In Jesus' name we pray. Amen.

C. Thought to Remember
God has called us out of fear and into His love and power.

Involvement Learning

Enhance your lesson with KJV Bible Student *(from your curriculum supplier) and the reproducible activity page (at www.standardlesson.com or in the back of the* KJV Standard Lesson Commentary Deluxe Edition*).*

Into the Lesson

Before class, write the following questions on the board: *1–Who from your early life had the greatest effect on the person you have become? 2–What did that person do or say that affected you the most?* Invite students to pair off (preferably not with a spouse) and answer the questions. After a few minutes of discussion, ask volunteers to share their answers with the class.

Alternative. Divide the class into pairs. Distribute paper and pen to each person. Give the pairs a few minutes to write down advice on ways to be confident. Allow pairs to share their answers with the whole group.

After either activity, lead into the Bible lesson by saying, "The people who influence us as children and youth have a profound effect on our character and spiritual life. Let's see how two of Timothy's family members and the apostle Paul influenced and encouraged Timothy."

Into the Word

Divide the class in half, designating one half as the **Family Group** and the other half as the **Family Friend Group**. Distribute handouts of the questions below (you prepare) for in-group discussions.

Family Group. Read 2 Timothy 1:5-7 and Acts 16:1-3. 1–Who were Lois and Eunice? *(Timothy's grandmother and mother.)* 2–What do we know about them? *(They were Jewish believers.)* 3–What influence did they have on Timothy? *(By their teaching and example, they helped bring him to a strong faith in Jesus Christ.)* 4–What do we know about Timothy's father? *(He was a Greek, so Timothy had never been circumcised.)* 5–How did Paul encourage Timothy, using the faith taught by his mother and grandmother? *(Have the confidence to grow in his gift of God's grace that he learned from his mother and grandmother.)* 6–Read 2 Timothy 1:13-14. How do these verses tie back to verse 5? *(Paul encourages Timothy to keep the faith and love of God that he was taught by his mother and grandmother.)*

Family Friend Group. Read 2 Timothy 1:3, 8-12 and Acts 16:1-4. 1–Who became Timothy's friend and mentor? *(The apostle Paul.)* 2–How well did Paul know Timothy's family? *(He met them in Lystra and was aware of their strong faith.)* 3–What action did Paul take to make Timothy more acceptable to other Jewish believers? *(He circumcised him.)* 4–What indication is there that Paul really cared about Timothy's welfare? *(He prayed for him day and night and longed to see him.)* 5–What are phrases Paul used to encourage Timothy in his ministry? *(stir up the gift of God [v. 6]; God gives us power, love, and a sound mind [v. 7]; do not be ashamed [v. 8]; He has saved us and called us to a holy calling [v. 9].)*

Alternative. Distribute copies of the "A Marvelous Mentor" exercise from the activity page, which you can download. Have learners work in small groups to complete as indicated. *Option.* Write the three categories on the board and have each verse read aloud. Then work together as a class to suggest an answer from each verse.

After calling time under either alternative, have groups present their findings in whole-class discussion. Use the commentary to correct misconceptions.

Into Life

Write on the board: *Hold fast the form of sound words.* Conduct a whole-class brainstorm about how to hold fast to sound doctrine. Jot ideas on the board.

Alternative. Distribute copies of the "Hold Fast" activity from the activity page. Have learners work in pairs to complete as indicated.

After either alternative, hand out index cards and pens. Invite learners to write out how they can be encouraged throughout the next week to hold fast to the faith and love that is in Christ Jesus.

Responsibility of Those Called

Devotional Reading: Amos 5:7-15
Background Scripture: James 2:1-12

James 2:1-12

1 My brethren, have not the faith of our Lord Jesus Christ, the Lord of glory, with respect of persons.

2 For if there come unto your assembly a man with a gold ring, in goodly apparel, and there come in also a poor man in vile raiment;

3 And ye have respect to him that weareth the gay clothing, and say unto him, Sit thou here in a good place; and say to the poor, Stand thou there, or sit here under my footstool:

4 Are ye not then partial in yourselves, and are become judges of evil thoughts?

5 Hearken, my beloved brethren, Hath not God chosen the poor of this world rich in faith, and heirs of the kingdom which he hath promised to them that love him?

6 But ye have despised the poor. Do not rich men oppress you, and draw you before the judgment seats?

7 Do not they blaspheme that worthy name by the which ye are called?

8 If ye fulfil the royal law according to the scripture, Thou shalt love thy neighbour as thyself, ye do well:

9 But if ye have respect to persons, ye commit sin, and are convinced of the law as transgressors.

10 For whosoever shall keep the whole law, and yet offend in one point, he is guilty of all.

11 For he that said, Do not commit adultery, said also, Do not kill. Now if thou commit no adultery, yet if thou kill, thou art become a transgressor of the law.

12 So speak ye, and so do, as they that shall be judged by the law of liberty.

Key Text

Hearken, my beloved brethren, Hath not God chosen the poor of this world rich in faith, and heirs of the kingdom which he hath promised to them that love him? —**James 2:5**

209

From Darkness to Light

Unit 3: God's Call
Lessons 10–13

Lesson Aims

After participating in this lesson, each learner will be able to:

1. Summarize why favoritism is incompatible with the Christ-honoring life.

2. Compare and contrast the biblical concept of favoritism with modern definitions of discrimination.

3. Propose a way to identify and correct occasions when his or her church does not treat people equally.

Lesson Outline

Introduction
    A. Playing Favorites
    B. Lesson Context: James, the Man
    C. Lesson Context: James, the Letter
I. Problem Identified (James 2:1-4)
    A. Partiality Forbidden (v. 1)
    B. Partiality Illustrated (vv. 2-3)
    C. Partiality's Implication (v. 4)
      The Good Girl
II. Problem Evaluated (James 2:5-7)
    A. God's Right Action (v. 5)
    B. Readers' Wrong Actions (vv. 6-7)
III. Problem's Solution (James 2:8-12)
    A. Fulfilling the Law (v. 8)
    B. Breaking the Law (vv. 9-11)
      No Irish Need Apply
    C. Liberation by Law (v. 12)
Conclusion
    A. Love, Not Favoritism
    B. Prayer
    C. Thought to Remember

Introduction

A. Playing Favorites

With regard to divisions among followers of Christ, a tendency has been to focus on doctrinal divides (example: meaning of the Lord's Supper). But it's easy to see that other reasons for division also weigh heavily. One of those involves race. In 1963, Dr. Martin Luther King, Jr. famously noted that eleven o'clock on Sunday morning was "the most segregated hour in this nation." Churches have made needed correctives in that regard over the ensuing 60 years, with more yet to be done.

Various demographics point to other divides among believers. Researchers occasionally note that denominational affiliation correlates with socioeconomic status. These observations are not airtight—there are exceptions. But they point to a truth of human nature: we tend to associate with people who are like us. The more differences that exist in a group—whether cultural, socioeconomic, or what have you—the greater the likelihood of instability in that group.

The problems faced by the readers of the book of James are readily recognizable as the selfsame problems we face in churches today. Likewise, the solutions James presents are just as applicable for us today.

B. Lesson Context: James, the Man

There are four or five men named James in the New Testament, so we should take care not to mix them up (see Mark 1:19-20; 15:40; Luke 6:15; Acts 1:13). Tradition has taken the phrase "James, a servant of God and of the Lord Jesus Christ" (James 1:1) to refer to the James who was the half brother of Jesus (see Matthew 13:55; Mark 6:3). Along with Jesus' other half brothers, James did not believe in Jesus before the resurrection (John 7:3-5). By the Day of Pentecost, however, Jesus' brothers had come to believe in Him (see Acts 1:14). Paul indicates that James had been a witness of the risen Jesus (1 Corinthians 15:7).

James had become a leader in the Jerusalem church by the mid–AD 40s (Acts 12:17; 15:13; 21:18). His exact role is not clear in the text, but Paul groups him with the apostles and lists him alongside Cephas (that is, Peter) and John as "pillars" of the church (Galatians 2:9; see 1:19). The significance of this is heightened when we consider the centrality of Jerusalem to the earliest Christians. The Jerusalem church was more than just one congregation among many. It was the mother church; what happened there mattered to all Christianity. We see the truth of this, as well as James's concrete impact, in the account of the Jerusalem council in Acts 15. There James gave the final, decisive word on a vital doctrinal matter after Peter and Paul had spoken their minds. The event portrays James as an observant Jew who expected Gentile converts to observe only certain foundational aspects of the Old Testament law (see Acts 15:19-20).

Outside of the New Testament, the Jewish historian Josephus (born around AD 37) dates the martyrdom of James to AD 62.

C. Lesson Context: James, the Letter

Given the details of James's life and death, a reasonable supposition is that the letter was written in the AD 50s, if not in the 40s. That makes it one of the earliest of the New Testament documents. Likely it was written from Jerusalem.

Structurally, the letter lacks certain typical features of an ancient letter, features that we see throughout Paul's letters. After opening with standard features of sender, recipients, and greeting, it lacks the typical thanksgiving and closing. The writer proceeds loosely from topic to topic, appealing to the Old Testament often. The tenor of the letter is thoroughly Jewish, having been written by a Christian of Jewish background to Christians of Jewish background—fellow believers under duress. These recipients of the letter are "scattered abroad," a reference to what is often called the Diaspora (James 1:1; compare John 7:35; 1 Peter 1:1-2).

I. Problem Identified
(James 2:1-4)
A. Partiality Forbidden (v. 1)

1. My brethren, have not the faith of our Lord Jesus Christ, the Lord of glory, with respect of persons.

Visual for Lesson 12. *Ask learners to silently consider this question for one minute before discussing the final set of questions together.*

The opening sentence of today's text is a plain thesis statement that introduces the subject to be discussed: *respect of persons.* Though the term *respect* may suggest to our ears a positive regard for others, it translates a word that indicates partiality or favoritism: showing attention and honor to some people and not to others. Such a practice cannot exist alongside faith in Jesus, the one who died for all.

God's own nature in this regard is seen in several places in the Old Testament. According to Deuteronomy 10:17, "the Lord your God is God of gods, . . . which regardeth not persons, nor taketh reward" (see also 2 Chronicles 19:7; compare 1 Samuel 16:7). The New Testament further confirms this truth about God (see Acts 10:34; Romans 2:11; Ephesians 6:9; Colossians 3:25). What is said of God himself is likewise commanded of the people: "Thou shalt not respect the person of the poor, nor honour the person of the mighty: but in righteousness shalt thou judge thy neighbour" (Leviticus 19:15; see also Proverbs 24:23; compare John 7:24).

How to Say It

Cephas	*See*-fus.
Diaspora	Dee-*as*-puh-ruh.
Josephus	Jo-*see*-fus.
Maccabees	*Mack*-uh-bees.
Samaritan	Suh-*mare*-uh-tun.

Per the custom of the era, the term *brethren* includes both men and women. This emphasizes that all Christians are part of a family that is drawn together by the blood of Christ, a tie stronger than earthly blood relationships (Luke 14:26). In this family there can be no favoritism.

B. Partiality Illustrated (vv. 2-3)

2. For if there come unto your assembly a man with a gold ring, in goodly apparel, and there come in also a poor man in vile raiment.

The word *if* translates a Greek word that is frequently used to introduce a hypothetical situation. Even so, the scenario described here seems realistic regarding situations that have taken place in the *assembly*. The Greek word behind this translation is not, as we might suppose, the word for "church." Rather, it is the word translated "synagogue(s)" dozens of times in the New Testament. If this comes as a surprise, recall that James is writing to Christians of Jewish background (see Lesson Context), members of "the twelve tribes which are scattered abroad" (James 1:1).

As we see throughout the Gospels, the synagogue was the usual place of worship and religious instruction for first-century Jews (Matthew 4:23; etc.). Trips to the temple in Jerusalem were reserved for major holidays and extraordinary circumstances. Christians of Jewish background apparently continued to refer to their gathering place(s) under the traditional name.

In the scenario that James presents, it is uncertain whether the two men who enter are visitors or regular attendees in the assembly. What is important to the teaching point is that one sports the *gold ring* of a well-to-do person, while the other is *a poor man*. Both men are described according to their clothing: *goodly apparel* and *vile raiment*. In the ancient world, clothing indicated one's role and status (Matthew 11:8; Acts 12:21). Clothing could also indicate gender (Deuteronomy 22:5), allegiance (nonbiblical 2 Maccabees 4:12), or widowhood (Genesis 38:19). We are to understand that the first man possesses considerable social status and the wealth that goes with it, while the second man has neither.

3. And ye have respect to him that weareth the gay clothing, and say unto him, Sit thou here in a good place; and say to the poor, Stand thou there, or sit here under my footstool.

To *have respect* means something like "show special regard for," and that is precisely what James condemned in James 2:1 (above). The believers had been looking at the clothing of each man and providing preferential treatment on that basis. The meaning of the word *gay* has, of course, changed since the *King James Version* came into being. Here it translates the same word rendered "goodly" in James 2:2 and means something like "shining," "resplendent," or "luxurious" (compare Acts 10:30; Revelation 15:6; 19:8).

The word translated *poor* is used in Revelation 3:17 in a context of spiritual poverty, but here the word occurs in a physical sense (also in James 2:2, 5-6). Note well that the offer to the poor man to *stand thou there, or sit here under my footstool* does not entail the same respect or consideration.

> **What Do You Think?**
> What examples of favoritism have you seen or experienced?
> **Digging Deeper**
> What are the potential consequences for the church's witness if these patterns are seen in God's gathered people?

C. Partiality's Implication (v. 4)

4. Are ye not then partial in yourselves, and are become judges of evil thoughts?

There are two accusations here that grow naturally out of the situation that James has presented. They are formed as rhetorical questions, and they both assume that the answer is "Yes!" Today we would express the idea of being *partial in yourselves* as "discrimination" or "showing prejudice."

The second phrase in the verse makes an equally pointed statement. *Judges of evil thoughts* means "judges who have evil thoughts." If judging is to be objective, based on law and not personal preference, then rich and poor are to be treated equally. Only an evil judge, perhaps one hoping for a bribe or favor from a rich person, shows partiality. Jesus condemned this kind of judging in John 7:24. To have evil thoughts is a matter of the heart (see Matthew 15:19). The evaluation criteria being used by those to whom James wrote is contrary to the very nature of God (compare James 4:11-12). In following customary patterns of responding to rich and poor, some first-century Christians were unwittingly denying the God whom they claimed to serve.

The Good Girl

Two sisters spent the day at their grandmother's house. They played outside on the small farm and swang on the tire swing in the shade of the big tree. Everything was fine, an idyllic afternoon in a pastoral setting, until the sisters started arguing. It was low-key to begin with—fussing over some tiny matter of disagreement. But before long, the sisters were yelling and fighting.

Inside the house, the grandmother heard their voices and went out to see what was happening. Grabbing the younger girl, the grandmother began to scold her fiercely. The older girl stood dumbfounded. Hadn't she herself also been part of the arguing and fighting? Why should her younger sister get all the punishment?

"Grandma! We were both fighting. It's my fault too!" the older girl protested. But her grandmother brushed her off. The older girl looked at her younger sibling, both with tears in their eyes at the injustice of it. There was no apparent reason for the favoritism. If this situation were played out on a regular basis, what consequences do you foresee for the older girl and her sister? What is revealed about the grandmother's heart?
—L. M. W.

II. Problem Evaluated
(James 2:5-7)
A. God's Right Action (v. 5)
5. Hearken, my beloved brethren, Hath not God chosen the poor of this world rich in faith, and heirs of the kingdom which he hath promised to them that love him?

James presents here the first of three arguments that indicate why showing partiality is wrong. The first argument points out that favoritism is inconsistent with the fact that *God* has *chosen the poor of this world*. It is presented in the form of a rhetorical question that expects the answer to be yes.

The way James frames his question might be jarring to our ears. What is so special about the poor? To answer, we might look again at the numerous Old Testament texts that address this; Psalms 9:18; 10:14; 18:27; and Isaiah 11:3-4 are just a few. To these we add New Testament texts such as the song of Mary in Luke 1:46-55 (lesson 4), particularly verses 52 and 53. James's position is entirely consistent with these.

B. Readers' Wrong Actions (vv. 6-7)
6a. But ye have despised the poor.

James's outlook might be foreign for those of us today who live comfortable lives and attend churches that are not always very welcoming of the poor (whether intentionally or not). This was at least partly the case for those among James's original readers who had *despised the poor*. Some of those readers had done so by the overt discriminatory treatment noted in James 2:2-3 (above). This brings us to James's second argument, next.

6b. Do not rich men oppress you, and draw you before the judgment seats?

James's second of three arguments is also framed as a rhetorical question that expects an affirmative answer. Favoritism is not only inconsistent with the nature of God; it is also downright illogical, given that it is the *rich* who are a source of oppression (Mark 12:38-40; etc.). Even so, deference toward the rich seems to be a human tendency. We are so drawn in by wealth and status (celebrity) that we will compromise our convictions if given the chance to be close to wealth and status, even if it's harmful to us.

The irony in this is obvious when we are speaking of other people. But have we examined ourselves for these tendencies? How prone are we to join in to the cult of celebrity that idolizes the extremely wealthy and famous? This even happens in the church. Consider the rise (and fall) of celebrity writers and megachurch ministers in recent decades; in such cases, believers have at times bent over backwards to accommodate someone who very likely cared very little about them or their situation. James confronts readers yet today in order to snap us out of such behavior.

7. Do not they blaspheme that worthy name by the which ye are called?

This can be seen as James's third argument or an extension of the second argument. By their behavior, the rich who oppress (and not all did back then or do so today) pretend to godliness (again, see Mark 12:40). Such pretense amounts to blasphemy against the *worthy name* of Jesus (see Romans 2:17-24, quoting Isaiah 52:5 and Ezekiel 36:22).

III. Problem's Solution

(James 2:8-12)

A. Fulfilling the Law (v. 8)

8. If ye fulfil the royal law according to the scripture, Thou shalt love thy neighbour as thyself, ye do well.

This is the only place in the Bible where the phrase *the royal law* is found. James immediately reveals what he means by this in identifying it with Leviticus 19:18: "*Thou shalt love thy neighbour as thyself.*" The vital importance of this imperative is seen in Jesus' declaration that it was one of the two greatest commandments (Matthew 22:34-40; Mark 12:28-34; compare Romans 13:8-10; Galatians 5:13-14).

Loving one's neighbor excludes partiality and prejudice. Jesus illustrated this truth by telling a story in which a Samaritan—the kind of person despised by much of His audience—generously cared for a victim of a crime (Luke 10:25-37). The Law of Moses itself is clear in its exclusion of partiality. Unlike other legal codes of the ancient world, that law did not provide different levels of protection for different classes of people. Kings and servants, the wealthy and the poor, Israelites and foreigners are subject to the same standards (examples: Exodus 23:3; Numbers 15:15-16; Deuteronomy 1:16-17).

> **What Do You Think?**
> What benefit is there in learning to love yourself?
>
> **Digging Deeper**
> How does loving others help keep self-love from becoming a sinful preoccupation?

B. Breaking the Law (vv. 9-11)

9. But if ye have respect to persons, ye commit sin, and are convinced of the law as transgressors.

Here James is as explicit as he can be: to *have respect to persons* (partiality, favoritism, discrimination) is to *commit sin.* The older use of the word *convinced* is to be understood in the sense of "convicted"—as in a trial one is convicted of a crime by *the law* that has been violated. Discrimination is a failure to love, and love is at the core of the law of Christ (compare 1 Corinthians 9:21; Galatians 6:2). James expected his readers to grasp this fact.

> **What Do You Think?**
> How do personal preferences regarding personality, etc., affect your treatment of others?
>
> **Digging Deeper**
> What do you (or can you do) to prevent these preferences from yielding sinful results?

No Irish Need Apply

From the mid-1800s to the early 1900s, discrimination against Irish immigrants in the United States ran high. They were stereotyped as lazy, hot-tempered, and clannish alcoholics. This stemmed from a lengthy discrimination against the Irish in Europe, where they were seen as troublemakers. Favoritism could be seen in the hiring practices of many businesses. Signs advertising open jobs often used the phrase "No Irish need apply." This led many people of Irish descent to try to get ahead by hiding their cultural identity.

Today discrimination toward those of Irish descent seems minimal. Even so, solving racial or cultural discrimination has been uneven at best. Progress (or lack thereof) is often in the eye of the beholder. Discrimination (which is unequal treatment without a rational basis) seems minimal unless *you* have been the one discriminated against!

Countries try to solve the problem of unequal treatment through enactment and enforcement of laws. The effectiveness of such laws in changing behavior and practices is a topic best debated elsewhere. But what may be beyond question is their ineffectiveness in changing *hearts*. Without the healing grace of Jesus in our lives, we will still be vulnerable to harboring attitudes of favoritism. And what grows in one's heart eventually makes itself known in behavior (Mark 7:20-23; James 1:14-15). Here's a question you may not have considered: In what ways have you tacitly approved of discrimination by accepting preferential treatment yourself? —L. M. W.

10. For whosoever shall keep the whole law, and yet offend in one point, he is guilty of all.

To show the seriousness of this matter, James makes an argument familiar to his readers of Jewish background. The Law of Moses presents itself not as a collection of individual commands but as a unified whole. It is both many laws and a single unit of law. The standard that God gave His people was not so that they would obey some or much of it, but all of it. So the failure to keep *one* part is the failure to keep the law in its entirety. To break *a* law is to break *the whole law*.

11. For he that said, Do not commit adultery, said also, Do not kill. Now if thou commit no adultery, yet if thou kill, thou art become a transgressor of the law.

James illustrates the point just made with an easily grasped example, drawn from the Ten Commandments (see Exodus 20:1-17; Deuteronomy 5:6-21).

C. Liberation by Law (v. 12)

12. So speak ye, and so do, as they that shall be judged by the law of liberty.

Knowing and understanding all this, James's readers should *speak* and *do* in accordance with it. We naturally think of laws in terms of restrictions. But this *law of liberty* is freeing (also James 1:25; compare Romans 8:2; 1 Peter 2:16). This law is another way of expressing the concept behind the royal law (James 2:8, above). As the readers contemplated God's law, they should have experienced fear because disobedience invites judgment. But they should also have had hope because obedience brings true freedom.

Conclusion
A. Love, Not Favoritism

Today's text is justly famous for the specific sin that it identifies and condemns. Discrimination grows out of our fallen human nature—a nature that is drawn to wealth and status, or at least proximity to it. Everyone is subject to its allure, and we all can think of instances when the temptation has been present for us. James's teachings are, therefore, for us as well as for his initial readers. May we take this lesson as an encouragement to examine the patterns of our lives and to root out prejudice, replacing it with love.

> **What Do You Think?**
> What idea in this lesson is most challenging to you?
> **Digging Deeper**
> How will you seek God's guidance on this issue in the coming week?

B. Prayer

Father, may Your Holy Spirit teach us to see those who walk the earth with us as You see them. As we do, deliver us from the sins of partiality, prejudice, and preference. In Jesus' name we pray. Amen.

C. Thought to Remember

God doesn't play favorites, and neither should we.

Involvement Learning

Enhance your lesson with KJV Bible Student *(from your curriculum supplier) and the reproducible activity page (at www.standardlesson.com or in the back of the* KJV Standard Lesson Commentary Deluxe Edition*).*

Into the Lesson

Before class, prepare six slips of paper. On the first slip, write the name of a wealthy person your class will recognize. Write the name of an important athlete in your area on the second slip. On the third slip, write the name of a celebrity that your group will quickly identify with. On each of the three other slips, write the name of a person whom your group would identify as not being important or known to society at large. Arrange the chairs in your room so that some seats appear a little more "premier" than others.

Ask participants to create a seating chart for each of the celebrities on the slips of paper by setting the slips of paper on the chosen seats. This might require someone to move. Repeat for the slips of paper of people who were identified as not important or known. Allow a few minutes of discussion as to why people were seated where they were. Be sure to give everyone the opportunity to openly express their feelings about such hypothetical favoritism.

Alternative. Distribute copies of "The Dangers of Favoritism" exercise from the activity page, which you can download. Have learners work in pairs to complete as indicated.

After either activity, give the group time to talk about favoritism. Lead into the Bible study by saying, "Favoritism can be dangerous to society and in our own lives. In today's text, James gives us a warning against allowing favoritism within the church."

Into the Word

Use the "Lesson Context: James, the Man" section of the commentary to briefly talk about the context and the James who wrote today's letter.

Divide the class into three small groups, designating one group as the **Respect of Persons Group**, the second group as the **Truly Wealthy Group**, and the third group as the **Royal Law Group**. Distribute handouts of the questions below (you prepare) for in-group discussions.

Respect of Persons Group. Read James 2:1-4. 1–What is different about the two main characters in these verses? 2–How differently are they treated? Why? 3–Describe how their treatment might make them feel about being part of that congregation.

Truly Wealthy Group. Read James 2:5-7. 1–How is dishonoring the poor wrong? 2–What is wrong with honoring the rich? 3–How does God treat the rich and the poor compared to how society usually treats them?

Royal Law Group. Read James 2:8-12. 1–What does James identify as the "royal law"? 2–Why does this law make respect of persons, or favoritism, a sin? 3–How does the "law of liberty" contrast with the Old Testament law?

After calling time, have groups present their findings in whole-class discussion. Use the commentary to correct misconceptions.

Into Life

Write the following on the board: *"There is no respect of persons with God"* (Romans 2:11). Conduct a whole-class brainstorming session by first talking about what the verse means, then challenging learners to suggest ways Christians should treat other people based on how God views them. Distribute index cards and pens to the learners. Invite everyone to write one way they pledge to treat people during the week. It should be based on how God views people.

Alternative. Distribute copies of the "Welcoming Newcomers" activity from the activity page. Have learners complete it individually (in a minute or less) before discussing conclusions in small groups.

After calling time under either alternative, have small groups talk about how you, as a church, might improve in not showing favoritism in your congregation. Close with a prayer.

Results of the Call

Devotional Reading: 1 Thessalonians 5:1-10
Background Scripture: 1 Peter 2:1-25

1 Peter 2:1-10

1 Wherefore laying aside all malice, and all guile, and hypocrisies, and envies, and all evil speakings,

2 As newborn babes, desire the sincere milk of the word, that ye may grow thereby:

3 If so be ye have tasted that the Lord is gracious.

4 To whom coming, as unto a living stone, disallowed indeed of men, but chosen of God, and precious,

5 Ye also, as lively stones, are built up a spiritual house, an holy priesthood, to offer up spiritual sacrifices, acceptable to God by Jesus Christ.

6 Wherefore also it is contained in the scripture, Behold, I lay in Sion a chief corner stone, elect, precious: and he that believeth on him shall not be confounded.

7 Unto you therefore which believe he is precious: but unto them which be disobedient, the stone which the builders disallowed, the same is made the head of the corner,

8 And a stone of stumbling, and a rock of offence, even to them which stumble at the word, being disobedient: whereunto also they were appointed.

9 But ye are a chosen generation, a royal priesthood, an holy nation, a peculiar people; that ye should shew forth the praises of him who hath called you out of darkness into his marvellous light:

10 Which in time past were not a people, but are now the people of God: which had not obtained mercy, but now have obtained mercy.

Key Text

Ye are a chosen generation, a royal priesthood, an holy nation, a peculiar people; that ye should shew forth the praises of him who hath called you out of darkness into his marvellous light. —**1 Peter 2:9**

From Darkness to Light

Unit 3: God's Call
Lessons 10–13

Lesson Aims

After participating in this lesson, each learner will be able to:

1. Identify the stone that causes people to stumble.

2. Explain why certain thoughts and actions are incompatible with status as a member of a holy priesthood.

3. State to the class which of the four identifications in 1 Peter 2:9a is most convicting to him or her, and why.

Lesson Outline

Introduction

A. Questions of Identity

We live in a time when questions of identity predominate. Who are we in terms of politics and consumer tastes? Which relationships define us? Are these markers static, or are they fluid? The questions multiply from these starting points.

As the New Testament writers amply attest, Jews from the religious leadership class all the way down to the common person found their identity in God and in the specific religious practices of the Law of Moses. When we read the New Testament today, we sometimes lose sight of the fact that becoming a Christian was a huge step in that cultural and religious context (compare Luke 14:26; etc.). Beginning with the apostles, Christian leaders worked tirelessly to help new believers come to see themselves in a new light. They had a new identity in Christ.

B. Lesson Context

Peter was undoubtedly the most prominent among the original 12 apostles. He is named first in listings (Matthew 10:2-4; Mark 3:16-19; Luke 6:13-16; Acts 1:13). His denials of Jesus and subsequent reinstatement are significant markers of his life (John 18:15-17, 25-27; 21:15-17). Some commentators use those and other indicators to see Peter's life in terms of four chronological segments. The following texts in that regard are not exhaustive but representative:

1. Early ministry . . . . .Mark 1:21, 29-30; Luke 5:1-7; John 1:40-42
2. With Jesus . . . . Matthew 16:18; Mark 1:16-20; Luke 9:28; John 1:42; 21:15-17
3. Post-ascension . . . . Acts 4:13; 5:29; 10:1–11:18; 12:1-19
4. Later Life . . . . John 21:18-19; 1 Corinthians 9:5; Galatians 2:11-14; 2 Peter 1

The 27 books of the New Testament include 2 that are ascribed to the apostle Peter. The first of these two is particularly thick with citations from and allusions to various Old Testament passages. By one count, 1 Peter is tied for second place with Hebrews in having the highest percentage of verses (69 percent of its 105 verses) that reflect Old

Testament passages; only Revelation has a greater percentage. Peter was particularly fond of drawing from the book of Isaiah (examples: 1 Peter 2:6a, 8-9a, below).

We should wonder who Peter's primary intended audience was. Were the addressees mainly Christians of Jewish background, Christians of Gentile background, or a significant percentage of both? Supporting the theory of a Jewish-Christian audience is the opening verse, which notes the letter addressed "to the strangers scattered throughout Pontus, Galatia, Cappadocia, Asia, and Bithynia" (1 Peter 1:1). The word translated "scattered" is *diaspora*, mentioned in last week's Lesson Context (see James 1:1; compare John 7:35). The Diaspora is a technical term for Jews who were dispersed among Gentiles as predicted in Deuteronomy 4:25-27; 28:64-68. And Jews certainly did live in the areas listed (compare Acts 2:5, 9-11), provinces located in modern-day Turkey.

On the other hand, supporting the theory of an audience of predominantly Gentile background are certain indicators in 1 Peter 1:14, 18; 2:9-10, 25; and 4:3-4. Proponents of this theory argue that Diaspora, or dispersion, should not be taken literally as applying strictly to Jews, but figuratively as applying to Gentile believers.

I. As Newborn Babies
(1 Peter 2:1-3)
A. Exhortation (vv. 1-2a)

1. Wherefore laying aside all malice, and all guile, and all hypocrisies, and envies, and all evil speakings.

The opening *wherefore* is a conjunction that gives the implication of what has just been said in terms of necessary action to be taken (compare Ephesians 4:25). Peter's audience—the members of the congregations to which he wrote—had received the gospel of Jesus Christ willingly. They had obeyed the truth (1 Peter 1:22), had purified their souls (1:22), and had been born again (1:23). Consequently, they must resolve to live in a way that was consistent with those facts (compare Romans 13:12).

Let your life be built on Christ.

Visual for Lesson 13. *Before closing with prayer, ask the class to consider what actions or inactions can hinder them from building their lives on Christ.*

What follows is called a "vice list" of five items in three groupings (compare Matthew 15:19; Galatians 5:19-21; Colossians 3:5, 8-9; 1 Timothy 1:9-10; 2 Timothy 3:2-4; 1 Peter 4:3). *Malice* constitutes the first grouping. It carries the sense of evil actions in general. Such actions can be motivated by greed, spite, jealousy, or other moral failings; the resulting action intends to harm another person.

The second grouping consists of attitudes or personality traits that present themselves in behavior. *Guile* is an orientation of general dishonesty. *Hypocrisies* characterize a person who will play whatever role is most beneficial to him or her. *Envies* characterize a bitter, restless spirit that begrudges the success or possessions of others. Envy is the opposite of gratitude, of contentment with what God has given (see 1 Timothy 6:6-8).

The third grouping is the spiritual poison of *evil speakings*. This word is translated

How to Say It

alpha privative	al-*fuh* **priv**-*uh*-tiv.
Bithynia	Bih-*thin*-ee-uh.
Cappadocia	Kap-uh-*doe*-shuh.
Diaspora	Dee-*as*-puh-ruh.
Galatia	Guh-*lay*-shuh.
Pontus	*Pon*-tuss.
Septuagint	Sep-*too*-ih-jent.

"backbitings" in 2 Corinthians 12:20. Such behavior is what results from the previous three: a deceitful person feigning innocence and friendship yet harboring deep resentment and envy. Such persons work behind the scenes to damage the reputation of others.

All this reveals Peter's concern for congregational solidarity. A congregation under pressure tends toward bickering and division (again, 2 Corinthians 12:20).

> **What Do You Think?**
> Are there any aspects of your life in which you give yourself a pass to indulge in the vices named in 1 Peter 2:1?
>
> **Digging Deeper**
> What risks are there in engaging in such, especially when the person speaks or acts anonymously?

2a. As newborn babes, desire the sincere milk of the word.

As there are different levels of spiritual maturity, there are different foods that are appropriate for those levels. These are described in more detail in 1 Corinthians 3:1-4 and Hebrews 5:11–6:3. There is nothing wrong with the *milk of the word;* it is necessary and desirable for those who are infants, spiritually speaking. But its ingestion should lead to something important (1 Peter 2:2b, next).

There is a play on words in the original text that is difficult to bring across in English. The words translated "guile" in 1 Peter 2:1 and *sincere* here are the same word, with the letter *a* added to the beginning of the second occurrence. This additional letter, known technically as an alpha privative, expresses negation. We often express negation the same way in English (compare the opposites *historical* and *ahistorical*). Thus, human guile and the sincere Word of God are seen as complete opposites.

B. Expectation (v. 2b)
2b. That ye may grow thereby.

There are two extremes to avoid when it comes to the milk of the word as spiritual nourishment.

One extreme is to become so attached to that milk that the believer becomes satisfied and never moves on to spiritual meat; the other is to avoid that milk altogether. Either extreme yields the same eventual outcome: stunted (or no) spiritual growth. The point of the "newborn babes" (1 Peter 2:2a, above) metaphor is not to illustrate helplessness or sinlessness. Rather, it frames and illustrates the need to *grow* in holiness.

> **What Do You Think?**
> How do you experience being completely reliant on God?
>
> **Digging Deeper**
> What other biblical illustrations are helpful when considering both your reliance on God and your responsibility to take initiative in your spiritual walk?

C. Explanation (v. 3)
3. If so be ye have tasted that the Lord is gracious.

The phrasing *if so be ye have* sounds strange to our modern ears. The *King James Version* elsewhere translates the underlying word as "though" (1 Corinthians 8:5) and "seeing it is" (2 Thessalonians 1:6), implying "since." Thus Peter was appealing to his readers' past experience with *the Lord.*

In so doing, Peter draws on Psalm 34:8: "O taste and see that the Lord is good." What the ancient psalmist advised is what Peter's audience had done. This created the obligation noted in 1 Peter 2:2a, above. The obligation, if recognized and implemented, would help Peter's audience grow out of the perilous state of spiritual infancy. Hebrews 6:4-6 expands on this danger.

II. As Living Stones
(1 Peter 2:4-8)
A. Model (v. 4)

4. To whom coming, as unto a living stone, disallowed indeed of men, but chosen of God, and precious.

The focus of the discussion now shifts from the

believers to whom Peter was writing to the Lord himself. Peter accomplished this by drawing on Psalm 118:22, the first of several Old Testament texts used as proof (see Lesson Context, above). Jesus applied this passage to himself in Matthew 21:42. Peter also used it in his earliest preaching (see Acts 4:11; compare Isaiah 28:16; 1 Corinthians 3:11; Ephesians 2:20). As the focus shifts, so does the metaphor: from infants needing to be desirous of milk to a *stone* evaluated in different ways.

To whom coming speaks of our approaching Jesus in obedience and worship. On the basis of what God has done in Christ, we as baptized believers have the privilege of approaching the throne of God in worship, praise, and petition (compare Hebrews 10:19-22). The words *approaching* and *coming* help us think about how the New Testament writers understand worship.

B. Result (v. 5)

5. Ye also, as lively stones, are built up a spiritual house, an holy priesthood, to offer up spiritual sacrifices, acceptable to God by Jesus Christ.

As rapidly as Peter shifted the focus away from his readers, so now he shifts back to them. One stone does not a building make, no matter how immense that stone may be. God's spiritual house requires numerous other *lively stones*. Their identity is not in doubt, as witnessed by the opening *ye also*.

The nature of this structure is also not in doubt: it is *a spiritual house,* not a physical one (2 Corinthians 6:16; Ephesians 2:20-22; etc; compare 1 Corinthians 6:19). The way Peter phrases things in the verse before us, this spiritual house consists of *an holy priesthood.* In the Old Testament era, priests went to the physical temple to offer physical sacrifices that included animals; in the New Testament era, the priests (all Christians) are

the temple, and they *offer* living *spiritual sacrifices* of themselves (also Romans 12:1-2). The physical temple building of the Old Testament era is not to be equated with physical church buildings of the New Testament or modern eras. The concepts of priesthood and temple have not been done away with; rather, they have been transformed (compare Revelation 1:6; 5:10; 20:6). Christians do not need a priest as the ancient Israelites did, because we now are priests ourselves as we serve under the great high priest, *Jesus Christ* (Hebrews 4:14).

Stones

Outside the town of Bethlehem, I saw a stone threshing floor. On top of Mount Masada, I saw the stone fortress where the Jews made their last stand against the Romans in AD 70. In Jerusalem, I marveled at the huge stones that had been the foundation for Solomon's temple. The small stones along the shore of the Sea of Galilee reminded me of Peter—a pebble compared to Jesus. A particularly moving sight was "the Pavement" (John 19:13) in Jerusalem, which tradition says caught the blood of Jesus during one of His trials. What "stones" in your life call Jesus to the front of your mind?

—C. R. B.

C. Prophesied (vv. 6-8)

6a. Wherefore also it is contained in the scripture.

Peter demonstrates the value of *scripture* as he begins to weave together several Old Testament texts. The particular reference here is Isaiah 28:16 (compare Romans 9:33; 10:11). The quotes don't read quite the same in our English version of Isaiah because Peter quoted from the ancient Greek version of the Old Testament, known as the Septuagint.

6b-7. Behold, I lay in Sion a chief corner stone, elect, precious: and he that believeth on him shall not be confounded. Unto you therefore which believe he is precious: but unto them which be disobedient, the stone which the builders disallowed, the same is made the head of the corner.

Sion is, of course, Zion, which is Jerusalem (see the words used as parallel expressions in Psalm 102:21; etc.). The Greek phrase translated *corner stone* or some variant of it occurs seven times in the New Testament (see Matthew 21:42; Mark 12:10; Luke 20:17). The second of the two uses here (*head of the corner*) quotes from Psalm 118:22. The two occurrences in today's text are entirely consistent in identifying this cornerstone as Jesus (compare Acts 4:11; Ephesians 2:20).

8. And a stone of stumbling, and a rock of offence, even to them which stumble at the word, being disobedient: whereunto also they were appointed.

The first two phrases are parallel expressions from Isaiah 8:14. In Hebrew poetry, parallel lines of poetry often describe only one thing but use two phrases with synonyms to do so. Thus the *stone of stumbling* and the *rock of offence* are two different ways of describing the same thing.

Much has been made of the fact that the Greek word for "offence" is *skandalon*, the source of our English word *scandal*. That is true, but it can also be misleading since the way we use the word *scandal* may not be the same as the way *skandalon* was used in the first century AD. The way the New Testament uses the parallel word translated *stumbling* comes to our rescue here. In 1 Corinthians 1:23, the apostle Paul is most direct in identifying the crucified Christ as this stumbling block. All devout Jews expected the Messiah (the Christ) to come, but no one expected Him to be crucified. The concept was downright offensive.

It is worthy of comment here that we do not often (or ever) present Jesus as *a stone of stumbling* or *a rock of offence*. We tend to prefer more appealing images, and quite often our evangelism bypasses the truth embedded in these phrases. Not everyone will believe when presented with the gospel; the crucifixion of Jesus can be incomprehensible for many.

The flip side of believers being "elect" (1 Peter 1:1-2), or destined to salvation, is that those who reject Christ are destined for destruction. Peter understood that God in His foreknowledge was aware that the enemies of the cross would reject the gospel, thus *they were appointed* to this. We can be sure, however, that Peter's heart longed for the salvation of his nation (compare Romans 9:1-3).

III. For a New Beginning
(1 Peter 2:9-10)
A. Identity, Part 1 (v. 9a-b)

9a. But ye are a chosen generation, a royal priesthood.

Chosen generation draws on the ancient Greek version (Septuagint) of Isaiah 43:20. The church as a chosen generation has not been granted that status because of its accomplishments, but because God selected it to be *a royal priesthood* (see discussion on 1 Peter 2:5, above; also compare wording in Exodus 19:6). In ancient Israel, those of royal lineage were separate and distinct from those in the priesthood. That changes in the New Testament era. Believers are royalty because of our relationship with King Jesus, but we're also priests in that we minister to one another.

I, the Priest

In my previous role as a hospital chaplain, I encountered an elderly man who was Roman Catholic. That tradition along with its religious terminology was deeply ingrained in him. That made it necessary for me to be creative in finding common ground on which to base my ministry to him.

My greatest challenge, however, was the fact that he was functionally blind and had extreme hearing loss. When I arrived for my weekly visit, his caregiver would announce, "The chaplain is here!" His response was always, "Who?" With more volume, she would then say, "The minister!" "WHO?" "THE *PRIEST!*" "Oh!" As he finally understood, a smile would cross his face.

I could have tried to correct his doctrinal error

in calling me a priest (as he had been taught to understand the matter). But my concern was more about bringing him closer to the Lord in his final days. I *was* a priest as I mediated Christ to him. When was the last time you mediated Christ to someone in your own role as a priest? —C. R. B.

9b. An holy nation, a peculiar people.

These two concepts draw on promises given to Israel. God told the people in Exodus 19:5-6 that they were to be unlike any other people on the earth in their dedication and service to God and in God's favor to them (compare Deuteronomy 7:6; 14:2). In the older English of the *King James Version*, the word *peculiar* has the sense of being a "unique possession" (compare Titus 2:14). God does not share the church with any other god. He is a jealous God (see Exodus 34:14). These descriptions and titles speak of the church as a collective of believers rather than merely as individuals who share the same beliefs.

B. Task (v. 9c)

9c. That ye should shew forth the praises of him who hath called you out of darkness into his marvellous light.

The contrast between spiritual *darkness* and *light* is a key New Testament theme (Matthew 4:16; Acts 26:17-18; among many others). We are not only *called . . . into his marvellous light*; we are indeed light, as the apostle Paul points out in Ephesians 5:8. The nature of our light sets us apart from unbelievers. To the degree that we fail to use that light to *shew forth the praises of him*, we lose the countercultural power of the Christian faith.

C. Identity, Part 2 (v. 10)

10. Which in time past were not a people, but are now the people of God: which had not obtained mercy, but now have obtained mercy.

The descriptions and titles Peter bestows on the baptized believers are all the more amazing when we consider the place from where the Jewish element of his audience had come. *In time past* they had forfeited their status as God's *people*, as seen in some of the lines Peter draws on from Hosea 1:6, 9-10; 2:1, 23. These speak of Israel's adulterous

faithlessness toward God. The Gentiles, for their part, had never been God's people just by definition. But in Christ the reversal for both was complete: believers are *the people of God* and recipients of His *mercy*. In light of that, no persecution or suffering at the hands of enemies of the cross can ultimately prevail.

> **What Do You Think?**
> In what ways would you describe being part of God's people as an example of His mercy?
> **Digging Deeper**
> What difference does it make to experience mercy in the context of community instead of solely as an individual?

Conclusion

A. Identity Redeemed

The question of identity is at the center of today's text. In the face of persecution and suffering, the believers to whom Peter wrote seemed to have had their doubts. In our contemporary world, the issue of our identity as Christians is just as important. Our world bombards us with endless identity options. These options in and of themselves range from the harmless to the sinful. But what all of these have in common is that they must give way before our allegiance to King Jesus.

Christians serve that king as members of royalty. Do we act like royalty in the best sense of the word? Do we treat fellow Christians as if they are princes and princesses alongside us? Most of all, do we honor King Jesus in all we do as His obedient servants? May we honor that role in the year 2023 and beyond as we work toward the unity of believers as the holy, royal nation of King Jesus.

B. Prayer

Lord God, help us to remember our identity in Your Son as we live out that identity. In Jesus' name we pray. Amen.

C. Thought to Remember

Our ultimate identity is to be found in Christ alone.

Involvement Learning

Enhance your lesson with KJV Bible Student *(from your curriculum supplier) and the reproducible activity page (at www.standardlesson.com or in the back of the* KJV Standard Lesson Commentary Deluxe Edition*).*

Into the Lesson

Before class, prepare individual slips of paper that contain one phrase on each slip: *Wearing brown shoes; Has blue eyes; Had breakfast today; Has a dog; Wears glasses only for reading; Is wearing a belt; Came to church in a truck; Is wearing a watch; Has brown hair; Has a younger brother; Owns a musical instrument; Has not answered yes so far; Was one of the first people in class today; Age is an even number; Has an older sister; Is wearing something blue.*

Randomly choose and read each slip while learners keep tally of the items to which they can answer yes. After reading all the slips, determine who has the highest score. Follow up by asking, "How do these answers show who you are?"

Alternative. Distribute copies of the "Which Category?" exercise from the activity page, which you can download. Have students complete it as directed.

After either activity, say, "Our identity is composed out of many facets of personality and experience. In today's text, Peter gives us metaphors for categories that help us better understand our identity as Christians."

Into the Word

Divide the class into three groups, designating one as the **Newborn Babies Group**, another one as the **Stones Group**, and the last as the **Royal Priesthood Group**. Distribute handouts (you create) of the questions below for in-group discussions.

Newborn Babies Group. Read 1 Peter 2:1-3. 1–Since they've been "born again," what activities should these new Gentile Christians be laying aside (1 Peter 1:23)? 2–Just like babies, what should these believers desire? 3–What are some activities that help new Christians grow? 4–By "tasting" the Word, what will they learn about the Lord?

Stones Group. Read 1 Peter 2:4-8. 1–Who is the living stone, rejected by men, but chosen by God? 2–What is our job as "lively stones" in Christ's "spiritual house"? 3–What does Peter teach us about Jesus by quoting Isaiah 28:16? 4–In what way is Jesus "a stone of stumbling" to unbelievers?

Priesthood Group. Read 1 Peter 2:9-10. 1–What are the four categories that describe Christians? 2–In what ways do Christians act as priests for other believers? 3–Explain how each of these four categories emphasizes community rather than individuality. 4–How does Peter use Hosea 2:23 to show the change in status these Gentile Christians were experiencing?

After allowing time for discussion, ask for volunteers from each group to share their answers. Then ask, "For Christians to be part of a 'holy priesthood,' what should they be doing? What thoughts and actions should they avoid?"

Into Life

Write Peter's four descriptive phrases for Christians on the board: *A chosen generation | A royal priesthood | A holy nation | A peculiar people.* Then write these new phrases beside the previous ones: *Be grateful | Be helpful | Be holy | Be unique.* Challenge learners to suggest ways the second set of phrases relates to the first set. (*Possible response:* As the chosen, we are to thank God for the honor of being His children. As priests, we are to help others get closer to the Lord. As a holy nation, we are to be holy people. As a peculiar people, we should be different from unbelievers.) Have students pair off and discuss which is the most difficult to live out. End with a challenge to choose one phrase to live out, throughout the week, as their identity in Christ.

Alternative. Distribute copies of the "Set Apart" activity from the activity page. Encourage students to finish the activity as a take-home.

Spring 2023
King James Version

Jesus
Calls Us

Special Features

Lessons

Unit 1: Called from the Margins of Society

Unit 2: Experiencing the Resurrection

Unit 3: The Birth of the Church

Quarterly Quiz

Use these questions as a pretest or as a review. The answers are on page iv of This Quarter in the Word.

Lesson 1

1. Which son asked for a portion of the father's goods? (older son, younger son, stepson) *Luke 15:12*

2. When the son returned to his father's house, the father ran to him. T/F. *Luke 15:20*

Lesson 2

1. The disciples asked, "Who is the _____ in the kingdom of heaven?" *Matthew 18:1*

2. Jesus told the disciples that unless they became like little children, they would never enter the kingdom of Heaven. T/F. *Matthew 18:3*

Lesson 3

1. The Samaritan woman asked if Jesus was "greater than" whom? (Abraham, Isaac, Jacob?) *John 4:12*

2. Jesus promised that He gave water "springing up into _____ life." *John 4:14*

Lesson 4

1. The man with an unclean spirit lived "among the _____." *Mark 5:3*

2. The spirits left the man and went into a herd of goats. T/F. *Mark 5:13*

Lesson 5

1. How did the women respond when they saw the two men? (bowed, prayed, fled) *Luke 24:5*

2. Mary Magdalene was among the women who found the Jesus' tomb empty. T/F. *Luke 24:10*

Lesson 6

1. The two travelers were going to what village? (Ephesus, Emmaus, Jerusalem) *Luke 24:13*

2. The travelers said that they believed that Jesus would redeem the world. T/F. *Luke 24:21*

Lesson 7

1. The fishing net was filled with how many fish? (40, 72, 153) *John 21:11*

2. Nathanael asked Jesus who He was. T/F. *John 21:12*

Lesson 8

1. How many times did the risen Jesus ask Peter, "Lovest thou me?" (1, 3, 7) *John 21:17*

2. Jesus commanded Peter, "_____ me!" *John 21:19*

Lesson 9

1. While John baptized with water, Luke promised a forthcoming baptism of the _____. *Acts 1:5*

2. The view of Jesus' ascension was blocked by a cloud. T/F. *Acts 1:9*

Lesson 10

1. In response to accusations of the crowd's drunkenness, Peter's quoted from the prophet _____. *Acts 2:16*

2. To receive the gift of the Holy Ghost, Peter told the crowd to do what? (choose two: sacrifice, repent, be baptized, be circumcised) *Acts 2:38*

Lesson 11

1. The temple gate to which the man was being carried was called _____. *Acts 3:2*

2. Peter had silver and gold to give the man at the temple gate. T/F. *Acts 3:6*

Lesson 12

1. Philip heard the man in the chariot reading from the prophet _____. *Acts 8:30*

2. After the eunuch was baptized, he took Philip to the next city in his chariot. T/F. *Acts 8:39*

Lesson 13

1. The Lord told Ananias to visit the house of _____. *Acts 9:11*

2. Ananias called Saul by what title? (Brother, Friend, Anointed?) *Acts 9:17*

Quarter at a Glance

What does it mean to be a citizen of the kingdom of Heaven? The lessons this quarter explore some of the most basic principles of Christian faith: that Christ's invitation is open to *all* people, that His resurrection changed everything, and that those who put their faith in Jesus and anticipate their own resurrections are Jesus' chosen community. These truths have much to reveal about what it means to live in the kingdom of Heaven, both in the present and in the glorious future we anticipate.

Open to All

Our first unit highlights accounts in which Jesus disregarded artificial societal barriers, choosing instead to reach people on the margins. Emotions, biases, and ignorance can stand in the way of accepting people as Jesus did. But the welcome of the prodigal son in Jesus' parable (Luke 15:11-24) sets the scene for all sorts of surprising people who can find their place in the kingdom of Heaven. Humble children (Matthew 18:1-9), foreigners, women, and even the formerly demon-possessed (Mark 5:1-13, 18-20; John 4) can find their place within Jesus' community.

How often are we unable to hear God's call, to perceive God's choice, because we are blinded by our own incomplete knowledge and conditional love? These lessons call us to examine our hearts and motives in order to see who we might think to be excluded from the kingdom . . . but whom Jesus himself has called to join Him.

Our New Reality

While we live in God's kingdom on earth and pray for its fullness "in earth, as it is in heaven" (Matthew 6:10), our hope is for nothing if Jesus has not been raised from the dead (1 Corinthians 15:1-19). As amazing as His resurrection remains, our second unit invites us to remember how difficult it was for Jesus' disciples to grasp that Jesus was raised back to life (Luke 24)—and how difficult it might be to continue to follow Him (John 21).

> The Spirit remains at work in us.

These lessons invite us to grapple with fear in the life of faith. Is it not often the case that we need to be reminded that we have been slow to understand (Luke 24:25), in part due to lingering fear? Are we not tempted, like Peter, to deny our Lord, even though we yearn to prove our love to Him (John 21:15-19)? Jesus' resurrection defines the kingdom of Heaven, and it is a kingdom intended to overcome not only death but also fear.

Our Heavenly Community

The work begun with Jesus' ministry and transformed by His death and resurrection continues in the community He chose: the church. The third unit takes us back to the earliest days of the church, which was and is God's instrument for the inbreaking of His kingdom. Jesus promised that the Holy Spirit would come (Acts 1:1-11); and ever since He did, God's kingdom has been transformed. Pentecost is one dramatic example of this (Acts 2). The same Spirit who empowered the disciples that day continued to work miracles for the sake of God's kingdom. These included healing (3:1-11), welcoming people into the community who had been excluded before (8:29-40), and recreating the heart of a man who zealously tried to destroy this emerging kingdom (9:9-17).

The gospel poses a threat to our ideas of status, esteem, security, and the way things ought to be. The Spirit was at work in the apostles and in the growth of the early church. And the Spirit remains at work in us, citizens of the kingdom of Heaven who continue to grow in faith, love, and hope.

Get the Setting

by Mark S. Krause

Societies contain barriers that marginalize certain people. These barriers come with all sorts of negative consequences for those being marginalized. Beyond a lack of resources or opportunities, marginalized groups often find that their contributions to society are not valued highly or that they don't even receive proper credit for their contributions! Many people in Jesus' day experienced marginalization to one degree or another, and this quarter will focus on some of their stories.

Roman and Jewish Margins

The Roman Empire was vast, and distance from its central city in many ways correlated with distance from its cultural heart. Devout Jews, especially those who resisted adopting Greco-Roman culture or continued to reside in the region that had been ancient Israel, were looked down on by their pagan neighbors. Jewish traditions such as circumcision, Sabbath-keeping, and ritual cleanliness laws were considered silly, even offensive, to Romans.

Jews from Galilee—like Jesus and several of His disciples—were marginalized even by fellow Jews who wielded influence from Jerusalem. Galilean Jews were seen as uneducated bumpkins in the urban center of Jerusalem (see John 7:41, 52; Acts 2:7-8). And their proximity to the Gentiles who settled in the region made these Jews only more suspect to Jerusalem's religious elite.

By the first century AD, many Gentiles had settled in Galilee (see Matthew 4:15). Strong Gentile cities such as Tiberias exerted influence throughout the region. Tiberias had become the capital city of Herod Antipas, the ruler of Galilee. The first-century Jewish historian Josephus records that Tiberias was built on a graveyard, perhaps a deliberate ploy by Antipas to discourage Jews from entering or settling in the city (see Numbers 19:11).

Gender Margins

In the first-century Jewish world, being a woman was considered no great honor. A rabbinical prayer dating to about this time reads in part, "Blessed art thou, O God, for not making me a Gentile, slave, or woman." Women were not permitted to take up the mantle of synagogue leadership nor given access to the inner courts of the Jerusalem temple. Women could not become sons of the covenant through circumcision. The witness of women in legal proceedings was considered highly unreliable. Though some women came to prominence in Rome, Jewish women were less likely to obtain power or influence outside of their homes.

Margins of Age

While the Jews had a higher view of children (particularly sons) than the Gentiles held, youngsters were still seen as more burden than blessing. The best thing about children was that they eventually grew up to be adults. This process was hastened in many ways. The rabbis of Jesus' time saw boys as entering manhood at age 12 or 13, now called the "bar mitzvah" (son of the covenant), thus beginning adulthood at the onset of puberty. In rural settings, young children were expected to work the fields, care for animals, and do household chores. Jewish parents were given responsibility to teach their children the ways of the law (Deuteronomy 4:9-10; 6:7).

Yet Jesus included women in His traveling band of disciples (Luke 8:2-3), and some of those women were the first witnesses to His resurrection (24:1-10)! One of His most dramatic healings was the resurrection of a girl, the daughter of Jairus (Mark 5:35-43). And, strikingly, Jesus did not use His fame to win favor among the Gentiles. Jesus understood His mission as being directed to "the lost sheep of . . . Israel" (Matthew 15:24). We have much to learn from Jesus' ministry to the marginalized.

This Quarter in the Word

Mon, Feb. 27	Lord, Hear My Prayer	Psalm 28
Tue, Feb. 28	Come to Me, You Weary	Matthew 11:25-30
Wed, Mar. 1	Jesus Shows Compassion	Matthew 14:13-21
Thu, Mar. 2	I Take Refuge in the Lord	Psalm 71:1-12
Fri, Mar. 3	I Will Proclaim God's Work	Psalm 71:13-24
Sat, Mar. 4	Heavenly Rejoicing!	Luke 15:1-10
Sun, Mar. 5	A Rebellious Son Restored	Luke 15:11-24
Mon, Mar. 6	Jesus Heals a Gentile Girl	Matthew 15:21-28
Tue, Mar. 7	Let the Little Children Come	Matthew 19:13-22
Wed, Mar. 8	Learn Wisdom, My Child	Proverbs 1:7-16
Thu, Mar. 9	Teach Your Children God's Laws	Deuteronomy 4:7-14
Fri, Mar. 10	Consecrated from the Womb	Jeremiah 1:1-10
Sat, Mar. 11	The Praises of Children	Matthew 21:12-17
Sun, Mar. 12	The Greatest in the Kingdom	Matthew 18:1-9; Mark 10:15
Mon, Mar. 13	Rivers of Living Water	John 7:37-43
Tue, Mar. 14	Worship God Alone	2 Kings 17:24-34
Wed, Mar. 15	Handling Opposition to God's Plans	Ezra 4:1-8, 11b-16
Thu, Mar. 16	Water on a Thirsty Land	Isaiah 44:1-8
Fri, Mar. 17	Jesus Offers Living Water	John 4:1-15
Sat, Mar. 18	Worship in Spirit and Truth	John 4:16-26
Sun, Mar. 19	Jesus, the Savior of the World	John 4:27-42

Mon, May 15	The Witness of Stephen	Acts 6:8-15
Tue, May 16	The First Martyr	Acts 7:48–8:2
Wed, May 17	The Far Countries Wait for God	Isaiah 60:9-14
Thu, May 18	Many People Will Come	Zechariah 8:1-8, 20-23
Fri, May 19	God Is Present Everywhere	Psalm 139:1-10
Sat, May 20	Samaritans Embrace the Gospel	Acts 8:4-17
Sun, May 21	The Spirit Guides Us	Acts 8:26-40
Mon, May 22	The Heavens Tell God's Glory	Psalm 19
Tue, May 23	Responding to the Gospel	Galatians 1:10-24
Wed, May 24	Only Christ Matters	Philippians 3:1-14
Thu, May 25	Our Citizenship Is in Heaven	Philippians 3:15-21
Fri, May 26	Blinded by the Light	Acts 9:1-9
Sat, May 27	Saul Preaches Jesus	Acts 9:10-22
Sun, May 28	Saul Escapes to Jerusalem	Acts 9:23-31

Answers to the Quarterly Quiz on page 226

Lesson 1—1. younger son. 2. True. **Lesson 2**—1. greatest. 2. True. **Lesson 3**—1. Jacob. 2. everlasting. **Lesson 4**—1. tombs. 2. False. **Lesson 5**—1. bowed. 2. True. **Lesson 6**—1. Emmaus. 2. False. **Lesson 7**—1. 153. 2. False. **Lesson 8**—1. 3. 2. Follow. **Lesson 9**—1. Holy Ghost. 2. True. **Lesson 10**—1. Joel. 2. repent, be baptized. **Lesson 11**—1. Beautiful. 2. False. **Lesson 12**—1. Esaias. 2. False. **Lesson 13**—1. Judas. 2. Brother.

Map Feature

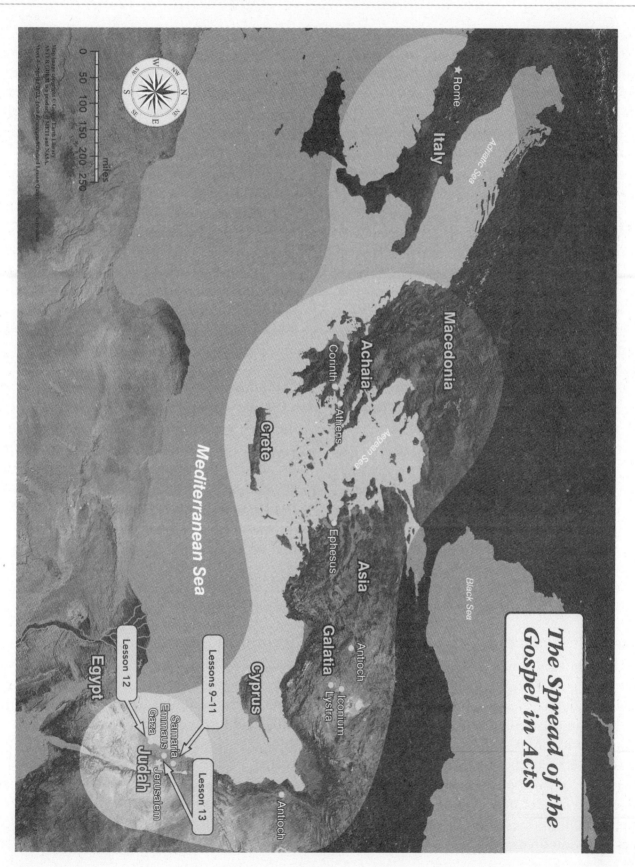

The Spread of the Gospel in Acts

Rome

Italy

Adriatic Sea

Macedonia

Achaia

Corinth

Athens

Aegean Sea

Crete

Black Sea

Mediterranean Sea

Ephesus

Asia

Galatia

Antioch

Iconium

Lystra

Cyprus

Antioch

Egypt

Samaria

Emmaus

Gaza

Judah

Jerusalem

Lesson 12

Lessons 9–11

Lesson 13

0 50 100 150 200 250

miles

Break It Up!

Teacher Tips by Mary T. Lederleitner

Your learners' ability to concentrate likely depends on the task on which they are concentrating. However, teacher beware! Lecture time is not always the best teaching style. Learning a few other strategies to intersperse with lecturing can result in more dynamic learning opportunities. So what other strategies can you try? Here are a few ideas to get you started!

Get Buy-In

Getting the buy-in of your learners is one of the best ways to help them stay focused. The best way to do this is by asking questions regarding their perspective on the topic being taught. You might consider asking why they think this topic is important. How will their lives will be affected positively or negatively by the main point? By asking these kinds of questions early in your teaching time, you will find that learners become more motivated to pay attention. With the relevance bar now raised high, they are primed to learn deeply.

Lecture in Small Segments

As you prepare your lesson, consider what key points you want your learners to retain. Try limiting lecture to no more than 10 minutes at a time. Focus these chunks of time on covering the main ideas you identified, before moving to activities that reinforce these key points.

Use Multimedia Presentations

Using images, songs, and story within lecture time engages different regions of the brain than having students merely listen to you. Having more of the brain engaged, in turn, creates avenues for long-term retention of material. When using a visual presentation, be sure to include an image on every slide or two; you may even choose to make slides with no text, only images. Using images to support your lecture breaks up your message and makes it a multisensory experience.

During lecture, tell a story. It does not have to be your own; consider using the Verbal Illustrations provided in each lesson! Or play a relevant song or video clip (with permission) that further explains or demonstrates your teaching point.

Imagining Exercises

Engaging the imagination is another way to stimulate more brain centers and increase the likelihood of lasting learning. Provide a time of personal reflection of no more than five minutes. Ask learners to spend the time considering how they might follow a key application point in their various spheres of influence. After time has passed, ask a few volunteers to share the results of their imagining exercise.

Buzz Moments

Short so-called buzz moments can be immensely effective at maintaining the focus of your learners. The practice consists of getting your learners "buzzing" as they quickly share what they are learning with other learners. Begin the exercise by asking class members each to turn to one other student and share one point from the class that they feel is most important. Another possible way to create a buzz moment would be for learners to share what most inspires or excites them about the topic of the day.

Planning for Growth

Giving learners opportunities to plan for growth helps keep them engaged beyond class time. At the beginning of class, give your learners a handout for note-taking. At the top of the handout, have the following questions printed: "What will you do to act on what you have learned?" "Who will you ask for accountability in this regard?" These two questions will give learners the opportunity to reflect on how they will apply what they have learned.

The Prodigal Son

Devotional Reading: Psalm 28
Background Scripture: Luke 15:11-32

Luke 15:11-24

11 And he said, A certain man had two sons:

12 And the younger of them said to his father, Father, give me the portion of goods that falleth to me. And he divided unto them his living.

13 And not many days after the younger son gathered all together, and took his journey into a far country, and there wasted his substance with riotous living.

14 And when he had spent all, there arose a mighty famine in that land; and he began to be in want.

15 And he went and joined himself to a citizen of that country; and he sent him into his fields to feed swine.

16 And he would fain have filled his belly with the husks that the swine did eat: and no man gave unto him.

17 And when he came to himself, he said, How many hired servants of my father's have bread enough and to spare, and I perish with hunger!

18 I will arise and go to my father, and will say unto him, Father, I have sinned against heaven, and before thee,

19 And am no more worthy to be called thy son: make me as one of thy hired servants.

20 And he arose, and came to his father. But when he was yet a great way off, his father saw him, and had compassion, and ran, and fell on his neck, and kissed him.

21 And the son said unto him, Father, I have sinned against heaven, and in thy sight, and am no more worthy to be called thy son.

22 But the father said to his servants, Bring forth the best robe, and put it on him; and put a ring on his hand, and shoes on his feet:

23 And bring hither the fatted calf, and kill it; and let us eat, and be merry:

24 For this my son was dead, and is alive again; he was lost, and is found. And they began to be merry.

Key Text

The son said unto him, Father, I have sinned against heaven, and in thy sight, and am no more worthy to be called thy son. —**Luke 15:21**

Jesus Calls Us

Unit 1: Called from the Margins of Society
Lessons 1–4

Lesson Aims

After participating in this lesson, each learner will be able to:

1. Identify the younger son's choices and the outcome of each choice.

2. Identify who each figure in the parable represents in real life.

3. Make a plan to confront his or her own resistance to receiving grace and forgiveness.

Lesson Outline

Introduction

A. Family Reunions

Did you look forward to your most recent family reunion, or did the thought of attending bring dread? For many families, these occasions are joyous as multiple generations assemble for conversation, celebration, and recollection, frequently over a cherished family meal.

However, other family situations are more complicated and painful. At best, the relationships within those families might feel cold or be difficult to tolerate. At worst, those relationships might be characterized by cruelty, mean-spiritedness, or even abuse. In such a family system, whole and harmonious relationships seem unattainable.

Shame or selfishness is often at the root of broken families. Scripture describes families who experienced conflict for these reasons (Genesis 21:1-20; 27; 37; etc.). Would Jesus' depiction of a broken family repeat these themes? Could He use these themes to change the hearts of His audience?

B. Lesson Context

The meaning and implications of parables have been greatly debated. The Greek word translated "parable" (Matthew 15:15; Mark 4:13; Luke 8:9; etc.) is also translated as "proverb" (4:23). In the Septuagint, the ancient Greek translation of the Old Testament, a form of the same Greek word is used regarding a proverb (Ezekiel 18:2) or a song of warning (Micah 2:4).

At their core, biblical parables compare something familiar—like an object or experience—to a truth about God and His work. Parables function on two levels: their literal reference and their spiritual implications. Jesus taught with parables to challenge His audience to consider what assumptions or attitudes of theirs were at odds with God's work (compare Matthew 13:10-15).

Today's Scripture is frequently called the parable of the prodigal son. While modern audiences sometimes use the designation "prodigal" to speak of the rebellion of the younger son, the word's meaning is associated with reckless waste and spending.

This parable is the third in a series in Luke 15. The other parables describe a lost sheep (15:3-7) and a lost coin (15:8-10). All three parables include similar themes: (1) something valuable is lost, (2) the lost thing is found, and (3) celebration ensues.

Jesus told these parables as a response to criticism from Pharisees and scribes. These groups were upset because Jesus "receiveth sinners, and eateth with them" (Luke 15:2). Throughout His ministry, Jesus associated with people whom the religious leaders considered unclean.

These people included "publicans" (Luke 5:30; 15:1), Jews who collected taxes for the ruling powers. Tax collectors were hated and regarded as having betrayed their people because they assisted the Roman Empire and acted corruptly (see 3:12-13).

Another group that Jesus frequently associated with was "sinners" (Matthew 9:11; Luke 7:34; 15:2). This title applied to people who had failed to follow the Law of Moses as interpreted by the religious leaders of the day.

Jesus' association with these people was not limited to the public gatherings. He shared meals with them before they had sought the proper means of forgiveness and restitution as prescribed by the law. His association with them was critical to His mission to seek those who are lost (see Luke 19:10) and bring repentance and salvation (5:29-31).

I. The Dishonorable Son
(Luke 15:11-19)
A. Shameful Demand (vv. 11-12)

11. And he said, A certain man had two sons.

The characters in Jesus' parables were generally left unnamed (examples: Luke 14:16; 16:1; 20:9; contrast 16:20, 23). This practice hinted to the audience that He was teaching by way of a parable and not speaking of real individuals. Jesus' introduction of *a certain man* and his *two sons* contin-

ues that trend. Today's lesson, however, will only focus on the interactions between the younger son and the father. The narrative of the older son (15:25-32) will not be included.

12a. And the younger of them said to his father, Father, give me the portion of goods that falleth to me.

Children traditionally did not receive their father's inheritance until the father's death (see Numbers 27:8-11). The *younger* son's request for his *portion* of the inheritance was effectively saying, "*Father*, I wish you were dead."

12b. And he divided unto them his living.

Each son would have received part of the father's property in the inheritance. Jesus does not describe the measures by which the father *divided* the inheritance. Based on the Law of Moses, the oldest son would have received a double portion (see Deuteronomy 21:15-17). Either son's portion could have included land (see Genesis 48:21-22), a house (see Proverbs 19:14), and other items of wealth (see 2 Chronicles 21:3).

The son's request implied tremendous dishonor toward the father and exhibited a rebellious attitude toward the family. The Law of Moses prescribed harsh consequences for a son who displayed stubbornness and rebellion toward his family (see Deuteronomy 21:18-21). Rather than respond according to the letter of the law, though, this father responded with mercy and grace. The father sought no retribution, despite his son's vile and dishonorable request.

B. Selfish Decisions (vv. 13-16)

13a. And not many days after the younger son gathered all together, and took his journey into a far country.

CONFESS YOUR SINS. DON'T STAY MIRED IN THE MUCK!

Visual for Lesson 1. *Discuss reasons why a person might stay "mired in the muck" without even realizing the need to repent.*

It was one thing for *the younger son* to demand his portion of the inheritance. However, for him to gather *all* that he had and leave the land of his family added further insult. By leaving nothing behind as he left for *his journey* implied that he did not intend to return. The parable does not reveal the name or location of the *far country*. Jesus wanted to keep the focus of the parable on the attitudes and actions of the son, not identify the country to which he relocated. Not only did the son want nothing to do with his father; the son physically distanced himself through his own relocation.

13b. And there wasted his substance with riotous living.

The son did not lose the *substance* of his inheritance through shrewd-but-failed investments. Instead, he *wasted* it through undisciplined behavior as he "devoured [the resources] with harlots" (Luke 15:30). The son piled shame upon shame; he brought further disgrace to his father and family name—all for gluttonous, *riotous living* (compare Proverbs 28:7).

14. And when he had spent all, there arose a mighty famine in that land; and he began to be in want.

Famines were frequent in biblical times, just as they are in parts of the world today. These famines would occur when crops failed because of drought (see 1 Kings 18:1-2; Jeremiah 14:1-6) or an infestation of insects (see Joel 1:2-10). Famine also resulted when fields went unharvested because of warfare (see 2 Kings 6:24-25; 25:1-3). The effect of the *mighty famine*, not its cause, was most important for the teaching point of the parable.

During a famine, people relied on the generosity of their relatives, neighbors, and leaders (examples: Genesis 41:56–42:2; 45:9-11; 2 Kings 8:1-2; Ruth 1:1). But the younger son had no such social network to provide care during this crisis.

Not only did he lack social connections, but *he had spent all* his money. These resources would have sheltered him from experiencing much of the effects of the famine. His survival would depend on his savvy actions, not his wealth.

15. And he went and joined himself to a citizen of that country; and he sent him into his fields to feed swine.

The son's desperation led him to take degrading work as the hired hand of *a citizen* of the famine-inflicted *country*. *Swine* (pigs) were considered unclean by the Law of Moses (Leviticus 11:7-8). Jesus' Jewish audience would have considered this job to be humiliating. Because the citizen owned swine, *he* was likely a Gentile (a non-Jew). The son's work would remind him the extent of his abandonment of his family and their heritage.

The son suffered three levels of shame: he wasted his wealth, became a servant, and took a job feeding swine. For Jesus' audience, the son had received the appropriate consequences for his dishonorable acts. He had brought shame to his father and household, and now multiple levels of shame were heaped on him. The parable seemed to fulfill an ancient proverb: "The righteous eateth to the satisfying of his soul: but the belly of the wicked shall want" (Proverbs 13:25; compare 13:18).

16. And he would fain have filled his belly with the husks that the swine did eat: and no man gave unto him.

Any food provided (if at all) was so unappealing that it made the food *that the swine did eat* seem desirable. The exact nature of *the husks* is unknown, but students have proposed that they came from the pods of a carob tree. The swine received better care than the son. He was without support or hope. The son lived up to (or down to) the designation "prodigal" (see Lesson Context).

C. Sorrowful Direction (vv. 17-19)

17a. And when he came to himself, he said.

The son had to come to the point of desiring pig food to realize his foolishness; he had wasted the material blessings that he had received. Though he had yet to repent, the statement *he came to himself* implied the first step of repentance. He recognized the faulty direction of his life and felt sorrow as a result (see 2 Corinthians 7:10).

17b. How many hired servants of my father's have bread enough and to spare, and I perish with hunger!

The son's sorrow and regret were based on his firsthand knowledge of his *father's* generosity. While the son desired pig food, he remembered that his father provided lavishly. All in the father's house had more than *enough* to eat.

As a result, the son viewed his father's generosity from the perspective of the *hired servants*. Because he had demanded his share of the inheritance, he experienced shame. But even worse than shame, he had forfeited his position as a son. If he were to receive generosity from his father, it would not be as a privileged son. Instead, he could only imagine receiving the same level of generosity that a hired worker received (compare Luke 12:35-38).

18. I will arise and go to my father, and will say unto him, Father, I have sinned against heaven, and before thee.

The son planned his way forward, based on his knowledge of his father's generosity and his own unworthy and shameful status. The first step would be to leave the foreign land where he had squandered his wealth.

The second step involved showing repentance for the ways that he had *sinned*. Recognizing sin and confessing guilt are the first steps of repentance (see Leviticus 5:5). The son acknowledged his sin: he had rebelled against his father, thus breaking the fifth commandment (Exodus 20:12). The son's rebellion was also directed *against* God since *heaven* is the place where God resides.

By confessing his sin, the son hoped to receive mercy from his father (see Proverbs 28:13). However, that response was not certain, given the stubborn and rebellious actions of the son (see Deuteronomy 21:18-21).

> ### What Do You Think?
> How do feelings of shame or sorrow lead a person to repentance?
> ### Digging Deeper
> How do 1 Corinthians 6:1-11; 2 Corinthians 7:8-11; and 2 Thessalonians 3:14-15 inform your answer?

19. And am no more worthy to be called thy son: make me as one of thy hired servants.

The son did not expect to be restored to his former status in his father's household. He hoped that perhaps the father would show mercy and grant him a place of service in the household, *as one of* the *hired servants*. In this role, the son would at least receive wages for his work (compare Matthew 20:1-15). However, working every day for his father would remind the son of his shameful acts.

II. The Compassionate Father
(Luke 15:20-24)

A. Emotional Reconciliation (vv. 20-21)

20. And he arose, and came to his father. But when he was yet a great way off, his father saw him, and had compassion, and ran, and fell on his neck, and kissed him.

The statement that the son was seen while he was still *a great way off* indicates that at the very least *his father* had been scanning the horizon. Despite the disrespect that the father had endured, he hoped that his lost and prodigal son would return. That return is an act of repentance even before the son could express such repentance in words.

The father disregarded any perceived indignity as he *ran* toward his son. Reunion was immediate! Physical displays of affection, such as how the father wrapped his arms around his son's *neck*

How to Say It

Gentile	*Jen*-tile.
parable	*pair*-uh-buhl.
prodigal	*prod*-i-guhl.
Septuagint	Sep-*too*-ih-jent.

and *kissed* him, were not uncommon at the time. Family members exhibited such affection regularly (Genesis 27:26-27; 48:10), even toward those members previously estranged (33:4; 45:14-15). The father's response revealed his heart of grace, mercy, and forgiveness.

Jesus intended that the father's forgiveness reveal the *compassion* of God. When God's people rebel, He responds with mercy (examples: Nehemiah 9:17-18; Daniel 9:9). His compassion is like that of a loving father toward his children (Psalm 103:13). But we realize at the same time that God's mercy has limits; He will not tolerate unrepentant, unending rebellion (example: 2 Kings 22:10-17; 24:2-4).

21. And the son said unto him, Father, I have sinned against heaven, and in thy sight, and am no more worthy to be called thy son.

The son remained committed to his plan of repentance and humility (see Luke 15:18-19, above). Despite the affection that he received, the son maintained his intentions to surrender his position in his father's house and offer himself as a hired servant.

What Do You Think?

In what ways is biblical repentance more than saying "I'm sorry"?

Digging Deeper

How will you ensure that future repentance will be followed by appropriate action (see Matthew 3:8; Acts 26:20)?

All-Encompassing Forgiveness

John watched his life spiral out of control. He had rebelled against his parents and disregarded the commitments that he had made as a believer. Because of anger, neglect of relationships, and substance abuse, John squandered his life and ignored his relationship with God.

However, John reconnected with a Christian friend who treated him with compassion and gentleness. Through this patient friendship, John realized the importance of showing repentance—to God and other people—for his previous misdeeds. John trusted that God would forgive him, and he recommitted his life to being a disciple of Jesus.

John's account and the example of the younger son in today's parable should encourage you to trust the all-encompassing nature of God's forgiveness. There is no situation too shameful for God to forgive. Can the same be said of how you react to others who have wronged you? (See Matthew 18:23-35; Ephesians 4:32.)   —C. R. B.

B. Gracious Celebration (vv. 22-24)

22. But the father said to his servants, Bring forth the best robe, and put it on him; and put a ring on his hand, and shoes on his feet.

The father interrupted his son's plan with a plan of his own. The son no longer needed to suffer humiliation; he would be restored to a position of honor. Fine clothing and rings were signs of authority and power (examples: Genesis 41:41-43; Esther 3:10-12; compare and contrast James 2:2-4). By receiving *the best robe* and *a ring*, the once-shamed son again shared in his father's wealth and authority.

23. And bring hither the fatted calf, and kill it; and let us eat, and be merry.

Slaughtering a *fatted calf* was not a frequent occurrence in Jesus' time. Not only would its meat need to be eaten quickly, but the animal was more than one family could consume. Neighbors would join the family to *eat* of it and celebrate the return of the lost son (compare Genesis 18:6-8).

The other parables in Luke 15 depict celebrations that occurred after the recovery of something lost (Luke 15:5-6, 9). These celebrations were intended to teach Jesus' audience of heavenly celebrations that follow repentance (15:7, 10).

24. For this my son was dead, and is alive again; he was lost, and is found. And they began to be merry.

The *son* had previously treated his father as if he were dead to him (see commentary on Luke 15:12, above). And by abandoning his family, the son had effectively become *dead* to his father. Despite the son's previously selfish actions, he was restored and considered *alive* to the father—a reason for the father *to be merry* and celebrate.

In this parable, Jesus' audience of publicans, sinners, Pharisees, and scribes (Luke 15:1-2) heard echoes of God's promise. To obey God leads to life, but to rebel against Him leads to destruction (Deuteronomy 30:15-18). The implications are profound. For the publicans and sinners, the promise is one of renewed acceptance upon their repentance. For the Pharisees and scribes, the promise is one of warning, a warning made more explicit in Matthew 21:28-32, another parable about two sons.

God promised to be generous and patient; celebration with joy and gladness would come when His people returned to Him (see Isaiah 35:9-10). God's people have confidence that He will show mercy and provide spiritual life, even when they are dead in their sin (see Ephesians 2:1-10).

The parable, however, does not end with the father's display of generosity and mercy. In its second part, Jesus focused on the anger of the older brother regarding the father's treatment of the younger brother (Luke 15:25-30). The parable's focus on mercy and generosity can be summarized by the father's response to the older brother: "We should make merry, and be glad: for this thy brother was dead, and is alive again; and was lost, and is found" (15:32).

What Do You Think?

In what ways can the life of a believer give evidence that new life from God lives within them?

Digging Deeper

How can believers celebrate regarding the spiritual transformation that they have experienced?

Plotlines

After watching numerous romantic comedy movies, I've noticed that many of these films have similar plotlines. These plotlines include a blossoming romance, mistaken motivations, the return of a former lover, conflict between all parties, and a "happily ever after" ending. I'm now at the point where I can almost always predict the plot.

The original audience of today's parable likely thought that they could predict its plot. The son had brought shame and dishonor to his father. The audience was prepared to hear that the son received harsh consequences from his father,

just as the law had prescribed. The parable's plot appeared so predictable.

However, Jesus inverted such expectations. The father's demonstration of kindness and generosity toward his lost son went beyond what was expected. In what other ways do Jesus' teachings upend your expectations?　　　　—C. R. B.

Conclusion
A. Lost and Found

Today's parable invites all people to embrace the upside-down nature of the family of God. In this family, God offers and desires reunion where broken relationships exist. We may feel shamefully unworthy, as the parable's younger son felt. However, like the parable's father, God is generous and merciful. His generosity has been displayed for centuries (see Numbers 14:8; Deuteronomy 28:11; Ephesians 3:16; James 1:5; etc.). Like a shepherd who cares for his flock, God cares for His people and provides for their needs (see Psalm 23:1; 1 Timothy 6:17). Such actions give testimony to all people of God's generosity and faithfulness (Acts 14:17).

God welcomes all people to become His beloved children in His family. He desires His people to feel hope and not shame (see Romans 5:5; 1 John 3:1). "And now, little children, abide in him; that, when he shall appear, we may have confidence, and not be ashamed before him at his coming" (2:28).

B. Prayer

Heavenly Father, You are loving, merciful, and kind. We rejoice that You accept us into Your family and love us. Help us reveal Your kindness and generosity to others. In Jesus' name. Amen.

C. Thought to Remember

Do you need to return to God?

Visuals FOR THESE LESSONS

The visual pictured in each lesson (example: page 236) is a small reproduction of a large, full-color poster included in the *Adult Resources* packet for the Spring Quarter. Order No. 3629122 from your supplier.

Involvement Learning

Enhance your lesson with KJV Bible Student *(from your curriculum supplier) and the reproducible activity page (at www.standardlesson.com or in the back of the* KJV Standard Lesson Commentary Deluxe Edition*).*

Into the Lesson

Give each learner an index card to write down a decision that a person might make. After one minute, collect the cards, shuffle them, and redistribute the cards to learners. Ensure that learners do not receive their own card. Have learners silently read their card. After one minute, ask for volunteers to share what might be an appropriate consequence for the decision written on their index card. Based on the consequence provided, give the whole class three guesses regarding the decision written on the card.

Alternative. Distribute copies of the "Would You Rather?" exercise from the activity page, which you can download. Have learners complete it individually in a minute or less before discussing conclusions in whole-class discussion.

After either activity, lead into the Bible study by saying, "All decisions have consequences. As we read the parable in today's Scripture, consider how your decisions would be similar to or different from the decisions made by each character."

Into the Word

Divide the class into two groups: the **Father Group** and the **Younger Son Group**. Allow time for the groups to read Luke 15:11-13 and write a diary entry from the perspective of their group's character. Instruct groups to use their "sanctified imagination" to fill in the gaps of their entries regarding their character's thoughts and feelings. After several minutes, ask a volunteer from each group to read their group's diary entry to the whole class.

Alternative. Distribute copies of the "If You Ask Me" activity from the activity page. Have learners complete prompts 1 and 2. After one minute, discuss responses in whole-class discussion.

Have the groups read Luke 15:14-19 and write a second diary entry based on their character's perspective in these specific verses. Encourage groups to consider the consequences of their character's decisions, using their "sanctified imagination" where necessary. After several minutes, ask a volunteer from each group to read their group's diary entry to the whole class.

Alternative. Have learners complete prompts 3 and 4 on the "If You Ask Me" activity page. After one minute, invite volunteers to share their responses and explain how the responses are similar to or different from the parable's narrative.

Have the groups read Luke 15:20-24 and write a third diary entry based on their character's perspective in these specific verses. Encourage groups to consider their character's treatment of the other character, using their "sanctified imagination" where necessary. After several minutes, ask a volunteer from each group to read their group's diary entry to the whole class.

Alternative. Have participants complete prompts 5 and 6 on the "If You Ask Me" activity page. After one minute, invite volunteers to share their responses and how the responses best connect with the characters or events of the parable.

Into Life

In whole-class discussion, make a list of attitudes, mindsets, and experiences that can cause a person to encounter resistance to receiving grace and forgiveness. Write responses on the board.

Distribute an index card to each learner. In one minute or less, have learners write down which of the responses is most true for them personally regarding their own resistance to receiving grace and forgiveness. Have learners flip over the index card and write a plan to confront the attitude, mindset, or experience that can cause resistance. Allow no more than one minute to complete this second part.

Conclude class by encouraging learners to consult their index card throughout the week to be encouraged by God's continued work in them.

The Greatest in the Kingdom

Devotional Reading: Matthew 19:13-22
Background Scripture: Matthew 18:1-9; Mark 10:15

Matthew 18:1-9

1 At the same time came the disciples unto Jesus, saying, Who is the greatest in the kingdom of heaven?

2 And Jesus called a little child unto him, and set him in the midst of them,

3 And said, Verily I say unto you, Except ye be converted, and become as little children, ye shall not enter into the kingdom of heaven.

4 Whosoever therefore shall humble himself as this little child, the same is greatest in the kingdom of heaven.

5 And whoso shall receive one such little child in my name receiveth me.

6 But whoso shall offend one of these little ones which believe in me, it were better for him that a millstone were hanged about his neck, and that he were drowned in the depth of the sea.

7 Woe unto the world because of offences! for it must needs be that offences come; but woe to that man by whom the offence cometh!

8 Wherefore if thy hand or thy foot offend thee, cut them off, and cast them from thee: it is better for thee to enter into life halt or maimed, rather than having two hands or two feet to be cast into everlasting fire.

9 And if thine eye offend thee, pluck it out, and cast it from thee: it is better for thee to enter into life with one eye, rather than having two eyes to be cast into hell fire.

Key Text

Whosoever therefore shall humble himself as this little child, the same is greatest in the kingdom of heaven. —**Matthew 18:4**

Jesus
Calls Us

Unit 1: Called from the Margins of Society
Lessons 1–4

Lesson Aims

After participating in this lesson, each learner will be able to:

1. Summarize Jesus' view of greatness.

2. Compare and contrast Jesus' view of greatness with that of the disciples.

3. State one way that he or she will practice childlike humility in the coming week.

Lesson Outline

Introduction
    A. What a Child Wants
    B. Lesson Context
I. Measure of Greatness (Matthew 18:1-5)
    A. Presumptive Question (v. 1)
       GOAT
    B. Perplexing Example (vv. 2-3)
    C. Primary Position (vv. 4-5)
       Learning from Children
II. Warning of Sin (Matthew 18:6-9)
    A. Regarding Little Ones (vv. 6-7)
    B. Regarding the Self (vv. 8-9)
Conclusion
    A. Humility and Self-Control
    B. Prayer
    C. Thought to Remember

Introduction

A. What a Child Wants

Children can't wait to grow up! They think that "growing up" means experiencing a life of unchecked freedom and complete autonomy. Ask any child how they would act as a grown-up, and their answers will reflect an expectation for freedom. For example, as a child, I anticipated that I would express my grown-up freedom by eating a container of cake frosting whenever I desired. However, I have yet to do that as an adult!

Although children want agency and power, they depend on caretakers to provide for their needs and wants. For this reason, the world does not customarily regard children as examples of greatness and power. But that did not prevent Jesus from using a child to teach His followers.

B. Lesson Context

By the time of today's text, Jesus' disciples had witnessed His divine power through His acts of healing (Matthew 14:35-36) and exorcism (15:21-28; 17:14-18), miraculous provision (14:15-21; 15:32-38), and control over creation (14:22-33). The apostles Peter, James, and John witnessed Jesus' power personally as they observed Jesus transfigured before them (17:1-13; Mark 9:2). Later, Peter interpreted the transfiguration as showing Jesus' divine honor and glory (2 Peter 1:16-18). In that event, God's power was revealed in and through Jesus Christ.

Peter acknowledged Jesus as "the Christ, the Son of the living God" (Matthew 16:16). The title *Christ* is the Greek equivalent of the Hebrew word *Messiah* (John 1:41). Both designations refer to the anointed one of God, a phrase describing God's chosen king (see 1 Samuel 16:1, 12-13; 2 Samuel 7:8-16).

When acknowledging Jesus as the Christ, Peter had certain expectations regarding Christ's work. Hebrew Scripture, also called the Old Testament, traces the contours of God's anointed one's liberating His people, sitting on God's throne, and ruling in righteousness (compare Genesis 49:10; Psalms 110:1; 132:11-12; Isaiah 16:5; Micah 5:2; etc.). Jews assumed that the Messiah would come with power and strength as the anointed servant of God (see Isaiah 42:1-4). They did not desire or expect a suffering and humbled Messiah (see Matthew 16:21-22; compare 20:25-28).

The Gospel writers use different names for God's rule on earth as inaugurated by the Christ. All four Gospels include the designation "kingdom of God" (Matthew 12:28; Mark 12:34; Luke 9:2; John 3:5; etc.). However, Matthew's Gospel includes a second designation: the "kingdom of heaven" (Matthew 3:2; 4:17; etc.). The reason for Matthew's unique designation is unknown, but students propose that Matthew used it to avoid writing the holy name of God. Both designations refer to the eternal kingdom established by God where He rules (see Psalms 145:11, 13; 103:19; compare John 18:36).

Jesus' teaching and ministry prepared people to receive this kingdom (see Matthew 4:17; Luke 8:1). To receive the kingdom requires that people be born again (John 3:3-8) and obey the will of God (Matthew 7:21). Today's Scripture reveals a third condition to enter God's kingdom. Parallel texts to today's lesson are Mark 9:33-37 and Luke 9:46-48.

I. Measure of Greatness
(Matthew 18:1-5)

A. Presumptive Question (v. 1)

1. At the same time came the disciples unto Jesus, saying, Who is the greatest in the kingdom of heaven?

Jesus had been teaching on the practices of "the kings of the earth" (Matthew 17:25). Although He was not teaching regarding God's kingdom, His *disciples* began considering *at the same time* their own position in that promised *kingdom*. The 12 disciples had been arguing regarding *who* from among them would be the *greatest* (Luke 9:46). Their discussions and arguments regarding their position continued, even as they shared the last meal with Jesus before His arrest (see 22:24). If the Messiah were to rule in the same manner as an earthly ruler, then the Messiah would require positions of lesser authority in His kingdom. The disciples assumed that they would fill such roles.

Jesus had previously shown special regard for Peter (see Matthew 16:17-19) along with James and John (17:1). At that time, the three saw Jesus transfigured before them (17:2-13). They were told to remain silent regarding what they had seen (17:9), and they obeyed (Luke 9:36). The separation of these three from the rest of the Twelve might have accelerated possible conflict among members of the entire group (compare the later episode of Matthew 20:22-24).

Had the disciples comprehended Jesus' previous teachings, they would have understood how inappropriate their question was. Jesus had already defined the character of a person considered great in the kingdom *of heaven* (Matthew 5:19-20; compare 11:11). The disciples were unaware that this kingdom was already in their midst (Luke 17:20-21).

> **What Do You Think?**
> When is it appropriate for Christians to concern ourselves with greatness?
> **Digging Deeper**
> In what situations can a focus on greatness become a distraction or even an idol?

GOAT

Who's the goat? No, I'm not referring to the ruminant farm animal. Instead, I'm referring to the "Greatest of All Time"—the GOAT. This title is bestowed on people regarded as the greatest in their field of work or performance. Conversations regarding a GOAT in professional sports leagues can turn heated. Among sports fans, there are numerous metrics for defining who is the GOAT. However, fans acknowledge that success and the prestige it brings are necessary for an athlete to be designated the GOAT in his or her sport.

An assumption of prestige and success was central to the disciples' question. They believed that Jesus would define *greatest* in a manner consistent with the world's assumptions. Do you seek worldly measures of success and prestige so that you might be great by the world's expectations? Or, instead, can you practice faithful and humble service to the Lord who is "great . . . and greatly to be praised" (Psalm 145:3)?   —T. Z. S.

B. Perplexing Example (vv. 2-3)

2. And Jesus called a little child unto him, and set him in the midst of them.

Jesus did not answer the disciples' question directly. Instead, He incorporated a visual teaching aid to make His forthcoming point more vivid. During His earthly ministry, Jesus used a variety of teaching methods, including parables (examples: Luke 15:1–16:15; see lesson 1) and physical illustrations (examples: Mark 12:41-44; John 13:3-17). Jesus' use of these teaching methods was one reason that His hearers were "astonished" about His authoritative teaching (Matthew 7:28-29).

3a. And said, Verily I say unto you, Except ye be converted.

To *be converted* in this verse does not refer to a person's conversion to salvation. Instead, Jesus was teaching of a general conversion of thought: a person's process of changing his or her consideration on a matter. The underlying Greek word occurs some two dozen times in the New Testament, and it is almost always translated as some variation of the word *turn* (examples: Matthew 5:39; 7:6); that is the sense here.

3b. And become as little children, ye shall not enter into the kingdom of heaven.

Jesus did not imply that His followers should *become* like immature or naïve *little children* (compare Matthew 10:16; 1 Corinthians 13:11; 14:20). Rather, what is implied is having a sense of being guileless and without pretense. The world's definitions of power and acclaim do not apply to God's kingdom (compare Mark 10:31).

What Do You Think?

What positions of status or influence do you hold? If following Jesus required you to renounce them, how would you do it?

Digging Deeper

What would leadership look like based on being childlike?

C. Primary Position (vv. 4-5)

4. Whosoever therefore shall humble himself as this little child, the same is greatest in the kingdom of heaven.

The disciples desired that Jesus would indicate who among them would be greatest. Jesus, however, responded with a teaching applicable to everyone. *Whosoever* lived in the manner that Jesus prescribed would find prestige in the kingdom. To *humble* themselves and each become as a *little child* meant that the disciples would need to take on an attitude of trust and dependence. Children demonstrate humility by trusting others for their survival and flourishing. They can do little for themselves in this regard.

Jesus demonstrated a life of humility during His time on earth (see Mark 10:45; Philippians 2:5-8; 1 Peter 2:23). Because of His humility, He received exaltation from His heavenly Father (see Acts 5:30-31; Philippians 2:9-11). He yet today commands followers to humble themselves (see Matthew 11:29-30; Luke 14:7-11; John 13:12-17).

When followers of Jesus live with humility, they will be lifted and considered *greatest in the kingdom of heaven* (compare James 4:10). Such people may not meet the world's standards of power, celebrity, status, or influence. But when believers live with humility, they will receive a greatness beyond what the world can provide (see Proverbs 3:34; Luke 1:52; James 4:6; 1 Peter 5:6). The disciples needed to change their assumptions of greatness from the world's criteria to that of God's kingdom.

Learning from Children

Laughs and giggles drew my attention to a nearby playground where a grandfather and his two young grandchildren were playing. The grandchildren adored their grandfather, and he loved spending time with them. When I asked the grandfather if he was having fun, he responded with a toothy grin, "I sure am!" I mentioned my own grandchildren and the joy they provide our family. He and I agreed that we don't need to pretend to be great for our grandchildren. Instead, the main things that grandchildren want from their grandparents are love and attention.

Though the world considers children insignificant, they can reveal to adults the power of love and humility. How will you be attentive to how children reveal the attitudes that God requires of His people? —C. R. B.

5. And whoso shall receive one such little child in my name receiveth me.

One such little child does not likely refer to an actual child, but a believer who shows the required childlike innocence. When Jesus' followers *receive* others through practices of hospitality, they demonstrate the required life of humility. Although this verse teaches hospitality toward other believers, God's people are to show hospitality toward all people (see Romans 12:13; Hebrews 13:2; 1 Peter 4:9). Believers receive their reward through humbling and hospitable acts that indicate the presence of genuine faith (see Matthew 10:40-42; Luke 14:12-14; compare Matthew 16:27). The resulting reward does not consist of worldly acclaim or wealth, but of Christ and the life that He offers (see 1 John 5:12).

II. Warning of Sin
(Matthew 18:6-9)
A. Regarding Little Ones (vv. 6-7)

6a. But whoso shall offend one of these little ones which believe in me.

The subject of this verse (*whoso*) is a parallel to the "whosoever" of Matthew 18:4 (above). Jesus continued with a universally applicable teaching.

The word *offend* translates a Greek word from which we derive our word *scandal*. It can refer to something that causes a person to trip, as in a "stumblingblock" (Romans 11:9). However, it can also refer to something more serious: an obstacle that breaks fellowship and causes sin (see Matthew 13:41).

Offense in this verse is not a cause for mere difficulty or dislike. Additionally, it is not a response of disgust, like how a person might respond to a bad odor or foul language. Rather, Jesus meant this in a much stronger sense: something that results in another person's transgressing God's law.

In Matthew's Gospel, Jesus uses the phrase *little ones* when speaking of His followers (here and in Matthew 10:42; 18:10, 14). Two possibilities exist regarding the identity of *these* little ones. They could be other believers in general (see commentary on 18:5, above), or they may specifically describe believers in less powerful positions. Jesus' warning works for both possibilities.

6b. It were better for him that a millstone were hanged about his neck, and that he were drowned in the depth of the sea.

Jesus illustrated His teaching by referring to an item that His audience would easily recognize: *a millstone*. These stones were critical to turn grain into usable flour (compare Matthew 24:41). Such stones varied in size. Some could be held in a hand, while other larger stones could only be moved by beasts of burden.

These stones would come in pairs (see Deuteronomy 24:6). The upper stone would rotate on the lower, stationary stone. Grains like barley or wheat would be poured between the stones. As the upper stone rotated over the lower stone, it would crush and grind the grains into usable flour.

One can imagine the horror on the disciples' faces as they imagined one of the larger millstones tied around a person's *neck*. The image of being *in the depth of the sea* with this "necklace" implied certain death by drowning. A dramatic point resulted from the illustration: causing entrapment and sin in others would lead to swift and unavoidable judgment. Followers of Jesus should not cause other believers to sin, and they should not abuse any authority that they might have. Either would lead to swift and certain judgment.

7. Woe unto the world because of offences! for it must needs be that offences come; but woe to that man by whom the offence cometh!

In the Old Testament, a statement of woe was proclaimed for several situations and several kinds of audiences. First, it was a lament for sin (example: Lamentations 5:16). Second, it warned people who had turned their backs on God and His commands (examples: Isaiah 10:1-2; Hosea 7:13).

How to Say It

hyperbole	hai-*pur*-buh-lee.
Messiah	Meh-*sigh*-uh.
Pharisees	*Fair*-ih-seez.

Matthew's Gospel directs most of its proclamations of woe toward the scribes and the Pharisees regarding their hypocrisy (examples: Matthew 23:13-36).

The scribes and the Pharisees were not the intended audience of this particular teaching. Instead, Jesus' first *woe* was directed at *the world*, the present evil age that leads people to stumble and sin (see Galatians 1:4; 1 John 2:15-16). Jesus' followers must not be tempted to adopt a position of worldly greatness and disregard the world's abuses. Even so, such abuses and *offences* would continue to *come* and "wage war against the soul" (1 Peter 2:11).

While Jesus directed the second *woe* at *that man*, He was not referring to a specific person. Rather, He was directing the woe to any person who would cause another to suffer *offence* and to stumble into sin. While evil is unavoidable, a person has no excuse for causing another to sin.

What Do You Think?
When you stumble, what steps can you take to mitigate the "offence" that you caused to others?

Digging Deeper
What Scripture passages give insight into the stakes of *not* taking care when you might cause "offence"?

B. Regarding the Self (vv. 8-9)

8a. Wherefore if thy hand or thy foot offend thee, cut them off, and cast them from thee.

Jesus did not state the kinds of actions that would *offend* a person and cause him or her to sin. However, the inclusion of multiple body parts indicates various possibilities that might lead to sin.

A person's *hand* or hands might grasp something that is not theirs to take (Exodus 20:15), create idols (2 Chronicles 32:19), or shed innocent blood (Proverbs 6:17). On *foot*, a person might walk from God's will (2 Kings 21:22) and step toward deceit (Job 31:5) or evil (Proverbs 4:27).

Jesus' command to *cut . . . off* any offending body parts is a metaphor and hyperbole. Although a pointed command, He was not advocating for

physical self-mutilation. After all, sin can still be committed in one's heart when the physical opportunity or ability to do so is absent (Matthew 5:27-28). Jesus used exaggerated language to impress on His listeners the seriousness of sin. He wanted His followers to remove and *cast* away the things that would cause it.

What Do You Think?
What radical life changes might help you live a more Christ-centered life?

Digging Deeper
What barriers prevent you from making either radical or minute changes for the sake of Christ?

8b. It is better for thee to enter into life halt or maimed, rather than having two hands or two feet to be cast into everlasting fire.

Matthew's Gospel elsewhere describes fire as a form of punishment (Matthew 3:10, 12; 5:22; 7:19; 13:40, 42, 49-50; 18:9). Matthew uses this imagery more than any other New Testament book besides Revelation. However, this verse is only one of three uses in the New Testament of the Greek phrase translated as *everlasting fire* (see also 25:41; Jude 7). It would be *better for* people to experience *life halt* (life with an impairment) *or maimed*, and without the things that cause sin, than to suffer eternal punishment (also Matthew 5:29-30). Part of this punishment includes separation from the Lord's presence and His power (see 2 Thessalonians 1:9).

Jesus desired that His followers evaluate whether their actions (or inactions) cause sin in themselves or others (compare Romans 14:19-21; 1 Corinthians 8:9-13). If such actions are continual and willful, then judgment will occur.

9. And if thine eye offend thee, pluck it out, and cast it from thee: it is better for thee to enter into life with one eye, rather than having two eyes to be cast into hell fire.

With the *eye*, a person might commit lust (Matthew 5:28; 1 John 2:16), show hateful intentions (Psalm 35:19), or refuse to look on a person in need (Proverbs 28:27). Eyes and vision are a means for temptation (see Genesis 3:6; Matthew

4:8-9). Jesus' inclusion of an eye with a hand and foot highlights the numerous ways that a person might sin—intentionally or unintentionally (Luke 12:47-48; John 9:41; James 4:17).

Matthew's Gospel uses the words *eye* and *eyes* more than any other New Testament text. Frequently, Matthew describes the healing of physical eyes (examples: Matthew 9:29; 20:33-34). However, his Gospel also shows greater concern for spiritual sight to see Jesus' work in the world (examples: 13:15-16; 15:14). People's spiritual vision and their spiritual health are connected (see 6:22-23).

The command to *pluck . . . out* one's eye *and cast it from thee* was not a command requiring forced blindness. As in the previous verse, Jesus taught His followers to take strong measures to remove temptation. The psalmist reflected a similar feeling: "I will set no wicked thing before mine eyes" (Psalm 101:3). If willful and unrepentant sin continued, then people would experience eternal punishment in *hell fire* (see also Mark 9:47-48; compare Isaiah 66:24). Jesus' language is almost identical to His teaching found in Matthew 5:29.

Are you humble like a child?

Visual for Lesson 2. *Pose this question for silent reflection after discussing the questions associated with verse 3 and before moving to verse 4.*

What Do You Think?
How do you discern not just what is sinful for you to see but what does not edify you (1 Corinthians 10:23)?

Digging Deeper
What role does your responsibility toward other believers play in deciding where you will rest your gaze?

Conclusion

A. Humility and Self-Control

Most people, at some time or another, desire to have power and be seen as great by the world. We are bombarded with messages and images that celebrate people who appear powerful, prestigious, and famous—great by the standards of the world.

The response to these messages requires that believers immerse themselves in Jesus' teaching regarding the required attitudes toward greatness. Through the power of the Holy Spirit, followers of Jesus must learn to embrace Jesus' definition of greatness—it must include childlike humility.

Further, followers of Jesus must remove those things that would cause themselves or others to stumble in sin. This includes disregarding the world's messages of greatness, power, and prestige. Believers should also remove the temptations to sin in the things that they see, hear, and do. These are the parts that make up a believer's actions and habits. Do your actions shape you to desire the world's definition of power and status? Do your habits lead you to sin or cause others to sin? If so, remove those causes of sin and adjust your habits!

Finally, followers of Jesus must embrace an attitude of humility and trust. This is not a sense of naivety, but confidence that God will provide for His people and show mercy consistent with His nature. When we embrace this attitude, we will likely not receive worldly glory. Instead, we will share in the promised—and far superior—glory from God (Romans 8:17).

B. Prayer

Heavenly Father, transform our hearts and minds so that we will continue to seek the kind of greatness that is required in Your kingdom. Orient our hearts toward the actions and habits that mark citizens of Your kingdom. In Jesus' name. Amen.

C. Thought to Remember
True greatness results from a life of humility and self-control.

Involvement Learning

Enhance your lesson with KJV Bible Student *(from your curriculum supplier) and the reproducible activity page (at www.standardlesson.com or in the back of the* KJV Standard Lesson Commentary Deluxe Edition*).*

Into the Lesson

Write the word *CHILDLIKE* in the middle of the board, and invite the whole group to share what words or phrases (good or bad) that come to mind when they see this word. Write their responses around the main word.

Alternative. Divide participants into three groups. Distribute copies of the "What to Remove" exercise from the activity page, which you can download. Have groups work to complete as indicated.

After either activity, lead into the Bible study by saying, "Being 'like a child' can mean different things. In today's text from Matthew, we consider which of these ideas Jesus meant when He was teaching His followers."

Into the Word

Ask a volunteer to read Matthew 18:1-5. If you used the first activity above, have the class identify the words on the board that most closely connect with what they believe Jesus meant in these verses. If you didn't use the activity, ask students to name some childlike qualities that Jesus values, and write them on the board. Invite clarification, if needed, for words or phrases. Invite participants to discuss and explain how these descriptions or behaviors should look in a person who comes to Jesus.

Alternative. Distribute copies of the "Like a Child" exercise from the activity page. Have learners work in pairs to complete as indicated. Instruct that not all boxes need to have entries.

After either alternative ask: 1–Why do you think Jesus values these qualities? 2–How are they relevant to the disciples' question on who is the greatest in the kingdom of Heaven?

Ask another volunteer to read Matthew 18:6-7. Divide learners into pairs. Point out that in several games, the strategy is to block, stump, or trick an opponent—to cause them to stumble and even-

tually lose the game. Have pairs discuss real-life ways that people can be blocked, stumped, or tricked—and that can keep them from putting their trust in Jesus.

Ask a third volunteer to read Matthew 18:8-9. Point out how in the previous verses the enemy is an outside person, but in these verses the enemy is ourselves. Give participants blank sheets of paper and ask them to draw a line down the middle of the page. Ask learners to write five things in the left-hand column that they do and that cause them to stumble in their walk with the Lord. In the right-hand column, ask them to write five things they do that strengthen their walk with the Lord.

Into Life

Write on the board *Childlike Humility* as a header. Underneath the header write the subheads *To Do* and *To Avoid*. Conduct a whole-class brainstorming session, encouraging learners to suggest ways to show childlike faith and humility to others. Then ask participants to choose one way of living childlike faith that they want to practice and strengthen in the coming week. Divide learners into pairs. Encourage partners to talk together about what will be practiced, as well as how to lovingly hold each other accountable to their plans. Invite pairs to spend time in prayer for each other, encouraging them to display the childlike qualities that Jesus desires, to embolden others who are trying to follow Jesus, and to get rid of things that cause them to stumble.

Alternative. Distribute copies of the "Humble Behavior" activity from the activity page. Have learners complete it individually (in a minute or less) before dividing into pairs. Give pairs time to pray for each other's plan to show humility throughout the week.

At the beginning of the next lesson, ask volunteers to share what happened when they practiced humble behavior during the week.

Jesus Talks with a Samaritan

Devotional Reading: Isaiah 44:1-8
Background Scripture: John 4:1-42

John 4:7-15, 28-30, 39-41

7 There cometh a woman of Samaria to draw water: Jesus saith unto her, Give me to drink.

8 (For his disciples were gone away unto the city to buy meat.)

9 Then saith the woman of Samaria unto him, How is it that thou, being a Jew, askest drink of me, which am a woman of Samaria? for the Jews have no dealings with the Samaritans.

10 Jesus answered and said unto her, If thou knewest the gift of God, and who it is that saith to thee, Give me to drink; thou wouldest have asked of him, and he would have given thee living water.

11 The woman saith unto him, Sir, thou hast nothing to draw with, and the well is deep: from whence then hast thou that living water?

12 Art thou greater than our father Jacob, which gave us the well, and drank thereof himself, and his children, and his cattle?

13 Jesus answered and said unto her, Whosoever drinketh of this water shall thirst again:

14 But whosoever drinketh of the water that I shall give him shall never thirst; but the water that I shall give him shall be in him a well of water springing up into everlasting life.

15 The woman saith unto him, Sir, give me this water, that I thirst not, neither come hither to draw.

28 The woman then left her waterpot, and went her way into the city, and saith to the men,

29 Come, see a man, which told me all things that ever I did: is not this the Christ?

30 Then they went out of the city, and came unto him.

39 And many of the Samaritans of that city believed on him for the saying of the woman, which testified, He told me all that ever I did.

40 So when the Samaritans were come unto him, they besought him that he would tarry with them: and he abode there two days.

41 And many more believed because of his own word.

Key Text

Many of the Samaritans of that city believed on him for the saying of the woman, which testified, He told me all that ever I did. —**John 4:39**

Jesus Calls Us

Unit 1: Called From the Margins of Society

Lessons 1–4

Lesson Aims

After participating in this lesson, each learner will be able to:

1. Identify the barriers that Jesus ignored when talking with the Samaritan woman.

2. Explain the significance of Jesus' discussion with the woman in light of the prevailing cultural, political, and religious taboos He ignored.

3. Identify elements of Jesus' approach to evangelism that he or she will use.

Lesson Outline

Introduction

A. The "Wrong" Neighborhood

As a small child, I lived in a mobile home park characterized by ethnic diversity and lower-income families. When I learned that my friends who lived across the street from the mobile home park were not allowed to come over and play with me, I was hurt and embarrassed. Apparently I lived in the "wrong" neighborhood.

Yet I remember ministers, Sunday school teachers, and youth ministers. They would take me to church services, out to eat, to baseball games, and even to a rodeo! I do not know where I would be today if they hadn't disregarded social barriers in order to invest time in a kid like me.

Today I'm humbled at the opportunity to spread the gospel to other communities and individuals who might otherwise be barred from meeting Jesus. In today's text Jesus himself modeled breaking barriers in ministry. What would be the impact of reaching into the "wrong" neighborhood?

B. Lesson Context

The Gospel of John was written later than those of Matthew, Mark, and Luke, probably in the AD 80s or 90s. The Apostle John likely wrote his Gospel from Ephesus, according to long-held church tradition. John's authorship is established primarily by his identification as the beloved disciple (John 13:23; 19:26; 20:2; 21:7, 20, 24; see lessons 7 and 8).

As our text in John 4 begins, Jesus and His disciples had left Judaea and were heading to Galilee (John 4:3), where He made the headquarters of His ministry (Matthew 4:13-16). For this journey, Jesus chose not to take one of two longer routes in order to avoid Samaria (John 4:4), as some Jews would do (compare and contrast Luke 9:51-53; 17:11). Samaria was the central region of what had been the kingdom of Israel, with Judaea to the south and Galilee to the north. Travel between Jerusalem and the region of Galilee would take about three days on the reliable Roman roads that ran through Samaria.

I. The Stranger
(John 4:7-15)

A. Physical Need (vv. 7-9)

7. There cometh a woman of Samaria to draw water: Jesus saith unto her, Give me to drink.

At the sixth hour (midday), Jesus came to this well that was known to have belonged to Jacob (John 4:5-6, not in our printed text; see commentary on 4:12, below). It was uncommon for anyone to be at the well at that hour, as the day was at its hottest. From ancient times, women journeyed *to draw water* as a group in the morning or the evening (example: Genesis 24:11; contrast 29:7). *A woman of Samaria* came alone, likely indicating she was outcast from her community, especially from other women (consider John 4:16-18, not in our printed text). *Give me to drink* does not seem an unusual request at a well. But John 4:9 (below) reveals several levels on which this was a very surprising request.

8. (For his disciples were gone away unto the city to buy meat.)

Jesus and *his disciples* sometimes carried funds to buy what they needed along the way (example: John 13:29), though other times they depended on other means for their sustenance (examples: Matthew 10:9; Mark 6:8; Luke 10:4). This journey took them through Samaria, specifically *the city* Sychar (John 4:5, not in our printed text; see commentary on 4:28, below). Ancient Jewish tradition suggests that the disciples would have been careful about ritual purity and social boundaries when procuring *meat* (the word indicates any kind of food) from Samaritans. Ordinarily they would not accept food as a gift from Samaritans, but allowed for the need to buy from Samaritans.

9a. Then saith the woman of Samaria unto him, How is it that thou, being a Jew, askest drink of me, which am a woman of Samaria?

The reasons Jesus' request was surprising are given here (see commentary on John 4:7, above). One was a gender issue. Women were often viewed as "less than" by men in the ancient Roman world. For a Jewish man, this would be especially true for any non-Jewish woman. Samaritan women were doubly stigmatized because of the animosity between Judah and Samaria. (On the barriers between Jews and Samaritans, see commentary on 4:9b, below.)

Within this conversation, the *woman of Samaria* would be amazed that Jesus knew about her several marriages *and* the man she was living with at the time (John 4:16-19, not in our printed text). Both Jews and other Samaritans would consider this pattern suspicious, if not downright sinful. We do not know why she'd been married so many times. But the implication of living with a man she had not married suggests there were less than pure reasons for the ending of the other relationships.

9b. For the Jews have no dealings with the Samaritans.

The antagonism between *the Jews* and *the Samaritans* dated back over 700 years, to the Assyrian conquest of the northern kingdom of Israel. The 10 tribes of Israel living there were taken captive in 722 BC, including the people living in the region called Samaria (2 Kings 17:1-6). The Assyrians habitually moved conquered people around the empire, so some Israelites remained while many foreign people settled in the land. When Israelites mingled with foreign peoples, the result was a syncretistic religion in which the Lord was worshipped in addition to other gods (17:24-33, 41).

All this religious turmoil resulted in a Samaritan religion that revered only the books of Moses (the first five books of the Bible, called the Pentateuch). Samaritans excluded any history, poetry, or prophecy that was written later. The Samaritans

How to Say It

Askar	*Haz*-kar.
Ebal	*Ee*-bull.
Gerizim	*Gair*-ih-zeem or Guh-*rye*-zim.
Hyrcanus	Hehr-*cayn*-uhs.
Manasseh	Muh-*nass*-uh.
Pentateuch	*Pen*-ta-teuk.
Samaria	Suh-*mare*-ee-uh.
Sychar	*Sigh*-kar.
syncretistic	sihng-creh-*tis*-tihk.

believed that God should be worshipped on Mount Gerizim (see Deuteronomy 11:29; 27:12), *not* in Jerusalem. They also expected a Messiah like Moses, not David (see John 4:29, below).

The Samaritans opposed the rebuilding of Jerusalem's temple and the city walls following the exiled Jews' three waves of return that began in 538 BC (Ezra 4:8-24; Nehemiah 4:1-2). Later, the Jewish historian Josephus (AD 37–100) recorded that the Samaritans were not forced to devote their place of worship to Jupiter (as the Samaritans claimed), but instead willingly did so between 175 and 164 BC. Josephus's account likely reflects more about his bias than any voluntary Samaritan complicity. John Hyrcanus (174–104 BC) was the high priest and ruler in Judea who briefly achieved Jewish independence by throwing off Syria and creating an alliance with Rome. In his leadership of the Jewish people, Hyrcanus destroyed the Samaritan place of worship on Mount Gerizim (112/111 BC). Josephus also notes that between AD 6 and 9, Samaritans attempted to defile the temple in Jerusalem during Passover by sneaking in and scattering dead men's bones on the temple grounds (compare Leviticus 21:1, 11; Numbers 5:2; 9:6-7; 19:13).

Even with all this historic hostility (examples: Hosea 7:1; 8:5-6) continuing in Jesus' lifetime (example: Luke 9:51-54), He typically did not avoid Samaritans and even spoke well of them (10:30-37; 17:11-19; contrast Matthew 10:5). This tendency is in keeping with Jesus' habit of associating himself with outcasts and sinners (Mark 2:15-17; Luke 7:36-39). And even more, Jesus never treated people as their stereotypes—in this case, a Samaritan and a woman. He saw the person before Him and valued that person, no matter their circumstances.

What Do You Think?

What hurdles does your congregation face when reaching out to a community that might be mistrustful of your motives?

Digging Deeper

How can your congregation prepare to overcome these obstacles?

B. Spiritual Bounty (vv. 10-15)

10. Jesus answered and said unto her, If thou knewest the gift of God, and who it is that saith to thee, Give me to drink; thou wouldest have asked of him, and he would have given thee living water.

The gift of God refers to the Holy Spirit (compare John 7:38-39), consistent with other New Testament usage and nuance. Looking at Old Testament uses of "springing water" (the nearest Hebrew equivalent to *living water*) offers useful insight. This is fresh, flowing water as opposed to bitter or salty water (Numbers 5:18-27; Jeremiah 23:15; James 3:11)—or no water at all. Spiritually and physically, God provides good water for His people to live (compare Numbers 24:7; Psalm 36:9; Isaiah 49:10; Jeremiah 2:13; 17:13; Ezekiel 47:12).

This Samaritan woman, however, had no knowledge of this gift in a spiritual sense or of Jesus' true identity. Already in John's Gospel, Jesus has been identified as "the Lamb of God, which taketh away the sin of the world" (John 1:29), "the Son of God" (1:34), and "the Messias, . . . the Christ" (1:41). But this knowledge was not widely accepted (1:9-11).

What Do You Think?

Are any of your prayers "small" compared to what Jesus offers you?

Digging Deeper

How do you balance "small" requests for "daily bread" with the "big" petition for God's "kingdom [to] come" (Matthew 6:10-11)?

11a. The woman saith unto him, Sir, thou hast nothing to draw with.

The woman had not yet caught on that Jesus was speaking about spiritual truths rather than about physical realities. Jesus should need something *to draw with,* or else water would not come out of the well. One would take a bucket or jar and lower it down the well with a rope to access the water. She likely assumed Jesus had no way of drawing the water for himself, or else this Jewish man would not have spoken with the Samaritan woman.

11b-12. And the well is deep: from whence

then hast thou that living water? Art thou greater than our father Jacob, which gave us the well, and drank thereof himself, and his children, and his cattle?

The well itself had long been associated with *father Jacob*, who lived about 2,000 years prior to the encounter of today's text. Jacob had bought the land of Shechem, eventually deeding it to his son Joseph (Genesis 33:18-19; 48:22; Joshua 24:32), although no well was mentioned.

The Samaritans traced their lineage through Joseph's sons, Ephraim and Manasseh. But because of the divergence of Israel's ten tribes from the southern two, collectively known as Judah, the Jews thought of Samaritans as foreigners (Luke 17:16-18). This well can still be visited today. It is over 100 feet *deep* and was possibly even deeper in Jesus' time. Even if Jesus had something with which to draw water, how could He possibly reach the *living water* at the bottom, which supplied the well?

Like the Jews, the Samaritans had great respect for Abraham, Isaac, and Jacob; and the woman thought that Jesus could not be greater (see commentary on John 4:29, below; compare 8:52-58). This question presupposes a negative answer and might even be considered mocking. But based on her faith, the woman rightly questioned whether Jesus could be *greater than* the patriarchs.

13-14. Jesus answered and said unto her, Whosoever drinketh of this water shall thirst again: but whosoever drinketh of the water that I shall give him shall never thirst; but the water that I shall give him shall be in him a well of water springing up into everlasting life.

Thirst is an apt metaphor for spiritual need. Just as any person or creature dies without the water they need, so too we die without the spiritual care we need. Psalm 42:1-2 pictures the soul panting for God as a hart pants for water. Isaiah depicts one who would "draw water out of the wells of salvation" (Isaiah 12:3; compare 55:1; 58:11). And Jesus states that those who hunger and thirst after righteousness are blessed and will be filled (Matthew 5:6; compare John 6:35). *Springing up* suggests especially vital properties in the living, spiritual *water* Jesus referred to. We could give a formula here: *everlasting life* comes only as a gift

JESUS PROVIDES LIVING WATER IN ANY DESERT.

Visual for Lesson 3. *Ask learners to reflect on their own desert experiences. What difference did Jesus' provision make for them?*

of the Father through accepting the invitation of Jesus and the daily work of the Spirit.

Much More

My friend drove for a ride-share company, and many of his customers requested rides to the nearest major airport, 70 miles away. His car was satisfactory, but he was looking for something more. A big part of his desired upgrade was a car that would lower his fuel costs. Still, his car was serviceable, so he waited for the opportune moment to make a purchase, knowing he'd also be taking on monthly car payments again.

Sitting at a red light, my friend was rear-ended, his car totaled. The "something more" suddenly became more necessity than mere desire. And my friend was delighted at how *much more* his new car gave him due to technological advances, especially in fuel efficiency. The downside—those pesky car payments.

What the world offers always has a downside. But with Jesus there are no downsides. The living water Jesus promised to the Samaritan woman was much more than she could have anticipated. What has been your experience of Jesus' *much more*?
—C. R. B.

15. The woman saith unto him, Sir, give me this water, that I thirst not, neither come hither to draw.

The woman's request demonstrated her

confusion about Jesus' words. She was in search of literal, physical *water* to meet her immediate needs. But even with her misunderstanding, she admirably continued her inquiry and search for understanding.

The dialogue in John 4:16-27 (not in our printed text) continued between Jesus and the woman. She rapidly progressed from considering Jesus to be a prophet to wondering if He might be someone even greater than that (see commentary on 4:29, below).

II. The Promised One
(John 4:28-30, 39-41)
A. Question of Identity (vv. 28-30)

28a. The woman then left her waterpot, and went her way into the city.

Leaving *her waterpot* behind indicated that *the woman* left in a rush (see commentary on John 4:30, below). *The city,* Sychar, sat in proximity to both Mount Gerizim and Mount Ebal (see commentary on 4:9b, above). Its only mention by name occurs in John 4:5 (not in our printed text). Though its location is unclear, there is reason to associate it with the modern village Askar. The village's proximity to Jacob's well—about one-half mile—as well as to both mountains lends credence to this supposition (see commentary on 4:11b-12, above). The name Sychar might also indicate a close relationship with Shechem, a better-known settlement in the same area. First mentioned as Abram entered Canaan (Genesis 12:6-7), the land became part of Ephraimite territory in northern Palestine (Joshua 17:8-10).

28b-29a. And saith to the men, Come, see a man, which told me all things that ever I did.

The woman's invitation to *Come, see* is reminiscent of Jesus' invitation when He called His first followers in John 1:39. Describing Jesus' knowing about her marriages and current living situation as having *told* her *all things that* she *did* reveals something about the culture this woman was living in. Her life's summary (at least in her mind, and likely in the mind of her community as well) could be told in terms of the men she had associated with (see John 4:16-18, not in our printed text). Instead of using this information to shame her, Jesus used

it to further her understanding regarding His identity. He was at least a prophet (4:19), and even more (see commentary on 4:29b, below).

In confirming Jesus' accurate and supernatural knowledge of her life story, the woman's testimony reveals that she was fully impressed by Him. Given the culture, one would not expect a woman to go into town and address the public the way she did. Her reputation would seem to make her a bad witness—not someone who would be taken seriously (compare Luke 7:36-50; see commentary on John 4:30, below).

"Come and See"

When my grandson Jesse was about 3 years old, we were walking from his house to the park nearby. Jesse ran ahead, then turned and ran back to me, shouting, "Grampa, come and see what I see! It's a hot dog stand! I think we ought to get a hot dog!" With a level of enthusiasm I didn't feel, I responded, "That's a great idea, Jesse!"

With hot dogs in his near future, Jesse said, "Grampa, you've got a good know-er brain, but I've got a good think-er brain." He was aware that my many years of life had given me more knowledge than he had, but he was proud of his ability to think of new ideas.

The Samaritan woman recognized that the man she had met was also a "know-er." Her "think-er" brain led her to introduce Jesus to her community. How often do you let it be known to your acquaintances that you think they need to meet Jesus? What holds you back?   —C. R. B.

29b. Is not this the Christ?

The woman anticipated a positive response (contrast John 4:12, above), partly based on Jesus' own assertion that He is *the Christ* (4:25-26, not in our printed text). The Samaritan expectations of the Christ differed from Jewish expectations because of their adherence only to the first five books of the Old Testament (see Lesson Context; commentary on 4:9b, above). Jesus fulfilled prophetic and kingly expectations, though not in the way either Samaritans or Jews had imagined (examples: 6:15, 41-42; 7:25-27, 52; Acts 1:6).

30. Then they went out of the city, and came unto him.

One cannot help but notice the contrast between the disciples who went into the town to bring back food and this woman who brought *out* the people *of the city* to meet the Christ.

B. Revelation of Identity (vv. 39-41)

39. And many of the Samaritans of that city believed on him for the saying of the woman, which testified, He told me all that ever I did.

In Jesus' ministry, people living on the margins sometimes made the biggest influence on their communities (examples: Matthew 9:9-13; Luke 19:1-10). This ostracized woman turned evangelist reached out to her community, which resulted in *many of the Samaritans of that city* believing that Jesus was the Christ (see commentary on John 4:29, above). Significantly, her testimony was that Jesus *told me all that ever I did*—a significant claim when looking for a prophetic Christ.

40-41. So when the Samaritans were come unto him, they besought him that he would tarry with them: and he abode there two days. And many more believed because of his own word.

Staying with *the Samaritans* was a significant break in Jewish custom (see commentary on John 4:9b, above). As a result of Jesus' time and preaching the gospel in Sychar (see commentary on 4:28a, above), *many more believed*. As the Samaritans encountered Jesus for themselves, they confessed that Jesus really is "the Saviour of the world" (4:42, not in our printed text).

One cannot help but ponder on how large the community of faith grew in Sychar. In Acts 8:4-25, the gospel spread in the land of Samaria through the work of Philip the evangelist, the groundwork for that success undoubtedly prepared by events in today's text.

What Do You Think?
How did others' testimony influence your early love for Jesus?
Digging Deeper
How do you continue to seek intimacy with Jesus?

Conclusion
A. Every Neighborhood

Jesus' earthly ministry did not include limits based on typical human barriers. His encounter with the Samaritan woman is a prime example. In Jesus' presence, many of the boundaries that we have put up or that others have put up around us disappear (Romans 3:22; 10:12; Galatians 3:28-29; Ephesians 2:11-22; contrast 5:11; 1 Timothy 4:7; 2 Timothy 3:1-5; Titus 3:10). As we find our identity in Jesus, we can become the conduit of mercy and grace to those we encounter. The living water Jesus gives us is available now and will continue to well up in us until we reach the age to come. The gift we find in Jesus is not a stagnant thing; it moves us from old to new, death to life, lost to found, enslaved to free; it means we are saved!

What Do You Think?
What encouragement can you find in today's passage?
Digging Deeper
What challenge do you find in the passage?

B. Prayer

Father, forgive us for the times when we have allowed barriers to prevent us from inviting others to see You. Help us to see those around us the way that You see them; help us demonstrate Your love and holiness to them. This we pray in Jesus' name. Amen.

C. Thought to Remember
Take *every* opportunity to offer Jesus' living water.

Involvement Learning

Enhance your lesson with KJV Bible Student (from your curriculum supplier) and the reproducible activity page (at www.standardlesson.com or in the back of the KJV Standard Lesson Commentary Deluxe Edition).

Into the Lesson

Hand an index card to each learner. Ask learners to write down, without sharing, the name of a famous person who has lived during the past 100 years. Collect the cards, shuffle them, and hand them back out to learners. Divide the whole group into pairs. Direct one person in each pair to ask his or her partner 10 questions in order to identify the name on the partner's card. The partner must answer the questions with words and actions of the person on the card, without directly revealing the name. After 10 questions have been asked, names can be revealed. Then switch roles to reveal the name on the other card.

Gather the whole group back together to discuss: 1–How difficult was it to guess your partner's identity? 2–What questions yielded the best clues? 3–What questions do you wish you had asked? Lead into the Bible study by saying, "Sometimes we don't know what to ask because we don't know who we're talking to. In this week's lesson, notice how people respond to each other, based on what they know of each other."

Alternative. Divide learners into small groups. Distribute the "Satisfaction Guaranteed" exercise from the activity page, which you can download. After allowing a couple of minutes for groups to complete as directed, reveal the correct answers.

Into the Word

Write the heading *Jews vs. Samaritans* on the board. Share some of the lesson information regarding Jews and Samaritans. Based on your presentation, have the class list different barriers and boundaries of the two groups.

Ask a volunteer to read John 4:7-10. Divide the class into small groups. Give them time to discuss: 1–What barriers and boundaries did Jesus "break" while interacting with the Samaritan woman? 2–How did Jesus' actions give hope to the woman?

Invite another volunteer to read John 4:11-15. Allow the group to talk through how Jesus' words satisfied the woman's deep desires and needs.

Ask a third volunteer to read John 4:28-30, 39-41. Invite groups to talk through: 1–How did Jesus approach telling the woman and His disciples who He was? 2–How did the woman share what she learned about Jesus?

Bring the groups back together. Give them time to identify ways Jesus approached evangelism in this story. List the ways on the board.

Into Life

Referring to the list from the previous exercise, ask, "What groups do not associate with each other today?" Write a few responses on the board. As a class, expand that list to barriers and groups that exist within your community. Invite small groups to review today's text one more time and consider these questions: 1–What did Jesus do to connect with the woman? 2–Why did He do this? Have the group create a second list of how Jesus approached evangelism.

Divide the group into pairs. Distribute index cards and pens to each learner. Challenge learners to create a fusion of the lists by choosing one of the barriers or groups listed on the board and then, as pairs, choosing one aspect of Jesus' evangelistic method from this story to apply to their lives this week. (Example: Overcome a social barrier by asking for help.)

Alternative. Distribute copies of the "Evangelistic Elements" activity from the activity page. Have learners work in small groups to complete as indicated. Not all answers need to be filled out. Encourage participants to finish the sheet at home during the week, to be discussed at the beginning of class next week.

Conclude by reading aloud John 4:42 and having small groups pray that their witness would have this effect on others.

Jesus Overpowers Legion

Devotional Reading: 2 Corinthians 10:1-6
Background Scripture: Mark 5:1-20 (cf. Luke 8:26-39)

Mark 5:1-13, 18-20

1 And they came over unto the other side of the sea, into the country of the Gadarenes.

2 And when he was come out of the ship, immediately there met him out of the tombs a man with an unclean spirit,

3 Who had his dwelling among the tombs; and no man could bind him, no, not with chains:

4 Because that he had been often bound with fetters and chains, and the chains had been plucked asunder by him, and the fetters broken in pieces: neither could any man tame him.

5 And always, night and day, he was in the mountains, and in the tombs, crying, and cutting himself with stones.

6 But when he saw Jesus afar off, he ran and worshipped him,

7 And cried with a loud voice, and said, What have I to do with thee, Jesus, thou Son of the most high God? I adjure thee by God, that thou torment me not.

8 For he said unto him, Come out of the man, thou unclean spirit.

9 And he asked him, What is thy name?

And he answered, saying, My name is Legion: for we are many.

10 And he besought him much that he would not send them away out of the country.

11 Now there was there nigh unto the mountains a great herd of swine feeding.

12 And all the devils besought him, saying, Send us into the swine, that we may enter into them.

13 And forthwith Jesus gave them leave. And the unclean spirits went out, and entered into the swine: and the herd ran violently down a steep place into the sea, (they were about two thousand;) and were choked in the sea

18 And when he was come into the ship, he that had been possessed with the devil prayed him that he might be with him.

19 Howbeit Jesus suffered him not, but saith unto him, Go home to thy friends, and tell them how great things the Lord hath done for thee, and hath had compassion on thee.

20 And he departed, and began to publish in Decapolis how great things Jesus had done for him: and all men did marvel.

Key Text

He departed, and began to publish in Decapolis how great things Jesus had done for him: and all men did marvel. —Mark 5:20

257

Jesus
Calls Us

Unit 1: Called from the Margins of Society
Lessons 1–4

Lesson Aims

After participating in this lesson, each learner will be able to:

1. List some key elements in Jesus' encounter with the demoniac.

2. Explain the messianic secret and how this story breaks with this theme in Mark's Gospel.

3. Share testimony about Jesus' intervention in his or her life.

Lesson Outline

Introduction
A. An Unfair Fight

Some years ago I took up historical fencing (swordsmanship) as a hobby for fun and to stay in better shape. I took to it quickly. My natural agility quickly elevated me to become one of the better fencers in our club. In a one-on-one match, I usually defeated my opponent.

One day the club decided to play a game, and I found myself fencing two people at once. I had beaten both of them individually. But it was a great challenge to fight two. Despite my aptitude and skill, I could not defend myself for long against two—and went down in defeat. Our game was an unfair fight in which I was outnumbered and lost. Today's passage tells of a similar scenario with a very different outcome.

B. Lesson Context

Mark's Gospel was likely written between AD 60 and 62, certainly before Matthew, Luke, or John. With Matthew and Luke, the book of Mark rounds out the Synoptic Gospels, so called because of their similar records of Jesus' earthly ministry. Today's text from Mark 5 is one example of the books' shared material, with parallels in Matthew 8:28-34 and Luke 8:26-39. Differences between the accounts say less about the historical *accuracy* of the event than about the faith *perspectives* the writers brought to the details.

A somewhat perplexing characteristic of the Gospel of Mark is also on display in this account: Jesus' tendency throughout the first half of the book to tell people whom Jesus had healed to keep quiet about the matter (Mark 1:44; 7:36; 8:30). This has been called the messianic secret.

Many theories have been proposed for this counterintuitive command to silence. One such is that Jesus did not want the people to become invested in wrong ideas about what it meant for Him to be the Messiah. While the people were looking for a political Messiah to deliver them from Roman imperialism, Jesus used the time of secrecy to teach about the larger role of the Messiah—beyond Israel and its politics. Jesus also wanted His ministry to be defined as a preaching and teaching ministry more than a healing and miracles ministry (Mark 1:35-39). The constant needs of people around Him and of crushing crowds looking for healing could have taken all His time if Jesus had not guarded it carefully. His preaching ministry was supported by the miracles, not the other way around. This suggests an element of crowd control (see 1:43-45).

The account of the Gadarene demoniac occurs during Jesus' preaching ministry in Galilee. This story is in a section of Mark that contains several other accounts focusing on Jesus' power and authority (see 4:35-41; 5:21-34).

I. Arrivals
(Mark 5:1-5)
A. Jesus (v. 1)

1. And they came over unto the other side of the sea, into the country of the Gadarenes.

They refers to Jesus and His disciples (Mark 4:35). *The other side of the sea* is the east side of the Sea of Galilee (see commentary on 5:20, below). This region was broadly called the Decapolis, meaning "10 cities" (see commentary on 5:20, below). Pinpointing exactly where in *the country of the Gadarenes* Jesus and the disciples landed is difficult. The region is associated with the cities Gadara and Gerasa, potentially confusing the matter. Gerasa can be ruled out because of its 40-mile distance from the sea. This distance would prohibit the incident from playing out as recorded (see 5:13, below). A town called Gergesa has been suggested as a likely site, though its location is unknown. Gadara is the most likely location, as the city was only five to six miles from the coastline (consider Matthew 8:28).

B. The Demoniac (vv. 2-5)

2-3a. And when he was come out of the ship, immediately there met him out of the tombs a man with an unclean spirit, who had his dwelling among the tombs.

Context makes clear that *he* who came *out of the ship* refers to Jesus (Mark 4:38-41; see commentary on 5:6, below). In typical fashion in his

Gospel, Mark gets straight to the action with the word *immediately* (examples: 1:42; 2:8; 6:27, 50; 10:52; 14:43).

The man's coming *out of the tombs* and *dwelling among the tombs* were cause for instant concern. These tombs would be caves or carved into rock, forming a necropolis: city of the dead. To have *an unclean spirit* indicates supernatural possession (compare Mark 1:23-27). Any Jew approaching the demoniac would consider him unclean because of his continual proximity to dead bodies (Numbers 19:11, 13, 16). Nowhere in this account does Jesus express concern about ritual uncleanness, however. Jesus' teachings about Sabbath (example: Matthew 12:9-12) and other holiness issues (example: 23:25-28) align with His greater concern for wholeness in the Lord than with outer, ritual uncleanness.

> **What Do You Think?**
> What is today's equivalent of living among tombs?
>
> **Digging Deeper**
> How can you introduce Jesus to those living in such situations?

3b-4. And no man could bind him, no, not with chains: because that he had been often bound with fetters and chains, and the chains had been plucked asunder by him, and the fetters broken in pieces: neither could any man tame him.

Once the possessed man lost control of himself, his community tried to step in. Though binding him *with chains* may once have worked, the demon within (see commentary on Mark 5:9, below) granted such perverse strength that the demoniac *plucked asunder* those restraints. His strength was matched by a wildness that no *man*

How to Say It

Decapolis	Dee-*cap*-uh-lis.
Gadara	*Gad*-uh-ruh.
Gergesa	*Gur*-guh-suh.
Scythopolis	Sith-*op*-uh-lus.
Synoptic	Sih-*nawp*-tihk.

could *tame*. The image is of a dangerous, undomesticated beast. The best course of action for the community was to be wary and hope the demon-possessed man would not come among them and cause harm.

5. And always, night and day, he was in the mountains, and in the tombs, crying, and cutting himself with stones.

A healthy person generally makes decisions that maintain his or her overall well-being. Even if another doesn't agree with those decisions, the logic behind the choices can be explained and understood by others. It seems, however, that one characteristic of demon possession is a loss of control over self-preservation. For instance, a healthy boy would not choose to burn himself or drown. But a demon within him could overwhelm him and put him in circumstances where burning or drowning were likely to occur (Matthew 17:14-18).

In the demoniac's case, he had lost so much control that even his instinct to care for himself was overridden. In his settlement *in the mountains*, he was given to self-harm. No one could prevent his hurting others *or* himself. And though his *crying* could have been a result of *cutting himself with stones*, the Greek verb is more in keeping with an animal's cry than with human sorrow. Once again, the demon reduced the man to a beastly station.

What Do You Think?
How have you heard demon possession explained in relationship to mental health issues?

Digging Deeper
What pitfalls can you anticipate in either overspiritualizing mental health or failing to recognize that demon possession can occur?

The Power of the Demon

Addiction's symptoms can include altered mental states; criminal activity such as theft or battery; isolation from loved ones; feelings of rage, hopelessness, or worthlessness; and suicidal thoughts or actions. Though we often think of addictions related to drugs and alcohol, we might consider at least some of the symptoms in relation to the media we consume, how we participate in politics, and many other everyday activities.

The demoniac's own circumstance sounds eerily similar to that of many with substance abuse issues: separation from those who cared for him, living in the shadowy recesses of society, bound by restraints that he shrugged off, feelings of deep anguish, and slowly destroying his own body. Addiction and spiritual possession are different issues. But the solution must always call on Jesus as the healer. Is that the *first* step you take, or do you do so only after everything else fails?
—C. R. B.

II. Confrontation
(Mark 5:6-13)

A. Pleading (vv. 6-13a)

6-7a. But when he saw Jesus afar off, he ran and worshipped him, and cried with a loud voice, and said, What have I to do with thee, Jesus, thou Son of the most high God?

Given that this happened in "the country of the Gadarenes" (Mark 5:1, above), the chances are slight that a man off the street would know *Jesus* by name, let alone recognize Him on sight. In context, it is clear that *worshipped* does not refer to religious veneration, since a demon would not worship Jesus. Instead, it refers to the act of bowing. This idea is used of worshipping God or idols, of bowing in obeisance before a king, or even welcoming an honored guest. Ironically, this man's question—the result of the demon's knowledge—answers the question the disciples posed only a few verses before: "What manner of man is [Jesus]?" (4:41). Demons well know who Jesus is (example: 1:34) and are rightly terrified of their coming judgment.

In keeping with what has been described about the Gadarene demoniac (see Mark 5:2-5, above), the demon was actually doing the talking. No human had yet acknowledged Jesus to be the *Son* of God, another clue that the demon knew what others did not. The title *most high God* emphasizes God's absolute rule over the heavens and the earth and under the earth, including every creature within those realms—supernatural or not (Philippians 2:10; Revelation 5:13).

7b-8. I adjure thee by God, that thou torment me not. For he said unto him, Come out of the man, thou unclean spirit.

It is not yet clear how effective the *unclean* spirit's begging was (see commentary on Mark 5:13b, below). The demon was subject to Jesus and His commands, just as the waves and the wind were on the journey across the sea (4:39, 41). Jesus could have cast the demon out immediately—could even *torment* the demon (see 5:10, below). But perhaps for our edification, Jesus chose to allow more information to come to light.

9. And he asked him, What is thy name? And he answered, saying, My name is Legion: for we are many.

Legion ordinarily referred to a Roman military unit consisting of approximately 6,000 foot soldiers plus a mounted attachment. While no legions were stationed in Palestine at the time of our text, Roman legions were found in Egypt and Syria during the time of Christ. They were a symbol (and source) of Roman imperial strength and power. In giving this *name*, the demons not only stated that they were *many* but also implied that they were strong. The word is used in the New Testament to refer to large numbers of spiritual forces, whether demonic or angelic (see Matthew 26:53). This makes it impossible to know how many demons were present, only that it was a huge, formidable horde.

Ancient people often believed that invoking the name of a spiritual being granted some power over that being (example: Acts 19:13-16). But Jesus needed no tips or tricks to obtain power over the demons (see Mark 5:13, below). Instead, Jesus was preparing to teach the disciples a lesson of the utmost importance: no matter how the powers of evil stacked against Him, Jesus was always in charge.

What's in a Name?

Romeo was a Montague and Juliet a Capulet. A generations-old feud between their families had to be observed at all costs. But on falling in love with her family's enemy, Juliet expressed her dismay, saying, "What's in a name? That which we call a rose / By any other name would smell as sweet."

As a tool for organizing human life, names *are* important. And the many languages in the world prove that a rose by another name really does smell as sweet! But Jesus' name, no matter what dialect we speak, always conveys His power and authority. Do not be distracted by the "legions" arrayed against you; trust in Jesus' name and follow in His ways.   —C. R. B.

10. And he besought him much that he would not send them away out of the country.

Jesus could send the demons to the into the deep (see Luke 8:31), which seems to be a place of punishment for demons preceding the final judgment (see Revelation 20). Perhaps this is what Legion was hoping to avoid by begging not to be sent *away out of the country.*

11. Now there was there nigh unto the mountains a great herd of swine feeding.

Because *swine* were unclean for Jews to eat (Leviticus 11:7-8), their presence was a reliable indicator of a Gentile population in a settlement (see commentary on Mark 5:1, above; 5:20, below). Much as goats or sheep were to shepherds in Judaea, these animals were key to their keepers' livelihood. They were acceptable sacrificial animals in pagan religious ceremonies, so they served that additional function as well.

12-13a. And all the devils besought him, saying, Send us into the swine, that we may enter into them. And forthwith Jesus gave them leave.

The devils were firmly within Jesus' jurisdiction (Mark 1:39); all creation is under His rule (Colossians 1:15-20). Having come face-to-face with the Son of God, Legion knew Jesus would not allow them to remain in the man any longer. This image of the "militant" demons (see commentary on Mark 5:9, above) might remind us of the faithful centurion who compared Jesus' power to a commander's over soldiers (Luke 7:1-9). They recognized that Jesus was in complete control. But perhaps Legion hoped to linger in the unclean

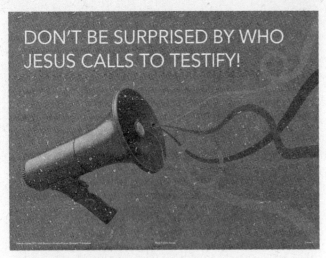

DON'T BE SURPRISED BY WHO JESUS CALLS TO TESTIFY!

Visual for Lesson 4. *Have learners pair up and discuss why their own calls to testify might be surprising.*

swine; then when Jesus had left the region, they could reenter the man (compare Matthew 12:43-45) or find a new victim. With Jesus' *leave*, Legion might have thought they had succeeded in outwitting the Son of God.

B. Stampede! (v. 13b)

13b. And the unclean spirits went out, and entered into the swine: and the herd ran violently down a steep place into the sea, (they were about two thousand;) and were choked in the sea.

What *the unclean spirits* experienced here was a foretaste of the defeat that Satan would experience following Jesus' crucifixion and resurrection. Though Satan looked for victory over Jesus, what the devil experienced was an unexpected (to him) and thorough defeat (Hebrews 2:14-15). Similarly, the demons' sudden entering *the herd* of *swine* wasn't even a partial victory, since the panicked animals immediately stampeded to their deaths. Given how the demons overwhelmed the faculties of an apparently otherwise rational person, we are not surprised at the pigs' fearful reaction.

Though we might think of a one-to-one correlation—that is, one demon per pig—clearly this is an unnecessary inference. The Gadarene demoniac had been host to Legion, a name that suggests several thousand. In theory, the numbers involved should have put Jesus at a disadvantage.

However, even though Jesus seemed outnumbered, there was never any doubt about His victory in this encounter.

Because the swine *choked in the sea*, the demons were deprived of both a human body and the animals' bodies. This was not a final defeat for the demons, as Jesus had apparently acknowledged it wasn't yet time for their ultimate demise. But this was a foretaste of what was coming to them: banishment from the torment they inflicted on *any* of God's creation.

But the herdsmen didn't see this extraordinary sign of God's goodness and victory over evil. Instead, they only felt fear. This explains why the community asked Jesus to leave the area after this encounter (Mark 5:14-17, not in our printed text).

III. Departures
(Mark 5:18-20)
A. Parting Ways (vv. 18-19)

18. And when he was come into the ship, he that had been possessed with the devil prayed him that he might be with him.

He that had been possessed with the devil knew what a miracle his healing was, and he appropriately hoped to follow Jesus and continue to learn from Him. And there was precedent for the man to join Jesus. As with "worshipped" in Mark 5:6 (above), *prayed* refers primarily to asking without religious overtones. The Greek word is usually translated as some form of the word *besought* in Mark's Gospel. When Mary Magdalene was delivered from seven demons (Luke 8:2), she became one of Jesus' most dedicated followers (see commentary on Mark 5:19, below). This man contrasts with his countrymen who begged Jesus to depart the area.

19. Howbeit Jesus suffered him not, but saith unto him, Go home to thy friends, and tell them how great things the Lord hath done for thee, and hath had compassion on thee.

In contrast to Mary's joining Jesus' traveling ministry (see commentary on Mark 5:18, above), *Jesus suffered him not* to join. Furthermore, Jesus' command to the man was different than we might expect. Throughout Mark's Gospel, Jesus frequently told people to stay quiet about what He did for them. Given that we know Jesus ultimately wanted the gospel to spread throughout the world (Matthew 28:18-20), why would He tell people He'd healed to stay quiet?

Maintaining what has been called the messianic secret seems to have been Jesus' practice in Jewish regions, particularly earlier in His ministry (see Lesson Context). But in this Gentile region, Jesus' concerns were different. Perhaps because Jews had the Old Testament, and especially the prophets, to point to Jesus, the secrecy could have been a temporary measure to allow Jesus' ministry to grow in its own time. But because Gentiles did not have the Scriptures to refer to or learn from, eyewitness accounts of the Jewish teacher and healer would prepare the soil for faith to come. Though not exactly the same (partly because Samaritans did follow Mosaic law), the story of the Samaritan woman's witness illustrates the potential power of a firsthand account (John 4:1-42; see lesson 3).

What Do You Think?
What roadblocks are you experiencing in your efforts to spread the gospel?
Digging Deeper
How can you discern whether to try harder in that endeavor or pivot to a different focus?

B. Homecoming (v. 20)

20. And he departed, and began to publish in Decapolis how great things Jesus had done for him: and all men did marvel.

The *Decapolis* refers to a group of about 10 Gentile cities located east of the Sea of Galilee (with the exception of Scythopolis, which was west of the sea). Today this region is located in northwest Jordan and southern Syria. Though the cities were not officially allied, they shared cultural and economic ties as well as a desire for relative independence from Rome, which they were granted to a degree. Later in Mark's Gospel, Jesus would perform another miracle there (Mark 7:31-37). In Matthew's Gospel, the Decapolis was named as evidence that Jesus' reputation was spreading among Gentiles (Matthew 4:25).

This man gave thanks by obeying Jesus and letting others know what *great things Jesus had done for him* (see Mark 5:19, above). The cities of the Decapolis included Damascus—famous as the city where Saul (later Paul) regained his sight and became a follower of "this way" (Acts 9:1-20)—and Philadelphia, one of seven cities to receive a letter as described in John's vision (Revelation 3:7-13). Who knows how the former demoniac prepared the way for the gospel!

What Do You Think?
Who has benefited from your witness to Jesus' work in your life?
Digging Deeper
What might you say or do to help "marveling" grow into lasting faith?

Conclusion
A. From Death to Life

We too have been delivered by Jesus. And like the *former* demoniac, we have stepped out of a life that was more like death (Ephesians 2:1-10; Colossians 2:13-15). We too are called to share the story of what Jesus has done for us, to prepare our own communities to meet Christ and come to new life (Matthew 28:18-20). No matter the legions aligned against us, Jesus is in control! All we have to do is place our faith in Him, with joy and obedience.

What Do You Think?
What most challenges you about today's passage?
Digging Deeper
What will you do to respond to that challenge?

B. Prayer

Heavenly Father, may we remember Your Son's mighty power and be quick to ask for deliverance. May we as Your servants show our gratitude by proclaiming to others the good things You have done for us. In Jesus' name we pray. Amen.

C. Thought to Remember
Jesus has the power. Will you cry out to Him?

Involvement Learning

Enhance your lesson with KJV Bible Student *(from your curriculum supplier) and the reproducible activity page (at www.standardlesson.com or in the back of the* KJV Standard Lesson Commentary Deluxe Edition*).*

Into the Lesson

Invite participants to name some television shows or advertisements that reveal "before and after" images to show positive transformation results (for example, home renovation, weight loss, hair care, makeovers, or antique restoration). Continue the discussion with the following questions: 1–What is the most interesting kind of improvement to see? 2–Why do we enjoy seeing the beginning and end in comparison? 3–What would our reactions be if the after picture was not an improvement on the before?

Alternative. Bring to class three sets of "before and after" printed pictures (from the examples listed above) which you find with an internet search. Divide the class into three groups. Hand each group a set of pictures to study while discussing the following questions: 1–What are the specific differences you see in the details of these pictures? 2–What is the most significant change?

After either activity say, "We are fascinated with dramatic transformation. In today's story, imagine what the 'before and after' pictures would look like for the man who encountered Jesus."

Into the Word

Ask a volunteer to read Mark 5:1-5. Divide the class into three groups, designating one as **Verse 3**, another as **Verse 4**, and the last as **Verse 5**. Invite the groups to study their verse and write down a list of adjectives that might describe the man, based on these details of how he lived. Challenge the groups to include words that the townspeople would attribute to the man, as well as words that Jesus would use. If any in the group are artistically inclined, suggest that they sketch a picture of what the man might have looked like.

Alternative. Distribute copies of the "The Ultimate Spiritual Makeover" exercise from the activity page, which you can download. Have learners complete as directed in one minute or less before discussing with their small groups.

After either activity, ask a volunteer to read Mark 5:18-20. Direct small groups to look back at the list of adjectives they made from the first section of verses. Instruct them to create a Venn diagram (two overlapping circles). The first circle should include words from the previous activity describing the demon-possessed man before Jesus' intervention. The second circle should contain words about the man after Jesus intervened. Decide together what descriptors are true before *and* after Jesus' intervention, and write those in the overlap between the two circles. (Possibilities here include that the man was and remained beloved of God, still a Gentile, etc.) Discuss together what the overlaps from the man's life while possessed by demons and his life after possession suggest about the nature of redemption and salvation in Christ.

Into Life

Transition by asking: 1–If there was a "before and after" picture of your life, what would it look like? 2–What is one of the most noticeable transformations that has happened to you because of Jesus? Invite volunteers to briefly give a testimony to the whole group.

Alternative. Distribute the "Before and After" activity page to each participant. Encourage them to take it home to complete this week. Ask volunteers to be prepared to share their testimonies at the beginning of the next lesson.

Divide the class into small groups. Encourage learners to discuss a plan for sharing their "before and after" testimonies with at least one person this week.

Conclude class time by praying for opportunities, courage, and wisdom to share these testimonies. Be sure to allow time next week for learners to share their experiences.

The Empty Tomb

Devotional Reading: Psalm 22:20-31
Background Scripture: Luke 24:1-12

Luke 24:1-12

1 Now upon the first day of the week, very early in the morning, they came unto the sepulchre, bringing the spices which they had prepared, and certain others with them.

2 And they found the stone rolled away from the sepulchre.

3 And they entered in, and found not the body of the Lord Jesus.

4 And it came to pass, as they were much perplexed thereabout, behold, two men stood by them in shining garments:

5 And as they were afraid, and bowed down their faces to the earth, they said unto them, Why seek ye the living among the dead?

6 He is not here, but is risen: remember how he spake unto you when he was yet in Galilee,

7 Saying, The Son of man must be delivered into the hands of sinful men, and be crucified, and the third day rise again.

8 And they remembered his words,

9 And returned from the sepulchre, and told all these things unto the eleven, and to all the rest.

10 It was Mary Magdalene, and Joanna, and Mary the mother of James, and other women that were with them, which told these things unto the apostles.

11 And their words seemed to them as idle tales, and they believed them not.

12 Then arose Peter, and ran unto the sepulchre; and stooping down, he beheld the linen clothes laid by themselves, and departed, wondering in himself at that which was come to pass.

Key Text

They said unto them, Why seek ye the living among the dead? He is not here, but is risen.

—Luke 24:5b-6a

Jesus
Calls Us

Unit 2: Experiencing the Resurrection
Lessons 5–8

Lesson Aims

After participating in this lesson, each learner will be able to:

1. List important facts surrounding the discovery of the empty tomb.

2. Compare and contrast the women's expectation of the tomb versus its reality.

3. Identify his or her personal expectations that Jesus might upend.

Lesson Outline

Introduction
A. Some Good News

In the early months of 2020, people around the world were desperate to receive some good news. Shutdowns related to the coronavirus pandemic had begun, creating in some people a sense of unease and uncertainty. Further, many people were unable to see their families and friends for an extended season because of concerns about exposure to the virus. Loneliness and sadness were unavoidable.

Enter actor and filmmaker John Krasinski. While the global news cycle repeated bad news, John felt that it was the perfect time to share good news. On March 29, 2020, his web video series *Some Good News* premiered. Each episode, about 20 minutes long, was filmed in his house and was posted across various social media platforms. The episodes highlighted several positive, feel-good stories from the previous week.

By the time of this writing in late 2021, there have been over 70 million views of the nine-episode run of *Some Good News*, evidence that many people want good news. However, just because people *hear* good news does not always mean that they will *believe* that good news.

B. Lesson Context

Today's Scripture follows after the narrative of Jesus' crucifixion and death (Luke 23:26-46). Torture and execution by crucifixion was one way that the Roman Empire demonstrated the power of the state over its subjects. The brutal process of crucifixion slowly killed its victims as they bled, became dehydrated, and suffered shock and asphyxiation. That Jesus died after only several hours on the cross was a surprise (see Mark 15:44). Making a public exhibition of a prolonged and humiliating death was the primary aim of crucifixion.

The bodies of those crucified frequently remained on the crosses for several days after death as a spectacle and as a passive threat to all who would oppose the ruling powers. However, such a display did not occur for Jesus' body. Joseph, a man from the city of Arimathaea and a member of the council of the Sanhedrin, received Pilate's permission to take Jesus' body (Matthew 27:57-58; Mark 15:43-45; Luke 23:50-52; John 19:38). Joseph had certain wealth, enabling him to own a rock-hewn tomb (Matthew 27:60). That Jesus was buried in this man's tomb indicated a level of love that Joseph had for Jesus; strangers were not generally buried in the tomb of another family.

Jesus' body was wrapped in burial clothes as it was entombed (Matthew 27:59; Luke 23:53; compare John 11:44). Aromatic spices were placed with the burial clothes and in the tomb to cover the stench of decay (19:40; compare 11:39). Because Jesus was buried the evening before Sabbath (Mark 15:42), additional burial spices would have to wait to be administered until after the Sabbath (Luke 23:55-56).

Joseph's tomb was like many others that were carved in rock. Chiseled niches allowed for several bodies to be buried in one tomb. A large, flat stone would seal the tomb's entrance and prevent thieves from stealing valuable artifacts or even bodies. Tombs remained sealed until all that remained of a body were its bones. Family would then enter the tomb and place the bones in a box called an ossuary.

Many first-century Jews believed in the physical resurrection of the dead, the Sadducees being a notable exception (see Acts 4:1-2; 23:8). This doctrine can be traced to Old Testament texts (Job 19:25-27; Isaiah 26:19; Daniel 12:1-2, 13). Other Jewish texts describe a physical resurrection of the righteous dead (see 2 Baruch 50–51; 2 Maccabees 7:9, 14, 23). By the time of the first century AD, the doctrine of the resurrection of the righteous dead had been accepted by several parties of Judaism, especially the Pharisees (see Acts 23:6-8).

During His earthly ministry, Jesus had prophesied regarding His death, burial, and resurrection (Matthew 17:22-23; Mark 8:31; 9:30-31; Luke 9:22, 44; 18:31-33; John 2:19). However, the concept of a suffering and resurrected Savior was incomprehensible to many people, even Jesus' own disciples (Luke 9:45; 18:34).

Matthew 28:1-20, Mark 16:1-8, and John 20:1-29 are parallel texts to today's Scripture. Each Gospel writer included certain details found only in his specific narrative. Examples include a "great earthquake" (Matthew 28:2), a "young man . . . clothed in a long white garment" (Mark 16:5), the women's silence (16:8), the women's interaction with the resurrected Jesus (Matthew 28:9-10), and Mary Magdalene's experience at the tomb (John 20:1-2). These differences do not invalidate the Gospel accounts; they highlight the different emphases that each Gospel writer wanted to stress.

I. Early-Morning Discovery
(Luke 24:1-7)
A. Empty Tomb (vv. 1-3)

1. Now upon the first day of the week, very early in the morning, they came unto the sepulchre, bringing the spices which they had prepared, and certain others with them.

Those who *came unto the sepulchre* were "the women . . . which came with [Jesus] from Galilee" (Luke 23:55). These women had supported Jesus during His final season of ministry. After He had died, they went to the tomb and had observed "how his body was laid" (23:55).

By necessity, the women arrived at the tomb *in the morning* on Sunday, *the first day of the week*. The Law of Moses prevented anyone from working on the Sabbath (Exodus 20:10; Leviticus 23:3). All work ceased by the beginning of the Sabbath at sundown on Friday. The *early* morning would have provided adequate sunlight for safe travel.

How to Say It

Arimathaea	*Air*-uh-muh-**thee**-uh (*th* as in *thin*).
Chuza	*Koo*-za.
Herod Antipas	*Hair*-ud *An*-tih-pus.
Magdala	*Mag*-duh-luh.
Magdalene	*Mag*-duh-leen or *Mag*-duh-*lee*-nee.
omnipotent	ahm-*nih*-poh-tent.
omniscient	ahm-*nish*-unt.
Sanhedrin	*San*-huh-drun or San-*heed*-run.
Sadducees	*Sad*-you-seez.
Pontius Pilate	*Pon*-shus or *Pon*-ti-us *Pie*-lut.

More than "Do No Harm"

My work as a hospital chaplain allows me to observe firsthand" the dedication of the hospital's employees. They prepare treatments, clean rooms, bring food, and provide comfort to patients and their families. The workload is difficult, but the staff rarely complain. These caretakers go above and beyond the health-care principle of "Do no harm." They achieve this by giving individualized care, no matter how long the patient's stay.

While death—the greatest physical harm—had come to Jesus, the women wanted to care for His body. They desired to serve Jesus, even if for the last time (in their perspective). Can you view your service to God and others as an act of worship?

—L. M. W.

2. And they found the stone rolled away from the sepulchre.

After the body was placed in the tomb, a large *stone* was rolled in front of the tomb's entrance (Mark 15:46). Because of the concerns of the chief priests and the Pharisees that Jesus' disciples might attempt to remove Jesus' body, Pontius Pilate allowed for the tomb to be made more secure (Matthew 27:62-65). The chief priests and the Pharisees secured the tomb with a sealed stone and a guard at the tomb's entrance (27:66). The stone prevented robbers and animals from coming into the tomb. And the removal of this stone was no easy task; such stones were immense and required several strong adults to move them.

3. And they entered in, and found not the body of the Lord Jesus.

The Law of Moses warned that if a living person touched a dead body, then that person would be considered unclean for one week (Numbers 19:11)—potentially a major disruption to one's life. This might explain why one disciple did not enter the tomb (see John 20:5). The possibility of a state of uncleanliness did not hinder the women; they *entered* the opened tomb.

Because grave robbing was a frequent occurrence, distress and uncertainty likely overtook the women when they *found not the body*. If robbers had taken His body, it would have been yet another humiliating dishonor to their *Lord Jesus*.

B. Two Strangers (vv. 4-7)

4. And it came to pass, as they were much perplexed thereabout, behold, two men stood by them in shining garments.

Seeing an empty tomb did not fit the women's expectations. They had come to the tomb to show respect and care for the body of their friend. Instead, they had become witnesses to what appeared to be a grave robbery. The women were *perplexed* and unable to explain the empty tomb.

To further the women's confusion, two figures appeared and *stood* before *them*. Although this verse describes the figures as *two men*, they are later described as "angels" (Luke 24:23; see lesson 6). Further, Matthew's Gospel tells of an angelic presence at the tomb: "the angel of the Lord" (Matthew 28:2). Despite variations in the Gospels regarding the number and identity of the individuals at the tomb, we can assume that these individuals were angelic. Elsewhere, Luke the writer describes an angelic visitor appearing as a man (Acts 10:30-31). This description has parallels in the Old Testament (example: Joshua 5:13-15). The appearance of these *men in shining garments* further confirms their heavenly identities (compare Luke 9:29-30; Acts 1:10-11).

5. And as they were afraid, and bowed down their faces to the earth, they said unto them, Why seek ye the living among the dead?

Luke's Gospel describes how people *were afraid* when seeing God's messengers (Luke 1:11-12, 26-30; 2:9-10), experiencing God's power (8:24-25, 32-35; 9:34-36), and meeting the resurrected Christ (24:37-39). The women recognized that they were in the presence of God's messengers. With a combination of fear and honor, the women *bowed*.

In Matthew's account of this event, the women were told to "fear not" (Matthew 28:5; compare Luke 1:13, 30; 2:10). Luke's account, however, does not include this statement of comfort. Instead, the women are asked a question that amounts to the following: "*Why* do you *seek* the *living* Savior *from among the dead*?" The women understandably had sought Jesus' body in the tomb. But the angels provided a corrective to the women: Jesus was no longer dead but was alive in both body and spirit; He walked with the living (see Revelation 1:18)!

6. He is not here, but is risen: remember how he spake unto you when he was yet in Galilee.

The underlying Greek verb behind *risen* is in passive voice. One might assume that this fact means that Jesus was raised from the dead through a power beyond His own. The totality of Scripture, however, provides a more nuanced perspective: Jesus' resurrection resulted from the power of the entire triune Godhead. All three persons of the Trinity—Father, Son, and Holy Spirit—resurrected Jesus (see John 2:18-19; 10:17-18; Acts 2:24; Romans 8:11; 1 Peter 3:18).

When Jesus ministered *in Galilee*, He had taught His disciples in private regarding His upcoming death and resurrection (Luke 9:18-22; compare Matthew 16:21; Mark 8:31). The women presumably received similar teachings from the disciples (see Luke 18:31-33) or from Jesus' public statements (see 17:20-25). The fulfillment of His prophecy shows that Jesus is both omniscient (all-knowing) and omnipotent (all-powerful). At no point was He surprised or were His plans thwarted.

What Do You Think?

In what ways are believers guilty of forgetting that which has already been taught to them regarding the faith?

Digging Deeper

How will you guard against this tendency?

She Is Not Here

I had been overtaken by fear: my young daughter had gone missing. She had accompanied me and my husband to our jobs at a small college. We had left her in the college's student center. However, as the afternoon turned to evening, she was no longer there. A quick search of the student center and the surrounding buildings revealed nothing—we had lost her!

I panicked and fearfully considered all possible outcomes. About that time, I opened the door to a small conference room and found her there, writing on a whiteboard. I can't describe my relief as we made our way back home that evening.

Imagine the women's fear and panic when they

For us and for our salvation Jesus suffered, was buried, and rose again on the third day.

Visual for Lesson 5. *Show this image as you review the discussion questions associated with Luke 24:7.*

saw that Jesus' body was no longer in the tomb. The angels' promise to the fearful women remains just as true to us today: He *is* risen!   —L. M. W.

7. Saying, The Son of man must be delivered into the hands of sinful men, and be crucified, and the third day rise again.

For the benefit of the women, the angels repeated the main points of Jesus' teachings regarding His suffering and resurrection. The message of the angels is not based on any one particular teaching of Jesus. Instead, it blends several of His teachings found in Luke's Gospel (see Luke 9:22, 44; 18:32-33).

The title *Son of man* is found primarily throughout the Gospels and on the lips of Jesus. Its roots are not immediately clear, although many students believe that the title comes from the book of Daniel. There, the prophet Daniel describes a figure, "one like the Son of man" (Daniel 7:13), who was given all divine authority and power (7:14). Jesus used this title when referring to His divine authority (Luke 5:24) and power (Matthew 25:31; 26:24; Mark 13:26), but also to His humility (Matthew 8:20; Luke 9:58), especially regarding His suffering and death (9:22, 44; 18:31). Jesus showed His divine authority by defeating the forces of sin and death. This occurred only as He "took upon him the form of a servant" and "humbled himself, and became obedient unto death" (Philippians 2:7-8; compare Mark 9:12-13; 10:45).

II. Bearing Witness
(Luke 24:8-12)

A. The Message Proclaimed (vv. 8-10)

8-9. And they remembered his words, and returned from the sepulchre, and told all these things unto the eleven, and to all the rest.

The women *remembered* Jesus' teaching regarding His death and resurrection (see Matthew 16:21-28; 17:22-23; Luke 9:43b-45). While they acknowledged His teaching, it remained to be known whether they understood the *why* behind what He taught.

Part of Jesus' ministry focused on the marginalized of society (see Luke 4:18-19). He showed special attention toward people with physical ailments (example: 5:12-15), people suffering from demon possession (example: Mark 1:21-28), children (example: Matthew 19:13-15), and women (example: Mark 5:21-43). Such people were promised the presence of God's blessing (see Luke 6:20-22). The revelation of the empty tomb continued the trend of showing special attention to those people marginalized by the world. Women, regarded by society as unreliable, received the blessing of being the first human witnesses to Jesus' resurrection.

The women's recall of Jesus' teaching led them to action, and they *returned* to the other followers of Jesus (contrast with Mark 16:8). These women became the first to proclaim the good news of Jesus' resurrection. Their mission field first consisted of *the eleven* remaining apostles of Jesus (see Luke 6:12-16; compare Matthew 27:1-5), then expanded to include *all the rest* of Jesus' followers in Jerusalem. This larger group of Jesus' followers likely included Cleopas and his traveling compan-

ion (see Luke 24:13-18; lesson 6) and some who would later be counted among the 120 believers on the Day of Pentecost (Acts 1:15). Through the unlikely witness of the women, the apostles were presented with the news of Jesus' resurrection.

10. It was Mary Magdalene, and Joanna, and Mary the mother of James, and other women that were with them, which told these things unto the apostles.

Luke previously described the first *Mary* as having been delivered from seven demons (Luke 8:2). *Magdalene* indicates that she came from Magdala (Matthew 15:39), a town northwest of the Sea of Galilee. In John's Gospel, she is the first to see the resurrected Christ (see John 20:11-18; compare Mark 16:9). *Joanna* was the wife of Chuza, the steward of Herod Antipas's household (Luke 8:3). Though her husband's position in Herod's house likely afforded her certain privilege, her support of Jesus would have alienated her from the house.

Elsewhere, the second *Mary* is identified as *the mother of James* (and perhaps Joses; Matthew 27:56; Mark 15:40; compare 15:47). By one proposal, she was Jesus' mother (see Mark 6:3). However, Luke's identification of her by way of Jesus' half brother is unexpected (compare Acts 1:14).

These three, along with the *other women*, proclaimed the good news of the empty tomb to Jesus' followers designated as *apostles*. Luke uses the title for the disciples chosen by Jesus during His earthly ministry (Luke 6:13-16; Acts 1:1-2) or for those who met the criteria in Acts 1:21-26. The title applied not only to the original Twelve (see Luke 9:10; 17:5; 22:14; Acts 2:37; 4:33) but also to certain others (see 14:14; 1 Thessalonians 1:1; 2:6). Luke's point was to show the immediate results of their receiving the women's message. Those apostles, who would eventually be sent to proclaim the resurrected Christ, first received that message from these women!

B. The Message Verified (vv. 11-12)

11. And their words seemed to them as idle tales, and they believed them not.

The Law of Moses did not prohibit the testimony of a woman. However, by the first century AD, Jewish historian Josephus wrote that a woman's testimony was disallowed. Regardless of who the message came from (see John 20:24-25), the apostles doubted the validity of an empty tomb and a resurrected Jesus; such occurrences *seemed . . . idle tales*. Numerous attestations regarding the resurrection would do little to persuade them (see Mark 16:11-14; compare John 20:9).

What Do You Think?

How would you respond to the statement that the accounts of Jesus' resurrection are only "idle tales" (Luke 24:11)?

Digging Deeper

What would be the most effective way to encourage nonbelievers to investigate the Gospels' claims in this regard?

---

12. Then arose Peter, and ran unto the sepulchre; and stooping down, he beheld the linen clothes laid by themselves, and departed, wondering in himself at that which was come to pass.

Peter (along with John; see John 20:3-10) wanted to verify the women's message. Peter is not portrayed as being lackadaisical or disinterested. Instead, he *ran* to *the sepulchre*, ignoring any personal indignity associated with his running. On arrival, *he beheld* that the tomb was not empty: burial garments *laid by themselves*. A robber would not have unwrapped *the linen* burial *clothes* from the body and left them behind in the tomb.

Seeing the tomb without Jesus' body did not lead to an immediate response of faith for Peter. Instead, he *departed* from the tomb and was left *wondering* what had happened to the body of his Lord. Peter's journey of faith had come to another critical juncture. He had once expressed faith that Jesus was God's Messiah (Luke 9:18-20) but then,

under pressure, had denied knowing Jesus (22:54-62). Peter now faced the challenge of the women's message. Would he believe that Jesus' teachings regarding His resurrection had come to pass?

Conclusion

A. The Good News, the Best News

For the women at the tomb, the angels brought true good news. Jesus had defeated death as He had been raised from the dead. As a result, He is now the resurrected King who rules over all creation.

Although other disciples initially doubted the women's witness, those same disciples would eventually see their resurrected Lord. As they received and believed in that good news, they were called to proclaim it to the whole world (see Matthew 28:16-20). The good news of the resurrection began with the women's witness and went out to all nations.

We believers have a role to play in proclaiming that very same good news! Followers of Jesus are called to proclaim the good news of Jesus' resurrection to the world. Are you merely *believing* in that good news ,or are you also *proclaiming* that good news to the world?

What Do You Think?

What steps will you take in the upcoming days before Easter to proclaim the good news that Jesus is alive?

Digging Deeper

How will you prepare now for possible rejection or dismissal when proclaiming this good news?

B. Prayer

God, we rejoice because we have the same good news that was first given to the women at the tomb: Jesus is risen! Show us new ways that we might share this news with others. Give us patience when the message is not received. In the name of the resurrected Jesus. Amen.

C. Thought to Remember

Rejoice in the good news: Jesus is risen!

Involvement Learning

Enhance your lesson with KJV Bible Student *(from your curriculum supplier) and the reproducible activity page (at www.standardlesson.com or in the back of the* KJV Standard Lesson Commentary Deluxe Edition*).*

Into the Lesson

Distribute blank sheets of paper to learners and have them write down a time when their reality differed (for better or worse) from their expectations. If they have a difficult time coming up with an example, provide the following ideas: tasting a new food, learning a new activity, receiving an online purchase, meeting a famous person, going on a long-awaited vacation.

Allow one minute for learners to write about the experience. Then have them form pairs to discuss what they wrote down. Have learners each share with his or her partner how they responded when reality was different from expectations. After three minutes, ask for volunteers to share their responses before the whole class.

Alternative. Distribute copies of the "Multiple Lenses" exercise from the activity page, which you can download. Have learners work in groups of four to complete as indicated.

After either activity, transition to Bible study by saying, "Today's Scripture will examine the nature of human expectations and the reality of when those expectations are not met—for the better!"

Into the Word

Begin Bible study by saying, "Today's Scripture is filled with instances of various expectations and surprising emotions. How do we convey our emotions to others?" After learners answer this question, talk briefly about emojis, the digital images used in electronic messages to express an emotion. State that while emojis appear trite, they can summarize and convey common emotions.

Divide the class into three groups.

Women Group: Mary Magdalene, Joanna, Mary the mother of James, and the other women

Angels Group: the two men in shining clothes

Disciples Group: the apostles, especially Peter

To each group, distribute markers and handouts (you prepare) with the verse numbers from Luke 24:1-12 spaced out along the left side of the paper. As you (or a volunteer) slowly read Luke 24:1-12, pause after each verse and have the groups draw emojis depicting the presumed emotions and expectations felt by their group's characters. (If desired, groups can write down the emotions and expectations.) Not every group will have a reaction for each verse. Repeat the process for each verse. After reading through all verses, ask for a volunteer from each group to share their group's emojis (or list of emotions) and explain what they thought their group's characters were expecting or feeling.

For whole-class discussion, ask why it took more than the empty tomb to convince the women and the disciples that Jesus had risen from the dead. Continue discussion by asking what preconceived expectations informed the beliefs of the women and the disciples.

Alternative. Distribute copies of the "What's the Story?" exercise from the activity page. Have learners work in groups to complete as indicated.

Into Life

Write on the board *Expectations Transformed*. Beneath that title, write *Then / Now* as the headers. Conduct a brainstorming session by challenging learners to fill in the *Then* column with expectations in the time period of the Gospels that were transformed by Jesus' resurrection. Then have the class reflect on how Jesus' resurrection transforms expectations of today's world. Write those ideas under the *Now* column.

Divide the class into pairs. Ask learners to share with their partners regarding an upcoming experience that will have a perceived challenge. Have pairs determine how Jesus' resurrection will change thoughts and behaviors in that experience. After five minutes of discussion, ask pairs to pray with each other, asking God for openness to the ways that Jesus' resurrection will transform challenging situations in the upcoming week.

Disciples Believe the Resurrection

Devotional Reading: John 20:11-18
Background Scripture: Luke 24:13-49

Luke 24:13-27, 30-31

13 And, behold, two of them went that same day to a village called Emmaus, which was from Jerusalem about threescore furlongs.

14 And they talked together of all these things which had happened.

15 And it came to pass, that, while they communed together and reasoned, Jesus himself drew near, and went with them.

16 But their eyes were holden that they should not know him.

17 And he said unto them, What manner of communications are these that ye have one to another, as ye walk, and are sad?

18 And the one of them, whose name was Cleopas, answering said unto him, Art thou only a stranger in Jerusalem, and hast not known the things which are come to pass there in these days?

19 And he said unto them, What things? And they said unto him, Concerning Jesus of Nazareth, which was a prophet mighty in deed and word before God and all the people:

20 And how the chief priests and our rulers delivered him to be condemned to death, and have crucified him.

21 But we trusted that it had been he which should have redeemed Israel: and beside all this, to day is the third day since these things were done.

22 Yea, and certain women also of our company made us astonished, which were early at the sepulchre;

23 And when they found not his body, they came, saying, that they had also seen a vision of angels, which said that he was alive.

24 And certain of them which were with us went to the sepulchre, and found it even so as the women had said: but him they saw not.

25 Then he said unto them, O fools, and slow of heart to believe all that the prophets have spoken:

26 Ought not Christ to have suffered these things, and to enter into his glory?

27 And beginning at Moses and all the prophets, he expounded unto them in all the scriptures the things concerning himself.

30 And it came to pass, as he sat at meat with them, he took bread, and blessed it, and brake, and gave to them.

31 And their eyes were opened, and they knew him; and he vanished out of their sight.

Key Text

Their eyes were opened, and they knew him; and he vanished out of their sight. —**Luke 24:31**

Jesus
Calls Us

Unit 2: Experiencing the Resurrection
Lessons 5–8

Lesson Aims

After participating in this lesson, each learner will be able to:

1. Summarize the conversation that took place on the road to Emmaus.

2. Compare and contrast the disciples' experiences of Jesus when they did *not* and then *did* recognize Him.

3. Write a prayer for his or her eyes to be opened to Jesus' presence during personal "road to Emmaus" times.

Lesson Outline

Introduction

A. The Resurrection Revolution

What do you think of when you hear the term *revolution*? Perhaps you think of socio-political revolutions, like the American Revolution. But other, much less bloody revolutions have since occurred. These revolutions have provided a similar sense of cultural change and upheaval in their wake.

Beginning with the creation of the transistor in the mid-twentieth century, the Digital Revolution has changed the way people engage with the world. From the transistor came the ability for more advanced computers and, ultimately, the internet.

By the twenty-first century, millions of transistors could be placed on a single microchip. These microchips are the computing power behind modern electronic devices. Because of the Digital Revolution and the resulting ease of access to computers, everyday life has changed in one way or another. Any person who has access to the internet can experience a life previously thought unattainable. All this has resulted in humanity's transition into a new era of history: the Information Age.

The story of Scripture comes to one climax with a revolution: the resurrection of Jesus. This revolution overthrew the reign of death and brought the possibility of new life, one free from fear and despair (Romans 5:12-21). Today's Scripture reveals the surprising nature of that revolution.

B. Lesson Context

Today's Scripture follows after the women discovered the empty tomb (Luke 24:1-8; see lesson 5). Two apostles wanted to see the empty tomb for themselves (24:12; compare John 20:3-10).

Many first-century Jews believed in the bodily resurrection of the righteous dead. This doctrine is rooted in certain Old Testament prophetic texts (see Daniel 12:1-3, 13; etc.). Jewish texts from the period between the Old and New Testaments developed this doctrine further (see the nonbiblical 2 Maccabees 7:13-14; 12:43; etc.). Not all Jews, however, believed in the resurrection (see Acts 23:8). Jesus' followers, though skeptical of the empty tomb, would not have entirely denied the possibility.

I. The Journey Begins
(Luke 24:13-16)

A. Distressed by Death (vv. 13-14)

13. And, behold, two of them went that same day to a village called Emmaus, which was from Jerusalem about threescore furlongs.

These *two* travelers were some of Jesus' followers who had heard the women's report regarding the empty tomb (see Luke 24:9). The travelers began their journey to *Emmaus* on the *same day* that the women had seen the tomb: "the first day of the week" (24:1). Scripture does not indicate the reason for their journey.

One possibility is that the two had come to *Jerusalem* for the observance of Passover, which had been during the previous week (see Luke 22:1; John 13:1). Jews were required to travel to Jerusalem to participate in that annual event (see Deuteronomy 16:5-6; compare Luke 2:41-42). Since the observance of Passover had passed (see Matthew 26:17; Luke 22:7), plus the fact that the Sabbath was over (see 23:54-56), the two travelers could have been returning home.

A furlong measures a little over 200 yards. A score is a measure of 20, so *threescore furlongs* is 60 furlongs. With these facts, we can estimate that the distance between Emmaus and Jerusalem was approximately seven miles. Two travelers without bulky loads could complete the journey to Emmaus in under a day. This verse is the only mention in the New Testament of *a village* named Emmaus, and its exact location is unknown.

14. And they talked together of all these things which had happened.

At a normal walking pace of two miles per hour, the journey provided ample time for contemplation and conversation regarding what *had happened* during the previous week. The primary attention-getters had been, of course, Jesus' arrest (Luke 22:47-54), trials (22:66–23:25), crucifixion (23:26-46), and burial (23:50-55). In their perspective, the final chapter of Jesus' life and ministry had been written. However, the women who visited Jesus' tomb had described a different reality (see 24:1-12). Was there any way for the two men to make sense of *all these things*?

B. Joined by Jesus (vv. 15-16)

15. And it came to pass, that, while they communed together and reasoned, Jesus himself drew near, and went with them.

The word translated *reasoned* is used elsewhere by Luke the author to suggest strong debate (see Luke 22:23; Acts 6:9; 9:29). The emphatic statement *Jesus himself* stresses that it was Jesus and no one else who appeared *and went with* the two.

16. But their eyes were holden that they should not know him.

The fact that the *eyes* of the two *were holden* could mean either that God obscured their vision in some way or that Jesus' physical appearance was somewhat changed from before His burial.

Another possibility is that the two were so engaged in conversation that they failed to recognize Jesus. The two had no reason to think that this other traveler would special have insight regarding the previous week's events. Later, other followers of Jesus would also fail to recognize Him in their midst (see John 20:14-15; 21:4).

II. The Travelers Lament
(Luke 24:17-24)

A. Despair (vv. 17-21)

17. And he said unto them, What manner of communications are these that ye have one to another, as ye walk, and are sad?

As the all-knowing Son of God, Jesus knew the reason for the two travelers' discussion and resulting sadness (compare Mark 2:8). Thus Jesus' question was intended to start a conversation, not to gain knowledge.

18. And the one of them, whose name was Cleopas, answering said unto him, Art thou only a stranger in Jerusalem, and hast not

known the things which are come to pass there in these days?

Luke identifies *one of* the two as *Cleopas*. It is highly unlikely that this individual was the same as "Cleophas" in John 19:25. Perhaps Luke identified this individual because he was still alive when Luke wrote his Gospel. If this were the case, the Gospel's original audience could corroborate the story.

Cleopas was surprised that the other traveler was unaware of the week's events. Jesus had taught openly at the Jerusalem temple (Luke 21:37). Crowds had gathered at His trial (23:13-23) and crucifixion (23:27). Therefore, Cleopas assumed that the traveler was *only a stranger* and was clueless as to what had happened in *Jerusalem*. But Cleopas's response could even be read as a sarcastic retort. Even a stranger coming to Jerusalem for Passover would have *known* what happened to Jesus.

Ironically, the person who seemed to be a stranger was the only person who fully understood the week's events. Cleopas assumed that the stranger was unaware at best and ignorant at worst. However, it was Cleopas who was in the dark.

19a. And he said unto them, What things?

Jesus did not immediately reveal His knowledge regarding the *things* that had occurred over the previous week. To start a conversation with the two travelers, Jesus asked them to recount the week's events as they understood them.

19b. And they said unto him, Concerning Jesus of Nazareth.

The designation *Jesus of Nazareth* occurs 17 times in the New Testament, functioning as an identifier of His earthly origin. Nazareth was the town where He grew up (see Luke 2:39-40). Jesus' followers invoked this designation when they did miraculous works in the name and power of Jesus (see Acts 3:6-8; 4:8-11).

What Do You Think?

Under what circumstances should we invoke Jesus' name today?

Digging Deeper

How do Acts 3:6, 16; 9:27-28; 16:18; Colossians 3:17; and James 5:14 help frame your answer?

19c. Which was a prophet mighty in deed and word before God and all the people.

As Jesus showed His might and proclaimed Scripture, people considered Him to be at least *a prophet* of God (see Matthew 21:10-11; Luke 7:16-17; 9:18-19). In addition to foretelling and forth-telling, prophets like those in the Old Testament did miraculous works in the name of the Lord (example: 1 Kings 18:30-38).

To the two, Jesus' power was evident through His teaching and miraculous deeds. However, even Moses was "mighty in words and in deeds" (Acts 7:22). Did the travelers believe that Jesus was more than a prophet and was truly the Son of God?

20. And how the chief priests and our rulers delivered him to be condemned to death, and have crucified him.

Jesus had warned His disciples about His arrest, specifically that the Jewish leadership would reject Him and instigate the process leading to His *death* (Luke 9:22; compare 19:47; 20:19). This was fulfilled when Pilate "called together *the chief priests* and the *rulers* and the people" (23:13) to determine what would happen to Jesus after His arrest.

No first-century Jew anticipated that God's Messiah would have been *condemned to death* and *crucified*. The Roman Empire used crucifixion as a tool to terrorize its subjects and assert its authority. Jesus' followers expected Him to overcome the Roman Empire and free God's people from oppression.

21a. But we trusted that it had been he which should have redeemed Israel.

The reason that the travelers were distraught was because they had (rightly) believed that Jesus was the anointed deliverer from God, the Messiah. Hebrew Scriptures promised that God's anointed deliverer would be a descendant of David to redeem and rule over *Israel* (see 2 Samuel 7:10-16; compare Luke 20:41-44). Many Jews anticipated that this would be a political redemption, freeing the people from oppressive foreign occupation (see Acts 1:6).

By saying *should have redeemed Israel*, the travelers likely shared this viewpoint. They had hoped and *trusted that* Jesus would free their people from foreign oppression. To see Jesus put to death in a horrifying manner brought them disappointment. For a deeper study on the concept of redemption and expectations of the redeemer, see Exodus 6:6; 2 Samuel 7:23; Psalm 130:8; Isaiah 43:1; 44:6; 49:7; Luke 1:68; 2:38; 21:25-28.

What Do You Think?

How should believers respond when God's plans turn out differently than they had expected?

Digging Deeper

How does prayer (see Philippians 4:6-7) prepare you to deal with those situations?

21b. And beside all this, to day is the third day since these things were done.

The two may have heard of the promise that Jesus made to His disciples regarding His resurrection on *the third day* (see Luke 9:22; 18:31-33; compare 13:32). On this, the promised third day, the two left Jerusalem without having experienced the fulfillment—or so they thought.

B. Skepticism (vv. 22-24)

22-23. Yea, and certain women also of our company made us astonished, which were early at the sepulchre; and when they found not his body, they came, saying, that they had also seen a vision of angels, which said that he was alive.

The two were part of "all the rest" (Luke 24:9) who had received the report from the *women* regarding the empty *sepulchre* (see lesson 5).

24. And certain of them which were with us went to the sepulchre, and found it even so as the women had said: but him they saw not.

The women's report had been confirmed by others. Peter had visited the empty tomb (Luke 24:12). John's Gospel indicates that another disciple—John himself—joined Peter in investigating (John 20:1-10). Both men confirmed what *the women had said*, but the men did not see their resurrected Lord. Jesus' followers had to live in faith, trusting Jesus' promises without having immediate evidence to their fulfillment (compare 20:26-29).

Unexpected Appearances

I sat across from my roommate in our dorm room as we talked about a mutual friend. Mid-conversation the door opened, and that mutual friend walked into our room. We wondered how much of the conversation our friend had heard!

News of Jesus' arrest, trial, crucifixion, and burial, along with the women's claim regarding the tomb, were all that the two men could talk about. They had questions and felt confusion regarding it all. What does our resurrected Lord think of your conversations? Do you proclaim Him in a way that invites others to proclaim Him also?   —L. M. W.

III. The Stranger Responds
(Luke 24:25-27, 30-31)
A. Corrective Teaching (vv. 25-27)

25. Then he said unto them, O fools, and slow of heart to believe all that the prophets have spoken.

By calling the two travelers *fools*, Jesus followed in the tradition of Hebrew wisdom literature that called out the folly of fools (Proverbs 13:16; etc.). Paul used the same underlying Greek word when he rebuked people who were being led astray by false teaching (see Galatians 3:1, 3).

The rebuke came because the two were *slow* to accept and *believe* the teachings regarding the promised Messiah. Jesus previously had brought together His Twelve Apostles and proclaimed that "all things that are written by the prophets concerning the Son of man shall be accomplished" (Luke 18:31). He followed with a prediction of His arrest, death, and resurrection (18:32-33).

How to Say It

Cleopas	*Clee*-uh-pass.
Cleophas	*Klee*-o-fus.
Emmaus	Em-*may*-us.
Ketuvim (*Hebrew*)	*Ket*-you-vim.
Maccabees	*Mack*-uh-bees.
Messiah	Meh-*sigh*-uh.
Nazareth	*Naz*-uh-reth.
Nevi'im (*Hebrew*)	*Neh*-vih-im.
Pentateuch	*Pen*-ta-teuk.
Pilate	*Pie*-lut.
Tanakh (*Hebrew*)	Tah-*nahkh*.
Torah (*Hebrew*)	*Tor*-uh.

Although these two were not among Jesus' Twelve Apostles, they had received the teaching of *the prophets* regarding the Messiah. Such teachings likely included Isaiah's proclamation regarding the suffering servant (Isaiah 52:13–53:12; etc.). Further, Jesus also might have referred to the prophet Daniel regarding the promised reign of "one like the Son of man . . . the Ancient of days" (Daniel 7:13-14).

The two were slow to believe, but they were not incapable or ill-prepared. The prophets' teachings, the women's testimony, and even the words of Jesus himself provided ample evidence of God's work.

26. Ought not Christ to have suffered these things, and to enter into his glory?

This simple question expressed a central part of God's eternal plan. Jesus had previously attested to the ways that the "Son of man" would suffer (Luke 9:22, 44; 17:22-25; 18:31-34). He then related that to the suffering experienced by *Christ*. The title "Christ" is the Greek equivalent of Messiah (see John 1:41), both titles meaning "the anointed one." God's plan of salvation required that Christ suffer before being glorified. As a result, salvation is available (see Acts 5:30-31; Hebrews 2:10).

27. And beginning at Moses and all the prophets, he expounded unto them in all the scriptures the things concerning himself.

Jesus referred to Hebrew Scripture, what Christians call the Old Testament, to prove His point. Its contents in Jesus' day are traditionally seen in three categories. First are the writings of *Moses*, the first five books of the Old Testament. These five are often referred to as the five books of law, the Pentateuch, or Torah. Two passages Jesus may have discussed from this section include Genesis 3:15 and Deuteronomy 18:15.

The second section is called *Nevi'im*, which is the Hebrew word for *prophets*. Some passages Jesus may have cited from this section include Isaiah 7:14; 9:6; Ezekiel 34:23; and Malachi 3:1. The third section, not mentioned in the verse before us, is called *Ketuvim*, which refers to all the other books of the Old Testament that are not in the writings of Moses or the prophets. The author Luke does not refer to this third category, but he does do so in Luke 24:44 by using the phrase "the psalms" loosely as a catchall category.

Taking the first letter of each word *Torah*, *Nevi'im*, and *Ketuvim* and adding vowels yields the word *Tanakh*, used to describe the entirety of the Old Testament. This three-fold division is rather different from the division most often used today: 5 books of law, 12 of history, 5 of wisdom and poetry, 5 of major prophets, and 12 of minor prophets.

What Do You Think?

How would you respond to someone who says that the Old Testament is not valuable for Christian faith and life?

Digging Deeper

What Old Testament Scriptures would be a particularly good starting point for making a gospel presentation?

B. Revealing Meal (vv. 30-31)

30. And it came to pass, as he sat at meat with them, he took bread, and blessed it, and brake, and gave to them.

As the travelers neared their destination, they invited Jesus to stay with them for the night (Luke 24:28-29, not in today's printed text). Their invitation did not imply that they were aware of the stranger's identity. They were just extending hospitality to the unknown traveler. Traveling at night was dangerous, so demonstrations of this type of hospitality were common (examples: Genesis 19:2; Judges 19:20).

The act of sharing a meal was an obvious way for the travelers to show hospitality. One of the two travelers would presumably serve as the meal's host. However, Jesus himself took the role of host when *he took bread* and *blessed it*. This act paralleled aspects of His final meal with His disciples (Matthew 26:26; Mark 14:22; Luke 22:19).

What Do You Think?

How can table fellowship be an opportunity for you to introduce the gospel to unbelievers?

Digging Deeper

Who among your unbelieving neighbors will you invite to your table?

31. And their eyes were opened, and they knew him; and he vanished out of their sight.

This meal not only met the travelers' physical needs, but it was also the moment in which Christ's presence was revealed to them (compare Luke 24:36-43; John 21:9-14; see also Hosea 6:1-3). The passive voice of the phrase *their eyes were opened* serves as the counterpart to the passive voice of "their eyes were holden" in Luke 24:16, above. The result in both cases is to stress what happened, not what or who caused it to happen.

Jesus did not linger with the two. The fact that Jesus could be seen and recognized and yet vanish *out of their sight* indicates both a continuity and a discontinuity with His physical body after the resurrection (see also Luke 24:36-43; John 20:19-29).

The interaction left the two realizing that *they knew* the resurrected Christ. Their previously saddened hearts had burned within them (Luke 24:32). Only after they knew Jesus could they explain the sensation in their hearts. The two returned to Jerusalem and told the other disciples of their experience with the resurrected Christ (24:33-35). Despite the presence of unbelief, the revolution of the resurrected Christ was underway.

"Ordinary" Hospitality

When our children were young, our family prioritized eating dinner together. This meant juggling dinnertime between work, school, and extracurricular activities. As our children grew older, eating dinner together each night became more difficult. But we remained committed to the tradition.

Certainly it would have been easier for our family to eat separately. We recognized, however, that mealtime was the best time to intentionally reconnect with each other. The ordinary acts of serving food and sharing meals deepened our family's relationships.

The two travelers thought they had lost relationship with Jesus. At some point during the meal, however, they realized with whom they were eating. They had unknowingly shown hospitality to the risen Lord! Make time to share a meal with your friends and neighbors. You might be surprised about what comes from those ordinary measures of hospitality (see Hebrews 13:2). —L. M. W.

Visual for Lesson 6. *Pose this question for whole-class discussion before you review the Conclusion as a class.*

Conclusion

A. Personal Revolution

The Digital Revolution has provided great advances for humanity (examples: improved productivity, rapid communication). Only time will tell if these benefits will be outweighed by the costs of this revolution (example: issues related to online privacy and personal addictions).

The travelers in today's Scripture experienced a Resurrection Revolution that brought a personal revolution. Their saddened outlook was transformed when they shared a meal with the resurrected Lord.

This revolution brought the two travelers joy, enthusiasm, and peace. It also meant reordered priorities; they received a correction and were reminded of how Scripture pointed to Christ's resurrection and the resulting revolution. Are you attentive to the ways the resurrection can change your expectations—and your life?

B. Prayer

Heavenly Father, Jesus' resurrection has changed the world. Show us how we might better teach Your Word for other people to believe in You. In the name of the resurrected Jesus. Amen.

C. Thought to Remember

Jesus' resurrection brings a revolution.
Are you living in it?

Involvement Learning

Enhance your lesson with KJV Bible Student *(from your curriculum supplier) and the reproducible activity page (at www.standardlesson.com or in the back of the* KJV Standard Lesson Commentary Deluxe Edition*).*

Into the Lesson

Ask for three volunteers to come to the front of the class. Each volunteer will give one true and two untrue statements about themselves. (The statements should be unusual and difficult to immediately verify.) The class will ask five questions of the first volunteer, trying to determine the true fact. Then the class will vote by a show of hands, and the volunteer will reveal the true fact. Repeat with the other volunteers. Lead a discussion about how people ask questions and seek evidence when hearing of something unusual.

Alternative. Distribute copies of the "Did It Happen?" exercise from the activity page, which you can download. Have learners work in pairs to complete as indicated.

After completing either activity, lead into Bible study by saying, "Last week's lesson was the first of two parts. This week we'll continue the story and consider how some of Jesus' followers were provided with an unexpected answer."

Into the Word

Announce a Bible-marking activity. Provide copies of Luke 24:13-27, 30-31 for those who do not wish to write in their own Bibles. Provide handouts (you create) with these instructions:

- Draw a circle around words or phrases that describe the concepts of vision or recognition.
- Draw a rectangle around words or phrases that describe the concept of disappointment.
- Underline the words or phrases from Jesus that address the travelers' disappointment.
- Write an exclamation point next to any verse that references another Scripture.
- Draw a question mark around any word or phrase that you find difficult to understand.

Read the Scripture aloud (or ask a volunteer to do so) slowly two to four times. As the Scripture is read, learners are to mark their copies in the ways noted.

Divide the class into three groups and distribute handouts (you create) of the following questions for in-group discussion.

Vision Group. 1–What is the significance of vision and recognition in today's Scripture? 2–What impediments prevent people from having spiritual "eyes" to see God's work? 3–How should believers respond once their "eyes" are opened to God's work?

Disappointment Group. 1–What is the significance of the travelers' disappointment, and how did Jesus address their disappointment? 2–What causes believers to experience spiritual disappointment? 3–What is the appropriate response to hearing another believer's spiritual disappointment?

Scripture Group. 1–How were other Scriptures used by the people in today's text? 2–How does their usage of Scripture inform our own usage? 3–What steps can believers take to better grasp the whole narrative of Scripture?

Alternative. Distribute copies of the "Extra! Extra!" exercise from the active page, which you can download. Have learners work in pairs to complete as indicated. After 10 minutes, have pairs present their articles to the whole class.

Into Life

Divide the class into pairs and have each pair discuss the following questions that you will write on the board: 1–Describe a time when you had a moment of spiritual insight regarding the presence of Jesus. 2–How did God use that insight to deepen your faith? 3–What situations or experiences—like the travelers' experience on the road to Emmaus—can prevent a believer from noticing Jesus' presence?

Have each learner write a prayer for his or her eyes to be opened to Jesus' presence during a "road to Emmaus" time. Encourage learners to put this prayer in a location where they will see it often.

Jesus Cooks Breakfast

Devotional Reading: Psalm 30
Background Scripture: John 21:1-14

John 21:1-14

1 After these things Jesus shewed himself again to the disciples at the sea of Tiberias; and on this wise shewed he himself.

2 There were together Simon Peter, and Thomas called Didymus, and Nathanael of Cana in Galilee, and the sons of Zebedee, and two other of his disciples.

3 Simon Peter saith unto them, I go a fishing. They say unto him, We also go with thee. They went forth, and entered into a ship immediately; and that night they caught nothing.

4 But when the morning was now come, Jesus stood on the shore: but the disciples knew not that it was Jesus.

5 Then Jesus saith unto them, Children, have ye any meat? They answered him, No.

6 And he said unto them, Cast the net on the right side of the ship, and ye shall find. They cast therefore, and now they were not able to draw it for the multitude of fishes.

7 Therefore that disciple whom Jesus loved saith unto Peter, It is the Lord. Now when Simon Peter heard that it was the Lord, he girt his fisher's coat unto him, (for he was naked,) and did cast himself into the sea.

8 And the other disciples came in a little ship; (for they were not far from land, but as it were two hundred cubits,) dragging the net with fishes.

9 As soon then as they were come to land, they saw a fire of coals there, and fish laid thereon, and bread.

10 Jesus saith unto them, Bring of the fish which ye have now caught.

11 Simon Peter went up, and drew the net to land full of great fishes, an hundred and fifty and three: and for all there were so many, yet was not the net broken.

12 Jesus saith unto them, Come and dine. And none of the disciples durst ask him, Who art thou? knowing that it was the Lord.

13 Jesus then cometh, and taketh bread, and giveth them, and fish likewise.

14 This is now the third time that Jesus shewed himself to his disciples, after that he was risen from the dead.

Key Text

Jesus saith unto them, Come and dine. And none of the disciples durst ask him, Who art thou? knowing that it was the Lord. —**John 21:12**

Jesus Calls Us

Unit 2: Experiencing the Resurrection
Lessons 5–8

Lesson Aims

After participating in this lesson, each learner will be able to:

1. List key points of the disciples' third encounter with the resurrected Christ.

2. Provide reasons as to why the disciples did or did not recognize Jesus.

3. Write a prayer asking for eyes that recognize Jesus at work this week.

Lesson Outline

Introduction

A. The Post-Wedding Brunch

For couples who want to spend more time celebrating with their guests on the wedding weekend, the post-wedding brunch is a popular option. Because it ordinarily happens the day after the wedding, it can be relatively low-key. For those guests who can linger, this meal offers time to offer final well wishes and say a proper goodbye, to laugh and chat in a more casual environment. And the brunch offers guests who need to leave quickly for a flight a grab-and-go meal they don't have to find for themselves. They get the satisfaction of having as much time with the bride and groom as possible—the whole reason those guests traveled in the first place!

The events leading to the meal in today's lesson are like that wedding brunch: another opportunity to spend time with dear friends and celebrate the bond between them.

B. Lesson Context

Some scholars have suggested that John 21 was not originally a part of John's Gospel. The evidence for this can be summarized as being based on (1) the fact that John 20:30-31 contains a natural conclusion to the Gospel; (2) perceived differences in language, style, and content compared to the rest of the Gospel; and (3) a supposed divergence from the story John told before chapter 21. Despite these observations, those who don't think John 21 is original generally argue that it was added by close associates of John very shortly after the Gospel was completed. The thinking, in part, is that John 21:20-23 seemed to suggest John would not die. When he did die, however, the death may have caused distress and shaken the faith of some in the community, which the epilogue was meant to alleviate.

Against the idea that John 21 is not original is the fact that the earliest manuscripts we have all include the epilogue. There is no reason to believe that the Gospel ever circulated without it. And such epilogues can be found in other ancient writings, showing that this is not a particularly remarkable literary characteristic. Arguments about supposed differences in language and style can be explained by differences in the material that make up the story. The epilogue also ties up loose ends of the Gospel, particularly Peter's redemption after his denial of Jesus, and adds further evidence of John's faithful witnessing of Jesus' life and teaching. Further, the epilogue fulfills Jesus' promise that He would meet the disciples in Galilee (Matthew 26:31-35; 28:5-10).

I. Gone Fishin'

(John 21:1-6)

A. The Disciples Fail (vv. 1-3)

1. After these things Jesus shewed himself again to the disciples at the sea of Tiberias; and on this wise shewed he himself.

John used the Greek verb translated *shewed* at various points when God or His glory was revealed (examples where the same Greek word is translated with a form of *manifest*: John 2:11; 9:3; 17:6). This post-resurrection appearance certainly fits with that pattern.

The sea of Tiberias is another name for the body of water more commonly called the Sea of Galilee (see John 6:1). The city of Tiberias was constructed by Herod Antipas in honor of Emperor Tiberius about AD 20. It became Herod Antipas's capital city, strategically placed on the western coast of the sea with major roads leading north, west, and south from it. The coastline offered good natural protection from attack as well as sweeping views of Galilee. Though the city was of strategic importance for Herod Antipas, Tiberias is named in the New Testament only once (6:23).

2a. There were together Simon Peter.

The double name *Simon Peter* occurs more often in John than in any other Gospel (John 1:40; 6:68;

Visual for Lesson 7. *Allow one minute for learners to reflect on and give thanks for meals that have had spiritual significance for them.*

20:2, 6; etc.). No explanation is given for this, but we could imagine it as a subtle way to remind readers both of Simon's natural life and his calling from Jesus to be Peter (Matthew 16:18). Before Jesus' death, Peter seemed to oscillate between two poles: first having great spiritual insight, then becoming blinded by his own expectations (examples: 16:13-16, 21-23). Peter was probably named first because he was an unofficial leader among the disciples (see commentary on John 21:3a, below; also lesson 8), even when his boldness in leadership failed him (example: Matthew 14:25-31).

2b. And Thomas called Didymus.

Both *Thomas* (Aramaic) and *Didymus* (Greek) mean "twin," though who that twin was remains unknown. While the other Gospels acknowledge Thomas was an apostle, only John provides any further information about the man. After Jesus received the news that His friend Lazarus had died, Thomas was the one who suggested the disciples go with Jesus to mourn, even if it meant their deaths (John 11:8, 14-16). After Jesus' resurrection, Thomas was absent when Jesus appeared to the others and remained skeptical about their experience until Jesus appeared to him too (20:24-29).

2c. And Nathanael of Cana in Galilee.

The Gospel of John names *Nathanael* as a disciple, while the other Gospels do not. Where we might expect to find him in the list of apostles, instead there is "Bartholomew" (Matthew 10:2-4; Mark 3:16-19; Luke 6:14-16; Acts 1:13). These two men could be one and the same, as the prefix *Bar-* (meaning "son of") would not necessarily be the only name the "son of Tolmai/Talmai" was known by. But there is no evidence that requires this.

In any case, Nathanael was one of Jesus' earliest followers (John 1:45). His hometown *Cana* was located *in Galilee*, a significant location in the Gospel of John. Here Jesus performed His first two miraculous signs (2:1-11; 4:46-54). Mentioning the town could be intended as a reminder of Jesus' work in Cana, or it could simply differentiate this Nathanael from someone else who was known to believers.

2d. And the sons of Zebedee.

The *sons of Zebedee* were James and John (see Matthew 4:21). The Gospel of John names neither of them as such. But the other Gospels portray them, along with Peter, to be Jesus' inner circle within the Twelve (17:1; Mark 5:37; 9:2; Luke 8:51). The omission of their names in John's Gospel has contributed to the view that the beloved disciple (John 21:20) was James or John. He could not be James, however, since Herod killed him in about AD 44 (Acts 12:1-2) —before this Gospel was written. Thus we assume the beloved disciple was none other than John, who chose not to identify himself or his brother by first name in his own Gospel account (John 13:23; 20:2; 21:7, 20).

2e. And two other of his disciples.

The *two other of his disciples* are commonly thought to be Andrew and Philip (Matthew 10:2-4). Some disciples can be eliminated rather easily. For instance, Matthew's work as a tax collector makes it unlikely he was out fishing with the others (9:9; see commentary on John 21:3a, below). Judas Iscariot can be dismissed outright, as he had committed suicide after betraying Jesus (Matthew 27:3-5). In their favor, both Andrew (Simon Peter's brother) and Philip have strong associations with the region of Galilee (John 1:40-45).

3a. Simon Peter saith unto them, I go a fishing. They say unto him, We also go with thee.

Simon Peter, Andrew, James, and John were fishermen (Mark 1:16-20). Some have considered Peter's plan to go *fishing* an abandonment of his discipleship. However, this is not a necessary conclusion, and several indicators suggest it was not the case. First, the disciples' presence in Galilee itself demonstrates obedience to Jesus (see Lesson Context).

Second, it seems incongruous that Peter would be opting out of discipleship after the post-resurrection events he had been privy to. He was the first disciple go inside the empty tomb (John 20:6-7). Later that evening, Jesus came to the disciples in a locked room; He did so again one week later (20:19-20, 26-27). Peter's actions and presence during Jesus' appearances point to renewed dedication.

Third, those who accuse Peter of jettisoning his apostleship must assert the same for the disciples who went fishing with him on this particular occasion. Yet no one seems inclined to make this assertion.

Fourth, multiple times Jesus had said that He was going to His Father (examples: John 14:12, 28; 16:28), but He had given little specific content about what the disciples' post-resurrection role would be. But He *had* told them He would meet them in Galilee—whether because Jesus knew they would naturally go home to fish, or as a sort of permission to visit home before receiving their commission.

Fifth and finally, Jesus had not told them exactly when He would appear. While home in Galilee, waiting on Jesus to come, there was no reason for Peter and the others to sit around idle. They did better to work as they waited—rather than to stare out a window, twiddling their thumbs.

3b. They went forth, and entered into a ship immediately; and that night they caught nothing.

Fishermen typically worked at *night* on the Sea of Galilee (see Luke 5:5). Fish would come up to

How to Say It

Antipas	*An*-tih-pus.
Cana	*Kay*-nuh.
Didymus	*Did*-uh-mus.
Emmaus	Em-*may*-us.
Tiberias	Tie-*beer*-ee-us.
Zebedee	*Zeb*-eh-dee.

the surface to feed at night, then dive deeper as the sun warmed the surface of the water throughout the day. This rendered nets useless, as they did not sink far enough into the water to catch fish in the warm daylit water (see commentary on John 21:6, below).

What Do You Think?
Which spiritual practices help you to persist when your efforts seem to end in failure?
Digging Deeper
What verses encourage you to depend on God when you have failed?

B. Jesus Provides (vv. 4-6)

4. But when the morning was now come, Jesus stood on the shore: but the disciples knew not that it was Jesus.

Mary Magdalene at the tomb and, later, other disciples on the road to Emmaus did not immediately recognize *Jesus* (Luke 24:13-16, 30-31; John 20:13-16). How could all these people not recognize Jesus when faced with Him? In the previous examples, it could be that something about Jesus' resurrected appearance had shifted, making Him less immediately identifiable by physical sight. Or perhaps because these people were not expecting to see Jesus after He had died, their eyes simply did not accept the clear evidence before them.

For *the disciples* here, the distance and quality of light could be contributing factors. *When the morning was now come* does not necessarily mean that the sun had risen; it could be that the light was that of predawn, enough to see nearby but not in detail far off (see commentary on John 21:8, below). Furthermore, the disciples were tired from their work night, a condition that does not facilitate clear sight.

5. Then Jesus saith unto them, Children, have ye any meat? They answered him, No.

Jesus' question assumed a negative answer. In context, it is clear that *meat* refers specifically to fish. Greco-Roman literature often used *children* in the context of education. It was a term of endearment from teacher to student that communicated affection deeper than mere collegiality (see also 1 John 2:18). In choosing this word, *Jesus*

positioned himself as a benevolent authority over the disciples and a caring mentor (see commentary on John 21:6, below).

6. And he said unto them, Cast the net on the right side of the ship, and ye shall find. They cast therefore, and now they were not able to draw it for the multitude of fishes.

Luke 5:1-11 recounts how Jesus met Simon Peter one morning after a similarly unsuccessful night of fishing. On that occasion, Jesus commanded Peter to go cast the nets for a catch, at which time Peter and the sons of Zebedee caught so many fish that the nets began to break. Why the men obeyed now when the night was over (see commentary on John 21:4, above)—whether they had an inkling this was Jesus, or they remembered that incident—is unclear. But the resulting *multitude of fishes* is the same.

II. "It Is the Lord"
(John 21:7-14)
A. First Responders (v. 7)

7a. Therefore that disciple whom Jesus loved saith unto Peter, It is the Lord.

John 21:20, 24 indicate that the *disciple whom Jesus loved* was the author of this Gospel. Early church tradition unanimously identified this as John. Moreover, multiple factors indicate this disciple as John, the son of Zebedee. Elsewhere John appears in tandem with Peter, as he does here (Luke 22:8; John 20:2; Acts 3:1–4:23; 8:14).

The Greek word translated *Lord* has a range of uses. It could be the polite address "sir" (John 12:21), but it could also designate the "lord" over a slave (15:20). The Septuagint (the Greek translation of the Old Testament) utilized this Greek word to translate *Yahweh*, a use reflected in New Testament references to God (6:68-69; 11:27; etc.). Who did *that disciple* think the man on the shore was? Simon Peter's quick action makes clear both fishermen understood the man on shore to be Jesus (compare 20:3-9).

7b. Now when Simon Peter heard that it was the Lord, he girt his fisher's coat unto him, (for he was naked,) and did cast himself into the sea.

Ancient art and literature depictions of those who fished with nets indicate that they often worked *naked*, or at least lightly clad. In deeper waters, fishermen could utilize nets that required a diver to bring one end toward the other, trapping fish inside before funneling them into the seacraft. This would obviously be safer and easier without any garments to weigh a man down. Peter donned his outer garment before diving into the water. Appearing naked before Jesus would have been an act of disrespect (compare Exodus 20:26). Peter would have *girt his fisher's coat* around his waist to free his legs for swimming (compare John 13:4-5).

> ### What Do You Think?
> How might your possessions be preventing you from seeking to close the distance between you and Jesus?
> ### Digging Deeper
> What would it take for you to shed those things that prevent a closer relationship with Jesus?

So Happy to See You!

It was late at night when I pulled my car into the space in front of our apartment building. I'd been gone for weeks. When I looked up to the third floor, I saw a light glowing in the window, indicating that my roommate and our dog were home. As I unpacked my car, I heard paws scrambling down the concrete steps toward me. I turned in time to see a black furry blur burst through the door to greet me.

Like my excited dog, Peter could not wait to see his Lord. Peter jumped into the water and swam to shore, too impatient to wait. Do you look forward to meeting Jesus one day? How does that excitement permeate into your daily walk with Him? How *should* it?   —L. M. W.

B. Second-Wave Disciples (vv. 8-9)

8. And the other disciples came in a little ship; (for they were not far from land, but as it were two hundred cubits,) dragging the net with fishes.

The *little ship* here is a contrast to the number of fish the *disciples* caught (see commentary on John 21:10-11, below). A cubit was about 18 inches in length, so the disciples were approximately 300 feet from shore. It is usually assumed that the six other disciples (21:2) arrived on shore after Peter, since he was likely a strong swimmer, and their haul of fish likely made the ship move slowly with drag in the water.

9a. As soon then as they were come to land, they saw a fire of coals there.

Peter had stood beside *a fire of coals* when he denied Jesus (John 18:18). It was here that Jesus would reaffirm Peter (21:15-19; see lesson 8).

9b. And fish laid thereon, and bread.

The presence of *fish* and *bread* likely evoked memories among the disciples of when Jesus converted five loaves and two fish into a filling lunch for 5,000 (John 6:1-13). After all, they had no idea where He had procured them from this time! But there was Jesus, and there were the bread and fish. They needed no other explanation. Jesus' presence and power were sufficient.

C. Jesus' Provision (vv. 10-13)

10-11. Jesus saith unto them, Bring of the fish which ye have now caught. Simon Peter went up, and drew the net to land full of great fishes, an hundred and fifty and three: and for all there were so many, yet was not the net broken.

In contrast to asking *Simon Peter* and his fellow fishermen to drop their nets and follow *Jesus* (Matthew 4:18-20), this seems to be an invitation to finish the task before joining Him. It could also be that eating some of *the fish* they had just *caught* was a way to celebrate the bounty Jesus had just provided.

Unsurprisingly, Simon Peter responded first. Though many have tried to find special significance in the number 153, it's more important as an indication that *so many* fish were caught, in contrast with the "nothing" caught earlier (see commentary on John 21:3b, above). There is a sense of marvel that *the net* did not break (contrast Luke 5:6-7). This detail points not only to Jesus' power to give abundantly but also to provide in such a way that His followers benefit from the abundance. Nothing is lost, nothing is broken when Jesus gives greatly.

What Do You Think?

When have you experienced Jesus' accepting what you bring to Him, even though He has provided more than enough for you?

Digging Deeper

What applications does Jesus' hospitality have in your own practice?

12. Jesus saith unto them, Come and dine. And none of the disciples durst ask him, Who art thou? knowing that it was the Lord.

Whenever *Jesus* ate with *the disciples*, they recognized Him (example: Luke 24:30-32, 40-43). In John 6:35, Jesus said, "I am the bread of life: he that cometh to me shall never hunger." Both the miracle of the fish and Jesus' sitting down to *dine* with these fishermen confirmed Jesus' identity as *the Lord* (see commentary on 21:7a, above).

13. Jesus then cometh, and taketh bread, and giveth them, and fish likewise.

Although this meal bears similarity to Jesus' institution of the Lord's Supper (Mark 14:12-26), it is unlikely that John intended us to understand it in a similar way. The emphasis is on Jesus' presence and the sharing of life that is signified in the sharing of a meal (John 6:26-40). The resurrected *Jesus* would send the Spirit to be present with His disciples as they embarked on the mission He would give them (15:26; Acts 1:4-8; 2:1-4; etc.).

A Soul Well Fed

I was stuck in the late-Soviet-era Moscow airport with a team of missionaries on our way to Ukraine. Being new to the country and unfamiliar with how things worked, we had only the food we had brought with us on the flight, which was very little.

It was late on our second night when our leader found us a hotel. And beyond beds, there was *food*. Needless to say, we ate ravenously. Two days with just crackers and cereal bars had left us hungry. Even the unfamiliar Russian foods looked and tasted better than anything I'd ever eaten before.

Hard work had whetted the disciples' appetites. But something else also fed them that morn-

D. Jesus' Third Appearance (v. 14)

14. This is now the third time that Jesus shewed himself to his disciples, after that he was risen from the dead.

In tandem with John 21:1 (above), this verse bookends the passage, emphasizing Jesus' post-resurrection appearances to eyewitnesses. John, of course, was counting based on the appearances he recorded, not what other Gospels also noted. We might quickly skip over the fact that all this happened *after . . . he was risen from the dead*—but that was the whole point! The grave could not contain *Jesus*; He had risen just as He said. And with this meal, Jesus was preparing *his disciples* for the work He would leave for them.

Conclusion

A. An Acted-Out Parable

Jesus is not waiting for Sunday to spend time with His disciples today. While you're at work—whatever that looks like for you—Jesus still invites you to experience His abundance and spend time with Him. How can you ensure that you don't miss these opportunities?

What Do You Think?

What groups are you a part of in which you all intentionally seek time with Jesus?

Digging Deeper

How do you experience Jesus differently in the presence of other believers than in your solitary devotion time?

B. Prayer

Our Father, we marvel at the abundance of life we find in Jesus. And we thank You for sending Him to us! We give thanks in Jesus' name. Amen.

C. Thought to Remember

Recognize the Lord and receive His abundance.

Involvement Learning

Enhance your lesson with KJV Bible Student *(from your curriculum supplier) and the reproducible activity page (at www.standardlesson.com or in the back of the* KJV Standard Lesson Commentary Deluxe Edition*).*

Into the Lesson

Provide breakfast food and drinks to enhance the opportunity for group fellowship. As you're enjoying the snack, gather around in a circle and brainstorm the distinctions and overlaps between "fellowship" and "friendship." Invite group members to share their perspectives on why it's important to differentiate between the two. Say, "Today's Bible study helps us understand how Jesus and His friends were in fellowship."

Alternative. Distribute copies of the "Word for Word" exercise from the activity page, which you can download. Have learners complete it individually in one minute or less before discussing in small groups. Transition to the Bible study by saying, "Today's lesson will show us how the concepts of trust, belief, faith, and obedience are interrelated."

Into the Word

Write on the board *Trust / Belief / Faith / Obedience* as the headers of four columns. Ask learners to define each of these words. Jot responses under column headings as they are offered.

Read John 21:1-14. Have the group discuss how the four words are interconnected in the Scripture passage as they consider the symbolic invitation of Jesus standing on the shore.

Distribute blank paper and pens for writing and drawing. Ask students to each divide the page into four equal parts. Read the passage a second time, pausing to give the following instructions for their indicated verses. Do not read the words in parentheses.

Verses 1-2—In the first square, illustrate seven men in a fishing boat on the Sea of Galilee; Jesus had instructed them to meet Him there. *(Obedience)*

Verses 3-6—In the next square, illustrate the fishermen catching fish on the right side of the boat, trusting Jesus' instructions. *(Trust)*

Verses 7-8—In the third square, show Peter casting himself into the sea to greet the Lord, and the others following behind in a little boat. *(Belief)*

Verses 9-14—In the final square, draw the disciples readily accepting Jesus' invitation to "come and dine." *(Faith)*

Remind learners of the headings on the board. Challenge the class to assign each of the four words as a label to their four drawings. Discuss their responses as a group. Allow learners to support their answers.

Alternative. Write these words on the board: *Who? What? Where? When? Why? How many?* Divide learners into pairs. Assign each pair one or more verses from the text, making sure all the verses are covered. Invite pairs to read their verses and, based on their reading, answer as many of the questions on the board as possible. After a few minutes, go through the verses in order as the groups share their questions and answers.

Ask participants to think again about relationships as you reread verses 12-13. Invite the learners to brainstorm reasons that the disciples recognized Jesus.

Into Life

Ask learners to share experiences in which they sensed that Jesus was at work. As a whole class, create a word cloud on the board with ways of recognizing Jesus at work. (A word cloud is a collection of words or phrases. The bigger and bolder a word or phrase is, the more times it is mentioned or is important.) Be sure to include everyday experiences.

Alternative. Distribute copies of the "I See Jesus" exercise from the activity page. Have learners complete it as directed.

After either activity, invite learners to write a prayer for eyes to recognize Jesus at work. Encourage participants to refer to their prayer throughout the week.

Jesus Reinstates Peter

Devotional Reading: 2 Corinthians 7:1-11
Background Scripture: John 21:15-25

John 21:15-19

15 So when they had dined, Jesus saith to Simon Peter, Simon, son of Jonas, lovest thou me more than these? He saith unto him, Yea, Lord; thou knowest that I love thee. He saith unto him, Feed my lambs.

16 He saith to him again the second time, Simon, son of Jonas, lovest thou me? He saith unto him, Yea, Lord; thou knowest that I love thee. He saith unto him, Feed my sheep.

17 He saith unto him the third time, Simon, son of Jonas, lovest thou me? Peter was grieved because he said unto him the third time, Lovest thou me? And he said unto him, Lord, thou knowest all things; thou knowest that I love thee. Jesus saith unto him, Feed my sheep.

18 Verily, verily, I say unto thee, When thou wast young, thou girdedst thyself, and walkedst whither thou wouldest: but when thou shalt be old, thou shalt stretch forth thy hands, and another shall gird thee, and carry thee whither thou wouldest not.

19 This spake he, signifying by what death he should glorify God. And when he had spoken this, he saith unto him, Follow me.

Key Text

When they had dined, Jesus saith to Simon Peter, Simon, son of Jonas, lovest thou me more than these? He saith unto him, Yea, Lord; thou knowest that I love thee. He saith unto him, Feed my lambs. —**John 21:15**

Jesus
Calls Us

Lesson Aims

After participating in this lesson, each learner will be able to:

1. Summarize the conversation between the risen Jesus and Peter and the reason(s) for it.

2. Explain the relationship between loving Jesus and caring for His sheep.

3. Describe one way he or she will act on that relationship in the coming week.

Lesson Outline

Introduction

A. Redemption

A hockey team may struggle mightily for two periods but turn the game around at the end to earn a comeback win. A runner may experience a painful injury only to finish the race with grim determination and an indomitable spirit. A redemption story depends on early failure but is defined by a finish that makes what came before pale in comparison.

Popular culture loves these stories, especially because of the self-determination that is required for redemption. The redemption story features characters who change their attitudes, make different decisions, and perform more nobly in the end. They redeem themselves.

Our story today is also one of redemption. But it is not the story of a man who failed and then brought himself to a redemptive success. Instead, it is the story of the Lord who called the man to accept redemption.

B. Lesson Context

This lesson picks up immediately where the previous lesson left off (see commentary on John 21:15a, below). For this reason, the context from lesson 7 is immediately relevant to the events of John 21:15-19. We note that the focus narrows from the disciples in general to Peter specifically. But keep in mind that as Jesus and Simon Peter speak, they are still in the presence of the others, including John (see commentary on 21:2e in lesson 7).

The New Testament testifies in various ways to Peter's unique and ongoing role in Jesus' ministry and in the earliest life of the church. Along with Paul, Peter stands out among the apostles in terms of his fame and influence. Peter (also known as "Cephas"; John 1:42) was one of three apostles considered by Paul to be "pillars" of the church (Galatians 2:9). Peter emerged early on as a leader, bold in word and deed (examples: Acts 2:14-41; 3:1-10). He was among the first to recognize that when Jesus told His followers to "go ye therefore, and teach all nations" (Matthew 28:19), He really did mean to go to Gentiles without requiring them to take up Jewish practices before accepting

Him (Acts 10:9–11:18; 15:6-11). Peter's influence resounded throughout the church. The impact of the events of today's text are therefore incalculable.

I. Jesus Questions Peter
(John 21:15-17)
A. Round One (v. 15)

15a. So when they had dined, Jesus saith to Simon Peter, Simon, son of Jonas.

So when they had dined refers to John 21:12-13 (see lesson 7). *Simon Peter, Simon, son of Jonas* is an attention-getting greeting; we might compare it to a mother calling her son by his first, middle, and last names. Simon's nickname *Peter* was a form of the Greek word that means "rock" (Matthew 16:18; John 1:42). Son of Jonas suggests a certain formality in the greeting. It might also be a subtle contrast to Jesus' own identity as "the Son of God" (1:49; 5:25; 11:27; etc.).

15b. Lovest thou me more than these?

Peter had overtly denied Jesus while Jesus was on trial (Matthew 26:69-75; Mark 14:66-72; Luke 22:54-62; John 18:15-18, 25-27). One explanation for Jesus' question (see commentary on 21:16-17, below) is simple redemption. This understanding was widespread in ancient Christian interpretation. Jesus was giving Peter the opportunity to repent of his betrayal and reaffirm his love for and devotion to Jesus.

Jesus' question as a call to repentance and redemption also largely refutes the idea that Jesus required affirmation from Peter, as though Jesus did not *know* if Peter loved Him, or that Jesus was feeling insecure regarding Peter's lasting loyalty. However, God's testing of Abraham regarding the sacrifice of Isaac seems like an ancient parallel (Genesis 22:2-18). In that case, we might think that God was eliciting information from Abraham. But, as with Peter, perhaps we do better to consider the test as beneficial to Abraham's own faith. Knowing the lengths Abraham was willing to go to for the Lord, and why (22:8; Hebrews 11:19), was surely beneficial to the man in the years to come. The same would clearly be true for Peter, given the hardships ahead of him (see commentary on John 21:18-19, below).

Visual for Lesson 8. *Display this visual while the class discusses the questions associated with verse 15d.*

Dovetailing with the above two explanations is one more concerned with Peter's prominent role in the first-century church. Even though all of Jesus' disciples abandoned Him (with the notable exception of the beloved disciple; John 18:15; 19:26-27), Peter's denial stands out as particularly grievous. Peter had boldly proclaimed that he would not betray Jesus even if others did (Mark 14:29-31), making his denials stand out in greater relief. How, then, could Peter become arguably the most influential of the Twelve? How could he, who did not just run but verbally and emphatically denied Jesus, become a faithful leader? John's inclusion of the series of questions and answers between Jesus and Peter more than justifies the position that Peter would hold (Matthew 16:17-19; see commentary on John 21:18, below).

Though it is possible Jesus was asking whether Peter loved Him *more than* Peter loved the other disciples or even his fishing profession, these meanings are unlikely in context. The best explanation is that Jesus was asking whether Peter loved Him more than the other disciples did. More than a comparison between the states of their hearts—clearly a task Peter was not qualified to take on—the question was about the depth of Peter's own love. Did Peter's experience deepen his love for Christ, or shatter it? And if Peter loved Christ more than the others did, would Peter be prepared to do as Jesus would command? (See commentary on John 21:15d, below.) We might ask ourselves the same questions following sinful failures.

15c. He saith unto him, Yea, Lord; thou knowest that I love thee.

Peter's address of Jesus as *Lord* (see commentary on John 21:7 in lesson 7) communicates Peter's awareness of Jesus' power, insight, and authority. One might expect someone called Lord to demand fealty or groveling. Instead, Peter answers Jesus' question affirmatively, not in terms of mere loyalty but in terms of *love*.

Preachers and scholars have made much of the fact that Jesus and Peter use different words for love. Jesus asks using one Greek verb, while Peter responds with another. Attempts to characterize *agape*—the form Jesus used—as a more godly, divine love doesn't account for the evidence of actual usage. For example, Jesus used the same word in Luke 11:43 when He rebuked the Pharisees for loving the seats of honor in the synagogues; in Matthew's record of that same incident, Jesus used the same form that Peter responded with here (Matthew 23:6). Demas's love of the world uses the verb again (2 Timothy 4:10). This illustrates the interchangeability of these two Greek verbs that are translated "love."

When one surveys the use of these words, both in the Bible and outside of it, the evidence suggests that they were considered near synonyms. This should caution us about attempts to overemphasize their usage in this chapter. It is noteworthy that ancient Christian commentators who spoke Greek fluently make no note of the alternating words in this passage. We do well to think of it as a literary feature, of John choosing not to use the same verb over and over again in order to vary the dialogue and have a more dynamic story.

Though the word *repentance* is not used here, Peter's response clearly illustrates it. His response was an important step in repairing his relationship with Jesus. Note that Jesus approached Peter; similarly, Jesus approached us before we even knew Him (Romans 5:8). Peter may have felt himself on unsteady footing with Jesus—a feeling Jesus did not immediately take steps to alleviate (see commentary on John 21:17, below). But Jesus' question allowed Peter to affirm for himself and his companions the depth of his love and loyalty, despite his prior stumble. And Jesus' question to us—whether He will be Lord of our lives, whether *we* love Him—is also an opportunity to repent of whatever sins have prevented us from having the relationship we need with Him.

What Do You Think?

How do you reaffirm your love for Jesus in your personal devotional time?

Digging Deeper

What difference do those private affirmations make when you have opportunity to confess publicly?

15d. He saith unto him, Feed my lambs.

Jesus had identified himself as "the good shepherd" (John 10:1-16). In that discourse Jesus contrasted himself with Israel's current spiritual shepherds, who acted more like thieves than caregivers. Jesus' self-disclosure as Israel's shepherd was a claim of rightful leadership in ancient terms and even a fulfillment of God's promises.

For example, in Ezekiel 34 God rebuked Israel's "shepherds": the nation's political-religious leadership. As with corrupt leadership the world over, past and present, these authorities were more concerned with their own welfare and even luxury than with the lives of the people they were tasked with serving (Ezekiel 34:1-6). God promised to remove those shepherds and take up the job himself. He would seek and find the lost sheep; He would feed them and heal them (34:7-16).

In Jesus, God has fulfilled His promise. Jesus is the loving shepherd who feeds and protects His flock. He demonstrated this by healing the sick and feeding the multitudes (examples: John 5:1-9; 6:1-15). Jesus taught God's love for the lost sheep (Luke 15:1-7) and indicated His own role in seeking the lost (19:10). With Jesus' time on earth rapidly coming to a close, the task of shepherding His flock was still primarily His own. But Jesus would ensure that His disciples were empowered to care for the fledgling church (24:49; John 14–17)—and this work continues today.

While questioning Peter, Jesus implied that He

accepted Peter's answer. This is understood when we consider that Jesus would not leave Peter such an important task if Jesus did not trust Peter's renewed dedication. Furthermore, the command to *feed my lambs* would be an ongoing opportunity for Peter to demonstrate his love (see commentary on John 21:19b, below).

> ### What Do You Think?
> Who are Jesus' lambs?
> ### Digging Deeper
> What role do you play in caring for those lambs?

B. Round Two (v. 16)

16. He saith to him again the second time, Simon, son of Jonas, lovest thou me? He saith unto him, Yea, Lord; thou knowest that I love thee. He saith unto him, Feed my sheep.

In a somewhat surprising move, Jesus asked Peter the question a *second time*. Peter himself may have wondered why Jesus asked again. Nevertheless, he dutifully gave the exact same response, to which Jesus gave the same commission, worded slightly differently.

C. Round Three (v. 17)

17. He saith unto him the third time, Simon, son of Jonas, lovest thou me? Peter was grieved because he said unto him the third time, Lovest thou me? And he said unto him, Lord, thou knowest all things; thou knowest that I love thee. Jesus saith unto him, Feed my sheep.

Some see in Jesus' three questions a parallel to Peter's three denials (see commentary on John 21:15b, above). Symbolically, Jesus provided Peter with an opportunity to commit to Him as many times as Peter had previously denied Him. But *Peter* himself did not seem to understand it this way, as shown by the fact he *was grieved* to continue answering the same question. Perhaps Peter felt he was being tested and found wanting, since surely Christ *knowest all things*. If Jesus knew the answer and continued asking, could it be that Peter harbored some impurity that Jesus was encouraging Peter to recognize?

But still, Peter answered the same way, though more emphatically. Seeing that Jesus ended His questioning here could suggest that Peter passed the test—that no falsehood was found within him as he asserted his love for the *Lord*. Whatever the case, Jesus' response of *feed my sheep* once again echoes His previous responses to Peter.

Jesus has promised He will appear again, but we don't know when this will happen (Mark 13:32-37). In the meantime, do we wall ourselves off from society and proverbially sit at the window, waiting? No! We too have tasks to fulfill. We are not all called to be apostles or preachers or teachers (1 Corinthians 12:27-31). But we are all called to good works in Christ (Ephesians 2:10), and whatever other work we do—as parents and grandparents, as employees or bosses, as citizens in our communities—we do "as to the Lord" (Colossians 3:23-25). Until Jesus returns, we too can make the most of our time and feed Jesus' sheep (Matthew 25:31-46).

> ### What Do You Think?
> What evidence is there in your life that you truly love Jesus?
> ### Digging Deeper
> What Scriptures shape your thinking about what it means to love Jesus?

The Hikers Ahead

When my wife and I visited Glacier National Park, a friend suggested that we hike to Avalanche Lake. It was three miles up, the same three back out and down. We both were physically fit enough to walk six miles on a flat trail, but three miles *up*? The problem wasn't distance; it was elevation.

The trail turned out to be even steeper than we anticipated. Several times we thought about turning back. But then other hikers coming down the trail would urge us to keep going: "You can do it!" "It's worth it." And so it was. As we hiked back down, it was our turn to encourage other tired hikers. "Don't give up!" "It's worth it."

Jesus first calls us and then commissions us. He encourages us, telling us our reward is great when we follow Him, though the way is even more difficult than we thought. Do you in turn encourage other weary souls to keep climbing? —D. F.

II. Jesus Speaks Truth to Peter
(John 21:18-19)
A. Young Life (v. 18a)

18a. Verily, verily, I say unto thee, When thou wast young, thou girdedst thyself, and walkedst whither thou wouldest.

Verily, verily translates the Greek word that we have adopted into English as *amen*. Although Jesus always spoke the truth, statements He began in this way often revealed spiritual truth (examples: John 3:3-5; 8:58) or future events (examples: 13:21, 38). *When thou wast young* sets up a contrast (see commentary on 21:18b, below). In the past, Peter took care of himself and lived as he saw fit.

B. Old Age (vv. 18b-19)

18b. But when thou shalt be old, thou shalt stretch forth thy hands, and another shall gird thee, and carry thee whither thou wouldest not.

In light of what lay ahead for Peter, faithfulness to Jesus required a love so great that it could overcome the instinct for self-preservation. In Jesus' words, Peter's redemption is laid bare. The man loved Jesus, and he would show this through his own ministry and death. *Stretch forth thy hands* is an allusion to carrying one's cross to one's execution. *Another shall gird thee, and carry thee whither thou wouldest not* finishes the contrast begun in John 21:18a. Peter's life would not be his own. In this way, his life would parallel that of Jesus.

The earliest reference to Peter's death is found in a letter called 1 Clement, attributed to the writer known as Clement of Rome, at the end of the AD 90s. This letter is the oldest Christian writing in our possession outside of the New Testament. It states that Peter was martyred (1 Clement 5:4). Other early church traditions further date his death in the context of Emperor Nero's persecution of Christians in AD 64. These traditions state that Peter was crucified, perhaps even upside down, due to Peter's conviction that he

was unworthy to die in the same manner as his Lord. There is no reason to disbelieve these early Christian leaders, especially since their testimony affirms what Jesus himself said would happen.

> **What Do You Think?**
> What can be gained spiritually by having experiences you would not choose?
>
> **Digging Deeper**
> How can you prepare for undesired experiences so that they can bring spiritual growth?

19a. This spake he, signifying by what death he should glorify God.

Lest there be any ambiguity about what Jesus meant, John clarified that Jesus said these things to signify *by what death* Peter *should glorify God* (compare John 11:4; 12:23, 27-28; 13:31-32; 17:1-15). The idea that being crucified could be a glorious death is a Christian innovation. Crucifixion was intended as a public shaming, an ignoble end to a vile criminal. Following Jesus' death, the purely negative connotation was turned on its head for Jesus' followers, because Jesus flipped the script (Philippians 2:8-11). This radical reinterpretation of crucifixion led Jesus' followers to reinterpret what the world called shame as glory (1 Corinthians 1:18-31). What had always in the past been a final humiliation became for Christians an unexpected way in which God glorified himself.

> **What Do You Think?**
> What are you doing now to ensure that your eventual death will glorify God?
>
> **Digging Deeper**
> What would you like to change in order to leave behind a legacy that draws others to the Lord?

19b. And when he had spoken this, he saith unto him, Follow me.

Having warned Peter, Jesus called him again to *follow* (Matthew 4:18-20; John 1:40-42). This is not the same command as caring for Jesus' flock. But for Peter, following Jesus would certainly entail care for the flock (example: Acts 9:36-41). Indeed, the writings of 1 and 2 Peter continue to edify Jesus' followers to this day! The image of caring for Jesus' flock remained with Peter, as his admonitions to Christian leaders attest (example: 1 Peter 5:1-4).

Playful or Painful?

When my son was a teenager, he asked me to spend a day with him and his friends playing paintball. That sounded great to me, but I quickly learned that some weekend warriors take the game very seriously. And paintballs hurt— especially when you get shot at close range. I came home covered with bruises, thinking, "I will never do that again." From across the room, though, I heard my son telling his sisters, "Dad and I had a great time today. I'm glad we did it together!"

When you accepted Christ, maybe you thought, *This is going to be great! God will take care of all my problems.* Then after a while you wondered, *This hurts! What's going on?*

If you make it your goal to glorify God, your journey of faith may take you where you would rather not go. When you fight the good fight, don't be surprised when you get hurt. But when it is finally over, you may hear yourself saying, "I'm glad the Lord and I did this together."   —D. F.

Conclusion
A. Model Disciple

Peter stands out as a model disciple for a number of reasons. First, Peter was not unique in his need for redemption. All of us stand before Jesus needing redemption, being incapable of accomplishing it for ourselves. Just as Jesus did for Peter, so also Jesus does for us. He made the first move toward our redemption long ago on the cross and continues to invite us to accept His sacrifice as the atonement for our own sins (Romans 3:25). God's grace is magnified by the fact that Jesus himself, the offended party, initiated the process. This is consistent with the biblical story in which God, who is always the offended party, initiates reconciliation with sinful humanity.

Second, Peter's redemption resulted in com-

mission. Like Peter, we confess our love for our Lord and Savior. Doing so must result in our commitment to living lives that parallel Jesus' own: being more concerned about the will of the Father than with our own agendas (Matthew 16:24-27; John 14:23-24). Though how we each live out Jesus' commission varies based on our circumstances, each of us is called to the life of faith.

Third, our commission comes with knowledge of what our faithfulness can cost us. Like Peter, we accept the call with the clear understanding that because Christ suffered and we are His, we too expect the life of faith to entail suffering (John 15:18–16:4), just as Peter's did. Sometimes this means physical suffering or even death at the hands of the world (example: Acts 7:54-60). Sometimes it means enduring shame and torment for righteousness' sake.

Fourth, like Peter's pain, our own suffering comes with a promise. When we suffer like Christ and for godly purposes, we bring glory to the Lord—no matter how humiliating the world might believe our plight to be (Matthew 5:10-12).

None of us today have had an encounter with Christ like Peter did. But when you tell the story of how God has redeemed you, what role do believers like Peter play? In whose redemption story do you (or *should* you) play a role?

B. Prayer

Heavenly Father, thank You for making our redemption story possible. Help us to embrace living lives that parallel Jesus' life and bring glory to You, even in suffering. In Jesus' name we pray. Amen.

C. Thought to Remember

Do you love Jesus?
Follow Him.

How to Say It

Cephas	*See*-fus.
Clement	*Cleh*-muhnt.
martyr	*mahr*-ter.
Nero	*Nee*-row.

Involvement Learning

Enhance your lesson with KJV Bible Student *(from your curriculum supplier) and the reproducible activity page (at www.standardlesson.com or in the back of the* KJV Standard Lesson Commentary Deluxe Edition*).*

Into the Lesson

Divide the class into two teams. Distribute a large sheet of paper and a marker to each team. Ask one team to brainstorm a list of advantages of winning a game or coming in first. Ask the other team to list advantages of losing. After a couple of minutes, call time. Bring the class back together and post the two lists. Talk together about the lists and why people usually value winning more than they value losing.

Move to the next part of the lesson by saying, "We all know how bad it feels when we are considered a loser. In this lesson we'll see how Peter went from being the loser who denied Jesus to one who would serve Him faithfully to the end."

Alternative. Divide the class into small groups. Distribute copies of the "Sheep, Sheep, Shepherd" exercise from the activity page, which you can download. Have learners complete it individually in one minute or less before discussing questions with small groups. Bring the groups back together before transitioning to the Bible study by saying, "In today's lesson we'll discover what Peter learned about being a shepherd."

Into the Word

Using a concordance, find references to "shepherd(s)." Write discovered characteristics on the board. (Some passages to use are Matthew 9:36; Luke 15:1-7; and John 10:11-15.) Discuss what makes a compelling shepherd/leader, someone others want to follow.

Have students break into small groups of four or five people. Distribute handouts (you prepare) to each group with the following questions: 1–Read Matthew 26:69-75 and Luke 22:55-62. In what ways and how many times did Peter deny Jesus? How do we know he deeply regretted his denial? What is it about Luke's account that makes this especially poignant? 2–Read John 21:15-17. What's the significance of Jesus asking Peter three times if

Peter loved Him? How would this be a way to heal Peter's relationship with Jesus? What is the significance of Jesus telling Peter to feed His lambs/sheep? 3–Read John 21:18-19. What did Jesus reveal to Peter about Peter's death? How would this help prepare Peter? Why did Jesus say to him, "Follow me"?

Allow time for groups to work through the handout. Using what they discovered in their groups, along with the list on the board, lead a whole-class discussion on Jesus' forgiveness of Peter and on Peter's role changing from a sheep to a shepherd.

Into Life

Ask participants to consider what they might require of someone who wished to restore a relationship with them after a relational breach. How does this compare and contrast with what Jesus asked of Peter? Invite participants to tell ways they have experienced restored relationships. Contrast with Luke 14:26, in which God expects us to "hate" our own families and our own lives. Then ask: "How does the story of Peter (who denied Jesus at the very point of Jesus' death) and Peter's redemption provide us with another way of approaching those who have broken relationships—especially within the church?"

Distribute index cards and pencils. Encourage learners to use these for notes as you work through the following thinking and prayer time: 1–What does following Jesus because you love Him look like in your life? 2–Jesus welcomed Peter with open arms. For whom can you "stand on the shore" with open arms? What broken relationship can you restore in this way? 3–How does your relationship with Jesus serve as an invitation for others? 4–What is one way you can share that relationship with others this week?

Alternative. Distribute copies of the "Revised Hollywood Ending" activity from the activity page. Have learners complete as indicated.

Jesus Makes a Promise

Devotional Reading: Psalm 24
Background Scripture: Acts 1:1-11

Acts 1:1-11

1 The former treatise have I made, O Theophilus, of all that Jesus began both to do and teach,

2 Until the day in which he was taken up, after that he through the Holy Ghost had given commandments unto the apostles whom he had chosen:

3 To whom also he shewed himself alive after his passion by many infallible proofs, being seen of them forty days, and speaking of the things pertaining to the kingdom of God:

4 And, being assembled together with them, commanded them that they should not depart from Jerusalem, but wait for the promise of the Father, which, saith he, ye have heard of me.

5 For John truly baptized with water; but ye shall be baptized with the Holy Ghost not many days hence.

6 When they therefore were come together,

they asked of him, saying, Lord, wilt thou at this time restore again the kingdom to Israel?

7 And he said unto them, It is not for you to know the times or the seasons, which the Father hath put in his own power.

8 But ye shall receive power, after that the Holy Ghost is come upon you: and ye shall be witnesses unto me both in Jerusalem, and in all Judaea, and in Samaria, and unto the uttermost part of the earth.

9 And when he had spoken these things, while they beheld, he was taken up; and a cloud received him out of their sight.

10 And while they looked stedfastly toward heaven as he went up, behold, two men stood by them in white apparel;

11 Which also said, Ye men of Galilee, why stand ye gazing up into heaven? this same Jesus, which is taken up from you into heaven, shall so come in like manner as ye have seen him go into heaven.

Key Text

Ye shall receive power, after that the Holy Ghost is come upon you. —**Acts 1:8a**

Jesus Calls Us

Unit 3: The Birth of the Church
Lessons 9–13

Lesson Aims

After participating in this lesson, each learner will be able to:

1. State the initial sequence of the geographical progression of the gospel message.

2. Analyze what the disciples meant when they asked Jesus about the restoration of Israel.

3. Recommit to the work Jesus has given him or her in accomplishing the gospel mandate.

Lesson Outline

Introduction

A. Flashbacks

Serialized television shows often feature brief flashbacks at the beginning of each episode. These flashbacks typically condense the key parts of the previous episodes into 90 seconds or less. The resulting salient points help viewers make sense of the new installment. These are particularly important for those of us who watch only one episode at a time rather than binge-watch multiple episodes!

Unlike any other pair of books in the New Testament, Luke begins his second volume (the book of Acts) with a summary of the first volume (the Gospel of Luke). This is a little like a modern flashback, a highly condensed version of the previous "episode" as a key to understanding the installment at hand. That's how the book of Acts begins.

B. Lesson Context

We may find it surprising that a Gentile who was not an apostle wrote more of the New Testament than anyone else. We're talking about Luke the physician (Colossians 4:14). His writings of the Gospel that bears his name and the book of Acts total 37,932 words in Greek across 2,158 verses. By comparison, Paul wrote 32,408 words across the 2,033 verses of his 13 epistles.

The sheer volume of Luke's writing also explains why the Gospel of Luke and the book of Acts are separate. Writings were frequently on scrolls in Luke's day, and the maximum practical length of a scroll was about 10 yards. Luke's Gospel and the book of Acts have about two scrolls' worth of material, making a physical division necessary. Luke did this thoughtfully by dividing the books into his account of Jesus and his account of the church. The bridge between the two is the ascension of Jesus, found in Luke 24:50-53 and repeated in Acts 1:6-9.

Careful study of these two books shows that Luke maintained high standards for accuracy. Where we can corroborate his historical details, he has proven to be completely reliable. For example, Luke refers to the magistrates of the city of Thessalonica by the Greek word *politarchas* (Acts 17:6, 8), a term not found elsewhere in ancient literature. This had led earlier scholars to wonder if Luke made up this word. However, archaeological excavations have since found inscriptions that use this title, confirming Luke's attention to accurate detail.

I. Promise Number 1
(Acts 1:1-5)
A. Looking Back (vv. 1-3)

1a. The former treatise have I made, O Theophilus.

The Gospel of Luke (which is *the former treatise*) and the book of Acts are both addressed to a certain *Theophilus* (compare Luke 1:3). Some students have proposed that this person may have been Luke's patron—his financial backer for the resulting scrolls (see Lesson Context). Luke 1:3 refers to him as "most excellent" Theophilus. Such language was used of high governmental officials, somewhat like our addressing a judge as "Your Honor" or a queen as "Your Majesty." Luke records Paul's having used this honorific (or a variant) to address Felix and Festus, the Roman governors in Acts 23:26; 24:3; and 26:25.

Others propose that the name Theophilus doesn't refer to any specific person but to all those who would sincerely seek the truth by reading what Luke wrote. The basis of this theory is that the name *Theophilus* means "[any]one who loves God." An extension of the first theory above is that this general meaning could indicate that it was a code name intended to protect a particular person's identity. The bottom line is that we simply don't know.

How to Say It

Bethany	*Beth*-uh-nee.
Galilee	*Gal*-uh-lee.
Judas Iscariot	*Joo*-dus Iss-*care*-ee-ut.
Pentecost	*Pent*-ih-kost.
politarchas (*Greek*)	*pawl*-ih-**tar**-case.
Samaria	Suh-*mare*-ee-uh.
Theophilus	Thee-*ahf*-ih-luss (*th* as in *thin*).
Thessalonica	*Thess*-uh-lo-**nye**-kuh (*th* as in *thin*).

1b. Of all that Jesus began both to do and teach.

This summarizes the content of Luke's Gospel. (See the Lesson Context.)

2. Until the day in which he was taken up, after that he through the Holy Ghost had given commandments unto the apostles whom he had chosen.

Luke highlights how his Gospel ends. In so doing, he established a chronological connection point to where the book of Acts begins.

3. To whom also he shewed himself alive after his passion by many infallible proofs, being seen of them forty days, and speaking of the things pertaining to the kingdom of God.

Jesus' post-resurrection appearances to the apostles (the *to whom*; see previous verse) and others are attested in many places (see Matthew 28:17; Luke 24:34, 36; John 20:19, 26; 21:1, 14; and 1 Corinthians 15:5-8). Time periods involving the number 40 are significant in the Bible (see Genesis 7:4; Exodus 16:35; Ezekiel 4:6; Jonah 3:4; Mark 1:13; etc.). Those instances often have figurative associations. But the *forty days* in the text before us should be understood in conjunction with the 50 days between the Passover (when Jesus was crucified, suffering *his passion*; Matthew 26:2) and the Day of Pentecost (when the church was birthed; Acts 2:1). After Jesus' departure and before the outpouring of the Holy Spirit on Pentecost, there remained a brief-yet-intense week and a half period of waiting and anticipation.

> **What Do You Think?**
> How important is the evidence of history ("proofs") to your being a Christian?
> **Digging Deeper**
> How do passages such as John 14:11 and 20:30-31 establish that evidence is more important than personal testimony and personal experience in this regard?

B. Looking Forward (vv. 4-5)

4a. And, being assembled together with them, commanded them that they should not depart from Jerusalem.

We should remember that most of the disciples were from Galilee, many miles north of *Jerusalem* and Judaea. After Jesus departed, they might have been inclined to leave Jerusalem and return home. In fact, they had already made one such trip after Jesus' resurrection (see John 21).

The apostle Paul knew of several meetings Jesus held with His followers during this 40-day period. One of them included appearing to more than 500 followers (1 Corinthians 15:6). We do not know how many such gatherings took place in total. But it is evident that Jesus did not maintain a constant presence with His disciples as He had before.

The word translated *assembled together* can have the sense of sharing a meal. But the food per se would have been secondary. They gathered for another purpose: God had strategically chosen Jerusalem as the birthplace of His church (see lesson 10). We take this for granted today, but the choice would not have been self-evident to disciples like Peter, Andrew, James, and John. If the fellowship of Jesus' followers were to continue, why not out of the synagogue in Capernaum, surely a safer place? But this was not God's plan.

4b-5. But wait for the promise of the Father, which, saith he, ye have heard of me. For John truly baptized with water; but ye shall be baptized with the Holy Ghost not many days hence.

Here the promise of Jesus plays on the meaning of the word *baptized*. The water baptism practiced by *John* the Baptist was contrasted with a promise of pouring out of *the Holy Ghost* on the Day of Pentecost, which would arrive *not many days hence*. The Greek word translated baptized means to engulf or immerse completely. The outpouring of the Holy Ghost to come would be like that: an immersion involving body, soul, heart, spirit, and mind.

What Do You Think?
How do you discern God's will regarding whether to wait or act?

Digging Deeper
How will you be "transformed by the renewing of your mind" (Romans 12:2) so that you can be attentive to God's will?

II. Promise Number 2
(Acts 1:6-8)

A. Lingering Question (v. 6)

6. When they therefore were come together, they asked of him, saying, Lord, wilt thou at this time restore again the kingdom to Israel?

They likely refers to the core group of the 12, reduced at this time to 11 due to the demise of Judas (see Matthew 27:5). In this setting, a burning question comes out. Expanded, the intent of the question is something like this:

Lord, having thwarted the leaders of the Jews in Jerusalem, the Roman authorities, and death itself, wouldn't this be a good time to rally those who acclaimed Your entry into the city a few days ago? Why not lead them to form an army and drive the Romans out? Come on, Jesus, we could do it!

This question would be comic if the setting were not so serious. Jesus knew that only moments remained for His time on earth with His disciples. But after three and a half years of close association, the disciples still misunderstood what His mission among them was. Rather than see the potential of humankind's complete freedom from sin, they were willing to settle for freedom from Roman rule.

B. Exasperated Response (v. 7)

7. And he said unto them, It is not for you to know the times or the seasons, which the Father hath put in his own power.

Jesus did not chastise those gathered with "O ye of little faith" as He had before (Matthew 6:30; 8:26; 14:31; 16:8; Luke 12:28). Rather, He responded with patience and understanding, although we can imagine exasperation as well (compare John 14:9). Rather than answer the question about the kingdom of Israel, Jesus' reply regarding *the times or the seasons* refers to His return in glory and judgment. This future event is discussed extensively in the Gospel of Luke (see Luke 17:20-37).

Jesus revealed that the timing of the Day of Judgment was in the *power* of *the Father* alone. Even the Son did not know the exact timing of His own return (see Matthew 24:36; Mark 13:32). There is a warning here: if Jesus himself did not know, it would seem unwise for any human being to attempt to precisely determine the date of His return. These are things reserved for the power of the Father (compare Deuteronomy 29:29).

C. Worldwide Ministry (v. 8)

8. But ye shall receive power, after that the Holy Ghost is come upon you: and ye shall be witnesses unto me both in Jerusalem, and in all Judaea, and in Samaria, and unto the uttermost part of the earth.

This verse begins Luke's characteristic stress on the role and power of *the Holy Ghost* (compare Acts 2:4, 17; 4:8, 31; 5:3; etc.; see also Luke 4:1). Luke's Gospel and the book of Acts together total about 27.5 percent of the New Testament, yet feature 57 percent of the designations "Holy Spirit" or "Holy Ghost" (54 of the New Testament's 94 occurrences).

Jesus proceeded to explain what the baptism of the Holy Spirit (Acts 1:5, above) would accomplish. In speaking of the Spirit's accompanying *power,* Jesus used a different Greek word than the one translated "power" in the previous verse. The word translated that way in Acts 1:7 is often translated "authority" elsewhere (examples: Luke 7:8; 20:2, 8, 20; Acts 9:14). Differing translations of the two Greek words appear together in nine verses (see Luke 4:36; 9:1; 10:19; 1 Corinthians 15:24; Ephesians 1:21; 1 Peter 3:22; Revelation 12:10; 13:2; and 17:13). Modern English understands the word *authority* as "the right to do something," and *power* as "the ability to do something."

But there is some overlap in meaning since the Father's power regarding the timing of Christ's return reflects His authority to determine that date. Similar can be said of the power that was to be bestowed on the disciples; it was a divine gift necessary to carry out their mission of sharing the gospel. To evangelize to *the uttermost part of the earth* means that no person on earth would be overlooked.

These words of Jesus serve as an outline for the rest of the book of Acts. The public witness of the apostles began *in Jerusalem* on the Day of Pentecost (Acts 2). By the time we get to Acts 9, Luke can speak of the church throughout "Judaea and Galilee and Samaria" (9:31). If the purpose of the powerful coming of the Holy Spirit was to empower the spread of the message to the ends of the earth, we should be clear as to what the disciples were to be witnessing about: they were to give their eyewitness testimony about Jesus, especially concerning His resurrection from the dead.

All the subsequent messages in Acts include such testimony. That kind of testimony is different from what we call a "personal testimony" today. In this testimony, I may testify about my changed life, personal peace, acceptance in the church's fellowship, the love of God, and many other things. But if I do not pass along the testimonies about the objective fact of Jesus the Christ risen from the dead, then I have left out the most important thing (see Luke 1:2; 24:46-48; 2 Peter 1:16).

Be One or Support One?

It took five flights and a three-hour canoe ride for me to get from Dallas, Texas, to the village of Yar in Papua New Guinea. There I saw speakers of the Waran language celebrate the completion of the New Testament in their language. Another time I sat in an East African refugee camp with men who were translating the Bible into their Nilotic language.

As of the time of this writing in July 2021, there

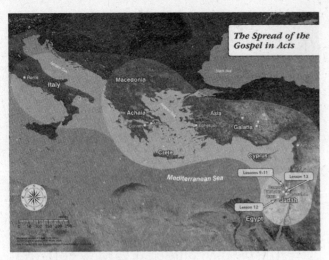

Visual for Lessons 9 & 10. *Show this map as you review the spread of the gospel as commanded in Acts 1:8.*

are 710 completed translations of both Old and New Testaments and 1,581 translations of the New Testament only. Further, efforts to translate the Bible into a whopping 2,753 languages are now underway. As great a blessing as that is, however, there are still more than 3,000 language groups who need Scripture, but no translation work is currently underway.

Think about it: What could be more foundational to achieving the mandates of Matthew 28:19-20 and Acts 1:8 than getting a readable Bible into people's hands? Today you have a choice: either *be* a Bible translator or *support* Bible translators. The eternal destinies of those whose native tongue is one of those 2,753 languages hang in the balance. —N. G.

III. Promise Number 3
(Acts 1:9-11)
A. Dramatic Departure (v. 9)

9. And when he had spoken these things, while they beheld, he was taken up; and a cloud received him out of their sight.

We recall that the word *they* refers to the 11 apostles of Acts 1:2. For Jesus to be *taken up* means He departed for Heaven, confirmed in Acts 1:10-11, below (see also Luke 24:51; compare 2 Kings 2:1, 11; contrast Numbers 11:25).

The text's wording with respect to how Jesus departed makes perfect sense in light of the ancient belief that Heaven is a physical space above Earth (compare Psalm 102:19; Luke 18:13; 2 Corinthians 12:2). But given our modern understandings of a massive, spherical planet Earth and a vast, empty outer space, we naturally wonder, *Where exactly did Jesus go?*

A key detail here is the presence of *a cloud* that *received him*. When the cloud did so, Jesus was *out of their sight*—He was no longer visible. This was not a random cloud parked in a handy place in the sky. Rather, it was a prepared, supernatural cloud. A cloud could be a sign of the presence of God (Luke 9:34-35), even a means of divine transport (see 21:27; 1 Thessalonians 4:17; Revelation 1:7; 11:12). Therefore, being received by the cloud in our text should be understood as being received by God.

The book of Acts reinforces this idea in the vision of the dying Stephen, where the martyr sees into Heaven and confirms that Jesus is standing by the throne of God (Acts 7:55). Stephen was not gifted with X-ray vision to look through the clouds; rather, his was a supernaturally granted view into the throne room of God in Heaven (compare Revelation 4:1; 20:11).

B. Angelic Urging (vv. 10-11)

10-11. And while they looked stedfastly toward heaven as he went up, behold, two men stood by them in white apparel; which also said, Ye men of Galilee, why stand ye gazing up into heaven? this same Jesus, which is taken up from you into heaven, shall so come in like manner as ye have seen him go into heaven.

While the apostles stare into the sky in stunned silence, *two men* enter the scene. Their *white apparel* and sudden appearance indicate that they are angels (compare John 20:12; see lesson 5). The apostles do not seem to notice them immediately, since the apostles' attention is still fixed skyward, *gazing up into heaven.*

The two speak, and this does get the disciples' attention. In essence, the angelic message is, "What's done is done. Now it's time to get busy." Although the angels knew that they were speaking to *men of Galilee* (compare Acts 2:7), we should remember that all this was taking place near Bethany (Luke 24:50), which was about two miles southeast of Jerusalem (John 11:18) and near the Mount of Olives (Acts 1:12). It was only 10 days until Pentecost, but Jerusalem—where the apostles were to wait (1:4, above)—was close by. Therefore a 75-mile walk from Galilee was not indicated. Those were not to be an idle 10 days. Certain preparations were needed, including gathering fellow believers in Jerusalem (1:13) and choosing a replacement for Judas Iscariot (1:21-26).

What was definitely *not* needed was a repeat of 2 Kings 2:16-18, where several days were wasted looking for Elijah after he was taken to Heaven. Rather, the apostles' task was to be busy witnessing for Jesus, beginning in Jerusalem and going outward to the ends of the earth.

What Do You Think?

How can believers be ready for Christ's return without disregarding what He has called His followers to do?

Digging Deeper

How do Matthew 24:36-51 and 1 Thessalonians 4:15–5:23 apply?

Why Not Right Now?

As my wife pushed the swing in which our 4-year-old sat, a natural back and forth rhythm developed. There weren't any other children on the playground to interrupt their conversation, which went something like this:

"Mom, what will it be like when Jesus comes back?"

"It will be wonderful, like a party, for those who love Him! We'll get to see Him and be with Him forever."

"I want Him to come back now!"

"Well, there are other people we need to invite. Many people don't know that He's coming, and we need to give them party invitations."

"Then why don't you call them and tell them right now?"

My son's response reminds me of the angel's question. Why procrastinate? We have work to do in sending out those invitations! Do you have anything to do in the week ahead that you consider to be more important than that?   —N. G.

Conclusion

A. Luke's Great Commission

When discussing the Great Commission given by Jesus, most Christians will think of Matthew 28:19-20, where Jesus said,

Go ye therefore, and teach all nations, baptizing them in the name of the Father, and of the Son, and of the Holy Ghost: teaching them to observe all things whatsoever I have commanded you: and, lo, I am with you alway, even unto the end of the world. Amen.

Luke's version of this is found in Acts 1:8, which could be summarized as, "Go to the ends of the earth and be my witnesses." There is no conflict between these versions. They are different ways of commanding the same thing. In both cases, the message is not confined to a small group of men who were physically present at Jesus' ascension, men who died some 2,000 years ago. Rather, these commands also apply to Christians today.

If we are truly Christ's disciples, we will be involved in spreading the saving testimony about Jesus to all the people of the earth. For some Christians, this involves strategic relocation to interact with people groups in countries that have no Christian witness. For other Christians, it means funding and supporting such cross-cultural evangelism. For all Christians, it involves ensuring that *talk* matches *walk* (Colossians 4:5; 1 Timothy 3:7; etc.).

The New Testament teaches that all Christians are to be involved in making disciples. This is to be motivated by our love for those who do not know Jesus, as well the need to obey His commands as our Lord (John 14:15). Jesus went to the cross out of His love for the world and His obedience to His Father's will. We should do no less.

B. Prayer

Heavenly Father, may we be the generation that finally fulfills Your desire to share our witness about Your Son with all the people of the earth. May Your Holy Spirit give us strength and courage to work toward this goal. In Jesus' name we pray. Amen.

C. Thought to Remember

The gospel must be spread *now*.

Involvement Learning

Enhance your lesson with KJV Bible Student *(from your curriculum supplier) and the reproducible activity page (at www.standardlesson.com or in the back of the* KJV Standard Lesson Commentary Deluxe Edition*).*

Into the Lesson

Write the heading *I love history because . . .* on a sheet of roll paper. Write the heading *I dislike history because . . .* on a second sheet of roll paper. Display the sheets in two opposite corners of the room.

As learners arrive, ask them to sit or stand by the paper that best describes their feelings regarding history. After all learners have arrived, allow two minutes for each group to compare within their group regarding why they chose that heading. Ask for a volunteer from each group to give an overview of their group's reasons. Encourage learners to respond respectfully to each other's reasoning. Discuss why the study of history is important, despite a person's likes or dislikes.

Alternative. Complete the previous activity as indicated, but write the headings on the board. Have students raise their hands to indicate which heading applies to them.

Transition to Bible study by saying, "Today begins five weeks of church history. Although the events that we will study happened about 2,000 years ago, each event is a remarkable story of God's work and what He wants from us now."

Into the Word

To each learner, distribute a handout (you create) with the following headings:

- What Jesus did . . .
- What Jesus said . . .
- What the disciples thought . . .
- What the disciples were promised . . .

Have learners make notes under each heading as a volunteer reads Acts 1:1-11 aloud two times.

Divide learners into groups of three to compare what they have written under each heading on their handouts. After five minutes, ask for volunteers to share their answers for the whole class.

Option 1. Distribute copies of the "In the Cloud" exercise from the activity page, which you can download. Have learners work in pairs to complete as indicated. Have pairs share with the whole class their answers to the last two questions.

Option 2. Display a map of the eastern Mediterranean region, like the map included on page 302. Highlight the locations of Jerusalem, Judah, and Samaria. Ask learners to describe the significance of Jesus' promise regarding the geographic spread of the gospel.

Into Life

Place learners in groups of four. Give each group a handout (you create) with the following prompts and have each group answer the prompts: 1–What are four modern-day equivalents that correspond to Jerusalem, Judaea, Samaria, and "the uttermost part of the earth" (Acts 1:8). 2–How is our congregation helping share the gospel in these places? 3–What are the members of our group doing to help to share the gospel in these places? 4–What attitudes, beliefs, or situations prevent believers from following the gospel mandate in Acts 1:8?

After five minutes, ask for a volunteer from each group to share their responses to the first two prompts. For whole-class discussion, ask why the congregation's influence seems to be stronger in some places than in others.

Ask for volunteers to share their responses to the third and fourth prompts. For whole-class discussion, ask how believers might overcome the attitudes, beliefs, or situations that prevent them from following the gospel mandate

Alternative. Distribute copies of the "Circles of Influence" activity from the activity page. Have learners work in small groups to complete as indicated.

End class by placing learners in pairs and having them pray for guidance for how they might rededicate themselves to the work that Jesus has given them to accomplish the gospel mandate.

The Day of Pentecost

Devotional Reading: Psalm 16
Background Scripture: Acts 2:1-42

Acts 2:1-8, 14-24, 37-39

1 And when the day of Pentecost was fully come, they were all with one accord in one place.

2 And suddenly there came a sound from heaven as of a rushing mighty wind, and it filled all the house where they were sitting.

3 And there appeared unto them cloven tongues like as of fire, and it sat upon each of them.

4 And they were all filled with the Holy Ghost, and began to speak with other tongues, as the Spirit gave them utterance.

5 And there were dwelling at Jerusalem Jews, devout men, out of every nation under heaven.

6 Now when this was noised abroad, the multitude came together, and were confounded, because that every man heard them speak in his own language.

7 And they were all amazed and marvelled, saying one to another, Behold, are not all these which speak Galilaeans?

8 And how hear we every man in our own tongue, wherein we were born?

14 But Peter, standing up with the eleven, lifted up his voice, and said unto them, Ye men of Judaea, and all ye that dwell at Jerusalem, be this known unto you, and hearken to my words:

15 For these are not drunken, as ye suppose, seeing it is but the third hour of the day.

16 But this is that which was spoken by the prophet Joel;

17 And it shall come to pass in the last days, saith God, I will pour out of my Spirit upon all flesh: and your sons and your daughters shall prophesy, and your young men shall see visions, and your old men shall dream dreams:

18 And on my servants and on my handmaidens I will pour out in those days of my Spirit; and they shall prophesy:

19 And I will shew wonders in heaven above, and signs in the earth beneath; blood, and fire, and vapour of smoke:

20 The sun shall be turned into darkness, and the moon into blood, before that great and notable day of the Lord come:

21 And it shall come to pass, that whosoever shall call on the name of the Lord shall be saved.

22 Ye men of Israel, hear these words; Jesus of Nazareth, a man approved of God among you by miracles and wonders and signs, which God did by him in the midst of you, as ye yourselves also know:

23 Him, being delivered by the determinate counsel and foreknowledge of God, ye have taken, and by wicked hands have crucified and slain:

24 Whom God hath raised up, having loosed the pains of death: because it was not possible that he should be holden of it.

37 Now when they heard this, they were pricked in their heart, and said unto Peter and to the rest of the apostles, Men and brethren, what shall we do?

38 Then Peter said unto them, Repent, and be baptized every one of you in the name of Jesus Christ for the remission of sins, and ye shall receive the gift of the Holy Ghost.

39 For the promise is unto you, and to your children, and to all that are afar off, even as many as the Lord our God shall call.

Key Text

The promise is unto you, and to your children, and to all that are afar off, even as many as the Lord our God shall call. —**Acts 2:39**

305

Jesus Calls Us

Unit 3: The Birth of the Church
Lessons 9–13

Lesson Aims

After participating in this lesson, each learner will be able to:

1. List the ways the Holy Spirit was active on Pentecost.

2. Explain why the Day of Pentecost was ideal for the birth of the church.

3. Write a prayer for empowerment by the Holy Spirit to follow Jesus more boldly.

Lesson Outline

Introduction
A. The Unholy Spirits Today
B. Lesson Context: The Holy Spirit
C. Lesson Context: The Jewish Calendar

I. The Spirit Comes (Acts 2:1-8)
A. Day and Place (v. 1)
B. Sound and Sight (vv. 2-4)
C. Diversity and Unity (vv. 5-8)
Language of the Heart

II. The Apostle Preaches (Acts 2:14-24)
A. Confrontation (vv. 14-15)
B. Proclamation (vv. 16-21)
C. Accreditation (vv. 22-24)

III. The Crowd Reacts (Acts 2:37-39)
A. Realization and Question (v. 37)
B. Imperatives and Promise (v. 38)
C. Who and Where (v. 39)
With or Without the Promise?

Conclusion
A. The Holy Spirit Today
B. Prayer
C. Thought to Remember

Introduction

A. The Unholy Spirits Today

The setting of one boy's encounter with an unholy spirit was the basement of a house owned by friends of his parents. Those present were only the preteen youth and his younger brother. The context was a combination of youthful curiosity, boredom, and a Ouija board discovered on a shelf. Setting the board up, the two boys wasted no time in asking "it" the inane and predictable questions.

To the boys' surprise, the board soon began responding as the triangular pointer upon which they had ever so lightly placed fingers became self-propelled. Each boy accused the other of moving it. But both instinctively knew that neither of them was moving the pointer.

Wondering how to prove or disprove the suspicion, the older boy quickly came up with an idea: the two of them would pose a question that neither of them knew the answer to but to which their mother (who was upstairs) did. The question agreed on was, "How old is Grandmother?" The board's response of "65" was quickly confirmed as correct after the boys raced upstairs to get their mother's answer. She wisely refused the boys' subsequent requests to have a Ouija board.

Similar means have long been used to contact the spirit world (example: Deuteronomy 18:10-12). Encounters of this sort are not to be sought and should be disturbing in any case (compare Mark 5:1-20; Acts 16:16-18; 19:13-16; etc.). But should encounters with the Holy Spirit be any less alarming in their own, holy way?

B. Lesson Context: The Holy Spirit

The descent of the Holy Spirit "like a dove" on Jesus at His baptism might suggest a picture of peace and acceptance (Luke 3:22). But the work of the Holy Spirit was not always a pleasant experience for those affected, since Jesus would baptize "with the Holy Ghost and with fire" (3:16). Imageries of fire in the Bible are associated with the destruction of God's enemies (Ezekiel 22:17-22, 31; Hebrews 10:26-27; 2 Peter 3:7; etc.) and the testing or purification of His people (Zechariah 13:8-9; 1 Corinthians 3:12-13; 1 Peter 1:6-7). The depiction in Luke 3:16 speaks of the power to do both, especially in light of the "fan" imagery of Luke 3:17.

C. Lesson Context: The Jewish Calendar

The most important observance on Israel's calendar was Passover. It was a time to remember deliverance from slavery in Egypt, when God's angel of death "passed over" Israelite households that had been marked with the blood of a lamb (Exodus 12).

Within a few weeks of leaving Egypt, the people of Israel arrived at Mount Sinai (Exodus 16:1; 31:18; etc.). There they entered into a covenant with God, agreeing to be His people while the Lord promised to be their God. For centuries thereafter, the Old Testament covenant people celebrated their deliverance on Passover and followed it 50 days later by celebrating God's giving of the law. Pentecost occurs seven weeks after the Passover Sabbath plus one day, which equals 50 days; it was one of the three great pilgrimage festivals (Deuteronomy 16:9, 16). This celebration is also called "the feast of harvest," "the feast of weeks," and "the day of the firstfruits" (Exodus 23:16a; 34:22a; Numbers 28:26).

The Jews in the time of Jesus had a marvelous temple in Jerusalem (see Mark 13:1). The city's economy centered on that structure, as the periodic influx of visiting Jews brought in money (compare John 2:14-15). We might say that the Jerusalem of the time had a tourist economy, and the height of the tourist season was the period from Passover to Pentecost. Many visitors would stay for the entire 50-day period between those two observances.

I. The Spirit Comes
(Acts 2:1-8)

The apostles continued to wait in Jerusalem as instructed by Jesus (Luke 24:49; Acts 1:4). These were the 11 apostles from the original 12, Judas Iscariot having committed suicide (Matthew 27:5; Acts 1:18). The followers grew to number about 120 (1:12-15).

A. Day and Place (v. 1)
1a. And when the day of Pentecost was fully come.

The day of Pentecost marked the final full day of the Passover-to-Pentecost season (see Lesson Context: The Jewish Calendar, above). Most who were visiting Jerusalem to attend these observances would begin returning home the next day.

1b. They were all with one accord in one place.

The fact that those gathered were *all with one accord* points to a common priority: that of intense, communal prayer (Acts 1:14). It had been 10 days since Jesus' departure, and the mood of those 120 was undoubtedly one of hopeful expectation. Seven weeks prior, the disciples had also been gathered together; but on that occasion they had gathered in fear (John 20:19). But being able to gather *in one place* was not to last long; soon enough, persecution would cause Jesus' followers to scatter (Acts 8:1).

B. Sound and Sight (vv. 2-4)
2. And suddenly there came a sound from heaven as of a rushing mighty wind, and it filled all the house where they were sitting.

It is important to read carefully what happened at this point, and not to rely solely on what we assume took place. This miracle and those that follow have been carefully documented by Luke, based on eyewitness interviews (Luke 1:2).

First comes a very unusual auditory phenomenon. The phrase *from heaven* signifies that we are intended to understand it as being of divine origin. There is no portent of danger in the phrase *a sound . . . as of a rushing mighty wind*. The text does not say that an actual wind was present, only the sound of wind.

3. And there appeared unto them cloven tongues like as of fire, and it sat upon each of them.

Second was a visual phenomenon: that of *fire*. Some have interpreted this as a river of fire coming out of the sky. The word translated *cloven* is translated "divided" in other places (Luke 11:17-18; 12:52-53), and that is the sense here. We should be careful to note that the phrase *like as of* indicates a figurative comparison, as the Greek word being translated indicates elsewhere (compare Matthew 9:36; Luke 22:44; Acts 6:15). This phenomenon did not injure as *it sat upon each of them*. Just as the sound of the wind had no moving air, these flames did not burn. Both were supernatural things from God.

4. And they were all filled with the Holy Ghost, and began to speak with other tongues, as the Spirit gave them utterance.

The sound and sight are followed by an act of empowerment as *the Holy Ghost* fills the followers of Jesus. The Spirit was active in Old Testament days, but only with a few of God's people (examples: Numbers 11:25-29; 1 Samuel 10:6, 10; 19:20, 23; Nehemiah 9:30). But now the promise of God is coming to fulfillment, the promise that He will pour His *Spirit* on His people (Isaiah 44:3-5; 32:15; Ezekiel 36:27; 37:14; Joel 2:28).

> **What Do You Think?**
>
> How can believers discern the source of seemingly miraculous events?
>
> **Digging Deeper**
>
> How do 1 Corinthians 2:6-16; Hebrews 5:11-14; and 1 John 4:1-6 inform your answer?

C. Diversity and Unity (vv. 5-8)

5-6. And there were dwelling at Jerusalem Jews, devout men, out of every nation under heaven. Now when this was noised abroad, the multitude came together, and were confounded, because that every man heard them speak in his own language.

The setting was clearly multilingual. The common, trade language of the day was Greek (see Acts 21:37). *Jews* of the *Jerusalem* area would also speak Aramaic (see Mark 5:41; John 20:16). The fact that the gathered Jews were *out of every nation under heaven* certainly would have included those whose native tongue was Latin (compare 19:20). Other languages are implied as well.

The fact that *every man heard them speak in his own language* is thus the third miraculous phenomenon. The word translated *confounded* implies confusion combined with a strong emotional reaction (see Acts 9:22; 19:32; 21:27, 31).

7-8. And they were all amazed and marvelled, saying one to another, Behold, are not all these which speak Galilaeans? And how hear we every man in our own tongue, wherein we were born?

The fact that those speaking were recognized as being *Galilaeans* is probably due to their accent (compare Matthew 26:73) and manner of dress. The multiplicity of native tongues that the crowd hears comes into sharper focus as provinces of origin are detailed in Acts 2:9-11 (not in today's text). We make sure not to miss the miracle here: those listening, who hailed from a dozen or more provinces, heard the message of the gospel in languages the speakers had not studied.

> **What Do You Think?**
>
> How would you respond to the statement that new Bible translations are not needed?
>
> **Digging Deeper**
>
> What steps can you take to partner with organizations that create Bible translations for unreached people groups?

Language of the Heart

"These people don't need the Bible in their own language. That promotes tribalism."

A district official spoke those words to us as we attended the wedding of a Bible translator in a small village. When the official found out that I helped facilitate Bible translation, he began to parrot his stance against local languages. He argued that everyone should use Swahili, the national language.

I asked what language group he came from, and he told me of his home in the north.

"Oh, did you know they just finished translating the Bible into your language?"

His face transformed from stern disapproval into one of surprised delight. "Really? They have the Bible in my language?!"

I've seen that delighted expression many times. When people hear their native language unexpectedly, they often radiate joy, even if the speaker knows only a phrase or two. How much more did the action of the Holy Spirit cause amazement on Pentecost!

Perhaps everyone you know speaks English but you're still having problems connecting with them. The reason may be that you're not tuned in to the "language" of their personality type, generational distinctives, etc. Try communicating with those factors in mind, and see what happens!   —N. G.

II. The Apostle Preaches
(Acts 2:14-24)

Even in the midst of miracles, there were always unbelievers and doubters (compare Luke 11:15). Likewise, some of those who experienced this particular miracle doubted. They even suggested that those speaking might be drunk (Acts 2:13).

A. Confrontation (vv. 14-15)

14-15. But Peter, standing up with the eleven, lifted up his voice, and said unto them, Ye men of Judaea, and all ye that dwell at Jerusalem, be this known unto you, and hearken to my words: for these are not drunken, as ye suppose, seeing it is but the third hour of the day.

Peter quickly discredited the charge of insobriety. *The third hour,* which is about 9:00 a.m., is a most unlikely time for drunkenness.

B. Proclamation (vv. 16-21)

16. But this is that which was spoken by the prophet Joel.

Moving immediately from what the phenomenon was *not* to what it *was,* Peter pointed to *the prophet Joel.* By some estimates, Joel prophesied in the eighth century BC, but exact dates are unknown. What he predicted had been a long time in coming to pass, but come to pass it had!

17a. And it shall come to pass in the last days, saith God, I will pour out of my Spirit upon all flesh.

Two things stand out regarding Peter's quote

How to Say It

apocalyptic	uh-*pock*-uh-lip-tik.
Diaspora	Dee-*as*-puh-ruh.
Sinai	*Sigh*-nye
	or *Sigh*-nay-eye.

of Joel 2:28-32. First is the announcement of the arrival of *the last days,* the final period of human history, as evidenced by the outpouring of God's *Spirit.* We understand this to mean that what remain are the events of the end of time: the return of Christ and the final judgment.

What Do You Think?

In what ways should Peter's conclusion change your priorities in life?

Digging Deeper

How do 1 Timothy 4:1; 2 Timothy 3:1-5; Hebrews 1:1-2; James 5:3; 1 Peter 1:5, 20; 2 Peter 3:3-7; 1 John 2:18; and Jude 18-19 help frame your response?

17b-18. And your sons and your daughters shall prophesy, and your young men shall see visions, and your old men shall dream dreams: and on my servants and on my handmaidens I will pour out in those days of my Spirit; and they shall prophesy.

Second, the validation for Peter's claim is the return of prophecy and the various methods by which prophecies come about. The Jews had not experienced prophecy for generations. Joel's language points to the pouring out of the *Spirit,* evoking the image of a deluge that cannot be contained.

19-20. And I will shew wonders in heaven above, and signs in the earth beneath; blood, and fire, and vapour of smoke: the sun shall be turned into darkness, and the moon into blood, before that great and notable day of the Lord come.

The imagery is also reflected in Isaiah 13:10; 34:4; Matthew 24:29-31; Mark 13:24-27; Luke 21:25-28; and Revelation 6:12-17. These passages help establish the meaning and significance of the apocalyptic depictions in the passage before us.

21. And it shall come to pass, that whosoever shall call on the name of the Lord shall be saved.

Peter ended his quotation of the ancient prophet with a shortened version of what he (Peter) went on to give in fuller form in Acts 2:38-39 (below).

C. Accreditation (vv. 22-24)

22. Ye men of Israel, hear these words; Jesus

of Nazareth, a man approved of God among you by miracles and wonders and signs, which God did by him in the midst of you, as ye yourselves also know.

Everyone present surely was aware of *Jesus of Nazareth* and His reputation as a miracle worker (compare Acts 26:26). Since working a miracle was a demonstration of divine power, Peter demanded acknowledgment that God was the source of such supernatural activity. The three Greek words translated *miracles*, *signs*, and *wonders* point to a larger reality—*God* himself. The same Greek words occur together in Acts 6:8; Romans 15:19; 2 Corinthians 12:12; 2 Thessalonians 2:9; and Hebrews 2:4.

23. Him, being delivered by the determinate counsel and foreknowledge of God, ye have taken, and by wicked hands have crucified and slain.

The crowd was also aware of the shameful death of Jesus seven weeks earlier *by wicked hands* (compare Luke 24:18-20). Peter saw no reason in this to doubt the plan of God, especially given what happened after the crucifixion.

24. Whom God hath raised up, having loosed the pains of death: because it was not possible that he should be holden of it.

God's plan did not terminate with Jesus' death, since *God* had *raised* Him *up* to live again. Surely many in the crowd had heard rumors about the appearances of the risen Lord!

III. The Crowd Reacts

(Acts 2:37-39)

In remarks that extend from Acts 2:25-35, Peter offered further proof "that God hath made that same Jesus, whom ye have crucified, both Lord and Christ" (2:36). This drew a notable reaction.

A. Realization and Question (v. 37)

37. Now when they heard this, they were pricked in their heart, and said unto Peter and to the rest of the apostles, Men and brethren, what shall we do?

We perceive the crowd as having believed Peter, accepting his interpretation of events as true. This terrified them. Thus their plea, *what shall we do?*

B. Imperatives and Promise (v. 38)

38a. Then Peter said unto them, Repent.

To *repent* is to turn away from sin and toward God in heart, mind, and lifestyle (compare Ezekiel 14:6; 18:30; Acts 3:19; 26:20). Throughout history there have been moments in which people were faced with the stark choice of either walking away from God or toward Him (Joshua 24:14-15; 2 Chronicles 7:14; etc.). A hard-hearted, prideful individual will not admit wrongdoing. But through repentance, that person can find peace with God.

38b. And be baptized every one of you in the name of Jesus Christ.

The apostle Paul later explained that to *be baptized* was to be "buried with [Jesus] . . . into death: that like as Christ was raised up from the dead . . . even so we also should walk in newness of life" (Romans 6:4; see also Colossians 2:12). He further noted that "as many of you as have been baptized into Christ have put on Christ" (Galatians 3:27).

There is nothing magical about the waters of baptism; rather, baptism is God's chosen time when regeneration and renewal happen (Titus 3:5; 1 Peter 3:21). As such, baptism is not a human work of merit (compare Ephesians 2:8-9); rather, it is a work of God.

38c. For the remission of sins.

Remission means "forgiveness," as the same Greek word is translated in Mark 3:29 and Acts 5:31. The most important thing for anyone upon reaching the age of awareness of having sinned against God is to have those sins forgiven. The wonderful thing is that God is willing to forgive us *and* to help us resist future sin. The former (known as "justification") happens through Christ; the latter (known as "sanctification") happens through the Holy Spirit (see 1 Corinthians 6:11; also see next).

38d. And ye shall receive the gift of the Holy Ghost.

With *the gift of the Holy Ghost,* Christians have the power to put off the works of the flesh and to bear the fruit of the Spirit (Galatians 5:22-25). Peter's sermon thus foreshadowed the church's submission to the leading of the Spirit.

C. Who and Where (v. 39)

39. For the promise is unto you, and to your children, and to all that are afar off, even as many as the Lord our God shall call.

Those who heard this sermon likely understood *all that are afar off* to refer to Jews who did not live in Israel. This reality was called the Diaspora (the dispersion of Jews beyond Israel). That dispersion was not limited to the exiles recorded in 2 Kings 17:6 and 25:21. The reality of the Diaspora in the first century AD was that Jews were living all over the Roman Empire (see Acts 2:9-11; James 1:1).

Chapters 8 and 10 of Acts record confusion and questioning about the scope of God's *call.* Christians of Jewish background initially believed that Jesus had come to redeem only Israel (compare Luke 24:21; Acts 11:18). But the book of Acts witnesses to the Spirit's leading of messengers to take the gospel to Gentiles as well.

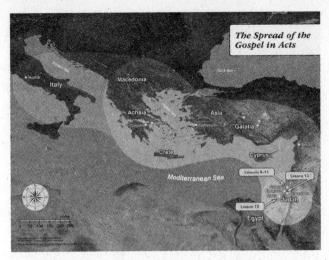

Visual for Lessons 9 & 10. *Keep this map posted throughout the quarter to give learners a geographic perspective.*

Peter's announced and permanent solution to sin and all unholiness—whether from unclean spirits (Acts 8:7; etc.) or personal choices—is the "gift of the Holy Ghost." That gift has been promised to those who repent and are baptized. Are you living *with* or *without* that promise right now?   —N. G.

> **What Do You Think?**
> How can you share the gospel to all people, even those who live far away?
>
> **Digging Deeper**
> How will you deal with perceived limitations that might add difficulty to sharing the gospel?

With or Without the Promise?

The elderly man waded out into the river that was near a remote African village. I watched as a younger man lowered him under the water in baptism and lifted him up. And as I stood next to a missionary, I heard him ask the soaking-wet man something in the local language.

The missionary translated the interchange for me: "I asked him why he waited until he was so old before he was baptized. He replied, 'Because no one ever told me.'"

Conclusion
A. The Holy Spirit Today

Acts 2 presents something fundamental: the Holy Spirit has come, and He has come with power. The long waiting period is over. We are in the last days, the era of Holy Spirit–empowered ministry. There is power in the gospel. When this message is preached faithfully, God's Spirit is active in the reception of it. This is true whether preaching from a pulpit or sharing with a friend. Whenever the gospel is communicated, God's Spirit is working with us to convict the hearer of His truth and bring that person to faith in Christ. How do you live out this reality?

B. Prayer

God, may we never doubt the power of Your Holy Spirit to change everything according to Your will. May Your Spirit work powerfully in our lives, as Jesus promised. We pray in His name. Amen.

C. Thought to Remember

Live the reality of the era of the Holy Spirit.

Involvement Learning

Enhance your lesson with KJV Bible Student (from your curriculum supplier) and the reproducible activity page (at www.standardlesson.com or in the back of the KJV Standard Lesson Commentary Deluxe Edition*).*

Into the Lesson

Write *POWER* on the board as learners arrive. Have them pair up and share with each other the most notable display of physical power that they have experienced. After three minutes, invite volunteers to share their experiences. Lead into the Bible study by saying, "Today we will consider a demonstration of power unlike anything you have experienced. As we study this Scripture, let's consider how followers of Jesus would have felt during this display of power."

Into the Word

Before class, recruit a class member to prepare a five-minute presentation on the Day of Pentecost, using material from the Lesson Context and other resources. The presentation should include information about the history of the day's observance, its significance to first-century Jews, and why it was an appropriate backdrop for the events in today's Scripture.

After the presentation, divide the class into groups of three. Distribute a handout (you prepare) to each group that contains the following sentences:

1–Jesus' followers were scattered throughout Jerusalem, and they came together only after the Day of Pentecost.
2–A tremendous windstorm, like a tornado, got the attention of everyone in the house.
3–People's eyes gleamed like a flame.
4–The disciples spoke in unfamiliar languages and interpreted their speech for the crowd.
5–Everyone was assumed to be of a sober mind.
6–Peter quoted Jesus regarding the last days.
7–Peter preached the importance of making sacrifices at the temple for the forgiveness of sins.

Instruct groups to mark whether each sentence is true or false. Then have groups check their answers by reading Acts 2:1-8, 14-24, 37-39. False statements should be rewritten to make them correct. (Note to teacher: Each sentence is false.)

Option. Distribute copies of the "Baptism in Scripture" exercise from the activity page, which you can download. Have learners work in small groups to complete as indicated.

Ask a volunteer to read today's Scripture passage aloud, pausing after each verse. Ask learners to raise their hands after each verse that includes a reference to the person or work of the Holy Spirit. Write these verse numbers on the board. Through whole-class discussion, review these verses and create a list of the ways that the Holy Spirit was active on the Day of Pentecost.

Into Life

Ask, "How is the Holy Spirit's influence evident throughout today's Scripture?" Then write the following continuum on the board:

The Holy Spirit's Influence

0	1	2	3	4	5
Never		Seldom			Daily

Each learner should share with their partner the extent of the Holy Spirit's influence over their lives by placing themselves somewhere on the continuum. Then have pairs answer the following questions: 1–What factors influence where you place yourselves on the continuum? 2–How can you be more attentive to the influence of the Holy Spirit?

Alternative. Distribute copies of the "Power, Power!" activity from the activity page. Have learners complete the activity in pairs before discussing answers in whole-class discussion.

After calling time for either activity, distribute index cards and pens to each learner. Ask learners to write a prayer based on the following prompt:

Lord, help me be attentive to the influence of the Holy Spirit. Empower me through the Holy Spirit to follow Jesus boldly this week as I . . .

Encourage learners to place the cards in a location where they will notice the prayers throughout the week.

Jumping for Joy

Devotional Reading: Luke 10:1-9
Background Scripture: Acts 3

Acts 3:1-11

1 Now Peter and John went up together into the temple at the hour of prayer, being the ninth hour.

2 And a certain man lame from his mother's womb was carried, whom they laid daily at the gate of the temple which is called Beautiful, to ask alms of them that entered into the temple;

3 Who seeing Peter and John about to go into the temple asked an alms.

4 And Peter, fastening his eyes upon him with John, said, Look on us.

5 And he gave heed unto them, expecting to receive something of them.

6 Then Peter said, Silver and gold have I none; but such as I have give I thee: In the name of Jesus Christ of Nazareth rise up and walk.

7 And he took him by the right hand, and lifted him up: and immediately his feet and ankle bones received strength.

8 And he leaping up stood, and walked, and entered with them into the temple, walking, and leaping, and praising God.

9 And all the people saw him walking and praising God:

10 And they knew that it was he which sat for alms at the Beautiful gate of the temple: and they were filled with wonder and amazement at that which had happened unto him.

11 And as the lame man which was healed held Peter and John, all the people ran together unto them in the porch that is called Solomon's, greatly wondering.

Key Text

He leaping up stood, and walked, and entered with them into the temple, walking, and leaping, and praising God. —**Acts 3:8**

Jesus Calls Us

Unit 3: The Birth of the Church
Lessons 9–13

Lesson Aims

After participating in this lesson, each learner will be able to:

1. Describe the life of the man who was lame.

2. Compare and contrast the people's reactions to the healing with reactions in Acts 4:1-22 and 14:8-13.

3. Write a prayer for discernment to recognize when to offer Jesus before offering material help.

Lesson Outline

Introduction

A. Uncompassionate Attitude

A few years ago, I helped lead a team of students on a missions week to a remote country. One of our team members was in a wheelchair, and the destination country's main airport was an obstacle for this teammate. As we went through the airport on our way home, our group was expected to get to the boarding area by using a narrow escalator, something our team member could not do.

We eventually found an elevator. But when we arrived at the gate level, we encountered a corridor blocked by a locked door. We eventually found someone who had a key to this door, but we were left with the impression that this airport employee believed that people in wheelchairs should not be traveling.

Followers of Christ agree that we should show respect and compassion to our neighbors who have a physical or mental disability, or both. However, this was not necessarily the outlook in Jesus' day. Many believed that suffering was God's punishment for sin (see Luke 13:1-5; John 9:2), and those people with disabilities were treated accordingly.

B. Lesson Context

Acts 2:42-47 summarizes the ongoing activities of the just-birthed church in Jerusalem, which included miraculous displays after the Day of Pentecost. Those ongoing displays are described as being "many wonders and signs . . . done by the apostles" (Acts 2:43). Hebrews 2:4 confirms God to be the one who authenticated the truth of the gospel preaching by "signs and wonders, and with divers miracles." Although miraculous healings obviously brought compassionate relief to the afflicted, their primary purpose was to validate the truth of Christianity in general and the person and work of Jesus in particular (see John 20:30-31). Today's lesson forms part of that larger tapestry.

We are not told exactly how long the events of today's lesson occurred after the Day of Pentecost, but it was probably several weeks later. The church had been busy, including a ministry of the selling of property to provide funds for relief of the poor (Acts 2:45). The apostles were still in Jerusalem, not having returned home to Galilee. They and the other followers of Jesus met daily in the spacious porticoes of the temple (2:46a). Activities included meeting in homes for "breaking bread"—fellowship meals that included celebration of the Lord's Supper (2:46b).

I. The Setting
(Acts 3:1-2)

A. Afternoon Prayers (v. 1)

1. Now Peter and John went up together into the temple at the hour of prayer, being the ninth hour.

We are presented with a daily custom of *prayer* that occurred at a specific time of day. We should remember that all the believers at this point were of Jewish background—there were no Gentile Christians until the events of Acts 10. Belief in Jesus and His resurrection did not cause *Peter and John* to abandon all Jewish practices; the same was true later for the apostle Paul (Acts 21:26; etc.).

Prayer had been important before, and it still was. Three traditional times for prayer at the temple were recognized: early morning when the priests made the daily sacrifice, in midafternoon, and at sunset (Exodus 29:38-39; Psalm 55:17). This is the second of those, *the ninth hour* being about 3:00 p.m. (see also Acts 10:3, 30).

The fact that Peter and John went *up . . . into the temple* indicates that its location in Jerusalem was at a higher elevation than the house where they were staying. These two apostles are mentioned together in the same verse a total of eight times in the book of Acts. Four of those times are in today's text; the other four are in Acts 1:13; 4:13, 19; and 8:14. Before their journey was interrupted, these two men surely recalled the words of Jesus: "My house shall be called of all nations the house of prayer" (Mark 11:17, citing Isaiah 56:7).

B. Daily Station (v. 2)

2. And a certain man lame from his mother's womb was carried, whom they laid daily at the gate of the temple which is called Beautiful, to ask alms of them that entered into the temple.

People suffering from disabilities were a common sight in the ancient world (compare Matthew 15:30), and no less so in Jerusalem (Acts 5:12-16; etc.). For someone to have been *lame from his mother's womb* indicates a congenital condition rather than a tragic accident (compare John 9:1, 32; Acts 14:8). The legs of this *certain man* had never been able to support his weight and allow him to walk.

Although his physical condition was terrible, he did have two things going for him. First, he had family members or friends who were willing carry him to the temple *daily*. Second, he had a prime, high-traffic place that seems to be recognized as his right; the exact opposite seems to be the case with the man in John 5:7. This particular *gate . . . called Beautiful* (again at Acts 3:10, below) is usually understood to have been on the eastern side *of the temple*. (Some see it as having been the eastern gate for the inner courtyard.)

> **What Do You Think?**
> What adjustments can your congregation make to ensure that people with disabilities can easily participate in worship in your meeting place?
>
> **Digging Deeper**
> Who should be recruited to help with appropriate follow through?

II. The Expectations
(Acts 3:3-6a)

A. Innocent Asking (v. 3)

3. Who seeing Peter and John about to go into the temple asked an alms.

The book of Acts sets up a collision course: two men going *into the temple* hear a beggar's request. This man confronted everyone who entered by this gate, just by his presence alone. *Peter and John* may have seen him before.

The Greek word translated *alms* occurs 13 times in the New Testament (Matthew 6:2, 3, 4; Luke 11:41; 12:33; Acts 3:2, 3, 10; 9:36; 10:2, 4, 31; 24:17); it refers to a duty-driven monetary gift to the poor and needy. Jesus never renounced the practice of giving to the poor, but He did condemn those who made a show of their giving to garner praise and honor (Matthew 6:2-4). Peter and John had no doubt given to beggars many times, both in Jerusalem and in their hometown.

B. Undivided Attention (vv. 4-5)

4-5. And Peter, fastening his eyes upon him with John, said, Look on us. And he gave heed unto them, expecting to receive something of them.

Peter, no longer the wishy-washy denier from Jesus' trials, spoke to the man with confidence. What Peter said first is interesting to compare with the previous verse, Acts 3:3. That verse indicates that the beggar had already seen the two apostles when Peter said, *Look on us*. Therefore the request by Peter wasn't for the man to do something entirely different but for him to do something more intensely. That extra intensity undoubtedly resulted in making eye contact. In any case, the two apostles gained the full attention of the man.

> **What Do You Think?**
> How can you practice being more attentive to people you might be tempted to ignore?
>
> **Digging Deeper**
> What kinds of people, if any, should believers not associate with? What Scriptures support your answer?

C. Forthright Admission (v. 6a)

6a. Then Peter said, Silver and gold have I none.

For unexplained reasons, neither *Peter* nor John had any coins. Peter expressed this in terms of precious metal coins (*silver and gold*), but we are given the impression that they did not have any copper coins either, not even a tiny bronze *lepton* (the "widow's mite" of Luke 21:2).

To shirk one's duty to care for the needy by not giving alms violated at least the spirit of the law, which required the people of Israel to care for those who were in need (see Deuteronomy 26:12). Others observing at this busy gate would have seen the apostles' failure to give alms as being shamefully unprepared.

III. The Wonder
(Acts 3:6b-11)
A. Invoked Name (v. 6b)

6b. But such as I have give I thee: In the name of Jesus Christ of Nazareth rise up and walk.

That is not the end of the story, though, for Peter did indeed have something precious to *give* this poor man: healing in the powerful *name of Jesus Christ of Nazareth*. Peter did not present himself as having miraculous powers (see also Acts 3:12; 10:26; 14:8-15). If the man were to *rise up and walk*, the power would come from his Lord.

Some have suggested that the man might not have wanted to be healed. They speculate that he was delivered daily to a prime spot for begging, perhaps a more lucrative gig than we might guess. This is to misunderstand the anguish of those with disabilities. Some do indeed rise above the limitations of their disability, but many with a disability would like to have it removed. It is important to acknowledge the unique stories of people with disabilities and not assume a universally applicable narrative.

> **What Do You Think?**
> In what ways does Peter's response set a precedent for believers? In what ways does it not?
>
> **Digging Deeper**
> How can you practice meeting a person's physical needs while also not ignoring his or her spiritual needs?

B. Cured Man (vv. 7-8)

7. And he took him by the right hand, and lifted him up: and immediately his feet and ankle bones received strength.

Remember, this man had been disabled from birth. Thus his disability was not from disease or injury. He was not being "healed" or "restored," technically speaking, since he was being made whole for the first time in his life.

The detail of the man's being *lifted* by *the right hand* lends the sense of an eyewitness testimony. We further note that the right hand can indicate honor as the left hand indicates dishonor (see Matthew 25:31-46). The book of Acts presents this miracle not as providing missing body parts, but as fully empowering the man's *feet and ankle bones*, the focal point of his disability.

8. And he leaping up stood, and walked, and entered with them into the temple, walking, and leaping, and praising God.

There is more here than having made this man's feet and ankles whole. He also learned to walk and jump instantly. Toddlers take months to learn to walk well and even longer to learn to hop about. Adults who have suffered traumatic injuries to the spine or legs can testify to the challenge of learning how to walk again. With this man on that day at the temple, the psychomotor controls in his brain instantly knew how to make his legs work. Not only could he walk; he could jump, which is an advanced stage of using legs and ankles. Leaping was not "stage two" for him; rather, it was the first thing he did!

The man's newfound physical abilities were accompanied by a sign of spiritual heath: as he was *walking* and *leaping*, the man praised *God*. This would be appropriate 100 percent of the times such a miracle happened, but surprisingly it did not (compare and contrast Luke 17:15-18).

> **What Do You Think?**
> How can you give praise to God through expressions of worship that are different from your normal expressions?
>
> **Digging Deeper**
> How will you use your unique skills and talents to praise God in this regard?

Jumping for a Better Future?

MIT's Mini Cheetah was the first four-legged robot to do a little backflip. Boston Dynamics' Atlas robot was the first two-legged humanoid robot to do a more intimidating backflip, militaristic in its precision. One website warns us to "be very afraid . . . robots can now do backflips." Will humanoid robots join us in creating an anticipated "better world"? Or will they become self-aware and turn on their creators as the Cylons did in the science-fiction show *Bat-*

tlestar Galactica? Life has been known to imitate art!

I've chosen to believe the backflipping robots are jumping for joy. One of my refrigerator magnets shows a humanoid robot jumping, and the custom caption I added says, "Jump for joy—robots now can for no reason."

The man in Scripture who had suffered from birth miraculously received motor skills that he had never before experienced—skills that most of us take for granted. His jumping bore witness to his healing and expressed his joy at this new experience. What are you neglecting to praise God for?

—C. E. R.

C. Amazed Crowds (vv. 9-11)

9-10. And all the people saw him walking and praising God: and they knew that it was he which sat for alms at the Beautiful gate of the temple: and they were filled with wonder and amazement at that which had happened unto him.

This man, now jumping about and happily *praising God*, was instantly recognized by those who frequented the temple courts. It is likely that he had only one set of clothes and one head covering. They had seen him many times, a beggar who had occupied a place *at the Beautiful gate* for years. They had seen him so often and for so long that there was no doubt in their minds that he truly had been disabled and was now doing physical things that defied his disability. This caused *wonder and amazement* for them, for this could only have been the work of God (see Luke 5:26; compare and contrast with Acts 4:1-22 and 14:8-13).

> **What Do You Think?**
> How can believers be attentive to the wonder and amazement of God's miraculous work in the world?
>
> **Digging Deeper**
> How would you respond to someone who says that miraculous occurrences can be explained by pagan gods (example: Acts 14:8-13) or natural measures?

11. And as the lame man which was healed

Visual for Lesson 11. *While discussing Acts 3:8, have this posted as you ask for examples of responding to God's miraculous work.*

held Peter and John, all the people ran together unto them in the porch that is called Solomon's, greatly wondering.

All the people who witnessed this miracle congregated in an area of the temple known as *Solomon's* Portico, or *porch.* This was a covered open-air area on the east side of the largest temple courtyard, the Court of the Gentiles. If the Beautiful Gate was on the outer wall (some think it is the eastern gate to the inner courtyard), then those entering the gate would turn left to access this area. Solomon's Porch is estimated to have been about 50 feet wide and maybe 100 to 150 feet long, with a wooden roof perched on marble columns that were 30 to 40 feet tall. The book of Acts presents this as a place where the Jerusalem church met at times (see Acts 5:12; compare and contrast 1 Kings 6:3; 7:12; John 10:23).

There is some debate about what kind of access those with disabilities would have had to the courts of the temple. We know that a priest serving in the inner courts could not be disabled according to the Law of Moses (Leviticus 21:17-23). Whether this prohibition extended so far as to prevent a disabled person from entering the temple cannot be determined with certainty. Imagine, though, if this were the case. The man had lain at the gate for years, but never been inside. His first move was not to return to his home and give the good news to his family, but to jump and leap his way into the house of the Lord, shouting

praises as he entered (Acts 3:8, above). It was his greatest day.

Why Be Healed?

How bad would your physical condition have to be for you to volunteer for experimental, unproven brain surgery? On December 22, 2016, I submitted to just such a surgery to relieve symptoms of Parkinson's disease. The surgery was experimental in that it was "no cut, no drill," using high-frequency focused ultrasound. The process required being inside an MRI tube for three and a half hours, much of the time awake.

I was age 61, and the symptoms had worsened over the 14 years I'd had the disease. During those years, I often wondered if I would be able to continue doing my job. Wouldn't it have been easier and safer just to go on disability?

The surgery resulted in a noticeable improvement of symptoms. As one of only about 30 in the clinical trial, I had beaten odds of thousands-to-one in being selected. Those odds combined with the nature of the technology might tempt one to declare the selection and results to be miraculous, but I think the term *providential* is more accurate.

Jesus' miracles were primarily intended to (1) authenticate Him as Messiah and Son of God so that (2) eternal life might result for those who believe (John 20:30-31). With the first option now established, our focus should be on the second.

The ultimate outcome we should pursue when God grants us extra quantity or quality of time on earth is spiritual healing—somehow—for those with whom we interact (see Mark 5:18-20; Acts 5:19-20; Colossians 4:3-4; compare Philippians 1:22-26). Is that what you expect from your prayers for physical healing? Or do you desire a longer life merely to enjoy more "rockin' chair time"?

Oh, I almost forgot to mention the job that the surgery allowed me to continue doing: it was as editor of the commentary that you and thousands of others are now reading.   —R. L. N.

Conclusion
A. The Ultimate Goal
Over half of Jesus' miracles recorded in the Gos-

pels involved people who were sick, blind, mute, deaf, or otherwise suffering a physical disability. This does not count summary statements where we are told Jesus "healed many" (see Mark 1:34). He cared deeply about those with physical disabilities. A word used several times to describe Jesus' attitude and actions in this regard is "compassion" (see Matthew 14:14; 15:32; 20:34; Mark 8:2).

Compassion is also seen in the first-century church's acceptance of responsibility to care for those among them who were unable to care for themselves fully (Acts 2:45; 4:32-35; 6:1-4; 2 Corinthians 8–9; etc.). The ministries extended to those whose disabilities caused them to be marginalized or ignored by others. The church of today continues to recognize and respond to such a challenge. It does so in a variety of ways; examples are the establishment of hospitals, the design of buildings that have no physical barriers restricting access, and distribution of food via pantries.

Peter and John's care for the man in today's text gained the attention of others who were then eager to hear Peter's gospel message. We must conclude that was the ultimate intended result, the most important part, not the healing in and of itself. Physical disabilities last only for this life; spiritual disabilities are eternal. A church's care for those who have physical challenges should make the church attractive to unbelievers who become open to hearing the gospel and can thereby gain eternal life.

B. Some Surprising Results

I once directed a Christmas Eve service at a church by using a traditional "lessons and carols" approach. This meant we listened to readings of Scriptures about the Christmas story, interspersed with songs and hymns about Jesus' birth. One of the members of that church was blind. He had been born without the ability to discern any level of light. We asked him to be our reader that year.

He eagerly and gratefully accepted. More than my merely lining up someone to participate in a ministry, the offer turned out to be an act of service to him; he had never been asked to do any act of service in that church. He and his family arranged to have braille copies of the selected texts. He practiced diligently for several weeks. The result was a magnificent and memorable witness as our ministry to him resulted in his ministry and witness to others.

Another church I served had a man who was severely disabled; he was confined to a wheelchair and was barely able to talk. Knowing him to be a person of great faith, we asked him to be on the schedule to do communion meditations. He too practiced extensively. He was somewhat difficult to understand, so we sometimes had his wife interpret his words to the congregation. Again, our ministry to him resulted in his ministry to others in ways few expected.

What guides you and your church in ministering to persons in your midst with disabilities? If you think you have no one like this, you are not looking hard enough. Don't just feel sorry for them. Find ways for them to serve! You will be surprised at the infectious nature of the bright smile of a greeter who is confined to a wheelchair. You will learn new things when a person with disabilities shares from Scripture. As you remember that such persons need the saving message of the gospel too, you will be surprised at how valuable the ministry *by* such persons is (compare Mark 5:18-20)! And you will be honoring the powerful name of Jesus.

C. Prayer

Heavenly Father, help us to anticipate great results as we minister to those who have unique needs. As we do, remind us that our compassion is not an end in and of itself. Rather, we make our obedience to Jesus complete by sharing the gospel, which leads to the eternal life that is available only through Jesus. We pray in His mighty name. Amen.

D. Thought to Remember
Offer spiritual healing as you meet physical needs.

How to Say It

Gentiles	Jen-tiles.
Messiah	Meh-sigh-uh.
Nazareth	Naz-uh-reth.
Pentecost	Pent-ih-kost.

Involvement Learning

Enhance your lesson with KJV Bible Student *(from your curriculum supplier) and the reproducible activity page (at www.standardlesson.com or in the back of the* KJV Standard Lesson Commentary Deluxe Edition*).*

Into the Lesson

At the front of the classroom, display a cardboard sign with the hand-drawn statement: "Will work for food." As learners arrive, note their reactions to the sign.

Begin the class by asking the following questions for whole-class discussion: 1–When did you last see someone holding a sign like this? 2–How does the sight of someone holding this kind of sign make you feel? 3–How do you usually respond when seeing a person with a sign like this? Acknowledge that some people may not feel comfortable sharing their answers. Encourage learners to respond and react with openness and gentleness throughout the discussion.

Make a transition to the lesson by saying, "Every community includes people who are poor or who experience a physical or mental disability. Today's Scripture describes an interaction between two apostles and a man who had been disabled since birth. Look for principles or examples that can guide our reaction to similar needs today."

Into the Word

Divide the class into three groups: **The Apostles Group, The Man with a Disability Group,** and **The Surrounding Crowd Group.** Have groups read Acts 3:1-11 and answer the following questions in their group regarding the actions of their group's namesake: 1–What did they want? 2–What did they do? 3–What was their reaction to others and God? 4–How might they have felt? After no more than 10 minutes, have a volunteer from each group give their findings.

Distribute a handout (you create) of a chart with these headings across the top: *Scripture, The Healer, The Miracle, The Reaction.* Below the *Scripture* heading, include three references: *Acts 3:1-11*; *Acts 4:1-22;* and *Acts 14:8-13.* Have groups compare these three events by completing the chart. After no more than 10 minutes, write the same chart on the board and ask for volunteers to complete the chart based on their group work.

Then write the following questions on the board for learners to discuss in their groups: 1–What were the major reactions of the people to each miracle? 2–Why do you think these miracles were performed? 3–Did the miracles accomplish their purposes?

Option. Distribute copies of the "Look Me in the Eye!" exercise from the activity page, which you can download. Have learners work together in pairs to complete as indicated.

Into Life

Ask for volunteers to state the perceived physical needs of members of your town or community. Write those needs on the board. Choose three needs and conduct a whole-class brainstorming session to determine how these needs can be addressed in your town or community. Then ask how your congregation could address these needs. (Note: Based on class interest, you may want to follow up with a community advocate or social worker to develop a plan of action for your congregation to advocate for and address the needs of your community.)

Alternative. Distribute copies of the "Signs of the Times" activity from the activity page. Have learners complete the activity in small groups before discussing conclusions with the whole class.

After either activity, distribute an index card and a pen to each learner. Have them write a prayer for the following needs; 1–Clarity for how to best meet the perceived needs of people in the community. 2–The desire to share the gospel with the people of your community. 3–Discernment to know how to do both.

Encourage learners to place these prayers in a visible location where they will be seen throughout the upcoming week.

An Ethiopian Is Baptized

Devotional Reading: Isaiah 60:9-14
Background Scripture: Acts 8:26-40

Acts 8:29-40

29 Then the Spirit said unto Philip, Go near, and join thyself to this chariot.

30 And Philip ran thither to him, and heard him read the prophet Esaias, and said, Understandest thou what thou readest?

31 And he said, How can I, except some man should guide me? And he desired Philip that he would come up and sit with him.

32 The place of the scripture which he read was this, He was led as a sheep to the slaughter; and like a lamb dumb before his shearer, so opened he not his mouth:

33 In his humiliation his judgment was taken away: and who shall declare his generation? for his life is taken from the earth.

34 And the eunuch answered Philip, and said, I pray thee, of whom speaketh the prophet this? of himself, or of some other man?

35 Then Philip opened his mouth, and began at the same scripture, and preached unto him Jesus.

36 And as they went on their way, they came unto a certain water: and the eunuch said, See, here is water; what doth hinder me to be baptized?

37 And Philip said, If thou believest with all thine heart, thou mayest. And he answered and said, I believe that Jesus Christ is the Son of God.

38 And he commanded the chariot to stand still: and they went down both into the water, both Philip and the eunuch; and he baptized him.

39 And when they were come up out of the water, the Spirit of the Lord caught away Philip, that the eunuch saw him no more: and he went on his way rejoicing.

40 But Philip was found at Azotus: and passing through he preached in all the cities, till he came to Caesarea.

Key Text

He commanded the chariot to stand still: and they went down both into the water, both Philip and the eunuch; and he baptized him. —**Acts 8:38**

321

Jesus Calls Us

Unit 3: The Birth of the Church

Lessons 9–13

Lesson Aims

After participating in this lesson, each learner will be able to:

1. Recite from memory the passage from Isaiah studied by Philip and the Ethiopian.

2. Analyze the importance of biblical knowledge for recognizing Christ as the Messiah.

3. List one or more hindrances to recognizing the Spirit's leading in cross-cultural evangelism and suggest ways to overcome them.

Lesson Outline

Introduction

A. Religious Tourism

The desire to travel to places of religious significance is ancient and yet still strong. Historically, we refer to travel to a sacred site as "making a pilgrimage." Many pilgrimage sites dot our world. For Christians these include St. Peter's Basilica in Vatican City, Mount Sinai in Egypt, and the locations around where Jesus is thought to have been crucified.

People often testify that a visit to a holy site had such an impact on them that they were changed forever. They never forget it. Our story today concerns a religious pilgrim who journeyed to Jerusalem to visit the temple some 2,000 years ago. His pilgrimage to Jerusalem may well have been a once-in-a-lifetime journey, taking many weeks. We know little of his lasting impressions of the holy city, but we learn of an encounter with Philip that changed his life forever, and he surely never forgot it.

B. Lesson Context: The Evangelist

A central figure in today's text is a man referred to as "Philip the evangelist, which was one of the seven" in Acts 21:8 (compare 6:3-5). That distinguishes him from "Philip the apostle"—they were not the same person. In addition to today's text, other passages that refer to Philip the evangelist are Acts 8:5-6, 12-13. On the other hand, passages that refer to the apostle of the same name are Matthew 10:3; Mark 3:18; Luke 6:14; John 1:43-46, 48; 6:5-7; 12:21-22; 14:8-9; and Acts 1:13. Regarding the designation *evangelist,* see also Ephesians 4:11 and 2 Timothy 4:5.

It's tempting to refer to this Philip as one of the first deacons of the church, as the noun is used in Philippians 1:1 and 1 Timothy 3:8, 12. But that noun does not appear in Acts 6:1-6, although variations of the Greek word do occur in 6:1 ("ministration"), 6:2 ("serve"), and 6:4 ("ministry").

Like his colleague Stephen, the Philip of today's lesson moved from a ministry of feeding widows (Acts 6:1-5) to preaching the gospel (compare 6:8–8:1a with 8:4-25). Philip was the first to take the gospel to the Samaritans in fulfillment of Jesus' directions in Acts 1:8. This happened as a result of persecution in Jerusalem (8:1b). During a highly productive ministry in Samaria (8:25), an angel of the Lord directed that Philip "go toward the south unto the way that goeth down from Jerusalem unto Gaza, which is desert" (8:26), the location of today's text.

C. Lesson Context: The Ethiopian

Acts 8:27-28 reveals several facts regarding the man whom Philip encountered in today's text.

First, he was from Ethiopia, a kingdom in Africa that is south of Egypt. This kingdom is also known as Cush (see Isaiah 11:11).

Second, he was a eunuch. Though some were born eunuchs or chose this status (Matthew 19:12), the word most commonly refers to a castrated man. Eunuchs were found in royal courts throughout the ancient world (compare 2 Kings 9:32; 20:18; Isaiah 39:7). The Greek historian Xenophon (430–355 BC) wrote that Cyrus the Great (about 600–530 BC; see Ezra 1:1; Isaiah 44:28–45:1; Daniel 1:21) preferred eunuchs in his court because he found them to be more reliable in general and trustworthy around women in particular. The Law of Moses restricted such men from participation in the assembly (Leviticus 21:16-23; Deuteronomy 23:1). One theory is that this individual had purchased a copy of Isaiah because of its promise of inclusion of eunuchs, those who sometimes described themselves as a "dry tree" (Isaiah 56:3-8).

Third, he was a servant to royalty. In particular, he served the queen of the Ethiopians as one having charge over the treasury. He was indeed a person of influence and wealth. He would have had to be wealthy to purchase a copy of Isaiah. The Great Isaiah Scroll, written in Hebrew and discovered among the Dead Sea Scrolls, measures about 9 inches in height and 24 feet in length!

I. Evangelist Running
(Acts 8:29-31)

A. Opportunity to Read (vv. 29-30)

29. Then the Spirit said unto Philip, Go near, and join thyself to this chariot.

The active role of the Holy *Spirit* is characteristic of the book of Acts (see the Lesson Context of lesson 10). Philip might have been intimidated by the splendor of the eunuch's *chariot* and thought any approach would be scorned. God's Spirit, though, knew that the heart of the man in the chariot had been prepared by his reading of Isaiah, and so prompted *Philip* to approach him.

The chariot, for its part, was not a vehicle designed for war, but for travel. It may have been more like what we would call a carriage or wagon, allowing the traveler some comfort while reading. Horses would have been pulling it at a walking pace, allowing Philip to run and catch up to it easily. It is unlikely the man intended to ride this all the way back to Ethiopia, hundreds of miles distant. It is more likely that he had purchased or hired the chariot to get him to a port on the Red Sea; there he would have been able to get a boat ride home.

30a. And Philip ran thither to him, and heard him read the prophet Esaias.

Philip could hear the man reading. This half verse tells us two things about the reading. First, the man was reading aloud even though there was no audience. People in the ancient world did not typically read silently to themselves like we would in a public setting. Reading, even for oneself, was done by voicing the words out loud. This was slower, but allowed for better understanding. Second, the man had a copy of *the prophet Esaias* (Isaiah), which indicates a high level of education to be able to read it and the wealth to purchase such a large scroll.

30b. And said, Understandest thou what thou readest?

How to Say It

Ashdod	*Ash*-dod.
Azotus	Uh-*zo*-tus.
Caesarea Maritima	Sess-uh-*ree*-uh Mar-uh-*tee*-muh.
eunuch	*you*-nick.
Gamaliel	Guh-*may*-lih-ul or Guh-*may*-lee-al.
Herod Antipas	*Hair*-ud An-tih-pus.
Septuagint	Sep-*too*-ih-jent.
Xenophon (Greek)	Zen-uh-*fun*.

Philip, trusting the Holy Spirit, interrupted the man with a simple question. To be able to read the text is one thing; to be able to comprehend it is another!

B. Failure to Understand (v. 31)

31. And he said, How can I, except some man should guide me? And he desired Philip that he would come up and sit with him.

Although the Ethiopian had traveled to Jerusalem to worship (Acts 8:27) and had some knowledge of Scripture, he was no master of the material. His plea for a guide indicated lack of in-depth schooling in interpretation as available in the great rabbinic schools of Jerusalem, such as Paul had with the school of Gamaliel (22:3; compare and contrast 4:13). The man's hunger to understand prompted him to invite a complete stranger into his carriage!

What Do You Think?

To whom do you turn for help with difficult Bible passages?

Digging Deeper

How can you be better prepared to be a faithful guide to others who are struggling with Scripture?

II. Gospel Preaching
(Acts 8:32-35)

A. Prophecy by Isaiah (vv. 32-33)

32. The place of the scripture which he read was this, He was led as a sheep to the slaughter; and like a lamb dumb before his shearer, so opened he not his mouth.

Comparing the differences of Isaiah 53:7-8 with its quotation here, we surmise that the reader had purchased a Greek translation of Isaiah, a version we call the Septuagint. As an official in a royal administration that had international dealings, it is not surprising that the man knew how to read Greek. He would have needed it for his business transactions.

In God's providence, the man's encounter with Philip coincided with his reading a passage from Isaiah that presents one of the clearest prophetic

visions of the coming Messiah! Verses from Isaiah 53 are quoted or alluded to nearly 40 times in the New Testament, making it a key text for understanding Jesus as the Messiah. The part before us is from Isaiah's fourth "Servant Song" (Isaiah 52:13–53:12). That text presents the Messiah as one who would suffer in accordance with God's will rather than serve as a military leader who would fight for the political independence of Israel (as many Jews expected; Acts 1:6).

The imagery of *sheep* and *lamb* depicts the suffering servant as one who would not fight or protest while on the way to death. Luke's account of Jesus' trials presents Him like this silent sheep, especially when He appeared before Herod Antipas (Luke 23:8-9; compare Mark 14:61).

What Do You Think?

What Old Testament passages do you find most helpful when witnessing about Jesus?

Digging Deeper

Given that "all scripture is given by inspiration of God" (2 Timothy 3:16), how do you celebrate the value of the *entire* Old Testament?

33. In his humiliation his judgment was taken away: and who shall declare his generation? for his life is taken from the earth.

The key to the Isaiah passage is the word *humiliation*, a blanket word to describe the horrendous treatment that Jesus would undergo during His trials and crucifixion. Jesus was denied fair *judgment*, or justice. Even though the Roman governor, Pilate, declared that there was no valid charge against Jesus (Luke 23:4), Pilate still consented to the execution. That made it a case of judicial murder (23:-2324). Jesus, as the suffering servant of Isaiah's prophecy, seemingly had no hope of being the father of a future *generation*.

B. Fulfillment by Jesus (vv. 34-35)

34. And the eunuch answered Philip, and said, I pray thee, of whom speaketh the prophet this? of himself, or of some other man?

In attempting to answer his own question, *the*

eunuch reasoned that Isaiah must be talking about a specific and identifiable person. In that light, *the prophet* may have been speaking *of himself.* That is possible, given that Isaiah sometimes spoke of his own experiences (compare Isaiah 6). But the Ethiopian probably realized that the passage under consideration did not quite fit the prophet's situation. Therefore he likely suspected *some other man* to be in view. His careful reading of Scripture brought him to the place where he was open to hearing about Jesus.

35. Then Philip opened his mouth, and began at the same scripture, and preached unto him Jesus.

The very verses that had puzzled the reader served as the springboard to preaching Jesus. We easily imagine *Philip* using other verses in this passage as part of that presentation—texts such as references to the Messiah as "a man of sorrows" (Isaiah 53:3), and one who has "borne our griefs" (53:4), as well as Isaiah's statement that God intended to "make his soul an offering for sin" (53:10).

The violence against the Messiah as predicted by Isaiah was a matter of historical record by the time of Philip's preaching. It is possible that the Ethiopian, as a recent visitor to Jerusalem, had heard some of these facts. But there is more to preaching Jesus than telling the story of the Good Friday crucifixion. We must say also that Jesus has risen from the dead, as Peter did in Acts 2:32, 36; that Philip did so as well is a safe assumption.

> **What Do You Think?**
> How can you prepare yourself to share Jesus with people who have some, if incomplete, knowledge of Him already?
>
> **Digging Deeper**
> What role does the Holy Spirit play in helping you know what to say (consult Matthew 10:18-20)?

A Ride to Remember

My first car was a 1966 Chevy Malibu, white with a black vinyl top. It looked sharp, but the windshield leaked. My then-future wife and I shared our first kiss in my second car—a rust-colored, rust-covered Plymouth Satellite. I proposed to her in that car.

Life-changing conversations can happen while in carriages, whether powered by engines measured in horsepower or by actual horses. Just ask the Ethiopian official! He and Philip discussed the Scriptures in depth. They talked about Jesus. As a result of their conversation, the Ethiopian believed and was baptized—one life changed for eternity. Or was it more than one life changed, as the Ethiopian returned home to spread this message?

The important issue of eternal destinies should lead us to examine what we most tend to talk about, whether in a traveling context or otherwise. Are you more able and willing to talk about your favorite sports team or about Jesus' death, burial, and resurrection? —D. F.

III. Water Baptizing
(Acts 8:36-40)
A. Believing (vv. 36-38)

36. And as they went on their way, they came unto a certain water: and the eunuch said, See, here is water; what doth hinder me to be baptized?

The assumption just mentioned, that Philip's presentation of the gospel included things like Peter's address in Acts 2, is supported here. *The eunuch* would not have inquired about what hindered him *to be baptized* had Philip not mentioned baptism before the carriage *came unto a certain water.* As with Peter on the Day of Pentecost, the story of Jesus' death and resurrection leads to a call for belief in Him (see next verse below), repentance from sins, and the cleansing of sins in baptism. The believer can rest assured that his or her sins are forgiven and that the presence of the Holy Spirit will be given (Acts 2:38; Titus 3:5).

37. And Philip said, If thou believest with all thine heart, thou mayest. And he answered and said, I believe that Jesus Christ is the Son of God.

Philip's response has a little "not so fast, my friend" to it. One thing had to be certain: that the man sincerely believed *that Jesus Christ is the*

Son of God (compare Matthew 16:16). This was indeed the man's confession of faith. It meant he acknowledged Jesus of Nazareth to be the Messiah, which is the Hebrew word rendered "Christ" in the Greek language (see John 1:41; 4:25); in English both words mean "anointed one." That is the irreducible content of the Christian faith, the belief that Jesus was God in the flesh, and that His atoning death was the proper mission of the Messiah as prophesied by Isaiah.

> ### What Do You Think?
> What concerns do you feel if someone makes a seemingly hasty decision to follow Jesus?
>
> ### Digging Deeper
> How does your answer shift, based on what you know of the person's background?

38. And he commanded the chariot to stand still: and they went down both into the water, both Philip and the eunuch; and he baptized him.

Only after *Philip* was assured of the Ethiopian's faith did he agree to baptize him. There is no mention of repentance, but we assume the man's familiarity with Scripture extended to knowledge that repentance precedes forgiveness (example: Jeremiah 36:3). Baptism is of no value without belief and repentance. An unrepentant unbeliever who is baptized is no more than a "wet sinner."

Although churches have different understandings of valid modes of baptism today, we see in the text before us the earliest mode of the baptismal action and one that is accepted by all churches even now: Philip and the man go down *into the water*. The precursors of Christian baptism, which were the ceremonial washings by the Jews of the day (see John 2:6), likewise were full-body experiences.

B. Rejoicing (vv. 39-40)

39. And when they were come up out of the water, the Spirit of the Lord caught away Philip, that the eunuch saw him no more: and he went on his way rejoicing.

The end of the story is surprising: *Philip* disappeared and *the eunuch saw him no more*. Rather than be terrified or regretful, the eunuch continued his journey home in a spirit of *rejoicing*. It is not illegitimate to attribute this to the Holy Spirit in his life, for the connection between the Spirit and joy is evident in Luke's books (Luke 10:21; Acts 13:52).

The Humbling Beauty of Baptism

I was the guest speaker at a retreat in Australia. During our recreation time the folks there wanted to play American-style football. They were not very familiar with the sport, and because I was from the United States, they considered me the expert. They even asked me to play quarterback! On the football field that day, I was large and in charge.

Later, though, the group decided to play cricket. And since I had never played that game, I didn't know what to do. Now I had to humble myself, admit my ignorance, display my awkwardness, and learn from the youngsters. I was no longer in charge.

A believer's baptism is both beautiful and humbling. Baptism requires humble surrender to the authority of Jesus Christ as one puts aside power, pride, and pretense and allows his or her body to be submerged in water by another.

If you haven't been baptized, when will you "stop the chariot" and submit to this step? If you have been baptized, does the memory of this beautiful event cause you to go on your way rejoicing even years or decades later?

—D. F.

> ### What Do You Think?
> How would you explain the significance of baptism to someone who wants to commit to following Jesus?
>
> ### Digging Deeper
> What other Scriptures would you reference to help this person better understand the importance of baptism?

40. But Philip was found at Azotus: and passing through he preached in all the cities, till he came to Caesarea.

Azotus was the Greek name of the ancient city

of Ashdod, located on the Mediterranean coastline of Israel. From there, Philip made a coastal tour all the way north *to Caesarea* Maritima, a trip of about 50 miles. When we next read of *Philip* (in Acts 21:8), he is in Caesarea. That was about 20 years later, so he may have made it his permanent residence after his ministry to the Ethiopian.

Conclusion

A. The Wonder of Fulfilled Prophecy

Many years ago, I heard Mildred Welshimer Phillips speak of her father, P. H. Welshimer. (His first name was Pearl, which explains the use of initials.) In the first decades of the twentieth century, Welshimer was the minister of the First Christian Church of Canton, Ohio. At its height, this congregation was often recognized as the largest church in the world, with a Sunday school attendance of 6,000 each Sunday.

One of Welshimer's more audacious public acts was to stage a debate with Clarence Darrow, the attorney who had won national recognition as the defender of evolution in the so-called Scopes Monkey Trial. Darrow was seen as the spokesman of a new kind of person in America, a public figure who was openly agnostic/atheist and who saw the Bible as nonsense, the church as a medieval relic, and Christian faith as preposterous.

The debate was inconclusive, as most of these sorts of things are, with Darrow rarely engaging the arguments of Welshimer. But, remarkably, the two became friendly after it was over. Darrow confessed that Welshimer presented one argument about the Bible that gave him pause: its record of prophecy and fulfillment.

Welshimer was doing nothing more and nothing less than what Philip did with the Ethiopian. The New Testament is loaded with quotations from the Old Testament that point to Jesus. This is not coincidental or accidental. The reader of Matthew cannot help but notice that he punctuates many of his stories of Jesus with the observation that this happened to fulfill Scripture (example: Matthew 1:22).

Presenting Jesus as the fulfillment of prophecy requires a high level of Bible knowledge. But as Welshimer's encounter with Darrow shows, there are opportunities to make gospel claims that are best framed by presenting Jesus as the fulfillment of prophecy. When Isaiah 53 is read in light of the events of Jesus' life, we should be struck by the remarkable fact that there are more than seven centuries between the two records! Those who have an inclination for deep, comprehensive knowledge of Scripture and its connections may be given opportunities to witness to unbelievers today in some manner like the Holy Spirit gave to Philip 2,000 years ago. Every generation of Christians must raise up those who are trained in understanding the Bible—their "Philips"—so they can explain it effectively and accurately to others.

B. Prayer

Our Father, You planned for Jesus to come, teach, heal, and to go to the cross for our salvation. You planned to raise Him from the dead. You even orchestrated the meeting of Philip with one who was eager to hear. We welcome Your plans that include using us as ones who are ready to preach Jesus. We pray in His name as we prepare ourselves. Amen.

C. Thought to Remember

Jesus fulfills prophecies in ways that cannot be explained—except as the providence of God.

Visual for Lesson 12. *While discussing verse 38, have learners spend one minute silently considering what faithful step they are putting off and why.*

Involvement Learning

Enhance your lesson with KJV Bible Student *(from your curriculum supplier) and the reproducible activity page (at www.standardlesson.com or in the back of the* KJV Standard Lesson Commentary Deluxe Edition*).*

Into the Lesson

Divide learners into groups of three. Ask group members to share a story about someone coming to their door unexpectedly. For example, they might remember a door-to-door salesman offering a household service, or a member of a religious group who appeared at their doorstep. What was their response to the unexpected visitor? Allow five minutes for group discussion before asking volunteers to share with the whole class.

Alternative. Distribute copies of the "Other Old Testament Prophecies" exercise from the activity page, which you can download. Have learners complete it individually (in a minute or less) before discussing conclusions in small groups.

Say, "Today we will consider an unexpected visit by a believer in Jesus to someone who did not understand the gospel."

Into the Word

Distribute handouts (you create) with the following questions: 1–Who was Philip? 2–Who was the eunuch? 3–What are Isaiah's "Servant Songs"? Choose one of these ways for working through these questions:

Mini lecture. Early in the week, recruit three class members to each speak for three minutes about one of the questions. Ask class members to jot notes on the handout as the volunteers share.

Research. Divide the class into small groups to use online or printed Bible-study resources to answer the same questions. After six to eight minutes, they should report to the whole group.

Then have today's text read aloud two times as class members listen for answers to these three questions: 4–What was the Holy Spirit's role in this conversion? 5–What did Philip learn from this experience? 6–What do we learn about baptism in this account?

Option. Distribute copies of the "One of Several Baptisms" activity from the activity page.

Have groups work together to complete as indicated before discussing their answer to the question posed there.

Ask learners to again look at Acts 8:32-33 from today's text and compare them with Isaiah 53:7-8. Discuss: 1–How did the Holy Spirit lead Philip to share about the passage? 2–How would you use Isaiah 53:7-8 to talk to someone about Jesus today? If time allows, work together as a class to memorize Isaiah 53:7-8. Start by repeating the verses, a phrase at a time, and pausing after each phrase to allow the whole class to repeat.

Into Life

Write on the board *Socially or Economically / Religiously / Ethnically* as the headers of three columns. Then write *Philip and the man of Ethiopia / Today* as two designations down the left side, to create two rows. Conduct a whole-class brainstorming session to fill out the first row of the chart. Talk about which differences created the biggest difficulty for Philip and the Ethiopian man to overcome, as well as who had to overcome that difficulty.

Then ask learners to name ways each of these barriers still keeps people from sharing the gospel today; record these in the second row of the chart. As a class, answer: 1–Which of these is the greatest impediment in our country? 2–Which is a bigger problem in our goal for worldwide evangelism?"

Distribute index cards and pencils. Give the class one minute of silence to think of someone they know who needs to hear the gospel. Have learners write that name on their cards along with a prayer for the Holy Spirit to overcome impediments that keep them from sharing about Jesus.

Close with prayers for the Holy Spirit to work in class members' lives to share the good news of Jesus with those who still need to hear it today.

Saul of Tarsus

Devotional Reading: Philippians 3:1-14
Background Scripture: Acts 9:1-31

Acts 9:9-17

9 And he was three days without sight, and neither did eat nor drink.

10 And there was a certain disciple at Damascus, named Ananias; and to him said the Lord in a vision, Ananias. And he said, Behold, I am here, Lord.

11 And the Lord said unto him, Arise, and go into the street which is called Straight, and enquire in the house of Judas for one called Saul, of Tarsus: for, behold, he prayeth,

12 And hath seen in a vision a man named Ananias coming in, and putting his hand on him, that he might receive his sight.

13 Then Ananias answered, Lord, I have heard by many of this man, how much evil he hath done to thy saints at Jerusalem:

14 And here he hath authority from the chief priests to bind all that call on thy name.

15 But the Lord said unto him, Go thy way: for he is a chosen vessel unto me, to bear my name before the Gentiles, and kings, and the children of Israel:

16 For I will shew him how great things he must suffer for my name's sake.

17 And Ananias went his way, and entered into the house; and putting his hands on him said, Brother Saul, the Lord, even Jesus, that appeared unto thee in the way as thou camest, hath sent me, that thou mightest receive thy sight, and be filled with the Holy Ghost.

Key Text

Ananias went his way, and entered into the house; and putting his hands on him said, Brother Saul, the Lord, even Jesus, that appeared unto thee in the way as thou camest, hath sent me, that thou mightest receive thy sight, and be filled with the Holy Ghost. —**Acts 9:17**

Jesus
Calls Us

Unit 3: The Birth of the Church
Lessons 9–13

Lesson Aims

After participating in this lesson, each learner will be able to:

1. Summarize Ananias's objection and the Lord's response.

2. Explain the significance of blindness as a possible spiritual metaphor.

3. Cultivate an attitude that seeks clearer spiritual sight.

Lesson Outline

Introduction
A. "I Once Was Blind . . ."

John Newton was an eighteenth-century Englishman who served as captain for ships that transported captured Africans to North America as slaves. The horrendous nature of that occupation included not only the acceptance of slavery but also the imposition of the inhuman conditions on the ships. To do this, one needed a callous soul.

In 1748, Newton was in a terrifying storm in a ship off the coast of Ireland. Fearing for his life, he began praying in a way that led to his conversion to Christ, eventually becoming a minister in 1764. He began writing about his faith, and in 1772 he published the words to "Amazing Grace," a semi-autobiographical account of how God had "saved a wretch like me."

One of the most memorable lines in the hymn is "[I] was blind, but now I see." While this phrase is drawn from the story of Jesus' healing of the blind man in John 9:25, it also fits the story of Saul in Damascus.

B. Lesson Context: Damascus

Even in Paul's day, Damascus was an ancient city, having been inhabited for at least 3,000 years (see Genesis 14:15). It figures prominently in Old Testament narratives, mentioned there 44 times in Hebrew. It lies about 150 miles north of Jerusalem.

As for the New Testament era, the book of Acts mentions the city of Damascus 13 times. It was a city of many ethnicities. It had become part of the Greek world after the conquest by the forces of Alexander the Great (356–323 BC). Under later Roman influence, Damascus was designated as one of the cities of the Decapolis, meaning "10 cities" (see Matthew 4:25; Mark 5:20; 7:31). Jesus performed miracles near those cities (Matthew 8:28-33; Mark 5:1-17; 7:31-37), although not in Damascus itself. Greco-Roman ruins are extant in Damascus today. These include a section of an impressive boulevard that is likely "the street which is called Straight" of Acts 9:11.

Damascus had many Jewish residents and synagogues in the first century AD. The historian

Josephus (AD 37–100) records that thousands of Jews were killed by the Romans in Damascus during the first Jewish Revolt (about AD 66). This testifies to a large presence with many houses of worship in that city. It is no wonder that Saul would travel there, expecting to find synagogues where Jews had embraced Christianity.

We are not told how or when the gospel message reached Damascus. A reasonable speculation is that it occurred as a result of the Day of Pentecost, as people returned home (see Acts 2:5-11). By the time of today's lesson, at least a couple of years had passed since that event, the stoning of Stephen, and the beginning of Saul's persecution. Acts 8:1 records that the Jerusalem church was scattered at that time, although only the destinations of Judaea and Samaria are mentioned there.

C. Lesson Context: Saul

We first meet Saul—later known as Paul, beginning in Acts 13:9—when he acted as a witness to the stoning of Stephen in Acts 7:58; 8:1 (see also 22:20). He is presented elsewhere as an ambitious young man who was building a career in the rabbinic tradition of Jerusalem and as a trusted servant of the temple officials and religious leaders (Galatians 1:14; Philippians 3:4-6). He could never have been a priest, because he was from the tribe of Benjamin rather than the priestly tribe of Levi (see Deuteronomy 18:1; Hebrews 7:5; etc.). But he could have become one of the greatest of the Pharisees, like his teacher Gamaliel (Acts 5:34; 22:3).

The climb up this career ladder accelerated when Saul oversaw a direct assault on the believers in Jerusalem, where he searched for them house to house and threw into prison those he found (Acts 8:3; 26:10). He apparently did effective work at that, for the high priest agreed to authorize him to go to Damascus to find Christians and bring them back to Jerusalem for trial and punishment (9:1-2; 22:19; 26:9-11). His ambitious trip to Damascus was the occasion of the resurrected Jesus appearing to Saul and asking, "Why persecutest thou me?" (9:4).

This Damascus Road story is told three times in Acts: once as narrated by author Luke (Acts 9:1-19) and twice as told by Saul/Paul himself (22:3-16; 26:9-18). As today's text opens, Saul had been struck blind by the Lord on that road. Subsequently, Saul was led by the hand into the city (9:1-8).

I. Saul's Waiting
(Acts 9:9-12)
A. Days of Fasting (v. 9)

9. And he was three days without sight, and neither did eat nor drink.

We certainly can imagine what Saul was thinking for these *three days without sight,* food, or *drink*! Acts 9:11 (below) fills this in, but only in general terms.

> **What Do You Think?**
> Do you practice fasting as a spiritual discipline? Why or why not?
>
> **Digging Deeper**
> What value do you experience or can you imagine from incorporating fasts into your spiritual walk?

B. Disciple of Damascus (v. 10)

10a. And there was a certain disciple at Damascus, named Ananias.

Luke, the author of the Gospel of Luke and the book of Acts, uses the word *disciple* dozens of times in his two works. In Luke's Gospel, a disciple is a dedicated student of Jesus the teacher. In Acts, a disciple is a committed follower of the risen Lord. In that regard, *Ananias* may be much like many Christians today who serve the Lord faithfully in relative anonymity.

We gain a bit more information about this *certain disciple* in Acts 22:12. There Paul (formerly the Saul of today's lesson) described Ananias as "a devout man according to the law, having a good report of all the Jews which dwelt there." We take care, of course, not to confuse this Ananias with two others by the same name in Acts 5:1 and 24:1.

Regarding the city of *Damascus,* see Lesson Context: Damascus, above.

10b. And to him said the Lord in a vision, Ananias. And he said, Behold, I am here, Lord.

How surprised *Ananias* must have been to experience *a vision* in which *the Lord* communicated with him personally! The word *vision* implies a supernatural origin. It involves seeing things not normally seen, but it may also consist of hearing things not normally heard, as in the calling of Samuel (1 Samuel 3:1-14). The same may be the case here. But unlike the calling of young Samuel, Ananias recognized what was happening immediately. So he answered *Behold, I am here, Lord.*

Responsive? Hiding? Fleeing?

When my youngest was a teenager, he would hide whenever some chore needed to be done. It didn't matter if it was cleaning his room, doing the dishes, or pulling weeds—I would call his name and get cricket chirps in return. My oldest son, however, was quite the opposite. More often than not, whenever I called his name, he would answer. And even though he really didn't want to do those chores, he would come running when I called him. It was responsiveness, plain and simple.

The Scriptures describe varying responses to calls from the Lord. The responses recorded in Exodus 4:13; Judges 6:15; 1 Samuel 10:21-22; Isaiah 6:8; Jeremiah 1:6; Jonah 1:3; Matthew 1:24; 2:14; Luke 1:34, 38, 46-55; and Acts 10:7-8 are quite instructive when compared and contrasted in their respective contexts. The Scriptures also tell of individuals who claimed to be obeying a call from the Lord when no such call existed; see Numbers 12:2; Jeremiah 14:14-16; 23:25-26; and Ezekiel 13 as examples.

Let's make clear at this point that there are two categories of callings by the Lord. First, there are the high-profile callings of specific individuals to specific tasks. Then there are the general callings given to all Christians; Matthew 28:18-20 and John 14:15 are examples. My child who hid from either kind of "calling" in a family-household sense always ended up with unwanted consequences for doing so. Similarly, it's easier (and better) in the long run to obey the Lord than it is to disobey (see Matthew 11:30).

Before concerning yourself with any specific calling you may be sensing from the Lord, how responsive are you to the general callings all Christians receive?

—P. M.

C. Directive by the Lord (vv. 11-12)

11a. And the Lord said unto him.

The Lord may refer to God in the general sense that does not distinguish among members of the Trinity. In this case, however, it refers to the risen Jesus in particular, as Acts 9:17b (below) makes clear.

11b. Arise, and go into the street which is called Straight, and enquire in the house of Judas for one called Saul, of Tarsus: for, behold, he prayeth.

The instructions are detailed—there can be no doubt regarding where and to whom Ananias is to go. *The street which is called Straight* is the grand boulevard of Damascus. This may indicate that this particular *Judas*, the homeowner, is a well-connected person of some wealth. His may have been the sort of place with whom a person authorized by the high priest for his task (like *Saul* was; Acts 9:1-2) might find lodging.

Saul's hometown of *Tarsus* was a well-known city about 250 miles north-northwest of Damascus and 355 miles due north of Jerusalem (straight line). Tarsus became the capital city for the Roman province of Cilicia in AD 72 (about 40 years after the events under consideration). Saul (as Paul) would later mention his civic pride in his hometown (Acts 21:39).

12. And hath seen in a vision a man named Ananias coming in, and putting his hand on him, that he might receive his sight.

With this information, *Ananias* learned he was

not the only one to have received *a vision*. Saul himself had preceded Ananias in that regard, even though Saul had been blinded (Acts 9:8-9). Ananias learned something else as well: he was to be God's chosen instrument for Saul to *receive his sight* back. The picture is remarkable: powerful Saul, a Roman "citizen of no mean city" (21:39; compare 22:26-29), in the house of wealthy Judas, praying and blind.

The outcome determined by the Lord could have been accomplished easily by the Lord himself in some other way. But He chose instead to work through a human as He often did—and still does (compare and contrast Ezekiel 22:30).

What Do You Think?
When have you been part of God's answer to someone else's prayers?

Digging Deeper
What texts suggest that God frequently desires to work through His people and not more supernatural interventions?

II. Ananias's Objection
(Acts 9:13-16)
A. Fear of Saul (vv. 13-14)

13-14. Then Ananias answered, Lord, I have heard by many of this man, how much evil he hath done to thy saints at Jerusalem: and here he hath authority from the chief priests to bind all that call on thy name.

Saul's reputation had preceded him—*Ananias* knew all about the notorious persecutor of the church and his plans. And Ananias was exactly the type of person Saul had come to arrest and haul back to *Jerusalem*.

We note in passing that Ananias referred to Jesus' disciples as *thy saints* and *all that call on thy name* rather than "Christians" at this point in time; the latter designation was not to become reality until Acts 11:26. Ironically, the designation *saints* eventually became a favorite of Saul's (when better known as Paul) when referring to Christians in his letters (see Romans 1:7; 1 Corinthians 1:2; Ephesians 1:1).

Acts 22:19 and 26:9-11 shed light on what *to bind all that call on thy name* entailed. Saul entered synagogues to find believers in Jesus in order to have them beaten, imprisoned, and/or put to death. So zealous was Saul that he went out of his way to punish this new and (to his prior way of thinking) heretical sect.

What Do You Think?
When have you acted timidly because of your knowledge of the risk involved in acting boldly?

Digging Deeper
What fears still hold you back from bold obedience to God?

B. Plans for Saul (vv. 15-16)

15. But the Lord said unto him, Go thy way: for he is a chosen vessel unto me, to bear my name before the Gentiles, and kings, and the children of Israel.

The Lord could have chosen to discipline Ananias for questioning the directive given to him. Instead, the Lord revealed part of His plans for Saul. Henceforth, Saul was to be *a chosen vessel unto* the Lord rather than a vessel of the religious authorities in Jerusalem. That reassignment would involve being the apostle to *the Gentiles* (see Acts 13:46; 14:27; 18:6; 22:21; Romans 11:13; 15:16; Galatians 1:16; 2:8; Ephesians 3:8), including their *kings* (Acts 25:13–26:23). The book of Acts ends with Paul's awaiting his hearing before the Roman emperor himself.

Even so, the regular practice of Saul (as Paul) would also be to try to convince his fellow Jews—*the children of Israel*—that Jesus was their promised Messiah (example: Acts 13:14-45). Indeed, preaching Jesus to fellow Jews would be his first order of business wherever Saul went (13:46-48; 18:5-6). By contrast, the task of the apostle Peter was something of a mirror image of that practice: Peter was the designated apostle to the Jews (Galatians 2:8-9), although he witnessed also to Gentiles (Acts 10:1–11:18).

As if receiving a vision from the Lord wasn't enough of a shock to Ananias in and of itself, the revealed mission to the Gentiles was probably

Visual for Lesson 13. *Ask volunteers to share their experience of receiving the Spirit and spiritual sight. In what ways is the experience ongoing?*

incomprehensible to him (compare Acts 11:18). Even more so was the predicted mission to kings, who were all Gentiles.

Heads Up!

One of our favorite pastimes when we were young was tossing a Frisbee while at the beach. The sea breeze was often strong enough to carry the plastic disc far afield from its intended destination. And there were usually so many people at the beach that the disc would sooner or later strike an unsuspecting beachgoer. It was not unusual to hear "Heads up!" shouted throughout the game. Some bystanders would hear and react appropriately. Others would turn around in confusion and look for the source of the warning first—and such bystanders would be the ones to experience an unwanted Frisbee to the head!

Surely Ananias didn't presume that the Lord lacked knowledge about Saul! But providentially, the Lord did not see fit to "throw a Frisbee" at Ananias's head. Instead, the Lord patiently provided an explanation that should have been unnecessary for Ananias's obedience.

The same may not be the case regarding you or me the next time we hesitate to obey. When God calls on you, will your obedience depend on receiving an answer you deem satisfactory, or will you obey without question? Remember: Ananias could have experienced the Lord's "Frisbee" to his head as did Zacharias in Luke 1:18-20. —P. M.

16. For I will shew him how great things he must suffer for my name's sake.

We continue to be in awe of God's revealing His plans for Saul to Ananias, a revelation that God was certainly not obligated to provide. The fulfillment of the prediction in this verse is seen in 2 Corinthians 6:3-10; 11:23-29; and elsewhere. Paul's suffering culminated in his execution (see 2 Timothy 4:6-7).

III. The Lord's Healing
(Acts 9:17)
A. Obedience (v. 17a)

17a. And Ananias went his way, and entered into the house; and putting his hands on him said.

The actions of *Ananias* in this half verse harmonize with actions required of him in Acts 9:11b, considered above.

B. Facts (v. 17b)

17b. Brother Saul, the Lord, even Jesus, that appeared unto thee in the way as thou camest, hath sent me, that thou mightest receive thy sight, and be filled with the Holy Ghost.

This half verse ties things together and clarifies. *The Lord* of the visions had been none other than *Jesus* himself. It was none other than He who had *appeared* to *Saul* on the road (compare Acts 9:5; 22:8; 26:15) and who had spoken to Ananias in Damascus.

As Saul was just about to *receive* back his *sight*, Ananias announced something we have not yet read about in the visions from the Lord: Saul was to *be filled with the Holy Ghost.* This phrase occurs eight times in the New Testament, all in the writings of Luke. Persons involved in the other seven cases are John the Baptist (Luke 1:15), his mother and father (1:41, 67), the apostles on the Day of Pentecost (Acts 2:4), Peter before the Sanhedrin (4:8), a gathering of believers (4:31), and Saul himself (13:9).

Saul's first action after having his sight restored was to be baptized, even before he broke his three-day fast from food (see Acts 9:18-19). He was strengthened in his soul and in his body.

Later texts tell us that others sought to kill Saul, even enlisting the support of the city's governor to arrest him (see 2 Corinthians 11:32). Instead, Saul's life was saved in a surprising way (see Acts 9:25; 2 Corinthians 11:33).

Regarding our current lesson, that final case is particularly interesting for at least two reasons. First, it was the time when Saul began to be referred to as Paul. Second, it is ironic in that the one who had been struck blind as an enemy of Jesus became the instrument by which a "child of the devil" and an "enemy of all righteousness" (Acts 13:10) was himself struck blind (13:11).

Conclusion

A. Conversion, Call, or Both?

The story of Saul's experience on the way to Damascus is usually portrayed as his "conversion." That is a valid description in that the episode shows a life transformed from an unbeliever into a believer, one who was baptized and received the Holy Spirit. But was that Luke's intent in documenting this story? Is Saul's conversion experience, with its spectacular visions and drama, intended to be some sort of model or expectation for conversions today?

Certainly many conversions over the centuries have been dramatically sudden and powerful. I have heard the stories, and so have you. But I have never heard of an unbeliever being called in a vision to the sort of mission to which Saul was called. He was a young man (Acts 7:58) whom Jesus simply had to have as His servant. Jesus did not have to stir up passion in Saul; he was already passionate. Jesus did not have to infuse Saul with a great knowledge of Scripture; he already had it. Jesus did not have to put an obedient spirit in Saul; he already had one. Unbeknownst to Saul, he had been preparing his whole life to be redirected and used by Jesus!

Jesus can still redirect a person's life while using all that person's life experiences in kingdom service. We should be on the lookout for such people —people whose life experiences, education, etc., could result in their being massively influential in service to the risen Lord! Which would be easier:

(1) to create zeal in an apathetic person or (2) to take an already zealous person and redirect that zeal for Christ? Think of people you know or have heard about whose lives were transformed by the gospel and redirected to do great things for Christ. How does your own story mesh with theirs? How might it?

> **What Do You Think?**
> What experiences illustrate the Holy Spirit's bringing you from spiritual blindness to sight?
>
> **Digging Deeper**
> What practices help you be aware of times when the Holy Spirit is at work further clarifying your vision?

B. Prayer

Heavenly Father, it is sobering to think how well You know us. Thank You for the inspiring stories of Your zealous ones! Empower and guide us to have similar zeal in doing great things for You. We pray in the name of Jesus Christ. Amen.

C. Thought to Remember

Christ calls us not only *to* Him
but also *for* Him.

How to Say It

Ananias	An-uh-*nye*-us.
Cilicia	Sih-*lish*-i-uh.
Damascus	Duh-*mass*-kus.
Decapolis	Dee-*cap*-uh-lis.
Gamaliel	Guh-*may*-lih-ul or Guh-*may*-lee-al.
Josephus	Jo-*see*-fus.
Judaea	Joo-*dee*-uh.
Levi	*Lee*-vye.
Pharisees	*Fair*-ih-seez.
Pentecost	*Pent*-ih-kost.
rabbinic	ruh-*bin*-ihk.
Sanhedrin	*San*-huh-drun or San-*heed*-run.
Tarsus	*Tar*-sus.
Zacharias	Zack-uh-*rye*-us.

Involvement Learning

Enhance your lesson with KJV Bible Student *(from your curriculum supplier) and the reproducible activity page (at www.standardlesson.com or in the back of the* KJV Standard Lesson Commentary Deluxe Edition*).*

Into the Lesson

Begin your session by using one of these ideas to explore the concept of blindness.

What is blindness? Prepare (or ask a class member to prepare) a brief presentation on blindness. How is blindness defined? What causes blindness? How many people live with blindness in your country? in the world? Can blindness be reversed? After your report, ask class members to share any experiences they have had with blindness in their family or among their acquaintances.

Blindman's buff. Play this updated version of the old game. Blindfold a volunteer to be "It." Ask the rest of the class to sit in a circle with It sitting in the middle. Everyone sitting in the circle changes places. It points to a participant who says, "Great things." It guesses who the participant is. If correct, that person becomes It. After a couple of rounds, encourage those who were It to share how they tried to figure out who talked.

After either activity, lead to Bible study by saying, "Blindness in everyday life is a serious problem. Today we'll read the story of one man who was blinded by God and another who was initially blind to God's plan and purpose. In both cases their blindness was reversed."

Into the Word

Divide the class into groups of four to six. Distribute a handout (you create) with the following instructions:

1–Read Acts 9:1-9. Consider Saul's dramatic experience. What do you imagine he was thinking about during the three days reported in verse 9?

2–Read Acts 9:10-12. What do we learn about Ananias? What can we surmise about the place where Saul was staying? Put yourself in the place of Ananias. What would you tell someone about what you just experienced?

3–Read Acts 9:13-14. What is Ananias's objection? How does his initial questioning compare with other examples of Bible heroes initially hesitant to answer God's call?

4–Read Acts 9:15-16. Do you believe Ananias was convinced by the Lord's answer? What about Saul's prophesied future is appealing? What is frightening?

5–Read Acts 9:17. What shows that Ananias believed what God had told him? How was Saul's blindness cured? How was Ananias also "healed of blindness"?

Read through today's text, stopping after each verse or group of verses indicated on the handout. Give two or three minutes for groups to answer each set of questions. Then move to the next verse(s) and questions, following this pattern until the class has worked through the text.

Option 1. To extend the above study, distribute copies of the "Before and After" exercise, which you can download. Have groups work to complete as indicated.

Option 2. Distribute copies of the "Called to Suffering" exercise from the activity page. Have small groups complete as indicated before sharing conclusions with the whole class.

Allow a few minutes for groups to share specific learnings about Saul with the whole class.

Into Life

Write the following jumbled sentence on the board: but blind now see was I once I.

The correct sentence is, "I once was blind but now I see." Divide the class into pairs to discuss how this statement applies to their own faith journeys. After several minutes, have the pairs give thanks for sight that has been received and petition the Lord for awareness of their blindspots and need for further vision correction. Ask volunteers to share any praises or petitions that come up in this exercise, which they would like the whole class to pray for in the upcoming week.

Summer 2023
King James Version

The Righteous
Reign of God

Special Features

Lessons

Unit 1: The Prophets Proclaim God's Power

Unit 2: Jesus Envisions the Kingdom

Unit 3: God's Eternal Reign

Quarterly Quiz

Use these questions as a pretest or as a review. The answers are on page iv of This Quarter in the Word.

Lesson 1

1. The feet that bring good tidings are called what? (beautiful, joyous, holy) *Isaiah 52:7*

2. Jerusalem is commanded to sing to God even though He has not yet redeemed it. T/F. *Isaiah 52:9*

Lesson 2

1. God promises to create new heavens and a new _____. *Isaiah 65:17*

2. The lion and the lamb will "feed together" on God's holy mountain. T/F. *Isaiah 65:25*

Lesson 3

1. The Lord promised that David would serve in what role for the unified people? (prophet, priest, king) *Ezekiel 37:24*

2. The Lord's covenant of peace will be an "_____ covenant." *Ezekiel 37:26*

Lesson 4

1. Zion can rejoice because the Lord has taken away _____. *Zephaniah 3:15*

2. The Lord will show joy by doing what? (singing, dancing, both) *Zephaniah 3:17*

Lesson 5

1. By way of the blood of the covenant, God will free prisoners from the pit. T/F. *Zechariah 9:11*

2. The saved people of God will be like the _____ of a crown. *Zechariah 9:16*

Lesson 6

1. The people asked if Jesus was the son of whom? (Joseph, Abraham, David) *Matthew 12:23*

2. The Pharisees said that Jesus worked by way of the power of Beelzebub. T/F. *Matthew 12:24*

Lesson 7

1. The seeds that fell among thorns were scorched by the sun. T/F. *Matthew 13:7*

2. The seeds that fell on good ground all produced the same yield of crop. T/F. *Matthew 13:23*

Lesson 8

1. The harvest represents the end of the _____. *Matthew 13:39*

2. The righteous will shine like "the _____ in the kingdom of their Father." *Matthew 13:43*

Lesson 9

1. The kingdom of Heaven is like a treasure found in a city market. T/F. *Matthew 13:44*

2. Who will come forth at the end of the world to separate the wicked and the just? (angels, prophets, Abraham) *Matthew 13:49*

Lesson 10

1. The entire law is _____ in the command to love your neighbor as yourself. *Galatians 5:14*

2. Those people who belong to Christ have done what to the flesh? (buried it, burned it, crucified it). *Galatians 5:24*

Lesson 11

1. The Lord promises that every knee will bow. T/F. *Romans 14:11*

2. Which of these is not listed as a matter of the kingdom of God? (righteousness, respectability, joy, peace) *Romans 14:17*

Lesson 12

1. The Lord "will bring to _____" things that are hidden in darkness. *1 Corinthians 4:5*

2. The kingdom of God is revealed in power, not in _____. *1 Corinthians 4:20*

Lesson 13

1. Mankind dies in Adam but is made alive in sacrifice. T/F. *1 Corinthians 15:22*

2. Who or what is the last enemy that God will destroy? (Satan, death, fear) *1 Corinthians 15:26*

Quarter at a Glance

by Mark S. Krause

Scientific discoveries continue to reveal the nature, expanse, and power of our universe. As a result, many believers are left struggling to understand the relationship that God has with His creation. The expanse of creation gives us a hint at the power and expanse of its Creator.

One way that Scripture describes the relationship between God and His creation is in terms of the relationship between a king and his kingdom. God is king! And the entire created order is under His rule. This quarter will explore the themes of God's rule, His kingdom, and the response of His people as revealed in the Old Testament prophets, the teachings of Jesus, and the letters of the apostle Paul.

A Kingdom of Peace

The prophet Isaiah's articulation of God as king began with his vision of the Lord on His heavenly throne (Isaiah 6:1-5). From that throne, the Lord would establish an eternal kingdom of justice (9:7). Isaiah's message reached a high point when he envisioned a messenger who proclaimed the good news: "Thy God reigneth!" (52:7, lesson 1).

Isaiah further described the kingdom as a time in the future when the Lord would establish His rule over a new heavens and a new earth. His rule will be a place where sorrow and need are no more and where harmony will be found in all places of the kingdom. The king's power will be on display in His kingdom, a place of peace where "the wolf and the lamb shall feed together" (Isaiah 65:25, lesson 2).

The Kingdom Is Like . . .

Central to Jesus' teaching was the proclamation that the kingdom of God had arrived (example: Mark 1:14-15). This kingdom is God's rule on earth. Jesus' power to deliver people from affliction signaled that God's kingdom had arrived (Matthew 12:28, lesson 6).

Jesus frequently taught by using parables, especially regarding the kingdom of God. He compared the kingdom to seed that produced crops, a treasure hidden in a field, a merchant looking for pearls, and a net cast into the sea. These parables revealed the urgency of the kingdom (Matthew 13:1-9, 18-23; lesson 7), the promised judgment in the kingdom (13:40-43, 49-52; lessons 8 and 9), and the ultimate value of the kingdom (13:44-48, lesson 9).

Kingdom Living

The teachings of the apostle Paul reveal the kingdom-living behavior required for believers. Such behavior is summarized in the command to love others and live a life filled with certain spiritual "fruit" (Galatians 5:13-26, lesson 10). Rather than tearing others down, living in light of God's kingdom calls believers to build up other believers (Romans 14:19, lesson 11).

> God is king! And the entire created order is under His rule.

Paul's letter to believers in Corinth reveals his deep concern regarding the seriousness of the kingdom. The Corinthians were reminded that the Lord, the king, would be the final judge regarding their behavior (1 Corinthians 4:5, lesson 12). Arrogance would have no place in God's kingdom (4:18-20).

Finally, Paul taught that the future bodily resurrection of believers would usher in the fulfillment of God's kingdom plans. At the return of Christ to earth and the moment of the promised resurrection of believers, Jesus will hand over the kingdom to God the Father (1 Corinthians 15:23-24, lesson 13). God's kingdom will reign in totality, without opposition (see 15:25-28). Only the Lord God who is omnipotent will reign and citizens of His kingdom will joyfully enter into His presence in worship.

Get the Setting

by Mark S. Krause

Monarchies—complete with kings, queens, and kingdoms—feel like relics of a bygone era. However, absolute monarchies where the king or queen has total control over the kingdom, though rare, still exist in our modern era.

Many such monarchies have been replaced with constitutional monarchies, in which the monarch's power is limited by an elected government. In this context, the monarch is little more than a figurehead or a ceremonial head of state. Some people may follow the developments of the royal family of the United Kingdom with interest, but this is closer to a fascination with celebrities than it is a concern for political power and leaders.

Total Authority

However, during the context of the writings of Scripture, most monarchs were absolute in power. Their word and will became the law of the land, often forcefully. Violence and brutality were frequently justified if such acts maintained the status quo desired by the monarch (see 2 Kings 15:16). Lying and cheating were encouraged, lest the monarch lose respect in the eyes of the people (see 1 Kings 21:1-16). Monarchs sometimes resorted to violence against their people to appease their pagan gods (see 2 Kings 17:31; 21:1-6).

Monarchs maintained their authority by way of a powerful military to protect the interests of the monarchy (example: 2 Kings 25). These military forces were expensive, so taxes and tributes were collected from the kingdom (see Esther 10:1) and from conquered peoples (see 1 Chronicles 18:2). Dishonest governance was excused, if for no other reason than that the end justified the means—with the "end" being the total rule of the monarch.

Temporary Rule

The nation of Israel in Scripture presents a mixed bag regarding the monarchs of its people. Kings were called and replaced. Such was the narrative of Saul, Israel's first king (see 1 Samuel 9:1–10:24; 15:1–16:13). At other times, kings followed God, and yet they still committed selfish atrocities. Such was the narrative of David, a "man after [God's] own heart" (Acts 13:22; see 1 Samuel 13:14); he committed sin with Bathsheba, which led to David's murder of her husband (2 Samuel 11).

Throughout the history of this people, their many kings (and divided kingdoms) revealed that not all kings desired to follow God. Some kings did, in fact, turn to the Lord and follow His commands (example: Josiah; see 2 Kings 23:1-25). But other kings disregarded the Lord and became idolaters who ignored God's law (example: Rehoboam; see 2 Chronicles 12:1). In many regards, these kings were no different than their contemporaries.

Scripture teaches that the ultimate king of Israel was the Lord himself (Isaiah 44:6), and His rule expands to include the whole world. All other authorities reign because they have been given that authority from God (see Daniel 4:17; Romans 13:1). When rulers recognize that they receive their authority from God, they rightly fulfill their role. However, not all rulers acknowledged God; some were worshipped as a god, such as Herod Agrippa of the first century AD (Acts 12:21-23).

The Righteous Rule of God

This quarter of lessons highlights the righteous rule of God. His kingdom and His rule are in contrast to the temporary rule of earthly monarchs and their kingdoms. Although earthly rulers can be weak or strong, selfish or benevolent, unwise or wise, God's rule over all creation—Heaven and earth—is totally and completely righteous.

God is the all-powerful king. He is not devious to gain power, because He has all the power. He is not desperate to retain power, for it cannot be taken from Him. He is righteous and just. All people—then and now—are invited to enter into His righteous rule.

This Quarter in the Word

Answers to the Quarterly Quiz on page 338

Lesson 1—1. beautiful. 2. False. **Lesson 2**—1. earth. 2. False. **Lesson 3**—1. king. 2. everlasting. **Lesson 4**—1. judgments. 2. singing. **Lesson 5**—1. True. 2. stones. **Lesson 6**—1. David. 2. True. **Lesson 7**—1. False. 2. False. **Lesson 8**—1. world. 2. sun. **Lesson 9**—1. False. 2. angels. **Lesson 10**—1. fulfilled. 2. crucified it. **Lesson 11**—1. True. 2. respectability. **Lesson 12**—1. light. 2. word. **Lesson 13**—1. False. 2. death.

The Parables of Matthew 13

From a ship on the Sea of Galilee, Jesus spoke to the crowd through parables . . .

- **The Parable of the Sower**
  vv. 1-23 (Lesson 7)

- **The Parable of the Good Seed**
  vv. 24-30, 36-43 (Lesson 8)

- **The Parables of the Small Things**
  vv. 31-35

- **The Parable of the Hidden Treasure**
  v. 44 (Lesson 9)

- **The Parable of the Pearl**
  v. 45 (Lesson 9)

- **The Parable of the Net**
  vv. 47-52 (Lesson 9)

Implicit and Explicit Curriculum

Teacher Tips by Mary T. Lederleitner

The field of education distinguishes between explicit and implicit curriculum. The former is the actual content of what is taught—the words we share, Scripture passages we quote, etc.; the latter is how we convey that information. Differences in ways people teach have formative consequences, even when the content remains the same.

The Power of Teaching Methods

When researchers studied schools in different communities, they realized that how teaching was done greatly affected learners. Even when teachers used the same explicit curriculum, students under some teachers learned to exercise personal agency, take risks, etc., but not under others. Students of the latter teachers did not take risks or initiative but simply did what they were told, etc.

The same has been found true in studies of congregations. When explicit and implicit messages align, tremendous spiritual growth occurs. However, when the messages do not align, people believe the implicit messages. These include messages embedded in how things are done in the congregation, the actions others model, what upsets people, how time and money are invested, etc. The implicit messages are what they will then integrate into their lives.

Both explicit and implicit curricula are critically important because of how they impact the discipleship process. Many times we do not step back and carefully consider what type of disciples the Lord wants. Does He want risk-takers who challenge hard issues, or does He want passive disciples who mainly just do what we say?

What Jesus Wanted in His Disciples

Jesus had an amazing discipleship agenda. He did and said only the things He saw and heard from His heavenly Father. He loved people in transformative ways, refusing to be trapped in legalism and judgmentalism. He also wholly fulfilled God's purposes by sacrificially giving His life to redeem us. He wanted His disciples to love God with all their heart, soul, mind, and strength. He also wanted them to love others as themselves, extend love to their enemies, and be His witnesses to the ends of the earth. Jesus' type of discipleship was a messy, risky process. But it changed the world.

Jesus' Implicit Curriculum

We easily see *what* Jesus taught in the pages of Scripture. But *how* did He teach? We see Him sharing meals. We see Him welcome diverse people and outcasts to follow Him. We see Him regularly ask questions about how His followers were making meaning of what they saw and experienced. He challenged them when they acted in ways that did not align with God's values, such as when they tried to keep children away or when they wanted to rebuke others who were casting out demons in His name.

In short, Jesus modeled faithful, genuine discipleship so His followers could see what it looked like day in and day out. He then sent them out to do for others what they had watched Him do. And He explained that when He left, the Holy Spirit would guide them.

Unpacking Your Implicit Curriculum

Most people who teach in churches are never taught about the power of implicit curriculum. They model how others taught them, or they implement teaching strategies that they watch others use. Many who teach have a nagging sense that perhaps there are better ways. If that is what you are sensing, begin taking risks and trying methods that Jesus used. Create a safe place where others can make mistakes and learn from them. Practice listening as much as talking. God will guide you too!

God Reigns

Devotional Reading: Colossians 3:8-17
Background Scripture: Isaiah 52:1-12

Isaiah 52:7-12

7 How beautiful upon the mountains are the feet of him that bringeth good tidings, that publisheth peace; that bringeth good tidings of good, that publisheth salvation; that saith unto Zion, Thy God reigneth!

8 Thy watchmen shall lift up the voice; with the voice together shall they sing: for they shall see eye to eye, when the Lord shall bring again Zion.

9 Break forth into joy, sing together, ye waste places of Jerusalem: for the Lord hath comforted his people, he hath redeemed Jerusalem.

10 The Lord hath made bare his holy arm in the eyes of all the nations; and all the ends of the earth shall see the salvation of our God.

11 Depart ye, depart ye, go ye out from thence, touch no unclean thing; go ye out of the midst of her; be ye clean, that bear the vessels of the Lord.

12 For ye shall not go out with haste, nor go by flight: for the Lord will go before you; and the God of Israel will be your rereward.

Key Text

How beautiful upon the mountains are the feet of him that bringeth good tidings, that publisheth peace; that bringeth good tidings of good, that publisheth salvation; that saith unto Zion, Thy God reigneth! —**Isaiah 52:7**

The Righteous
Reign of God

Unit 1: The Prophets Proclaim God's Power
Lessons 1–5

Lesson Aims

After participating in this lesson, each learner will be able to:

1. Identify the "good tidings."
2. Explain the reason for those good tidings.
3. Describe ways to proclaim good tidings today.

Lesson Outline

Introduction

A. The Power of Announcements

One of the more impactful inventions of the late 1800s, though not one we notice often, was the color poster. This was due to improvements in photography, papermaking, and printing. As a result, businesspeople, artists, preachers, and government leaders could suddenly advertise ideas and experiences to the general public in artistically interesting ways.

Today, many of those early posters are collectors' items, commanding six-figure prices at auction. But originally they simply made announcements in inviting ways: "Your country needs you" . . . "Buy our medicine" . . . "Come to the circus" . . . The message drew viewers into the world of the creators, passing along not just information but values, feelings, and obligations.

The ancient audience of the book of Isaiah never saw a poster, of course. But they did experience the power of announcements to motivate, precisely because the announcement contained more than information. The people were being invited to experience a new world, to feel differently about themselves, and to reclaim the values they thought they had lost. The good news being announced would radically change their lives and the lives of their descendants.

B. Lesson Context

In the ancient world, heralds traveled from the capital to smaller cities, reporting the decrees of the king or news of war and peace (example: Habakkuk 2:2). Isaiah 40 begins a large section (of which chapter 52, today's lesson, is part) with the image of a herald announcing good news. And in some sense the entirety of chapters 40–55 could be seen as one single announcement by just such a person. For the ancient hearers of the contents of this text, the auditory was more important than the visual, particularly if they were unable to read. But the power of the announcement was present either way. So we might think of these verses as a sort of audio poster, an announcement depicting a new world in which the audience could imagine themselves taking part.

Isaiah 52 falls into five sections: verses 1-2, 3-6, 7-10, 11-12, and 13-15. Each of the first four sections invites exiled Israelites to return home because Babylon is about to fall to the Persians under Cyrus the Great (see Isaiah 44:28; 45:1, 13). The poems in these four sections personify Zion as a woman, and depict the period of exile as one of slumber for the ancient city. A rebuilt Jerusalem would welcome home her returning children. The holy and ethical acts to which the prophets had always called the people could be embraced anew as Jerusalem was given another chance to live up to her calling and potential.

I. A Call to Rejoice
(Isaiah 52:7-10)

A. Chorus of Singers (vv. 7-9)

7a. How beautiful upon the mountains are the feet of him that bringeth good tidings, that publisheth peace; that bringeth good tidings of good, that publisheth salvation.

Paul quoted this verse in Romans 10:15 as part of his discussion about the relationship between preaching and faith. The good news affects the one announcing it as well as the hearers. The prophet's *feet* become *beautiful* inasmuch as the message is beautiful. In the book of Isaiah, however, the verse has a more specific reference: it describes the one announcing the good news of the return from Babylonian exile to the homeland of Israel and especially to Jerusalem.

The first part of the verse takes the reader back to chapter 40, the beginning of the book's celebration of the return from exile. The verse before us extols the proclaimer—here the same people invited to announce God's comfort to Jerusalem in Isaiah 40:1-3. They do so *upon the mountains* as in Isaiah 40:9, not only so they can be heard across the valleys, but also because the Israelite homeland was mountainous in contrast to the flat plains of Babylonia.

The message of *good tidings* has important content, namely *peace* and *salvation* (rescue). Israelites will experience the end of their suffering at the hands of the Babylonians in a way somewhat similar to the exodus from Egypt, which happened

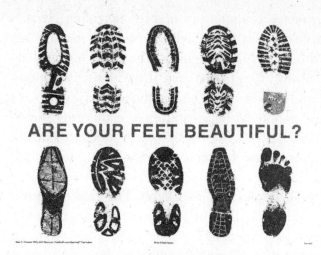

ARE YOUR FEET BEAUTIFUL?

Visual for Lesson 1. *Allow one minute for silent reflection on (and possible rededication to) learners' commitment to spreading the good news.*

hundreds of years earlier. The deliverance to come would (or should) lead to good, ethical behavior. Properly practiced, that behavior will result, in turn, in social harmony and fairness. But that would happen only if the people were to commit themselves to the message. For similar thoughts, see Nahum 1:15.

> **What Do You Think?**
> How do you celebrate within your congregation both the good news *and* those who proclaim it?
> **Digging Deeper**
> What are some practical ways to bless and encourage spiritual leaders who spread the good news?

On Giving and Receiving Good News

One summer a family friend found herself in the midst of a tragic close call while boating: her family's boat capsized in the path of a very large wake. She was frantic as she popped up from the water, searching for the members of her family. One was missing—her daughter. Her husband swam underneath the capsized boat three times, but always came up without her. As my friend yelled for help, one man dove in and came up with the little girl. She was alive! I can only imagine the relief they all must have felt.

There is much celebration when sharing a

message of hope, joy, and thanksgiving. That is true not only for the one receiving the message but also for the one bringing it. The man who saved my friend's little girl was overcome with such emotions.

Our lives could be so much more joyful were we to pray for opportunities to share the gospel—the gospel that rescues people from eternal death. Do you pray for such opportunities?   —P. M.

7b. That saith unto Zion, Thy God reigneth!

The last line of this verse summarizes the announcement as the coming of God's reign. As Psalms 93, 97, and 99 indicate, variations of the phrase *thy God reigneth* are found in the worship in the temple. In that worship expression, God's rule over the cosmos was celebrated and affirmed. People who believe that God reigns live in hope of the time when all the evils of the world will disappear and goodness will triumph.

Zion is another designation for the city of Jerusalem. This fact is seen in many passages where Hebrew poetry repeats thoughts by using related or synonymous words, a feature known as parallelism (examples: Isaiah 31:9; 64:10).

What Do You Think?
What practical results do you see when you fully trust that God reigns?

Digging Deeper
How do you cling to this same truth when it doesn't appear—in the moment—that God is reigning?

8a. Thy watchmen shall lift up the voice; with the voice together shall they sing.

The prophet imagines the city of Jerusalem after it is rebuilt and its staff of night *watchmen* put to work. The guards will not need to warn of approaching armies or other dangers, however. Instead, they will shout loudly about the salvation of the people and their ongoing return to the city.

Certain biblical texts refer to the prophets as watchmen (Jeremiah 6:17; Ezekiel 3:17; 33:7). Since the previous verse in our text speaks of the beautiful feet of the messengers, the verse at hand may have prophets-as-watchmen in mind. In that case, a prospective change in the prophets' mes-

sage would be in view. Instead of earlier prophets' messages of warning—criticisms that fell mostly on deaf ears—the prophets would lead with news of celebrations in the new era of redemption. We note in passing that false prophets can be seen as false watchmen (Isaiah 56:10).

8b. For they shall see eye to eye, when the LORD shall bring again Zion.

Eye to eye is a literal translation of the underlying Hebrew. But the expression does not have the same meaning in Hebrew that it normally does in English. For clarity, we can turn to Numbers 14:14, where the same Hebrew expression is translated "face to face," indicating clear and unhindered communication—visual as well as auditory. Everyone involved will see the miraculous deeds of God! The people of God will witness His work with all their senses.

When the Lord shall bring again Zion is also confusing at first glance. Clarity is found in other passages where the underlying Hebrew word for "bring again" is translated. One such is Jeremiah 44:14, where the same word is translated (twice) as "return." Whereas God had formerly abandoned Zion (see Ezekiel 10), things were to change when God returned and resumed full communion with the people.

9a. Break forth into joy, sing together, ye waste places of Jerusalem.

When the works of the Lord are recognized as such, there should be an appropriate response. Regarding the *waste places of Jerusalem,* Isaiah 35:1-2 is similar. The singing was to be done not just by the people, but by desolated Jerusalem itself. The prophet Isaiah mentions these waste places also in Isaiah 51:3 and 61:4, along with the parallel terms "wilderness," "desert," "desolations" (twice), and "waste cities." The rebuilding and repopulation of Jerusalem would turn the city into a place of celebration as the memory of God's saving work would come to the people's minds. Their songs—reversals of laments like Psalm 137—would echo off the stone walls that the people were to rebuild. About 140 years would elapse between the destruction of Jerusalem in 586 BC and the rebuilding of the city's walls in about 445 BC. When that event came to pass, the people did indeed celebrate with singing in a grandiose ceremony (Nehemiah 12:27-43).

9b. For the LORD hath comforted his people, he hath redeemed Jerusalem.

The comfort promised in Isaiah 40:1 is the rebuilding of the city. It was set in motion when Sheshbazzar led the first wave of returnees from Babylon back to Jerusalem in 538 BC, according to a decree by Cyrus, king of Persia (Isaiah 45:13; Ezra 1:1-11). They began a start-and-stop process of rebuilding that lasted through the time of Nehemiah, almost a century later.

B. Reason for Singing (v. 10)

10. The LORD hath made bare his holy arm in the eyes of all the nations; and all the ends of the earth shall see the salvation of our God.

The image of God's making *bare his holy arm* is an anthropomorphism—a description of something not human (in this case, someone) in terms of human characteristics. Since God is Spirit (John 4:24), He doesn't have a literal, physical arm. But the figure of speech is marvelously useful in communicating information about God's authority (the right to do something) and power (the ability to do something). His arm, along with mention of His "hand," occurs in several Old Testament texts that describe God's warfare against evil (examples: Exodus 15:16; Deuteronomy 4:34; Ezekiel 20:33-34). It also can indicate God's actions in pastoral care and protection (Isaiah 40:11; compare John 10:29).

Given the modifier of the word *holy* and the wider context, the warfare aspect is in view, here considered necessary to pastoral care. The verse at hand does not explicitly name God's foe to be defeated, though surely the Babylonian Empire is meant (see Isaiah 48:20). That empire met its end in 539 BC at the hands of Cyrus, the Lord's

chosen vessel (see Lesson Context). Working His will through human vessels seems to be God's preferred method. But if He can find no such vessel that is suitable, He will do it himself (59:16; Ezekiel 22:30-31).

The phrases *in the eyes of all the nations* and *all the ends of the earth shall see* might cause us to wonder how widespread the knowledge of Israel's experience of deliverance could have been in the sixth century BC. Jewish enclaves existed in various parts of the Babylonian Empire and in Egypt, and they could have spread news. Since Phoenician colonies existed around the Mediterranean, stories had a way of making the rounds via their trading routes (compare 1 Kings 10:6-7).

Even so, the fulfillment of this promise was generations into the future. As in the previous verse, the prophet was less concerned with a time line than he was regarding the final outcome and the people's response to it. Further, the imagery may also be intended as a type (depiction) of the deliverance we have in Christ, since we are to take the gospel of deliverance from sin to "all nations" (Matthew 28:19-20).

II. A Call for a New Exodus
(Isaiah 52:11-12)
A. Leaving Babylon (v. 11)

11a. Depart ye, depart ye, go ye out from thence.

The apostle Paul quotes this verse in 2 Corinthians 6:17, along with other Old Testament texts that call the people of God to cling to Him only. The command to *depart ye, depart ye, go ye out from* Babylon reminds the reader of the exodus from Egypt. That event, separated by some 900 years from the forthcoming departure, featured movement away from a place of suffering, thanks to God's merciful plans for His people.

11b. Touch no unclean thing; go ye out of the midst of her; be ye clean, that bear the vessels of the LORD.

The book of Leviticus, particularly chapters 11 and 13–15, specifies numerous *unclean* things that the Israelites were to avoid. Contact with such things rendered a person temporarily unable to participate in temple worship (2 Chronicles 23:19). Since the people would carry the temple *vessels* back to Jerusalem (Ezra 5:13-14; 7:19; 8:25-30), they needed to avoid anything other than absolute respect for those objects and the uses to which they would be put. The kings of Babylon had used these items for unholy purposes (1:7; Daniel 1:2; 5:1-4, 23), and that practice dare not be repeated. Paul's own reference to uncleanness points mainly to anything connected to idolatry, as does the wider context of today's passage in Isaiah (see commentary on Isaiah 52:11a, above).

The temple objects were to connect the Jews' future worship to what had gone before. The connection between verse 1 and verse 11 forms a complete idea: the people, the objects, and the entire city will become fit for the proper worship of God in a rebuilt temple.

What Do You Think?

What practices help you pursue purity from sin?

Digging Deeper

How will you strike a balance between remaining spiritually pure and actively witnessing to a sinful world (James 1:27)?

Are You Done?

When my children were young, to say they didn't mind getting dirty would be an understatement! They seemed to find all the mud puddles every time they played outside. When they came home covered in dirt, I would ask them one question: "Are you done?" The reason was simple: I didn't want to go through all the work of cleaning them up more than once.

When the Israelites received the good news of their pending return to their homeland, two departures were actually in view. One was physical, and the other was spiritual: their physical departure from Babylon was to be accompanied by the more important departure from sin (compare Isaiah 59:20).

God has paid a high price to cleanse us spiritually so that we might return to Him for all eternity. That price was the life of His Son. It's a price He won't pay twice, and it's a price that we dare not disdain (see Hebrews 6:4-6). We value that price properly when we decide that we are done with sin (see Romans 6:6-7; 1 Peter 4:1-3).

Can you say firmly and decisively today that you are done with sin?   —P. M.

B. Trusting God (v. 12)

12. For ye shall not go out with haste, nor go by flight: for the LORD will go before you; and the God of Israel will be your rereward.

The second exodus here promised contains both a departure from the past first exodus and a continuity with it. Before, the Israelites ate their food in *haste* because they needed to leave Egypt quickly (see Exodus 12:11). However, whereas the first exodus happened under the continued threat of a cruel ruler, the second exodus was to need no such vigilance, because the Babylonian Empire had collapsed. No hasty flight would be necessary. Careful planning could occur, and the departure would take place when all was ready.

Both cases, however, witness to God's protection. The phrase *the Lord will go before you* is reflected in Exodus 13:21; the idea of a supernatural *rereward* (rearguard) is seen in Exodus 14:19. Although the second exodus predicted by Isaiah would not be endangered by a pursuing army as

---

How to Say It

anthropomorphism	ann-thruh-puh-*more*-fizz-um.
Babylonian	Bab-ih-*low*-nee-un.
Cyrus	*Sigh*-russ.
Mediterranean	*Med*-uh-tuh-**ray**-nee-un.
Nehemiah	*Nee*-huh-**my**-uh.
Phoenician	Fuh-*nish*-un.

the first one was, the returnees would still need divine protection (Ezra 8:21-23).

God's ultimate future for those devoted to Him was to come about because of the work of the suffering servant, described in the three verses immediately after the verse before us (Isaiah 52:13-15). Relief for God's suffering people of the sixth century BC foreshadowed the ultimate and eternal relief from suffering by that servant —Jesus Christ.

Conclusion

A. Isaiah 52 Back Then

The prophetic poetry of Isaiah 40–55 has come a long way by the time we get to Isaiah 52. The section began with a distraught, heartbroken people living in a foreign land, subject to the whims of foreign rulers. They had given up hope in God's care for them since their ancestors' sins had brought an ongoing catastrophe upon them. But at the point of today's Scripture, they stood on the verge of a new and bright future. For the ancient audience of Isaiah 52, the call to return home involved a literal, physical movement from Babylonia to the land of Israel, more than 1,000 miles away. Yet the more important movement was not that of a four-month journey across the land, but that of an interior journey of faith, in mind and spirit.

The greatest enemy of faith is often traced to a loss of hope. This week's text called on the people of Israel to reclaim their hope so that they could act in faith toward the God who sought their trust, their obedience, and their love. The temptation to despair undoubtedly remained strong, and that is not something one can simply will away. But by refreshing memories of God's saving actions of the past, Isaiah's prophetic vision of the future could be believed and acted on. A renewed realization of God's presence is always in order!

But several things had to happen for that realization to take root. These included (1) affirming the value of the messengers; (2) trusting those messengers to do their jobs in speaking truth; (3) accepting the opportunity to transform ruins, both physical and spiritual, into places of rejoicing;

and (4) reintroducing of worship as God desires. All these foundational elements became reality as God set forth His plan of rescue. As such, the text takes a full-orbed view of the return (the new exodus), considering the actions and attitudes of all parties involved. Such a wide lens repeats the picture that appears in Isaiah 40, the opening of the "comfort section" of the book.

B. Isaiah 52 for Today

There can be no greater calling than that of bearing God's words of hope to people who are seemingly without hope. That is true whether we are talking about the sixth century BC or the twenty-first century AD. And just as the announcement of rescue to the ancient Israelites was to result in rejoicing, so also for us. The good news of God's saving work should always create a climate of gratitude, joy, desire to share the news, and generous acceptance of all who receive it.

Because God was in the picture, all was not lost for the Jews in Babylonian exile. The same is true today for those exiled spiritually in sin, enemies of God. Today's gospel messengers—all Christians —are to join God's work in spreading that message of eternal rescue (Matthew 28:19-20). The courage and faith required of the ancient Israelite is our must-have as well. Let us celebrate the good ways in which God can use us as His vessels to transform the lives of those around us.

C. Prayer

O God, who calls us to faith, empower us to leave the comfortable and familiar for places You would have the message of Your Son spread. We pray in the name of that Son. Amen.

D. Thought to Remember

Don't just celebrate the good news of the gospel— be its messenger!

Visuals FOR THESE LESSONS

The visual pictured in each lesson (example: page 347) is a small reproduction of a large, full-color poster included in the *Adult Resources* packet for the Summer Quarter. Order No. 4629123 from your supplier.

Involvement Learning

Enhance your lesson with KJV Bible Student *(from your curriculum supplier) and the reproducible activity page (at www.standardlesson.com or in the back of the* KJV Standard Lesson Commentary Deluxe Edition*).*

Into the Lesson

Give each learner an index card. Ask all to write down one piece of recent and true good news from his or her personal life without writing their name on the card. When everyone is finished, gather, shuffle, and redistribute the cards. Have learners take turns reading a random card aloud and making one guess of whose good news is on the card. If the guess is correct, the card is given back to its owner. If the guess is incorrect, allow a second guess before asking the person who wrote the card to reveal him- or herself.

After this activity, say, "Today's Scripture talks about bearing good news. As we read together, consider what is the very best news we can proclaim to others and how we can spread that news this week."

Into the Word

Divide participants into four groups: **A Greater Reality, Peace, Tidings of Future Events,** and **Salvation.** Ask a volunteer to read Isaiah 52:7-8. Instruct each group to discuss how their group name fits into verses 7 and 8 and to then find two other verses (outside of Isaiah 52) that focus on their topic. Indicate that groups can refer to Isaiah 52 for context for what God says will happen. Provide paper. Have groups write down their verses, then sum up the verses in one short exclamatory sentence.

After gathering the whole group together, ask a volunteer from each group to read their verses and statement in an excited voice, like this is the best news they have ever declared. *Option.* Have each group choose one of the passages associated with their topic and create an attractive poster display with it. Provide poster board, markers, and creative embellishments (glitter, crepe paper, etc.).

Alternative. Distribute copies of the "Exciting Announcement" exercise from the activity page, which you can download. Have pairs complete the exercise as indicated.

Ask a volunteer to read Isaiah 52:9-10. Challenge the original four groups to each think about a praise chorus that they could sing in response to these verses. If a group feels inclined, they can even write their own new chorus. Have each group lead/teach the class their chosen chorus to sing together. (*Option.* Provide hymnals or praise songbooks as reference tools.)

Ask a volunteer to read Isaiah 52:11-12. Write on the board *What to Take* and *What to Leave* as two headers. Ask the whole class what the verses say the people should leave or avoid from the land of their exile (expected answer: unclean things) and what they should take with them to return home (expected answer: vessels of the Lord). Write these things in their respective columns. Ask for examples of specific things these general terms might be referring to for the Israelites. Then challenge the class to name, in each category, items that would be relevant today.

Into Life

As a whole class, discuss how the word *gospel* means "good news" and how, as believers, we are called to live out and proclaim this good news to others. Ask how our spiritual experience relates to the experience the Israelites had in Isaiah 52.

Divide the class into pairs to discuss what it would look like for us to share the good news with our community this week. Ask pairs to come up with two or three ideas to share with the whole group. Close with partners praying together about sharing the good news throughout the week.

Alternative. Distribute the "Good News for Me" exercise from the activity page. Have learners complete it individually (in a minute or less) before discussing the sheet in small groups. End with the small groups praying together. Encourage participants to take the handout home to remind them to share the gospel this week.

God's Kingdom of Peace

Devotional Reading: John 16:20-33
Background Scripture: Isaiah 65:17-25

Isaiah 65:17-25

17 For, behold, I create new heavens and a new earth: and the former shall not be remembered, nor come into mind.

18 But be ye glad and rejoice for ever in that which I create: for, behold, I create Jerusalem a rejoicing, and her people a joy.

19 And I will rejoice in Jerusalem, and joy in my people: and the voice of weeping shall be no more heard in her, nor the voice of crying.

20 There shall be no more thence an infant of days, nor an old man that hath not filled his days: for the child shall die an hundred years old; but the sinner being an hundred years old shall be accursed.

21 And they shall build houses, and inhabit them; and they shall plant vineyards, and eat the fruit of them.

22 They shall not build, and another inhabit; they shall not plant, and another eat: for as the days of a tree are the days of my people, and mine elect shall long enjoy the work of their hands.

23 They shall not labour in vain, nor bring forth for trouble; for they are the seed of the blessed of the LORD, and their offspring with them.

24 And it shall come to pass, that before they call, I will answer; and while they are yet speaking, I will hear.

25 The wolf and the lamb shall feed together, and the lion shall eat straw like the bullock: and dust shall be the serpent's meat. They shall not hurt nor destroy in all my holy mountain, saith the LORD.

Key Text

The wolf and the lamb shall feed together, and the lion shall eat straw like the bullock: and dust shall be the serpent's meat. They shall not hurt nor destroy in all my holy mountain, saith the LORD. —**Isaiah 65:25**

353

The Righteous Reign of God

Unit 1: The Prophets Proclaim God's Power
Lessons 1–5

Learning Aims

After participating in this lesson, each learner will be able to:

1. State the reason why weeping will be undetectable.

2. Defend identifications of figurative imagery in the text.

3. Write a prayer of thanks to God for the future He plans for him or her.

Lesson Outline

Introduction

A. New Creation in This World?

During the pandemic that began in 2020, wild animals returned to various locations that had not seen them in generations. This was due to people's self-isolation. Creatures that had been pushed out of their habitats to the fringes of human civilization lost their fear and reemerged in search of food and shelter among suddenly less-threatening areas. These appearances lit up social media—one clear reminder of the consequences of our interactions (and lack thereof) with the larger world.

This reemergence might be seen as a new creation, albeit a very modest one. Such a scenario has intrigued people for a long time. The plot lines of many science-fiction and horror films focus on the disastrous results of human behavior (intentional or mindless) on the environment. Such plots usually result in a hero finding a solution to undo the effects of misguided actions. That's one approach to new creation. But it's not the approach taken by the prophet Isaiah.

B. Lesson Context

Isaiah 63–66 is identifiable as a unit of thought. These chapters echo the problem of human failings addressed in chapters 56–59, but they don't stop there. They go on to add elements of hope because of the power of God. In so doing, chapters 63–66 contrast human inability to *be* righteous with God's divine ability to *produce* righteousness.

The backdrop is again that of what the people in Babylonian captivity—several decades in the future from the time Isaiah prophesied—would need as hopeful assurances of better days (see lesson 1). When we speak of that exile, we take care to distinguish it from the Assyrian exile of the 10 tribes of northern Israel in 722 BC (2 Kings 17:6). The two tribes of southern Israel, collectively known as Judah, came under Babylonian dominance in about 609 BC (24:1-7). The Babylonians (also known as the Chaldeans) tightened the screws in 597 BC when Jerusalem surrendered after a siege and suffered a partial exile (24:8-20). The final straw was the wholesale deportation (exile) to Babylon in 586 BC.

The impact of that exile can be seen by piecing together the texts, among others, of 2 Kings 25; 2 Chronicles 36:15-21; Nehemiah 1:1-3; Psalm 137; Jeremiah 52; Lamentations; Ezekiel 4:1–24:14; Daniel 1:1-2; and 9:1-19. In particular, the last of these passages notes that (1) Jerusalem's desolation would last 70 years, (2) the people of Judah and Jerusalem had brought the destruction on themselves by refusing to obey God, (3) the curses poured out on the Judeans were exactly what had been predicted in the Law of Moses, and (4) God had kept His promise to inflict such punishment. The predictions of punishment via exile are found in Leviticus 26:27-33; Deuteronomy 4:25-28; and 28:64-68 (compare Nehemiah 1:8; Jeremiah 9:13-16; 15:1-2, 14; Ezekiel 12:15; 20:23-24; Zechariah 7:13-14).

I. Celebrating Newness
(Isaiah 65:17-19)

A. Source of Rejoicing (v. 17)

17a. For, behold, I create new heavens and a new earth.

The poem that begins here describes a radically different future reality. But does this refer to the ultimate new creation that God will bring about at the end of time? Similar wording in 2 Peter 3:13 and Revelation 21:1 tempts us to think so (compare and contrast Isaiah 66:22; Hebrews 12:25-27).

But the opening word *for* leads us to reconsider. This translates a Hebrew word that appears also Isaiah 26:3; 40:7; and 43:20, where the translation is "because," as in "here's the reason why." As such, this word connects the thoughts of the verse at hand with those of the previous verses. Those previous verses announce two things: (1) the end of foreign domination of Israel (see 48:14, 20 regarding Babylon and 52:4 regarding Assyria) and (2) the end of unholy rebellion by the Israelites (65:11-12). The end of imperial aggression would mark such a dramatic change that the language of new creation is appropriate for it. When added to the extreme language regarding elimination of unholiness, an end-times interpretation of the destruction and replacement of planet Earth is very inviting.

But two other options should be considered. One is that a double fulfillment is intended. The first fulfillment, focused on ancient Israel, sees the language as figurative and hyperbolic; the second fulfillment is then end-times literal. Another option is that the text features what is known as "prophetic foreshortening" (see explanation of this possibility in lesson 5, concerning Zechariah 9:9). The verses that follow will provide clues as to which interpretation is more likely the correct one.

17b. And the former shall not be remembered, nor come into mind.

Under any of the above possibilities, a feature of the new era will be a kind of forgetting. The Bible speaks of issues involving requests to remember and promises to forget—between people and God (examples: Isaiah 43:25; Jeremiah 15:15). The type of forgetting in view here is the kind when an event or experience fades into the background because something more important has replaced it. This is an image of the end of suffering.

B. Call for Rejoicing (v. 18)

18a. But be ye glad and rejoice for ever in that which I create.

An invitation to celebrate in worship occurs often in the psalter for times of communal festivity (examples: Psalms 32:11; 48:11; 149:2), especially following some action by God to bring about rescue or salvation (examples: 9:14; 13:5; 14:7; 35:9). This attitude is built into Old Testament religious expression. It is an attitude that rests on confidence in God's sure promises to overcome evil in its various forms. The wording *for ever* may automatically cause us to think in terms of eternity without end, but the underlying Hebrew may signify "age enduring," or to the end of the age (compare 132:12).

How to Say It

Assyrians	Uh-*sear*-e-unz.
Babylonians	Bab-ih-*low*-nee-unz.
Chaldeans	Kal-*dee*-unz.
Nehemiah	*Nee*-huh-**my**-uh.
Zechariah	*Zek*-uh-**rye**-uh.
Zephaniah	Zef-uh-*nye*-uh.

18b. For, behold, I create Jerusalem a rejoicing, and her people a joy.

The hope for rebuilding *Jerusalem* occupied the thoughts of the poets, prophets, and other leaders of the period (Nehemiah is an example). Because the city and its (destroyed) temple represented access to God, Jerusalem was (or should have been) a symbol of all that could be holy (compare Revelation 21:2).

C. Promise of Rejoicing (v. 19)

19a. And I will rejoice in Jerusalem, and joy in my people.

Celebration is not reserved for humans only—God himself can join the celebration (compare Zephaniah 3:17). The relationship between the people of Judah and God will have changed. The strains and mutual hostility brought on by the people's sin will have vanished, thanks to God's merciful forgiveness.

> **What Do You Think?**
> What biblical examples can you point to of God's rejoicing over His people?
>
> **Digging Deeper**
> What analogous examples do you see in your congregation?

19b. And the voice of weeping shall be no more heard in her, nor the voice of crying.

The voice of weeping is to disappear because of the forthcoming change of relationship between God and His people. The destruction of Jerusalem and other cities in the southern kingdom of Judah resulted in intense grief and mourning. Reversal of those facts seemed impossible from a human viewpoint, but not from God's (compare Isaiah 25:8; Revelation 7:17; 21:4).

II. The New Reality
(Isaiah 65:20-25)
A. Long Life (v. 20)

20a. There shall be no more thence an infant of days, nor an old man that hath not filled his days: for the child shall die an hundred years old.

The new reality to come is to differ from the old reality in important ways. One such way is a movement back toward an ideal of the first creation: long life (see Genesis 1–11). As we consider this change, we should take care to distinguish between humans' life span, which is 120 years (6:3), and life expectancy, which is 70 years (Psalm 90:10). The high rate of *infant* mortality in the ancient world meant that life expectancy on average was probably no more than 35 years. But if a person could make it to age 5, then the chances of reaching age 70 were pretty good. Therefore the change of life expectancy promised in the verse at hand is a major one (see also Zechariah 8:4)!

We also note that this verse provides a clue regarding the alternatives presented in commentary on Isaiah 65:17a, above; the "new heavens" and "new earth" predicted there are not the same as those predicted in 2 Peter 3:13 and Revelation 21:1, since the renewal in those two passages will feature an end to death altogether (Revelation 21:4). Even so, the newness promised in our lesson text may serve as a type, or pattern, of the ultimate, eternal reality to come (compare Matthew 11:13-14; Romans 5:14; Galatians 4:24; Colossians 2:17; Hebrews 9:24; 13:14).

A Promise to Inspire

I, the hospital chaplain, stood near the tiny cradle and looked at the perfectly shaped head of the newborn baby boy. His father stood silently as the mother, trying to smile, said, "I keep reminding myself that God is here in this storm. I try to remember that He will heal my baby and keep him safe in Heaven. But it's so hard when he's here with me, and all I want to do is snuggle him close forever." Her eyes brimmed with tears. I prayed for her baby that night, even though I knew the doctors said he would only live a few more days.

Isaiah 65:17-25 provides us with a launching point for anticipating the fulfillment of Revelation 21. God has promised to create a new heavens and new earth; absent will be weeping and death. How does that future reality influence how you think and live right now? How *should* it?

—L. M. W.

20b. But the sinner being an hundred years old shall be accursed.

This line is more difficult to understand. Clarity comes in the fact that the Hebrew verb translated *sinner* can also be translated "miss," as it is in Judges 20:16. Therefore the idea is that someone who misses the mark of reaching age 100 is to be considered *accursed*. In that case, the line would simply amplify the idea of the previous one rather than adding a new idea.

B. Housing and Sustenance (v. 21)

21. And they shall build houses, and inhabit them; and they shall plant vineyards, and eat the fruit of them.

The ruins of Jerusalem rendered stark testimony of disobedience long after the destruction of 586 BC (1 Kings 9:6-9; Jeremiah 19:8). Today's text, however, promises that those returning from that exile will regain stable, productive lives. The mention of *vineyards,* a word occurring more than 100 times in the Old Testament, reflects an important part of the diet and economy of the ancient Israelites (see also Ezekiel 28:26; Amos 9:14).

C. Safety and Security (vv. 22-23)

22a. They shall not build, and another inhabit; they shall not plant, and another eat.

This verse reminds us of the old saying "What goes around comes around." Hundreds of years before this text was written, God had granted the Israelites a new homeland where they took ownership of houses they hadn't provisioned, wells they hadn't dug, and vineyards they hadn't planted (Deuteronomy 6:10-12). This happened after the original owners forfeited their place in that land due to sin (Genesis 15:16).

That change of ownership came with a warning not to commit the sins of those ejected, lest the Israelites suffer the same consequences (Leviticus 18:24-28; Deuteronomy 28:15-68). But that's exactly what happened (1 Kings 21:25-26; 2 Kings 16:1-4; 21:10-16; compare Judges 6:1-6). Results of the exile of 586 BC included loss of houses and fields, which became occupied and tended by others (see Jeremiah 52:16). The devastation was so complete that areas of human habitation became again habitations of wild animals (9:11; 10:22). God kept His promise. But that reversal was to be itself reversed.

22b. For as the days of a tree are the days of my people, and mine elect shall long enjoy the work of their hands.

The theme of reversal continues as the imagery shifts to the longevity *of a tree*. Although trees are not immortal, they do often long outlive humans. The promise that *mine elect shall long enjoy the work of their hands* couples longevity of life with enjoyment of that life, creating a word picture of a *people* who will flourish (compare Psalms 1:3; 92:12-14).

A Permanent Home

During the time of Joseph Stalin (1878–1953), a certain newlywed couple was assigned free housing in the area known as Crimea. That area was in Ukraine when it was still part of the USSR. When the couple arrived at the assigned house, they found it fully furnished, with clothing in the dressers, dishes on the table, and food in the pantry.

An eerie feeling overcame the couple. What had happened to the previous inhabitants of the house? The neighbors whispered stories. But no one voiced questions in the post–World War II Soviet Union. So the couple suppressed their fear that something terrible had happened. Years later they learned that Stalin had deported an entire people group known as the Crimean Tatars. Having accused them of collaborating with Hitler, he herded them onto trains bound for central Asia. Then he brought people from other parts of the USSR to inhabit their empty houses (compare 2 Kings 17:24).

In this fallen world, we may suffer the consequences of our own actions or the actions of others—or not at all, given the (sometimes intentional) imperfections of human justice. But no one escapes the ultimate and perfect justice of God. Because He is perfect, He pursues everyone in love, wanting us all to enjoy His eternal, permanent home.   —L. M. W.

23. They shall not labour in vain, nor bring forth for trouble; for they are the seed of the blessed of the Lord, and their offspring with them.

This verse ties together the previous three verses in summarizing the people's new condition to come. The phrase *nor bring forth for trouble* may be confusing in that regard. Clarity is found in that the Hebrew word translated *bring forth* is the same translated "bring forth children" in Isaiah 23:4, and that is the sense here. The loss of sons and daughters was predicted as an anguish of the exile (Deuteronomy 28:32, 41), so again we have promise of reversal.

Isaiah 49:19-21 and 54:1-2 note surprise and joy at the uptick in the birthrate as the text predicts the situation of the postexilic era (that is, following 538 BC). During the 40-year penalty of wandering in the wilderness (about 1447–1407 BC), Israel had experienced a decline in population (compare Numbers 2:32 with 26:51). Nations obviously cannot survive, much less flourish, unless they bring new generations into the world. Children are a sign of hope and blessing (Psalm 128), tokens of God's presence both in the present and the promised future (Isaiah 61:9).

D. God Answers Prayers (v. 24)

24. And it shall come to pass, that before they call, I will answer; and while they are yet speaking, I will hear.

Perhaps the most significant promise in the list is right here. Whereas exile from their homeland would mean an estranged relationship between God and the people, the new era will see deep and immediate communication between the two. Thus we have another reversal (compare and contrast Jeremiah 7:16; 11:14; 14:11; Lamentations 3:8, 44).

The book of Isaiah opens with condemnations of the people because of their stubbornness and oppression. Their acts of piety were designed to cover up their sins rather than lead them to correct them (Isaiah 1:12-17), causing great offense to God. Since they would not defend the poor, the widows, or the orphans, God would not even give ear to their prayers (1:15).

The future, however, was to be one where God listens intently to their prayers. In extending mercy to the people, God has called them to make prayer an occasion for concern. When we pray properly, we become attuned to God's love for all human beings. We increasingly share that concern and act on the basis of it. Then God will listen.

> **What Do You Think?**
> When have you experienced God's anticipating your cares or concerns?
> **Digging Deeper**
> How would you respond to someone who points to God's foreknowledge as negating the need for prayer?

E. End of Violence (v. 25)

25. The wolf and the lamb shall feed together, and the lion shall eat straw like the bullock: and dust shall be the serpent's meat. They shall not hurt nor destroy in all my holy mountain, saith the Lord.

The final verse of the lesson reflects Isaiah 11:6-9, the so-called vision of the peaceable kingdom. The verse at hand applies that earlier vision to the time when Israel will have returned from Babylonian exile and resettled in its land (that is, after 538 BC). In doing so, the vision paints a strong contrast to what would become the actual experience of the people. Old problems would remain or resurface after the return (compare Ezra 10:10-15; Nehemiah 13; Haggai 1:1-11; etc.). Yet the sinful problems need not prevail. If the people turned to God fully, a new era of peace could ensue.

As in almost all prophetic speeches in the Old Testament, this verse intends to speak about a reality that should ideally come about. Yet that possibility remains always just beyond our grasp, as we do not yet live in the peaceable kingdom. Still, the text calls its readers to pursue righteousness and peace so that we may draw closer to the alternative reality—in which God reigns not just in the world as He always does, but also in our thoughts and actions, which He often does not.

> ### What Do You Think?
> What would you be willing to do to heal a relationship with an enemy, demonstrating the reality of God's "peaceable kingdom"?
>
> ### Digging Deeper
> What verses inform your understanding of the extent of your responsibility for peace?

Conclusion

A. Embracing Life

Isaiah 65 is a visionary text that should inspire its readers to see beyond both past failures and the seemingly valid temptations of the present. It invites us to imagine a different world than the one we inherited, a world in which old wounds will be healed and the God-given talents of all are used to bless others. This text offers a vision of a world in which the communication between God and humanity remains open, free, and life-giving.

Reading a visionary text means we have to think creatively in a biblical way. Such texts call us to use our imaginations so we can begin to see what God might be creating in our lives as individuals and churches. In such a vision, God is the one who does the recreating. The language of creation does not apply just to the beginning of time, but to a new era that can emerge when people who have experienced God's mercy embrace the possibilities of new and holy ways of life.

God's peace brings together all of creation!

Visual for Lesson 2. *Ask volunteers to offer other examples of reconciliation in nature that seem to be a foretaste of God's coming peaceful kingdom.*

The text of our lesson advances that move in a dramatic way. It does not portray the citizens of Jerusalem and Judah as being able, by their own power, to bring about the new world God seeks. Sometimes they fall back into the same sins that led their ancestors to lose their homeland. So if a new situation were to come about, God must be the one to bring it about.

This vision of an alternative world continues to exert enormous influence on Christians today. Texts like this remind us that the current reality is neither inevitable nor the full expression of God's plans for humankind. More is possible. Imagining that something more, and celebrating even small hints of its arrival in our everyday lives, makes the community of God's people what it is.

B. Prayer

Creator God, who made the heavens and the earth and everything in them, create in us new hearts, new hands, and new feet so that we may think as You think, do what You give us to do, and go where You call us. Take from us the tendency to think too small and to shrink back in fear. We ask this in the name of the one who has promised to usher in a new heaven and a new earth, Your Son, Jesus Christ. Amen.

C. Thought to Remember

Live as if the time of the new heaven and new earth were now.

Involvement Learning

Enhance your lesson with KJV Bible Student *(from your curriculum supplier) and the reproducible activity page (at www.standardlesson.com or in the back of the* KJV Standard Lesson Commentary Deluxe Edition*).*

Into the Lesson

Divide participants into three groups and give each group one of the following topics: 1–butterfly metamorphosis, 2–leaf color-change process, 3-plant growth stages. Provide information or have groups do an internet search for their topic. Be sure each group notes how long the full transformation takes and what the in-between steps look like. After a few minutes of research time, give groups time to report on what they learned.

Alternative. Distribute copies of the "Word Transformation" exercise from the activity page, which you can download. Have learners work in pairs to complete as indicated. *Option.* This exercise can be done as a race. Do as many rounds as time allows.

After either activity, say, "Transformation often happens in stages, but it can bring about dramatic changes. In today's lesson, look for the ways God promises to transform His creation."

Into the Word

Ask a volunteer to read Isaiah 65:17-19. On the board, make two columns and title them *Past* and *Future*. Divide the group in half and designate one as the **Past Team** and the other as the **Future Team**. Instruct the **Past Team** to study these verses in terms of what was in the past. Ask the **Future Team** to study the verses, looking for what will be in the future. Have a volunteer from each team write their findings on the board under their designated columns.

Ask a volunteer to read Isaiah 65:20-23. Have the **Past** and **Future Teams** add more points to the columns on the board, based on what they find in these verses. Then provide paper and colored pencils/markers to each group, along with the following instructions.

Past Team. Imagine and discuss what you might do to celebrate someone's 200th birthday. Summarize your discussion by creating a birthday party invitation. Be creative in your celebration!

Future Team. Imagine and discuss how you might celebrate a retirement from 200 years of fulfilling labor and create a retirement party invitation. Be creative in your celebration!

When they are completed, have the two groups share their invitations with each other.

Ask a volunteer to read Isaiah 65:24-25. Once more invite the **Past** and **Future Teams** to add any final points to their columns on the board. Then invite the teams to think of three to five concept words to summarize the columns. (Potential answers include: past—death, sorrow, violence; future—life, joy, peace.) Give teams an opportunity to study each other's list and give feedback. Then ask participants to consider what makes all these differences and changes possible. (Expected answer: The sacrifice of Jesus, which defeats the curse of sin and death.)

Alternative. Distribute copies of the "Reverse the Curse" exercise from the activity page. Have learners complete it individually (in one minute or less) before discussing conclusions with a partner. Allow additional time for pairs to share and discuss their responses and thoughts with the whole group.

Into Life

Distribute index cards. Have learners think about one item from these verses that they are especially looking forward to experiencing in God's eternal kingdom. Allow a time of discussion for participants to elaborate on why they are excited for this thing, or to share what they think it will be like to experience it. After the discussion, have learners write a prayer of thanks to God for the future He has planned for them. Invite learners to refer to their index cards frequently during the week. Close the lesson by dividing the group into pairs. Allow partners time to pray together, giving God thanks for His promises.

God's Servant-King

Devotional Reading: Isaiah 50:4-9
Background Scripture: Ezekiel 37:15-28

Ezekiel 37:21-28

21 And say unto them, Thus saith the Lord GOD; Behold, I will take the children of Israel from among the heathen, whither they be gone, and will gather them on every side, and bring them into their own land:

22 And I will make them one nation in the land upon the mountains of Israel; and one king shall be king to them all: and they shall be no more two nations, neither shall they be divided into two kingdoms any more at all:

23 Neither shall they defile themselves any more with their idols, nor with their detestable things, nor with any of their transgressions: but I will save them out of all their dwelling-places, wherein they have sinned, and will cleanse them: so shall they be my people, and I will be their God.

24 And David my servant shall be king over them; and they all shall have one shep-herd: they shall also walk in my judgments, and observe my statutes, and do them.

25 And they shall dwell in the land that I have given unto Jacob my servant, wherein your fathers have dwelt; and they shall dwell therein, even they, and their children, and their children's children for ever: and my servant David shall be their prince for ever.

26 Moreover I will make a covenant of peace with them; it shall be an everlasting covenant with them: and I will place them, and multiply them, and will set my sanctuary in the midst of them for evermore.

27 My tabernacle also shall be with them: yea, I will be their God, and they shall be my people.

28 And the heathen shall know that I the LORD do sanctify Israel, when my sanctuary shall be in the midst of them for evermore.

Key Text

My tabernacle also shall be with them: yea, I will be their God, and they shall be my people.
—Ezekiel 37:27

361

The Righteous Reign of God

Unit 1: The Prophets Proclaim God's Power
Lessons 1–5

Lesson Aims

After participating in this lesson, each learner will be able to:

1. State the identity of "my servant."
2. Defend that identification.
3. Make a plan to change one area of his or her life that is inconsistent with being one of God's people.

Lesson Outline

Introduction
  A. Establishing Trust Again
  B. Lesson Context

I. Return to the Land (Ezekiel 37:21-25)
  A. Regathering (v. 21)
    Together?
  B. Reunification (v. 22)
  C. Rededication (v. 23)
  D. Reign (v. 24)
  E. Residence (v. 25)

II. Covenant of Peace (Ezekiel 37:26-28)
  A. Permanent Sanctuary (vv. 26-27)
  B. Worldwide Knowledge (v. 28)
    When Healing Becomes Testimony

Conclusion
  A. Finding Life Again
  B. Prayer
  C. Thought to Remember

Introduction

A. Establishing Trust Again

There is an old story of a man who comes to two great teachers and demands of them, "Teach me the Law of Moses while I stand on one foot." The first one tells him that his request is unreasonable and sends him away. The second one tells him that the Law of Moses is about loving God and neighbor. "All the rest is commentary. Go and learn."

We remember that Jesus said much the same thing in Mark 12:29-31. But behind the elegant simplicity of that observation lies the hard fact that learning the ways of God requires work. And for that work to yield valid and fruitful results, the seeker must demonstrate honesty and open-mindedness. That gets to the heart of the matter: learning God's Word is about trusting Him. Learning to trust God requires a lifetime of effort. But a commitment to do so pays daily and everlasting dividends.

Hearing, accepting, and trusting God's Word involves more than just intellectual ability (again, Mark 12:30). It requires us to reorient our desires. We must want to trust, to hope, and to love. Today's text helps clarify this needed reorientation.

B. Lesson Context

Ezekiel lived at the time Jerusalem fell to the Babylonians in 586 BC (Ezekiel 1:1-2; 33:21). That destruction and accompanying exile was preceded by two other deportations. The first of those came in 605 BC, when Daniel and his friends were taken captive to Babylon (2 Kings 24:1-2; Daniel 1:1-6). Ezekiel's relocation to Babylon became part of the second deportation as he found himself among the 10,000 of the elite citizenry taken in 597 BC (2 Kings 24:12-14). Daniel and other Jews were taken to serve "in the king's palace" (Daniel 1:4), while Ezekiel found himself "among the captives by the river of Chebar" where "the hand of the Lord was there upon him" (Ezekiel 1:1, 3).

The book of Ezekiel features many astonishing word pictures. One of the most famous is that of the valley of dry bones, in Ezekiel 37:1-14. It is followed by the much less famous illustration of two sticks in 37:15-28. Both of these metaphors speak of the restoration of Israel while emphasizing different aspects of that reunification. Today's lesson explores the significance of the metaphor involving the two sticks. As our text opens, Ezekiel had just been directed to show to an audience the stick on which he had written "For Judah, and for the children of Israel his companions" and a second stick on which he had written "For Joseph, the stick of Ephraim, and for all the house of Israel his companions" (37:16). The explanation follows.

I. Return to the Land
(Ezekiel 37:21-25)
A. Regathering (v. 21)

21a. And say unto them, Thus saith the Lord God.

The beginning word *and* connects what follows with the previous verses that introduced imagery of two sticks (see the Lesson Context). The explanation, which now begins, is introduced by the familiar declarative phrase *thus saith the Lord.* This phrase and its variations occur hundreds of times in the Old Testament. That which follows the phrase is authoritative!

21b. Behold, I will take the children of Israel from among the heathen, whither they be gone, and will gather them on every side, and bring them into their own land.

This verse introduces a series of specific future realities that together paint a picture of a new life to come. The predicted reality of the Israelites being regathered *into their own land* had been stated before (Ezekiel 34:13) and would be stated again (39:25-28). It was a message that bore repeating! And indeed it was repeated by other prophets as well (examples: Isaiah 14:1-2; Hosea 11:10-11; Amos 9:15).

The dispersion and scattering of *the children of Israel*—commonly known as the Diaspora—continued into the time of Jesus (compare James 1:1). It seems unlikely, therefore, that the prophets expected each and every person of Israelite descent to return to Palestine. As the books of Ezra, Esther, and Daniel make clear, some Jews chose not to return to the homeland, and they continued to live in Gentile settings. There they

GOD DWELLS WITH HIS PEOPLE.

Visual for Lesson 3. *Allow one minute for silent reflection before asking volunteers to share what practical difference God's presence makes daily.*

continued to reflect deeply on how to maintain faith as a minority that was often persecuted. Even so, the return home and the rebuilding of the temple signaled to everyone the presence of God.

Together?

My grandmother grew up in a large, impoverished Appalachian family. As the oldest of 10 children, she watched her mother work hard to keep them all clothed and fed. That lifestyle produced in my grandmother a fierce loyalty to family, an intense work ethic, and a determination not to live the life her own mother had lived. So she turned down marriage proposals and made her way north to work in a factory during World War II. There she met and married my grandfather.

Driven to improve the economic status of her family of origin, she invited one sibling after another to live with her as they reached adulthood. They found jobs and spouses and settled down into a better life. Eventually even my grandmother's parents moved next door to her and my grandfather. Yet despite the improvements that the move brought to their lifestyle, this close-knit family mourned the loss of their community and connection.

No matter how much a family can mourn a loss of such connection, God's pain is so much the greater in that regard (Hosea 11:8; etc.)! Does this perhaps cause you to see a problem with all the divisions within Christianity today?   —L. M. W.

B. Reunification (v. 22)

22. And I will make them one nation in the land upon the mountains of Israel; and one king shall be king to them all: and they shall be no more two nations, neither shall they be divided into two kingdoms any more at all.

The *one nation* of Israel had split into *two nations* in 931 BC, following the death of King Solomon (1 Kings 11:41–12:24). That situation may have seemed permanent, given the facts of two exiles (Assyrian and Babylonian) and the passage of three and a half centuries. But Ezekiel expected the 12 tribes of Israel to be reunified nonetheless.

In that regard, the verse at hand offers us an opportunity to clarify the use of some tribal names of Ezekiel 37:15-20 (see Lesson Context). The 12 tribes of Israel were descended from the 12 sons of the patriarch Jacob (died about 1860 BC), who had his name changed to Israel (Genesis 32:28; 35:23-26).

Two of his 12 sons were Judah and Joseph. In the naming of the 12 tribal territories, one territory each is named after Jacob's 12 sons, with two exceptions: the tribe of Levi (which received no territory as an inheritance, per Deuteronomy 18:1) and the tribe of Joseph. In the latter case, two tribal territories were named after Joseph's two sons, Ephraim and Manasseh (Numbers 34:23-24; Joshua 14:4). In time, the names Israel and Ephraim became synonyms in referring to the 10 northern tribes, while Judah became the designation for the two southern tribes of Judah and Benjamin (2 Chronicles 11:1; 30:1; Jeremiah 3:8; Hosea 11:12; etc.).

When no longer divided between the northern kingdom of Israel and the southern kingdom of Judah, the people would enjoy a renewed unity. This reunification would happen under *one king,* in distinction to the two kings that had characterized divided Israel between 931 and 722 BC.

A difficulty here, of course, is that the monarchy was not restored after the return from Babylonian exile. Instead, the people had "governors" (Nehemiah 5:14-15; Haggai 1:1; Malachi 1:8). Promises such as Ezekiel's here came to be seen not as literal predictions of a singular human king ruling in a specific place, but as anticipating the Messiah, whose rule would encompass all things.

C. Rededication (v. 23)

23a. Neither shall they defile themselves any more with their idols, nor with their detestable things, nor with any of their transgressions.

The forthcoming restoration was also to be characterized by the end of idolatry in all its forms. The verse at hand features two words that refer to false gods. The first, translated *idols,* is Ezekiel's favorite in this regard; the underlying Hebrew appears 39 times in his book, out of 48 times in the Old Testament as a whole. The second word, translated *detestable things,* occurs 16 times in Ezekiel, out of 50 total Old Testament occurrences; this word is also translated "abomination(s)" in Daniel 9:27; 11:31; and 12:11.

The double impact of both Hebrew words together occurs only here and in Deuteronomy 29:17; 2 Kings 23:24; and Ezekiel 20:7-8. The worship of false gods was the prime reason for all of the Israelites' other problems. It had led to the defilement of the land in general and of the temple in particular (8:1-16). Cleaning the land and the temple of such religious filth would be important (compare 2 Kings 23:4-16). Cleaning idolatry from hearts would be all the more so (compare Ezekiel 14:2-7).

> **What Do You Think?**
> What in your life threatens to steal your attention and devotion away from God alone?
>
> **Digging Deeper**
> What people or practices help you identify and reject potentially idolatrous thoughts and behaviors?

23b. But I will save them out of all their dwellingplaces, wherein they have sinned, and will cleanse them.

However deep Israel's problem with idolatry had been in the past, Ezekiel prophesied that the future would be different. Ezekiel did not think that the people could completely purge idolatry by their own willpower. Rather, God was to *cleanse them.* The people would experience the sort of physical and spiritual purification necessary for anyone going to the temple to worship (see Psalm 24:3-4). The forthcoming purification would affect all of life—life with God and life with one another.

> **What Do You Think?**
> What other Scriptures encourage you that cleansing is God's work, not yours?
>
> **Digging Deeper**
> What are your responsibilities following being cleansed by God?

23c. So shall they be my people, and I will be their God.

The wholeness of the approach becomes clear in the last line of the verse. Instead of being alienated people suffering under divine judgment, the returning exiles will again become God's *people*. Given Ezekiel's priestly background (Ezekiel 1:3), the context of his thinking may be a text like Leviticus 26 or the similar Deuteronomy 28. Those texts expect expulsion from the promised land as the punishment for community-wide sin. But in connecting our verse's outcome with Deuteronomy 14:2, we see a further connection to the New Testament era in Titus 2:14 and 1 Peter 2:9.

D. Reign (v. 24)
24a. And David my servant shall be king over them.

This verse expands on Ezekiel 37:22, above, in specifying the "one *king*" to be *David*. Davidic kingship, not just monarchy in general, was being prophesied. Ezekiel did not expect the literal, physical reincarnation of that ancient ruler, dead for nearly 400 years by Ezekiel's day. Rather, the expectation was that of the rise of a new ruler who was to be like David in one or more ways.

An example of this kind of interpretation presents itself in the case of John the Baptist, whom Jesus declared to be "Elias [Elijah], which was for to come" (Matthew 11:14) as predicted in Malachi 4:5. John the Baptist was not literally the prophet Elijah resurrected. Rather, John the Baptist was the one who ministered "in the spirit and power" of that long-ago prophet (Luke 1:17; compare Matthew 11:14; 17:10-13).

24b. And they all shall have one shepherd.

Anyone who rules over God's people should function as a shepherd. That designation describes someone who protects others from harm. The *one shepherd* to come would stand in stark contrast to the worthless shepherds who had exploited the people (Jeremiah 23:1-6; Ezekiel 34:1-10). The contrast between good and bad shepherds continues into the New Testament (John 10:1-16; Acts 20:28; Hebrews 13:20-21; 1 Peter 5:1-4; Jude 12).

> **What Do You Think?**
> How do you experience Jesus' shepherding in your present circumstances?
>
> **Digging Deeper**
> How can you become more attuned to Jesus' leading?

24c. They shall also walk in my judgments, and observe my statutes, and do them.

This partial verse describes the behavior of the people that will result from the rule of the one shepherd-king to come. People tend to behave as their leaders do, and this fact was a driver of ending up in exile (Jeremiah 44:16-17). The shepherd-king will be a model of behavior that reflects the opposite. The result will be an era of justice, in which faithful people obey God's *judgments* and *statutes* fully.

E. Residence (v. 25)
25. And they shall dwell in the land that I have given unto Jacob my servant, wherein your fathers have dwelt; and they shall dwell therein, even they, and their children, and their children's children for ever: and my servant David shall be their prince for ever.

This verse summarizes promises already stated (compare Ezekiel 11:17; 28:25; etc.). But it also adds a new idea: *for ever*. The return to *the land* and the rule by the *servant David* will both be permanent in some sense. But as we noted in lesson 2, the Hebrew behind the wording *for ever* does not necessarily require us to think in terms of "eternity without end," since it may signify "age enduring" or "to the end of the age" (compare Psalm 132:12).

II. Covenant of Peace

(Ezekiel 37:26-28)

A. Permanent Sanctuary (vv. 26-27)

26. Moreover I will make a covenant of peace with them; it shall be an everlasting covenant with them: and I will place them, and multiply them, and will set my sanctuary in the midst of them for evermore.

In the Bible, a covenant indicated a long-term, usually permanent agreement between two parties, in which each party assumed a set of responsibilities. Leviticus 26 and Deuteronomy 28 describe the relationship between God and Israel as a covenant. When the Israelites violated the terms of the covenant, God gave them chances to repent. But when they refused, the punishments of the covenant were activated. The ultimate punishment involved Israel's expulsion from its own land (Leviticus 18:25, 28).

Ezekiel insisted that even after the catastrophe of exile, God would renew the covenant; this promise was nothing new (see Deuteronomy 30; 1 Kings 8:46-51). Ezekiel calls the new arrangement *a covenant of peace,* a designation he uses also in Ezekiel 34:25. This is a fairly rare phrase in the Bible, occurring elsewhere only in Numbers 25:12; Isaiah 54:10; and Malachi 2:5.

The focal point of the people's renewal (*multiply them*) was to be the (rebuilt) temple in Jerusalem (*my sanctuary*). That building was a symbol of God's abiding presence among the people (1 Kings 8:10-11).

The promised peace would therefore be more than a mere absence of conflict. Rather, it was to be a condition in which the people would flourish as God intended. Ezekiel insisted that this new arrangement would in some sense be permanent, given that the terms *everlasting* and *for evermore* are translations of the same word translated "for ever" in Ezekiel 37:25, above.

What Do You Think?

When have you experienced peace as more than just the absence of conflict?

Digging Deeper

As far as it depends on you, what can be done to share such peace with others?

---

27. My tabernacle also shall be with them: yea, I will be their God, and they shall be my people.

Paul quotes this verse in 2 Corinthians 6:16. There he uses "temple" in place of *tabernacle;* the two served the same function in the Old Testament, the temple being the successor and permanent version of the portable tabernacle. Paul's usage is in the wider context of Christians personally being "the temple of the living God."

The word translated *tabernacle* is also translated "habitation(s)" in Psalms 78:28; 132:5 and "dwellingplaces" in Jeremiah 30:18, which again underlines the idea of God's presence. The Israelites knew, of course, that God did not literally reside in a building in the same way that human beings do (see 1 Kings 8:27; compare Acts 7:48-50; 17:24). Yet the temple was a sort of magnet for the prayers of the faithful as they sought God's guidance and protection. A wrong view eventually came into thinking when the people held the temple in such high regard that they viewed it as something of a good-luck charm that made them immune from attack (Jeremiah 7:1-8). Even so, the verse at hand emphasizes the willingness of God to be among the people who were to return from exile and to aid them in various ways.

B. Worldwide Knowledge (v. 28)

28. And the heathen shall know that I the LORD do sanctify Israel, when my sanctuary shall be in the midst of them for evermore.

This section concludes by announcing the awareness of non-Israelites to God's intent for *Israel.* The Hebrew word behind the word *hea-*

How to Say It

Appalachian	A-puh-lay-chun.
Chaldean	Kal-*dee*-un.
Chebar	*Kee*-bar.
Ephraim	*Ee*-fray-im.
Judean	Joo-*dee*-un.
Manasseh	Muh-*nass*-uh.
patriarch	*pay*-tree-ark.

then is usually translated "nations" and sometimes "Gentiles" in the *King James Version,* perhaps with less negative overtones (examples: Isaiah 11:10; Ezekiel 4:13; 5:5). One might imagine that neither God nor the Israelites would care about the opinions of those outside the covenant of promise. However, the Old Testament, especially the book of Ezekiel, witnesses several references to God's concern for His reputation among non-Israelites (20:9, 14, 22; 36:20-23).

Having noted some possibilities regarding the term *for evermore* in Ezekiel 37:26 above, we should also take note of Revelation 21:3. That text and others promise a future when God will be immediately present to His people for all eternity.

What Do You Think?

What evidence can nonbelievers see in your congregation that God lives among you?

Digging Deeper

What, if any, congregational issues might distract nonbelievers from experiencing God's presence in your assembly times?

When Healing Becomes Testimony

The mother held her baby for the last time. Tears poured down her cheeks as she rocked the unconscious infant. Engulfed in her grief, she seemed oblivious to her husband's attempts to comfort her. Each of the other mothers present felt the stab of grief as if it were her own. When this mother rose to leave her baby's lifeless body, she paused at the door to look at him one last time, sure she could not live a whole life without him.

Several years later, this same woman organized a retreat for mothers grieving for the same reason. She had found comfort and healing in relationships with other moms who had lost children, and she determined to pass that comfort along. It's been said that "God never wastes your pain," and hers was not wasted.

The Scriptures witness frequently to God's promise to heal His people's pain. Those watching would know that God had extended great care to His people. How can God use your difficult experiences as a testimony to His greatness and salvation?

—L. M. W.

Conclusion

A. Finding Life Again

Rebuilding a community after any kind of disaster is difficult work. For progress to be made, those affected must acknowledge their pain, find resources for renewed hope, and take practical steps to build a new life. The Judean prophets, priests, and other leaders of the sixth century BC took precisely those steps during and after the Babylonian (Chaldean) exile. God made sure that they did!

Connecting practical steps with the values, commitments, and dreams of a congregation presents an ongoing challenge, as all church leaders know. We easily drift into saying, "We must do *something;* here is something; therefore, we must do this." Clear thinking about *why* we need to act in a certain way easily gets lost. Ezekiel made sure that his audience thought deeply about what to do and why. He held out the hope not just of reclaiming lost spaces and practices, but of reentering the deeper meaning of those very spaces and practices.

We need constant renewal in this regard. Before assuming that "God is on our side," we should ask, "Are we on His?" The latter question will invite a season of self-reflection and prayer. That in turn puts us in a position for being made "perfect in every good work to do his will . . . through Jesus Christ; to whom be glory for ever and ever" (Hebrews 13:20-21).

B. Prayer

God of all generations, who restores and renews us after catastrophes of our own making, grant us a deeper sense of Your presence in our lives. May Your church then become an example to all the world of what those created in Your image may be. In Jesus' name we pray. Amen.

C. Thought to Remember

Bless your successors by your own hope-filled obedience to God.

Involvement Learning

Enhance your lesson with KJV Bible Student *(from your curriculum supplier) and the reproducible activity page (at www.standardlesson.com or in the back of the* KJV Standard Lesson Commentary Deluxe Edition*).*

Into the Lesson

Divide learners into three groups. Give each group a bag of about 30 craft sticks or thin cards and instruct them to build a "dwelling" in five minutes or less. When they are finished, ask the whole class to analyze what each building's greatest strength is, as well as its greatest weakness. Then have groups dismantle their individual dwellings and combine all the materials together to form one bigger, better, and stronger dwelling.

Alternative. Distribute copies of the "What's in a Word?" exercise from the activity page, which you can download. Have learners work in pairs to complete as indicated.

After either activity, transition to the Bible study. Say, "In this week's lesson, notice how God brings His people together, gives them a dwelling place, and makes them strong."

Into the Word

Ask a volunteer to read Ezekiel 37:21-22. Have two volunteers read these additional verses: Deuteronomy 30:1-4 and Isaiah 43:5-7. Ask: "What are the common words and promises made in all three passages?" (Expected responses include: scattered, gather, bring back.)

Read Ezekiel 37:23-25 out loud. Then divide the class into three groups, designating one group as the **Jeremiah Group**, the second as the **Matthew Group**, and the third as the **Luke Group**. Based on Ezekiel 37:23-25, each group should identify how the new kingdom (1) will differ from all others and (2) will be superior to all others. Then have the groups answer this question based on their assigned additional text: "How do these verses clarify who the servant David is in Ezekiel's prophecy?"

Jeremiah Group. Read Jeremiah 23:3-6.
Matthew Group. Read Matthew 21:9-11.
Luke Group. Read Luke 1:31-33.

Bring the groups back together to discuss what they discovered in these additional verses. Then ask for other verses that come to mind regarding who the servant David of Ezekiel 37 is.

Ask a volunteer to read Ezekiel 37:26-28. Ask, "What words in these verses signify permanency?" Then assign one of these psalms of ascent to each of the three groups: Psalms 121, 131, and 133. Give learners time to read and discuss within their group what the theme of the psalm is. Bring the groups together and ask each group read the last verse of their psalm aloud to hear what the three psalms have in common. (Expected response: "Forever!")

Into Life

Allow a few moments for participants to imagine what it will be like to live in a kingdom as described in Ezekiel. Ask, "What words or phrases would you use to describe the people of God in this context?" Suggest that participants reread the verses to help them in this exercise. Write responses on the board. (Possible responses include: unified, at peace, thriving, secure, holy.) Then challenge participants: "Is there a word or phrase on the board that you don't think describes you? If so, spend some time this week praying for that thing to become more evident in your life." Divide participants into pairs to share their thoughts about this and pray for each other.

Alternative. Distribute copies of the "United Forever" activity from the activity page. Have participants work in pairs to complete as indicated. Then bring the class together to discuss how the various puzzle pieces work together. Have learners color in one piece that isn't an accurate description of his or her experience in God's kingdom. Ask the partners to pray for one another regarding the growth area(s) they both identified.

Renewed in God's Love

Devotional Reading: 2 Corinthians 5:12-21
Background Scripture: Zephaniah 3:14-20

Zephaniah 3:14-20

14 Sing, O daughter of Zion; shout, O Israel; be glad and rejoice with all the heart, O daughter of Jerusalem.

15 The LORD hath taken away thy judgments, he hath cast out thine enemy: the king of Israel, even the LORD, is in the midst of thee: thou shalt not see evil any more.

16 In that day it shall be said to Jerusalem, Fear thou not: and to Zion, Let not thine hands be slack.

17 The LORD thy God in the midst of thee is mighty; he will save, he will rejoice over thee with joy; he will rest in his love, he will joy over thee with singing.

18 I will gather them that are sorrowful for the solemn assembly, who are of thee, to whom the reproach of it was a burden.

19 Behold, at that time I will undo all that afflict thee: and I will save her that halteth, and gather her that was driven out; and I will get them praise and fame in every land where they have been put to shame.

20 At that time will I bring you again, even in the time that I gather you: for I will make you a name and a praise among all people of the earth, when I turn back your captivity before your eyes, saith the LORD.

Key Text

The LORD thy God in the midst of thee is mighty; he will save, he will rejoice over thee with joy; he will rest in his love. —**Zephaniah 3:17a**

The Righteous
Reign of God

Unit 1: The Prophets Proclaim God's Power
Lessons 1-5

Lesson Aims

After participating in this lesson, each learner will be able to:

1. Identify a reason for joy.

2. Contrast a reason for joy with a reason for sorrow.

3. Sing a hymn or praise chorus that reflects the text's mandate to do so.

Lesson Outline

Introduction

A. Nobody Wants to Do It!

A task that no one wants to do is to notify the next of kin that a loved one died in a traffic crash or a similar incident. A veteran of 30-plus years in law enforcement said that this was the worst part of his work. These situations are especially stressful when there are multiple deaths.

Old Testament prophets also had the unwelcome task of bringing bad news. Their task involved not news of deaths that had happened, but deaths that were to come. And reactions to the prophecies differed. At one extreme was wholesale repentance (example: Jonah 3:5-9). Much more common was the other extreme of rejection of the message and persecution of the prophet (example: Jeremiah 38:1-6).

Zephaniah was a prophet like others in bringing news both good and bad. How he was treated is unknown to us. But his prophecies bear study yet today.

B. Lesson Context

The instructor for a class on the Minor Prophets presented an imaginary conversation in Heaven. A person had recently arrived there, and one of the first persons he met introduced himself as Zephaniah. The new arrival was thrilled, for he assumed that this was the prophet who wrote book of the Bible by that name. So he asked his new friend if he had indeed written that book. The individual replied that he had, and then he asked the new arrival in Heaven what he thought of the little book of only three chapters. One of the students in the class reflected on that scenario and decided to write a term paper that would feature some aspect of the book of Zephaniah—just in case!

The prophet is identified in Zephaniah 1:1 in terms of the name of his father. That was a normal way to identify a person more specifically. But that designation is part of a listing found in no other writing prophet: the four generations of those who came before Zephaniah. The fourth one is Hezekiah (given as "Hizkiah" in the *King James Version*), the same name as one of the "good" kings of Judah (reigned about 727–699 BC; 2 Kings 18).

The information given by Zephaniah causes many to conclude that he is referring to that king. That is a conjecture, but it is usually understood that there is no reason to list the name unless it referred to that king, who reigned about 100 years earlier. Zephaniah was therefore a great-great-grandson of Hezekiah. The prophet rebuked members of the royal family (Zephaniah 1:8), and it has been suggested that his being of royal blood gave him more grounds to condemn his cousins.

Zephaniah 1:1 also features the name of "good" King Josiah, during whose reign (from 640 to 609 BC) Zephaniah prophesied. The flagrant iniquity that is condemned throughout most of the book seems to indicate that the reforms of Josiah had not yet taken place. The revival began after the Book of the Law was found in 622 BC by Hilkiah the priest while doing repairs to the temple (2 Chronicles 34:8-15). A possible time for the book of Zephaniah is, therefore, in the late 620s BC.

Judgment, punishment, and hope are three topics frequently found in the writings of the prophets. Judgment indicates that God has compared His announced expectations with the obedience of the people, nation, or nations being considered. Punishment is pronounced on those found guilty. Hope often follows when the punishment has accomplished its purposes. All three topics are present in the book of Zephaniah.

The prophet is primarily concerned with Judah's continued rebellion against God (see 2 Kings 22:1–23:28). The first two chapters of the book of Zephaniah describe a coming Day of the Lord, in which Judah is to face judgment and punishment for idolatry. The punishment promised was to be a tool of God for purifying His people.

The prophecy presents us with a sharp change of theme beginning in Zephaniah 3:9, where restoration of a remnant takes center stage. Today's study reviews the final verses of Zephaniah, where a hopeful theme resounds.

I. Praises to the Lord
(Zephaniah 3:14-17)
A. Calls to Sing (v. 14)

14. Sing, O daughter of Zion; shout, O Israel; be glad and rejoice with all the heart, O daughter of Jerusalem.

Hebrew poetry often repeats thoughts by using different words—a feature known as parallelism. That feature is present when the phrases in lines of poetry echo one another. Despite two (or more) different phrases, one thing or action is in view. Thus in the verse before us, the *daughter of Zion* being addressed is the same as both *Israel* and *daughter of Jerusalem*. The designation Zion originally referred to "the city of David" (2 Samuel 5:7); eventually Zion came to include the temple area just to the north (Joel 2:1). Zion often parallels (stands for) the city of Jerusalem in Old Testament poetry (example: Psalm 128:5), and that is the case here.

The prophets frequently refer to Jerusalem, Zion, or both in terms of a daughter (examples: Isaiah 37:22; Lamentations 2:13). This is a literary technique known as personification, in which the writer assigns the qualities of a person to something that isn't human. The name Israel, for its part, can take different references depending on historical context. Sometimes it refers to the entirety of the 12 tribes (example: 1 Kings 4:7). At other times it refers only to the 10 tribes of the northern kingdom of the divided monarchy (example: 2 Kings 3:1). At still other times it refers to the patriarch Jacob (example: Genesis 35:10). Here all the terms in our verse seem to refer to the faithful remnant.

The verse under consideration stands in sharp contrast to Zephaniah 3:11, which addresses wrongful rejoicing because of pride. Future rejoicing *with all the heart* was to have an entirely different basis as a response to the fulfilled promises of the Lord. God's people were not forgotten, and times of joy and happiness lay ahead. Indeed, when the first wave of returnees from Babylon laid

How to Say It

Chaldean	Kal-*dee*-un.
Hezekiah	Hez-ih-*kye*-uh.
Hilkiah	Hill-*kye*-uh.
Josiah	Jo-*sigh*-uh.
Zephaniah	Zef-uh-*nye*-uh.

the foundation for the second temple, their rejoicing was heard far away (Ezra 3:11-13).

What Do You Think?

What prevents you from singing and shouting for joy more frequently?

Digging Deeper

What other verses encourage you to overcome these barriers to more joyful worship?

B. Causes for the Rejoicing (v. 15)

15a. The LORD hath taken away thy judgments, he hath cast out thine enemy.

Here begins a listing of four reasons why the people were to sing, shout, and rejoice. First, the prophesied Day of the Lord and its attendant *judgments* would be a thing of the past (see Zephaniah 1:7-10, 14-16, 18; 2:2-3). Second, God will defeat (*cast out*) the *enemy* Babylon, thus ending the oppression Judah was yet to face. The oppression was the consequence of the nation's sinful choices, but God would not allow those consequences to destroy completely. Instead, like a parent considering a punishment to be sufficient, He will end it (compare Isaiah 40:1-2). God's affirmation of His faithful remnant in this regard is to be the cause for the joyful celebration just noted above.

What Do You Think?

Does accepting the reality that God has taken away judgment for your sins dismiss feelings of guilt? Why or why not?

Digging Deeper

How will you bear patiently the consequences of past behavior (examples: health issues, broken relationships, legal problems)?

15b. The king of Israel, even the LORD, is in the midst of thee.

We come to the third and most important of the four reasons for rejoicing: *the Lord*, the real *king of Israel*, will be with the people. In the ancient Near East, the presence of a king was essential to the well-being of his people. An absentee ruler could not judge disputes. People might think, *While the cat's away, the mice can play* (compare Matthew 24:48-49). A ruler who was present and active could be expected to provide some degree of protection and justice. So when Zephaniah describes God as a king present *in the midst of* His people, the prophet is telling a powerful story of God's protective rule (compare Isaiah 54:14; Zechariah 9:8-9). The text thus serves to provide encouragement for those who would be oppressed in the still-future Babylonian (Chaldean) exile.

This language of presence foreshadows significant New Testament themes. God's promise to dwell with His people was fulfilled in Jesus. As the incarnate Word, He physically lived among people (John 1:1-18). Before He ascended, Jesus promised that "where two or three are gathered together in my name, there am I in the midst of them" (Matthew 18:20). The indwelling of the Holy Spirit for the Christian is a blessed reality (Romans 8:9-11; 1 Corinthians 6:19; 2 Timothy 1:14). The promise here is also a reminder of Jesus' final words, as given in Matthew 28:20: that He would be with His people—always!

What Do You Think?

What spiritual practices do you lean into when you need to overcome fear or anxiety?

Digging Deeper

How does the assurance of God's presence ease the burden of overcoming these things on your own?

15c. Thou shalt not see evil any more.

When God is with His people, there is no room for *evil*. And that is the fourth reason for rejoicing. God was promising through Zephaniah to step into the situation in a new way. Although the nation of Judah as a whole had disobeyed and turned its back on God, He would not abandon the faithful remnant among His covenant people. The promised restoration in general and this verse in particular in no way suggest that God exempts His people from experiencing the natural consequences of their choices. The context, rather, is that of God's removal of those who *instigate* evil.

The promise of restoration does not end with

Zephaniah's prophecies to pre-exilic Judah (and the restoration that will result in a post-exilic remnant). In the Lord's Prayer, Jesus taught His disciples to pray for restoration in terms of God's kingdom coming and God's will being done (Matthew 6:10).

As Jesus proclaimed that coming kingdom, He did not consider the restoration to have been accomplished fully during His earthly ministry. Instead, restoration and the establishing of the kingdom of God were inaugurated. Fulfillment is in some sense both "now" and "not yet." Full restoration in terms of new life in Christ is consummated at His return (1 Corinthians 15:52-57; Revelation 22). In the meantime, we allow the Holy Spirit to transform us daily (Romans 12:2).

Visual for Lesson 4. *While discussing verse 17, ask learners for other images that come to mind when thinking of God's joy in His people.*

> ### What Do You Think?
> In what ways are you already experiencing the "now" of restoration in your relationship with God?
>
> **Digging Deeper**
> What aspects of life suggest that you are still living in the "not yet"?

Bearable Losses

Every year on her birthday, Meri Mion remembers her lost birthday cake. It happened when she turned 13, which was also the day Allied troops liberated her hometown in Italy during World War II. After a tense night, hiding as the retreating Germans shot at their house, Meri and her mother peeked out the next morning to discover that an American command post had been set up only 150 yards away!

In celebration of both Meri's birthday and the liberation, her mother used scarce supplies to bake a cake. But after leaving it outside the window to cool, it disappeared before Meri had a bite of it. But she reasoned that someone else—maybe even one of her liberators—needed it worse than she did. That reasoning made the sacrifice bearable.

We all face negative experiences as big as losing a loved one and as small as losing a birthday cake. What can help most in this regard is contrasting our losses with God's infinitely greater sacrifice when His Son died on the cross. When we are overwhelmed by joy and gratitude at the liberation Jesus has brought us, we can take our own losses in stride. As we do, we constantly remember that our current suffering (perhaps of our own making) is far outweighed by the eternal reward that awaits (2 Corinthians 4:16-18). How can you best stay focused on that perspective?   —A. W.

C. Confidences Expressed (vv. 16-17)

16. In that day it shall be said to Jerusalem, Fear thou not: and to Zion, Let not thine hands be slack.

When burdens are lifted, some people become cautious about moving forward—just in case another difficult blow is coming. God's people as a nation had experienced much suffering throughout their history. Here, however, a blessed assurance is repeated in different words, and *Jerusalem* —synonymous with *Zion*—is exhorted again to be confident and move ahead. It is time to be busy in the Lord's work. Caution can be wise, but too much caution results in accomplishing nothing.

17. The LORD thy God in the midst of thee is mighty; he will save, he will rejoice over thee with joy; he will rest in his love, he will joy over thee with singing.

The image Zephaniah paints is that of a victorious king. Having defeated the enemy, God's entire focus shifts to His utter *joy* over once again being with His people, providing and caring for them (compare Isaiah 62:4). The phrase *he will rest in his love* may seem curious at first. It should be understood as God's shifting from a mode of active wrath to one of steady love. In that mode, the Lord will no longer punish the people (compare Hosea 14:4). The cycle of joy is thereby complete: as God's people will celebrate their restored relationship with Him, God will celebrate being present with them.

> ### What Do You Think?
> How would you approach life differently if you wholeheartedly accepted that God rejoices over His people?
>
> ### Digging Deeper
> What prevents you from joining in God's joy over His people?

II. Promises of the Lord
(Zephaniah 3:18-20)
A. Comfort for the Sorrowful (v. 18)
18a. I will gather them that are sorrowful for the solemn assembly, who are of thee.

This verse presents some translation difficulties. Taken as a whole, however, the verse suggests that *the solemn assembly* that was instituted (whether part of an annual festival or a Sabbath observance) as an expression of faith either had or was to become a matter of shame instead. Another possibility is that because God calls the people to rejoice, He will remove those who choose to continue to wallow in sorrow; they will not be allowed to prevent others from expressing their joy.

18b. To whom the reproach of it was a burden.

The language of *reproach* brings another dimension to the promise of restoration. The same word is translated "shame" elsewhere (example: Isaiah 47:3), and that may be the sense here. Shame and honor In the time of the ancient Near East were more than simply matters of hurt feelings. Rather, those concepts spoke to how people identified and valued themselves. To be cast into exile would result in the Judeans no longer understanding who they were as a people (compare Psalm 74). This *burden* will be lifted when God reclaims His remnant.

B. Condemning the Oppressors (v. 19a)
19a. Behold, at that time I will undo all that afflict thee.

The phrase *at that time* links this promise to the previous verses. The consequences to be suffered for sin will come to an end as God removes the agents of judgment (*all that afflict thee*). Judah will no longer be known as the people who abandoned their God (compare Deuteronomy 29:24-25; Isaiah 60:18). What the Babylonians will have done to the people of God will become their own fate also.

C. Confirming the Restoration (vv. 19b-20)
19b. And I will save her that halteth, and gather her that was driven out; and I will get them praise and fame in every land where they have been put to shame.

In the ancient Near East, physical disabilities often were considered evidence of a deity's judgment (see John 9:2). The older English word *halteth* refers to a handicap related to walking. Similarly, enslavement by a hostile nation was thought to prove the inability of both king and deity to protect a people (compare Isaiah 14:1-8). Restored relationship with God removes and heals these purported signs of abandonment (see also Ezekiel 34:16; Micah 4:6). Physical healing, freedom, and return home are concrete ways God's justice and love will be announced.

Best Plan or Second-Best Plan?

"It was a combination of the saddest moment of my life but also the proudest." That's how Craig described meeting his son Sam for the first time.

It all started in 1969 when Craig was a young enlisted man stationed at an army base. His red convertible helped him attract a pretty girlfriend, but It didn't exactly suggest he was the marrying type. After completing military service and returning home, his former girlfriend called and congratulated him on being the father of a healthy baby boy—whom she had already placed for adoption.

Unable to find Sam or contest the adoption according to the laws of the time, Craig resigned himself to never seeing his son—such was a consequence of the immorality that preceded. But 52 years later, Sam tracked Craig down with the sad news that he was dying of cancer. Craig crossed the country to sit at Sam's side and catch up on the lost decades. On the drive back home, Craig received a phone call that Sam had passed away.

That was a bittersweet reunion. We too may find ourselves in long years of struggle over a relationship broken because of sin. Often when we are attempting to cope, we are actually searching for God's second-best plan, His best plan ("Don't sin!") having been rejected already (hence the heartache).

Which do you find yourself searching for most: God's best plan or His second-best plan?
—A. W.

20. At that time will I bring you again, even in the time that I gather you: for I will make you a name and a praise among all people of the earth, when I turn back your captivity before your eyes, saith the LORD.

The book of Zephaniah ends in a positive way. This is a vivid contrast to the first chapters of the book, which provide both a scathing denunciation and the promise of punishment. As Zephaniah again referred to *that time*, he reinforced the link between the promises. God's restoration of familial relationship goes hand in hand with restoring a sense of identity as God's covenant people. God's care is to be demonstrated in this renewed relationship and rediscovered identity.

The phrase *when I turn back your captivity* reemphasizes that the terrible judgments of the Day of the Lord were yet to occur, from the perspective of the original reader. And as the decades passed until they did, it would be easy to forget or outright dismiss the predictions of exile and return (compare 2 Peter 3; Revelation 2:4-5). Could there be anything sadder than to fail to be restored to relationship with God Almighty himself?

Conclusion

A. An Irony of Prophecy

Fulfilled prophecy is partly intended to validate a prophet and His message. In the Bible, however, quite often the original recipients of a prophecy did not live to see the fulfillment. That is the situation with the prophecies in today's lesson. The original recipients of this message lived in the time of Josiah (Zephaniah 1:1). He was slain in battle about 609 BC. The destruction of the temple did not take place until 586 BC and the return from exile did not begin until 538 BC. So the people who first heard this prophecy did not understand the significance of what was being promised. Later, the people in captivity in Babylon *did* understand, and they are described as weeping when they remembered Zion (Psalm 137:1).

The return of the captives from Babylon was a rare event in history. What happened to them was noticed by other nations: almost 50,000 people were so sincere in their faith that they made the four-month trip back to the land God had promised to their forefathers. The people who returned were never seriously tempted again by idolatry. The Babylonian captivity was not pleasant, but it had positive, long-lasting results. People finally learned that God meant what He had said in the first of the Ten Commandments: "Thou shalt have no other gods before me" (Exodus 20:3). Today's study is therefore a lesson about hope, and this hope is backed by the assurances of God himself.

Jesus promised that He would come again, and He added that the time is unknown (Matthew 24:36, 44). Almost 2,000 years have passed since Jesus made those statements. He then added that the important thing is to be ready. God keeps His word, so . . . be ready!

B. Prayer

Almighty God, we are thankful for the people who taught us about You. We are grateful for their examples of faithfulness and for the faith of others through the centuries. Today we rededicate ourselves to be faithful until the end—the end of our lives or the end when Jesus comes to gather His people. In Jesus' name we pray. Amen.

C. Thought to Remember

Resolve to stand on the promises of God—today and all the tomorrows!

Involvement Learning

Enhance your lesson with KJV Bible Student *(from your curriculum supplier) and the reproducible activity page (at www.standardlesson.com or in the back of the* KJV Standard Lesson Commentary Deluxe Edition*).*

Into the Lesson

Distribute sheets of paper and pencils. Ask learners to fold their papers vertically in half to create a crease, then open the papers again. Have them label the left side "Joy" and the right "Sorrow"; then allow one minute to list words and experiences that they associate with the two words.

Bring the class together to discuss these questions: 1–Did your lists display any overlaps? Where, or why not? 2–How can we be simultaneously joyful and sorrowful about something?

Explain that today's lesson challenges us to consider apparent contradictions in seemingly opposing truths: that God's judgment and discipline deliver us and give us hope; they restore us and are part of His plan for our salvation.

Into the Word

Ask a volunteer to read Zephaniah 3:14-20. Write *Joy* and *Sorrow* on the board as the headers of two columns (you will add a third column shortly). Conduct a discussion on how to fill in the columns, using the verses from Zephaniah. Refer to the Into the Lesson exercise to compare and contrast with the lists learners already created.

Add the third column with the header of *Punishment*. Challenge learners to consider how God's definitions differ from our worldly understandings. Ask: 1–What does this passage teach about God's attitude toward punishment? 2–What does this passage teach about God's attitude toward discipline?

Have participants form pairs (or groups of three), each with access to a Bible and a concordance. Distribute paper and pencils to the groups. Invite groups to identify other passages that seem to demonstrate similar and contrasting attitudes toward punishment and discipline, as well as how we reconcile the passages. As an example, together look at 1 John 4:18. Discuss how our cultural views of fear and love differ from this biblical mes-

sage. Challenge participants to consider how this cultural disconnect can cause people outside the church to misinterpret the message of the prophets. Then allow time for groups to find and make notes about other passages. After 15 minutes, bring groups together for discussion about their findings.

Alternative. Distribute copies of the "Power and Promises" exercise from the activity page, which you can download. Have participants work in groups of three or four to complete as indicated. After 15 minutes bring the class together to discuss their findings.

Into Life

Ask students to get into pairs as you cue up some background music with a peaceful message about renewal in Christ. Encourage them to consider how the passage in Zephaniah carries a timeless message about the temptations of idolatry and trusting in God to overcome its power over us. Display the following phrases as discussion prompts:

> *Your Life*
> *Your Neighborhood*
> *Our City*
> *Our Country*
> *The World*

Have pairs discuss: 1–Where is renewal happening in your life? in the other listed areas? 2–For each of these, did renewal look the way you expected? How did God surprise you? Individuals might look back at the joy and sorrow notes they wrote at the beginning of the lesson as they reflect on renewal here. Close by singing together a favorite praise song. Invite the group to spend time during the week rejoicing in God.

Alternative. Distribute copies of the "Viral Rejoicing" activity from the activity page. Have learners work in pairs or trios to complete as indicated.

Peace to the Nations

Devotional Reading: Isaiah 55
Background Scripture: Zechariah 9:9-17

Zechariah 9:9-13, 16-17

9 Rejoice greatly, O daughter of Zion; shout, O daughter of Jerusalem: behold, thy King cometh unto thee: he is just, and having salvation; lowly, and riding upon an ass, and upon a colt the foal of an ass.

10 And I will cut off the chariot from Ephraim, and the horse from Jerusalem, and the battle bow shall be cut off: and he shall speak peace unto the heathen: and his dominion shall be from sea even to sea, and from the river even to the ends of the earth.

11 As for thee also, by the blood of thy covenant I have sent forth thy prisoners out of the pit wherein is no water.

12 Turn you to the strong hold, ye prisoners of hope: even to day do I declare that I will render double unto thee;

13 When I have bent Judah for me, filled the bow with Ephraim, and raised up thy sons, O Zion, against thy sons, O Greece, and made thee as the sword of a mighty man.

16 And the LORD their God shall save them in that day as the flock of his people: for they shall be as the stones of a crown, lifted up as an ensign upon his land.

17 For how great is his goodness, and how great is his beauty! corn shall make the young men cheerful, and new wine the maids.

Key Text

The LORD their God shall save them in that day as the flock of his people: for they shall be as the stones of a crown, lifted up as an ensign upon his land. —**Zechariah 9:16**

The Righteous
Reign of God

Unit 1: The Prophets Proclaim God's Power
Lessons 1–5

Lesson Aims

After participating in this lesson, each learner will be able to:

1. Identify the biblical fulfillment of Zechariah's prophecy.

2. Explain the significance of that fulfillment.

3. State one reason why that fulfillment should make a difference in his or her life.

Lesson Outline

Introduction
   A. Extreme Preparations?
   B. Lesson Context: Zechariah the Prophet
   C. Lesson Context: Zechariah as Prophecy
I. The Lord's King (Zechariah 9:9)
   A. Rejoicing Commanded (v. 9a)
   B. Reasons to Rejoice (vv. 9b-c)
      A Surprising Nature
II. The Lord's Kingdom (Zechariah 9:10-13)
   A. Peace Secured (v. 10)
   B. Prisoners Released (v. 11)
   C. Promise of Plenty (v. 12)
   D. Promise of Power (v. 13)
III. The Lord's Care (Zechariah 9:16-17)
   A. The Lord Saves (v. 16)
      The 50-Cow Wife
   B. The Lord Supplies (v. 17)
Conclusion
   A. Play Money vs. Real Money
   B. Prayer
   C. Thought to Remember

Introduction

A. Extreme Preparations?

When overnight guests are expected, a host is faced with the decision of how to prepare for the visit. The preparations may vary according to the status of the visitor. At one extreme of preparation, a regularly used room may be vacated and receive a deep cleaning—windows washed, bedspreads laundered, carpet steamed, etc. At the other extreme are situations calling for little or no preparation, with the guest being expected to sleep on the couch; relatives or the kids' friends are more likely to experience no special preparation for their overnight stay.

A brief description of what was to be done to prepare for the arrival of the ultimate dignitary, the Lord God, is found in Isaiah 40:3-4. This passage is cited in the New Testament as being fulfilled in the ministry of John the Baptist (Matthew 3:3; Mark 1:2-3; Luke 1:76; 3:4-5; John 1:23). All this leads to the conclusion that the preparation was to be spiritual in nature, a preparation of the heart.

People reacted to John's message in various ways. At one extreme were reactions of sincere repentance by unlikely people (examples: Luke 3:7-14); at the other extreme were attempts to discredit John (example: Matthew 11:18). Only those at the proper extreme of heart preparation were able to recognize a prophetic fulfillment when it happened right before their eyes.

B. Lesson Context: Zechariah the Prophet

There are about 30 men in the Bible named Zechariah, and the passage Zechariah 1:1 allows us to identify the one of interest today. The names of the man's father and grandfather listed there point to the prophet whose work can be dated from 520 BC onward. He and his contemporary Haggai played a leadership role in rebuilding the temple following the return from Babylonian exile (Ezra 5:1; 6:14; Zechariah 1:7; 7:1). Zechariah joined Haggai with a general exhortation (1:1-6), followed by a series of eight visions that provided encouragement in the project of building a new temple. A tremendous assurance is given toward the end of the first vision when, the Lord declares that "my house shall be built" (1:16). In that regard, those two prophets lived during the time of King Darius of Persia, who reigned from 522 to 486 BC.

C. Lesson Context: Zechariah as Prophecy

The book of Zechariah is located in a section of the Old Testament known as the Minor Prophets. It is the longest of those 12 books, comprising about 22 percent of that section.

Following an introductory paragraph (Zechariah 1:1-6), the book falls into three major parts. The first part, Zechariah 1:7–6:15, features eight night visions, and the format is apocalyptic—vivid, unusual visions of future events. This type of literature seems to have its origins during the time that the Jews were captives in Babylon. Some text in the books of Daniel and Ezekiel also are examples.

Zechariah 7 and 8 constitute the second major part, revealed to the prophet about two years after the night visions (compare 1:7 with 7:1). This segment records responses by the Lord to observances of fasting that were asked by a delegation from Bethel. The Law of Moses prescribed only one day of fasting for the Israelites: the Day of Atonement. That fasting is inherent in the phrase "afflict your souls" (Leviticus 23:26-32; Numbers 29:7). But while the Jews were in Babylon, they had introduced more fasts into the calendar (Zechariah 7:3, 5; 8:19).

Zechariah 9–14, the third major part of the book, presents itself as two undated prophecies. The first prophecy, chapters 9–11, speaks of God's forthcoming actions of judgment and mercy; today's lesson text is part of this prophecy. The second prophecy, chapters 12–14, describes a coming Day of the Lord. The book of Zechariah is quoted seven times in the New Testament:

Zechariah 8:16 in Ephesians 4:25
Zechariah 9:9 in Matthew 21:5 and
    John 12:15
Zechariah 11:12-13 in Matthew 27:9-10
Zechariah 12:10 in John 19:37
Zechariah 13:7 in Matthew 26:31 and
    Mark 14:27

As Zechariah 9 begins, the first eight verses are believed to focus on events during the time of Alexander the Great (lived 356–323 BC). He defeated the Persian army under Darius III at the famous battle of Issus in 333 BC, near the northeastern corner of the Mediterranean Sea. Alexander then turned south, and the places named in Zechariah 9:1-8 parallel his route. Verse 8, which immediately precedes the text of today's lesson, is thought to refer to the fact that Alexander's Greek army did not attack Jerusalem but continued on to Egypt. God blessed and condemned empires and kings throughout the centuries. Each one had a role in God's plan that would ultimately bring the Messiah into the world at just the right time in history (Galatians 4:4). Alexander's conquests are considered very important, for they fulfilled what God intended!

If the time line references above are correct, it means that there is a gap of more than 300 years between the events predicted in verses 8 and 9, given how this text is seen to be fulfilled in Matthew 21:5 and John 12:15. Some students have called this literary feature "prophetic foreshortening": what appears at first glance to be prophecies that are to be fulfilled closely together in time turn out to be separated by centuries. Another example of prophetic foreshortening is found in Isaiah 61:1-2, given where Jesus stops His quotation of that text in Luke 4:16-19. The time gap between the utterance of the prophecy of Zechariah 9:9 and its fulfillment is even wider: at least 500 years.

I. The Lord's King
(Zechariah 9:9)

A. Rejoicing Commanded (v. 9a)

9a. Rejoice greatly, O daughter of Zion; shout, O daughter of Jerusalem: behold, thy King cometh unto thee.

Parallelism, a feature of Hebrew poetry, is seen when the writer repeats a thought by using words that are synonyms or are nearly so. We see two instances of parallelism before us: the words translated *rejoice* and *shout* both imply a celebration in this context; likewise, the designations *Zion* and

Jerusalem are parallel. Those two designations combine with the word *daughter* in nine instances in the Old Testament. One such is Zephaniah 3:14, which expresses an imperative that is virtually identical to the one in our text (see lesson 4). Recognizing parallelism keeps us from the error of seeing two actions, locations, etc., being described when in fact there is only one.

The celebration is to be in response to the arrival of a *King* in the city. This royal arrival is not one of conquest, given the commands to rejoice and shout. Monarchs sometimes came with armies to conquer or punish a rebellious group (2 Chronicles 36:17; etc.). But the arrival of this king is to be an occasion of rejoicing; the rest of verse 9, below, tells us why.

B. Reasons to Rejoice (vv. 9b-c)
9b. He is just, and having salvation.

To be *just* is to be righteous, which is how the same Hebrew word is translated in 2 Chronicles 12:6. This is definitely a quality that you want in your king! His righteousness is to be one hallmark of His reign. This king will rule for the benefit of the people, doing what is best for them. We see the ideas of being just and *having salvation* together in several other passages, especially Jeremiah 23:5-6.

9c. Lowly, and riding upon an ass, and upon a colt the foal of an ass.

Kings are often arrogant in wielding power. Amazingly, this king will be exactly the opposite! We see this trait of lowliness throughout the earthly life of Jesus, from birth to death. The animal that He chose to ride in His triumphal entry into Jerusalem is but one example. It was His city and His temple, but He entered it in the same way as thousands of others.

Each of the four Gospels tells of the fulfillment of this predicted event (Matthew 21:1-11; Mark 11:1-10; Luke 19:28-40; John 12:12-19). And all four Gospels refer to the animal on which Jesus rode into the city. A donkey was for common people; kings were expected to be on horses or in chariots (compare 2 Kings 9:21).

Matthew 21:4 affirms specifically that "all this was done, that it might be fulfilled which was spo-

ken by the prophet." John 12:14 is more succinct in declaring the fulfillment to be "as it is written."

A Surprising Nature

When my parents were newlyweds in the 1960s, they accepted a large loan from an elderly relative as a down payment on their first house. What appeared to be an unselfish act of generosity soon turned into misery for my parents, however. The anxious gentleman repeatedly called them to ask about repayment. He fretted to other relatives about the loan, even though my parents were making all their payments on time. My dad worked overtime hours in order to be able to repay the loan early and be freed from this emotional pit.

Thirty years later, my parents loaned money to me and my wife for the same purpose. But the loan actually turned out to be a gift because they ultimately refused to accept repayment. Which of these two accounts better illustrates the surprising nature of King Jesus? How should your conclusion be reflected in your service to Him?   —A. W.

II. The Lord's Kingdom
(Zechariah 9:10-13)
A. Peace Secured (v. 10)

10. And I will cut off the chariot from Ephraim, and the horse from Jerusalem, and the battle bow shall be cut off: and he shall speak peace unto the heathen: and his dominion shall be from sea even to sea, and from the river even to the ends of the earth.

Ephraim is the name of one of the 10 northern tribes of Israel (Numbers 1:33; etc.). As that designation is used here, however, it stands for the entire northern nation of divided Israel. Similarly,

Jerusalem in this context stands for the southern kingdom of divided Israel, sometimes called Judah. The intention is to show that the entirety of Israel is included in this promise (compare Isaiah 7:17; 11:13; Ezekiel 37:16; Hosea 5:12-14; 6:4).

Through the use of various images, Zechariah foretold the *peace* that the coming king was to bring to the nation. This peace would not be only for the nation of Israel, but for everyone—pictured as being *from sea even to sea* and *from the river* (perhaps the Euphrates River) to *the ends of the earth*. His reign will extend throughout the planet; no place will be exempt. There will be no small regional wars, no pockets of resistance. It will be peace, peace, peace, forever and ever!

This prediction calls again to mind the concept of prophetic foreshortening, discussed above. The events of Zechariah 9:9 have already occurred, but those of the verse before us are yet to happen in a physical sense and are still in progress in a spiritual sense. This peace is more than mere absence of conflict between humans. It is the peace of reconciliation between God and people.

This verse features a subtle change that is easy to overlook. Notice that the verse begins with what *I will* do with the chariots, and then it shifts to the fact that *he shall speak peace*. From our perspective in the year 2023, it is obvious that the reference in Zechariah 9:9 is to Jesus, so the *he* here in verse 10 refers to what the Son of God would do. Even so, Matthew 10:34-36 speaks of the conflict He brings as well.

Visual for Lesson 5. *Point to this visual as you ask learners how they have been "saved to shine" in light of this lesson's Scripture text.*

phrase *the blood of thy covenant* looking to the past (as in Exodus 24:8) or to the future (as in Matthew 26:28)? The context implies that the redemptive work of the Messiah is in view (compare Luke 4:16-19). Throughout history it was a hopeless situation to be sentenced to a *pit*. The additional description of such a place being waterless brings to mind the prophet Jeremiah, who as a prisoner was once confined in such a place (Jeremiah 38:6; compare Genesis 37:24). The shedding of Jesus' blood gave hope to the hopeless—those trapped in the bondage pit of sin.

Even so, a double reference may be intended. In that case, the physical release from Babylonian captivity (fresh in the memory of Zechariah's original audience) serves as a type (that is, a pattern) of spiritual freedom that Messiah was to bring.

C. Promise of Plenty (v. 12)

12. Turn you to the strong hold, ye prisoners of hope: even to day do I declare that I will render double unto thee.

Those who are *prisoners of hope* are commanded to go to a place of security. The original word being translated *strong hold* is difficult; this is the only place in the Old Testament where the Hebrew word occurs, so there are no other texts to compare it with. The most likely meaning is that it refers to Jerusalem. At the time Zechariah prophesied, Jerusalem's walls had not yet been rebuilt. So any safety experienced in that location would

---

What Do You Think?

How can your congregation promote peace among the nations as a sign of the coming eternal peace Jesus brings?

Digging Deeper

What local strategies can be employed in pursuit of this lofty goal?

B. Prisoners Released (v. 11)

11. As for thee also, by the blood of thy covenant I have sent forth thy prisoners out of the pit wherein is no water.

This verse raises an important question: Is the

have to come from God personally (compare and contrast Joel 3:16).

The imagery indicates that when one returns to God, He will give more than was expected. The ancient Israelites had received a *double* portion of God's wrath for their idolatry; but they could experience a double portion of God's blessing by returning to Him (compare Isaiah 40:2; 51:19; 61:7; Jeremiah 16:18; Revelation 18:6).

> **What Do You Think?**
> What areas of your life might you describe as a prison?
>
> **Digging Deeper**
> While you wait for deliverance, how do you demonstrate that you are also a "prisoner of hope"?

D. Promise of Power (v. 13)

13. When I have bent Judah for me, filled the bow with Ephraim, and raised up thy sons, O Zion, against thy sons, O Greece, and made thee as the sword of a mighty man.

On the extended references to *Judah* and *Ephraim* and the ultimate disposition of weapons of war, see on Zechariah 9:10, above. The phrase *against thy sons, O Greece* reverses the problem noted in Joel 3:6 (compare Daniel 8:21; 10:20; 11:2). Although the arrival of the Messiah is some 500 years beyond the time of Zechariah's prophecy, God promises to rescue His people during that (to the readers, uncertain) interval.

After Alexander the Great died in 323 BC, his Greek Empire was divided among four of his generals. The boundary between two of their territories ran through Palestine, which became a flash point for conflict. The Apocrypha, nonbiblical writings from the time between the Old and New Testaments, documents these conflicts. The most significant was the Maccabean Revolt of 167–160 BC. It wasn't until 152 BC that the Jews regained their autonomy. But it didn't last. By 63 BC, the land of Judah and surroundings were again under foreign domination: the Roman Empire. More details about God's plan to defend His people are found in Zechariah 12:1-9.

III. The Lord's Care
(Zechariah 9:16-17)
A. The Lord Saves (v. 16)

16a. And the Lord their God shall save them in that day as the flock of his people.

The figure of speech for the Lord's *people* changes from military action to the familiar picture of caring for a *flock* of sheep (compare Psalm 100:3). God's care had seemed distant or nonexistent during the Babylonian exile (Psalm 137; Lamentations 3:43-44; etc.). But the prophet expresses confident trust that such an outlook was to be temporary.

16b. For they shall be as the stones of a crown, lifted up as an ensign upon his land.

The imagery changes yet again. This promise reveals the great value that the Lord saw in the people; they were indeed as precious gemstones that adorn *a crown* (compare 2 Samuel 12:30; Isaiah 62:3). The nature of the blessings won't be hidden. Rather, they will be *lifted up as an ensign upon his land* as a witness for all to see.

> **What Do You Think?**
> Who in your life demonstrates an attitude befitting a stone in God's crown?
>
> **Digging Deeper**
> What prevents you from carrying yourself in a manner that communicates God's valuation of you?

The 50-Cow Wife

In a certain African tribe, it was the custom for a man to give a gift of cows to his bride's father as compensation for the father's expenses in rearing her. A particularly desirable match from a prominent family might fetch a brideprice of 20 or even 30 cows. Much more common was a gift of 10 cows or fewer, due to the poverty of the area.

A young man once came to a village with a vast herd of 50 cattle, and he offered a father the whole herd in exchange for his daughter—a plain, shy girl with dim marriage prospects. Shocked, the father hastily agreed.

The village did not hear from the couple for a year. But one day the man returned with a glowing, beautiful woman by his side. She was adorned like an African princess and was carrying a healthy baby. At first the people of the village thought he had taken a different wife. But looking closer, they realized she was the one from their village! "How did you know that she would actually become a beautiful woman?" they asked. He replied, "A woman's true beauty is found in the eyes of the man who values her most."

God values you more than anything—so much so that He purchased you at an astounding price. Are you willing for God to hold you up like a crown for the whole world to see how and why He values you?   —A. W.

B. The Lord Supplies (v. 17)

17. For how great is his goodness, and how great is his beauty! corn shall make the young men cheerful, and new wine the maids.

Two sudden praises are a response to the promises of the previous verse. God is *great*—all the time! The language goes back to the results of what God will do. The word *corn* in the *King James Version* is an older term for grain in general. Bread, made from grain, was a staple in the diet, so it was a blessing that would bring life and health. Food was not taken for granted. When the word *corn* occurs with *wine* (about 30 times in the Old Testament), the picture is either one of prosperity (example 2 Kings 18:32) or its opposite (example: Deuteronomy 28:51).

What Do You Think?
How does a time of feasting remind you of God's goodness?

Digging Deeper
Are these reminders limited to religious feasts (such as the Lord's Supper)? Why or why not?

Conclusion

A. Play Money vs. Real Money

Imagine a father playing a board game with his young son. The game involves buying and selling things with play money; thus the youngster learns quickly the value of the money in his hand. As the lad expresses his appreciation in that regard, his father responds, "Someday I'm going to give you thousands of dollars." The boy is eager to receive the gift, but what he doesn't realize is that his father is referring to real money. The father doesn't make the distinction at the time of the promise because his son hasn't yet reached the age where he can appreciate the difference. The son is focused on the apparent value of play money.

So it would seem with today's text. God is intent on bringing eternal life ("real money") to those created in His image. But He made promises to those under the old covenant in terms of physical, earthly deliverance ("play money") because that was their frame of reference. Even into the New Testament era, people had a hard time seeing the spiritual as surpassing the earthly, of seeing beyond the temporary to the eternal (Matthew 13:10-13; Acts 1:6; etc.).

Where are you in that regard?

B. Prayer

Almighty God, as we think about Jesus as king, we resolve that our goal every day will be to remember that our citizenship is in Heaven and to be the best citizens possible of His kingdom. In Jesus' name we pray. Amen.

C. Thought to Remember

Jesus' kingdom is superior to any alternative—now and forever.

How to Say It

apocalypse	uh-*pock*-uh-lips.
Babylonian	Bab-ih-*low*-nee-un.
Ephraim	*Ee*-fray-im.
Ezra	*Ez*-ruh.
Haggai	*Hag*-eye or *Hag*-ay-eye.
Judah	*Joo*-duh.
Mediterranean	*Med*-uh-tuh-**ray**-nee-un.
Zechariah	Zek-uh-**rye**-uh.
Zephaniah	Zef-uh-*nye*-uh.
Zion	*Zi*-un.

Involvement Learning

Enhance your lesson with KJV Bible Student *(from your curriculum supplier) and the reproducible activity page (at www.standardlesson.com or in the back of the* KJV Standard Lesson Commentary Deluxe Edition*).*

Into the Lesson

Start with an activity to get people thinking about gratitude. Draw a large heart on your board. Distribute small sticky notes and pencils. Invite participants to quickly write things they're grateful for (each on a separate note) and then attach them to the large heart. Read aloud some of the responses as you discuss together what people put in the large heart.

Alternative. Distribute copies of the "Attitude of Gratitude" exercise from the activity page, which you can download. Have learners complete it individually (in a minute or less) before revealing the answers.

After calling time on either alternative, invite responses to these questions: 1–What does gratitude do for us? 2–How is gratitude connected to worship? Transition by talking about how the group will be studying verses from Zechariah to discover that there is much to rejoice about and be thankful for!

Into the Word

Divide the participants into small groups. Distribute a handout (you create) of the questions below for in-group discussions. At the top put the heading *Prophecy Fulfilled.* Then include the instructions and questions with space for them to write answers. Do not to include the answers in italics: Read Zechariah 9:9 and answer the following questions. 1–At the time when Jesus lived on earth, what were the people's expectations about the Messiah? *(They thought He would be a king who would come in great power and conquer the Romans.)* 2–What was included in this prophecy that should have given them different expectations? *(It says He would be "lowly and riding upon an ass.")* 3–All four Gospels tell the story of Jesus' triumphal entry. What are the four references? *(Matthew 21:1-11; Mark 11:1-10; Luke 19:28-40; John 12:12-19)* 4–How is Zechariah's prophecy fulfilled by Jesus? *(He enters the city of Jerusalem riding on a donkey, and the people are praising Him and rejoicing.)* After calling time, ask groups to share their answers with the class.

Ask for a volunteer to read Zechariah 9:10-13, 16-17. Invite the group to describe what the coming king will be like. Write the descriptors on the board throughout the discussion. Use the following questions to help frame the discussion. Possible answers are in italics: 1–What word will He speak to the heathen? *(peace)* 2–How far will His dominion extend? *(from sea to sea and to the ends of the earth)* 3–How will He set prisoners free? *(by the blood of the covenant)* 4–What word does He give to the prisoners? *(hope)* 5–In what way will He be like a shepherd? *(He will save His flock.)* 6–Which image does he use to show how God will view His people? *(stones in a crown)*

Bring everyone back together for a whole-class discussion on how Jesus fulfilled the position of king as described by Zechariah. Write their ideas on the board.

Into Life

Have participants form their small groups again. Ask groups to discuss the wrong ideas many people today have about who Jesus is. Then ask groups to compare those wrong ideas with the description of Jesus as king. After allowing time for the groups to discuss, invite the whole group to share ideas about how to present Jesus as He really is.

Alternative. Distribute copies of "Play by the Rules" exercise from the activity page. Have participants work in groups of three or four to complete as indicated before sharing their rules with the larger group. Allow several minutes for groups to complete this activity.

In the remaining minutes, have participants each write a short prayer rejoicing and thanking God for the many wonderful qualities in Jesus, our king and Messiah.

The Kingdom Has Come upon You

Devotional Reading: Matthew 6:5-15
Background Scripture: Matthew 12:1-32

Matthew 12:22-32

22 Then was brought unto him one possessed with a devil, blind, and dumb: and he healed him, insomuch that the blind and dumb both spake and saw.

23 And all the people were amazed, and said, Is not this the son of David?

24 But when the Pharisees heard it, they said, This fellow doth not cast out devils, but by Beelzebub the prince of the devils.

25 And Jesus knew their thoughts, and said

unto them, Every kingdom divided against itself is brought to desolation; and every city or house divided against itself shall not stand:

26 And if Satan cast out Satan, he is divided against himself; how shall then his kingdom stand?

27 And if I by Beelzebub cast out devils, by whom do your children cast them out? therefore they shall be your judges.

28 But if I cast out devils by the Spirit of God, then the kingdom of God is come unto you.

29 Or else how can one enter into a strong man's house, and spoil his goods, except he first bind the strong man? and then he will spoil his house.

30 He that is not with me is against me; and he that gathereth not with me scattereth abroad.

31 Wherefore I say unto you, All manner of sin and blasphemy shall be forgiven unto men: but the blasphemy against the Holy Ghost shall not be forgiven unto men.

32 And whosoever speaketh a word against the Son of man, it shall be forgiven him: but whosoever speaketh against the Holy Ghost, it shall not be forgiven him, neither in this world, neither in the world to come.

Key Text

If I cast out devils by the Spirit of God, then the kingdom of God is come unto you. —**Matthew 12:28**

The Righteous Reign of God

Unit 2: Jesus Envisions the Kingdom
Lessons 6–9

Lesson Aims

After participating in this lesson, each learner will be able to:

1. Summarize Jesus' encounter with the Pharisees.

2. Explain why the logic used by the Pharisees was defective.

3. Identify an instance of false logic used against Christians today.

Lesson Outline

Introduction

A. Unforgiven

The 1992 film *Unforgiven* won four Academy Awards, including the award for Best Picture, in telling the story of an aging farmer who regressed into his previous occupation as a gunslinger. The appeal of the movie for popular audiences is its moral ambiguity. The film takes place in the so-called Wild West, an era depicted as a time when morality was in the eye of the beholder (compare Deuteronomy 12:8; Judges 21:25). During this time, it seemed that a person was only "forgiven" or "unforgiven" on the basis of self-rationalizations.

The Bible, however, is much clearer on what has to happen for a person to be forgiven. Even so, I once counseled a church member who was convinced that he had committed an unforgivable sin. He was in despair, deciding if to live a dissolute life because he would not receive forgiveness. The possibility of committing a sin that God will not forgive was troubling, even terrifying.

Understanding what Jesus taught concerning sin that will not be forgiven requires that we pay close attention to the setting and context of today's lesson.

B. Lesson Context

Although the Gospel of Matthew does not identify its author explicitly, the early church attributed it to Matthew, one of the original 12 apostles chosen by Jesus. His given name was Levi (Mark 2:14; Luke 5:27-29), being named after one of the 12 sons of Jacob (see Genesis 29:34; 35:23). Levi was the patriarch of the priestly tribe (Deuteronomy 18:1). The name Matthew is from the Hebrew language and means "gift of the Lord." Some believe this may have been a nickname given to him, perhaps even by Jesus (compare Matthew 16:18; Mark 3:16-17).

We know little about Matthew's family background, although he is once identified as a "son of Alphaeus" (Mark 2:14), creating the possibility that he was a brother of "James the son of Alphaeus" (Matthew 10:3), another of the 12 apostles.

Matthew's chosen profession was to be a publican (tax collector). This means that he worked for the hated foreign overlords, the Romans who occupied Palestine. His job was to squeeze taxes from his fellow Jews to appease the oppressors, and he was allowed to dip into this money flow to enrich himself (compare Luke 19:2, 8). Such tax collectors were seen as traitors. Indeed, the Gospels categorize them with "sinners" and "harlots" (Matthew 9:9-10; 21:32).

By contrast, the Pharisees of Jesus' day were regarded in a positive manner, zealous for scrupulously keeping the laws of the Jews (see Acts 26:5). Even in Galilee, far from Jerusalem, the Pharisees formed an elite brotherhood that demanded strict observance of their understandings of the law. They were identified by their mode of dress (Matthew 23:5). While influential, they were never numerous. Some estimate their numbers to have been fewer than 10,000 at the time of Jesus. They frequently appear in the Gospels as Jesus' critics and opponents, and He repeatedly pointed out their hypocrisies, teaching that the people needed another way to find God's favor than the way of the Pharisees (see 5:20; 23:13-32). Similar and parallel accounts to today's confrontation are Matthew 9:32-34; Mark 3:22-29; and Luke 11:14-23.

I. Kingdom and Healing
(Matthew 12:22-24)
A. Three Maladies Cured (v. 22)

22. Then was brought unto him one possessed with a devil, blind, and dumb: and he healed him, insomuch that the blind and dumb both spake and saw.

The account begins much as the one in Matthew 9:32 does: with a succinct setting of the stage of the controversy that followed. By this time, Jesus had already garnered widespread acclaim as a healer (Matthew 4:23-25; 12:15). The Greek word translated *healed* here is the source of our word *therapy*. It has the sense of a person being made whole or delivered from afflictions. The healing ministry of Jesus included casting out "devils," or demons (4:24; 8:16). In the case at hand, the man brought to Jesus suffered physical disability in two ways, in addition to being demonized. To be both *blind* and *dumb* is an unusual combination, because inability

to speak is more often associated with being profoundly deaf. Nevertheless, Jesus *healed him*, presumably also expelling the demon—with the result that the man could both see and speak.

What Do You Think?
In what ways can people lack spiritual "sight" because of sin?
Digging Deeper
What evidence is there that a person has received spiritual "sight" because of Jesus' work?

B. Two Reactions Provoked (vv. 23-24)

23. And all the people were amazed, and said, Is not this the son of David?

To proclaim Jesus to be *the son of David* was a way to acknowledge Jesus as the long-awaited Messiah of the Jews (see Romans 1:3). Some believed God's Messiah would have a divine gift of healing (Matthew 9:27-30). Jesus' mastery of both the oppressive demon and the physical issues caused *the people* to wonder if He was indeed the Messiah they had been waiting for. Not everyone recognized that possibility though (next verse).

What Do You Think?
How do the different titles of Jesus, such as "son of David," describe the various aspects of His person and work?
Digging Deeper
What title do you need to understand better, and how will you study it?

24. But when the Pharisees heard it, they said, This fellow doth not cast out devils, but by Beelzebub the prince of the devils.

Some *Pharisees*, not present at the healing, had a different explanation. They did not doubt the fact of the exorcism, but to explain it they attributed Jesus' power to an unholy, undivine source. In other words, they ascribed Jesus' command of the demons to His being in league with the demons themselves. Their logic was that Jesus' control over the minor demon that afflicted the man was due to the fact that Jesus was in league with a greater demon. The people had great respect for the

Visual for Lessons 6 & 9. *As the class discusses Matthew 12:28, ask them for examples of how God's kingdom is different from earthly kingdoms.*

Pharisees, so this slanderous accusation would be taken seriously. These religious leaders had made this charge before (Matthew 9:34), and their opposition to Jesus was becoming more entrenched.

Historically, the name *Beelzebub* is related to the name "Baal-zebub," the pagan god of the Philistine city of Ekron (2 Kings 1:2-3, 6, 16). The name means something like "lord of the dwelling," which relates to the account at hand. The Pharisees did not see Beelzebub as a pagan god, however. Rather, he was thought to be *the prince of the devils*, meaning the ruler of all the demons. Their charge against Jesus was that He was the opposite of the Lord's anointed one, the chosen Messiah. Jesus' power, they concluded, came not from God but from the satanic realm.

The Bible depicts demons as crafty and unified in their opposition to God's work and in their desire to deceive people (example: Genesis 3:1). Satan was the great deceiver and liar, and still is today (see Revelation 20:10). To lump the work of Jesus in with theirs surely takes one's breath away!

Calling Good Evil

In the first half of the twentieth century, Russian Communists did their best to stamp out Christianity in their country. Church buildings were demolished or otherwise "repurposed." Leaders were harassed, arrested, and killed. Religious holidays were canceled. According to the government, Christians were mentally deficient,

immoral, and unpatriotic traitors who cooperated with foreign spies. As a result, many believers met in secret, sometimes under the guise of having a birthday party.

The Pharisees of Jesus' day were not the first to call good evil (see Isaiah 5:20), and they won't be the last. However, no matter how powerful Jesus' opponents were, He was not afraid of them, and we should not be either (Matthew 10:28). The same Jesus who endured abuse has guided His church through difficult years of persecution, and He continues to do the same today. Whenever opposition comes, is your first thought to remember that He who is in you is greater than he who is in the world (1 John 4:4)? If not, why not? —A. W.

II. Kingdom and Unity
(Matthew 12:25-30)
A. Division's Result Is Failure (v. 25)

25. And Jesus knew their thoughts, and said unto them, Every kingdom divided against itself is brought to desolation; and every city or house divided against itself shall not stand.

Jesus was never deceived about the motives of His opponents. He saw into the hearts of people and *knew their thoughts* (Luke 6:8; etc.). In the case at hand, Jesus knew of the jealousy of these Pharisees that pushed them to wrongly interpret the healings as evil in origin.

When under personal attack, there are typically three ways for a person to react:

1. Don't react; say nothing
2. Defend yourself with words of correction
3. Launch a counterattack

Here we see Jesus responding with option 2 as He points out the logical absurdity of the Pharisees' conclusion.

Many people have heard about Abraham Lincoln's "House Divided" speech, delivered on June 16, 1858. But it should be remembered that Jesus used the phrasing first in pointing out that any *kingdom* or *city* or household that bickers and becomes *divided against itself* will fall. Turning against one's allies and fighting them is utter foolishness, for you are aiding and abetting your enemies.

B. Satan's Realm Is Unified (vv. 26-27)

26. And if Satan cast out Satan, he is divided against himself; how shall then his kingdom stand?

Jesus continues under option 2, above. Both Jesus and the Pharisees see the demonic realm as an organized *kingdom* (compare Ephesians 2:2; Revelation 2:13). This stronghold stands in opposition to the kingdom of Heaven, which was at the center of Jesus' preaching of good news (Matthew 9:35). Spiritual war exists between the kingdom of Satan and the kingdom of God, not as an internal strife within Satan's domain. No one thought Satan or the demons were fools in that regard; they would not work against themselves.

27. And if I by Beelzebub cast out devils, by whom do your children cast them out? therefore they shall be your judges.

Having destroyed the Pharisees' argument, Jesus now switches to option 3 as He counterattacks (see above). Jesus' response assumes the personhood of *Beelzebub*, tacitly agreeing with the Pharisees' claim that Beelzebub was "the prince of the devils" (Matthew 12:24, above). There is evidence in the Dead Sea Scrolls that the name Beelzebub was used as a synonym for Satan in Israel at the time, and we should understand it this way here. This is not a hypothetical entity for either Jesus or the Pharisees. Jesus therefore started from common ground to use their charge against Him —a charge that He was empowered by Satan and the demonic—to reveal their hypocrisy.

Ancient sources tell us that some Jews were known as exorcists in this period. One example we have is in Acts 19:13-16, the account of the seven sons of Sceva. These Jews were itinerant exorcists in the Ephesus region who failed spectacularly to drive out a demon when they used the name of Jesus inappropriately.

Jesus even hinted at a personal, family relationship between the accusing Pharisees and some local exorcists, their *children*. Jesus warned that if such local exorcists were summoned, they would serve as condemning *judges* against the Pharisees. This would defend Jesus' authority as coming from God, not Satan, further exposing the hypocrisy of the charge.

C. God's Spirit Unites (vv. 28-30)

28. But if I cast out devils by the Spirit of God, then the kingdom of God is come unto you.

Jesus used this occasion to announce a fulfillment of something that He had been preaching. He began His ministry by proclaiming that the people had to repent of their sins because God's kingdom was near (Matthew 4:17). He taught His disciples to pray for the coming of the kingdom of God (6:10). Here He cited His authority over *devils* as a confirmation of the arrival of *the kingdom*. God's reign on earth had overtaken Satan's rule (also John 12:31). No demon could withstand the one empowered *by the Spirit of God*! The work of God was evident in Israel, banishing the evil spirits that had crippled and tormented the people (see Luke 7:21; etc.).

> ### What Do You Think?
> What evidence have you seen of the work of the kingdom of God in your neighborhood or town?
> ### Digging Deeper
> How can believers remain confident in the ultimate victory of God, even when evil appears prevalent?

29. Or else how can one enter into a strong man's house, and spoil his goods, except he first bind the strong man? and then he will spoil his house.

Jesus offers one more analogy to show the absurdity of the Pharisees' charge. The analogy involves an "everyone knows" type of illustration. A thief who wishes to steal from *a strong man's house* knows that the homeowner must be neutralized before any thievery is possible; otherwise, the thief risks physical harm. One method the robber might use would be to *bind the strong man*. If tied up securely, the man could do nothing but watch as his house is burgled.

The lesson of the analogy is that Jesus' actions in casting out demons is to *spoil* Satan's house. It is to mess with Satan's plans and operations. Since Satan is powerful, how could this be? Only if Jesus were able to neutralize, or *bind*, Satan (see Revelation

20:1-3). Jesus could do this by "the Spirit of God" (Matthew 12:28, above), who is infinitely stronger than the strongest member of the demonic world, Satan himself. Jesus was not working for Satan. Instead, Jesus has overcome Satan/Beelzebub himself (compare Luke 10:18; Revelation 12:7-9).

30. He that is not with me is against me; and he that gathereth not with me scattereth abroad.

Jesus ended His comments with a warning. For a person not to recognize and appreciate His power to heal and cast out demons meant that person was *against* Him. Likewise, one who did not gather with Jesus was working against Him by scattering those Jesus would call to himself. There was no middle ground, no neutral zone. The disinformation campaign of the Pharisees had dire eternal consequences, for no one who was against Jesus would prevail. In the end, all will bow to Him in worship (Philippians 2:10-11).

What Do You Think?

How do you ensure that you do not live contrary to God and His will?

Digging Deeper

What spiritual tools (see Ephesians 6:10-18) do you use to fight the influence of evil?

Undivided Kingdom

Gandhi was rumored to have said, "I like your Christ; I do not like your Christians." Similarly, an acquaintance from social media recently posted a lengthy rant about the selfishness and intolerance of professing Christians and the corruption of the church. By contrast, he sang the praises of Jesus himself—as a friend of sinners who cared about all parts of the person, physical as well as spiritual. He described Jesus as a fearless radical who spoke hard truths to people in power, called out self-righteous religious people for their hypocrisy, and threw in His lot with the poor and oppressed.

I responded that I *agreed* with his conclusions about Jesus, and that is exactly why I am a Christian. More than anything, the world needs the *real* Jesus, who is all too often hard to see through the

smoke and mirrors that some believers throw in the way. God is not divided against himself, nor is His kingdom. Do you live in a way that helps His kingdom grow, so that unbelievers see your actions and attitude and want what you have?   —A. W.

III. Kingdom and the Spirit
(Matthew 12:31-32)
A. Blasphemy (v. 31)

31. Wherefore I say unto you, All manner of sin and blasphemy shall be forgiven unto men: but the blasphemy against the Holy Ghost shall not be forgiven unto men.

Several times the Bible refers to something that has been called the unforgivable sin, or the unpardonable sin (compare Exodus 23:21; Hebrews 6:4-6; 10:26-27; 1 John 5:16). The verse before us identifies such a sin as *blasphemy against the Holy Ghost*. Therefore, the text takes a very dark turn at this point: Jesus stated that His opponents were flirting with eternal disaster.

Blaspheme is a Greek-based word referring to an insult or slander intended to harm the reputation of a person. Against a human this can be forgiven if admitted with repentance. But consistent and repetitive slander against the reputation of God and His work is another matter. For Jesus, slander against the Holy Spirit is the same as an insult against God.

B. Opposition (v. 32)

32. And whosoever speaketh a word against the Son of man, it shall be forgiven him: but whosoever speaketh against the Holy Ghost, it shall not be forgiven him, neither in this world, neither in the world to come.

Remarkably, even speaking against Jesus, *the Son of man,* can *be forgiven.* Church history is replete with stories of powerful opponents of Jesus (such as the apostle Paul) who came to faith and served the cause of Christ. That is not what the Pharisees were doing. They were attributing God's divine work among humanity to Satan! This was not accidental or casual. It was deliberate (compare Numbers 15:30-31).

We should understand this verse as a warning

rather than a pronouncement of judgment. None of the Gospel accounts of this incident indicate that the Pharisees had committed full blasphemy against the Holy Spirit and therefore had entered into a state of eternal unforgiveness. But they were surely close. That Jesus would issue this grim warning revealed His underlying love and concern for them. He did not want them to cross the line and be committed followers and servants of Satan.

> ### What Do You Think?
> How will you respond to Christians who believe that they have committed an unforgivable sin?
>
> ### Digging Deeper
> How does a person's willful defiance of God versus their willful concern to follow the ways of God inform your response?

Conclusion
A. Evil, Be Thou My Good

In Book IV of *Paradise Lost,* author John Milton has Satan musing at length on his situation and prospects. Satan realizes that his rebellion against God has left him without hope for redemption; thus he utters, "Farewell, hope." Satan then reasons, "All good to me is lost." He had begun a journey away from God from which there was no return. Therefore, he decided, "Evil, be thou my good"—one of the most chilling lines in all of literature.

What does it take to commit an eternal sin, a sin that cannot be forgiven, ever? Are we in daily danger of this, always walking a tightrope between salvation and eternal damnation? Could a careless word or thought condemn us for eternity?

We should recognize that some Christians fear the possibility of committing an unpardonable sin. However, we are probably not in a position to evaluate for sure whether it has been committed. Paul speaks of those who have a "seared" conscience (1 Timothy 4:2), referring to those who will not and so cannot repent. They have willingly reversed the order of good and evil in the universe, becoming like those Isaiah condemns when he says, "Woe unto them that call evil good, and

good evil; that put darkness for light, and light for darkness" (Isaiah 5:20). These are the ones who have agreed with Milton's Satan: "Evil, be thou my good." Some would say today that evil and depravity are celebrated more than good. But we must not turn our backs on the unrepentant people in our community, just as Jesus did not abandon the Pharisees without a warning.

In the end, it is for God, not us, to judge whether or when the unforgivable sin has been committed. The old rule of thumb is that if you are concerned about it, you have not yet committed it, for you still have a conscience that discerns good from evil. God and His Word call us constantly to repent. If you still sense the stirring in your heart to get right with the Lord, even if the stirring is weak, you must do so.

Jesus' words remain a lesson for today's church. Opponents of Christianity will always seek to discredit Jesus and divide His followers. Once confronted with the gospel, it is impossible to remain neutral. To reject Jesus is to be against Him. This may done subtly, however. If we're not careful, we may end up working against Jesus to divide and scatter His followers, bringing disunity to the body of Christ.

B. Prayer

Heavenly Father, we want to rely even more on the power of the Holy Spirit for good works and to please You. May we never be intimidated by those who refuse to recognize You and Your power in their midst. We pray in the name of the one who loves us, Jesus our Lord. Amen.

C. Thought to Remember
Learn from the Pharisees' mistakes.

How to Say It

Alphaeus	Al-*fee*-us.
Beelzebub	Bih-*el*-zih-bub.
Levi	*Lee*-vye.
Messiah	Meh-*sigh*-uh.
patriarch	*pay*-tree-ark.
Pharisees	*Fair*-ih-seez.
Sceva	*See*-vuh.

Involvement Learning

Enhance your lesson with KJV Bible Student *(from your curriculum supplier) and the reproducible activity page (at www.standardlesson.com or in the back of the* KJV Standard Lesson Commentary Deluxe Edition).

Into the Lesson

Write the following statement on the board:

What are the worst crimes?

Ask learners to brainstorm responses to the question and write their responses on the board. After responses are provided, work together as a whole class to rank the crimes from the perceived worst to perceived least bad.

Alternative. Distribute copies of "Seven Deadly Sins?" activity from the activity page, which you can download. Have learners work in pairs to complete as indicated. Allow volunteers to share with the class how they answered.

Make a transition to the lesson by saying, "Today we are going to study a passage of Scripture that can be difficult to understand. In it we will look at a certain deadly stance toward God and His work."

Into the Word

Ask a volunteer to read aloud Matthew 12:22-30. Divide the class into four groups and distribute a handout (you prepare) with the questions below. Each group should answer the question from the perspective of their group's namesake.

Healed Man Group: 1–What was it like to be possessed by a demon? 2–How did it affect your life? 3–In what ways did your life change after Jesus cast out the demon?

All the People Group: 1–What was your reaction when you saw Jesus heal the demon-possessed man? 2–In light of this healing, what did you think was Jesus' true identity?

Pharisees Group: 1–What upset you about Jesus' act of healing? 2–What accusation did you make against Jesus?

Jesus Group: 1–How did you answer the Pharisees? 2–What was especially illogical about their claims?

After five minutes, ask a volunteer from each group to present their group's responses.

Ask a volunteer to read aloud Matthew 12:31-32. Then distribute an index card to each learner. Say, "Most people would admit that they don't have a very clear understanding of the meaning of blasphemy against the Holy Spirit. I've used information from the lesson commentary to write some true-false statements about this subject."

Say the following statements and have each learner write down true or false for each statement. (Note: The correct answers are in italics.) After each question, review the answers with the class.

1. Blasphemy against the Holy Spirit will be forgiven. *False; "it shall not be forgiven." (v. 31)*

2. Jesus warned the Pharisees that by accusing Him of working with Satan, they were in danger of this blasphemy. *True.*

3. Slandering the reputation of another person is bad, but slandering or blaspheming God's reputation is more serious. *True.*

4. Speaking against Jesus is an unforgivable offense. *False; "whosoever speaketh a word against the Son of man, it shall be forgiven him." (v. 32)*

5. This sin of blasphemy against the Holy Spirit occurs when someone knowingly attributes the work of God's Spirit to Satan. *True.*

Into Life

Divide learners into pairs and have them use the internet on their smartphones to research examples of a faulty logic that is used against the Christian faith. After 10 minutes, ask volunteers for their findings and write the examples on the board. Have learners share ideas of how they would respond to each example. Close with a prayer, asking God for courage in the upcoming week to share the good news of Jesus in challenging situations.

Alternative. Distribute copies of the "Arguments Against" activity from the activity page. Have learners work in small groups to complete as indicated.

The Sower and the Seed

Devotional Reading: Psalm 95
Background Scripture: Matthew 13:1-23; Mark 4; Luke 8:5-15

Matthew 13:1-9, 18-23

1 The same day went Jesus out of the house, and sat by the sea side.

2 And great multitudes were gathered together unto him, so that he went into a ship, and sat; and the whole multitude stood on the shore.

3 And he spake many things unto them in parables, saying, Behold, a sower went forth to sow;

4 And when he sowed, some seeds fell by the way side, and the fowls came and devoured them up:

5 Some fell upon stony places, where they had not much earth: and forthwith they sprung up, because they had no deepness of earth:

6 And when the sun was up, they were scorched; and because they had no root, they withered away.

7 And some fell among thorns; and the thorns sprung up, and choked them:

8 But other fell into good ground, and brought forth fruit, some an hundredfold, some sixtyfold, some thirtyfold.

9 Who hath ears to hear, let him hear.

18 Hear ye therefore the parable of the sower.

19 When any one heareth the word of the kingdom, and understandeth it not, then cometh the wicked one, and catcheth away that which was sown in his heart. This is he which received seed by the way side.

20 But he that received the seed into stony places, the same is he that heareth the word, and anon with joy receiveth it;

21 Yet hath he not root in himself, but dureth for a while: for when tribulation or persecution ariseth because of the word, by and by he is offended.

22 He also that received seed among the thorns is he that heareth the word; and the care of this world, and the deceitfulness of riches, choke the word, and he becometh unfruitful.

23 But he that received seed into the good ground is he that heareth the word, and understandeth it; which also beareth fruit, and bringeth forth, some an hundredfold, some sixty, some thirty.

Key Text

He that received seed into the good ground is he that heareth the word, and understandeth it; which also beareth fruit, and bringeth forth, some an hundredfold, some sixty, some thirty. —**Matthew 13:23**

The Righteous Reign of God

Unit 2: Jesus Envisions the Kingdom
Lessons 6-9

Lesson Aims

After participating in this lesson, each learner will be able to:

1. Summarize the parable of the sower.
2. Describe the fruit to be brought forth.
3. State which soil in Matthew 13:19-21 he or she is most like and suggest a plan for change.

Lesson Outline

Introduction
  A. Teaching Methods
  B. Lesson Context
 I. Teaching by the Shore (Matthew 13:1-3a)
  A. Setting (v. 1)
  B. Audience (v. 2)
  C. Method (v. 3a)
 II. Sowing of Seed (Matthew 13:3b-9)
  A. On Hardened Soil (vv. 3b-4)
  B. On Shallow Soil (vv. 5-6)
  C. On Thorny Soil (v. 7)
  D. On Fertile Soil (vv. 8-9)
III. Explaining the Meaning (Matthew 13:18-23)
  A. Failure to Understand (vv. 18-19)
  B. Failure to Endure (vv. 20-21)
  C. Failure to Overcome (v. 22)
    Real-Life Weeds
  D. Fruitful Discipleship (v. 23)
    A Fertile Heart
Conclusion
  A. Four Types of Hearers
  B. Prayer
  C. Thought to Remember

Introduction

A. Teaching Methods

An internet search of "teaching methods" quickly leaves the researcher buried under an avalanche of claimed methods—100 or more. A struggle to narrow those down to manageable types or categories leads to the foundational distinction between teacher-centered methods and student-centered methods. In teacher-centered methods, the instructors are authority figures who deliver knowledge; this is sometimes described as being a "sage on the stage." In student-centered methods, teachers function more as facilitators; this is sometimes described as being a "guide on the side." The distinction seems simple enough. But complexity asserts itself anew when varying levels of technology are considered under each method.

Analyzing the teaching methods of Jesus would seem to be simpler because there is little or no technology factor to consider. Yet there is no consensus regarding the enumeration of His methods. One researcher identifies five teaching methods Jesus used, another says there were seven, while a third researcher identifies no fewer than nine! Even so, prominent in *every* such listing is teaching via the use of parables. Today's study considers one of the longest of Jesus' parables.

B. Lesson Context

A problem we encounter with parables is how to define what a parable is. One definition that many learned in Sunday school is that "a parable is an earthly story with a heavenly meaning." Another is that "a parable is a narrative of some real or imaginary event in nature or in common life which is adapted to suggest a moral or religious truth." The lack of consensus here means that there is also no agreement on the exact number of parables recorded in the New Testament. An example is Luke 16:19-31 concerning the rich man and Lazarus. Many students say that this is not a parable since there is no other parable of Jesus in which a character is named.

Are you confused yet? If so, you're not alone! Jesus' disciples themselves had a hard time comprehending both the *why* and *what* of Jesus' use of figurative language in general and parables in particular (see Matthew 13:10-15; 15:15; 16:5-12; Luke 8:9; 12:41; John 16:29)—much to the consternation of Jesus himself (Mark 4:13; 7:18).

By the time we get to chapter 13 in the Gospel of Matthew, Jesus has used figurative language several times (Matthew 5:14-16; 7:1-6; 9:16-17; 12:24-30; see lesson 6). This yields a rather complex picture of Jesus when considered alongside the revealing of His supernatural authority over nature in stilling a storm (8:26) and over spirits (8:28-32). The previous lesson shows that while the people loved Jesus and His teachings, He had made enemies among the Pharisees and other Jewish elites.

Matthew 13 has been called "the parable chapter" because it has the greatest concentration of parables in the book; this chapter witnesses the first of 17 times that the words *parable* and *parables* are used in this Gospel account. The chapter begins with Jesus teaching the sower parable. In some ways this is the "paradigm parable"—the one that shows Jesus' disciples how to understand His parable illustrations correctly, as He intended them to be understood.

I. Teaching by the Shore
(Matthew 13:1-3a)

A. Setting (v. 1)

1. The same day went Jesus out of the house, and sat by the sea side.

The opening sentence is reasonably understood to have Jesus located near the Sea of Galilee. This body of water is the freshwater lake that dominates northern Palestine. *The house* was likely located in the village of Capernaum, a center for Jesus' activities at this time in His ministry (Matthew 4:13). When combined with the time indicator *the same day*, the picture is that of Jesus' shifting teaching locations so that more would be able to hear (compare the previous location in 12:46-49).

B. Audience (v. 2)

2. And great multitudes were gathered together unto him, so that he went into a ship, and sat; and the whole multitude stood on the shore.

Good soil produces an abundant crop.

Visual for Lesson 7. *Point to this visual as you ask learners for examples of the types of spiritual crops that result from good spiritual soil.*

A teaching stage was improvised. The water made a natural barrier for crowd control, so a small *ship* was available to serve as a floating podium. An added benefit was the excellent acoustic properties of the surface of the water. This allowed *the whole multitude* to hear Jesus' voice clearly.

A location of Capernaum makes it likely that the boat belonged to one of the disciples who had been engaged in commercial fishing (see Matthew 4:18-22). In 1986, the remains of a fishing boat dating from this period were recovered from the mud on the shore of the Sea of Galilee. It measured 27 feet in length and over 7 feet in width, making it a substantial vessel. Depictions of this scene that show Jesus sitting in a small rowboat likely underestimate the size of the boat in the text.

C. Method (v. 3a)

3a. And he spake many things unto them in parables.

This general statement implies that what follows is but a smattering of Jesus' teachings. Considering His ministry of about three years, figuring a few hours per week, the implication is that He spent hundreds of hours in teaching, surely repeating himself many times. The use of *parables* was a favorite method for this master teacher. Mark goes so far as to say that Jesus did not teach the crowds without using parables (Mark 4:34).

Scholars identify about 50 teachings in the Gospels that could be categorized as parables, although not all are called parables by the authors of the Gospels (see the Lesson Context). Several of them appear (with slight variations) in Matthew, in Mark, and in Luke. The parable of the sower and its interpretation are also found in Mark 4:1-20 and Luke 8:4-15. Variations are to be expected because we can assume Jesus reused His material and adjusted it to the situation. Jesus' parables were illustrations drawn from rural village life, close to the lives of His crowds.

What Do You Think?

In what ways can telling a story—fictitious or not—communicate the gospel message more clearly?

Digging Deeper

How can the true story of your own salvation inspire others to follow Jesus?

II. Sowing of Seed
(Matthew 13:3b-9)
A. On Hardened Soil (vv. 3b-4)

3b. Saying, Behold, a sower went forth to sow.

Modern farming has become precise and technical when it comes to getting seeds into the ground. Today, seeds produced solely for planting are available commercially. This was not the case in Jesus' day. An appropriate amount of grain was set aside at harvest to be used for the next year's planting. Seeds were a precious commodity, and planting day required preparation. The soil had to be tilled to receive the seeds. After planting day, the soil needed to be moist and warm enough to allow the seeds to germinate and begin to grow. In the few words *a sower went forth to sow*, Jesus created a word picture that resonated instantly with the agrarian life experiences of His audience. All was ready, and the sower headed out to do his job.

4. And when he sowed, some seeds fell by the way side, and the fowls came and devoured them up.

No matter how experienced the sower, the method of casting the seeds by hand could not be perfect. Some *seeds* would fall on *the way side*, the hard-packed soil of the paths in the field. Birds'

(*fowls*) eating of seeds is always problematic for farmers. But seeds having no cover have little hope of sprouting and growing. They are just bird food.

B. On Shallow Soil (vv. 5-6)

5. Some fell upon stony places, where they had not much earth: and forthwith they sprung up, because they had no deepness of earth.

The second word picture is that of soil characterized as lacking depth because it is *stony*—too many rocks. Fields in the hilly terrain of Galilee could have varying depths of topsoil. Hard bedrock might be but an inch or two under the surface, with none of the *deepness* the seeds needed to become productive crops. A competent sower would not knowingly spread seeds on this type of soil, but there would be few clues as to the depth of soil based on its surface appearance.

6. And when the sun was up, they were scorched; and because they had no root, they withered away.

In times of little rain, the moisture of the soil recedes from the surface. Deep roots can still tap the water necessary for healthy growth even in times of no rain, but shallow soil can lose almost all its water content. Seeds might germinate and sprout if they fell on wet, rocky ground that was covered by a thin layer of dirt. But lack of rain and a hot *sun* would cause them to be *scorched* and wither *away*.

C. On Thorny Soil (v. 7)

7. And some fell among thorns; and the thorns sprung up, and choked them.

A third type of soil the sower could encounter is dirt having noxious weeds already embedded. Modern farmers treat their fields with genetically specific herbicides that kill most noxious weeds without damaging the crop. But the farmers of Jesus' day had no such advantage. A bare field could have good topsoil that was full of weed seeds, and the rich dirt would benefit both the weeds and the crop seeds.

There could be several plants to fit the description of having *thorns*. One possibility is the spiky thistle plants known to this region. When a thistle appears, it must be pulled by the roots or else it will grow back again. Cutting it down is merely a temporary solution. The soil that Jesus envisages might have dormant thistle plants (already rooted) or the seeds of such plants in the soil, ready to germinate. The sower's wheat or barley seeds must compete with these thorny bushes, and his crop will be *choked*, producing puny growth and little grain.

> **What Do You Think?**
> What are the kinds of spiritual "soil" that you experience in your community?
>
> **Digging Deeper**
> How will you adjust your proclamation of the gospel to account for the challenges of that "soil"?

D. On Fertile Soil (vv. 8-9)

8. But other fell into good ground, and brought forth fruit, some an hundredfold, some sixtyfold, some thirtyfold.

All is not lost, though, because some seed is cast *into good ground.* This is soil that is not hard-packed, not shallow, and not full of weeds. The wheat or barley would grow quickly and produce a great return.

The stated return at harvest would have been amazing to Jesus' hearers. We estimate that even the best years in Palestine might have yielded a ten-fold harvest, with most years being six- or seven-fold. Jesus projected multiples of the yields of the best years His crowds could remember! This highlights the illustrative nature of the parable. Such a marvelous harvest could only be miraculous, accomplished through the blessing of God.

9. Who hath ears to hear, let him hear.

Jesus closes with what became a signature saying to end a teaching (see Matthew 11:15). We understand it better when we hear it again from the risen Christ in the book of Revelation. There we find the statement, "He that hath an ear, let him hear what the Spirit saith unto the churches" (Revelation 2:7, 11, 17, 29; 3:6, 13, 22). Jesus looks for those who have "spiritual ears," able to discern the spiritual truths He is teaching. In this case it would mean that some of the hearers (those with *ears to hear*)

were not left puzzling over this story about farming. They understood a deeper message, a spiritual message that Jesus wanted them to know.

III. Explaining the Meaning
(Matthew 13:18-23)

A. Failure to Understand (vv. 18-19)

18. Hear ye therefore the parable of the sower.

In the intervening text of Matthew 13:10-17 (not in today's lesson), the disciples came to Jesus for more information about His parables. They did not understand what His point was, and maybe they did not have the required spiritual hearing. The parable's meaning was important for them to know, though, so Jesus proceeded to explain *the parable of the sower* in detail.

19. When any one heareth the word of the kingdom, and understandeth it not, then cometh the wicked one, and catcheth away that which was sown in his heart. This is he which received seed by the way side.

Mark's version of Jesus' explanation is more direct than Matthew's, beginning, "The sower soweth the word" (Mark 4:14). This fits here too, for the main character in the little drama Jesus presented is not intended to be seen as a literal farmer, but as a preacher of *the word of the kingdom.* No one fits this description better than Jesus himself, for He had come preaching the good news about the kingdom of God (see 1:14-15). His preaching was met with various reactions.

Some hearers were (and are) like the hardened soil, with hearts and minds that do not understand even the basics of what Jesus was (and is) trying to communicate. The result: being like seeds that never even sprout. There can be no faith if there is no understanding. The attack comes not from literal birds, but from *the wicked one*—Satan

How to Say It

Capernaum	Kuh-*per*-nay-um.
Galilee	*Gal*-uh-lee.
Lazarus	*Laz*-uh-rus.
Pharisees	*Fair*-ih-seez.

himself. It is he who encourages people to dismiss the pleadings and warnings of Jesus as nonsense.

B. Failure to Endure (vv. 20-21)

20. But he that received the seed into stony places, the same is he that heareth the word, and anon with joy receiveth it.

A second type of soil is the hearer who is initially thrilled by the good news heard in Jesus' message about the kingdom. That message is understood and creates *joy* and hope in this person.

21. Yet hath he not root in himself, but dureth for a while: for when tribulation or persecution ariseth because of the word, by and by he is offended.

Despite this joyous reception, though, there are some who do not take this message to heart in a lasting way. They do not have an enduring faith. Jesus had taught that the kingdom must be received in repentance (Matthew 4:17), a change in orientation toward God and away from sin. Some are buoyed by the joy they experience, but they do not have a change in heart. When there is *tribulation or persecution*, their shallow faith will not survive. They will be like the shallowly rooted plants that cannot endure the scorching sun.

> **What Do You Think?**
> How will you offer discipleship to enthusiastic new believers to help their spiritual "roots" grow deeply?
>
> **Digging Deeper**
> What encouragement will you offer new believers who may face discouragement regarding their spiritual growth?

C. Failure to Overcome (v. 22)

22. He also that received seed among the thorns is he that heareth the word; and the care of this world, and the deceitfulness of riches, choke the word, and he becometh unfruitful.

The third type of reception of Jesus' message is found among those who do not forsake their worldly desires for service in the kingdom (example: 2 Timothy 4:10). Jesus would later say that to be His disciple, one has to "deny himself, and take up his cross, and follow me" (Matthew 16:24).

Believers cannot have divided loyalties. We cannot serve two masters equally (Matthew 6:24). A person who is still attached to the god of money may give the appearance of being a disciple, but he or she will be an *unfruitful* disciple. A wheat plant that competes with weeds and thorns for water, soil nutrients, and sunlight will not flourish or produce.

Real-Life Weeds

My daughter's friend Jenny spent much of one summer at our house. The two were inseparable—laughing in my daughter's room, going on walks to the park, and texting or video-calling friends. As part of the summer's activities, Jenny went to youth group with my daughter. We began picking her up for church on Sundays, and she expressed interest in knowing Jesus better. We loved Jenny and wanted her to know Jesus too.

In the winter, Jenny began to drift away from my daughter. There was no falling out, but my daughter felt like Jenny was distracted by other friends. Plus, Jenny's family started struggling and her parents separated. Even though we reached out to her and tried to help her feel loved and accepted by our family, she eventually stopped coming over altogether. My daughter said, "Mom, she does this sometimes. She gets to know people and then starts feeling like they don't like her, even when they do. So she pushes them away."

The challenges of Jenny's life and her anxiety about relationships seemed to affect her relationship with Jesus. These challenges were like weeds that choked her spiritual growth. How do you deal with the "weeds" that affect your relationship with Jesus?

—L. M. W.

D. Fruitful Discipleship (v. 23)

23. But he that received seed into the good ground is he that heareth the word, and understandeth it; which also beareth fruit, and bringeth forth, some an hundredfold, some sixty, some thirty.

Three things will happen when Jesus' message falls on those with "ears to hear." First, the people will listen sincerely and earnestly. They will truly hear *the word* of salvation. Second, they will understand the basis of the message and the personal consequences for disbelieving it. Third, this understanding and the faith that follows will be demonstrated in these persons bearing *fruit*. They will be disciples who make other disciples, who do good works as service to Christ and His church. Those who seek to serve with sincere hearts will have astounding results.

What Do You Think?
    How can believers focus on the *process* of bearing spiritual fruit and not get caught up in the *amount* of spiritual fruit produced?
Digging Deeper
    How do you remove the spiritual "birds," "stones," and "thorns" that prevent you from bearing spiritual fruit?

A Fertile Heart

A childhood friend came from an unbelieving home. Not only were her parents nonbelievers, but they filled her home with anger and criticism. Her mother yelled at her, berated her in front of her friends, and treated her with contempt. Her father came home drunk and cussed her out. Her friends knew this was happening, but what could they do? They were children also. Needless to say, my friend suffered from doubt, depression, and anxiety—as a child and as a young adult.

Somewhere along the way, this girl began going to church with another friend. At church she learned about a God who loved her just as she was, whose love did not wax and wane with a volatile moodiness. She learned she had a family of God who cared about her and were there for her when she struggled. And she learned about a loving Jesus, whose death and resurrection brought her the opportunity for new life.

Confronted with the irresistible love of God, she flourished. Not that she didn't struggle; she did. She faced traumas and many deep wounds, but the seed of the gospel landed on her fertile heart and grew there. She realized her need for Jesus and willingly accepted Him.

Is your heart fertile ground for the gospel? If so, who around you needs for you to share it with them?
—L. M. W.

Conclusion
A. Four Types of Hearers

A common application for the sower parable is to ask, "What kind of soil are you?" While this question may cut to the heart of being a disciple and give us pause for self-examination, the parable is more about the sower than the soils, about Jesus and other preachers who spread the divine seed of God's Word. Preachers and teachers who faithfully communicate the gospel will meet many reactions, just as the seed encountered several soils.

We will not always be able to know the hearts and minds of those with whom we share the gospel. Even so, the wise and talented sower spreads the seed widely, ever knowing that some seed will not produce fruit. The wise preacher keeps preaching, and the wise teacher keeps teaching—always looking for opportunities to share the gospel. Faith is sometimes kindled and brought to a blazing fire in unlikely people. The most passionate and bitter enemy of the church may be but a few steps away from the walk of a joyous believer.

God empowers our gospel proclamation. We offer words, but God touches those having "spiritual ears" and draws them to faith. We pray for those with "ears to hear" and faithfully proclaim the gospel to "let them hear."

What Do You Think?
    How will you apply the parable's example of faithful and generous gospel-sowing in the upcoming week?
Digging Deeper
    What new steps will you take to further sow seeds of the gospel among your unbelieving neighbors and friends?

B. Prayer

Lord of the harvest, may we remain faithful to the task of proclaiming the gospel. May we not prejudge potential hearers. Instead, we trust that Your Spirit will work to bring others to faith. We pray in Jesus' name. Amen.

C. Thought to Remember
Producing kingdom fruit is not optional.

Involvement Learning

Enhance your lesson with KJV Bible Student *(from your curriculum supplier) and the reproducible activity page (at www.standardlesson.com or in the back of the* KJV Standard Lesson Commentary Deluxe Edition*).*

Into the Lesson

Bring to class a coconut, a jar of sunflower seeds, and a jar of mustard seeds, keeping the items concealed. (*Option*: Use pictures if the items are not readily available.)

As you reveal each item, ask learners to guess the number of seeds "in" each item. Reveal the coconut first; the correct answer is one. Second, reveal the jar of sunflower seeds and give all learners a chance to guess the number of seeds. Whoever gets closest to the actual number (pre-counted by the teacher) is correct. Finally, reveal the container of mustard seeds and give all learners a chance to guess. After all the guesses, acknowledge that the mustard seeds are too small to count with ease; therefore there is no easy way to determine the correct answer.

In whole-class discussion ask how the planting process might be different for these different seeds. Describe how larger seeds, such as the coconut, might require more space or depth than would be required by the other seeds. Ask how the size of the seed might affect the way in which that seed could be sown. Lead into the lesson by saying, "In today's lesson we will see the connections between planting seeds, harvesting crops, and the message of the gospel."

Into the Word

Option. If you have an experienced gardener in your class, before today's class ask him or her to present a brief talk regarding the different types of soil, frequent problems with soil, and ways to improve soil. If the gardener allows, have learners ask questions regarding the topic.

Assign learners to perform a skit illustrating the parable from Matthew 13:1-9. Assign the following parts: (1) a narrator/Scripture reader; (2) a sower; (3) seed that fell on the hardened soil; (4) seed that fell on the shallow soil; (5) seed that fell on the thorny soil; (6) seed that fell on the fertile soil.

Depending on the class size, other students may be involved as the sun, rocks, birds, or thorns. As the narrator reads Matthew 13:1-9, encourage learners to act out expressively and humorously the description of the fate of the various seeds in Jesus' parable.

Alternative 1. Divide learners into four groups: **Hardened Soil Group**, **Shallow Soil Group**, **Thorny Soil Group**, and **Fertile Soil Group**. Have each group retell the parable in front of the whole class from the perspective of their namesake.

Alternative 2. Distribute copies of the "Matching Soil" exercise from the activity page, which you can download. Have participants work in pairs to complete as indicated.

Write on the board the following headers: *Type of Soil | Type of Faith Life | Modern Life*. Ask a volunteer to read Matthew 13:18-23. As a whole class, complete the first two columns based on the Scripture reading and the lesson commentary. The third column will be completed in the next section.

Into Life

Complete the third column (*Modern Life*) by asking the following questions for whole-class discussion: 1—How can people become hardened to the gospel? 2—What "rocks" create obstacles or hardships that can cause people to fall away from their faith? 3—What "thorns" choke out the message of Scripture and make it unproductive in the lives of people? 4—What "cares" can help the fertile soil to become productive?

Distribute an index card and pencil to each learner. Ask learners to write down which kind of soil found in verses 19-21 best represents their life, and what they will do to make any changes to improve that soil.

Alternative. Distribute copies of the "Paradise Gardening Service" activity from the activity page. Allow one minute for learners to complete it.

Weeds Among the Wheat

Devotional Reading: 2 Corinthians 13:1-10
Background Scripture: Matthew 13:24-43

Matthew 13:24-30, 36-43

24 Another parable put he forth unto them, saying, The kingdom of heaven is likened unto a man which sowed good seed in his field:

25 But while men slept, his enemy came and sowed tares among the wheat, and went his way.

26 But when the blade was sprung up, and brought forth fruit, then appeared the tares also.

27 So the servants of the householder came and said unto him, Sir, didst not thou sow good seed in thy field? from whence then hath it tares?

28 He said unto them, An enemy hath done this. The servants said unto him, Wilt thou then that we go and gather them up?

29 But he said, Nay; lest while ye gather up the tares, ye root up also the wheat with them.

30 Let both grow together until the harvest: and in the time of harvest I will say to the reapers, Gather ye together first the tares, and bind them in bundles to burn them: but gather the wheat into my barn.

36 Then Jesus sent the multitude away, and went into the house: and his disciples came unto him, saying, Declare unto us the parable of the tares of the field.

37 He answered and said unto them, He that soweth the good seed is the Son of man;

38 The field is the world; the good seed are the children of the kingdom; but the tares are the children of the wicked one;

39 The enemy that sowed them is the devil; the harvest is the end of the world; and the reapers are the angels.

40 As therefore the tares are gathered and burned in the fire; so shall it be in the end of this world.

41 The Son of man shall send forth his angels, and they shall gather out of his kingdom all things that offend, and them which do iniquity;

42 And shall cast them into a furnace of fire: there shall be wailing and gnashing of teeth.

43 Then shall the righteous shine forth as the sun in the kingdom of their Father. Who hath ears to hear, let him hear.

Key Text

Let both grow together until the harvest: and in the time of harvest I will say to the reapers, Gather ye together first the tares, and bind them in bundles to burn them: but gather the wheat into my barn. —**Matthew 13:30**

The Righteous Reign of God

Lesson Aims

After participating in this lesson, each learner will be able to:

1. Summarize the parable of the weeds.

2. Compare and contrast the parable of the weeds with the parable of the sower (last week's lesson).

3. Explain one personal challenge of being a stalk of wheat living among weeds.

Lesson Outline

Introduction
    A. How Long?
    B. Lesson Context
 I. Weeds with the Wheat (Matthew 13:24-30)
    A. Two Sowers (vv. 24-25)
    B. Two Crops (vv. 26-27)
    C. Two Harvests (vv. 28-30)
 II. Wicked with the Righteous
                (Matthew 13:36-43)
    A. Private Audience (v. 36)
    B. Cast of Characters (vv. 37-39)
       You're Different
    C. Final Sorting (vv. 40-43)
       The Forgetful Gardener
Conclusion
    A. The Wicked Among the Holy
    B. Prayer
    C. Thought to Remember

Introduction

A. How Long?

It seems that daily I am reminded of the wickedness in the world. I'm sure you are reminded of the same when you turn on the television or check your social media feed. I hear stories of terrorists who use violence to bring horror and suffering to others, human traffickers who prey on the most vulnerable members of society, powerful people who dishonestly accumulate massive wealth, and companies who ravage God's creation in order to increase production.

Does the Bible have a word of warning for the wickedness in the world? Or, instead, can we only resort to the lament, like that of the prophet Habakkuk, "How long shall I cry, and thou wilt not hear! even cry out unto thee of violence, and thou wilt not save?" (Habakkuk 1:2).

B. Lesson Context

The phrase "kingdom of heaven" occurs 32 times in the Gospel of Matthew. This is equivalent to the phrase "kingdom of God" as used dozens of times in the Gospels of Mark, Luke, and John but rarely in Matthew (see Matthew 12:28; 19:24; 21:31, 43). The kingdom of Heaven/kingdom of God is not defined by territory or government apparatus. It does not levy taxes or conscript people for military service. This kingdom is where God reigns as king; it is the dominion of His authority. There is no limit to this potential, for, as the psalmist taught, "The Lord . . . is a great King over all the earth" (Psalm 47:2; compare 83:18; 97:9). The psalmist affirms the nature of God with the repeated acknowledgment that "the Lord reigneth" (Psalms 93:1; 96:10; 97:1; 99:1).

Both John the Baptist and Jesus called people to repentance and preparation for the coming of this kingdom; they warned that it was "at hand" (Matthew 3:2; 4:17). Later, Jesus stated that His ministry of casting out demons signaled that the kingdom had come into the midst of humanity (12:28; see lesson 6). The arrival of the kingdom was something for which Jesus and His disciples had prayed (6:10).

Jesus' disciples often heard Him speak about the kingdom of Heaven/kingdom of God, and they were astonished and confused by His descriptions of its nature (example: Matthew 19:23-25). Much of their reaction can be traced to the fact that Jesus' kingdom parables were metaphorical (figurative) in nature regarding aspects of the kingdom (see the Lesson Context, lesson 7). Characteristically, these kingdom parables begin, "The kingdom of heaven is like . . ."; the majority of those are found in Matthew 13. Today's lesson text of the parable of the weeds among the wheat is the first time Jesus uses this introductory phrase in the Gospel of Matthew.

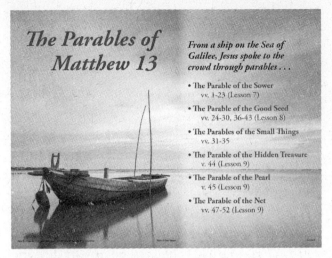

The Parables of Matthew 13

From a ship on the Sea of Galilee, Jesus spoke to the crowd through parables . . .

- The Parable of the Sower vv. 1-23 (Lesson 7)
- The Parable of the Good Seed vv. 24-30, 36-43 (Lesson 8)
- The Parables of the Small Things vv. 31-35
- The Parable of the Hidden Treasure v. 44 (Lesson 9)
- The Parable of the Pearl v. 45 (Lesson 9)
- The Parable of the Net vv. 47-52 (Lesson 9)

Visual for Lesson 8. *Point to this visual as you discuss the Lesson Context and the other parables from Matthew 13.*

I. Weeds with the Wheat
(Matthew 13:24-30)

A. Two Sowers (vv. 24-25)

24. Another parable put he forth unto them, saying, The kingdom of heaven is likened unto a man which sowed good seed in his field.

This *parable* involves sowing *seed*, as did the first parable in this chapter of Matthew 13 (see lesson 7). The practice of sowing seed in a preindustrial era involved spreading it by hand. Wheat and barley were the staple grains planted in this way.

25. But while men slept, his enemy came and sowed tares among the wheat, and went his way.

An *enemy* of the farmer now appears in the story. The *tares* that the enemy *sowed* translates a Greek word that refers to a weed known as darnel (technical name: *Lolium temulentum*). It looks very much like wheat until it matures. These are not weeds that merely threaten the growth of the crop; rather, these are weeds easily confused with the crop itself. Ingesting darnel can cause nausea, leading some to call it "poison wheat."

Wheat was a vitally important field crop in the ancient world, being the primary ingredient of bread—the dietary staple (see Deuteronomy 32:13-14; Psalm 147:12-14). Further, it was also used in trade (Ezekiel 27:17) or for payment (Luke 16:1-7; Revelation 6:6). Wheat's importance is signaled by images of heads of wheat on

ancient coins. The Bible refers to wheat dozens of times, the earliest being in the time of the patriarch Jacob (Genesis 30:14), many centuries before Jesus. Representations of ancient wheat fields in Egypt depict a taller plant than we experience today, reaching shoulder height at maturity. Galilean farmers grew wheat not only to meet their own households' needs but also as a cash crop to sell. That seems to be the case here, for the farming operation is more than a single family; the *men* who slept worked for the landowner.

There is nothing negligent implied about the men being asleep. Jesus' point is that the second sower comes at night so that he can work in darkness and secret as criminals tend to do (compare 1 Thessalonians 5:2). The introduction of this enemy's "bad seed" would have been undetectable at this point in the planting and harvest cycle.

B. Two Crops (vv. 26-27)

26-27. But when the blade was sprung up, and brought forth fruit, then appeared the tares also. So the servants of the householder came and said unto him, Sir, didst not thou sow good seed in thy field? from whence then hath it tares?

At first, the two kinds of plants seem identical. But their differences become more apparent with time. Eventually *the servants of the householder* discern that their *field* is infested with weeds (*tares*). Unlike in the parable of the sower (Matthew 13:1-

9, 18-23; see lesson 7), all the soil in this parable is fertile; it has readily received both *good seed* and bad. Not until the *fruit* (the grain head) appears do the servants recognize the weeds among the wheat. Some weeds might be expected, of course, so the servants' alarm indicates the presence of a large number of unwanted plants. As Jesus tells the story, the servants do not inform the householder about the weeds in so many words. Rather, they ask how the situation has arisen.

C. Two Harvests (vv. 28-30)

28. He said unto them, An enemy hath done this. The servants said unto him, Wilt thou then that we go and gather them up?

The householder knows what has happened. The servants' response is in line with conventional wisdom: there's no room for nonchalance where weeds are concerned. Every hour they live means that they are drawing water and nutrients away from the good plants, in addition to blocking sunlight. Surely the master will agree that the weeds must be dealt with immediately!

29-30a. But he said, Nay; lest while ye gather up the tares, ye root up also the wheat with them. Let both grow together until the harvest.

The wise householder rejects the servants' suggestion. He knows that the roots of the plants are now entangled. Therefore pulling out *the tares* risks inadvertently pulling out a substantial number of *wheat* stalks at the same time—weeding is bound to cause collateral damage. It is best to wait.

30b. And in the time of harvest I will say to the reapers, Gather ye together first the tares, and bind them in bundles to burn them: but gather the wheat into my barn.

The householder does have a plan, though. *The reapers*, who will conduct the *harvest*, are to fol-

How to Say It

Capernaum	Kuh-*per*-nay-um.
Lolium temulentum	Low-*lie*-um
	tem-you-*len*-tum.
Thessalonians	*Thess*-uh-**lo**-nee-unz
	(*th* as in *thin*).

low the distinctive instructions we see here. The instructions are stated not only in terms of the final dispositions of *the tares* and *the wheat*, but also of a certain sequence as evidenced by the word *first*.

Some students connect this verse with Jesus' other teachings on the return of the Son of Man (compare Matthew 13:37, below), the second coming of Christ to earth. Reading this parable in light of those teachings implies that the one who is "taken" in Matthew 24:40-41 and Luke 17:34-35 is a member of the weeds and the one who is "left" in those passages is part of the wheat.

Many in Jesus' audience undoubtedly found this to be surprising. They expected that when God's king brings God's kingdom into the world, both evil and evildoers would be judged and eliminated immediately. But Jesus sketches a very different picture: the breaking in of God's kingdom and the final judgment on evil are separated by a period of time. During that interval, the people of the kingdom live alongside evildoers. A separation will indeed come, but only at the harvest.

> **What Do You Think?**
> How does this parable change your thinking and presuppositions regarding the nature of God's kingdom?
>
> **Digging Deeper**
> How does this parable illustrate that God's kingdom has *already* arrived, but that it has *not yet fully* come?

II. Wicked with the Righteous
(Matthew 13:36-43)

A. Private Audience (v. 36)

36. Then Jesus sent the multitude away, and went into the house: and his disciples came unto him, saying, Declare unto us the parable of the tares of the field.

Having already been given a private interpretation of the meaning of the sower parable (Matthew 13:18-23), the *disciples* realized that there was a deeper meaning to *the parable of the tares of the field*. With *Jesus* having *sent the multitude away*, they are back in *the house*, perhaps in Capernaum (see 13:1-2, lesson 7).

B. Cast of Characters (vv. 37-39)

37. He answered and said unto them, He that soweth the good seed is the Son of man.

Jesus' interpretation reveals that the parable is an intended allegory, a story in which each character or action may have a second identification that is divorced from the setting that appears at first glance. An allegory uses a carefully constructed story as a way to present another matter, and that other matter is the primary focus of the teaching (compare Galatians 4:24). The point of this parable is not about farming. It is about preaching the gospel and its reception.

Jesus began His explanation by saying that the sower *is the Son of man*—a self-identification that occurs dozens of times in the four Gospels. But in contrast to the parable of the sower, *the good seed* is not exactly the Word of God. (See the next verse.)

38. The field is the world; the good seed are the children of the kingdom; but the tares are the children of the wicked one.

The field upon which both good and bad seed falls is not a local plot of land, but rather is global in scope (compare John 3:16). This has inspired and motivated countless evangelists and missionaries in the history of the church. The idea that the field *is the world* means there are no limits on the need for evangelistic endeavors. Even the most closed countries, those with laws that make Christian evangelism illegal, are still the "field" where the word must be preached.

As the allegory proceeds, we learn that *the good seed* is not exactly the Word of God as "the seed" is in Matthew 13:23. Rather, the good seed *are the children of the kingdom*. These believers are sown throughout the world in order that a harvest might result. But the Word of God is definitely involved since it is through the proclamation of the Word that people become the children of the kingdom.

The contrast between the two categories of children mentioned here is examined further in 1 John 3:10. The methods and motives *of the*

wicked one, whose identity is revealed next, are discussed in greater detail in John 8:44.

> **What Do You Think?**
> How will you support evangelists and missionaries in sowing the gospel message throughout the "field" of the world?
> **Digging Deeper**
> What specialized training do you need in order to support this work or take part in the work yourself?

You're Different

I was just a rural farm boy from a small town when I enrolled as an undergraduate student at a major university. The multicultural environment of the university was exciting, but also intimidating. Students, faculty, and staff came from all walks of life and followed every philosophy and religious faith (and non-faith) imaginable.

To help pay my bills during that time, I took a job in the library, working for a supervisor who lived a worldly lifestyle and embraced a variety of New Age beliefs. At first I was too intimidated to discuss my faith with coworkers, except for an elderly lady named Marlene. My supervisor, Karley, once said to me in Marlene's earshot, "There's something different about you. I can't quite place my finger on it, but you're different." Marlene quickly retorted, "He's got purity, Karley, and you wouldn't know anything about that!"

Being a stalk of "wheat" in what seems to be a field of "weeds" can be lonely and even intimidating, as we imagine how others might criticize us. However, we are called to be faithful witnesses to God's kingdom, to whomever God puts in our path. We have been given the opportunity to work with fellow "stalks of wheat" to witness to "weeds" that they might become "wheat" (see 2 Peter 3:9). How can you better take advantage of those opportunities?   —A. W.

39. The enemy that sowed them is the devil; the harvest is the end of the world; and the reapers are the angels.

Three more identifications are now stated. *The*

devil is the great adversary of God and humanity (2 Corinthians 4:4; 11:14; Ephesians 6:11; 1 Peter 5:8). *The harvest* as *the end of the world* is also described as such in Revelation 14:15; that passage, as here, affirms *the reapers* to be *angels*. The Greek word being translated *world* can refer to an age ,or era, as it is translated in Ephesians 2:7 and Colossians 1:26.

C. Final Sorting (vv. 40-43)

40. As therefore the tares are gathered and burned in the fire; so shall it be in the end of this world.

This verse summarizes what the next two state in more detail. The verbal image of sheaves of weeds being *burned* corresponds to the judgment of "the children of the wicked one" (Matthew 13:38, above). The angels will deliver them to eternal punishment (Revelation 14:16-20). This final judgment is more than an event scheduled for the end of a *period* of time. It is *the end of* time!

41-42. The Son of man shall send forth his angels, and they shall gather out of his kingdom all things that offend, and them which do iniquity; and shall cast them into a furnace of fire: there shall be wailing and gnashing of teeth.

In contrast to the concept of a rapture of believers before the end of the world, Jesus presents His angels' first move as roaming the entire earth and removing *all things that offend* as well as *them which do iniquity*. The physical tools of sin (such things as pornography, weapons of cruelty, and artistic representations that defy and mock God) will be no more. Likewise, the evildoers will be gathered by the *angels*. And *the Son of man* (Jesus) will be in charge of this time of reaping and judgment (Revelation 14:14-20; etc.).

This answers the age-old question: Why do the righteous seem to suffer and the wicked prosper? (see Jeremiah 12:1; Ecclesiastes 7:15). The answer: the wicked will not prosper forever. The way of the wicked will come to a dramatic end at the final judgment. They will join the devil and his angels in the eternal fire prepared for them (Matthew 25:41), the second death of the lake *of fire* (Revelation 20:10-15).

No one would desire this eternity, for it will be a place of *wailing* in pain and despair. Jesus dramatized this as a time of *gnashing of teeth,* a tight grimace of the mouth as a way to endure agony (compare Matthew 8:12). But there will be no relief. Satan, his demonic angels, and his earthly followers will experience eternal banishment from the presence of God at the final judgment.

> **What Do You Think?**
> How would you respond to someone who said that this parable describes a capricious and spiteful God?
> **Digging Deeper**
> How can you dig deeper into the nature of God, nature of man, and the nature of sin—with Scriptures like Isaiah 55:6-7?

43a. Then shall the righteous shine forth as the sun in the kingdom of their Father.

The future for the wheat—the children of the kingdom—stands as completely different. They will not suffer eternal, punishing fire, but will have an inner glory, an eternal fire that allows them to *shine forth as the sun* (compare Daniel 12:3). They will be rewarded with a place in the final fellowship of the saved, *the kingdom of their Father.* This will be the eternal community in which there is no mixing of wheat and weeds, righteous and wicked. Only the *righteous* will find this resting place.

The Forgetful Gardener

Nebraska is an overlooked gem in the United States. The wind sweeps over the prairies and makes the grass ripple like waves. Enormous thunderstorms roll up in the spring, looking for all the world like dark tidal waves coming over the horizon. The coyotes yip and howl at night like rowdy teenagers. And in the late summer, wild sunflowers spring up along the highways and fencerows.

Being a transplant from the East Coast, I find the landscape fascinating. I once stopped by a highway and pulled up a small sunflower by the roots to transplant in my backyard—where it promptly died. I soon wrote it off as a failed experiment and forgot about it.

Fast-forward to a year later. Lo and behold, an

unfamiliar plant started growing in my flower bed! I almost pulled it out, but something told me to wait and see what it was. I let it grow all summer. When it finally bloomed, the secret was revealed: yes, it was that sunflower (or seed from it) making a reappearance.

Perhaps you've had the same experience in your garden; but more importantly, perhaps you've had that experience in God's harvest field as well. You may have planted a seed in someone's life and didn't think much about what you said or the kind deed you did. But those words and actions can make a bigger impression than we might imagine. Maybe in this life, maybe in the next, don't be surprised if someone comes up to you and says, "Hey, thank you for the seed you planted in my life. Look at the beautiful harvest that came from it!"   —A. W.

43b. Who hath ears to hear, let him hear.

Jesus ends with a admonition that occurs dozens of times in Psalms, the Prophets, and the New Testament. Jesus is not referring to physical ears on the sides of one's head, but to hearts attuned for hearing, believing, and obeying spiritual truth. The ones who *hear* in this manner will be like the wise man who chose a foundation of rock for his new house (Matthew 7:24-25).

> **What Do You Think?**
> How can believers prioritize the health of their "spiritual ears"?
>
> **Digging Deeper**
> How can believers transition from hearing Scripture to obeying Scripture (see James 1:19-27)?

Conclusion
A. The Wicked Among the Holy

The parable of the weeds among the wheat explains one of the greatest mysteries of the kingdom: why God allows the wicked to prosper alongside His holy people. The parable teaches us that God is aware of wickedness but He chooses to leave such wickedness unjudged for the time being. God is neither oblivious to wickedness nor

does His allowing the wicked to continue indicate His tacit approval.

To followers of God who are mixed among those who reject God, the point of the parable of the weeds among the wheat must not be lost: the presence of the wicked among us is temporary. We, like the prophet Habakkuk, wonder at the silence of the Lord when "the wicked devoureth the man that is more righteous than he" (Habakkuk 1:13).

Even so, Jesus taught in this parable that God is not oblivious to these injustices. But we should not be in more of a hurry for the wicked to be punished than He is (2 Peter 3:9; Revelation 6:10). We should remember that if God took immediate vengeance on a person with every sin committed, we, the children of the kingdom, would be punished on a daily basis. God's timing is just that: a plan that He determines and controls in ways beyond our understanding. The "harvest" of the wicked and the righteous will come in God's good time.

We must hope and pray for final, ultimate justice. We must be diligent that we and all whom we love are harvested as wheat, not weeds.

> **What Do You Think?**
> How would you retell this parable for a modern audience? What would you need to adjust for your specific audience?
>
> **Digging Deeper**
> What advantages are there in communicating eternal spiritual truths through stories and analogies?

B. Prayer

Lord of the harvest, may we be workers in the field of Your world. May we be ones who are unwilling to give up on those who seem wicked. May we not despair when evil seems to win the day. We believe the promise that Your time of final judgment will allow the righteous to shine as the sun. We look forward to that day with faith and anticipation. We pray in the name of Jesus. Amen.

C. Thought to Remember

You're either wheat or weed.
There is no in-between!

Involvement Learning

Enhance your lesson with KJV Bible Student *(from your curriculum supplier) and the reproducible activity page (at www.standardlesson.com or in the back of the* KJV Standard Lesson Commentary Deluxe Edition*).*

Into the Lesson

Write the words *Treat* and *Trash* on the board as headers to two columns. Distribute a list (you prepare) of random jelly bean flavors. (For ideas, search the internet for "best and worst flavors of jelly beans.") Include some flavors that many people would find delicious (example: grape) and flavors that many people would find disgusting (example: sardine).

Ask for volunteers to read aloud the jelly bean flavors. As they do so, have the class vote by raising hands to indicate whether each flavor should go under the *Treat* column or the *Trash* column.

Option. Show pictures of different flavored jelly beans. Have learners indicate which column each flavor would go under.

Alternative. Distribute copies of the "Survival Recipes" activity from the activity page, which you can download. Have learners work in pairs to complete as indicated.

After either activity, lead into Bible study by saying, "It can be hard for us to judge what things are good and what things are bad, just from outward appearances. Discerning another person's character and heart is even more difficult. Let's see what Jesus had to say about His timing regarding judging the hearts of people."

Into the Word

Ask a volunteer to recap the parable of the sower (Matthew 13:1-9, 18-23; see lesson 7). Ask the volunteer to recall the four types of soil as described in that parable. Ask a different volunteer to read aloud Matthew 13:24-30. Then ask the whole class to compare and contrast the thorns in lesson 7 with the "tares" (weeds) from this week's lesson.

Ask the following questions for whole-class discussion: 1–Was the householder's decision to wait a good strategy? Why or why not? 2–What other alternatives might the householder have had? 3–What might have been the results of those alternatives?

Ask another volunteer to read aloud Matthew 13:36-43. Ask the following questions for whole-class discussion: 1–Why does God wait some time before separating the "children of the kingdom" from the "children of the wicked one" (Matthew 13:38)? 2–Does the interpretation of the parable describe a literal reality? Why or why not? 3–How does having "tares" among the "wheat" help the "wheat" live out their faith? 4–What is required of the "wheat" as they live among the "tares"?

Into Life

Ask for volunteers to name perceived challenges that believers may face as they live among unbelievers in the world. Write the responses on the board.

Divide students into small groups and have groups discuss actual situations that would involve the listed challenges. Invite groups to discuss handling these situations in a way that helps them remain fruitful "children of the kingdom" while also being a witness of Christ Jesus to those who may be "children of the wicked one."

Distribute an index card to each learner. In light of this week's Bible study and small-group conversation, have each learner explain one challenge of being a stalk of wheat living among the weeds.

Option. Distribute copies of the "Whole Wheat Living" activity from the activity page. Have participants work in small groups to complete as indicated. If time allows, ask for representatives from each group to state their group's responses to the questions.

Close class with a prayer asking God to help the class both to grow and be fruitful as wheat in God's field.

Finding and Gathering

Devotional Reading: Job 28:1-2, 12-19
Background Scripture: Matthew 13:44-52

Matthew 13:44-52

44 Again, the kingdom of heaven is like unto treasure hid in a field; the which when a man hath found, he hideth, and for joy thereof goeth and selleth all that he hath, and buyeth that field.

45 Again, the kingdom of heaven is like unto a merchant man, seeking goodly pearls:

46 Who, when he had found one pearl of great price, went and sold all that he had, and bought it.

47 Again, the kingdom of heaven is like unto a net, that was cast into the sea, and gathered of every kind:

48 Which, when it was full, they drew to shore, and sat down, and gathered the good into vessels, but cast the bad away.

49 So shall it be at the end of the world: the angels shall come forth, and sever the wicked from among the just,

50 And shall cast them into the furnace of fire: there shall be wailing and gnashing of teeth.

51 Jesus saith unto them, Have ye understood all these things? They say unto him, Yea, Lord.

52 Then said he unto them, Therefore every scribe which is instructed unto the kingdom of heaven is like unto a man that is an householder, which bringeth forth out of his treasure things new and old.

Key Text

Then said he unto them, Therefore every scribe which is instructed unto the kingdom of heaven is like unto a man that is an householder, which bringeth forth out of his treasure things new and old. —**Matthew 13:52**

The Righteous
Reign of God

Unit 2: Jesus Envisions the Kingdom
Lessons 6–9

Lesson Aims

After participating in this lesson, each learner will be able to:

1. Identify the analogies Jesus used.
2. Compare and contrast those analogies.
3. Identify a proper and improper use of analogies today.

Lesson Outline

Introduction

A. Unexpected Treasure

On an episode of *Antiques Roadshow,* a man came with a beautiful violin to be appraised by one of the show's experts. It had been in his family for years and had a label inside with the year 1519, supposedly the year it was made. The violin was unusually ornate with extra carvings, inlaid wood, and even an oil painting on the back. Rather than having a carved scroll at the end of the pegbox, it had a detailed carving of a bearded man's head, a rare feature for such an instrument.

The owner seemed confident that such a sixteenth-century instrument would be very valuable. But the appraiser quickly disabused him of this notion. The appraiser judged the violin to have a false date on the label, the instrument being a glitzy commercial product of a nineteenth-century French shop. But since it was old and of good quality, the appraisal was given to be in the range of $3,000 to $4,000—still far below what the owner expected.

But then the episode took an unexpected turn. In the violin case was an accompanying bow of more recent vintage, from the 1940s. The bow looked bad because it needed to be rehaired. The expert identified the bow as having been made by French master craftsman Eugène Sartory. Consequently, the bow was appraised at $14,000 to $15,000, about four times what the violin was worth! And this may have been a modest estimate—a Sartory bow sold at auction in 2017 for $214,000!

The man had a treasure without realizing it. If he had sold the violin in its case and unwittingly included the bow, he might have received much less than he could have. To have discerning eyes and ears is indeed important.

B. Lesson Context: The Two Horizons

A primary challenge we have in applying the New Testament properly to our lives is that of bridging the gap between what is called "the two horizons." The first horizon is the historical context in which the New Testament was written; the second horizon is the modern context in which the twenty-first-century reader stands. Today's lesson requires that we grapple with this challenge—and consider what people in the first century AD valued as they accumulated wealth or were unable to do so.

In the ancient world, a person's wealth was recognized in terms of physically possessing tangible assets such as livestock, precious metals, or luxurious attire (examples: Genesis 13:2; Joshua 22:8; Job 1:1-3; Luke 15:8; 16:19; James 2:2). A person considered wealthy in the modern day might possess such things as well. But it is just as likely, or even more so, that a person's wealth today would be measured—among other things—in terms of his or her investments in futures or trades in exchange-traded funds involving precious metals. The challenge of valid interpretation of the New Testament is obvious: to best determine proper and valid application, we should first try to see things through the eyes of the original, ancient audience.

The challenge is similar when it comes to preserving wealth. In both the ancient and modern worlds, cattle can be rustled, gold can be stolen, and attire can wear out (examples: Joshua 7:21; Job 1:17; Matthew 6:19; James 5:2). Today, however, we are more likely to think in terms of threats to wealth that come via electronic means: phone calls from dishonest telemarketers, ransomware attacks, and wire fraud from criminal hackers. To protect accumulations of gold and silver in the ancient world involved securing those precious metals on one's person or hiding them somewhere (examples: 2 Kings 7:8; Matthew 25:18, 25). Protecting wealth today is much more likely to involve keeping one's computer antivirus and firewall up-to-date and being cautious about using public Wi-Fi, since modern-day wealth is largely stored in computer memory banks.

C. Lesson Context: Parables

We now move to the third of three lessons on parables of Jesus. In that regard, the Lesson Contexts of lessons 7 and 8 apply here as well.

The parables of Jesus come to us in various forms. Some are developed stories; in these we can identify several that have a beginning (sets a scene), a middle (involves a crisis), and an ending (the crisis is resolved). The parables considered in lesson 7 (Matthew 13:1-9, 18-23) and lesson 8 (13:24-30, 36-43) fit this category.

But there are also extremely brief parables, which have recently been called a form of flash fiction. A popular example of such fiction is only six words long: "For sale: baby shoes, never worn." The imagination of the reader is left to fill in the likely tragic details of this story.

Another modern standard is to tell a story in a so-called microblog or a tweet, realizing that Twitter limits the length of tweets to 280 characters (including spaces). As far as today's lesson goes, the parable of the treasure in the field has (in the *King James Version*) 189 characters, the parable of the pearl of great price has 142 characters, the parable of the net has 175 characters (not including its interpretation), and the parable of treasures old and new has 173 characters. These are lengths that would have allowed Matthew to tweet them out if he'd had our technology!

These parables include enough detail to make a point while allowing the reader to imagine other details. Jesus' parables are usually sparse on details, including only what was necessary to make His point(s). Today's lesson includes four of these mini narratives that are only found in the Gospel of Matthew. These are descriptions of first-century life in a few words that make a powerful point.

> **What Do You Think?**
> How can you use a mini narrative to describe God's kingdom in a way that a modern audience would find helpful?
>
> **Digging Deeper**
> What steps will you take in the coming week to proclaim the message of God's kingdom?

I. Selling Everything
(Matthew 13:44-46)

A. Parable 1: Hidden Treasure (v. 44)

44. Again, the kingdom of heaven is like unto treasure hid in a field; the which when a man hath found, he hideth, and for joy thereof goeth and selleth all that he hath, and buyeth that field.

GOD'S KINGDOM IS DIFFERENT.

ARE YOU READY?

Visual for Lessons 6 & 9. *Point to this visual and allow the learners one minute to consider how they need to ready themselves for God's kingdom.*

In this first parable, the burial of a certain *treasure* was not the result of an exotic pirate adventure, but reflected a situation with which Jesus' original audience would have been familiar. Burying wealth was not the practice of an eccentric miser as it might be today, but was a common practice (see Lesson Context; see also Proverbs 2:4).

The *field* in the parable is a farming plot, not the site for a house. The Greek word here is *agros,* from which we get our word *agriculture.* Such a field was likely secluded, away from others. This gives the sense that the treasure was uncovered while the man was alone, with no witnesses. This hoard had been forgotten, so only the finder knew its location.

The means of discovery of the treasure is not stated, but it seems to be random. Perhaps it resulted from inspecting the field for possible purchase or from the inadvertent tripping over a large rock. In any case, we are wise to focus on what the parable *does* say, not on what it *does not* say.

Jewish law from this period stipulated that if such treasure was lifted from the ground, it would belong to the current owner of the field. The man apparently covered the treasure, hiding it again, so there was nothing illegal about his actions.

What should he have done? If he were unscrupulous, he might have merely taken the treasure and left, enriching himself with little chance of detection. But that would be stealing. Instead, he decided to purchase the field, thus becoming the rightful owner of the treasure within it.

In Jesus' story, buying this field was not a simple thing for the man. He had no ready supply of sufficient money; he ended up selling *all that he hath.* He was taking risks. The risks were (1) that he had reckoned that the treasure was worth more than all his personal wealth and (2) that the treasure would still be there after the purchase. In taking these risks, he invested all his earthly possessions in his hopeful expectations regarding the outcome of this transaction!

The point of the parable is that *the kingdom of heaven* is of superlative, inestimable value. But it requires the commitment of everything for those who would be part of it. This surely resonated with Jesus' disciples. Peter later asserted that they had left everything to follow Him (Matthew 19:27). That is more than figurative language! These men gave up their businesses, their livelihoods, and, eventually, their lives to serve and follow the Lord. When we follow Jesus, the rewards are far greater than what we sacrifice.

What Do You Think?

How can you discern what you need to give up in order to more seriously pursue a flourishing life in God's kingdom?

Digging Deeper

Who will you ask to be an accountability partner regarding this discernment?

B. Parable 2: Costly Pearl (vv. 45-46)

45. Again, the kingdom of heaven is like unto a merchant man, seeking goodly pearls.

The second parable's narrative compares *the kingdom of heaven* to the work of a pearl *merchant.* Pearls are unique as gems because living creatures, the lowly oysters, make them. A pearl is formed when a foreign object (such as a shell fragment) is trapped within the oyster's shell. The oyster secretes a substance (mother-of-pearl) to make the sharp fragment smooth and nonirritating.

Pearls are treasured because they are delightful to hold and look at. They come in various colors, with black pearls being among the rarest. Some historians claim that pearls were seen as the highest treasure in the ancient world, valued above gold, silver, or precious gemstones. The high value of pearls is reflected in their use in the apostle John's vision of the heavenly city (see Revelation 21:21).

A business that involves trading in such a valuable commodity has the potential for great risk and great reward. This man sought *goodly pearls,* the finest. We can assume that he was an expert who could quickly and accurately tell the grade of a pearl that might be offered for sale. Oysters were considered unclean for eating, according to the Law of Moses (see Leviticus 11:9-10), but that doesn't mean that possessing pearls was forbidden.

46. Who, when he had found one pearl of great price, went and sold all that he had, and bought it.

The man became obsessed as his keen and experienced eye beheld *one pearl of great price.* We should understand this not so much as sticker shock about how much money the pearl's seller wanted but, rather, as the potential buyer's appraisal. It was a pearl unlike any he had ever seen, its value likely due to a combination of spherical perfection, luster, color, and size. His business savvy kicked into high gear. He must have this pearl!

Like the man with the field in the previous parable (Matthew 13:44, above), the merchant *sold all that he had, and bought it.* Were he traveling, this would mean, at least, everything he could sell for cash right then—maybe his camel or donkey, his extra clothes, all the pearls or gems he had already purchased, any jewelry on his person, and even his bags or satchels. At most it would mean returning home to liquidate property holdings.

The point of the parable is similar to the previous one: to enter the kingdom of Heaven requires relinquishing our control over everything. Spiritually, we must give up all our ungodly ways and submit fully to the Lord. Materially, nothing we own can be held back if we are fully committed to serve in the kingdom. Everything becomes the Lord's. This involves a shift of mindset from "I own" to "I am a steward." The treasure we receive is worth it!

Achieving Focus, Finding Gems

Visitors to the Crater of Diamonds State Park in Arkansas get to search for rocks, minerals, various gemstones, and real diamonds. The park is one of the few places where people can keep what they find. In May 2021, Christian Liden brought his homemade mining equipment and searched the crater. On the third day, he found a 2.2-carat diamond! He was so excited when he found it that he asked his friend to pick it up for him because his hands were shaking so much.

Mining for diamonds involves, among other things, a single-minded focus that disregards look-alike diamond wannabes. So does our search for the kingdom of Heaven. What would have to happen for you to have that focus?   —L. M. W.

II. Catching and Rejecting
(Matthew 13:47-52)

A. Parable 3: Good & Bad Fish (vv. 47-50)

47-48. Again, the kingdom of heaven is like unto a net, that was cast into the sea, and gathered of every kind: which, when it was full, they drew to shore, and sat down, and gathered the good into vessels, but cast the bad away.

The narrative of the third parable is quite different, as Jesus likens *the kingdom of heaven* to a commercial fishing situation. His hearers were familiar with fishing in the Sea of Galilee, a large, productive, freshwater lake. Commercial fishing was done using *a net* (see Matthew 4:18; Mark 1:16; Luke 5:2)—here a large, open mesh of rope that was woven at regular intervals. It would have both floats and weights suitable for dragging the net between two boats, catching all fish in its area of coverage. The use of such nets results in indiscriminate fishing: they do not differentiate between species of fish that are likely to be near the surface and those that thrive at a depth.

If the net is filled with fish, it would be too heavy to load onto one of the fishing boats. Instead, the bottom of the net would be lifted to trap the fish, and the boats would be sailed or rowed back *to shore,* beaching the haul of fish (John 21:6-11). There, the fish would be sorted with *good* fish being thrown *into vessels,* probably

How to Say It

Messiah   Meh-*sigh*-uh.

large baskets used to take them to the market. The *bad* fish would be *cast* aside, either back into the lake or, perhaps, left on the beach for consumption by scavenger birds or roving dogs.

By one estimate, there are 24 species of fish in the Sea of Galilee today, although it is impossible to know how many there were in the time of Jesus. The Law of Moses stipulated that only fish with fins and scales were considered clean and could be eaten (Leviticus 11:9-12). This made animals such as eels (no scales), various types of catfish (smooth skin, no scales), and any shellfish (neither scales nor fins) unclean and therefore of no commercial or personal value.

> **What Do You Think?**
> How will you cast a wider "net" to evangelize to a variety of people?
>
> **Digging Deeper**
> In what ways can you incorporate your hobbies and interests as a means to meet different people?

49-50. So shall it be at the end of the world: the angels shall come forth, and sever the wicked from among the just, and shall cast them into the furnace of fire: there shall be wailing and gnashing of teeth.

The reader of the Gospel of Matthew is expected to make connections between this parable and the earlier parable of the wheat and the weeds (Matthew 13:24-30). Fishermen, somewhat like farmers, were "harvesting" the fish of the lake. Like the earlier parable, the harvest of fish must be sorted, discarding bad fish (like the weeds), and keeping the good fish (like the wheat).

To leave no doubt, Jesus explained the significance of this parable. Ultimately, it is not about fishers, fish, or nets. Rather, it is an allegory about the "harvest" *at the end of the world* (Matthew 13:40), the time of final judgment. The point of the parable is about the eternal destinies. At the final judgment, the sorting will separate the *wicked from . . . the just* (righteous). Like sheaves of weeds are burned, the wicked will be consigned to *the furnace of fire*, eternal punishment (Revelation 21:8). The imagery of *wailing and gnashing of teeth*

is one of desiring relief that never comes (compare Matthew 8:12; 13:42; 22:13; 24:51; 25:30).

Sorting Rice from Sand

While a missionary in Ukraine, I sat in the dimly lit home of a woman who had very few worldly possessions. Her two-room hut was on a rutted dirt road in a village on the outskirts of a metropolitan area. She lived with her son and his family, and she spent much of her day cooking on a camping stove and trying to keep their home clean and warm.

As I sat in her kitchen, I watched as she spread a scoop of rice over the kitchen table. She sorted through each grain of rice slowly and painstakingly in order to separate the rice from rocks and grains of sand. I commented on the tedious nature of the task. In my life in the United States, rice does not come mixed with pebbles!

In reply, she shrugged her shoulders and smiled as if to say, "Someone has to do it." To that idea of sorting we could add—in light of today's lesson —"and everyone will have it done to them." Do you live daily with that future reality in mind?

—L. M. W.

B. Interlude (v. 51)

51. Jesus saith unto them, Have ye understood all these things? They say unto him, Yea, Lord.

The setting for these parables is still the house where Jesus was speaking privately with the disciples (*them*; see Matthew 13:36). These parables (*all these things*) combine to provide crucial insights into the nature of the kingdom of Heaven. First, it will cost them a great deal: all that they have. Second, the reward they receive by being part of the kingdom of Heaven is far greater than what they give up. Third, there is great warning. What if the man had not given everything to purchase the field and claim the treasure? What if the merchant had not sold everything to purchase the great pearl? What if their possessions were more important than following Jesus? In that case, they will also lose the greatest reward, that of being counted part of the kingdom of Heaven.

Jesus pushed them by asking, "*Have ye under-*

stood all these things?" Implied in this is the deeper question, "Are you ready to give up everything to follow me?" The response *Yea, Lord* may reveal more than a hint of bravado (compare Matthew 20:22; 26:35).

C. Parable 4: Old & New Treasures (v. 52)

52. Then said he unto them, Therefore every scribe which is instructed unto the kingdom of heaven is like unto a man that is an householder, which bringeth forth out of his treasure things new and old.

Not all students of the text consider our fourth example to be a parable. But it does teach about *the kingdom of heaven* through use of an analogy.

A *scribe* was a literate person who made copies of Scripture painstakingly by hand and thus was an expert in the Law of Moses (compare Ezra 7:6; Matthew 2:4; 23:2; etc.). For such a person to be depicted as a *householder, which bringeth forth out of his treasure things new and old* indicates several things. First, the "new" and "old" in this context refer to the new treasure of Jesus and the old treasure of the Law of Moses.

Second, since scribes were experts in the old treasure of the Law, they should have eagerly embraced the new treasure of the Messiah when He arrived on the scene (see Matthew 2:3-6; etc.). Instead, Jesus found it necessary to criticize, even condemn, the scribes and their allies, the Pharisees, for their failure in this regard (see numerous examples in Matthew 23). But not all the scribes opposed Jesus (Mark 12:28-34). Some were willing to find a new treasure in Jesus' teachings about the kingdom of Heaven, seeing it as an extension of their old treasure of the Jewish Scriptures.

Third, for a householder to bring treasure out of its hiding place would be to display that treasure for others to see. We can imagine the old valuables to be those the man inherited—family heirlooms, accumulated precious metals and gems, etc. The new treasures would be those he has acquired himself, perhaps jewelry he has purchased or gold coins he has earned through hard work. But this is not about a wealthy householder who wants to show off. Rather, it's about a willingness to share what the householder has discovered.

Conclusion

A. Giving Up What You Cannot Keep

Jim Elliot, a missionary, was killed in Ecuador on January 8, 1956, while attempting to bring the gospel to the indigenous Huaorani people. The death of Elliot and his missionary companions has made him one of the most well-known Christian martyrs of the twentieth century. In 2006, his story came to the silver screen with the release of the movie *End of the Spear.*

Something Elliot wrote in his journal in 1949 epitomized his passion for serving Jesus: "He is no fool who gives what he cannot keep to gain that which he cannot lose." This speaks to the core point of the parables in today's lesson. To remain dedicated to the kingdom of Heaven is a treasure far beyond any material possessions. But its cost is a willingness to give up what we have to follow Jesus.

B. Prayer

Father, grant us the wisdom to recognize the priceless nature of Your kingdom! And give us the courage to yield all that we have for it. We pray in the name of Jesus. Amen.

C. Thought to Remember

The kingdom of Heaven is of ultimate value.

Involvement Learning

Enhance your lesson with KJV Bible Student *(from your curriculum supplier) and the reproducible activity page (at www.standardlesson.com or in the back of the* KJV Standard Lesson Commentary Deluxe Edition*).*

Into the Lesson

Divide learners into pairs and have them discuss the following scenario:

Imagine that your house is on fire. Your family and pets are safe, but you have time to grab one item as you escape. What would you grab, and why?

One of the firefighters has a chance to save one item for you. What would they think was the most valuable item in your house?

Ask volunteers to share their answers for both questions.

Alternative. Distribute copies of "Kingdom Teaching" activity from the activity page, which you can download. Have learners complete it individually (in a minute or less).

After calling time under either activity, have pairs discuss how easy it can be for people to place value on the wrong things. Transition to the lesson by saying, "Jesus played on people's inaccurate perceptions of value as He taught them using parables regarding that which has ultimate value."

Into the Word

Ask a volunteer to read aloud Matthew 13:44-46. Ask, "What does it mean to give up *everything* to follow Jesus?" Distribute pens and index cards to learners and ask them to list as many things as possible that they have had to give up to follow Christ. Remind learners to consider their relationships, material possessions, lifestyle, personality traits, and future plans. Give them the opportunity to discuss their responses in small groups. (Note: Some learners may prefer to keep their responses private.)

Option. Distribute copies of the "Inventory of Everything" activity from the activity page. Have learners complete it individually (in a minute or less) before discussing conclusions in small groups, but with no pressure to reveal private information.

Upon completion of either activity, allow vol- unteers to share with the class some of the things that they have chosen to give up to follow Jesus.

Ask another volunteer to read aloud Matthew 13:47-52. Based on information found in the lesson commentary, remind learners how Jesus used analogies and parables to teach others regarding the kingdom of God. Ask, "What analogies might Jesus use today to teach on the kingdom of God?" Distribute index cards with the following prompt (you prepare) to help learners get started:

The kingdom of God is like . . .

Encourage learners to complete the prompt, and remind them that there is not a right or wrong answer. (Note: You may need to prepare possible responses before class.)

Into Life

Lead the class in a discussion regarding how believers might use analogies as they share their faith with nonbelievers. Ask the following questions for whole-class discussion: 1–What analogies have you heard (or used) regarding aspects of the Christian faith? 2–How do you discern whether an analogy is faithful to what God has revealed in Scripture? 3–How do you discern that an analogy is appropriate for the audience? 4–What possible drawbacks are there to using analogies in your teaching about Scripture?

Distribute an index card and pen to each learner. Ask them to write a brief parable for the kingdom of Heaven; then have learners share their parables with the whole class. Then have learners write the name of one individual with whom they will share their parable during the upcoming week.

End class with a time of silent prayer. Ask learners to pray for the opportunity and wisdom to share their parables with others. Conclude the time of prayer with praise and thanks for God's heavenly kingdom.

Inheriting the Kingdom

Devotional Reading: Isaiah 44:21-28
Background Scripture: Galatians 5:13-26

Galatians 5:13-26

13 For, brethren, ye have been called unto liberty; only use not liberty for an occasion to the flesh, but by love serve one another.

14 For all the law is fulfilled in one word, even in this; Thou shalt love thy neighbour as thyself.

15 But if ye bite and devour one another, take heed that ye be not consumed one of another.

16 This I say then, Walk in the Spirit, and ye shall not fulfil the lust of the flesh.

17 For the flesh lusteth against the Spirit, and the Spirit against the flesh: and these are contrary the one to the other: so that ye cannot do the things that ye would.

18 But if ye be led of the Spirit, ye are not under the law.

19 Now the works of the flesh are manifest, which are these; Adultery, fornication, uncleanness, lasciviousness,

20 Idolatry, witchcraft, hatred, variance, emulations, wrath, strife, seditions, heresies,

21 Envyings, murders, drunkenness, revellings, and such like: of the which I tell you before, as I have also told you in time past, that they which do such things shall not inherit the kingdom of God.

22 But the fruit of the Spirit is love, joy, peace, longsuffering, gentleness, goodness, faith,

23 Meekness, temperance: against such there is no law.

24 And they that are Christ's have crucified the flesh with the affections and lusts.

25 If we live in the Spirit, let us also walk in the Spirit.

26 Let us not be desirous of vain glory, provoking one another, envying one another.

Key Text

Brethren, ye have been called unto liberty; only use not liberty for an occasion to the flesh, but by love serve one another. —**Galatians 5:13**

The Righteous Reign of God

Unit 3: God's Eternal Reign
Lessons 10–13

Lesson Aims

After participating in this lesson, each learner will be able to:

1. List the fruit of the Spirit.

2. Contrast the fruit of the Spirit with the works of the flesh.

3. Make a plan to identify and eliminate one unhealthy fruit in his or her life.

Lesson Outline

Introduction
    A. Already Having What We Seek
    B. Lesson Context
I. Living in Freedom (Galatians 5:13-18)
    A. Fulfilling God's Law (vv. 13-15)
    B. Choosing God's Side (vv. 16-18)
    Focus Control
II. Rejecting Selfishness (Galatians 5:19-21)
    A. Deadly List (vv. 19-21b)
    B. Deadly Consequences (v. 21c)
III. Pursuing Godliness (Galatians 5:22-26)
    A. A List of Life (vv. 22-23)
    What Fruit Is This?
    B. A Life to Live Out (vv. 24-26)
Conclusion
    A. Forgiveness Plus
    B. Prayer
    C. Thought to Remember

Introduction

A. Already Having What We Seek

A man walks through his home, searching. *Where are my keys?* he asks himself repeatedly. Then he reaches in his pocket. His keys are there.

A woman rummages through her car, searching. *Where are my glasses?* she wonders. Then she touches her head. Her glasses are there.

Sometimes we already have what we are looking for. Today's text is like that.

B. Lesson Context

Our text is from Paul's letter to the Galatians, written to address a controversy among churches founded on his first missionary journey. He wrote in response to some people's belief that Christians of Gentile background had to obey stipulations in the Law of Moses in order to belong to God's people (Galatians 1:6; 5:2-6; see Acts 15:1-5).

But Paul pointed out that faith in Jesus, not the completion of the works of law, is the true identifier of God's people (Galatians 2:15-16; 3:1-6). God gave the Israelites the Law of Moses to guide them until He brought the fulfillment of His promises (3:23-25). That fulfillment was Jesus. His death and resurrection made it possible for people of every nation to be welcomed into God's family. Works of law in general (3:10-12) and circumcision in particular (5:2-6) had not resulted in the people living as God called them to live: fully devoted to Him in holiness. But in Jesus and through the Holy Spirit, there was freedom and empowerment to do so.

I. Living in Freedom
(Galatians 5:13-18)

A. Fulfilling God's Law (vv. 13-15)

13a. For, brethren, ye have been called unto liberty.

The nature of the controversy indicates the presence of *brethren* from both Jewish and Gentile backgrounds. These disparate groups had been made into a family by God's call. That call is the good news that in Jesus, God had come in the flesh, had submitted to death, and rose to new life.

The result of that call is *liberty* (see also 2 Corinthians 3:17; Galatians 2:4). That term would have reminded Paul's Jewish readers of Israel's exodus from Egypt. Marking the end of their enslavement, the exodus began the journey to freedom in the promised land. But beset by sinful disobedience generation after generation, Israel lived more under oppression than in true freedom. That state led eventually to exile and captivity in a foreign land. God promised that true freedom means an end to being exiled from His presence; in the gospel, that promise is fulfilled (compare Revelation 7:15-17).

13b. Only use not liberty for an occasion to the flesh, but by love serve one another.

But *liberty* is not license. Some might have thought that because the requirements of the law were fulfilled, then their freedom meant that they could do as they pleased. Paul negated this thought. Using freedom to repeat the sinful rebellion that led to exile in the first place would hardly be an expression of faith in Jesus, who was unwaveringly faithful to God the Father.

Jesus' faithfulness was expressed in His loving service for others (Mark 10:45). His followers are compelled to exercise Christian liberty in the same way: *by love* serving *one another*. To do otherwise would be to provide *an occasion to the flesh*. The term translated "occasion" suggests something like a base of operations (also Romans 7:11).

We should consider how Paul uses the word *flesh* here. In some places, he uses this word to refer to the physical body (example: Romans 4:1). In other places, he uses this word to refer to unholy physical desires (example: Ephesians 2:3). But here the focus seems to be a perspective that is entirely self-centered, not acknowledging God's rule or others' significance.

14. For all the law is fulfilled in one word, even in this; Thou shalt love thy neighbour as thyself.

Many Jewish teachers, including Jesus (Mark 12:28-34) and Paul, saw the entire Law of Moses as pointing to two great obligations: to love God and *love* others (compare Leviticus 19:18; Deuteronomy 6:5). Because the Galatian churches faced division, Paul emphasized loving others as the law's focus. If motivated by their love for God as revealed in Jesus, the Galatian Christians could

love one another despite long-standing divisions of their respective heritages.

15. But if ye bite and devour one another, take heed that ye be not consumed one of another.

The alternative to the love just described was self-defeating division. Each side attacked the other, like flesh-eating animals. In such a conflict, both sides would be eaten up. In the Cold War that followed World War II, the United States had a policy of nuclear deterrence known as "mutual assured destruction"—appropriately known as MAD for short. It would indeed be madness for the Galatians to undercut *one another* since that would only result in mutual destruction.

We might wonder whether a solution would be for the Galatian churches to divide into all-Jewish and all-Gentile congregations. For Paul, such a division was unthinkable. The singularity of the gospel and of God himself must be reflected in the unity of His people (Ephesians 4:1-6). A divided church will be a devoured church.

The two groups had to come to terms with the truth that they both belong to God's people through their faith in Jesus rather than through their obedience to the Law of Moses. This did not mean ignoring their differences in background or experience; but it *did* mean uniting across those differences with Christlike love.

B. Choosing God's Side (vv. 16-18)

16. This I say then, Walk in the Spirit, and ye shall not fulfil the lust of the flesh.

But what can give the power to live such a life of loving service? The answer, Paul says, is what only faith in Jesus can provide: God's own Spirit, the Holy Spirit. In Old Testament times, God had sent His Spirit to a few individuals—notably the prophets, who proclaimed His message authoritatively. But God had promised that in the age to come, He would pour out His Spirit without that limit (Joel 2:28-32). All believers could be thereby empowered

How to Say It

Galatians	Guh-*lay*-shunz.
Gentiles	*Jen*-tiles.
Philippians	Fih-*lip*-ee-unz.

to live prophetically in the sense of their lives testifying to the true God and His rule over the world.

With Christ's death, resurrection, and ascension, that promise is fulfilled. Those who believe in Jesus as God's true king are promised that God's Holy Spirit will live within them (Acts 2:38). Thereby they are empowered to do what Israel had failed to do before: live genuinely as God's people.

Paul did not need to tell his readers to receive the Spirit, because they already had. But the Spirit's direction and power can be resisted (Acts 7:51). So the Galatians needed to be reminded to *walk* (or live) *in the Spirit*. In so doing, they would fulfill God's will as summarized in the command to love. Such a life is the opposite of the life *of the flesh*; that is, the life of sinful selfishness. The flesh provokes desire, or *lust*, meaning not just sexual desire but any selfish motivation.

What Do You Think?

What steps will you take to ensure that you continue walking in step with God's Spirit?

Digging Deeper

Who is a mature believer you can ask for accountability in this regard?

Focus Control

What do you think about your job, your family, or your financial situation? Each topic brings up both positive and negative aspects to ponder. Perhaps you were passed over for a promotion. But the promotion would have meant working for a supervisor who was not as caring as your current supervisor. You have a choice as to what you'll focus on: you can be angry that someone else received the promotion, or you can choose to see the blessing that resulted in remaining where you are.

This type of choice is critical because thoughts can lead to actions. Walking in the Spirit reveals a focus on the things of Christ. And when we're focusing on Him, we aren't thinking about the things we could have had, the things that went wrong, or the people who wronged us. What does all this say about your choice of focus?   —P. M.

17. For the flesh lusteth against the Spirit, and the Spirit against the flesh: and these are contrary the one to the other: so that ye cannot do the things that ye would.

These two sets of desires, those of *the flesh* and of *the Spirit*, are fundamentally opposed to each other. We are either motivated by our self-interest or filled with the Holy Spirit who directs us toward Christlike loving service for others.

Romans 6–8 (especially 7:24–8:1) offers us Paul's own extended commentary on the phrase *so that ye cannot do the things that ye would*. What we truly want is to be God's people, to fulfill the purpose for which God created us. But the selfishness that pervades our hearts prevents that. However, we receive the power to become the people we desire to be—people who reflect God's holiness—through the gift of God's Holy Spirit (see 8:10-11).

18. But if ye be led of the Spirit, ye are not under the law.

Paul clarifies that there was nothing inherently wrong with *the law* in and of itself. But the Law of Moses did have its limitations (see Romans 7:7; 1 Timothy 1:8). The Jewish constituents among Paul's original audience were especially challenged to shift their thoughts, speech, and behavior toward a life directed by *the Spirit*.

II. Rejecting Selfishness
(Galatians 5:19-21)
A. Deadly List (vv. 19-21b)

19a. Now the works of the flesh are manifest, which are these.

For purposes of contrast, Paul reminded his readers what life in *the flesh*, the self-ruled life, was like as he began what we call a vice list. There are many such lists in Paul's letters (examples: Romans 1:29-31; Colossians 3:5). We should keep in mind, however, that even collecting all the vices from all of Paul's lists would not include everything that could be named. For the list at hand, the vices fall into four groupings across three verses.

19b. Adultery, fornication, uncleanness, lasciviousness.

These terms encompass all forms of sexual activity that occur outside of a marriage relationship. In addition to hurting others, these acts also harm the guilty person (see 1 Corinthians 6:12-20).

Uncleanness speaks to guilt through such activity. *Lasciviousness* refers to behavior that is shocking to public decency. Even cultures far from godly standards uphold some standards of sexual propriety (see 1 Corinthians 5:1). But a life of selfishness will find a way to shock any society. Life in the Holy Spirit is directly opposed to the life of flagrant sexual sin (1 Thessalonians 4:3-8).

20a. Idolatry, witchcraft.

The list then shifts the focus to false religious practices. *Idolatry* exalts the created above the Creator, reducing God to something much less than He is. *Witchcraft* is the attempt to use physical objects and rituals to manipulate the spiritual world.

20b. Hatred, variance, emulations, wrath, strife, seditions, heresies.

Next, Paul lists attitudes and actions that work against self-sacrificial love, threatening the church's unity. *Hatred* refers to hostility toward those we identify as enemies. *Variance* is divisiveness, making differences greater rather than seeking to overcome them. *Emulations* are strong passions that resent the success of others.

Wrath refers to strong anger. God's wrath is the expression of His holiness against human evil. But human anger is often driven not by holiness but by selfishness. *Strife* is the forming of mutually hostile groups to advance selfish interests; *seditions* intensify that unholy tendency. *Heresies* later became a term for false beliefs accepted by some Christians, but here it is another expression for hostile division and partisanship.

> ### What Do You Think?
> How does the world's inclination for hatred, strife, and cruelty affect the church's display of sacrificial love?
> ### Digging Deeper
> How might James 1:19-27 inform the church's response to such inclinations?

21a. Envyings, murders.

Envyings and *murders* conclude the grouping of sins of selfishness. These two refer to the desire to deprive others of what they have—even life itself!

21b. Drunkenness, revellings, and such like.

Paul concludes with two terms that represent public displays of the self-destructiveness produced by selfishness. *Drunkenness* (intoxication from alcohol) suggests individual self-destruction. Drunkenness is part of the wild, party-like atmosphere of *revellings*, a context which includes unrestrained immorality (contrast Romans 13:13-14; 1 Peter 4:3).

B. Deadly Consequences (v. 21c)

21c. Of the which I tell you before, as I have also told you in time past, that they which do such things shall not inherit the kingdom of God.

All these evils are contrary to *the kingdom of God*—that is, to the reign of God brought about by Christ, now and in eternity. If these behaviors had become the mode of the Galatians' lives, they showed themselves to have returned to rebellion against God's rule. Those whose lives are characterized by these vices would have no eternal inheritance except death (see Revelation 22:14-15).

III. Pursuing Godliness
(Galatians 5:22-26)
A. A List of Life (vv. 22-23)

22a. But the fruit of the Spirit is love, joy, peace.

The fruit of the Spirit stands in sharp contrast to the works of the flesh. The word *fruit* is an apt term because like a farmer who plants a crop and reaps a harvest, what the Holy Spirit produces is what God seeks in His people. Since Paul's focus is on doing good toward others, perhaps this is why the word *fruit* is singular: all these characteristics belong together as one fruit, not many fruits.

As with the previous list, this list groups similar characteristics. It begins with three foundational aspects of the Christ-follower's character: love, joy, and peace. The kind of *love* Paul has in mind is not conditioned on how deserving of love the other person is. Rather, the kind of love in view flows from grace that blesses the undeserving. It

Visual for Lesson 10. *Show this visual as you discuss the Digging Deeper question associated with Galatians 5:22b.*

is the kind of love that God demonstrates toward us (John 3:16). *Joy* is an inner disposition of well-being, but it always is expressed outwardly and shared with others (see 2 Corinthians 8:2).

The word *peace* reminds us of Old Testament statements about the peace that God granted His people (Numbers 6:26; Psalm 29:11; Isaiah 9:6-7). More than the end of hostility, such peace means positive goodwill and fellowship. As God has made whole our relationship with Him, His Spirit empowers us to make relationships whole with others (see 2 Corinthians 13:11).

22b. Longsuffering, gentleness, goodness.

The second grouping consists of characteristics that undergird relationships. *Longsuffering* is patience regarding the failings of others, including wrongs that others commit. As God is patient with us, His Spirit empowers our patience toward others (compare Romans 2:4).

Gentleness names the attitude that seeks to do positive good to others in all circumstances. It serves to nurture and protect others. Again, because God treats His people in this way, His Spirit enables them to treat others likewise (see Colossians 3:12-13). *Goodness* further develops the idea of gentleness, putting the attitude into action. Those empowered by the Spirit do not simply want the good; they actually do good things for others. The Spirit compels us to be loyal to fellow Christians, committed to their welfare no matter what.

What Fruit Is This?

We moved into a new house several years ago, and I was amazed at the beauty of the landscaping. The lawn was lush green, every brick-lined planter had blooms, and the backyard was lined with trees.

Visitors would ask us what kind of trees we had. The problem was, I had no idea. It wasn't until the trees began to produce fruit that I could identify them. We were fortunate to have an orange tree, a lemon tree, a fig tree, and two pomegranate trees! One of the things that I loved about having those trees, besides their delicious fruit, was the fact that I learned how to recognize those trees because of their fruit-bearing properties.

However, there were some seasons when the pomegranate fruit never sweetened and turned red. The seeds stayed tasteless and white. Sometimes they'd be rotten right there on the vine, and you didn't know it until you cracked one open.

Jesus had pointed things to say about bearing fruit (see Matthew 7:15-20; 12:33-37; Luke 13:6-9), and Paul drilled down to specifics. Bad fruit may or may not immediately be visible. But sooner or later, the nature of what the tree produces becomes known (compare 1 Corinthians 3:12-15). It's impossible to go half-and-half on this (see James 3:12). Think of your most recent "fruit"—was it one of those listed in Galatians 5:22-23?   —P. M.

> **What Do You Think?**
> How do the Spirit's gifts (Romans 12:6-8; 1 Corinthians 12:4-11) empower you to seek the welfare of others?
>
> **Digging Deeper**
> How will you continue to develop never-failing love (1 Corinthians 13) so that you can be attentive to others?

22c-23. Faith, meekness, temperance: against such there is no law.

The list concludes with three characteristics that are to undergird all the believer's actions. *Faith* in this context refers to a willingness to practice without fail what one believes. As God has been devoted and persistent to fulfill the promises that He has made, so also His Spirit empowers us to be persistently devoted.

A second feature undergirding Spirit-filled action is *meekness*. The meek do not seek to assert rights or privileges. As Christ emptied himself of privilege in becoming human, so also do those empowered by His Spirit (compare Ephesians 4:2).

The word translated *temperance* is also (with variations) found in Acts 24:25; 1 Corinthians 7:9; 9:25; and 2 Peter 1:6. It refers to the ability to keep desires in check. This was a characteristic admired in Paul's time but not widely practiced.

The Galatian Christians could be criticized by their Jewish neighbors for abandoning the Law of Moses and by their pagan neighbors for abandoning the customs of pagan worship. But Paul reminds them that if they live as the Spirit directs, they will produce a fruit that *no law*—Jewish or Roman—stands *against*.

B. A Life to Live Out (vv. 24-26)

24. And they that are Christ's have crucified the flesh with the affections and lusts.

Believers in Christ are joined to Him in His death and so are raised to a new life (Romans 6:1-14). This does not mean that our old desires and habits disappear instantly. But it means that over time the Spirit replaces them with Christlikeness. This requires our cooperation to assure that the old life remains dead and buried.

> **What Do You Think?**
> How would you explain to a new believer what it means to have "crucified the flesh" (Galatians 5:24)?
>
> **Digging Deeper**
> How might Romans 7:22–8:17 help inform your explanation?

25. If we live in the Spirit, let us also walk in the Spirit.

The new life the Galatians had in Christ carried an obligation: to put that life into practice. The phrase *walk in the Spirit* could also be translated as "get in line with the Spirit." It means deliberately reordering one's life to reflect what God has done. It is bearing the fruit of the Spirit as routine practice.

26. Let us not be desirous of vain glory, provoking one another, envying one another.

The Spirit's work can be destroyed easily by persistent selfishness, the key characteristic of the life of the flesh. If Paul's original audience chose to seek attention for themselves, then the result would be to disregard and disrespect others. That would destroy the fellowship that the Spirit sought to build. Christians are saved by a Lord who was worthy of glory but chose lowliness to serve others (Philippians 2:1-11). Following His way by the Spirit's power directs the Christian to a better way through loving others.

Conclusion

A. Forgiveness Plus

Paul begins and ends his vice list with the commonly named pagan vices but devotes most of his attention in the middle to matters of hostility and disunity. He is driving home a point to Galatian church members that needs to be heard through the ages: When we divide the body of Christ for self-serving reasons, we serve the flesh. We might tend to minimize such acts by pointing to the blatant evils of the ungodly world around us, but our selfish hostility is just as evil. We paganize ourselves when we refuse to love one another. Do you want a kingdom life, the life that God always intended for His people? Then let the Holy Spirit bear His fruit.

> **What Do You Think?**
> In what ways will you serve a neighbor in the upcoming week?
>
> **Digging Deeper**
> How will the fruit of the Spirit (Galatians 5:22-23) inform your acts of neighborly love?

B. Prayer

Thank You, God, for Your incomparable blessing of freedom and life in the Spirit. We rely on the power of Your Spirit so that we can be people who reflect our Lord's resurrection. Amen!

C. Thought to Remember

Freedom means becoming what God made us to be.

Involvement Learning

Enhance your lesson with KJV Bible Student *(from your curriculum supplier) and the reproducible activity page (at www.standardlesson.com or in the back of the* KJV Standard Lesson Commentary Deluxe Edition*).*

Into the Lesson

Before class, prepare slips of paper, each containing one letter from the words *license* and *liberty*. Have learners gather in small groups. Make enough slips to give the letters of one word to each group. Challenge the groups to arrange the letters to make a word.

After groups discover their word, ask the following questions for whole-class discussion: 1–What is the difference between *license* and *liberty*? 2–How are the two sometimes confused with each other? 3–Which one is more difficult to practice? 4–Which should Christians prefer? Why?

Lead to Bible study by saying, "In today's text the apostle Paul deals with both ideas. Let's discover specific examples of license that he condemns and the possibility for true liberty that he lifts up."

Into the Word

Divide the class into small groups. Distribute a handout (you prepare) with two charts. Half of the groups will complete the first chart, while the other half will complete the second.

The first chart will have three headings: *Works of the flesh / How this attribute harms others / How this attribute can lead to division.* Have groups read Galatians 5:19-21 and complete the chart.

The second chart will have three headings: *Fruit of the Spirit / How this fruit demonstrates neighborly love / How this fruit can lead to unity.* Have groups read Galatians 5:22-23 and complete the chart.

After 10 minutes of small-group work, call the groups together and lead a whole-class discussion on what learners discovered.

Write the following statements on the board:
A divided church will be a devoured church.
Love your neighbor as yourself.

Ask a volunteer to read aloud Galatians 5:13-26 as learners decide how the Scripture underscores the truth of each statement. Ask learners briefly to respond.

Alternative. Distribute copies of the "Acts to Avoid" exercise from the activity page, which you can download. Have learners work in pairs to complete as indicated.

Into Life

Distribute blank paper and ask each learner to write the days of the week in a column on the left side of their paper. Then ask them to write instances during the last week when they exhibited a fruit of the Spirit. Next, ask learners to write instances during the last week when they exhibited an "act of the flesh" (Galatians 5:19).

Have learners turn over their papers and write again the days of the week in a column on the left side. At the bottom of the page, have each learner make a plan to identify and eliminate one unhealthy fruit in his or her life. Ask them to keep this page as a journal to record how they see the fruit of the Spirit at work in their lives during the upcoming week.

Alternate. Display the following self-rating scale on a poster for the class to read:

0–Don't see it
1–I have seen it in the past
2–I have seen it often
3–I have seen it this week
4–This is a daily part of who I am

Ask participants to decide how they see each fruit of the Spirit in their lives. Distribute paper for each learner to list each fruit with their self-rating score beside it. Have volunteers share ways to submit to the Spirit in order to identify and eliminate things that prevent them from developing the fruit in their lives.

Option. Distribute copies of the "Yield to the Spirit" activity from the activity page. Have learners work together in pairs to complete it. After 10 minutes, bring the groups together to discuss their conclusions.

The Nature of the Kingdom

Devotional Reading: Proverbs 2:1-11
Background Scripture: Romans 14:10-23

Romans 14:10-23

10 But why dost thou judge thy brother? or why dost thou set at nought thy brother? for we shall all stand before the judgment seat of Christ.

11 For it is written, As I live, saith the Lord, every knee shall bow to me, and every tongue shall confess to God.

12 So then every one of us shall give account of himself to God.

13 Let us not therefore judge one another any more: but judge this rather, that no man put a stumblingblock or an occasion to fall in his brother's way.

14 I know, and am persuaded by the Lord Jesus, that there is nothing unclean of itself: but to him that esteemeth any thing to be unclean, to him it is unclean.

15 But if thy brother be grieved with thy meat, now walkest thou not charitably. Destroy not him with thy meat, for whom Christ died.

16 Let not then your good be evil spoken of:

17 For the kingdom of God is not meat and drink; but righteousness, and peace, and joy in the Holy Ghost.

18 For he that in these things serveth Christ is acceptable to God, and approved of men.

19 Let us therefore follow after the things which make for peace, and things wherewith one may edify another.

20 For meat destroy not the work of God. All things indeed are pure; but it is evil for that man who eateth with offence.

21 It is good neither to eat flesh, nor to drink wine, nor any thing whereby thy brother stumbleth, or is offended, or is made weak.

22 Hast thou faith? have it to thyself before God. Happy is he that condemneth not himself in that thing which he alloweth.

23 And he that doubteth is damned if he eat, because he eateth not of faith: for whatsoever is not of faith is sin.

Key Text

Let us therefore follow after the things which make for peace, and things wherewith one may edify another.
—Romans 14:19

The Righteous Reign of God

Unit 3: God's Eternal Reign
Lessons 10–13

Lesson Aims

After participating in this lesson, each learner will be able to:

1. Identify the danger of sitting in judgment on others.

2. Explain the concept of mutual edification.

3. Examine his or her position on tolerance and intolerance in light of the text.

Lesson Outline

Introduction
A. Something Bigger than Myself
B. Lesson Context

I. On Inappropriate Judging (Romans 14:10-13)
A. Current Problem (v. 10a)
B. Future Accounting (vv. 10b-12)
C. Necessary Conclusion (v. 13a)
D. Required Actions (v. 13b)

II. On Personal Convictions (Romans 14:14-18)
A. Issues of Conscience (v. 14)
B. Result of Behavior (vv. 15-18)
 Chasing a Baseball Cap

III. On Vital Imperatives (Romans 14:19-23)
A. Peace and Edification (vv. 19-21)
 A Dose of Vitamin E-Squared
B. Faith and Sin (vv. 22-23)

Conclusion
A. Peace, Not Conflict
B. Prayer
C. Thought to Remember

Introduction

A. Something Bigger than Myself

Have you ever had a day to do just what you wanted, only to feel let down afterward? Maybe it was a day off from work. Maybe friends gave you a break from your normal duties. Somehow we often experience disappointment at the end of such times.

Why does that happen so often? Perhaps it is, to some extent, because we long to be part of something bigger than ourselves. "Me time" sounds great, but God has put in us a desire that our lives matter for others.

The church is too often (because even once is too often!) the place where people seem most devoted to their own preferences. Churches have become infamous for the pettiness of their arguments over matters of opinion. We all grieve this fact, but it is likely that we all have been part of the problem at times. Today's lesson will be the uncomfortable mirror in which we see ourselves in this regard.

B. Lesson Context

Our text comes from Paul's letter to the Romans. The letter addresses a church divided between Jewish and non-Jewish (Gentile) followers of Jesus. While we cannot know the exact circumstances, it appears that each group looked down on the other for the way it practiced life in God's kingdom.

Paul wrote the letter to show each group that they belong to God's kingdom on the same terms: faith in Jesus in response to God's good news about Him (Romans 1:5; 10:5-17). So Paul says "to the Jew first, and also to the Greek" (1:16) that each group has the same status (3:9; 10:12). All have sinned, both Jews and Gentiles (3:22-23). Paul's addressees belong to God's kingdom not by observances of the Law of Moses, which defined the Jewish people. Rather, they belong by faith in Jesus, who died that all might live eternally.

This equality of status must be practiced. Jews were accustomed to keeping the laws of clean and unclean laid out in the Law of Moses (see Leviticus 11; Deuteronomy 14:3-20). In a city like Rome, finding meat that was ceremonially clean was probably difficult. Add to that the fact that much meat had been offered in sacrifice to pagan idols, and it appears that many Jews in Rome had simply given up meat altogether.

Meanwhile, Christians from a Gentile background had been brought into God's kingdom by their faith in Jesus, being formerly excluded because they did not belong to the people of Israel (compare Ephesians 2:11-13). They had never been subject to the laws of clean and unclean. For Jewish followers of Jesus, dietary restrictions had always been a sign of devotion to God. But for Gentile followers of Jesus, these rules seemed strange and unnecessary.

Different practices with food matter little when we are with our own group. But the fellowship of the church brought these two groups together, and shared meals were a vital part of that fellowship. Whose rules should prevail?

I. On Inappropriate Judging
(Romans 14:10-12)

A. Current Problem (v. 10a)

10a. But why dost thou judge thy brother? or why dost thou set at nought thy brother?

Paul introduced two disputes at the beginning of Romans 14: one about eating certain foods (Romans 14:2) and the other about the sacredness of certain days (14:5). In the verse before us, we see him ask pointed questions to clarify what is at stake regarding these issues. He has shown the readers over many chapters that both Jews and Gentiles are guilty of sin but that both can be restored to God's kingdom by expressing faith in Jesus. Therefore, no Christian, regardless of background identity, can *judge* another's status on other criteria. To *set* a fellow Christian *at nought* is to treat him or her as less important than oneself (see also Luke 23:11; Acts 4:11). To do so over the foods that others eat is most unfitting for a follower of Jesus!

B. Future Accounting (vv. 10b-12)

10b. For we shall all stand before the judgment seat of Christ.

This verse in context implies two reasons for not passing judgment on others in the manner above. First, if any judging is to be done with regard to practices of dietary choices, that will be Christ's prerogative, not ours. Second, we will be called to account on the last day for all judgments we formulate (see Romans 14:12, below; see also 2 Corinthians 5:10).

11. For it is written, As I live, saith the Lord, every knee shall bow to me, and every tongue shall confess to God.

To stress that God alone is judge, Paul quotes from Isaiah 45:23. This text promised the Israelites that God would not only restore them to their homeland after exile in Babylon, but He would also bring salvation to all the earth (Isaiah 45:22).

Now through Jesus' death and resurrection, God had ended the deeper exile of sin and has made salvation available to all nations. As a result, no human group or category has privilege over another. *Every knee shall bow* and *every tongue shall confess to God* as ultimate king (see also Philippians 2:10-11).

12. So then every one of us shall give account of himself to God.

God's forthcoming judgment defines our responsibility, and His Word stresses human accountability (Matthew 12:36; Romans 3:19). Popular culture likes to quote Matthew 7:1-2 as a prohibition against any and all judgments that Christians may express. However, that practice ignores the context in which Jesus uttered that warning. At certain times and in certain situations, making judgment is indeed valid and necessary (examples: Matthew 7:15-20; 1 Corinthians 5), but those cases are not in view here.

Sometimes membership with a certain group can seem to justify judging others. After all, if everyone in "my group" sees others in the same way, then our judgment of them seems justified. That may have been the situation for the Roman Christians. But judging with a group is no better than judging as an individual (Exodus 23:2).

What Do You Think?

How do you decide when, if at all, believers should show judgment?

Digging Deeper

How do Romans 16:17-18; 1 Corinthians 5:11–6:5; 1 Timothy 6:3-5; and Titus 1:10-16 inform your answer?

C. Necessary Conclusion (v. 13a)

13a. Let us not therefore judge one another any more.

This statement serves as a transition from what Paul's readers were no longer to do, to the positive action of what they should do instead.

D. Required Actions (v. 13b)

13b. But judge this rather, that no man put a stumblingblock or an occasion to fall in his brother's way.

Judging fellow believers is to give way to caring for them. Paul uses figures of speech to describe such caring: *a stumblingblock* is something in a roadway that can make someone trip (see also 1 Corinthians 8:9); *an occasion to fall* is an obstacle that blocks a path or causes a misstep. The two may be seen as synonyms. Paul uses similar figures of speech in Romans 9:33, reflecting the Hebrew parallelism of Isaiah 8:14. Paul further discusses this in Romans 14:20 (below).

II. On Personal Convictions
(Romans 14:14-18)

A. Issues of Conscience (v. 14)

14a. I know, and am persuaded by the Lord Jesus, that there is nothing unclean of itself.

The phrase *nothing unclean* points to the issue of eating food, which Paul introduced in Romans 14:2. Now he reaffirms the new distinction between clean and unclean foods: there is no distinction. This reflects what *the Lord Jesus* declared in Mark 7:14-23: purity is not about food but about a person's inner character (compare Matthew 15:11). Israel's rules regarding clean and unclean food were always intended by God not as definitions of right and wrong behavior for all people, but as cultural boundaries that defined Israel as a distinct nation. Good and evil have always been about our inner dispositions that drive our actions.

How to Say It

antonyms   *ann*-tuh-**nimz**.
Ephesians   Ee-*fee*-zhunz.

14b. But to him that esteemeth any thing to be unclean, to him it is unclean.

Romans 14:2 establishes that the one who *esteemeth any thing to be unclean* is the one "who is weak" in the Christian faith. Such a person hasn't yet reached the point of fully accepting the truth that external things, like food, do not make a person unclean. Years or decades of avoiding unclean foods can be a practice that is hard to let go of! If such a person's conscience still considers a food unclean, then *to him it* [still] *is unclean.*

B. Result of Behavior (vv. 15-18)

15. But if thy brother be grieved with thy meat, now walkest thou not charitably. Destroy not him with thy meat, for whom Christ died.

Apparently, what the Jewish Christians in Rome were seeing Gentile Christians eat was causing problems. Considering the nature of the "stumblingblock" and "occasion to fall" (Romans 14:13b, above), the word *grieved* in this verse indicates something more serious than mere sadness or irritation. This conclusion is backed up by the implications of the word *destroy.* Acting in a visible way that violates another person's conscience can result in spiritual destruction of someone for whom Christ died. This is no minor matter. It goes to the core of the gospel. We are called to have a high regard for the conscience of fellow believers—higher regard than we have even for our own. Paul has more to say on this issue in 1 Corinthians 8:7-13.

> **What Do You Think?**
> How will you show love toward believers who may have a stricter conscience than yours regarding behavior not prohibited by Scripture?
>
> **Digging Deeper**
> How will you decide to forgo something in consideration for that believer?

16. Let not then your good be evil spoken of.

Those in Rome who understood that Christ had set aside the rules of clean and unclean had an accurate grasp of God's truth. They were ready to act on it as an expression of their faith. Theirs was a *good* position. But to act without concern for those who had not yet grasped this truth was to invite good actions to be *spoken of* as *evil*. That phrase is also translated as a form of the word "blaspheme" in Romans 2:24 and 1 Timothy 1:20. It is a strong term for an insult, especially directed to someone of high standing. The implication is that we can provoke slander that can extend even to Christ himself if we get careless in regard to what Paul is saying.

17. For the kingdom of God is not meat and drink; but righteousness, and peace, and joy in the Holy Ghost.

Rules and practices regarding food are among the most obvious ways that groups of people mark their differences from other groups. Food preferences are central to a people's culture. Even apart from Israel's rules of clean and unclean, those rules were important to the Israelites because they were observed constantly (compare Acts 10:14; 11:8). But Paul reminds us that God's *kingdom* is not merely about what is easily seen. Food is nothing compared to what God has done in Christ, what now defines His people as subjects of His kingdom.

Paul's three terms that characterize that kingdom are important. The Greek word translated *righteousness* occurs about 100 times in the New Testament, and one-third of those are in Romans. Quite simply, the word *righteousness* refers to that which is right and just.

The word translated *peace* is also a favorite of Paul's in Romans. Its usage occurs in the greeting at the beginning (Romans 1:7) and in a word of assurance at the end (16:20). God's peace is not just a cessation of strife. It is harmony in loving, caring relationships. The gospel calls us not just to get along but to work for one another's benefit.

The word translated *joy* also occurs dozens of times in the New Testament. About one-third are in Paul's letters but only three times in Romans (here and Romans 15:13, 32). Joy flows from the abiding sense of confidence that God is making things right as He establishes His kingdom.

Despite the high frequency of each of the three terms in the New Testament, Romans 14:17 is the only place where all three occur together. This says something about Paul's concern! Peace and joy are among the fruit of the Holy Spirit (Galatians 5:22, lesson 10). Here Paul ascribes them along with righ-

teousness as being associated with the Spirit. The Spirit's presence, not our adherence to food laws, marks us as belonging to God's people (compare Ephesians 1:13). In identifying us as God's righteous people, the Spirit empowers us to love others and so to surrender our own preferences. Life in the Spirit is better than even your favorite food.

> **What Do You Think?**
> How should a believer respond to rules or preferences that seem uncomfortable, but not against Scripture?
> **Digging Deeper**
> How will you live with righteousness, peace, and joy in your above response?

Chasing a Baseball Cap

I was wearing my favorite baseball cap as I rode a ski lift to the top of a mountain. About three-fourths of the way up the hill, the cap blew off my head, and I watched it fall to the ground below.

Stepping off the lift, I could see my cap lying on the ground about 100 yards downslope. It didn't look too far away, so I set out to retrieve it. The problem was, the slope was steeper than it looked; and gravity took over as I carefully began to make my way down the hill. I picked up speed, and soon I was involuntarily running down the hill—on the verge of losing control. Just in the nick of time, I grabbed a tree that kept me from tumbling down the steep slope.

After I successfully retrieved my treasured possession, I reflected on the foolishness of my decision. I had risked serious bodily injury for the sake of a silly baseball cap! Why did I go to so much trouble for something that is relatively unimportant? Now whenever I wear that cap, it reminds me to choose my priorities wisely.

In the Christian life, there's a danger of majoring in minors, of becoming preoccupied with lesser things. How will you ensure that you don't make that mistake? —D. F.

18a. For he that in these things serveth Christ is acceptable to God.

Deferring to others' needs and concerns is at the

Visual for Lesson 11. *Show this visual as you discuss the lesson commentary associated with Romans 14:19.*

very core of kingdom life, and Christ himself was the supreme example of one who did so (see Philippians 2:3-8). Christ did the will of His Father, so to serve *Christ* is to do what is *acceptable* and pleasing *to God* the Father. Indeed, service to Christ is of much greater importance to God than focusing only on a person's observance of rules about food.

18b. And approved of men.

Deferring to others' concerns even gains human approval. In the social structures of the first century AD, Jewish Christians stood apart from the larger Jewish communities because of their acceptance of Gentiles as God's people. Gentile Christians, for their part, had abandoned the pagan worship that required loyalty to the Roman Empire. If these two "renegade" groups became known for their arguments over food, their credibility would suffer all the more. But if they could demonstrate love, their example could shine (John 13:34-35). When the church fights, a vile reputation results. When its members love as Christ did, we become the salt and light of the world (Matthew 5:13-16).

III. On Vital Imperatives
(Romans 14:19-23)
A. Peace and Edification (vv. 19-21)

19. Let us therefore follow after the things which make for peace, and things wherewith one may edify another.

The peace of God's kingdom is a gift of God.

But putting peace into practice is not automatic. Returning to stating imperatives, Paul tells his readers to *follow after*, or pursue, *peace* (compare 1 Peter 3:11). They must apply diligent effort to make sure that everyone in Christ's body is respected, included, and loved. Conflict will be necessary when confronting doctrinal defection, moral defection, or divisiveness (see Romans 16:17-18; 1 Corinthians 5:11–6:5; 1 Timothy 6:3-5; Titus 1:10-16; 3:10). But such conflict should serve the greater good in protecting the integrity of the church.

More than just absence of conflict, peace means edifying one another, or building one another up. The noun *edification* and the verb *edify* compare human relationships to constructing a building (an edifice). Our aim is to make others stronger, their faith more resilient. Paul has much more to say on this subject in Romans 15:2; 1 Corinthians 14:3-26; 2 Corinthians 12:19; and Ephesians 4:11-13, 29.

What Do You Think?
Who will you edify through your God-given sense of peace?
Digging Deeper
What steps will you take to avoid being a "stumblingblock" (Romans 14:13) to that person?

A Dose of Vitamin E-Squared

Every November, his letter catches me by surprise. You'd think I would be expecting it, because the same thing has happened more than 20 years in a row. Yet when I see the envelope in my mailbox and recognize the sender's name, my heart jumps.

It all started more than two decades ago when Robert began attending our church. Later he admitted that he had come reluctantly, mainly to satisfy his young son, who had asked, "Dad, why don't we go to church?" Robert sat in the back, preparing to be bored. To his surprise, he was greeted kindly, and the minister's message about Christ was more compelling than Robert had expected. Soon he attended a class that I was teaching on the basics of the Christian faith, and a few weeks later, he confessed his faith in the Lord and was baptized on a November evening.

He has sent me a letter on the anniversary of his baptism ever since. In these letters he tells me about his growth as a follower of Christ, and he always thanks me for helping him find the Lord. These letters reveal what can result from a dose of spiritual vitamin E-squared: "encouraging edification" —initially from me to him, now from him to me. To whom can you offer such a vitamin this week?
—D. F.

20-21. For meat destroy not the work of God. All things indeed are pure; but it is evil for that man who eateth with offence. It is good neither to eat flesh, nor to drink wine, nor any thing whereby thy brother stumbleth, or is offended, or is made weak.

Paul repeats his observations from Romans 14:14 (see above), but more forcefully. The opposite of "edify" in 14:19 is *destroy*. In modern English, we may take the words *offence* and *offended* to mean something like "irritate" or "insult." But the Greek being translated is stronger than that; the idea is to be a cause of spiritual stumbling.

B. Faith and Sin (vv. 22-23)

22. Hast thou faith? have it to thyself before God. Happy is he that condemneth not himself in that thing which he alloweth.

The word *faith* is used here in the sense of what believers are allowed to do. And in certain cases, the truth of that faith must be kept between oneself and God to avoid creating a stumbling block. The phrase *condemneth not himself* points to avoidance of a second area of destruction: as the "weak" (Romans 14:1-2; 15:1b) end up stumbling, the "strong" (15:1a) do so as well.

The Greek behind the word *happy* is translated "blessed" in many other passages (examples: Romans 4:7-8), and that is the sense here.

23. And he that doubteth is damned if he eat, because he eateth not of faith: for whatsoever is not of faith is sin.

Paul continues with a comparison of opposites (antonyms) as he affirms a doctrinal principle. For those with the *faith* to affirm that all foods are clean, the important matter is not food but the consciences of fellow believers. Some whose faith is weaker, who still believe some foods to be unclean, may follow others' examples and eat foods still thought (but wrongly so) to be unclean. And if they act against their own consciences in this way, they have sinned since actions that do not come from faith are *sin* by nature.

Conclusion
A. Peace, Not Conflict

Up to the point of today's lesson text in Romans, Paul had spent many chapters reminding the Christians in Rome that no group had any preference before God. Faith in Jesus—not being in a certain biological lineage or doing better works—is what brings sinners of every ethnicity into God's kingdom. United with Him in death and resurrection, they are now dead to sin. They live a new life, empowered by God's Spirit, transformed to love and serve one another (Romans 6:1-14).

But can we bring that truth to shared meals? Can we exercise our faith in such a way as to defer to one another on matters of conscience? Can we be patient with one another as we learn to use our freedom for the benefit of others, not ourselves? The concern of those with strong faith should be for the welfare of those with weaker faith. The former must support the latter, both in what consciences direct and in the growth of faith toward greater understanding. Of such love, grace, patience, and edification is the kingdom of God.

> **What Do You Think?**
> Which concept or imperative in today's lesson do you have the most trouble coming to grips with? Why?
> **Digging Deeper**
> How will you resolve this problem?

B. Prayer

Gracious Father, we thank You for our freedom in Christ! Lead us to use that freedom to build up others, never to tear down. May we be instruments of Your peace in the name of Your Son. Amen.

C. Thought to Remember
Be strong enough to serve the weak.

Involvement Learning

Enhance your lesson with KJV Bible Student *(from your curriculum supplier) and the reproducible activity page (at www.standardlesson.com or in the back of the* KJV Standard Lesson Commentary Deluxe Edition*).*

Into the Lesson

Ask the class to list behaviors or social norms that they follow every day. Allow two minutes for learners to call out responses while you write those responses on the board. (Some examples might include brushing teeth, tipping the local barista, stopping for traffic lights, etc.)

Ask the following questions for whole-class discussion: 1–Which of these are mandated rules and which are socially accepted norms? 2–How do you tell the difference? 3–How do you respond if someone does not follow either? 4–How does your understanding of love inform your response?

Transition to the Bible study by saying, "Today's text challenges Christians about how to respond when the behaviors or choices of others do not match what we are accustomed to. Sometimes these differences are matters of faith, and sometimes they're matters of opinion. We'll find guidelines for coping with them as we study today."

Into the Word

Before class, ask a learner to prepare a five-minute presentation on the context of today's Scripture text. The presentation can include information from the Lesson Context portion of the commentary or outside resources.

Ask a volunteer to read aloud Romans 14:10-13. Ask the following questions for whole-class discussion: 1–How does the Scripture context inform your understanding of these verses? 2–Why did the Roman church struggle with passing judgment?

Divide the class into small groups. Distribute a handout (you create) with the following headers written across the top: *Behaviors to Avoid | Behaviors to Adopt | Results That God Wants*. Ask the groups to read Romans 14:14-23 and write down the reference of every verse from that passage under at least one column. Then write a paraphrase for each instruction given.

Option. Distribute copies of the "Building and Encouraging Love" exercise from the activity page, which you can download. Have participants work in pairs to complete as indicated.

After calling time under either alternative, have the class present their findings for discussion.

Into Life

Write each of the following statements on a separate index card. (Note: You may also make a photocopy of this page and cut out the paragraphs.)

- With many people suffering from diabetes and other lifestyle-related disease, I'm offended that our congregation offers a vast assortment of donuts and pastries each week. Christians should not be contributing to such health problems.
- I used to think that he was a wonderful Christian, but then I heard him talking about the jokes and memes that he posts on his social media accounts. Many of these so-called jokes make fun of people he disagrees with regarding political or social issues. I can't believe that a Christian would make fun of another person in that way.
- My dad was an alcoholic, and I can't begin to describe the chaos created in our family by his drinking habit. I was offended when a preacher once said that a flourishing relationship with Jesus is like enjoying a sip of the finest wine.

Divide the class into three groups and give each group one of the cards. Ask each group to respond to their given statement in a way that reflects the principles taught in today's study.

Discuss the following questions in whole-class discussion: 1–What does it mean for Christians to edify each other? 2–How should our attitudes toward tolerance or intolerance be shaped by the teaching in today's Scripture text?

Option. Distribute copies of the "Weighing All the Angles" activity from the activity page. Have participants complete it individually (in a minute or less) before discussing conclusions in small groups.

Judgment in the Kingdom

Devotional Reading: Isaiah 41:1-14
Background Scripture: 1 Corinthians 4:1-21

1 Corinthians 4:1-6, 17-21

1 Let a man so account of us, as of the ministers of Christ, and stewards of the mysteries of God.

2 Moreover it is required in stewards, that a man be found faithful.

3 But with me it is a very small thing that I should be judged of you, or of man's judgment: yea, I judge not mine own self.

4 For I know nothing by myself; yet am I not hereby justified: but he that judgeth me is the Lord.

5 Therefore judge nothing before the time, until the Lord come, who both will bring to light the hidden things of darkness, and will make manifest the counsels of the hearts: and then shall every man have praise of God.

6 And these things, brethren, I have in a figure transferred to myself and to Apollos for your sakes; that ye might learn in us not to think of men above that which is written, that no one of you be puffed up for one against another.

17 For this cause have I sent unto you Timotheus, who is my beloved son, and faithful in the Lord, who shall bring you into remembrance of my ways which be in Christ, as I teach every where in every church.

18 Now some are puffed up, as though I would not come to you.

19 But I will come to you shortly, if the Lord will, and will know, not the speech of them which are puffed up, but the power.

20 For the kingdom of God is not in word, but in power.

21 What will ye? shall I come unto you with a rod, or in love, and in the spirit of meekness?

Key Text

Judge nothing before the time, until the Lord come, who both will bring to light the hidden things of darkness, and will make manifest the counsels of the hearts: and then shall every man have praise of God. —1 Corinthians 4:5

The Righteous
Reign of God

Lesson Aims

After participating in this lesson, each learner will be able to:

1. Identify why Paul sent Timothy to Corinth.

2. Compare and contrast the issue of judgment in this week's lesson with last week's lesson and 1 Corinthians 5.

3. Recruit an accountability partner for the mutual purpose of avoiding being "puffed up."

Lesson Outline

Introduction

A. "You're Not the Boss of Me"

No one likes to be bossed around. We like to get our own way. We like to get credit for good outcomes. And we especially like others to do what we tell them. For some people, "You're not the boss of me" has become a catchphrase, expressing their resistance to authority.

But a personal desire to be independent is paradoxical for Christians. As followers of Jesus, we are to submit to the Lord Jesus, who died and rose for us; to God the Father, who sent His Son for us; and to the Holy Spirit, who directs and empowers us. Christians do have a boss, the boss of bosses, the King of kings. We also have leaders in the church to whom we are to submit (Hebrews 13:17). At the same time, those leaders set an example of humility (1 Corinthians 11:1; Philippians 3:17; compare John 13:12-17) that we emulate as we submit to one another in the church (see 1 Corinthians 16:15-16; Ephesians 5:21). We are to submit to the world's governing authorities (Romans 13:5) even as we reject the world's principles (2 Corinthians 10:3-4; Colossians 2:20-23).

An individual Christian may have a mistaken, distorted view of what it means to follow and submit to Jesus. We rely on the understanding and correction of others to help us overcome our mistakes and distortions. At the same time that the Lord is the ultimate judge of any human, we are called by our Lord to help one another overcome our misunderstandings and failings—and identifying such issues involves judgment (Matthew 12:33; 1 Corinthians 5; etc.). Our text today brings this paradox into focus. Paul writes to a church with a host of problems.

B. Lesson Context

The apostle Paul planted the church in the city of Corinth while on his second missionary journey of AD 52–54 (Acts 18:1-8). Indeed, he spent the majority of that time with this one church (18:11). But after Paul left town for Ephesus and locations farther east (18:18-23), problems in the Corinthian church became known to him.

The problems in Corinth had become many and serious. They included factionalism (1 Corinthians 1:10-17; 3:1-9), gross sexual immorality (5:1-13; 6:12-20), lawsuits between believers (6:1-11), misunderstandings about marriage and singleness (7:1-16, 25-40), divisions over foods (8:1-13; 10:14-33), selfish behavior in the worship assembly (11:2-22), improper understanding and exercise of spiritual gifts (12:1-31; 14:1-25), a focus on self-glory to the exclusion of love (13:1-13), and false views of resurrection (15:1-58).

Paul spoke directly, eloquently, and with authority on these issues, leaving no doubt regarding the way forward on each one. As he did, a common thread that ran through all the Corinthians' problems could be seen. The solution to that poisonous thread is the subject of today's lesson.

I. Faithful Servants
(1 Corinthians 4:1-6)

The immediate foreword to today's text establishes how the message of the gospel runs counter to what people generally understand as wisdom (1 Corinthians 3:18-20). And since Christian leaders are to take no personal credit for their message or their success, there is no place for factionalism in the church (3:21-23). Thus, as 1 Corinthians 4 opens, Paul has come full circle regarding his opening salvo addressing such "I am of . . ." divisions (see 1:10-17).

A. Divine Trust (vv. 1-2)

1. Let a man so account of us, as of the ministers of Christ, and stewards of the mysteries of God.

Paul's difficult life as an apostle seems to have been hard for the believers in Corinth to comprehend (2 Corinthians 6:3-10; 11:22-33). They did not regard him as a fluent public speaker. Although they considered his letters to them to be "weighty and powerful," his physical presence was "weak" and his speech was "contemptible" (10:10). But in light of the gospel, how should they have regarded Paul?

Paul answers this unstated question with two phrases. First, we notice the phrase *the ministers of Christ* to be similar to the wording of Acts 26:16, where Paul (as Saul) received his apostolic commission from Jesus himself. The Greek word translated "ministers" is also translated "servants" in John 18:36, and that is the sense here.

Second, the phrase *stewards of the mysteries of God* challenges Paul's audience to recognize the sacredness of his task (see also 1 Corinthians 3:5; 9:17; compare Galatians 2:7; Colossians 1:25). A steward manages the possessions of another (compare Luke 12:42; 16:1-12). When Paul went on to write his letter to the Romans a few years later, he explained that his gospel preaching was "according to the revelation of the mystery, which was kept secret since the world began, but now is made manifest" (Romans 16:25-26).

One could say much about the importance of someone like the apostle Paul. But Paul saw his role as lowly. That lowly role must be respected, though, for it is lowly service that imitates Christ himself.

2. Moreover it is required in stewards, that a man be found faithful.

Jesus told stories about masters leaving servants in charge of wealth while the master was away (Matthew 24:45-51; 25:14-30; Luke 19:11-27). As Paul penned this letter more than two decades after Jesus' resurrection, such teaching almost certainly undergirds Paul's statement. His faithfulness to his stewardship role should have been a model for the Corinthians.

> **What Do You Think?**
> What new steps will you take to be a faithful steward of the gospel message?
> **Digging Deeper**
> How does 1 Peter 4:1-11 inform the actions and attitudes of such stewards of the gospel message?

To Be Entrusted

I once received a phone call from a man who was going to spend the summer helping with mission work overseas. The reason for the call was that he needed someone to leave his car with for the summer. We had a large driveway, so I said, "Sure, we'll be glad to help."

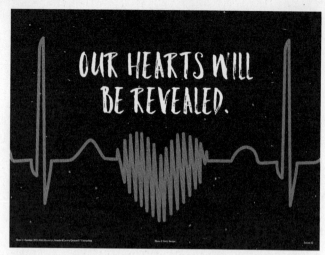

Visual for Lesson 12. *Allow one minute for silent personal reflection on this truth after discussing the commentary associated with verse 5.*

Soon he and his wife arrived at our house. He tossed me the keys and said, "Feel free to drive my car while we're gone"—and the car was a shiny new Lincoln Continental! It was quite a contrast with my own car, a worn-out Ford Fiesta.

I did drive the Lincoln several times that summer, but I was very careful how I drove it and where I parked it. I wouldn't let my kids eat in the back seat. I was more careful with my friends' car than I would have been if I had owned it myself. I felt a keen responsibility to be a faithful steward and take good care of property that belonged to someone else.

What level of care should we give to things that belong to God, which He has entrusted to us?

—D. F.

B. Clear Conscience (vv. 3-5)

3-4. But with me it is a very small thing that I should be judged of you, or of man's judgment: yea, I judge not mine own self. For I know nothing by myself; yet am I not hereby justified: but he that judgeth me is the Lord.

Paul recognized that he was indeed being wrongly *judged* by some or many in the Corinthian church. But he was committed to living only to please *the Lord*. Paul needed no one else's approval. He didn't even trust his self-evaluation! The phrase *I know nothing by myself* may be confusing. The word being translated as "know"

is related to the word translated "conscience" in 1 Corinthians 8:7, 10, 12; 10:25, 27-29. So Paul was acknowledging that nothing was bothering his conscience regarding the issue of being judged.

But having a clear conscience didn't mean that Paul was therefore automatically without fault before God. And so he said, *yet am I not hereby justified*. After all, there are evil people whose consciences don't bother them at all when they do wrong. Such people have "given themselves over" to their evil actions (Ephesians 4:19) because they have a "conscience seared with a hot iron" (1 Timothy 4:2). Paul was confident that the Lord knew his heart and actions better than Paul himself or the Corinthians did.

5. Therefore judge nothing before the time, until the Lord come, who both will bring to light the hidden things of darkness, and will make manifest the counsels of the hearts: and then shall every man have praise of God.

The phrase *judge nothing* may seem to conflict with the judgment that 1 Corinthians 5:9-13 prescribes. The key is context. *Judge nothing* in the context at hand refers to things that can't be seen, such as *the hidden things of darkness* and *the counsels of the hearts*—whether Paul's or anyone else's. By contrast, the case in chapter 5 involves an obvious and flagrant sin that was visible to all. To fail to exercise proper judgment in that case would be to allow a cancerous sin to grow in the church.

Again Paul echoed the teaching of Jesus, who spoke of the judgment at His return as revealing (making *manifest*) what had been hidden before (Matthew 25:31-46; Luke 12:2-3). As all of humanity is assembled before God in judgment when Christ returns, all will hear and know the rightness of His judgment (Psalm 9:8; Acts 17:31). So Paul entrusted himself entirely to God's evaluation.

C. Leaders' Examples (v. 6)

6. And these things, brethren, I have in a figure transferred to myself and to Apollos for your sakes; that ye might learn in us not to think of men above that which is written,

that no one of you be puffed up for one against another.

Paul proceeded to explain further his responsibility to trust God's judgment alone. The intent was to provoke his readers to ponder their own trust in that regard. As they did so, they would refrain from judging the motives not only of apostles such as Paul but also of other leaders such as *Apollos* (see Acts 18:24–19:1). Members of the church had taken sides as to who they followed, exalting their favorites as something like heroes (1 Corinthians 1:10-17). But when the Corinthians exalted their favorite leaders, they were in fact exalting themselves. The Corinthians were acting as if their choices were better and that approval in this regard was important. In this they were being *puffed up* with pride *one against another*.

The issue of pride was central to the other problems that the Corinthian church was experiencing. Such pride inevitably produces conflict, as each proud person tries to rise above all others. The conflict at Corinth may have seemed as if it were about the popularity of preachers, but in fact it was about the pride of church members. Ironically, when pride is behind an attempt to rise above others, the result is the opposite. In that case, "destruction" and "a fall" are unavoidable (Proverbs 16:18).

> **What Do You Think?**
> How can a church congregation oppose prideful attitudes through their love for one another (see Romans 12:9-21)?
>
> **Digging Deeper**
> What steps will you take to avoid a prideful attitude that will eventually lead to destruction (see Proverbs 16:18)?

II. Faithful Correction
(1 Corinthians 4:17-21)

In the intervening verses of 1 Corinthians 4:7-16 (not in today's lesson), Paul addressed the Corinthians with sharp sarcasm and exaggerated language. He pointed out that they exalted themselves while disparaging Paul and the others who brought them the Christian message. While the Corinthians imagined themselves to be wise and strong, Paul was living in lowliness and suffering, reflecting the attitude of Christ. As Paul finished this section, he changed his tone, addressing his readers as a father speaks to his children (4:14-16). He wanted what was best for them. Like obedient children, they were to follow his example.

A. Timothy's Instructive Example (v. 17)

17. For this cause have I sent unto you Timotheus, who is my beloved son, and faithful in the Lord, who shall bring you into remembrance of my ways which be in Christ, as I teach every where in every church.

Paul could not be at Corinth personally to set things straight; his letters were substitutes for his personal presence. He sent these letters with trusted associates, who could listen, observe, explain, encourage, and then report back to Paul. For this letter, Paul *sent* Timothy as his representative.

The person *Timotheus* is referred to by that name 17 times in the *King James Version* but also 7 times as "Timothy." His name is most familiar to us by means of the two letters Paul wrote to him, namely those we call 1 Timothy and 2 Timothy. Those letters reveal that the relationship between them was that of mentor and protégé. The phrase *who is my beloved son* is to be taken not in a physical, biological sense, but in a spiritual sense (see Acts 16:1; 1 Timothy 1:2). Paul speaks of Timothy's faithfulness not just to commend him as reliable but to put him forward as an example of Christlikeness, like Paul himself.

> **What Do You Think?**
> What steps will you take to prepare to be a mentor to a spiritual "child" regarding his or her spiritual growth and formation?
>
> **Digging Deeper**
> How does Paul's relationship with Timothy (see 2 Timothy 3:10–4:8; etc.) help inform this mentoring relationship?

B. Paul's Stern Warning (vv. 18-21)

18. Now some are puffed up, as though I would not come to you.

Puffed up is Paul's expression for arrogant pride (compare 1 Corinthians 4:6 [above], 19 [below]; 5:2; 8:1; 13:4). Every Christian should be committed not to live with pride but to be filled with edification: the building up of one another's faith for a true life of witness to the reign of God (10:23; 14:3-5, 12, 17, 26).

In their puffed-up state, some of the Corinthians believed that Paul, whom they perceived as "base" and "weak" (2 Corinthians 10:1, 10), *would not* return. Thus they would have free reign to do as they pleased. This assumption was not merely a denial of Paul's strength but of Christ's. Would their Lord forever let them rebel against His rule of humility and justice? Would there be no consequences? Paul could bring warning and correction under the Lord's direction, but eventually the moment comes when all stand before the Lord to give an account (see 5:10).

What Do You Think?

How is the judgment that a person might receive different from or similar to the consequences that a person might receive for their actions?

Digging Deeper

What Scriptures come to mind regarding temporary and eternal consequences?

The Smartest Guy in the World?

When I graduated from high school in 1973, I thought I was just about the smartest guy in the world. Anticipating college, I told myself, *When I get to that college, I'm going to teach them a thing or two!* But when I graduated from college four years later, I realized that I was not as smart as I thought I was. Over the course of those four years, it gradually dawned on me that for every new thing I learned, there were dozens or hundreds of other things I didn't know.

Since those days in college, I have gone on to earn three more degrees, each experience more humbling than the one before. I have come to realize that although a person's growth in knowledge is important, how that knowledge—real or claimed—is wielded is no less vital. As Paul will say a bit later in his letter, "Knowledge puffeth up, but charity edifieth" (1 Corinthians 8:1).

In what ways can you ensure that your self-image of "I know better" gives way to "I am no better"? —R. L. N.

19. But I will come to you shortly, if the Lord will, and will know, not the speech of them which are puffed up, but the power.

Timothy's visit and Paul's letter were but the first steps in Paul's plan to correct the problems in the Corinthian church. Paul himself planned to visit. Yet even with the confidence that Paul had—both in his calling as an apostle and in the necessity of this plan—he deferred ultimately to *the Lord*. His plan would come to pass only if God allowed it, only if it was in accord with God's will (compare James 4:13-15).

Paul was aware that in this situation he could end up being as arrogant as his opponents, but he avoided being so. So the confrontation to come would not be a test of who had the most persuasive words, but of who had the legitimate *power*. When Paul confronts his opponents with the triumph of Christ's resurrection and the truth of His present and eternal rule, will they be as *puffed up* then as they were in Paul's absence? Will their power rival that of the risen Christ? When we see the real issue, we know the answer to the question.

20. For the kingdom of God is not in word, but in power.

Human talk cannot compete with the *power* of *the kingdom of God*. This power does not operate as does the world's power, which derives from human talk. Kingdom power is expressed in the resurrection of Jesus, who surrendered to death for the sake of His unworthy people. Kingdom power comes through the Holy Spirit (Romans 15:13). And that power was the antidote to the pride that infected the Corinthian church.

21. What will ye? shall I come unto you with a rod, or in love, and in the spirit of meekness?

The Corinthian Christians faced a choice.

If they would acknowledge their pride and its inconsistency with the gospel, Paul could *come* to them expressing fully the love of Christ that they shared. Such a visit would be in a spirit of the *meekness*, or gentleness, that should characterize Jesus' followers (Matthew 5:5). It is an attitude that does not assert its own supposed rights, privileges, or entitlements.

But if Paul's opponents persisted in the path they were on, he would have to come *with a rod*. This is a stark metaphor (compare Revelation 2:27). When contrasted with a visit *in love*, a visit with a rod refers to retributive correction. Taken together, these possibilities imply three possible outcomes:

1. The Corinthians would have successfully corrected their attitudes and actions before Paul's return visit.
2. Paul himself would successfully correct those attitudes and actions when he returned.
3. Paul would be unsuccessful in correcting those attitudes and actions when he returned, resulting in his disfellowshipping the rebels (compare 1 Corinthians 5; 1 Timothy 1:20).

Which of the three possible outcomes would come to pass was up to the Corinthians. As we say, the ball was in their court.

Unlike many New Testament letters, we have a glimpse of how the readers of 1 Corinthians responded to the letter. In another letter to the church, Paul mentioned that he did not want to make another painful visit (2 Corinthians 2:1). It appeared that when Paul visited the church, as he said in our text he would, he was met with considerable resistance, perhaps even hostility.

But that experience was not the end of the story. As time went on and as other influences came to bear, many in the church repented of their behavior (2 Corinthians 2:5-11). As Paul wrote 2 Corinthians, he reflected on the pain of their relationship but also on the joy he had that the Corinthian Christians were indeed still growing and maturing in their faith and expressing it with greater consistency. The love of Christ, even if expressed with a corrective "rod," bore fruit in greater humility and love.

Conclusion
A. A Difficult Calling

Paul's language toward the Corinthians is sharply and appropriately judgmental. This helps us understand why Paul wrote as he did, helping us understand what it means to live in God's kingdom.

God is our ultimate judge. But God calls us into a kingdom in which His subjects, answering only to Him, nevertheless humbly and lovingly nurture one another toward greater Christlikeness. This happens even as we acknowledge our own weaknesses and submit to those who help us to grow. It is a calling that is as difficult as it is rewarding.

B. Prayer

God, we come to You in repentance of the arrogance that we all have been guilty of at times. May we abandon our focus on our supposed entitlements and focus instead on the entitlements Jesus voluntarily gave up so that we might live with Him eternally. In His name we pray. Amen!

C. Thought to Remember
With God as our judge,
the church lives in humble fellowship.

How to Say It

Apollos	Uh-*pahl*-us.
Colossians	Kuh-*losh*-unz.
Corinth	*Kor*-inth.
Corinthians	Ko-*rin*-thee-unz (*th* as in *thin*).
Ephesus	*Ef*-uh-sus.

Involvement Learning

Enhance your lesson with KJV Bible Student *(from your curriculum supplier) and the reproducible activity page (at www.standardlesson.com or in the back of the* KJV Standard Lesson Commentary Deluxe Edition*).*

Into the Lesson

Open class by asking learners to call out as many answers as possible to this question: "What's the first word that comes to your mind when I say the word *judge*?" Write their responses on the board. After one minute, evaluate responses by drawing a circle beside the responses that have a negative connotation and a star beside the ones that have a positive connotation.

Divide the class into pairs to discuss the following questions: 1–Give an example of a time when a judgment passed was accurate or helpful. 2–Give an example of a time when a judgment passed was incorrect or hurtful.

Transition to the Bible study by saying, "This is not the first time that we've discussed passing judgment; it was central to the last class discussion. Let's learn about what Paul says on this topic."

Into the Word

Divide the class into small groups. Ask each group to read 1 Corinthians 4:1-6, 17-21 and answer the following questions: 1–What is Paul's stance on passing judgment? 2–When does Paul say that passing judgment is wrong, and for what reason(s)? 3–In what situation does Paul say that passing judgment is the right thing to do, and for what reason(s)? After five minutes, have the groups share their responses with the whole class.

Alternative. Distribute copies of the "Judging Paul's Faithfulness" exercise from the activity page, which you can download. Have learners work in pairs to complete as indicated.

Distribute a sheet of paper with the following headers to each group: *The Corinthian Situation / Paul's Teaching / Scripture Reference.* Ask each group to reread 1 Corinthians 4:1-6, 17-21 and make a list under the first heading to answer the question, "What was the Corinthian situation that prompted Paul to write this?" Groups should then make a list under the second heading, summariz-ing Paul's teaching regarding passing judgment. Finally, under the third column, groups are to list the Scripture references that support their findings in the first two columns. After 10 minutes, have groups present their findings with the whole class.

Option. Start a discussion comparing and con-trasting this week's lesson with last week's lesson on Romans 14:10-23. Ask the class how each Scripture teaches believers about passing judgment.

Option 2. Distribute copies of the "The Lord, Our Judge" activity from the activity page. Have learners work in small groups to complete as indicated.

Into Life

Discuss the following questions as a whole class: 1–Why is humility not held in high regard today? 2–Give an example of a time when humil-ity received a poor response from others. 3–How does living with humility keep a person from pass-ing judgment on others?

Distribute a sheet of paper to each learner and ask them to write a personal response to this prompt that you will write on the board:

When am I "puffed up" with pride and a judgmental spirit?

After one minute, invite volunteers to talk about how sharing their responses with a trusted friend would help them develop an attitude of humility. (*Note*: Remind learners that they don't have to dis-close their responses at this time. Rather, learn-ers should focus on how accountability can help shape their attitudes in this regard.)

Close class by challenging learners to write down the name of a friend (or two) who could be an accountability partner for the mutual purpose of developing humility instead of pride. End with a prayer asking God to give each learner courage to speak with their accountability partner regard-ing humility.

God's Kingdom Will Be All in All

Devotional Reading: Isaiah 6:1-8
Background Scripture: 1 Corinthians 15:1-28; Ephesians 1:15-23

1 Corinthians 15:20-28

20 But now is Christ risen from the dead, and become the firstfruits of them that slept.

21 For since by man came death, by man came also the resurrection of the dead.

22 For as in Adam all die, even so in Christ shall all be made alive.

23 But every man in his own order: Christ the firstfruits; afterward they that are Christ's at his coming.

24 Then cometh the end, when he shall have delivered up the kingdom to God, even the Father; when he shall have put down all rule and all authority and power.

25 For he must reign, till he hath put all enemies under his feet.

26 The last enemy that shall be destroyed is death.

27 For he hath put all things under his feet. But when he saith all things are put under him, it is manifest that he is excepted, which did put all things under him.

28 And when all things shall be subdued unto him, then shall the Son also himself be subject unto him that put all things under him, that God may be all in all.

Key Text

When all things shall be subdued unto him, then shall the Son also himself be subject unto him that put all things under him, that God may be all in all. —**1 Corinthians 15:28**

The Righteous
Reign of God

Unit 3: God's Eternal Reign
Lessons 10–13

Lesson Aims

After participating in this lesson, each learner will be able to:

1. Summarize the roles of Adam, Jesus, and God the Father.

2. Explain why death is an enemy.

3. State why he or she looks forward to resurrection and why.

Lesson Outline

Introduction
  A. Unveiling the Masterpiece
  B. Lesson Context
I. Guaranteed Victory (1 Corinthians 15:20-22)
  A. Firstfruits (v. 20)
  B. Reversal (vv. 21-22)
II. Plan for Victory (1 Corinthians 15:23-26)
  A. Assured Sequence (v. 23)
    A "What," Not a "When"
  B. Enemy Defeated (vv. 24-26)
    No Compromise!
III. Total Victory (1 Corinthians 15:27-28)
  A. All but One (v. 27)
  B. All in All (v. 28)
Conclusion
  A. The Promise of Resurrection
  B. Prayer
  C. Thought to Remember

Introduction

A. Unveiling the Masterpiece

Few artists share their creative processes. They paint or sculpt or compose or write in private. Only when their work is first shown, at an unveiling or a performance, does the audience witness what the artist has created. Even then, what is often unveiled is only the masterpiece itself, not the process that brought it into being.

The universe is God's creative masterpiece, and humanity is its focus (Genesis 1:26-27). The processes of creation are slowly being discovered via many tools such as space telescopes, microscopes, and advanced computers. But it is the masterpiece itself that speaks loudest (Psalm 19:1-6).

But we humans have derailed God's intentions for His masterpiece (Romans 1:18-23). The story of God's response to human rebellion is the story of the Bible. In that response, God re-creates the world and re-creates humanity to be what He has always intended.

B. Lesson Context

Our text comes from the next-to-last section of Paul's first letter to the Corinthians. It could almost be said that Paul was saving the most important part of his letter for last: his teaching about the resurrection.

We should clarify at the outset what we mean by the word *resurrection*. Some students take that word to refer primarily to the immediate life after death: when someone who belongs to Jesus dies, that person's spirit remains alive in the Lord's presence. To be in the presence of the Lord after death is an important biblical idea, affirmed by Paul himself (2 Corinthians 5:1, 6; Philippians 1:20-24). The Lord is faithful: He will never abandon His people, even in death. But this is not the meaning of *resurrection*.

Life in Heaven as disembodied spirits is not the final status of the Lord's people. From the outset, humans were intended to be a combination of body and spirit. As the Creator of everything that is seen and unseen, God's intent is to reclaim His entire creation (see Romans 8:22-23). This means that when Christ returns to complete God's saving work, God will raise the dead so that they are alive as a unity of body and spirit. They will be in fellowship with those who are still alive at Christ's second coming (1 Thessalonians 4:13-18). This final act in God's plan will mark the ultimate victory of God.

For reasons that are uncertain, some members of the church of Corinth had begun to dismiss the idea that God will raise the dead. In light of Paul's emphasis on the church's "puffed up" pride (see lesson 12), it may be that some found the idea of God's raising dead bodies to be distasteful or bizarre. This view would have been compatible with pagan Greek philosophy, which viewed the body as a prison from which one's spirit desired to escape; the Greek play on words for this belief was *sōma sēma* ("the body, a tomb"; compare Acts 17:32). Another error is to equate resurrection with reincarnation, the latter being part of a never-ending cycle of reward and punishment.

Paul argued that God does indeed raise the dead because God raised Christ from the dead. He recounted to the Corinthians the gospel as they first heard it: focused on Jesus' death, burial, and resurrection, all "according to the scriptures" (1 Corinthians 15:3-4). Then he recounted the many who saw Jesus after His resurrection, alive in His body that had been dead and entombed (15:5-7). Paul considered himself as the last of these witnesses (15:8), reminding readers that the Lord Jesus appeared to him in bodily form on the road to Damascus (Acts 9:3-9). It is Jesus' resurrection, Paul says, that demonstrates not only that God *can* raise the dead but that He *will* raise the dead.

I. Guaranteed Victory
(1 Corinthians 15:20-22)
A. Firstfruits (v. 20)

20. But now is Christ risen from the dead, and become the firstfruits of them that slept.

Having discussed the overwhelming testimony of witnesses to Christ's resurrection (see Lesson Context), Paul began to apply that historical event to the question at hand: Does God raise the dead? Christ's resurrection proved that God can and has. But more than that, Paul says, it guarantees that He will do so in the future.

All creation is under the King.

Visual for Lesson 13. *Display this visual as you ask the discussion questions associated with 1 Corinthians 15:25.*

Paul uses the term *firstfruits* to describe this idea. For ancient Israel, the day of firstfruits (also known as the Feast of Weeks or Feast of Harvest) involved a sacrifice of the produce of the land. The firstfruits were brought at the beginning of the harvest, expressing that all that was harvested came from God and was dedicated to God (Leviticus 23:15-21; Numbers 28:26-31; Deuteronomy 26:1-10). With this offering, the faithful pledged to God not just this one offering but the entirety of their harvest.

Regarding resurrection, however, God is the one who has offered the firstfruits. He did so by making a promise to His people that what He has begun with Christ's resurrection, He will complete with theirs. (See more on this role reversal below.)

Prior to the resurrection of Jesus, most Jews believed that God would indeed raise His people from the dead (Daniel 12:2; John 11:24; contrast Mark 12:18). That event would mark the end of one era and the beginning of another. In so doing, God would right the injustices of the present age and welcome all His people from every period of history to enjoy the fullness of His blessings.

Jesus' resurrection modified this expectation for Jesus' followers. They came to realize that by raising Jesus, God was taking the promises commonly associated with "the end" and pulling them, in part, back to the middle, so to speak. Paul's readers were already enjoying the blessings of the age to come through their forgiveness in Christ. Further blessings were the indwelling of God's Holy Spirit and their fellowship as God's people.

But all that is still not the end! God has more for His people: what Christ's resurrection did to give us a down payment is the guarantee of full payment to come (2 Corinthians 1:21-22; 5:5; Ephesians 1:13-14). Because Christ is raised, the Christian's faith has hope for the future, hope that is more than wishful thinking. Even when faith seems futile, Christ's resurrection tells us that God is not finished. We have much to look forward to.

B. Reversal (vv. 21-22)

21. For since by man came death, by man came also the resurrection of the dead.

Paul places Christ's resurrection in the setting of the entire biblical story, from its very beginning. God intended to sustain people's lives as they depended on Him (Genesis 2:9). But rebellion severed that relationship and separated humans from God's sustaining power (3:22-24; Romans 5:12). In this way humanity brought *death* upon itself, both the loss of physical life and the ruin of God's goodness in our lives.

Resurrection, however, is a reversal of all this. Those who turn from rebellion to faith, submitting to God's rule in His kingdom, are promised the king's life-giving provision. Someone first brought the death that all received in their rebellion, but someone else has brought life. That someone is Jesus of Nazareth, whom God raised from *the dead.*

What Do You Think?

How does the resurrection of Christ encourage you regarding death?

Digging Deeper

How will you answer another believer who may be worried and fearful regarding death?

---

22. For as in Adam all die, even so in Christ shall all be made alive.

The phrase *in Adam all die* brings up an issue of "fairness": Why is it fair for me to die because of what Adam did without my consent? Paul's response negates such a question because what *Christ* has done has canceled the result of Adam's sin. Death is reversed in that *all* will *be made alive.*

We should note that the two uses of the word *all* are absolute; neither use is limited to a specific group. All humanity is in view in both usages. Christ's death and resurrection has canceled any eternal punishment that might be projected from Adam onto everyone else. The forthcoming bodily resurrection applies to everyone! This fact is not, however, to be equated with the false doctrine of universal salvation/universalism; people will still be held accountable for their own personal sins. Paul lays this out in greater detail in Romans 5:12-21 (compare Daniel 12:2).

II. Plan for Victory
(1 Corinthians 15:23-26)
A. Assured Sequence (v. 23)

23a. But every man in his own order: Christ the firstfruits.

Paul offers a sequence of events to show how God's plan unfolds. The basis of this sequence is the fact that God the Father raised *Christ* on the third day after His crucifixion. Again, the mention of *firstfruits* brings to mind the fact that the whole harvest belongs to God. (See again the issue of role reversal, above.)

23b. Afterward they that are Christ's at his coming.

The word *afterward* establishes the next event in the sequence. In this text, the word *they* could refer to (1) the dead in Christ who are raised *at his coming* or (2) those still alive when Christ returns or (3) both. A more detailed sequence in that regard is found in 1 Thessalonians 4:13-18 and

How to Say It

Damascus	Du-*mass*-kus.
Deuteronomy	Due-ter-*ahn*-uh-me.
Gethsemane	Geth-*sem*-uh-nee
	(*g* as in *get*).
Thessalonians	Thess-uh-**lo**-nee-unz
	(*th* as in *thin*).

2 Thessalonians 1:5-10; 2:1-12, but that detail is not important to Paul's purposes here.

Christ's return to earth will be from Heaven, where He will have reigned at God's right hand since the ascension (Acts 1:9-11; 2:32-36; 7:55-56; Ephesians 1:20). The crucified Christ was not just restored to life by His resurrection. He has been exalted to rule. When He returns, He comes as king to make His rule full and final over all creation.

We should pause to stress that although Paul has sketched a sequence, he has not even hinted at a time line. Many readers of this commentary will remember the failed prediction of the booklet *88 Reasons Why the Rapture Will Be in 1988*. All attempts to establish a time line regarding the return of Christ are bound to fail (Matthew 24:36, 42-44; Acts 1:7). As one commentator has said regarding Christ's return, "We're on the welcoming committee, not the planning committee."

A "What," Not a "When"

Our group was studying the book of Daniel. Our leader was an avid follower of several Christian "prophecy experts" who proclaimed with assurance that the "soon return" of Jesus was just around the corner. Parroting those views, our leader boldly affirmed that the "signs of the times" strongly indicate Christ's imminent return.

I sat quietly for a time, and then I suggested that various biblical passages do indeed assure us of the Lord's return, but they give us no time line as to when it will happen. I referred to Matthew 24:36-42; Acts 1:6-8; and others.

Some of my friends—who seem to have spent more time listening to "prophetic" preachers than studying the Bible—had difficulty with my responses. Even so, Paul and Jesus remind us that it's far more important for Christians to tell the world that Jesus is coming again than it is for us to speculate about when and how it will happen.

How do you ensure that you stay focused on *the what* rather than *the when*?　　　—C. R. B.

B. Enemy Defeated (vv. 24-26)

24. Then cometh the end, when he shall have delivered up the kingdom to God, even the Father; when he shall have put down all rule and all authority and power.

Paul now explains what the sequence of divine actions will accomplish. *The end* refers to the end of this present age, in which sin and evil seem to prevail. Notice how the New Testament contrasts the current era with the one to come (Matthew 12:32; Mark 10:29-31; 1 Timothy 6:19; Titus 2:11-13). Christ's ability to *put down all rule and all authority and power* certainly includes the powers of the unseen spiritual world that empower earthly rebellions against God.

Ephesians 1:19-21 is a particularly important passage on this topic:

> . . . and what is the exceeding greatness of his power to us-ward who believe, according to the working of his mighty power, which [God] wrought in Christ, when he raised him from the dead, and set him at his own right hand in the heavenly places, far above all principality, and power, and might, and dominion, and every name that is named, not only in this world, but also in that which is to come.

Christ's work will be utterly complete. Its completion is guaranteed by the great act already accomplished: His resurrection from the dead. With His return and the renewal of creation (2 Peter 3:10; Revelation 21:1), God's will shall indeed be done in full on earth as it is in Heaven (Matthew 6:10).

Christ's return is not something for the faithful to fear. It means resurrection life! It means the defeat of evil in all its manifestations. It means the end of suffering. It means joy. It means peace. We have a foretaste of all that now since the baptism of believers signals a spiritual resurrection from the dead (Romans 6:1-14; Colossians 2:11-13).

What Do You Think?

How would you respond to someone who sensationalizes and evokes fear in believers regarding the Bible's message of Christ's return?

Digging Deeper

How does Revelation 19:11-21 inform your response?

25. For he must reign, till he hath put all enemies under his feet.

To support his point, Paul drew on Psalm 110:1. This verse is quoted or alluded to some 18 times in the New Testament (here; Matthew 22:44; 26:64; Mark 12:36; 14:62; 16:19; Luke 20:42-43; 22:69; Acts 2:34-35; Romans 8:34; Ephesians 1:20; Colossians 3:1; Hebrews 1:3, 13; 8:1; 10:12, 13; 12:2).

The *he* is Christ, the risen one who reigns on the throne following His death, burial, resurrection, and ascension. His rule is focused on defeating *all enemies*—evil in all its forms. In the meantime, His subjects join Him in His current work of overcoming evil as it coexists with good (see Matthew 13:24-30, 37-43). But as we do so, we know that we will see the complete defeat of evil only when Christ returns as king.

What Do You Think?

What new steps will you take to join Christ's work of overcoming evil in the world?

Digging Deeper

How do 2 Corinthians 6:6-7; 10:3-5; and Ephesians 6:10-17 inform those steps?

26. The last enemy that shall be destroyed is death.

God's victory at Christ's return is comprehensive. It leaves no enemies standing. *Death* itself is among those enemies and is *the last* to be defeated. God pronounced death as the punishment for sin (Genesis 2:17; Romans 6:23). But with sin's punishment paid for on the cross, God's holy nature is satisfied. This expression reminds us of how thoroughly God loves and supports His people (8:31-39).

The victory of God means the end of death. God destroys death by raising His people from the dead, uniting their spirits with resurrected bodies, and bringing them into eternal, unbroken fellowship with God and with one another (see 2 Timothy 1:9-10; Revelation 21:4).

No Compromise!

World War I was called "the war to end all wars." It wasn't, as the advent of World War II demonstrated. That war's end was hoped to "make the world safe for democracy." It didn't, as the ensuing Cold War and its "iron curtain" showed. Major regional conflicts continue to this day.

Wars sometimes end in a negotiated peace, sometimes in unconditional surrender. Neither outcome applies to our spiritual war against the forces of darkness. What is promised, rather, is the total destruction of sin and its deadly consequences when Christ returns. What spiritual guardrails can you erect to ensure that you do not attempt any kind of compromise with the enemy until that return?　　　　—C. R. B.

III. Total Victory
(1 Corinthians 15:27-28)
A. All but One (v. 27)

27. For he hath put all things under his feet. But when he saith all things are put under him, it is manifest that he is excepted, which did put all things under him.

Paul's reference to Psalm 110:1 continues. In that passage, God promises to defeat the enemies of His anointed one. In so doing, those enemies end up being trodden underfoot. This will be justified punishment for those enemies who have dared attempt to do the very same thing to the Son of God (Hebrews 10:29)!

The defeat of the enemies means that *all things* are subject to God's king, the Christ, with but one exception: God the Father, the one who brings the enemies *under* the king's authority. God the Father and God the Son effectively share reign over the new creation that is fully subject to the divine authority of the triune God (Colossians 2:9-10).

B. All in All (v. 28)

28. And when all things shall be subdued unto him, then shall the Son also himself be subject unto him that put all things under him, that God may be all in all.

Paul takes a step beyond Psalm 110:1 to describe the completion of God's plan. First, God the Father subjects *all things* to His anointed one, the Christ, His *Son*. When that grand plan is complete, the Son in turn willingly subjects himself to the Father, placing himself and all that is subjected to the Son *under* the Father's authority. In this way, Paul says, *God* becomes *all in all,* the ruler of all, the victor over all.

It is important to recognize here that Christ willingly subjects himself to the Father. There is no hint in what Paul says that the Son is lesser than, or inferior to, the Father. In Christ "dwelleth all the fulness of the Godhead bodily" (Colossians 2:9). Paul also wrote that even though Christ was fully equal with God, Christ refused to use that equality for His own advantage. Instead, He willingly became a servant to do the will of the Father, a will that was also His. Christ was then exalted to the highest place by the Father (Philippians 2:6-11).

We see the willing subjection of the Son to the Father in the story of Jesus' prayer in Gethsemane (Matthew 26:36-42). We should always remember that we submit to the Christ, who himself submitted to God the Father. This reveals that submission is the true way of life. So it is fitting that the last act of the divine plan is that the Son submits himself and all creation to God the Father. The decisive act of salvation was in the Son's submission, and so the story comes to its climax.

> **What Do You Think?**
> How does Jesus' submission to God the Father remind you that submission to God is an act of worship?
>
> **Digging Deeper**
> How will you remove any perceived roadblocks that prevent you from following Jesus' example in this regard?

Conclusion

A. The Promise of Resurrection

Because we mortal humans live so close to death, a Christian's mind often goes to the promise of God that death is followed by life with God in Heaven. That promise is real, true, important, and a real comfort as we consider our mortality.

But today's passage reminds us that there is

even more to look forward to. As one writer put it, life after death is followed by "life after life after death." It will be a life that makes us again a body-spirit unity, as we are fitted for a new existence. Resurrection from the dead is integral to the end of history to come. Without resurrection, the "all things" over which God rules would leave out the most precious elements of God's creation: His people. But raised from the dead, God's people are made whole. We shall be brought together in living fellowship, and made new for a neverending life in the new heavens and earth that God has prepared for us.

That life to come will bring us together with all of God's people from across the ages. It will be a life in which we inhabit the new heavens and earth, able to do the things in creation for which we were ourselves created. We can only imagine what God has in store for us—and wonder at His wisdom and love that has made it all possible.

We should not forget that the world we live in now and the bodies that are currently ours are temporary, to be replaced by the permanent. That truth should sanctify our every action. This is what inspires hope even in the worst of trials. This is what God has promised us, now and eternally.

> **What Do You Think?**
> How has your perspective on the resurrection and life after death changed in light of today's study?
>
> **Digging Deeper**
> How will your response to human ethical issues be informed by Scripture's teaching on Christ's return and the promised resurrection of believers?

B. Prayer

Great God, Your ways are far above our ways. Your promises to us are more than we can imagine. May we live in the light of Your promised kingdom. We look forward to seeing the promise of resurrection fulfilled. In Jesus' name we pray. Amen!

C. Thought to Remember

God's final victory will make us eternally whole.

Involvement Learning

Enhance your lesson with KJV Bible Student *(from your curriculum supplier) and the reproducible activity page (at www.standardlesson.com or in the back of the* KJV Standard Lesson Commentary Deluxe Edition*).*

Into the Lesson

Ask learners to raise a hand if they agree with any of the following statements:

1–Authority and submission to authority are necessary for a properly functioning society.

2–It's easier for people to *have* authority than *submit* to authority.

3–I would rather *have* a boss than *be* the boss.

4–Jesus presents us with the best example of submitting to authority.

5–All authority is temporary.

Pause after each statement to allow learners a chance to explain why they agree or disagree with the statement.

Alternative. Distribute copies of the "Define Authority?" exercise from the activity page, which you can download. Have learners work in pairs or small groups to complete as indicated. After calling time, have volunteers share their responses with the class.

Lead into Bible study by saying, "Determining a proper response to authority is a problem for some people. Today's Scripture shows how this problem is resolved for followers of Jesus."

Into the Word

Distribute a handout (you create) that contains the following statements. Do not include the numbers in parentheses.

1–Christ is raised from the dead. (2)

2–God's people are raised from the dead. (4)

3–Through Adam, death enters the world. (1)

4–Christ destroys all earthly rule, authority, and power. (3)

5–Death itself is destroyed. (5)

6–Through His submission, Christ's authority is seen forever. (6)

Put learners into pairs and ask them to read 1 Corinthians 15:20-28, then arrange the statements in correct order, reflecting the order that they have happened or will happen. (The numbers in parenthesis show the correct order of the statements.)

Alternative. Distribute copies of the "Main Characters" activity from the activity page. Have learners work in pairs to complete as indicated.

After calling time under either activity, ask the following questions for whole-class discussion: 1–What are the roles of Adam, Jesus, and God the Father as described in 1 Corinthians 15:20-28? 2–How is God's authority demonstrated and explained in this passage?

Into Life

Ask students to gather into five small groups. Give each of the groups a slip of paper containing one of the following statements:

• "I saw how my mother suffered during the last stages of her disease, and frankly, I don't want to go through that. I have to admit I'm afraid to die."

• "Death is a blessing. To sink into silent oblivion, with no more worries. With as much trouble and pain as I'm experiencing now, I'm eager to die."

• "I'm my own person, and I do what I want! I'm focused on my career and I'm preparing to enjoy my retirement years. I'm going to make that happen, and God won't have anything to do with it."

• "Two years ago, my brother had a heart attack, and my neighbor told me that he was praying. My brother recovered, so I'm willing to believe that God had something to do with it."

• "My young daughter died unexpectedly. I can't believe in a God who would allow the kind of suffering that my family has experienced."

Ask the groups to prepare a response to their prompt, based on today's Scripture. Encourage groups to discuss how the promise of resurrection informs the situation. Allow groups time to talk before calling on them to report back to the whole class. End class by asking volunteers to explain why they look forward to the resurrection.